DICTIONARY OF LEGAL BIOGRAPHY

1845-1945

DICTIONARY OF LEGAL BIOGRAPHY

1845-1945

by

A.B. Schofield

Barry Rose Law Publishers Ltd.
Chichester

ISBN 1 872328 87 3

Barry Rose Law Publishers Ltd.
Little London
Chichester

Printed by the Alden Group, Oxford

CONTENTS

PREFACE

A short explanation is necessary concerning the scope of this volume. As indicated, it covers the years between 1845 and 1945 (inclusive). The individual entries relate to all those who within that period held office or rank as follows:

> Lord Chancellor
> Judge of the Superior Courts
> Attorney-General
> Solicitor-General
> Recorder of London
> Common Serjeant
> Judge of Mayor's and City of London Court
> (or its predecessors)
> County Court Judge
> Serjeant-at-Law
> Queen's Counsel
> Metropolitan magistrate

It will be appreciated that a subject is often eligible by more than one of these criteria.

A natural, but acceptable consequence of this arrangement is that the period under consideration is, in a sense, extended. Some of those still living in 1845, had careers which began in the previous century, and some who had qualified for entry by 1945, remained professionally active well beyond that date. Indeed two of the latter are still with us at the present time.

For information supplied, my thanks are due to Mr. G.F. Holborn, Lincoln's Inn Librarian, Mrs. Theresa Thom, Gray's Inn Librarian, Mr. Ian Murray, Inner Temple Archivist, and Mr. Malcolm Macgregor of Claygate, Surrey. I must also acknowledge the considerable assistance given over many hours by my wife, Stephanie.

A.B.S.

ABBREVIATIONS

AA & QMG	Assistant Adjutant and Quartermaster General
AAG	Assistant Adjutant-General
ADC	Aide-de-Camp
Adj.	Adjutant
ADJAG	Assistant Deputy Judge Advocate-General
AJAG	Assistant Judge Advocate-General
AMICE	Associate Member of Institution of Civil Engineers
ARIBA	Associate of Royal Institute of British Architects
ARIC	Associate of Royal Institute of Chemistry
ARSM	Associate of Royal School of Mines
ASC	Army Service Corps
BCS	Bengal Civil Service
BEF	British Expeditionary Force
BRCS	British Red Cross Society
CA	County Alderman; Chartered Accountant
CB	Companion of Order of the Bath
CBE	Commander of Order of British Empire
CC	County Council
CE	Civil Engineer
CH	Companion of Honour
Chan.	Chancellor
CIE	Companion of Order of Indian Empire
CIV	City Imperial Volunteers
CJ	Chief Justice
CMG	Companion of Order of St. Michael and St. George
Comm.	Commission

CP	Common Pleas
CSI	Companion of Order of Star of India
CStJ	Commander of Order of St. John of Jerusalem
CVO	Commander of Royal Victorian Order
DAAG	Deputy Assistant Adjutant-General
DAG	Deputy Adjutant-General
DAQMG	Deputy Assistant Quartermaster-General
DCLI	Duke of Cornwall's Light Infantry
DJAG	Deputy Judge Advocate-General
DL	Deputy Lieutenant
DLI	Durham Light Infantry
DPP	Director of Public Prosecutions
DSO	Companion of Distinguished Service Order
FBA	Fellow of British Academy
FCA	Fellow of Institute of Chartered Accountants
FCS	Fellow of Chemical Society
FGS	Fellow of Geological Society
FIArb.	Fellow of Institute of Arbitrators
FIOB	Fellow of Institute of Builders
FISE	Fellow of Institute of Sanitary Engineers
FLS	Fellow of Linnean Society
FPS	Fellow of Pharmaceutical Society
FRAS	Fellow of Royal Astronomical, or Asiatic, Society
FRCI	Fellow of Royal Colonial Institute
FRGS	Fellow of Royal Geographical Society
FRI	Fellow of Royal Institution
FRIBA	Fellow of Royal Institute of British Architects
FRIC (formerly FIC)	Fellow of Royal Institute of Chemistry
FRMS	Fellow of Royal Microscopical Society
FRS	Fellow of Royal Society
FRSA	Fellow of Royal Society of Arts
FRSan.I.	Fellow of Royal Sanitary Institute

FRSE	Fellow of Royal Society of Edinburgh
FRSL	Fellow of Royal Society of Literature
FSA	Fellow of Society of Antiquaries
FSI	Fellow of Royal Institution of Chartered Surveyors
FSS	Fellow of Royal Statistical Society
GBE	Knight Grand Cross of Order of British Empire
GCB	Knight Grand Cross of Order of the Bath
GCIE	Knight Grand Commander of Indian Empire
GCMG	Knight Grand Cross of St. Michael and St. George
GCSI	Knight Grand Commander of Star of India
GCVO	Knight Grand Cross of Royal Victorian Order
G.I.	Gray's Inn
HAC	Honourable Artillery Company
HEICS	Honourable East India Company's Service
HLI	Highland Light Infantry
ICE	Institution of Civil Engineers
ICS	Indian Civil Service
IMS	Indian Medical Service
Intern.	International
ISO	Imperial Service Order
I.T.	Inner Temple
JAG	Judge Advocate-General
KB	King's Bench
KBE	Knight Commander of Order of British Empire
KCB	Knight Commander of Order of the Bath
KCIE	Knight Commander of Indian Empire
KCMG	Knight Commander of St. Michael and St. George

KCSI	Knight Commander of Star of India
KCVO	Knight Commander of Royal Victorian Order
KG	Knight of Order of the Garter
KH	Knight of Hanover
KOSB	King's Own Scottish Borderers
KOYLI	King's Own Yorkshire Light Infantry
KStJ	Knight of Order of St. John of Jerusalem
KSLI	King's Shropshire Light Infantry
KT	Knight of Order of the Thistle
LC	Lord Chancellor
LCB	Lord Chief Baron
LCC	London County Council
LCJ	Lord Chief Justice
L of A	Lord of Appeal
L.I.	Lincoln's Inn
LJ	Lord Justice
MBE	Member of Order of British Empire
MC	Military Cross
MCC	Marylebone Cricket Club
MCS	Madras Civil Service
MGC	Machine Gun Corps
MICE	Member of Institution of Civil Engineers
MIChemE	Member of Institution of Chemical Engineers
MIME	Member of Institution of Mining Engineers
MINA	Member of Institution of Naval Architects
MLA	Member of Legislative Assembly
MR	Master of the Rolls
MRI	Member of Royal Institution
MRIA	Member of Royal Irish Academy
M.T.	Middle Temple
MVO	Member of Royal Victorial Order
OBE	Officer of Order of British Empire
OM	Order of Merit

OStJ	Officer of Order of St. John of Jerusalem
OTC	Officers' Training Corps
PC	Privy Councillor
PD & A	Probate Divorce and Admiralty
Pres.	President
QB	Queen's Bench
RA	Royal Artillery; Royal Academician
RAeS	Royal Aeronautical Society
RAMC	Royal Army Medical Corps
RAOC	Royal Army Ordnance Corps
RASC	Royal Army Service Corps
RE	Royal Engineers
RFA	Royal Field Artillery
RFC	Royal Flying Corps
RGA	Royal Garrison Artillery
RI	Royal Institute of Painters in Water Colours
RNAS	Royal Naval Air Service
RSI	Royal Sanitary Institute
TD	Territorial Decoration
TF	Territorial Forces
V-C	Vice-Chancellor
VC	Victoria Cross
VD	Volunteer Officers' Decoration
WS	Writer to the Signet
Yeo.	Yeomanry

PRINCIPAL SOURCES

Alumni Cantabrigienses (to 1900). Venn
Alumni Dublinenses (to 1846)
Alumni Oxonienses (to 1886). Foster
Annual Registers
Armorial Families. Fox-Davies. 1929-30
Army Lists
Biographica Juridica. Foss. 1870
Burke's Family Index. 1976
Burke's Handbook to the Order of the British Empire. 1921
Burke's Landed Gentry
Burke's Peerage
Cambridge University War Register 1914-18
Cambridge University Calendars
Debrett's House of Commons and Judicial Bench
Debrett's Peerage
Dictionary of Indian Biography. Buckland. 1905
Dictionary of National Biography
Dod's Parliamentary Companion
Dod's Peerage
Gentleman's Magazine
Gray's Inn Admission Registers, 1889
Inner Temple Admission Registers (unpublished)
Inner Temple, Masters of the Bench, 1883
Inner Temple, Masters of the Bench (supplement), 1901
Kelly's Handbook of the Titled Landed and Official Classes
Law Journal
Law Lists
Law Magazine
Law Times
Lincoln's Inn Admission Registers, 1896
List of English Law Officers, King's Counsel etc. Sainty, 1987

List of Judges of Superior Courts of England 1272-1990. Sainty,
    1993
Men at the Bar. Foster, 1885
Middle Temple Admission Registers, 1949
Middle Temple Bench Book, 1937
Modern English Biography. Boase, 1851-1900
Oxford University Calendars
Oxford University War Roll 1914-19
Registers of Births, Deaths, and Marriages
School Registers
Solicitors' Journal
The Times
Walford's County Families of the United Kingdom
Who Was Who

CROSS-REFERENCES

ABERCONWAY, Lord see McLaren
ALVERSTONE, Lord see Webster
AMULREE, Lord see Mackenzie
BIRKENHEAD, Lord see Smith, F.E.
BLANESBURGH, Lord see Younger
BRAMPTON, Lord see Hawkins
CALDECOTE, Lord see Inskip
CHELMSFORD, Lord see Thesiger
COTTENHAM, Lord see Pepys
CRAIGHILL, Lord see Millar
CRAIGMYLE, Lord see Shaw
CRANWORTH, Lord see Rolfe
DANESFORT, Lord see Butcher
DUNEDIN, Lord see Murray
DUNROSSIL, Lord see Morrison
EDMUND-DAVIES, Lord see Davies
ESHER, Lord see Brett
FAIRFIELD, Lord see Greer
GLENAVY, Lord see Campbell
GORELL, Lord see Barnes
GRIMTHORPE, Lord see Beckett
HAILSHAM, Lord see Hogg
HALSBURY, Lord see Giffard
HANWORTH, Lord see Pollock
HATHERLEY, Lord see Wood
ILFORD, Lord see Hutchinson
KILBRACKEN, Lord see Godley
KILLANIN, Lord see Morris
KINGSDOWN, Lord see Pemberton-Leigh
KINROSS, Lord see Balfour
LANGDALE, Lord see Bickersteth
LLANDAFF, Lord see Matthews

LOCHEE, Lord see Robertson
LOREBURN, Lord see Reid
LUDLOW, Lord see Lopes
LYNDHURST, Lord see Copley
MAENAN, Lord see Taylor
MERRIVALE, Lord see Duke
MERSEY, Lord see Bigham
MONKSWELL, Lord see Collier
OXFORD & ASQUITH, Lord see Asquith
PARMOOR, Lord see Cripps
PENZANCE, Lord see Wilde
READING, Lord see Isaacs
ROWLEY, Lord see Henderson
ST. HELIER, Lord see Jeune
ST. LEONARDS, Lord see Sugden
SELBORNE, Lord see Palmer
SELBY, Lord see Gully
SILSOE, Lord see Eve
STERNDALE, Lord see Pickford
STOW HILL, Lord see Soskice
STRATHCARRON, Lord see Mapherson
STUART, Lord see Wortley
SUMNER, Lord see Hamilton
SWINFEN, Lord see Eady
THANKERTON, Lord see Watson
TREVETHIN, Lord see Lawrence
TREVETHIN & OAKSEY, Lord see Lawrence
TRURO, Lord see Wilde
WALSINGHAM, Lord see De Grey
WENSLEYDALE, Lord see Parke
WESTBURY, Lord see Bethell
WRENBURY, Lord see Buckley
WYNFORD, Lord see Best

ABADY, Jacques

s. of Abram Jacques Abady, Manchester, and head of Intelligence Dept. Suakim, Egypt. b. 2nd Oct. 1872. educ. Manchester Gr. Sch.; Birkbeck Inst. Consulting engineer. M.T. July 1905. KC 1935. Bencher 1942. Parliamentary draftsman; Mayor of Westminster 1927-28; JP London; MInst. Mech.E.; gold and silver medallist at Inst. of Gas Engineers. Author of Clauses and Precedents in private bill legislation, and Gas Analyst's Manual. d. 15th April 1964.

ABDY, John Thomas

s. of Col. James Nicholas Abdy, HEICS. b. Madras, 5th July 1822. educ. Proprietary Sch. Kensington; Trinity Hall, Camb. LLB 1847, LLD 1852, Fellow 1850-54. Regius prof. of civil law, Camb. 1854-73; prof. of civil law, Gresham Coll., London 1858-96. I.T. Jan. 1850. Recorder of Bedford 1870-93; Cty. Ct. judge 1871-93; JP Essex and Hertfordshire. Author of works on Roman law, and edited Kent's Commentary on International Law 1866. d. 25th Sept. 1899.

A'BECKETT, Gilbert Abbot

s. of William A'Beckett, Golden Sq., London, barrister. b. 9th Jan. 1811. educ. Westminster. G.I. Jan. 1841. Metrop. magistrate, Southwark 1849-56; proprietor of numerous newspapers and periodicals; dramatic critic of the Weekly Despatch; one of the original staff of Punch; leader writer for Times and Morning Herald. Author of Comic Blackstone 1846, Comic History of England 1847-48, Comic History of Rome 1852; wrote more than fifty plays. Brother of Sir William A'Beckett, CJ Victoria, 1851. d. Boulogne, 30th Aug. 1856.

ACLAND, Sir Reginald Brodie Dyke

s. of Sir Henry Wentworth Acland Bt. KCB, MD (d. 1900). b. 18th May 1856. educ. Winchester; University Coll. Oxf. BA 1878, MA 1883. I.T. June 1881. KC 1904. Bencher 1913. Junior counsel to the Admiralty 1897-1904; Recorder of Shrewsbury 1901-03, of Oxford 1903-24; Judge-Adv. of the Fleet 1904; counsel for G.B. in North Sea Inquiry 1905; member of bar council; member Royal Comm. on Legal Delay 1913; Chmn. Berkshire Quarter Sess. 1916; Chmn. Hospital Saturday Fund 1890-98; Knight 1914; JP Berkshire. d. 18th Feb. 1924.

ACTON, Sir Edward

s. of Henry Morell Acton, Bowden, Cheshire, an editor of Manchester Guardian. b. 6th Nov. 1865. educ. Uppingham; Wadham Coll. Oxf. BA 1889. I.T. April 1891. Bencher 1920. Lecturer in law at Manchester Univ.; Cty. Ct. judge 1917-20; KB judge 1920-34 the first promotion from Cty. Ct. bench; Knight 1920; made reliable decisions which generally stood on appeal.
d. 17th Nov. 1945.

ADAMS, Arthur Robarts

s. of Henry Cadwallader Adams, JP, DL, Anstey Hall, Warwickshire. b. 16th Aug. 1812. educ. Merchant Taylors'; St. John's Coll. Oxf. BCL 1835, DCL 1840, Fellow 1835-77. M.T. Jan. 1839. QC 1869. Bencher 1870. Reader 1875. Recorder of Birmingham 1866-77; Assessor of Chancellor's Ct., Oxford 1871-76. d. 13th Dec. 1877.

ADAMS, John

s. of Simon Adams, Anstey Hall, Warwickshire, barrister. b. 1786. educ. Fotheringay Sch.; St. John's Coll. Camb. 1806. M.T. Nov.

1812. Serjeant 1824; patent of precedence 1834. Chmn. of Middlesex magistrates 1836; the first paid assistant judge at Middlesex Sess. 1844-56. Author of a treatise on ejectment 1812. d. 10th Jan. 1856.

ADDAMS, Jesse

s. of Richard Addams, Rotherhithe, shipbuilder. b. 1st Jan. 1786. educ. Merchant Taylors'; St. John's Coll. Oxf. BCL 1810, DCL 1814. Advocate Doctors' Commons Nov. 1814. QC 1858. Reported cases in Doctors' Commons 1823-26. d. 25th May 1871.

ADDISON, John

s. of John Addison, Preston, barrister (d. 1837). b. 21st April 1791. educ. Blanchard's Sch., Nottingham. Articled to solicitor in Preston. I.T. Feb. 1818. Recorder of Clitheroe 1837-59; Cty. Ct. judge 1847-59; Mayor of Preston 1833 and 1843. Brother of Thomas Batty Addison (I.T. 1808) Recorder of Preston. d. 14th July 1859.

ADDISON, John Edmund Wentworth

s. of Lt. Col. Henry Robert Addison. b. Bruges, 5th Nov. 1838. educ. Trinity Coll. Dublin. BA 1859. I.T. April 1862. QC 1880. Bencher 1883. Recorder of Preston 1874-90; MP Ashton-under-Lyne 1885-95; Cty. Ct. judge 1895-1907; JP Lancashire and Chmn. Quarter Sess. d. 22nd April 1907.

ADKINS, Sir William Ryland Dent

s. of William Adkins JP, Springfield, Northampton. b. 11th May 1862. educ. Mill Hill; University Coll. London B.A.; Balliol Coll. Oxf. 1882. I.T. Jan. 1890. KC 1920. Junior counsel to P.O. on Midland circuit 1908; Recorder of Nottingham 1911-20, of

Birmingham 1920-25; MP Lancashire (Middleton) 1906-23; Chmn. Northamptonshire CC 1920; Chmn. Cty. Councils Assoc.; Knight 1911; DL, JP Northamptonshire. d. 30th Jan. 1925.

ADOLPHUS, Jahn Leycester

s. of John Adolphus, barrister and historian (d. 1845). b. 11th May 1795. educ. Merchant Taylors'; St. John's Coll. Oxf. BA 1815, MA 1819. I.T. June 1822. Bencher 1851. Sol-Genl. Cty. Palatine of Durham; Cty. Ct. judge 1852-62; reported, (with R.V. Barnewall), cases in KB 1830-34, and (with T.F. Ellis), cases in KB and QB 1834-52. d. 24th Dec. 1862.

ADRIAN, Alfred Douglas

s. of Emperor Adrian, Charrington St. London N.W., and Local Govt. Board. b. 1845. educ. London Univ. BA. M.T. June 1869. KC 1904. Asst. Secy. to Local Govt. Bd. 1883-99, legal adviser 1899-1910; CB 1895. d. 18th April 1922.

ALCHIN, Gordon

s. of Alfred Head Alchin MINA, Rust Hall, Kent. b. 1894. educ. Tonbridge; Brasenose Coll. Oxf. BCL, MA. WWI 2nd Lieut. RFA, RFC. M.T. May 1922. Cty. Ct. judge 1940-47. RAF (VR) 1940; AFC. d. 14th May 1947.

ALDERSON, Sir Edward Hall

s. of Robert Alderson, Recorder of Norwich (d. 1833). b. 11th Sept. 1787. educ. Scarning Sch. Norfolk; Bury St. Edmunds' Gr. Sch.; Charterhouse; Caius Coll. Camb. BA 1809, Senior Wrangler and First Chancellor's medallist, MA 1812, Fellow 1809-23. I.T. June 1811. A commr. for amendment of the law 1828; judge of Common

Pleas 1830-34 (on the number of judges being increased from 12 to 15); Knight 1830; Exch. Baron 1834-57; tried Goodman for the Running Rein fraud (Derby won by substituted horse); one of the judges summoned to assist H of L in Cadell v. Palmer (rule on perpetuities); reported, (with R.V. Barnewall), KB cases 1817-22. Father of Edward Pakenham Alderson (I.T. 1851), Recorder of Faversham, and Sir Charles Henry Alderson (1831-1913), Chief Charity Commr. (I.T. 1855). d. 27th Jan. 1857. Notes on his life by Charles Henry Alderson, 1858.

ALEXANDER, David Lindo

s. of Joshua Alexander, London, solicitor. b. 1842. educ. City of London Sch.; Trinity Hall Camb. BA 1864, 30th Wrangler. L.I. June 1866. QC 1892. Bencher 1895. Equity draftsman and conveyancer; JP London; Pres. Jewish Bd. of Deputies. d. 29th April 1922.

ALEXANDER, Sir William John, Bt.

s. of Sir Robert Alexander, Bt. b. 1st April 1797. educ. Trinity Coll. Dublin. BA 1817; Trinity Coll. Camb. BA 1825, MA 1825. L.I. Feb. 1825. QC 1844. Bencher (M.T.) 1845. Reader 1851. Att-Genl. to Prince of Wales 1853; one of the Council of Prince of Wales 1864; 3rd. baronet 1859. d. 31st March 1873.

ALLEN, Sir Carleton Kemp

s. of Rev. William Allen, Sydney, New South Wales. b. 7th Sept. 1887. educ. Newington Coll. Sydney; Sydney Univ.; New Coll. Oxf. BA 1912, MA 1919, DCL 1932. WWI Capt. and Adjt. Middlesex Regt., MC. L.I. May 1919. KC 1945. Hon. Bencher. Law lecturer Univ. Coll. Oxf. 1919; Stowell Civil Law Fellow Univ. Coll. 1920, Dean 1922-26; junior proctor 1924-25; prof. of jurisprudence Oxf. 1929-31; delivered Tagore lectures, Calcutta 1926; Oxf. Secy. of Rhodes Trustees; Warden of Rhodes House 1930-52; Knight 1952; FBA 1944; FRSL 1951; JP Oxford; Hon. LLD Glasgow. Author of

Law in the Making 1927, Bureaucracy Triumphant 1931, Law and Orders 1945, The Queen's Peace 1953, Aspects of Justice 1958, Legal Duties 1931, Law and Disorders 1954, Administrative Jurisdiction 1956. d. 11th Dec. 1966.

ALLEN, Henry George

s. of John Hensleigh Allen MP, Cresselly, Pembrokeshire. b. 29th July 1816. educ. Rugby; Christ Church Oxf. BA 1837, MA 1840. L.I. May 1841. QC 1880. Bencher 1881. Recorder of Andover 1857-72; MP Pembroke 1880-86; DL, JP Haverford West; JP Pembrokeshire and Carmarthenshire; Chmn. Pembrokeshire Quarter Sess. d. 25th Nov. 1908.

ALLEN, Robert

s. of Samuel Allen LLD, FSA., Paris and Bath. b. 1801. Was an actor and schoolmaster. G.I. Nov. 1835. Serjeant 1845; patent of precedence 1850; FSA. d. 17th Feb. 1854.

ALLEN, Sidney Scholefield

s. of Joseph William Allen, Prenton, Birkenhead (d. 1951). b. 3rd Jan. 1898. educ. Birkenhead Inst.; Liverpool Univ. LLB 1922. WWI commissioned in RFA 55th (West Lancashire) Divn. G.I. Jan. 1923. KC 1945. Member of Manx bar; Pres. Merseyside Fabian Socy. 1933; Chmn. Birkenhead branch, League of Nations Union 1934-45; MP Cheshire (Crewe) 1945-73; Hon. Freeman of Crewe 1968; Recorder of Blackburn 1947-69; delegate at annual meetings of Inter-Parliamentary Union, at Rio de Janeiro and other venues 1958-68; ViceChmn. Br. Branch of that Union; Vice-Chmn. legal committee of Council of Europe 1960; Vice-Chmn. Parliamentary Labour Party Commonwealth & Colonies Group from 1964; JP Cheshire. d. 26th March 1974.

ALLEN, Wilfred Baugh

s. of George Baugh Allen DL, JP, Cilrhiw, Pembrokeshire (d. 1898). b. 14th Nov. 1849. educ. Rugby; Trinity Coll. Camb. BA 1873. I.T. June 1882. Cty. Ct. judge 1903-17; JP Pembrokeshire, Nottinghamshire and Yorkshire. d. 10th June 1922.

ALLEN, William

s. of William Shepherd Allen MP, DL, JP, Woodhead Hall, Staffordshire (d. 1915). b. 1870. educ. Rydal Mount, Colwyn Bay; Emmanuel Coll. Camb. 1890. Capt. South Australian Mounted Rifles in South African War 1900-01. I.T. Nov. 1905. KC 1930. Bencher 1937. Head of Agricultural Branch, Min. of Nat. Service 1917-19; Recorder of Ludlow 1928-32, of Newcastle-under-Lyme 1932-45; MP Newcastle-under-Lyme 1892-1900, Stoke-on-Trent (Burslem) 1931-35; member Royal Comm. on Licensing; Charity Commr. 1935-36; Tithe Commr. 1937; JP Staffordshire. d. 11th Sept. 1945.

ALLSEBROOK, George Clarence

s. of William Pole Jones Allsebrook JP, Wollaton, Nottinghamshire (d. 1906). b. 12th Aug. 1877. educ. Nottingham High Sch.; Trinity Coll. Oxf. BA 1915, MA 1919. Mining engineer 1896-1909. I.T. Nov. 1913. WWI Capt. Derbyshire Yeo., later seconded to Min. Of Munitions; Br. arbitrator in Commission Arbitrale des Litiges Miniers au Maroc 1919-21; Cty. Ct. judge 1934-50; member Royal Comm. on safety in coal mines 1935-38; Chm. Cumberland Quarter Sess. 1945-53; JP Cumberland and Northumberland. d. 2nd Dec. 1957.

AMBROSE, William

s. of Richard Ambrose, Chester. b. 1832. educ. privately; London

Univ. 1849. L.I. Jan. 1859 (Cert. of Hon.) QC 1874. Bencher (M.T.) 1881, Reader 1891, Treasurer 1898. MP Harrow 1885-99; member Council of Legal Educ. 1889; Att-Genl. Cty. Palatine of Lancaster 1895-99; Master in Lunacy 1899. Joint author of Ambrose and Ferguson on Land Transfer Act 1898. d. 18th Jan. 1908.

AMOS, Andrew

s. of James Amos, London, Russia merchant. b. India 1791. educ. Eton; Trinity Coll. Camb. BA 1813, 5th Wrangler, MA 1816, Fellow 1815-23. L.I. Nov. 1818. Recorder of Banbury, Nottingham and Oxford; prof. of English law, London Univ. 1829-37; member of first criminal law comm. 1834-43; fourth ordinary member of Supreme Council of India 1837-43; Cty. Ct. judge 1847-52; Downing prof. of laws of England, Camb. 1849-60; JP Hertfordshire. Author of treatise on fixtures 1827. d. 18th April 1860.

AMOS, Sir Percy Maurice Maclardie Sheldon

s. of Prof. Sheldon Amos, appeal judge in Egypt (d. 1886), and g.s. of Andrew Amos, Cty. Ct. judge. b. 15th June 1872. educ. privately; Trinity Coll. Camb. BA 1895, MA 1904. I.T. May 1897. KC 1932. Licencié en droit, Paris Univ. 1899. Judge of Cairo native ct. 1903, native ct. of appeal 1906-12; director, Khedivial Sch. of Law 1913-15; with Min. of Munitions 1915-17; judicial adviser to Egyptian Govt. 1917-25; member of Lord Balfour's mission to U.S.A. 1917; Quain prof. of comparative law, London 1932-37; chief Br. delegate to Intern. Committee of experts on private aerial law 1933-40; KBE 1922; Hon. LLD Lausanne; Grand Cordon, Order of the Nile. Author of The English Constitution 1930, Introduction to French law (with F.P. Walton) 1935, The American Constitution 1938. d. 10th June 1940.

AMPHLETT, Richard Holmden

s. of Samuel Holmden Amphlett, Birmingham, surgeon (d. 1857), and nephew of Amphlett, Baron of Exch. b. 24th April 1847. educ. Eton; Trinity Coll. Camb. BA 1870, MA 1873. L.I. June 1871. QC 1896. Bencher 1903. Recorder of Worcester 1891-1908; Cty. Ct. judge 1908-25; Vice-Chmn. Worcestershire Quarter Sess. 1892; JP Worcestershire and Warwickshire. d. 23rd Nov. 1925.

AMPHLETT, Sir Richard Paul

s. of Rev. Richard Holmden Amphlett, Hadsor, Worcestershire (d. 1842). b. 24th May 1809. educ. Brewood Gr. Sch.; St. Peter's Coll. Camb. BA 1831, 6th Wrangler, MA 1834, Fellow 1832-40, Hon. Fellow 1882. L.I. June 1834. QC 1858. Bencher 1858. Practised in VCs' Cts.; MP East Worcester 1868-74; Exch. Baron 1874-76; Knight 1874; LJ 1876-77; PC 1876; Pres. of Legal Educ. Assoc. 1872; Vice-Chmn. Worcestershire Quarter Sess.; DL, JP. d. 7th Dec. 1883.

ANDERDON, Thomas Oliver

s. of John Procter Anderdon, Beech House, Ringwood, Hampshire. L.I. Nov. 1822. QC 1841. Bencher 1841. Equity draftsman and conveyancer. d. 31st July 1856, age 70.

ANDERSON, Charles Henry

s. of Rev. Richard Anderson, Bedale, Yorkshire. b. 22nd April 1838. I.T. Jan. 1867. QC 1885. Lecturer on common law, Inc. Law Socy. 1867-69; MP Elgin and Nairn 1886-89. Author of digest of common and criminal law, conveyancing, equity, and bankruptcy 1865. d. Johannesburg, 25th Aug. 1889.

ANDERSON, James

s. of David Anderson, Bellfield, Edinburghshire. b. 1802. educ. Edin. High Sch.; Edin. Univ. Scottish bar 1828. M.T. June 1839. QC 1851. Bencher 1852, Reader 1855, Treasurer 1860, Senior Bencher 1880-88. Examr. to Inns of Ct. 1864-72; member Council of Legal Educ. 1872-87; examr. in Ct. of Chancery 1873-76; Official Referee, High Ct., 1876-86. d. 22nd June 1888.

ANDREWS, Biggs

s. of Joseph Andrews, Mildenhall, Suffolk. b. 1794. M.T. Nov. 1819. KC 1837. Bencher 1837, Reader 1840, Treasurer 1845. Commr. in Bankruptcy 1858-69. d. 28th April 1880.

ANSTIE, James

s. of James Overbury Anstie, Devizes. b. 1836. educ. London Univ. BA 1856. L.I. Nov. 1859 (Cert. of Hon.). QC 1882. Bencher 1886. Reporter for Inc. Council of Law Reporting 1865; examr. in common law and evidence, London Univ. 1881-83; a Charity Commr. 1884. d. 30th Sept. 1924.

ARCHER, Francis Kentdray

s. of R.K. Archer, South Australia. b. 1882. educ. St. Peter's, Adelaide; London Univ. LLB. L.I. May 1912 (Cert. of Hon.). KC 1923. Bencher 1929. Equity draftsman and conveyancer; member of bar council 1934-37; Cty. Ct. judge 1937-54. d. 23rd June 1962.

ARCHIBALD, Sir Thomas Dickson

s. of Samuel George Williams Archibald LLD, Speaker of the House of Assembly, Nova Scotia. b. Truro, Nova Scotia 1817. educ. Picton Presbyterian Coll. Attorney and barrister, Nova Scotia 1837. Special pleader in London 1844-52. M.T. Nov. 1852. Drafted framework for Petition of Right Act (Bovill's Act) 1860; junior counsel to Treasury 1868-72; assisted Serjeant Petersdorff with his Abridgment of the Common Law; QB judge 1872-75; Knight 1873; judge of Common Pleas 1875-76. Brother of Sir Edward Mortimer Archibald (1810-84) Adv-Genl. Newfoundland. Father of Sir William Frederick Alphonse Archibald (I.T. 1874), Master in KB Divn. d. 18th Oct. 1876.

ARMSTRONG, John Warnford Scobell

s. of John Scobell Armstrong, Nancealverne, nr. Penzance. b. 1st March 1877. educ. abroad. I.T. July 1905. WWI with Directorate of Mil. Intell. (postal censorship). Asst. legal adviser Foreign Office 1919-20; legal adviser Reparation Claims Dept., Bd. of Trade 1920-22; CBE 1920; Cty. Ct. judge 1940-50; Chmn. Cornwall Quarter Sess. 1945-53; JP Cornwall; Officier d'Académie 1920. Author of War and Treaty Legislation 1914-21, The Taxation of Profits 1937, Yesterday (autobiog) 1955. d. 2nd March 1960.

ARMSTRONG, Robert Baynes

s. of John Armstrong, Lancaster, merchant. b. 1785. educ. Clitheroe and Sedbergh Schs.; St. John's Coll. Camb. BA 1807, MA 1810, Fellow 1809-17. I.T. June 1814. QC 1840. Bencher 1840, Reader 1851, Treasurer 1852. Recorder of Hull 1836-37, of Leeds 1837-39, of Manchester and Bolton 1839-65; MP Lancaster 1848-53. d. 15th Jan. 1869.

ARNOLD, Thomas James

s. of Samuel James Arnold, theatre manager. b. 1803. educ. St. Paul's; Göttingen Univ. L.I. Nov. 1829. Commr. in Bankruptcy, Liverpool; metrop. magistrate 1847, finally at Westminster 1851-77; FSA 1869. Author of treatise on law of municipal corporations 1852. d. 20th May 1877.

ASHER, Alexander

s. of Rev. William Asher DD, Inveravon, Banffshire. b. 1835. educ. Elgin Acad.; King's Coll. Aberdeen; Edin. Univ.; Hon. LLD Aberdeen 1883, Hon. LLD Edin. 1891. Scottish bar 1861; advocate-depute 1870; QC 1881; Sol-Genl. for Scotland 1881-85, 1886, 1892-94; Dean of Faculty of Advocates 1895; MP Elgin Burghs 1881-1905; DL Edin. d. 5th Aug. 1905.

ASHLEY, Anthony John

s. of 6th Earl of Shaftesbury. b. 21st Dec. 1808. educ. Eton; Christ Church Oxf. BA 1829. I.T. June 1836. QC 1866. Conveyancer; MP Gatton 1831-32; DL, JP Essex. d. 1st Jan. 1867.

ASHTON, Arthur Jacob

s. of Walter Ashton, Warrington, Lancashire. b. 4th Feb. 1855. educ. Manchester Gr. Sch.; Balliol Coll. Oxf. BA 1879. I.T. Jan. 1881. KC 1906. Bencher 1914. Recorder of Manchester 1914; judge of Appeal, Isle of Man 1921-25. d. 23rd March 1925.

ASKE, Sir Robert William, Bt.

s. of Edward Aske, Hull. b. 29th Dec. 1872. educ. London Univ. LLD 1900. Solicitor 1894, practised in Hull. M.T. Nov. 1914 (Cert. of Hon.). KC 1934. Bencher 1940. WWI Lt. Col. commdg. 1/5 Battn. East Yorkshire Regt., TD. Dep. Sheriff of Hull 1906-08; MP Newcastle-on-Tyne (East) 1923-24, 1929-45; Knight 1911; Baronet 1922; JP Surrey. Author of the Law of Customs of Trade. d. 10th March 1954.

ASKWITH, George Ranken (Lord Askwith)

s. of Gen. William Harrison Askwith RA (d. 1897). b. 17th Feb. 1861. educ. Marlborough; Brasenose Coll. Oxf. BA 1884, MA 1887, Hon. DCL 1912, Hon. Fellow 1919. I.T. and M.T. Nov. 1886. KC 1908. Counsel to HM Commrs. of Works; High Steward of Manor of the Savoy 1899; Comptroller-Genl. Commercial Statistical and Labour Dept., Bd. of Trade 1909-11; Chmn. Fair Wages Advisory Committee 1909; Chief Industrial Commr. 1911-19; Chmn. Govt. Arbitration Committee 1915-17; Chmn. Royal Socy. of Arts 1922-24; Pres. British Science Guild 1922-24; Chmn. Malta Royal Comm. 1931; Chmn. parliamentary delegation to Bermuda 1932; Pres. Instit. of Arbitrators 1933-41; Hon. Freeman City of London; Mayor of St. Ives, Hunts. 1913; CB 1909, KCB 1911, Baron Askwith of St. Ives 1919; Order of the Crown of Belgium, and Legion of Honour. Author of Industrial Problems and Disputes 1920, British Taverns, their history and laws 1928, Lord James of Hereford 1930. d. 2nd June 1942.

ASPINALL, Butler Cole

s. of Butler Cole Aspinall, Att-Genl., Melbourne, Victoria (d. 1875). b. 1861. educ. London Univ. BA 1881. M.T. Nov. 1884. QC 1899. Bencher 1907, Reader 1919, Treasurer 1929. Practised mainly in arbitrations; counsel for Bd. of Trade in Titanic Inquiry 1912; Chmn. Naval Prize Procedure Committee 1913, and of Release of Cargoes Committee 1914; represented Canadian Pacific Ry. at inquiry into loss of Empress of Ireland 1914, and Cunard Co. at inquiry into loss of Lusitania 1915; Wreck Commr. on loss of Egypt 1922, and Vestris 1929; Chmn. Br. and American Joint Arbitration Bd. 1920. d. 15th Nov. 1935.

ASPINALL, James Perronet

s. of John Bridge Aspinall QC b. 18th July 1844. educ. St. Cuthbert's Coll., Durham; Ushaw Coll; Trinity Coll. Camb. London Univ. BA

1864. M.T. June 1867. QC 1892. Bencher 1891. Member of bar council 1896-98; leader at Admiralty bar; reporter for Law Times in Privy Council 1872-82, and in Ct. of Appeal 1882-92; drew up rules for govt. to be used in Prize Cts. of England and colonies; reported maritime law cases 1870-99; JP Suffolk. d. 29th Nov. 1898.

ASPINALL, John Bridge

s. of Rev. James Aspinall, Althorpe, Lincolnshire. b. 12th Dec. 1818. educ. Rugby. M.T. Nov. 1841. QC 1864. Bencher 1864, Reader 1868, Treasurer 1877. Dep. Recorder of Liverpool 1857, Recorder 1862-86; Att-Genl. Cty. Palatine of Durham 1872-86; Pres. Royal Comm. of inquiry into corrupt election practices in City of Gloucester 1880-81. Uncle of Butler Cole Aspinall QC. d. 6th Feb. 1886.

ASPLAND, Lindsey Middleton

s. of Robert Brook Aspland MA, Unitarian pastor, Hackney (d. 1869). b. 9th April 1843. educ. London Univ. MA 1863, LLD 1867. M.T. Jan. 1868 (Cert. of Hon.). QC 1886. Member of bar committee 1883-91; member Council of Univ. Coll. London 1874-80. d. 6th May 1891.

ASQUITH, Cyril (Lord Asquith)

s. of Earl of Oxford and Asquith. b. 5th Feb. 1890. educ. Summer Fields; Winchester; Balliol Coll. Oxf. BA 1914, MA 1920, Hon. Fellow 1947, Fellow of Magdalen Coll. 1913-20. I.T. April 1920. KC 1936. Bencher. WWI Capt. Queen's Westminster Rifles and Min. of Munitions. Asst. Reader in common law to Council of Legal Educ. 1925-38, member of Council 1938-53; appointed to Law Revision Committee 1934; Recorder of Salisbury 1937; KB judge 1938-46; Knight 1938; attached to General Claims Trib. 1939; Chmn. Advisory Committee on Aliens 1940, Comm. on Higher

Educ. in Colonies 1943-44, Comm. on Equal Pay 1944-46; LJ 1946-51; PC 1946; declined Lord Chancellorship 1951; L of A 1951-54; Baron 1951; Chmn. Political Honours (Scrutiny Committee) 1952. Author of Trade Union Law for Laymen 1927, Outlines of Constitutional Law (with D. Chalmers); wrote biography of father (with J.A. Spender) 1932. d. 24th Aug. 1954.

ASQUITH, Herbert Henry (Lord Oxford and Asquith)

s. of Joseph Dixon Asquith, Croft House, Morley, Yorkshire. b. 12th Sept. 1852. educ. City of London Sch.; Balliol Coll. Oxf. BA 1874, Fellow 1874-82. L.I. June 1876. QC 1890. Made his name as junior counsel for Charles Stewart Parnell 1888. MP East Fife 1886-1918, 1920-24; Home Secy. 1892-95; Chanc. of Exchequer 1905-08; Prime Minister 1908-16; obtained passage of Parliament Act 1911, abolishing H of L power of veto; formed coalition cabinet with Unionists 1915; forced out by Lloyd George 1916. PC 1892; KG 1925; Earl 1925. d. 15th Feb. 1928.

ASTBURY, Sir John Meir

s. of Frederick James Astbury JP, Hilton Park, Prestwich, Lancashire, chartered accountant (d. 1901). b. 14th June 1860. educ. Manchester Gr. Sch.; Trinity Coll. Oxf. BA 1882, Vinerian scholar 1884, BCL and MA 1886, Hon. Fellow 1923. M.T. June 1884. QC 1895. Bencher 1903, Reader 1915, Treasurer 1925. Practised in Manchester until 1895; specialised in patent cases; MP South West Lancashire (Southport) 1906-10; Chancery judge 1913-29; PC 1929; Knight 1913; judge in bankruptcy 1921; his judgment that General Strike of 1926 was illegal, became material factor in its collapse. d. 21st Aug. 1939.

ASTON, James Jones

s. of Benjamin Richard Aston, London, coal merchant. b. 12th Dec. 1822. M.T. Nov. 1846. QC Cty. Palatine of Lancaster 1867 (the last appointed). QC 1880. Assessor to Sheriff of Lancashire. Author of Chancery Practice of Cty. Palatine of Lancaster 1852. d. 17th Jan. 1885.

ASTON, Theodore (also known as Theophilus)

s. of Thomas Aston, Handsworth, Staffordshire, schoolmaster. bapt. 21st Jan. 1827. educ. St. John's Coll. Camb. BA 1847, MA 1850. L.I. Nov. 1853. QC 1872. Bencher 1872. Specialist in patent law. d. 24th Oct. 1910.

ATCHERLEY, David Francis

s. of David Francis Jones, Cymmau, Flint, solicitor. b. 13th June 1783. educ. King's Sch. Chester; Gr. Schs. at Ludlow and Oswestry. L.I. July 1810. Serjeant 1827; patent of precedence 1830. Att-Genl. Cties. Palatine of Lancaster and Durham 1835; Recorder of Chester 1814-20; auxiliary judge Norfolk, Western and Oxford circuits 1842; FRS; FSA; assumed name of Atcherley 1834. d. 6th July 1845.

ATHERLEY-JONES, Llewellyn Archer

s. of Ernest Charles Jones, Chartist leader, poet and barrister, Broughton, Manchester (d. 1869). b. 1851. educ. Brasenose Coll. Oxf. BA 1874. I.T. April 1875. QC 1896. Bencher 1907, Treasurer 1927. Recorder of Newcastle-on-Tyne 1906-29; judge of Burgess and Non-Burgess Cts. of Record, Newcastle 1909; MP Durham (North West) 1885-1914; judge of City of London Ct. 1914-29; JP Berkshire. Author of The Miners' Handbook to the Coal Mines Regulation Act 1887, Commerce in War, A Treatise on International Law, The Law of Children and Young Persons, Looking Back, 1925. d. 15th June 1929.

ATHERTON, Sir William

s. of Rev. William Atherton, Battle Bridge, Middlesex. b. Oct. 1806. Special pleader 1832-39. I.T. Nov. 1839. QC 1851. Bencher 1851. Leader on Northern circuit. QC Cty. Palatine of Lancaster 1851-60; MP Durham 1852-64; Judge-Adv. of the Fleet and counsel to the Admiralty 1854-59; Sol-Genl. 1859; Att-Genl. 1861-63; Knight 1860. d. 22nd Jan. 1864.

ATKIN, James Richard (Lord Atkin)

s. of Robert Travers Atkin, Fernhill, Cork (formerly MLA in Queensland). b. Brisbane, 28th Nov. 1867. educ. Christ Coll. Brecon; Magdalen Coll. Oxf. BA 1889. G.I. Jan. 1891. KC 1906. Bencher 1906, Treasurer 1914, Vice-Treasurer 1917. KB judge 1913-19; Knight 1913; judge of Munitions Tribs. Appeal Ct. 1916-19; Chmn. War Cabinet Committee on Women in Industry 1918-19; member committee on Br. and Foreign legal procedure 1918-19; Chmn. Council of Legal Educ. 1919-34; LJ 1919-28; PC 1919; Chmn. LC's Committee on Crime and Insanity 1922-23; L of A 1928-44; Baron Atkin of Aberdovey 1928; Pres. Medico-Legal Socy. 1923-27; FBA 1938; govr. of Charterhouse; member Councils of Bradfield Coll. and Univ. Coll. of Wales. d. 25th June 1944. Biog. by Geoffrey Lewis, 1983.

ATKINSON, Sir Cyril

s. of Leonard William Atkinson, Altrincham, Cheshire. b. 9th May 1874. educ. privately; London Univ. LLD 1899. LI. June 1897. KC 1913. Bencher 1920, Treasurer 1942. Equity draftsman and conveyancer; Referee, 1921-24, under Safeguarding of Industries Act 1921; MP Cheshire (Altrincham) 1924-33; KB judge 1933-48; Knight 1933; member Church Assembly 1950-55. Father of Sir Fenton Atkinson, QB judge 1968-71. d. 29th Jan. 1967.

ATKINSON, Sir Edward Tindal

s. of Henry Tindal Atkinson, Cty. Ct. judge. b. 1847. educ. Felsted. M.T. June 1870 (Cert. of Hon.). QC 1886. Bencher 1892, Reader 1902, Treasurer 1913. Presided at Worcester Election Comm. 1906; Recorder of Leeds 1897-1919; Att-Genl. Cty. Palatine of Durham 1901-15, Chancellor 1915-30; Ry. and Canal Comm. 1919-30; Knight 1926. d. 2nd Sept. 1930.

ATKINSON, George

s. of John Atkinson, Long Marton, Westmoreland. b. 24th Nov. 1809. educ. Charterhouse; Queen's Coll. Oxf. BA 1830. I. T. June 1840. Serjeant 1854; Treasurer 1868. Acting judge of High Ct. Bombay 1869. Author of treatise on sheriff law 1839, and other works; editor of Shipping Laws of the British Empire 1854. d. Bombay, 8th Nov. 1891.

ATKINSON, Henry Tindal

s. of George J. Atkinson, London. b. 1818. M.T. Jan. 1844. Serjeant 1864. Cty. Ct. judge 1870-88. d. 4th Feb. 1890.

ATKINSON, Henry Tindal

s. of Henry Tindal Atkinson, Cty. Ct. judge. b. 1841. educ. Felsted Sch. M.T. Jan. 1865. Bencher 1896, Reader 1908. Cty. Ct. judge 1901-18; JP Hertfordshire. Father of Sir Edward Hale Tindal Atkinson (1878-1957), Dir. of Public Prosecutions. d. 14th March 1918.

ATKINSON, John (Lord Atkinson)

s. of Edward Atkinson MD, JP, Glenwilliam Castle, co. Limerick.
b. 13th Dec. 1844. educ. Royal Belfast Academical Inst.; Queen's
Coll. Galway LLB 1865. Irish bar 1865. QC 1880. Bencher 1885.
Practised on Munster circuit. I.T. Jan. 1890. Bencher 1906.
Sol-Genl. Ireland 1889-92, Att-Genl. 1892, and 1895-1905; MP
North Londonderry 1895-1905; PC (Ireland) 1892; L of A 1905-28;
Baron and PC 1905. Father of Cecil Thomas Atkinson (I.T. 1912),
puisne judge Bihar and Orissa 1915. d. 13th March 1932.

AUSTIN, Charles

s. of Jonathan Austin, Creeting Mill, Suffolk, Govt. contractor. b.
26th Mar. 1799. educ. Bury St. Edmund's Gr. Sch.; Jesus Coll.
Camb. BA 1824, MA 1827. M.T. May 1827. QC 1841. Recorder
of Hastings 1836-39, of Rye 1837-39; leading parliamentary
counsel; High Steward of Ipswich; Chmn. East Suffolk Quarter Sess;
retired from practice 1848; a brilliant conversationalist.
d. 21st Dec. 1874.

AUSTIN, James Valentine

s. of Rev. John Valentine Austin, St. Nicholas Olave, City of
London. b. 26th June 1850. educ. Tavistock Gr. Sch.; Trinity Coll.
Oxf. BA 1872. I.T. Jan. 1876. Cty. Ct. judge 1892-1914; member
of various arbitration and trade conciliation committees; JP
Somerset. d. 3rd June 1914.

AVORY, Sir Horace Edmund

s. of Henry Avory, solicitor, clerk of arraigns at Central Criminal
Ct. (d. 1881). b. 31st Aug. 1851. educ. King's Coll. London; Fellow
1912; Corpus Christi Coll. Camb. LLB 1874; captain of Boat Club;
Hon. Fellow and Hon. LLD 1911. I.T. Jan 1875. KC 1901. Bencher
1908, Treasurer 1929. Junior counsel to Treasury at Central

Criminal Ct. 1889, senior counsel 1899; Recorder of Kingston-upon-Thames 1902-10; Commr. Of Assize, South Eastern circuit 1909, Northern circuit 1910; KB judge and knighted 1910; senior judge 1923-35; PC 1932; famous as criminal lawyer and judge. d. 13th June 1935. Biog. By Gordon Lang 1935.

BACON, Francis Henry

s. of Bacon, V-C. b. 7th Oct. 1831. educ. King's Coll. Sch.; Balliol Coll. Oxf. BA 1854, MA 1856. L.I. June 1856. Secy. to Giffard LJ 1868-70, and to Bacon V-C. 1870; Cty. Ct. judge 1878-1911. d. 10th June 1911.

BACON, Sir James

s. of James Bacon, barrister (d. 1815). b. 11th Feb. 1798. Newspaper journalist. G.I. may 1827, L.I. 1845. QC 1846. Bencher 1846, Treasurer 1869. Equity draftsman and conveyancer. Under-secy. and secy. of causes to MR 1859; leader in V-C Stuart's Ct.; Commr. in Bankrupcy for London District 1868-69; chief judge in bankruptcy 1870-83, when office abolished; V-C 1870-75; Knight 1871; Chancery judge 1875-86; PC 1886. d. 1st June 1895.

BADCOCK, Isaac

s. of Henry Badcock JP, Wheatleigh, Taunton, Somerset, banker (d. 1888). b. 1842. educ. Fordington Vicarage, Dorchester; Trinity Coll. Oxf. BA 1863, MA 1867. M.T. April 1867. QC 1899. Bencher 1895. d. 15th Dec. 1906.

BADEN-POWELL, Henry Warington Smyth

s. of Rev. Prof. Baden Powell FRS, Oxford and Langton, Kent (d. 1860). b. 3rd Feb. 1847. Served at sea 1860-73. I.T. June 1876. QC

1897. Practised mainly in admiralty cts.; Lieut. RNR. Author of works on naval subjects. d. 24th April 1921.

BAGGALLAY, Claude

s. of Baggallay LJ. b. 26th Oct. 1853. educ. Blackheath Sch.; King's Coll. London; Trinity Hall Camb. LLB 1878, LLM 1881. L.I. July 1878. QC 1897. Bencher 1904. d. 13th July 1906.

BAGGALLAY, Ernest

s. of Baggallay LJ. b. 11th July 1850. educ Marlborough; Caius Coll. Camb. BA 1872, MA 1875. L.I. April 1873. Counsel to P.O. 1877-87; MP Brixton 1885-87; metrop. magistrate 1887, finally at Lambeth 1910-14; JP London and Home Counties. d. 9th Sept. 1931.

BAGGALLAY, Sir Richard

s. of Richard Baggallay, Kingthorpe House, Upper Tooting, merchant (d. 1870). b. 13th May 1816. educ. Hambledon, Hants. (Rev. J.L. Barton); Caius Coll. Camb. BA 1839, 14th Wrangler, MA 1842, Fellow 1842-47, Hon. Fellow 1880-88. L.I. June 1843. QC 1861. Bencher 1861, Treasurer 1875. Lecturer on conveyancing at Inc. Law Socy. 1854-56; practised in Rolls Ct.; counsel to Camb. Univ. 1869; MP Hereford 1865-68, Mid-Surrey 1870-75; Sol-Genl. 1868 and 1874; Knight 1868; Att-Genl. 1874-75; piloted Judicature Act 1875; LJ 1875-85; PC 1875; member of Merchant Taylors' Co. 1839, Warden 1853, Master 1863; JP Surrey and Herefordshire. Father of Richard Baggallay (L.I. 1872). d. 13th Nov. 1888.

BAGSHAWE, Henry Ridgard

s. of Sir William Chambers Bagshawe, Sheffield, physician (d. 1832). b. 1st Nov. 1799. educ. Oakham and Richmond Gr. Schs.;

Trinity Coll. Camb. BA 1821, MA 1824. M.T. Nov. 1825. QC 1854. Bencher 1855, Reader 1858, Treasurer 1864. Cty. Ct. judge 1861-70; JP Glamorganshire, Camarthenshire, Pembrokeshire and Cardiganshire. d. 16th May 1870.

BAGSHAWE, William Henry Gunning

s. of Henry Ridgard Bagshawe QC. b. 18th Aug. 1825. educ. Univ. Coll. Sch.; St. Mary's Coll. Oscott; London Univ BA 1843. M.T. Nov. 1848. QC 1874. Bencher 1875, Reader 1885, Treasurer 1894. Joint examr. in equity and real property at London Univ.; Cty. Ct. judge 1881-1901; JP Northamptonshire, Bedfordshire and Huntingdonshire. d. 4th Nov. 1901.

BAILEY, William Frederick

s. of John Bailey, Blagdon, Somerset. b. 1820. M.T. Nov 1845. QC 1880. Bencher 1882. d. 20th Dec. 1887.

BAILHACHE, Sir Clement Meacher

s. of Rev. Clement Bailhache, secretary of Baptist Missionary Socy. (d. 1878). b. 2nd Nov. 1856. educ. City of London Sch.; London Univ. LLB 1877. Solicitor 1877, practised in Newport, Monmouthshire. M.T. Nov. 1889. KC 1908. Bencher 1913. Specialised in commercial law; KB judge 1912-24; Knight 1912; dealt with many cases in commercial ct. during WWI; pres, of committee to inquire into efficiency of planes supplied to RFC, and the administration of the Corps 1916. d. 8th Sept. 1924.

BAILY, John

s. of John Baily, London, FRCS. b. April 1805. educ. Merchant Taylors'; St. John's Coll. Camb. BA 1828, 2nd Wrangler, MA 1831,

Fellow 1830. L.I. May 1832. QC 1851. Bencher 1851. Leader in V-C. Kindersley's Ct.; counsel to Camb. Univ. 1857-67. d. 19th June 1877.

BAIN, Edwin Sandys

s. of Lt. Col. William Bain, Livelands, nr. Stirling. b. 1804. educ. in Twickenham, Middx.; Trinity Coll. Camb. BA 1820, MA 1824. M.T. June 1829. Serjeant 1845. d. 30th Dec. 1874.

BAINES, Mathew Talbot

s. of Edward Baines MP, Leeds. b. 17th Feb. 1799. educ. Richmond Gr. Sch.; Trinity Coll. Camb. BA 1820. I.T. May 1825. QC 1841. Bencher 1841, Reader 1854, Treasurer 1855. Recorder of Hull 1837-47; MP Hull 1847-52, Leeds 1852-59; Pres. Of Poor Law Board 1849-52 and 1853-55; PC 1849; Chan. of Duchy of Lancaster 1855-58. d. 22nd Jan. 1860.

BAIRSTOW, Arthur William

s. of James Bairstow, Halifax, woollen merchant. b. 24th Sept. 1855. educ. Huddersfield Coll.; University Coll. London; Trinity Hall Camb. BA 1878. I.T. Nov. 1878. KC 1908. Bencher 1915, Treasurer 1937. Sol-Genl Cty. Palatine of Durham 1915-18; Recorder of Scarborough 1917-18; Cty. Ct. judge 1918-28. d. 28th Mar. 1943.

BAKER, Sir George Sherston, Bt.

s. of Henry Sherston Baker, barrister. b. 19th May 1846. M.T. and L.I. Nov. 1871. Recorder of Helston 1886-89, of Barnstaple and Bideford 1889-1923; examr. to Inns of Ct. 1895-1901; Cty. Ct. judge 1901-23; Associate of Instit. De Droit International 1879, member 1921; standing counsel to Hon. Socy. of the Baronetage 1898-1901;

JP Lincolnshire; succeeded cousin 1877, as 4th baronet. Editor of Law Mag. and Review 1895-98; author of treatises on municipal and international law. d. 15th March 1923.

BALFOUR, John Blair (Lord Kinross of Glasclune)

s. of Rev. Peter Balfour, Clackmannan. b. 11th July 1837. educ. Edin. Acad.; Edin. Univ. Hon. LLD 1882. Scottish bar 1861; MP Clackmannan 1880-99; Sol-Genl. for Scotland 1880; Lord Advocate 1881-85, 1886 and 1892-95; Lord Pres. of Ct. of Session 1899; QC 1880; Dean of Faculty of Advocates 1885 and 1889; PC 1883; Baron 1902. d. 22nd Jan. 1905.

BALGUY, John

s. of John Balguy, Darwent Hall, Derbyshire, barrister. b. 14th Sept. 1782. educ. St. John's Coll. Camb. M.T. June 1805. KC 1833. Bencher 1833, Reader 1837, Treasurer 1840. Recorder of Derby 1830-58; Commr. in Bankruptcy, Birmingham 1842-58; Chmn. Derbyshire Quarter Sess. 1837; DL, JP Derbyshire. d. 16th Dec. 1858.

BALGUY, John

s. of John Balguy, QC. b. 16th Dec. 1821. educ. Repton; Eton; Merton Coll. Oxf. BA 1844. M.T. May 1848. Metrop. magistrate Greenwich and Woolwich 1874-86; JP Derbyshire, Staffordshire, Kent. d. 5th Dec. 1886.

BALLANTINE, William

s. of William Ballantine, Fulham, London, merchant. Lt. Reay Fencible Infantry 1798-1802. Lt. North Lincoln Militia 1803-1807. I.T. Feb. 1813. Metrop. magistrate Thames St. 1821-48; JP Middlesex. d. 14th Dec. 1852, age 73.

BALLANTINE, William

s. of William Ballantine, metrop. magistrate. b. 3rd Jan. 1812. educ.
St. Paul's. I.T. June 1834. Hon. Bencher 1878. Serjeant 1856; patent
of precedence 1864. Treasurer of Serjeant's Inn 1872-77. Counsel
for pros. of Franz Muller 1864, for pros. of Madame Rachel 1868;
counsel for Tichborne claimant 1871; the original Mr. Chaffanbrass
in Trollope's "Orley Farm". Author of Some Experiences of a
Barrister's Life 1882. Father of William Henry Walter Ballantine
MP (I.T. 1871). d. 9th Jan. 1887.

BANKES, George

s. of Henry Bankes MP, Kingston Hall, Dorset (d. 1834). b. 1788.
educ. Westminster; Trinity Hall Camb. LLB 1812, Fellow 1814-22.
I.T. April 1813. MP Corfe Castle 1816-23, 1826-32, Dorset 1841-
56; Commr. in Bankruptcy 1822; Recorder of Weymouth 1823;
Secy. to Bd. of Control 1829-30, Commr. of Bd. 1830; junior lord
of Treasury 1830; Judge Adv-Genl. 1852; Cursitor Baron of the
Exch. 1824-56, when office abolished; PC 1852. d. 6th July 1856.

BANKES, Sir John Eldon

s. of John Scott Bankes DL, JP, Soughton Hall, Flintshire (d. 1894).
b. 17th April 1854. educ. Eton; University Coll. Oxf. BA 1877, Hon.
Fellow. I.T. Nov. 1878. KC 1901. Bencher 1899, Treasurer 1923.
Chan. of diocese of St. Asaph 1908-10; KB judge 1910-15; Knight
1910; LJ 1915-27; PC 1915; GCB 1928; Chmn. Royal Comm. on
Traffic in Arms 1935; Chmn. Flintshire Quarter Sess. for thirty-three
years; JP Flintshire; MA Lambeth; Hon. LLD Wales 1921,
Manchester 1923; Fellow of Eton Coll. Father of Robert Wynne
Bankes CBE (I.T. 1911). d. 31st Dec. 1946.

BANKES, Ralph Vincent

s. of John Scott Bankes DL, JP, Soughton Hall, Flintshire. (d.1894). b. 17th Mar. 1867. educ. Winchester; University Coll. Oxf. BA 1889. I.T. June 1890. KC 1910. Metrop. magistrate, South Western, 1917-21. Father of Ralph George Scott Bankes (I.T. 1924). d. 25th Oct. 1921.

BANKS, Sir Reginald Mitchell

s. of Sir William Mitchell Banks, MD, LLD, FRCS, Liverpool (d. 1904). b. 1880. educ. Rugby; Christ Church Oxf. BA 1903. I.T. July 1905. KC 1923. Bencher 1930. WW1 Lieut. 1/5 Gurkha Rifles. Recorder of Wigan 1928-34; MP Swindon 1922-29 and 1931-34; Cty. Ct. judge 1934-40; Knight 1928. d. 9th July 1940.

BARBER, Charles Chapman

Cty. Ct. judge Feb. 1874, resigned March 1874 to resume practice.

BARBER, Charles Henry

s. of John Barber, barrister. b. 9th July 1782. educ. Charterhouse. G.I. July 1810. KC 1834. d. 22nd Aug. 1849.

BARBER, William

s. of Joseph Barber, Brighouse, Yorkshire. b. 12th Nov. 1833. educ. Worcester Coll. Oxf. BA 1856, MA 1859; Fellow of Radley Coll. 1856-60. L.I. Jan. 1862. QC 1882. Bencher 1885. Prof. of law of real and personal property, Council of Legal Educ. 1880-85; Cty. Ct. judge 1889-92. An editor of Dart's law of vendors and purchasers of real estate 1871-88. d. 29th Mar. 1892.

BARKER, John Edward

s. of Edward Barker, Bakewell, Derbyshire. b. 9th April 1832. educ. Eton; Exeter Coll. Oxf. BA 1855, MA 1857. I.T. Nov. 1862. QC 1891. Recorder of Leeds 1880-96; Chmn. Derbyshire Quarter Sess. 1894-97; JP Derbyshire. d. 20th Aug. 1912.

BARKER, John Henry

s. of Thomas Barker, Ashford Hall, Derbyshire. b. 1806. educ. Christ Church Oxf. BA 1829, MA 1834. L.I. May 1836. Metrop. magistrate 1860, finally at Clerkenwell 1863-74. d. 28th Jan. 1876.

BARNARD, Sir Henry William

s. of William Tyndall Barnard KC. b. 18th April 1891. educ. Wellington; Merton Coll. Oxf. BA 1912, MA 1920. WWI Capt. 5th Battn. Royal West Kent Regt. G.I. Jan. 1913. KC 1939. Bencher 1939, Treasurer 1953. P D and A judge 1944-59; Knight 1944; judge of the Cinque Ports 1967. d. 20th July 1981.

BARNARD, William Tyndall

s. of William Tyndall Barnard, South Hornsey, London, barrister. b. 1855. educ. Aldenham Sch. G.I. Jan. 1879. KC 1905. Bencher 1896, Treasurer 1905. P D and A Registrar 1915-23. d. 30th Sept 1923.

BARNES, John Gorell (Lord Gorell)

s. of Henry Barnes, Liverpool, shipowner (d. 1865). b. 16th May 1848. educ. privately; Peterhouse Camb. BA 1868, MA 1874, Hon. Fellow 1898, Hon. LLD 1898. Articled to solicitor in Liverpool. I.T. Jan. 1876. QC 1888. Bencher 1896. Special Pleader; succeeded to large junior practice of Sir J.C. Mathew 1881; P D and A judge 1892-1905; Knight 1892; Pres. P D and A Divn. 1905-09; PC 1905;

27

Baron 1909; Chmn. Cty. Cts. Committee 1909, Copyright Committee (leading to Act of 1911), Royal Comm. on divorce 1909; Chmn. East Suffolk Quarter Sess. Father of Henry Gorell Barnes, 2nd Baron DSO (I.T. 1906) and Ronald Gorell Barnes, 3rd Baron, CBE, MC (I.T. 1909). d. 22nd April 1913.

BARRATT, John Arthur

s. of J.A. Barratt. b. 15th Nov. 1857. educ. Coll. of City of New York, MA; Columbia Univ. LLB 1880. At New York bar, U.S. Supreme Ct. 1880-98. I.T. Jan. 1901. KC 1923. Member American Bar Assoc.; Vice-Pres. Intern. Law. Assoc.; Vice-Pres. Intern. Law Confce., The Hague 1921, Vienna 1926; a founder of The Pilgrims, and Vice-Pres. 1925; Officer of the Order of the Crown of Belgium. Author of English Law for Americans, American company law, Jurisdiction in Divorce, Monroe Doctrine. d. 1st March 1944.

BARRINGTON-WARD, Frederick Temple

s. of Rev. Canon Mark James Barrington-Ward DD, Duloe, Cornwall. b. 30th Aug. 1880. educ. Westminster; Hertford Coll. Oxf. BA 1902, MA 1905, BCL 1905. Vinerian Law Scholar 1904; Fellow, All Souls Coll. 1904-11. L.I. May 1905. KC 1919. Bencher 1923. Recorder of Hythe 1914-28, of Chichester 1928-30; metrop. magistrate, Lambeth 1930-38; Chmn. West Sussex Quarter Sess. 1928-30; Capt. City of London Vol. Regt. d. 22nd Feb. 1938.

BARROW, Francis

s. of Rev. Francis Barrow, Cranbrook. b. 15th Mar. 1821. educ. Wadham Coll. Oxf. BA 1841, MA 1844. L.I. Nov. 1844. Recorder of Rochester 1867-88; Cty. Ct. judge 1876-83; FRAS 1870, Treasurer 1878-84; JP Kent. d. 13th May 1888.

BARRY, Sir Patrick Redmond Joseph

s. of Rt.Hon. Redmond Barry, LC Ireland (d. 1913). b. 4th Sept.
1898. educ. Downside; RMC; Balliol Coll. Oxf. BA 1921. WWI
Lieut. and acting adjutant Irish Guards, MC. I.T. June 1922. KC
1938. Bencher 1946. Practised in Manchester. WWII Capt. Irish
Guards and Lt.Col. General Staff. Recorder of Oldham 1942-50;
judge of Appeal, Isle of Man 1946-50; KB judge 1950-66; Knight
1950; Chmn. Advisory Council on the Treatment of Offenders 1958;
member of Radcliffe Trib. of Inquiry into the Vassall spying case
1962. d. 6th May 1972.

BARSTOW, Thomas Irwin

s. of Thomas S. Barstow, Fulford, Yorkshire. b. 10th Nov. 1818.
educ. Shrewsbury; Trinity,Coll. Camb. BA 1842, MA 1845. I.T.
June 1845. Commr. for inquiry into corrupt election practices at
Lancaster 1866, at Beverley 1869; member Royal Comm. of inquiry
into trade union outrages at Sheffield 1867, at Manchester 1868;
metrop. magistrate 1874, finally at Dalston 1888-89; JP Middlesex
and Home Counties. d. 21st July 1889.

BARTLEY-DENNISS, Sir Edmund Robert

s. of Edmund Pinnock Denniss, Chelsea, London. b. 9th April 1854.
educ. Christ's Hosp.; Hertford Coll. Oxf. 1874; Sidney Sussex Coll.
Camb. Assumed additional name of Bartley 1922. In legacy duty
office, Somerset House. M.T. Nov. 1879. KC 1922. MP Oldham
1911-22; member Commercial Committee of H. of C.; member
London Ct. of Arbitration, and Council of London Chamber of
Commerce; Hon. Treas. Air League of Br. Empire; Pres. Harrow
and Hendon Conservative Assocs.; Knight 1922; Freeman, City of
London. Cousin of George Hamson Denniss CBE (M.T. 1890). d.
20th March 1931.

BARTON, Wilfrid Alexander

s. of Sir Edmund Barton, prime minister of Australia (d.1920). b. 9th Oct. 1880. educ. Sydney Gr. Sch.; Sydney Univ.; Magdalen Coll. Oxf. (Rhodes Scholar) BA 1906. G.I. Jan. 1908 (Cert. of Hon.); I.T. 1928. KC 1937. WWI Capt. King's Liverpool Regt, and at GHQ (despatches). d. 18th March 1953.

BATESON, Sir Alexander Dingwall

s. of William Gandy Bateson, Allerton, Liverpool, solicitor. b. 1866. educ. Rugby; Trinity Coll. Oxf. BA 1888. I.T. Jan. 1891. KC 1910. Bencher 1920. Junior counsel to Admiralty 1909-10; P D and A judge 1925-35; Knight 1925. Father of Sir Dingwall Latham Bateson (1898-1967), Pres. of Law Society. d. 11th Jan. 1935.

BATESON, Owen Latham

s. of Bateson J. b. 24th July 1900. educ. Rugby; Wadham Coll. Oxf. I.T. May 1925. KC 1945. Junior counsel to Admiralty 1936. Brother of Sir Dingwall Latham Bateson (1898-1967), Pres. of Law Socy. d. (accident at home) 24th March 1947.

BATT, Francis Raleigh

s. of Henry Ellis Batt, Heavitree, Exeter. b. 9th June 1890. educ. Mount Radford Sch. Exeter; Wales Univ. LLM. Solicitor 1911. G.I. Jan. 1917. Asst. lecturer in law Univ. Coll. Aberystwyth 1911-13; lecturer in law Sheffield Univ. 1913-19; prof of commercial law Liverpool Univ. 1919-42; Dean of Law Faculty Liverpool Univ. 1925-42, hon. prof. of common law 1942-45; Pres. Socy. of Public Teachers of Law 1939-46; Asst. Recorder of Liverpool 1940-42; Cty. Ct. judge 1942-61; Dep. Chmn. Lancashire Quarter Sess.; JP Cheshire and Lancashire. Author of Law of Master and Servant 1928, Law of Negotiable Instruments 1931; edited Chalmer's Bills of Exchange. d. 25th March 1961.

BATTEN, James Winterbotham

s. of John Batten, Cheltenham, merchant. b. 3rd June 1831. educ. Millhill Gr. Sch. Articled to solicitor in Stroud. I.T. Jan. 1872. QC 1899. Brother of James Brend Batten, solicitor and parliamentary agent. d. 3rd June 1901.

BATTEN, Lauriston Leonard

s. of Rayner Winterbotham Batten FRCP, Gloucester. b. 26th July 1863. educ. Amersham Hall, Oxfordshire; Trinity Coll. Camb. BA and LLB 1884. I.T. Nov. 1886. KC 1905. Bencher 1914. Special pleader. WWI Capt. Royal Gloucestershire Hussars Yeo. and Major RAF 1918. Specialised in admiralty cases; JP Gloucestershire. d. 31st July 1934.

BAYFORD, Robert Augustus

s. of Augustus Frederick Bayford LLD, Prin. Registrar, Ct. of Probate. b. 13th March 1838. educ. Kensington Gr. Sch.; Trinity Hall Camb. BA 1860, 36th Wrangler, MA 1867; cricket blue. I.T. June 1863. QC 1885. Bencher 1891, Treasurer 1912. Registrar of Probate and Matrimonial Cts.; JP Hampshire. d. 24th Aug. 1922.

BAYFORD, Robert Frederic

s. of Robert Augustus Bayford KC. b. 24th Sept. 1871. educ. Eton; Trinity Hall. Camb. BA 1895. I.T. Nov. 1895. KC 1919. Bencher 1925. Member of bar council 1923; Recorder of Portsmouth 1929-44; Dep. Chmn. Hampshire Quarter Sess. 1938-47; JP Hampshire; OBE 1920, for services as Commander, Metrop. Special Constabulary. d. 5th June 1951.

BAYLEY, Francis

s. of Sir John Bayley Bt. KB judge, and Exch. Baron. b. 6th Feb. 1803. educ. Eton; Trinity Coll. Camb. M.T. June 1827. Cty. Ct. judge 1849-93; FSA. Author of treatise on fines and recoveries 1828; edited father's Summary of the law of Bills of Exchange 1830. d. 4th May 1893.

BAYLIS, Thomas Henry

s. of Edward Baylis, Harrow. b. 22nd June 1817. educ. Harrow; Brasenose Coll. Oxf. BA 1838, MA 1841. Special pleader 1840-56. I.T. Jan. 1856. QC 1875. Bencher 1877, Reader 1898, Treasurer 1899. Judge of Liverpool Ct. of Passage 1876-1903; Lt Col. retd. 18th Middlesex Rifle Vol.; VD. Author of The Temple Church and Chapel of St. Anne 1893, and a treatise on law relating to domestic servants 1857. Father of Thomas Erskine Baylis, barrister 1874. d. 4th Oct 1908.

BAZALGETTE, Evelyn

s. of Louis Bazalgette, Chiswick, Middlesex. b. 1802. educ. Balliol Coll. Oxf. BA 1823, MA 1825. L.I. May 1827. QC 1858. Bencher 1858, Treasurer 1877. d. 21st July 1888.

BEADON, William Frederick

s. of Richard Beadon, Fitzhead, Somerset. b. 1808. educ. Eton; St John's Coll. Camb. BA 1829, MA 1833. I.T. May 1835. Registrar of Dioc. of Bath and Wells; metrop. magistrate 1847, finally at Marlborough St. 1856-62. d. 30th March 1862.

BEALE, Sir William Phipson, Bt.

s. of William John Beale, Bryntirion, Merionethshire, solicitor. b. 29th Oct 1839. educ. in Heidelberg and Paris. L.I. Jan. 1867. QC 1888. Bencher 1892. MP South Ayrshire 1906-18; Baronet 1912; JP Ayrshire; FGS; FCS. d. 13th April 1922.

BEALES, Edmund

s. of Samuel Pickering Beales, Newnham, Cambridge, merchant. b. 3rd July 1803. educ. Eton; Trinity Coll. Camb. BA 1825, MA 1828. M.T. June 1830. Equity draftsman and conveyancer; Cty. Ct. judge 1870-81; Pres. National League for independence of Poland 1863; Pres. Reform League 1865-69. Political author. d. 26th June 1881.

BEAMES, John

s. of John Beames, Clifton, Gloucestershire. L.I. May 1811. KC 1832. Bencher 1832. Commr. in Lunacy 1821-23; Commr. in Bankruptcy 1823-30; DL Hamp-shire. Author of works on equity and bankruptcy. d. 17th Oct 1853, age 72.

BEASLEY, William Cole

s. of Capt. William Beasley, Surfleet, Lincolnshire. b. 5th July 1816. educ. Boston and Fotheringay Gr. Schs.; Lincoln Coll. Oxf. BA 1836, MA 1838. I.T. April 1853. Bencher 1876. QC 1880. Senior counsel to HM Customs; Treasury counsel at Central Criminal Ct. 1859-77; Recorder of Warwick 1874, of Kingston-upon-Hull 1874-87. d. 10th Jan. 1888.

BEAUMONT, Sir John William Fisher

s. of Edward Beaumont, barrister. b. 4th Sept. 1877. educ.

Winchester; Pembroke Coll. Camb. BA 1899, MA 1904, Hon. Fellow 1946. L.I. May 1901. KC 1930. Bencher 1943, Treasurer 1963. WWI Lieut. RGA. Equity draftsman and conveyancer; CJ Bombay 1930-43; acting judge of Federal Ct. of India 1942-43; Knight 1931; PC 1944, and member of judicial committee; Master of Cutlers' Co. 1951-52. d. 8th Feb. 1974.

BEAZLEY, Sir Hugh Loveday

s. of Robert Clover Beazley, Liverpool (d. 1925). b. 16th Oct. 1880. educ. Cheltenham Coll.; Oriel Coll. Oxf. BA 1901, MA 1932. I.T. July 1905. Bencher 1941. WWI Capt. Kings' Liverpool Regt., (despatches). Member of bar council 1924-27; Cty. Ct. judge 1927-37; judge of Mayor's and City of London Ct. 1937-42; Common Serjeant 1942-53; Knight 1953; Dep. Chmn. Hertford Petty Sess.; JP Hertfordshire. d. 17th July 1964.

BECKETT, Edmund (Lord Grimthorpe)

s. of Sir Edmund Beckett, Bt. b. 12th May 1816. educ. Doncaster Gr. Sch.; Eton; Trinity Coll. Camb. BA 1838, 30th Wrangler, MA 1841, LLD 1863. L.I. Nov. 1841. QC 1854. Bencher 1854, Treasurer 1876. Equity draftsman and conveyancer; leader of parliamentary bar; retired from practice 1880; designer of clocks, including the one for the Houses of Parliament 1859; Pres. of Horological Inst. 1868; involved in matters of ecclesiastical architecture; Chan. and Vicar-Genl. of York 1877-1900; dropped his original name of Denison in 1872, when his father succeeded to the baronetcy; Baron 1886. d. 29th April 1905. Much litigation concerning his will.

BEDWELL, Francis Alfred

s. of Francis Robert Bedwell, Chancery registrar. b. Ist March 1828. educ. Clapham Gr. Sch.; St John's Coll. Camb. BA 1851, 21st Wrangler, MA 1854. L.I. April 1855. Equity draftsman and conveyancer; Cty. Ct. judge 1874-98; JP Yorkshire East Riding. d.

27th June 1898.

BELLASIS, Edward

s. of Rev. George Bellasis, Basildon, Berkshire. b. 14th Oct. 1800. educ. Christ's Hospital. I.T. July 1824. In parliamentary practice 1836-66; Serjeant 1844; Steward of manors of Duke of Norfolk in Norfolk and Suffolk 1863; one of the three Commrs. who reported upon the College of Arms 1870. d. Hyères, France, 24th Jan. 1873.

BENEY, Frederick William

s. of William Augustus Beney JP, Beckenham, Kent (d. 1924). b. 9th March 1884. educ. Mill Hill; New Coll. Oxf. BA 1906, MA 1909. I.T. Nov. 1909. KC 1943. Bencher 1948. Legal asst. in War Office 1914-20; Recorder of Rye 1942-44, of Norwich 1944-59; member departmental committee on Alternative Remedies 1944-46; Chmn. departmental committee on Nat. Insce. against Industrial Diseases 1953-54; Commr. of Assize South Eastern circuit 1959-61;, Western circuit 1961; Commr. at Central Criminal Ct. 1959-64; BBC broadcasting 1961-66; member Appeal Trib. Assoc. of Br. Travel Agents; CBE 1962. d. 5th April 1986.

BENJAMIN, Judah Philip

s. of Philip Benjamin. b. St Croix, West Indies, 1811. educ. Yale Coll. Connecticut. New Orleans bar 1832. Counsellor of Supreme Ct. New Orleans 1848; Senator for Louisiana 1852, expelled 1861; Att-Genl. of Southern Confederacy 1861; Acting Secy. of War 1861-62; Secy. of State 1862-65. L.I. June 1866. QC Cty. Palatine of Lancaster 1869. QC 1872. Bencher 1875. Had substantial Privy Council practice. Author of Digest of decisions of Supreme Ct. of New Orleans 1834, and treatise on law of sale of personal property 1868. d. Paris, 6th May 1884.

BENNETT, Sir Charles Alan

s. of Charles Hudson Bennett, Cooden Beach, Bexhill-on-Sea, solicitor. b. 9th May 1877. educ. Winchester. Employed in father's office 1894-97. L.I. Jan. 1900. KC 1923. Bencher 1928. Chancery judge 1929-43; Knight 1929. d. 20th Dec. 1943.

BENNETT, Eugene Paul

s. of Charles Bennett, Stroud. b. 4th June 1892. educ. Marling Sch. Stroud. WWI Capt. Worcestershire Regt, MC 1915, VC 1916 (despatches). M.T. June 1923. Metrop. magistrate 1935, finally at Marlborough St. 1946-61; pros. counsel to PO on South Eastern circuit 1931-35. d. Italy, 4th April 1970.

BENNETT, Sir Henry Curtis

s. of Rev. George Peter Bennett, Kelvedon, Essex. b. 11th May 1846. educ. in Kelvedon. M.T. June 1870. Metrop. magistrate 1886, finally at Bow St. 1908-13; chief magistrate and knighted 1913; JP Middlesex. and Home Counties. d. 2nd June 1913.

BENSON, Ralph Augustus

s. of Moses George Benson DL, JP, Lutwyche Hall, Much Wenlock (d. 1871). b. 11th Oct. 1828. educ. Winchester; Christ Church Oxf. BA 1850, MA 1864. I.T. Jan. 1854. Recorder of Shrewsbury 1866-67; Secy. to Royal Comm. on pollution of rivers 1867; metrop. magistrate 1867, finally at Southwark 1869-79; JP Shropshire. d. 11th March 1886.

BENSON, Williaim Denman

s. of Gen. Henry Roxby Benson CB (d. 1892). b. 21st March 1848. educ. Eton; Balliol Coll. Oxf. BA 1872, LLD; rowed for Univ. I.T. June 1874. Counsel to PO; Cty. Ct. judge 1907-19; JP

Glamorganshire. d. 19th Feb. 1919.

BERE, Montagu

s. of Montagu Baker Bere, barrister. b. 9th July 1824. educ. Cheam Sch.; Balliol Coll. Oxf. BA 1846. I.T. May 1850. QC 1869. Bencher 1870. Recorder of Penzance 1857-62, of Southampton 1862-70, of Bristol 1870-72; Cty. Ct. judge 1872-87; Chmn. Devon Quarter Sess. 1879-87; JP Cornwall and Devon. d. 19th Oct. 1887.

BERESFORD, Cecil Hugh Wriothesley

s. of William Beresford, Cty. Ct. judge. educ. Eton; Trinity Coll. Camb. BA 1875. M.T. June 1875. Cty. Ct. judge 1891-1912; JP Somerset. d. 14th Feb. 1912, age 61.

BERESFORD, Tristram de la Poer

s. of Cecil Hugh Wriothesley Beresford, Cty. Ct. judge. b. 29th Sept 1887. educ. United Services Coll. Westward Ho; Trinity Hall Camb. 1906. M.T. June 1909. KC 1936. Bencher 1943. WWI Capt RFC and RAF. Recorder of Folkestone 1939-62; member of departmental committee for revision of Army and Air Force courts-martial 1938; a chmn. for examination of Germans and Austrians for internment 1939-40; Chmn. West Kent Quarter Sess. 1946, East Kent Quarter Sess. 1947; member of bar council 1948; Chmn. Special Grants Committee, Min. of Pensions and Nat Insce. 1954-58; KStJ. d. 23rd Sept 1962.

BERESFORD, William

s. of Rev. Gilbert Beresford, Anglestone, Leicestershire. b. 19th Feb. 1817. educ. Rugby; King's Coll. London; St John's Coll. Camb. BA 1842. Special pleader 1843-58. M.T. Nov. 1858. Dep. judge at Whitechapel Cty. Ct.; Cty. Ct. judge 1877-91. d. 30th Jan. 1892.

BERRYMAN, Montague Levander

s. of Frederic John Berryman, Great Chesterford, Essex. solicitor (d. 1939). b. 21st July 1899. educ. Westminster. WWI 2nd Lieut. 3rd Battn. Royal Sussex Regt. and RAF. M.T. and I.T. Jan. 1921. KC 1945. Bencher (M.T.) 1953-66, Hon. Bencher 1966. Recorder of Gravesend 1945-47, of Dover 1947-62; member of bar council; Dep. Chmn. Hertfordshire Quarter Sess. 1950-59, Chmn. 1959-63; Chmn. Kent. Quarter Sess. 1962-71; Hon. Freeman, Borough of Dover 1963; JP Hertfordshire and Kent. Edited Elliott's Workmen's Compensation Acts. d. 25th June 1974.

BESLEY, Edward Thomas Edmonds

s. of Thomas Besley, prop. of Devonshire Chronicle and Exeter News. b. 11th Aug 1826. educ. Exeter Free Gr. Sch. Reporter for Morning Chronicle 1851-54, Times 1854-64. M.T. June 1859. QC 1894. Recorder of Bury St Edmunds 1892-1901; director of Lambeth Water Works and several Gas companies. d. 18th Sept. 1901.

BEST, William Draper (Lord Wynford)

s. of Thomas Best, Haselbury Plucknett, Somerset. b. 13th Dec. 1767. educ. in Crewkerne; Wadham Coll. Oxf. 1782. M.T. Nov. 1789. Serjeant 1800. MP Petersfield 1802, Bridport 1812; one of the managers on the impeachment of Lord Melville for malversation 1806; Recorder of Guildford 1806; Sol-Genl. to Prince of Wales 1813, Att-Genl. 1816; CJ of Chester 1818; KB judge 1818; Knight 1819; PC 1829; CJ of Common Pleas 1824-29; Baron Wynford 1829; a deputy speaker of H of L; strongly opposed the Reform Bill; DCL Oxf. 1834. Father of William Samuel Best (I.T. 1823), MP, 2nd Baron. d. 3rd March 1845.

BETHELL, Richard (Lord Westbury)

s. of Richard Bethell MD, Bradford-on-Avon, Wiltshire (d. 1831). b. 30th June 1800. educ. Bristol Gr. Sch.; Wadham Coll. Oxf. BA 1818, MA 1822, Vinerian law scholar, Fellow 1822-25, Hon. DCL 1860; a tutor in the univ. M.T. Nov. 1823. QC 1840. Bencher 1840, Reader 1844, Treasurer 1848. Leader of chancery bar; counsel to Oxf. Univ. 1846; MP Aylesbury 1851-59, Wolverhampton 1859-61; V-C of Cty. Palatine of Lancaster 1851-63; Sol-Genl. 1852-56; Knight 1853; first Pres. of Juridical Socy. 1855; Att-Genl. 1856-58 and 1859-61; introduced and carried Divorce Bill 1857, and Bankruptcy Bill 1861; declined judgeship in Probate and Divorce Ct. 1857; LC 1861-65; responsible for Statute Law Revision Acts 1861 and 1863; resigned following vote of censure in H of C, who regarded him as inattentive to public interests; Baron and PC 1861; continued to sit on appeals in H of L and Privy Council; Act of 1862 to facilitate proof of title and transfer of land, known by his name; an arbitrator in winding-up of European Assce. Socy. 1872. Father of Richard Augustus Bethell (M.T. 1853), 2nd Baron, bankruptcy registrar, Slingsby Bethell CB (M.T. 1857), clerk of committees H of L, and Walter John Bethell (M.T. 1868). d. 20th July 1873. Biog. by T. A. Nash, 2 vols. 1888.

BEVAN, Charles Dacres

s. of Lt. Col. Charles Bevan, Bath. b. 7th Nov. 1805. educ. Charterhouse; Balliol. Coll. Oxf. BA 1827, MA 1829. M.T. May 1830. Recorder of Dartmouth 1845-55, of Truro 1848-49, of Falmouth 1850-56, of Helston 1850-56, of Penzance 1855-57; Cty. Ct. judge 1857-72. Capt. 13th Duke of Cornwall Artillery Vol. d. 24th June 1872.

BEVAN, Stuart James

s. of William James Butler Bevan, Regent's Park, London, merchant. b. 31st March 1872. educ. St Paul's; Trinity Coll. Camb. BA and

LLB 1894. M.T. Nov. 1895. KC 1919. Bencher 1925. Lieut. Duke of Cornwall's Regt. 1890, Capt. 1896. Recorder of Bristol 1932-35; member of bar council 1934; MP Holborn 1928-35. d. 25th Oct 1935.

BEVIR, Edward James

s. of George Bevir, Cirencester, solicitor. b. 5th July 1817. educ. St Paul's; St. Mary Hall Oxf. BA 1837, MA 1840. LI. Nov. 1840. QC 1877. Bencher 1881. Chmn. Law Reversionary Interest Socy. 1884-96. d. 24th July 1896.

BEYFUS, Gilbert Hugh

s. of Alfred Beyfus, 69 Lincoln's Inn Fields, solicitor (d. 1914). b. 19th July 1885. educ. Harrow; Trinity Coll. Oxf. BA 1907. I.T. Jan. 1908 (Cert of Hon.) KC 1933. Bencher 1940. WWI Capt 3rd Battn (Res.) Duke of Wellington's Regt. (prisoner of war, despatches). Dep. Chmn. West Sussex Quarter Sess. 1950. Famous as a jury advocate in civil cases; known as "The Old Fox"; biography under that title by Iain Adamson 1963. d. 30th Oct 1960.

BICKERSTETH, Henry (Lord Langdale)

s. of Henry Bickersteth, Kirkby Lonsdale, Westmoreland, surgeon and apothecary (d. 1821). b. 18th June 1783. educ. Free Gr. Sch., Kirkby Lonsdale. Apprenticed to father 1797; studied medicine in London and Edin.; medical attendant to Earl of Oxford 1803. Caius Coll. Camb. BA 1808, Senior Wrangler, MA 1811, Senior Fellow 1814. I.T. Nov. 1811. KC 1827. Bencher 1827, Reader 1835, Treasurer 1836. Confined his practice to the Rolls Ct; refused to accept chief judgeship in bankruptcy, and Exch. Barony; declined appointment as Sol-Genl. 1834; MR 1835-51; Baron Langdale and PC 1835; in his capacity as MR, known as "the father of Record Reform." Declined to be LC, but was head of comm. for custody of

Great Seal 1850; head of registration and conveyancing comm.; frequently presided in Judicial Committee of PC; a trustee of Br. Museum. d. 18th April 1851. Memoirs by T.D. Hardy, 2 vols. 1852.

BIDDER, George Parker

s. of George Parker Bidder, civil engineer. b. 18th Aug. 1836. educ. King's Coll. Sch.; Edin. Univ.; Trinity Coll. Camb. BA 1858, 7th Wrangler, MA 1861. L.I. Nov. 1860. QC 1874. Bencher 1876. Leader at parliamentary bar; Secy. to Royal comm. on the wreck of the Megaera steamship 1871-72; a cryptographer; AICE 1861; FRAS 1868. d. 1st Feb. 1896.

BIGHAM, John Charles (Lord Mersey)

s. of John Bigham, Rodney St, Liverpool, merchant and shipowner (d. 1880). b. 3rd Aug. 1840. educ. Liverpool Inst; London Univ.; Berlin; Paris. M.T. June 1870. QC 1883. Bencher 1886, Reader 1896, Treasurer 1907. MP Liverpool (Exchange) 1895-97; QB judge 1897-1909; Knight 1897; chief judge in bankruptcy 1904; Pres. Ry. and Canal Comm. 1904-08; Commr. for revision of martial law sentences in South Africa 1902; Pres. P D and A Divn. 1909-10; PC 1909; Baron 1910; Commr. to inquire into loss of Titanic 1912, Empress of Ireland 1914, Lusitania 1915; presided at appeals from Prize Ct. during WWI; Pres. Intern. Confce. on Safety of Life at Sea 1913; Pres. Admiralty Transport Arbitration Bd. 1914; member of Civil Service Comm. 1914; Viscount 1916. Father of Sir Frank Trevor Roger Bigham, Dep. Commr. Metrop. Police (M.T. 1901). d. 3rd Sept 1929.

BINGHAM, Peregrine

s. of Rev. Peregrine Bingham, Edmundesham, Dourest. b. 1788. educ. Winchester; Magdalen Coll. Oxf. BA 1810. M.T. Nov. 1818. Recorder of Southampton 1830-40; of Portsmouth 1838-40; metrop. magistrate 1841, finally at Gt. Marlborough St. 1846-60; reported cases in Common Pleas and other Cts. 1824-41. Author of works on judgments and executions, and infancy and coverture. d. 1st Nov. 1864.

BINGLEY, Henry Campbell Alchorne

s. of Rev. Robert Mildred Bingley, JP, Brayesworth, Eye. b. 7th March 1862. educ. Charterhouse; Trinity Coll. Camb. BA 1884, LLM 1890. I.T. April 1888. Asst. Secy. Parnell Comm. 1889; Secy. to bar council 1896-1917; Commr. for Suffolk under Military Service (Civil Liabilities) committee 1916; metrop. magistrate 1917, finally at Marylebone 1926-34; JP London and Home Counties. d. 15th May 1939.

BIRCH, Thomas Jacob

s. of Wyrley Birch, Wretham Hall, near Thetford (d. 1866). b. 15th Oct. 1806. educ. Eton; Brasenose Coll. Oxf. BA 1828, MA 1831. I.T. Nov. 1831. Recorder of Thetford 1839-66; Cty. Ct. judge 1847-68; JP Norfolk and Mayo. Brother of Henry William Birch, solicitor. d. Mayo, 26th April 1868.

BIRKBECK, William Lloyd

s. of George Birkbeck, London, MD, FRS. b. 6th March 1807. educ. Charterhouse; Trinity Coll. Camb. BA 1830, 9th Wrangler, MA 1833, Fellow 1830-40. I.T. Nov. 1833. QC 1886. Downing prof. of Laws of England, Cambridge 1860-85; Reader in equity to Council of Legal Educ. 1852-73; examr. in civil law, Cambridge 1873-74; Master of Downing College 1885-88. Author of Historical Sketch of the distribution of land in England with suggestions for some improvement in the law 1885. d. 25th May 1888.

BIRKETT, William Norman (Lord Birkett)

s. of Thomas Birkett, Ulverston, Lancashire, draper (d. 1913). b. 6th Sept. 1883. educ. in Ulverston and Barrow-in-Furness; Emmanuel Coll. Camb. BA and LLB 1909, MA, Hon. Fellow 1946, Hon. LLD 1958. Apprenticed in father's business. I.T. June 1913. KC 1924. Bencher, Treasurer 1956. Medically unfit for service in WWI. Practised in Birmingham 1913-20; joined chambers of Sir Edward Marshall Hall 1920; MP East Nottingham 1923-24, and 1929-31; an outstanding advocate, particularly in criminal defences; Chmn. of Committee on Abortion 1937, of Home Office Committee regarding interned persons 1939; KB judge 1941-50; Knight 1941; alternate Br. judge at Nuremberg War Trials 1945; PC 1947; LJ 1950-56; Chmn. Phone Tapping Inquiry 1957; Baron 1958; Chmn. Buckinghamshire Quarter Sess. 1946-58; JP Buckinghamshire; Pres. of The Pilgrims 1958; Pres. National Book League; Chmn. Ct. of London Univ. 1946; four times Master of Curriers' Co.; Hon. LLD Liverpool, Hull, Birmingham. d. 10th Feb. 1962. Biogs. by D. Bardens 1962, H. Montgomery Hyde 1964.

BIRON, Sir Henry Chartres

s. of Robert John Biron, QC. b. 10th Jan. 1863. educ. Eton; Trinity Coll. Camb. BA 1884. L.I. Nov. 1886. Bencher 1930. Treasury counsel at London Sess; counsel to P.O. at Central Criminal Ct.; metrop. magistrate 1906, finally at Bow St. 1920-33; chief magistrate and knighted 1920. Author of Without Prejudice 1936, and Biron and Chalmers on Extradition. d. 28th Jan. 1940.

BIRON, Robert John

s. of Rev. Edwin Biron, Lympne, Kent. b. 25th March 1830. educ. King's Sch. Canterbury; Corpus Christi Camb. BA 1853. L.I. June 1854. QC 1882. Bencher 1886. Commr. for municipal election petitions 1869-83; Recorder of Hythe 1859-83, of Deal 1872-83, of Sandwich 1872-83; leading counsel for PO on South Eastern circuit

1883; metrop. magistrate, Lambeth, 1883-95; JP Middlesex and Home Counties. d. 18th March 1895.

BIRRELL, Augustine

s. of Rev. Charles Morton Birrell, Wavertree, Liverpool. b. 19th Jan. 1850. educ. Amersham Hall Sch.; Trinity Hall Camb. Hon. Fellow 1899. I.T. Nov. 1875. QC 1895. Bencher 1903. Quain prof. of law, Univ. Coll. London 1896-99; MP West Fife 1889-1900, North Bristol 1906-18; Pres. Bd. of Educ. 1905-07; Chief Secy. for Ireland 1907-16; established National Univ. of Ireland 1908; resigned after 1916 rebellion. Successful essayist. d. 20th Nov. 1933.

BISHOP, John

s. of Charles P. Bishop, Doly-garreg, S. Wales, solicitor. b. Nov. 1828. educ. in Bridgenorth; Caius Coll. Camb. BA 1852. I.T. April 1853. Stip. magistrate Merthyr Tydfil 1876-86; Cty. Ct. judge 1886-1910; DL, JP Carmarthenshire; JP Glamorganshire, Brecknockshire, Pembrokeshire, Cardiganshire. d. 27th April 1913.

BLACKBURN, Colin (Lord Blackburn)

s. of John Blackburn, Killearn, Stirlingshire (d. 1840). b. 18th May 1813. educ. Eton; Trinity Coll. Camb. BA 1835, 8th Wrangler, MA 1838. I.T. Nov. 1838. Hon. Bencher 1877. Able, but relatively unknown, when appointed QB judge 1859; Knight 1860; L of A 1876-86; a supreme exponent of the common law; PC 1876; Chmn. of Royal Comm. on draft criminal code 1878-79; Baron Blackburn of Killearn 1876; Hon. LLD Edin. 1870.; reported (with T.F. Ellis) cases in QB and Exch. Chamber 1852-58. Author of a treatise on the effect of the contract of sale on the legal rights of property and possession in goods, wares, and merchandise 1845. Lost the sight of one eye early in his career. d. 8th Jan. 1896.

BLAINE, Delabere Roberton

s. of Delabere Pritchard Blaine, Woodbridge, Suffolk. Solicitor in London. M.T. May 1846. Cty. Ct. judge 1871. FRGS 1854. Author of Laws of Artistic copyright and their defects 1853, Suggestions on the Copyright Bill 1861. d. 13th Dec. 1871, age 64.

BLAIR, James Kennedy

s. of James Blair, Weatfield, Belfast. b. 9th Dec. 1807. educ. Belfast Academical Inst.; Edin. Univ. L.I. Jan. 1835. Judge of Salford Ct. of Record; Cty. Ct. judge 1857-72; JP Lancaster. d. 1st Oct 1879.

BLANSHARD, William

s. of Richard Blanshard, Northallerton. b. 29th June 1802. educ. in Durham. Served as midshipman on "Carnatic" in East India Co's navy 1817-19. I.T. May 1828. Recorder of Ripon 1830-35; advocate in all the cts. of Archbishop of Canterbury, who appointed him MA 1839; Recorder of Doncaster 1857-70; Cty. Ct. judge 1863-71; JP Northumberland and Yorkshire West Riding. Author of treatise on statutes of limitation 1826. d. 28th Nov. 1872.

BLENNERHASSETT, Rowland Ponsonby

s. of Richard Francis Blennerhassett, Kells Park, Kerry (d. 1854). b. 22nd July 1850. educ. Christ Church Oxf. 1869. I.T. May 1878. QC 1894. Bencher 1903. MP Kerry 1872-85; JP Kerry. d. 7th April 1913.

BLISS, Henry

s. of Jonathan Bliss, New Brunswick, N. America. b. in New Brunswick. I.T. Feb. 1827. QC 1850. Bencher 1850, Reader 1863,

Treasurer 1864. Agent in England for Nova Scotia. Author of State Trials 1838, and other works. d. 31st July 1873, age 76.

BODEN, George

s. of John Boden, Edmaston Lodge, Derbyshire. b. 22nd Jan. 1816. educ. Rugby; Trinity Coll. Camb. BA 1841, MA 1845. I.T. April 1841. QC 1862. Bencher 1862, Reader 1876, Treasurer 1876. Recorder of Stamford 1855-59, of Derby 1859-80. d. 16th Feb. 1880.

BOMPAS, Henry Mason

s. of Serjeant Charles Carpenter Bompas (d. 1844). b. 6th April 1836. educ. Amersham Hall Sch.; University Coll. London LLB; St John's Coll. Camb. BA 1858,5th Wrangler, MA 1862. I.T. Jan. 1863. QC 1877. Bencher 1881, Treasurer 1905. Reporter in Ct. of Common Pleas 1865-75; Commr. to inquire into corrupt election practices at Knaresborough 1878; Recorder of Poole 1882, of Plymouth and Devonport 1884; Commr. of Assize, South Wales circuit 1891; Cty. Ct. judge 1896-1909; JP Yorkshire West Riding. Father of Cecil Henry Bompas 1868-1956, ICS, (I.T. 1889). d. 5th March 1909.

BOND, William

s. of Rev. William Bond, Tyneham, Dorset (d. 1852). educ. Wadham Coll. Oxf. BA 1821, MA 1824. I.T. Nov. 1824. Recorder of Poole 1834, of Wareham 1836; metrop. magistrate, Westminster 1842-46. Brother of Thomas Bond (L.I. 1833), Recorder of Wareham. d. 11th Oct. 1846, age 47.

BONSEY, Henry Dawes

s. of William Henry Bonsey, Slough, Buckinghamshire. b. 23rd July 1849. educ. St John's Coll. Camb. BA 1874. I.T. Nov. 1875. Reported QB cases for Law Times; Recorder of Bedford 1910-12; Cty. Ct. judge 1911-19. d. 12th May 1919.

BOSANQUET, Sir Frederick Albert

s. of Samuel Richard Bosanquet DL, JP, Dingestow Court, Monmouth, barrister (d. 1882). b. 8th Feb. 1837. educ. Eton; King's Coll. Camb. BA 1860, MA, Fellow 1859. I.T. June 1863 (Cert. of Hon.). QC 1882. Bencher 1889, Treasurer 1909. Junior counsel to Admiralty; Recorder of Worcester 1879-91, of Wolverhampton 1891-1900; Common Serjeant 1900-17; Knight 1907; Chmn. East Sussex Quarter Sess. 1912-21; Chmn. Inc. Council of Law Reporting 1909-17; JP Monmouth. Author, (with J.G.N. Darby), of treatise on Statutes of Limitations 1867. Known as "Bosey". d. 2nd Nov. 1923.

BOSANQUET, Sir John Bernard

s. of Samuel Bosanquet DL, JP, governor of Bank of England (d. 1806). b. 2nd May 1773. educ. Eton; Christ Church Oxf. BA 1795, MA 1800. L.I. May 1800. Counsel to East India Co., and Bank of England; Serjeant 1814; conducted numerous bank prosecutions for forgery; declined to be CJ of Bengal 1824; King's Serjeant 1827; Pres. Comm. to inquire into practice of common law cts. 1828-30; judge of Common Pleas 1830-42; Knight 1830; PC 1833; a Lord Commr. of the Great Seal, with Pepys and Shadwell 1835-36; arbitrated between Crown and Duke of Atholl concerning sovereignty of Isle of Man; reported (with C. Puller) cases in Common Pleas, Exch. and H of L 1797-1807. d. 25th Sept. 1847.

BOSANQUET, Sir Samuel Ronald Courthope

s. of Samuel Courthope Bosanquet, Dingestow Court, Monmouth, barrister (d. 1925). b. 6th Sept 1868. educ. Eton; Trinity Coll. Camb. LLB 1891. I.T. Jan. 1893. KC 1924. Bencher 1930. Recorder of Ludlow 1919-28, Walsall 1928-31; member of bar council 1926; Chan. of diocese of Hereford 1928; Official Referee of Supreme Ct. 1931-1943; Dep. Chmn. Monmouthshire Quarter Sess. 1913-35, Chmn. 1935-50; Knight 1942; JP Monmouthshire. d. 5th Nov. 1952.

BOTELER, William Fuller

s. of William Boteler FSA, Eastry, Kent. b. 12th April 1778. educ. Charterhouse; St. John's Coll. Camb. BA 1799, Senior Wrangler, MA 1802; Fellow of St. Peter's 1799. L.I. Nov. 1804. KC 1831. Bencher 1831, Treasurer 1843. Recorder of Canterbury, Sandwich, Hythe, New Romney and Deal; Commr. in Bankruptcy, Leeds 1844. Father of William Boteler 1810-67 (L.I. 1834). d. 23rd Oct 1845.

BOUSFIELD, William Robert

s. of Edward Tenney Bousfield, Bedford, engineer. b. 12th Jan. 1854. educ. Bedford Modern; Caius Coll. Camb. BA 1876, 16th Wrangler, MA 1879. I.T. June 1880. QC 1891. Bencher 1897, Treasurer. MP Hackney North 1892-1906; JP Middlesex; FRS 1916; AMICE. d. 16th July 1943.

BOVILL, Sir William

s. of Benjamin Bovill, Durnsford Lodge, Wimbledon (d. 1864). b. 26th May 1814. Articled to solicitor in London. Special pleader. M.T. Jan. 1841. QC 1855. Bencher 1855, Reader 1859, Treasurer 1866. Had large practice in patent and other commercial cases; MP Guildford 1857-66; Petition of Right Act, and Partnership Law Amendment Act became known as Bovill's Acts; Sol-Genl. for 5 months in 1866; Knight 1866; CJ of Common Pleas 1866-73; PC 1866; ordered Tichborne claimant to be indicted for perjury 1872; member of Judicature Comm. 1873; FRS 1867; JP Surrey; Hon. DCL Oxf. 1870. Father of William Channell Bovill (M.T. 1873), clerk of assize on Western circuit, and Archibald George Bovill (M.T. 1876), clerk of arraigns on Western circuit. d. 1st Nov. 1873.

BOVILL, William John

s. of William Bovill, Upper Tooting, Surrey, solicitor. b. Dec. 1810. educ. privately; St John's Coll. Camb. 1839. Solicitor in London 1833-46. M.T. Jan. 1847. L.I. Jan. 1850. QC 1872. Bencher 1872. Largely engaged in railway cases. FSS. Father of Sir Elliot Charles Bovill (1848-93), CJ of Straits Settlements. d. 3rd March 1882.

BOWEN, Charles Synge Christopher (Lord Bowen)

s. of Rev. Christopher Bowen, Winchester (d. 1890). b. 1st Jan. 1835. educ. in Lille; Rugby; Balliol Coll. Oxf. BA 1857, MA 1872, DCL 1883, Fellow 1857-62, Visitor 1885-94. Contributor to Saturday Review 1859-61. L.I. Jan. 1861. Bencher 1879. Commr. on working of Truck Acts, 1870; junior counsel against Tichborne claimant 1871-74; secy. to Totnes election comm. 1868; junior counsel to Treasury 1872-79; Recorder of Penzance 1872-76; QB judge 1879-82; Knight 1879; LJ 1882-93; PC 1882; L of A 1893-94; Baron Bowen of Colwood 1893; FRS 1885; a trustee of Br. Museum 1893. Author of "The Alabama Claims, and arbitration, considered from a legal point of view" 1868. d. 10th April 1894. Biography by Sir Henry Cunningham 1897.

BOWEN, David

s. of John Bowen, Pentre, Rhondda, Glamorganshire. b. 13th Feb. 1885. educ. privately; University Coll. Cardiff. Lecturer in geology, mining, and mine surveying at Sch. of Mines, Camborne, Cornwall

1908-09; asst prof. of mining, Leeds Univ. 1909-10, and head of Mining Dept. 1911-13; consultant mining and civil engineer 1911-14. WWI Capt. 8th West Yorkshire Regt. and seconded as Capt. RE (Tunnelling Companies); asst. commanding Cannock Chase 1917-19. L.I. April 1920. KC 1938. Bencher. Equity draftsman and conveyancer. Author of Vendors and Purchasers 1922, The Law relating to Fixtures 1923, and manuals on the Mines and Quarries Act 1923, and the Coal Act 1938. d. 27th Nov. 1950.

BOWEN, Ivor

s. of Rev. John Bowen Jones, Bedwellty, Monmouthshire. b. 25th Aug. 1862. Dropped the name of Jones 1883. G.I. July 1889. KC 1912. Bencher 1912, Treasurer 1923. Commd. in 2nd Vol. Battn. Welsh Regt. 1896; WWI Lt. Col. Royal Welsh Fusiliers. Recorder of Merthyr Tydfil 1914-15, of Swansea 1915-18; Cty. Ct. judge 1918-33. Editor of The Statutes of Wales, and Commons in Wales. d. 2nd Jan. 1934.

BOWEN, James William

s. of Lieut. Thomas Bowen, Carmarthen. b. 1820. educ. Shrewsbury. M.T. Jan. 1851. QC 1873. Bencher 1875, Reader 1885. Presided over Royal Comm. into corrupt election practices at Boston 1880; Recorder of Kidwelly 1875-88; DL, JP Camarthenshire and Cardiganshire. d. 8th Feb. 1888.

BOWER, George Spencer

s. of George Bower, St Neots, Huntingdonshire (d. 1911). b. 12th Oct 1854. educ. Winchester; New Coll. Oxf. BA 1877. I.T. June 1880. KC 1903. Bencher 1912. Author of works on defamation, misrepresentation, estoppel and res judicata. d. 4th Sept 1928.

BOXALL, William Percival Gratwicke

s. of William Percival Boxall JP, Brighton (d. 1898). b. 28th April 1849. educ. Emmanuel Coll. Camb. BA 1871, MA 1874. L.I. April 1873. KC 1902. Bencher 1908. Recorder of Rye 1905-11, of Brighton 1911-28; member of bar council; Chmn. West Sussex Quarter Sess.; JP West Sussex. d. 5th Dec. 1931.

BOYD, Edward Charles Percy

s. of Lt. Col. Alexander Boyd, St Andrews, Fifeshire. b. 3rd Sept 1871. educ. Fettes; Trinity Coll. Camb. BA 1893. I.T. June 1896. Junior Treasury counsel at Middlesex Sess. 1912, and at Central Criminal Ct. 1912-16; metrop. magistrate 1916, finally at Marlborough St. 1933-41. d. 30th May 1949.

BOYD, Hugh Fenwick

s. of Edward Fenwick Boyd, Moor House, Durham (d. 1889). b. 24th Dec. 1852. educ. Marlborough; Brasenose Coll. Oxf. 1871. I.T. Jan. 1880. QC 1896. Author, (with A.B. Pearson), of The Factors Acts 1823-77; edited, (with Pearson), Benjamin's Law of sale of personal property. d. 5th July 1898.

BOYLE, Sir Edward, Bt.

s. of Edward O'Boyle, CE, London. b. 6th Sept 1848. educ. privately for the army. Began practice as an architect 1870. FSI 1878. I.T. Nov. 1887. QC 1898. MP Taunton 1906-09; Director of the London and India Docks; Dep. Chmn. Imperial Life Office; Baronet 1904. Author of Principles of Rating, The Law of Compensation (Land Clauses Acts), Law of Railway and Canal Traffic. Father of Edward Gurney Boyle (I.T. 1902), later second baronet. d. 19th March 1909.

BRADBURY, James Kinder

s. of George Thomas Bradbury, Liverpool. b. 5th Nov. 1847. educ. Liverpool Coll.; Caius Coll. Camb. BA 1872, 10th Wrangler, MA 1875, Fellow 1875-85. I.T. Jan. 1875. Cty. Ct, judge 1900-13. d. France, 1st Feb. 1913.

BRADLEY, Francis Ernest

s. of Nathaniel Bradley, JP, FCS, Manchester. b. 16th April 1862. educ. Manchester Gr. Sch.; Manchester Univ. MA, M.Com., LLB London Univ. LLD 1895. G.I. Jan. 1889. Equity draftsman and conveyancer; lecturer in equity, Liverpool Univ. 1892-93; tutor in English law, Owen's Coll. Manchester 1892-99; Cty. Ct. judge 1921-33; JP Lancashire; FRSE; Master of Glaziers' Co. 1923-24. Author of works on company law. d. 3rd Sept. 1933.

BRADSHAW, Thomas Joseph Cavendish

s. of Joseph Hoare Bradshaw, London, banker. b. 17th Oct. 1824. educ. Eton; Christ Church Oxf. 1843. L.I. Nov. 1853. Secy. to Royal Comm. on judicature 1867-71; Cty. Ct. judge 1871-84. d. 17th Dec. 1884.

BRAMWELL, George William Wilshere (Lord Bramwell)

s. of George Bramwell, London, banker (d. 1858). b. 12th June 1808. educ. Palace Sch., Enfield. Clerk in father's bank. Special pleader 1834-38, and pupil of Fitzroy Kelly. L.I. May 1838, I.T. June 1838. QC 1851. Bencher (I.T.) 1851. Member of Common Law Procedure Comm. 1850; served on comm. which resulted in Companies Act 1862; Exch. Baron 1856-76; Knight 1856; member of Royal Comm. on Cts. of Law and Equity 1867-74; LJ 1876-81; PC 1876; FRS 1882; Baron Bramwell of Hever 1882; frequently sat in H of L on hearing of appeals; Hon. LLD Dublin 1887. d. 9th May

1892. "Bramwelliana" (The wit and wisdom of Lord Justice Bramwell) published 1892.

BRANDON, Harold Eustace

s. of Jonathan Brandon, West Kensington, London. M.T. Jan. 1897. KC 1926. Adopted name of Eustace in place of Ezekial, 1896. d. 17th Nov. 1927, age 57.

BRANDON, Woodthorpe

s. of Henry Brandon, London, merchant. b. 28th Nov. 1813. educ. St. Paul's. M.T. Nov. 1851. Registrar, Mayor's Ct. 1859; assistant judge 1873-87. Author of treatise on law of foreign attachment 1861, and notes on practice in Mayor's Ct. d. 17th March 1887.

BRANDT, Robert

s. of Charles Frederick Brandt, Manchester. educ. Oswestry Sch.; Trinity Coll. Camb. BA 1818, MA 1821. L.I. June 1821. Commr. in Bankruptcy; judge of Bury Ct. of Requests until 1847; Cty. Ct. judge 1847-62. d. 15th April 1862, age 65.

BRANSON, Sir George Arthur Harwin

s. of James Henry Arthur Branson, barrister. b. 11th July 1871. educ. Bedford Sch.; Trinity Coll. Camb. BA 1893; rowing blue. Articled to solicitor in London. I.T. April 1899. Bencher. Junior counsel to Treasury 1912-21; KB judge 1921-40; Knight 1921; PC 1940. Joint author of Schwabe and Branson on the Law of the Stock Exchange. Father of Edward James Branson (I.T. 1950), metrop. magistrate 1971. d. 23rd April 1951.

BRAY, Sir Edward

s. of Reginald Bray JP, FSA, Shere, Surrey, solicitor (d. 1879). b. 19th Aug. 1849. educ. Westminster (captain); Trinity Coll. Camb. BA 1873. L.I. June 1875. Cty. Ct. judge 1905-26; WWI Controller of Contracts, Army HQ, India; Knight 1919; played cricket for Surrey. d. 19th June 1926.

BRAY, Francis Edmond

s. of Bray J. b. 2nd March 1882. educ. Harrow; Trinity Coll. Camb. BA 1904, MA 1911; univ. shooting eight 1902-05. I.T. Nov. 1906. KC 1936. WWI with 5th Battn. Queen's Royal Regt, MC (despatches twice); retired as Lt.Col. 1926; TD. Chmn. Bd. of Referees 1939; DL Surrey. Author of British Rights at Sea, and a commentary on Trade Marks Act 1938. d. 8th May 1950.

BRAY, Sir Reginald More

s. of Reginald Bray, JP, FSA, Shere, Surrey, solicitor (d. 1879). b. 26th Sept. 1842. educ. Harrow; Trinity Coll. Camb. BA 1865, 12th Wrangler, MA 1869. I.T. Nov. 1868. QC 1897. Bencher 1891. Recorder of Guildford 1891-1904; KB judge 1904-23; Knight 1904; Lord of the manors of Shere, Gumshall and Coneyhurst; DL Surrey. d. 22nd March 1923.

BRETT, William Baliol (Lord Esher)

s. of Rev. Joseph George Brett, Hanover Chapel, Regent St, London (d. 1852). b. 13th Aug. 1815. educ. Westminster; King's Coll. London; Caius Coll. Camb. BA 1840, MA 1845, Hon. Fellow 1886; captain of Boat Club. L.I. Jan. 1846. QC 1861. Bencher 1861. Specialist in bankruptcy, mercantile and marine cases; leader in Admiralty Ct. and Liverpool Ct. of Passage; MP Helston 1866-68; Sol-Genl. and knighted 1868; concerned in prosecution of Fenians (plot to blow up Clerkenwell House of Detention) 1868; conducted legislation to abolish public executions; Judge of Common Pleas 1868-76; acted in Ct. for Crown Cases Reserved; LJ 1876-83; PC 1876; MR 1883-97; hon. freedom and livery of Salters' Co. 1876; Baron Esher 1885; Viscount 1897. d. 24th May 1899.

BRICE, Seward William

s. of William Brice, Stratton-on-the-Fosse, Somerset. b. 1846. educ. University Coll. London BA 1866, MA 1869, LLB 1871, LLD 1873. I.T. Nov. 1871. QC 1886. Bencher 1894. Author of works on public worship, patents, designs and trademarks, the doctrine of ultra vires, and tramways and light railways. Emigrated to practise in Johannesburg. d. 18th Dec. 1914.

BRIDGE, Sir John

s. of John H. Bridge, Longbredy, Dorchester. b. 21st April 1824. educ. Trinity Coll. Oxf. BA 1846, MA 1849. I.T. Jan. 1850. Bencher 1888. Metrop. magistrate 1872, finally at Bow St 1886-99; chief magistrate and knighted 1890; JP Berkshire, Middlesex and Home Counties. d. 26th April 1900.

BRISTOWE, Sir Henry Fox

s. of Samuel Ellis Bristowe DL, JP, Beesthorpe Hall, Nottinghamshire (d. 1855). b. 8th May 1824. educ. Trinity Hall Camb. 1845. M.T. June 1847. QC 1869. Bencher 1870, Reader 1875, Treasurer 1885. V-C. Cty. Palatine of Lancaster 1881-93; FRGS; Knight 1887. d. 20th Feb. 1893.

BRISTOWE, Samuel Boteler

s. of Samuel Ellis Bristowe DL, JP, Beesthorpe Hall,

Nottinghamshire (d. 1855). b. 5th Oct. 1822. educ. Trinity Hall Camb. BA 1845, MA 1848, Fellow 1850-56. I.T. June 1848. QC 1872. Bencher 1872, Treasurer 1891. Recorder of Newark-on-Trent 1869-70; MP Newark 1870-80; Cty. Ct. judge 1880-97; badly wounded when shot by a disappointed litigant. d. 5th March 1897.

BRODERIP, William John

s. of William Broderip, Bristol, surgeon. b. 21st Nov. 1789. educ. Seyer's Sch. Bristol; Oriel Coll. Oxf. BA 1812. L.I. May 1817. Bencher (G.I.) 1850, Treasurer 1851. Metrop. magistrate 1822, finally at Westminster 1846-55; reported (with P. Bingham) cases in Common Pleas and other cts. 1820-22; FLS 1824; FGS 1825; FRS 1828; a founder of the Zoological Socy. 1826. d. 27th Feb. 1859.

BRODRICK, William John Henry

s. of Rev. and Hon. Alan Brodrick, hon. canon of Winchester. b. 25th Jan. 1874. educ. Charterhouse; Corpus Christi Coll. Oxf. BA 1897, MA 1930. L.I. and I.T. Nov. 1899. Recorder of Bournemouth 1924-28; metrop. magistrate 1928, finally at Clerkenwell to 1944; OBE 1917; Chev. of Order of Crown of Belgium. Father of Norman John Lee Brodrick (QC 1960). d. 28th Oct 1964.

BROS, James Reader White

s. of Thomas Bros, Upper Clapton, Middlesex, barrister. b. 16th Nov. 1841. educ. Brighton Coll.; Rugby; St John's Coll. Camb. BA 1863. I.T. Nov. 1866. Recorder of Abingdon 1878-88; metrop. magistrate Clerkenwell 1888-1921; JP London and Home Counties. Brother of Thomas Kemmis Bros (1835-1922), Registrar Southwark Cty. Ct. d. 2nd Oct 1923.

BROUGHTON, Robert Edwards

s. of Rev. Thomas Broughton, Cotham, Gloucestershire. I.T. May 1825. Metrop. magistrate 1827, finally at Marlylebone 1854-60; FRS 1842. d. 29th June 1860, age 79.

BROWN, Douglas

s. of Jonathan Brown, Jamaica, merchant. b. 9th April 1820. educ. Edin. Acad.; Trinity Coll. Camb. BA 1843, MA 1846. L.I. May 1847. QC 1869. Bencher 1869. Recorder of King's Lynn 1869-85; DL, JP Yorkshire North Riding; FSA 1866. d. 29th June 1892.

BROWN, Joseph

s. of Joseph Brown, Camberwell, London, wine merchant. b. 4th April 1809. educ. Camberwell Gr. Sch.; Queen's Coll. Camb. BA 1830, MA 1833. Employed by West India merchants in London. Special pleader 1833. M.T. Nov. 1845. QC 1865. Bencher 1865, Reader 1869, Treasurer 1878. Initiated publication of the Law Reports 1865; Chmn. Incorp. Council of Law Reporting 1875-92; CB 1892; FGS. Author of The Dark Side of Trial by Jury, The Evils of Unlimited Liability for Accidents, and The Tichborne Case. d. 9th June 1902.

BROWN, Reginald

s. of Joseph Brown, CB, KC. b. 1846. educ. Brighton Coll.; Trinity Hall Camb. LLB 1868. M.T. April 1870. QC 1898. Cty. Ct. judge 1901-20; JP Cheshire. d. 18th Sept 1936.

BROWNE, George

s. of John Browne, Hall Court, Hertfordshire, Att-Genl. Jamaica (d. 1828). b. Jamaica 1825. educ. in Bridgnorth; Jesus Coll. Camb. BA

1848, MA 1877. I.T. May 1849. QC 1880. Recorder of Ludlow 1873-80. Author of treatises on practice in probate and matrimonial cts. d. 19th Sept, 1880.

BROWNE, John Hutton Balfour

s. of Dr. William Alexander Francis Browne, Crindan, Dumfries. b. 13th Sept 1845. educ. Edin. Univ. LLD. M.T. June 1870. QC 1885. Bencher 1890. Registrar and Secy. to Railway Comm. 1874-82; DL, JP. Author of works on jurisprudence of insanity, carriers, rating, usages and customs, railways, and compensation, also, 40 Years at the Bar 1916. d. 27th Sept. 1921.

BRUCE, Sir Gainsford

s. of John Collingwood Bruce LLD, Newcastle-upon-Tyne, schoolmaster (d.1892). b. 1834. educ. Glasgow Univ. M.T. June 1859. QC 1883. Bencher 1888, Reader 1897. Recorder of Bradford 1877-92; Sol-Genl. Cty. Palatine of Durham 1879-86, Att-Genl. 1886-87, Chan. 1887-92; MP Finsbury (Holborn) 1888-92; QB judge 1892-1904; Knight 1892; judge under Benefices Act, 1899-1904; PC 1904; DL and Hon. DCL Durham. Author of Life of John Collingwood Bruce 1906; joint author of Williams and Bruce's Admiralty Practice; edited Maude and Pollock on Shipping. d. 24th Feb. 1912.

BRUCE, Sir James Lewis Knight

s. of John Knight, Fairlinch, Devon (d. 1799). b. 15th Feb. 1791. educ. Bath Gr. Sch.; Sherborne. Articled to solicitor in London. L.I. Nov. 1817. KC 1829. Bencher 1829, Treasurer 1842, laid foundation stone of new hall and library 1843. Practised in Chancery; leader in Sir Lancelot Shadwell's Ct.; MP Bishop's Castle 1831-32; assumed by royal licence additional surname of Bruce 1837; V-C 1841; Knight and PC 1842; chief judge in bankruptcy 1842; LJ

1851-66; FRS 1829; Hon. DCL Oxf. 1834. d. 7th Nov. 1866.

BUCKLEY, Henry Burton (Lord Wrenbury)

s. of Rev. John Wall Buckley, St Mary's, Paddington. b. 15th Sept 1845. educ. Merchant Taylors; Christ's Coll. Camb. BA 1868, 9th Wrangler, MA 1871, Fellow 1868-82, Hon. Fellow 1901. L.I. June 1869. QC 1886. Bencher 1891. Member of bar committee and bar council 1883-98; Chancery judge 1900-06; Knight 1900; LJ 1906-15; PC 1906; Baron Wrenbury of Old Castle 1915; active in judicial and legislative functions of H of L, and in PC; instrumental in preparation of Income Tax Act 1918. Author of The Law and Practice under the Companies Acts 1873. Father of Bryan Burton Buckley, 2nd Baron (L.I. 1913) and Buckley LJ (b. 1906). d. 27th Oct. 1935.

BUCKMASTER, Stanley Owen (Lord Buckmaster)

s. of John Charles Buckmaster JP, Ashleigh, Hampton Wick, Middlesex (d. 1908). b. 9th Jan. 1861. educ. Aldenham Sch.; Christ Church Oxf. BA 1883, MA 1886, Hon. DCL, Hon. Student 1917. I.T. June 1884; L.I. 1902. KC 1902. Bencher 1910. Counsel to Oxf. Univ. 1911-13; member Council of Duchy of Lancaster 1912; MP Cambridge Borough 1906-10, Yorkshire West Riding (Keighley) 1911-15; Sol-Genl. 1913-15; Knight 1913; Director, Press Bureau 1914-15; LC and Speaker 1915-16; PC and Baron 1915; member Inter-Allied Confce. on Finance and Supplies; Chmn. Political Honours Review Committee 1924 and 1929; GCVO 1930; Viscount 1933; Chmn. of Govrs. of Imperial Coll. of Science and Technology 1923-24; JP Hertfordshire; Hon. LLD Toronto and Edin. Father of Owen Stanley Buckmaster, 2nd Baron (I.T. 1913). d. 5th Dec. 1934.

BUCKNILL, Sir Alfred Townsend

s. of Bucknill J. b. 15th Aug. 1880. educ. Cheam Sch.;

Charterhouse; Trinity Coll. Oxf. BA 1902, MA 1906, Hon. Fellow 1944. I.T. Nov. 1903. KC 1931. Bencher 1928, Treasurer 1951. WWI Major, Surrey Yeo. and on staff (DJAG), OBE 1919. Had extensive practice in admiralty cts. and shipping inquiries; P D and A judge 1935-45; Knight 1935; conducted inquiry into loss of Thetis submarine on trial dive 1939; Pres. trib. inquiring into escape of three German warships from Brest 1942; LJ 1945-51; PC 1945. Author of The Law relating to Tug and Tow, and The Nature of Evidence 1953. Father of Peter Thomas Bucknill (QC 1961). d. 22nd Dec. 1963.

BUCKNILL, Sir Thomas Townsend

s. of Sir John Charles Bucknill MD, FRS, East Cliff House, Bournemouth (d. 1897). b. 18th April 1845. educ. Westminster; Geneva. I.T. Nov. 1868. QC 1885. Bencher 1891. Recorder of Exeter 1885-99; MP Surrey (Epsom) 1892-99; QB judge 1899-1914; Knight 1899; Alderman Surrey CC 1889-92; JP Surrey; edited Abbott on Shipping, Cunningham's Reports (KB 1734-35), and Cooke's Common Pleas Reports (1706-47). Stepfather of Sir John Alexander Strachey Bucknill (1873-1926), CJ Straits Settlements. d. 4th Oct. 1915.

BULLER, Charles

s. of Charles Buller, HEICS. b. Calcutta, 6th Aug. 1806. educ. Harrow, tutored by Thomas Carlyle; Edin. Univ.; Trinity Coll. Camb. BA 1828. L.I. June 1831. QC 1846. MP West Looe 1830-31, Liskeard 1832-48; Secy. to Gov. Genl. of Canada 1838; Judge Adv-Genl. 1846; Chief Poor Law Commr. 1847; originated the Record Commission; declined to be PC. d. 29th Nov. 1848.

BULLOCK, Edward

s. of Edward Bullock, Jamaica. educ. Eton; Christ Church Oxf. BA 1822, MA 1825. I.T. Nov. 1824. Judge of Sheriff's Ct. of London and Commr. at Old Bailey 1840-50; Common Serjeant 1850-55. Father of Edward Bullock (I.T. 1858), Recorder of Buckingham. d. 27th Dec. 1857, age 57.

BULWER, James Benjamin Redfoord

s. of Rev. James Bulwer, Hunworth-cum-Stody, Norfolk. b. 22nd May 1820. educ. King's Coll. London; Trinity Coll. Camb. BA 1842, MA 1845. I.T. Jan. 1847. QC 1865. Bencher 1865, Reader 1880, Treasurer 1880. Recorder of Ipswich 1861-66, of Cambridge 1866-98; MP Ipswich 1874-80, Cambridgeshire 1881-85; Second Chmn. Norfolk Quarter Sess. 1882-99; Master in Lunacy 1886-99. Edited Law Reports, common law series 1865-85. Lt. Col. 2nd Vol. Battalion Rifle Brigade 1865. Lt. Col. 23 Middlesex Rifle Corps 1873-84. d. 4th March 1899.

BURCHAM, Thomas Borrow

s. of John Burcham, Scarning, Norfolk. educ. Norwich Sch.; Trinity Coll. Camb. BA 1830, MA 1833, Fellow 1832-69. I.T. Jan. 1843. Recorder of Bedford 1848-56; metrop. magistrate Southwark 1856-69. d. 27th Nov. 1869, age 61.

BURGE, William

s. of John Burge, Castle Cary, Somerset. educ. Blundell's; Wadham Coll. Oxf. BA 1806, MA 1830, DCL 1834. I.T. May 1808. KC 1834. Bencher 1835, Reader 1844, Treasurer 1844. Att-Genl. Jamaica; MP Eye 1831-32; Commr. in Bankruptcy, Leeds 1846; Recorder of Winchester 1844-47; FRS 1847; FSA. Author of Commentaries on Colonial and Foreign Laws, in their conflict with each other, and with the laws of England 1838, Commentaries on the Law of Suretyship 1847, The Temple Church, an Account of its Restoration 1843. d. 12th Nov. 1849, age 63.

BURGIS, Sir Edwin Cooper

s. of Edwin Burgis, Withington, Manchester. b. 1878. educ. Victoria Univ. LLB; Lincoln Coll. Oxf. BA 1901, MA 1904, BCL 1906. G.I. June 1904 (Cert. of Hon.). Lecturer in common and commercial law, Manchester Univ. 1906-14. WWI Major RGA. Cty. Ct. judge 1924-50; Dep. Chmn. Cheshire Quarter Sess. 1942; Chmn. Eddisbury Petty Sess.; Chmn. Cheshire Cty. Licensing Committee; DL, JP Lancashire; JP Cheshire; Knight 1948. d. 4th Feb. 1966.

BURKE, James Saint George

s. of John French Burke, London, merchant. b. Lisbon, 20th Dec. 1804. Solicitor 1829. M.T. Nov. 1846. QC 1862. Bencher 1863, Reader 1865. Counsel to London Chatham and Dover Ry. Co.; confined himself to parliamentary practice. d. 25th Feb. 1881.

BURKE, Peter

s. of John Burke, London, genealogist. b. 7th May 1811. educ. Caen Coll. Normandy. I.T. June 1838. QC Cty. Palatine of Lancaster 1858. Serjeant 1860. Director Socy. of Antiquaries of Normandy 1866-67. Author of Celebrated trials connected with the Aristocracy 1849, The Romance of the Forum 1852-61, Celebrated naval and military trials 1866. d. 26th March 1881.

BURNABY, John Dick

s. of Col. John Dick Burnaby, Rotherby Hall, nr. Melton Mowbray, Leicestershire (d. 1852). b. 19th April 1802. educ. Oakham; Emmanuel Coll. Camb. LLB 1826. I.T. Nov. 1828. Commr. in Bankruptcy; Cty. ct. judge 1847-55; Dep. Chmn. Leicestershire Quarter Sess.; DL, JP Leicestershire. Father of Sherard Beaumont James Burnaby (I.T. 1876) and William Augustus Burnaby, solicitor. d. 29th Dec. 1855.

BURRELL, John Palfrey

s. of Palfrey George Burrell, Alnwick, Northumberland. G.I. July 1805. Bencher 1829, Treasurer 1833. Metrop. magistrate 1833, finally at Vincent Sq. 1846-54. d. 11th July 1859, age 86.

BURRELL, Robert Eric

s. of John Burrell, London. b. 2nd Jan. 1890. educ. Merchant Taylors'; Trinity Hall Camb. BA and LLB 1911, MA, LLM; Berlin Univ. (Science) 1911-13. I.T. June 1913. KC 1937. Bencher 1945. WWI Lieut. Royal Welch Fusiliers, Capt. Army Cyclist Corps.; legal adviser, British legation Christiania, Norway 1917-19. Secy. Trade Marks, Patents and Designs Fedn. 1920-26; technical adviser and later vice-pres. Industrial Property Comm. of Intern. Chamber of Commerce, Paris 1921-55; delegate of Intern. Chamber at Diplomatic Confces. for Revision of Industrial Property Conventions, Hague 1925, London 1934; Pres. of Br. Group of Intern. Assoc. for Protection of Industrial Property 1928-29; Chmn. Trade Mark Committee of Intern. Law Assoc. 1946-51; hon. member Inst. of Trade Mark Agents. Father of Robert John Burrell (QC 1973). d. 25th July 1968.

BURROWS, Sir Roland

s. of John Henry Burrows, Solbys, Hadleigh, Essex. b. 12th Feb. 1882. educ. St. John's Coll. Southend; London Univ. LLB 1901, LLD 1903; Trinity Hall Camb. BA 1906, MA 1910, LLM, Hon. Fellow. I.T. Jan. 1904. KC 1932. Bencher. Priv. secy. to Sir Frederick Smith when Sol-Genl. and Att-Genl. 1915-19; asst. priv. secy. to Lord Birkenhead 1919-22; counsel to Food Controller 1916-19; Recorder of Chichester 1926-28, of Cambridge 1928-52; counsel in bankruptcy to Bd. of Trade 1927-32; Chmn. West Sussex Quarter Sess.; Dep. Chmn. Boundary Comm. for England; Chmn. London Regional Aliens Advisory Committee 1940-45; Chmn. London Licensing Planning Committee 1945-49; Pres. Medico-Legal Socy.

1942-45; Knight 1946; Reader in evidence, civil procedure, and criminal law at Inns of Ct. Author of The Interpretation of Documents; edited Phipson on Evidence, and Words and Phrases; consulting editor for All England Law Reports. d. 13th June 1952.

BURY, Ralph Frederic

s. of Charles James Bury DL, JP, CA, St. Leonard's House, Nazing, Essex (d. 1897). b. 22nd Dec. 1876. educ. Trinity Coll. Camb. BA 1898. L.I. June 1901. KC 1938. Served in TA 1900-10. WWI Capt. 9th Service Battn. Essex Regt., DAAG (Major), despatches, croix de guerre. Equity draftsman and conveyancer; Gold staff officer at Coronation 1911; Pres. Epping Divn. Conservative Assoc.; High Sheriff, Essex 1910-11; DL, JP Essex. d. 15th Jan. 1954.

BUSH, Francis Whittaker

s. of George Bush, Penleigh House, Wiltshire. b. 8th Jan. 1825. educ. Magdalen Hall Oxf. BA 1849, MA 1851. L.I. May 1851. QC 1885. Bencher 1888. JP Surrey and London. d. 21st March 1903.

BUSHBY, Henry Jeffreys

s. of Henry Turner Bushby HEICS. b. India, 4th Oct. 1820. educ. Eton; East India Coll.; Haileybury, gold medals in classics, law and political economy. Bengal Civil Service 1839-45; asst. to Gov. Genl.'s agent for Rajput States. I.T. Nov. 1851. Recorder of Colchester 1863-70; metrop. magistrate, Worship St. 1870-96; one of HM's Lieutenants for City of London; Commr. of Lieutenancy for London; JP Hertfordshire. Author of Widow Burning 1855, and other works. d. 27th Aug. 1903.

BUSHE, Seymour Coghill Hort

s. of Rev. Charles Bushe, Castlehaven, Cork, and g.s. of Bushe LCJ, Ireland. b. 5th April 1853. educ. Rathmines Sch. Dublin; Trinity Coll. Dublin BA. Irish bar 1879. QC 1892. Bencher King's Inns 1896. I.T. Nov. 1899. KC 1904. Senior Crown prosecutor for Cty. and City of Dublin 1901; JP Co. Cork. d. 27th Jan. 1922.

BUSZARD, Marston Clarke

s. of Marston Buszard MD, Lutterworth, Leicestershire. b. 13th July 1837. educ. Rugby; Trinity Coll. Camb. BA 1860, MA 1863, LLM 1873. I.T. Jan. 1862. QC 1877. Bencher 1880, Treasurer 1903. MP Stamford 1880-85; Recorder of Derby 1890-99, of Leicester 1899-1921; counsel to PO on Midland circuit; JP Leicestershire; Dep. Chmn. Leicestershire Quarter Sess. d. 11th Sept. 1921.

BUTCHER, John George (Lord Danesfort)

s. of Samuel Butcher, bishop of Meath (d. 1876). b. 15th Nov. 1853. educ. Marlborough; Trinity Coll. Camb. BA 1874, 8th Wrangler, Fellow 1875, MA 1877. L.I. May 1878. QC 1897. Bencher 1903. Member of bar council; MP York 1892-1906 and 1910-24; JP Yorkshire East Riding; Hon. Freeman City of York 1906; Baronet 1918; Baron Danesfort 1924. d. 30th June 1935.

BUTT, Sir Charles Parker

s. of Rev. Phelpes John Butt, Wortham Lodge, Bournemouth (d. 1883). b. 24th June 1830. educ. privately. L.I. Nov. 1854. QC 1868. Bencher 1869. Practised in consular cts. at Constantinople, where also correspondent for the Times 1870-80; MP Southampton 1880-83; P D and A judge 1883; Knight 1883; Pres. P D and A Divn. 1891-92; PC 1891; member Royal Comm. to investigate causes of loss of life at sea 1884. d. Wiesbaden, 25th May 1892.

BUTT, George Medd

s. of John Butt, Sherborne, Dorset. b. 1797. Special pleader. I.T. June 1830. Bencher 1845. QC 1845. Reader 1858, Treasurer 1859. MP Weymouth 1852-57. d. 11th Nov. 1860.

BYLES, Sir John Barnard

s. of Jeremiah Byles, Stowmarket, Suffolk, timber merchant. b. 11th Jan. 1801. Special pleader. I.T. Nov. 1831. Recorder of Buckingham 1840-58; Serjeant 1843; leader of Norfolk circuit; patent of precedence 1846; Queen's Serjeant, with Shee and Wrangham, 1857 (the last appointments); judge of Common Pleas 1858-73; Knight 1858; PC 1873. Author of A Discourse on the present state of the law of England 1829, A practical compendium on the law of bills of exchange 1829, Observations on the usury laws 1845, Free Trade and its so called sophisms, examined by a barrister 1850. Father of Walter Barnard Byles (L.I. 1865), Sheriff of Middlesex, and Maurice Barnard Byles (I.T. 1866). d. 3rd Feb. 1884.

BYRNE, Sir Edmund Widdrington

s. of Edmund Byrne, Westminster, solicitor. b. 30th June 1844. educ. King's Coll. London. L.I. Jan. 1867. QC 1888. Bencher 1892. Equity draftsman and conveyancer; member of bar committee 1891; MP Essex (Walthamstow) 1892-97; Chancery judge 1897-1904; Knight 1897; rarely reversed on appeal; tried numerous patent cases. Father of Lucius Widdrington Byrne (L.I. 1899). d. 4th April 1904.

BYRNE, Sir Laurence Austin

s. of William Austin Byrne, journalist. b. 17th Sept. 1896. WWI Lieut. Queen's Royal West Surrey Regt. Employed with LCC. M.T. April 1918. Bencher 1942, Reader 1954. Counsel to Mint at Central Criminal Ct. 1928-30; junior Treasury counsel at Central Criminal

Ct. 1930, second senior counsel 1937, senior 1942-45; Recorder of Rochester 1939-45; seldom appeared in civil cases; declined appointment as Director of Public Pros. 1944; P D and A judge 1945-47; Knight 1945; KB judge 1947-60; chmn. committee of inquiry into method of taking depositions in criminal cases; tried case in which Penguin Books were acquitted of publishing an obscene book, the unexpurgated Lady Chatterley's Lover, 1960; member Jockey Club committee set up concerning administration of drugs to racehorses. d. 1st Nov. 1965.

CADMAN, John Heaton

s. of Edwin Cadman, Westbourne House, Yorkshire. b. 24th July 1839. educ. Collegiate Sheffield; Worcester Coll. Oxf. BA 1862, MA 1865; Lycée Imperial, Versailles. I.T. Nov. 1864. Recorder of Pontefract 1877-89; Cty. Ct. judge 1889-1906; JP Yorkshire West Riding. d. 22nd Feb. 1906.

CAILLARD, Camille Felix Désiré

s. of Camille Timothée Caillard, officer in French army. b. 12th Sept. 1822. educ. privately. I.T. Nov. 1845. Cty. Ct. judge 1859-67; Chmn. Wiltshire Quarter Sess; DL, JP Wiltshire; JP Somerset. d. 1st May 1898.

CAIRNS, Hugh McCalmont (Lord Cairns)

s. of William Cairns, Cultra, Co.Down., Captain 47th Foot. b. 27th Dec. 1819. educ. Belfast Acad.; Trinity Coll. Dublin BA 1838, LLD, Chancellor 1867. M.T. Jan. 1844. QC 1856. Bencher (L.I.) 1856. MP Belfast 1852-66; introduced, in 1859, bills to simplify titles to real property, and to establish a land registry; Sol-Genl. 1858-59; Knight 1858; Att-Genl. 1866; LJ 1866-68; PC 1866; Baron Cairns of Garmoyle 1867; LC 1868 and 1874-80; Earl Cairns 1878. "A model of judicial excellence". LLD Camb. 1862; DCL Oxf. 1863.

d. 2nd April 1885.

CAIRNS, John Arthur Robert

s. of John Cairns, Belfast. b. 1874. educ. Royal Acad. Inst. Belfast; Royal Univ. of Ireland BA 1897. M.T. May 1908. Pros. counsel to PO on North Eastern circuit 1912-20; Dep. Chmn. London Sess. 1919-20; metrop. magistrate 1920, finally at Westminster to 1933; JP London and Home Counties. Author of The Loom of the Law, and Experiences and Reflections of a Metropolitan Magistrate. d. 10th Nov. 1933.

CALVERT, Frederick

s. of Genl. Sir Harry Calvert, Bt. b. 9th June 1806. educ. Harrow (captain); Christ Church Oxf. BA 1827, MA 1831; Fellow of Merton Coll. 1830-66. I.T. Jan. 1831. QC 1849. Bencher 1849, Reader 1861, Treasurer 1862. A leader at parliamentary bar; elected MP for Aylesbury 1850, but election declared void 1851; member of Bd. of Queen Anne's Bounty office 1869-91; DL, JP Buckinghamshire. Author of treatises on equity, and on the jurisdiction of the Inns of Ct. d. 6th June 1891.

CAMPBELL, James

Nephew of Lt. Genl. James Campbell, London. L.I. Feb. 1821. QC 1851, Bencher 1851. A Charity Commr. for England and Wales 1855-66. d. 2nd March 1866, age 67.

CAMPBELL, James Henry Mussen (Lord Glenavy)

s. of William Mussen Campbell, Prospect House, Terenure, Dublin. b. 4th April 1851. educ. Kingstown Sch.; Trinity Coll. Dublin BA 1874, Hon. LLD 1904. Irish bar 1878. QC 1892. Bencher 1894. G.I.

April 1899. KC 1906. Bencher 1901. MP St. Stephen's Green 1898-1900, Dublin Univ. 1903-16; Sol-Genl. Ireland 1901-05; Att-Genl. 1905 and 1916; PC (Ireland) 1905; LCJ, Ireland 1916-18; Baronet 1917; LC, Ireland 1918-21; Baron 1921; Chmn. Irish Free State Senate 1922-28. Father of Charles Henry Gordon Campbell, 2nd Baron, (G.I. 1911), and Sir Cecil James Campbell KBE, CMG (G.I. 1917). d. 22nd March 1931.

CAMPBELL, John (Lord Campbell)

s. of Rev. George Campbell, Cupar, Fife (d. 1824). b. 15th Sept. 1779. educ. Cupar Gr. Sch.; St. Andrews Univ. MA. Parliamentary reporter and dramatic critic for Morning Chronicle 1800-05. L.I. Nov. 1806. KC 1827. Bencher 1827, Treasurer 1834. Leader of Oxford circuit; Chmn. Real Property Comm. 1828; MP Stafford 1830-32, Dudley 1832-34, Edinburgh 1834-41; Sol-Genl. 1832-34; Knight 1832; Att-Genl. 1834 and 1835-41; LC of Ireland 1841; Baron Campbell of St. Andrews 1841; PC 1841; Chan. of Duchy of Lancaster 1846-50; LCJ 1850-59; tried William Palmer, the Rugeley poisoner 1856, and Achilli v. Cardinal Newman (libel) 1852; LC 1859-61; reported cases at nisi prius 1809-16. Author of The Lives of the Lord Chancellors 1846-47, The Lives of the Chief Justices 1849-57, Lives of Lord Lyndhurst and Lord Brougham 1869. Father of Dudley Campbell (1833-1900), barrister. d. 23rd June 1861. Biography by Mrs. Hardcastle (daughter), 2 vols. 1881.

CAMPBELL, Sybil

d. of Neill Graeme Campbell, Auchendarroch. b. 1889. educ. Dunardarigh, North Berwick; Girton Coll. Camb. MA. Inspector under Trade Boards Act 1914-18. M.T. Nov. 1922. A metrop. chmn. Cts. of Referees 1930-39; OBE 1942; metrop. magistrate Tower Bridge 1945-61. d. 29th Aug. 1977.

CAMPBELL, Wiliam Lawson Walford

s. of Robert Lee Campbell, Edinburgh. b. 5th July 1890. educ. Harrow; Magdalen Coll. Oxf. BA 1913; Trinity Hall Camb. MA 1939. L.I. Nov. 1914. WWI Lieut. 6th Battn. Black Watch. Cty. Ct. judge 1937-62; Chmn. Isle of Ely Quarter Sess. 1941-65; Acting Chmn. Soke of Peterborough Quarter Sess. 1942-65; Chmn. Cambridgeshire Quarter Sess. 1950-65; JP Isle of Ely; Dep. Chmn. National Advisory Council on training of magistrates 1964. d. 26th Sept. 1970.

CAMPION, Bernard

s. of Samuel Smith Campion DL, JP, Northampton. b. 1871. educ. Taunton Sch.; London Univ. LLB. G.I. June 1899. KC 1923. Bencher 1920, Treasurer 1935. Gilbart lecturer on Banking, King's Coll. London 1923-27; Recorder of Northampton 1927-28; metrop. magistrate 1928, finally at Tower Bridge to 1943. Father of John Cecil Campion (1907-71), metrop. magistrate. d. 10th March 1952.

CANCELLOR, Henry Lannoy

s. of Rev. John Henry Cancellor, Hamble, Hampshire. b. 1862. educ. Eton; University Coll. Oxf. BA 1884, MA 1887. I.T. April 1888. Metrop. magistrate 1914, finally at Marlborough St. 1924-29. Author of The Life of a London Beak 1930. d. 6th Oct. 1929.

CANDY, George

s. of Rev. George Candy, South Newington, Oxfordshire. b. Bombay, 14th Oct. 1841. educ. Islington Proprietary Sch.; Wadham Coll. Oxf. BA 1864, MA 1867. Schoolmaster. I.T. Nov. 1869. QC 1886. Author on procedure in Mayor's Ct. London, and on licensing justices. d. 25th Oct. 1899.

CANN, Sir William Moore

s. of Abraham Cann, Nottingham, solicitor. b. 6th July 1856. educ. Nottingham High Sch.; Shrewsbury; Clare Coll. Camb. BA 1880. I.T. Jan. 1883. Equity draftsman and conveyancer; Cty. Ct. judge 1914-31; Knight 1929. d. 18th April 1947.

CANTRELL, Joseph Thomas

s. of Joseph Cantrell, King's Newton, nr. Derby. b. 1802. educ. Repton Gr. Sch. L.I. Nov. 1831. Judge of Staffordshire Potteries Ct. of Requests; Cty. Ct judge 1847-62. d. 4th April 1862.

CAPEWELL, Arthur Adams

s. of Arthur Thomas Capewell, Sheffield. b. 15th Dec. 1902. educ. Shrewsbury; Gonville & Caius Coll. Camb. BA and LLB 1924. G.I. Jan. 1926. KC 1945. Member of Kensington BC 1932-38. WWII DAQMG West Lancashire Area, GSO2 Administrative Staff Sch.; DAQMG 44 Divn. Asst. secy. (legislation) Min. of Town and Country Planning 1943-44; counsel to Lord Chmn. of Committees, H of L 1944-46, to Ecclesiastical Committee of Parliament 1944-46; Chmn. Southern Rhodesian Royal Comm. on Planning, Incremental Values, etc. 1949; Dep. Chmn. Middlesex Quarter Sess. 1945-54; Dep. Chmn. Somerset Quarter Sess. 1950, Chmn. 1957; JP Somerset. d. 18th Oct. 1957.

CAPORN, Arthur Cecil

s. of Arthur Leason Caporn, South Africa and Nottingham. b. 16th April 1884. educ. South African Coll. Sch.; Trinity Hall Camb. BA 1906, LLB 1906. M.T. April 1907 (Cert. Of Hon.). WWI Capt. RFA and General Staff. MP West Nottingham 1931-35; Cty. Ct. judge 1939-53. d. 25th Nov. 1953.

CARPMAEL, Ernest

s. of William Carpmael, CE, London. b. 1844. educ. St John's Coll. Camb. BA 1867, 6th Wrangler, MA 1870, Fellow 1869. M.T. Nov. 1869. QC 1895. Engaged chiefly in patent cases; FRAS, FRGS, MRI. d. 4th Dec. 1921.

CARPMAEL, Kenneth Sydney

s. of Ernest Carpmael KC. b. 12th July 1885. educ. Dulwich. Entered accountant branch RN 1903; Lieut. 1917; Paymaster Cdr. (retd.) 1924. M.T. May 1919. KC 1935. Bencher 1942, Reader 1954, Treasurer 1961. Barrister and KC, Northern Ireland 1948; junior counsel to Admiralty 1931-35; on panel of Wreck Commrs. (England) under Merchant Shipping Acts, 1938; acting Cdr. RN 1940; member Admiralty Ferry Crew Organisation 1943-60; govr. Dulwich Coll. 1942, and James Allen's Girls' Sch. Dulwich 1946-58. d. 26th Nov. 1975.

CARR, Sir Arthur Strettell Comyns

s. of Joseph William Comyns Carr, dramatist (d. 1916). b. 19th Sept. 1882. educ. Winchester; Trinity Coll. Oxf. BA 1905. Journalist. Secy. to E.A. Strauss MP. G.I. Jan. 1908. KC 1924. Bencher 1938, Treasurer 1950. WWI with Mins. of Munitions and Reconstruction. MP Islington (East) 1923-24; Chief British pros. at Intern. Mil. Trib. for Far East; Chmn. Foreign Compensation Comm. 1950-58; Knight 1949. Part author of National Insurance 1912, Recent Mining Legislation 1931, Empire and World Currency 1932, Faraday on Rating. d. 20th April 1965..

CARR, Sir Cecil Thomas

s. of Thomas Carr, Twerton-on-Avon, Bath. b. 4th Aug. 1878. educ. Bath Coll.; Trinity Coll. Camb. BA 1900, LLB 1901, MA 1904,

LLM 1907, LLD 1920, Hon. Fellow 1963. I.T. June 1902. KC 1945. Bencher 1944. WWI 2nd Lieut. 4th Battn. Wiltshire Regt., and DAAG Poona, Bombay. Editor, Revised Statutes and Statutory Rules and Orders 1923-43; lecturer in USA 1935-40; member, Statute Law Committee 1943-65; counsel to the Speaker 1943-55; Chmn. Committee on Electoral Law Reform 1944-47; visiting lecturer, Univs. of Cape Town and Witwatersrand 1955; Pres. of Selden Socy. 1958-61; Chmn. of Athenaeum; Knight 1939; KCB 1947; FBA 1952; Hon. LLD Columbia 1940, London 1952, Queen's Univ. Belfast 1954. Author of Delegated Legislation 1921, Concerning English Administrative Law 1941, Law of Corporations 1905, Collective Ownership 1907, Select Charters of Trading Companies 1913, Clement's Inn Pension Book 1960. d. 12th May 1966.

CARROW, John Monson

s. of Rev. Richard Carrow, Redland, Lincolnshire. b. 14th Dec. 1807. educ. Westminster; Trinity Coll. Camb. BA 1831. I.T. Jan. 1834. A reporter of cases relating to railways and canals 1840-48, and New Sessions cases 1845-49; Recorder of Wells 1852-53; Cty. Ct. judge 1847-53. d. 8th May 1853.

CARSON, Edward Henry (Lord Carson)

s. of Edward Henry Carson CE, Harcourt St., Dublin, Vice-Pres. Royal Inst. of Architects. b. 9th Feb. 1854. educ. Portarlington Sch.; Dublin Univ. BA 1876, MA 1889, Hon. LLD 1901. Irish bar 1877. KC 1889. Bencher 1891. M.T. April 1893. QC 1894. Bencher 1900, Reader 1912, Treasurer 1922. Counsel to Att-Genl. of Ireland 1887-90; senior Crown prosecutor for Cty. and City of Dublin 1891-92; Sol-Genl. Ireland 1892; MP Dublin Univ. 1892-1918; PC (Ireland) 1896; recognised as brilliant orator after appearing in Oscar Wilde's libel action against Queensbury 1895; Sol-Genl. 1900-05; Knight 1900; PC 1905; gained for Archer-Shee, naval cadet, exoneration from charge of stealing postal order 1910; leader of Irish Unionists in H of C 1910, and of movement for prov. govt. in Ulster; Att-Genl. 1915-16; First Lord of Admiralty 1916-17, when he entered War Cabinet; resigned 1918, because of Lloyd George's intention to introduce Home Rule Bill for whole of Ireland; MP Belfast (Duncairn) 1918-21; resigned as leader of Ulster Unionists 1921; L of A 1921-29; Baron 1921; d. 22nd Oct. 1935. Principal biogs.: The Life of Lord Carson, Vol.1 by E. Marjoribanks 1932, Vols. 2 and 3 by I. Colvin 1934, 1936; by H. Montgomery Hyde 1953.

CARSON, Thomas Henry

s. of Rev. Joseph Carson DD, Vice-Provost, Trinity Coll. Dublin (d. 1898). b. 24th Nov. 1843. educ. Marlborough; Trinity Coll. Dublin BA 1866, MA 1867, gold medallist in classics and philosophy; Fellow 1866. L.I. Nov. 1869. KC 1901. Bencher 1907. Edited Gale on Easements, and Tudor's leading cases in real property and conveyancing. d. 30th June 1917.

CARTER, Albert Thomas

s. of Thomas Albert Carter MD, FRCP, Shottery Hall, Stratford-on-Avon. b. 1861. educ. in Leamington; Queen's Coll. Oxf. BA 1882, BCL and MA 1886, Hon. Fellow; Christ Church DCL 1893. I.T. July 1886. KC 1921. Adviser to HM's procurator-genl., and solicitor to Treasury 1915; Reader in constitutional law and legal history to Inns of Ct. 1898-1910; CBE 1917. Author of A History of English Legal Institutions. d. 29th July 1946.

CARTHEW, Thomas Walter Colby

s. of Thomas Carthew, Woodbridge, Suffolk. b. 1st July 1880. educ. Uppingham. South African War, Lieut. Northumberland Fusiliers 1899-1902. I.T. Jan. 1910. KC 1936. WWI Lt.Col. RFC and Bedfordshire Regt., DSO (despatches thrice), Croix de Guerre. Recorder of Maidstone 1936-51. WWII Wing Cdr. RAF; regional commandant, Eastern Region ATC 1941. d. 18th April 1955.

CARVER, Thomas Gilbert

s. of William Carver, Broomfield, Manchester, merchant (d. 1868). b. Gibraltar, 14th Nov. 1848. educ. Forest Sch. Snaresbrook; St. John's Coll. Camb. BA 1871, 8th Wrangler, MA 1874. L.I. and M.T. June 1873. QC 1897. Bencher 1904. Cty. Ct. judge 1906. Author of The Law relating to the Carriage of Goods by Sea 1885. d. 12th May 1906.

CASSEL, Sir Felix Maximilian Schoenbrunn, Bt.

s. of L.S. Cassel, Orme Square, London. b. 16th Sept. 1869. educ. Harrow; Corpus Christi Coll. Oxf. BA 1892, MA 1920, Hon. Fellow. L.I. April 1894. KC 1906. Bencher 1912, Treasurer 1935. Member LCC 1907-10; MP St. Pancras (West) 1910-16. WWI Capt. 19th Battn. London Regt.; American Distinguished Service Medal 1919. Judge Adv-Genl. 1916-34; member Council of Legal Educ.; Chmn. Departmental Committee on Compulsory Insce. 1936; member Departmental Committee on Courts-Martial 1938; Master of Musicians Co. 1939-44; High Sheriff, Hertfordshire 1942; JP Hertfordshire; Baronet 1920; PC 1937. Father of Sir Harold Cassel Bt. (QC 1970). d. 22nd Feb. 1953.

CASSELS, Sir James Dale

s. of Robert Cassels, Sheen, Surrey, clerk in civil service. b. 22nd March 1877. educ. Westminster City Sch. M.T. July 1908. KC 1923. Bencher 1929, Treasurer 1947. MP Leyton (West) 1922-29, Camberwell (North West) 1931-35; Recorder of Guildford 1927-28, of Brighton 1928-39; KB judge 1939-61; Knight 1939. Father of Francis Henry Cassels (M.T. 1932), circuit judge. d. 7th Feb. 1972.

CASSWELL, Joshua David

s. of Joshua Joyce Casswell, Wimbledon. b. 1886. educ. King's Coll. Sch. Wimbledon; Pembroke Coll. Oxf. BA 1910, MA 1928. M.T. Nov. 1910. KC 1938. Bencher 1947. WWI Commander V Divn. Metrop. Special Constabulary; Major ASC, horse transport (despatches). Recorder of Salisbury 1938-41, of Southampton 1941-51; Official Referee of Supreme Ct. 1951-59; Dep. Chmn. Surrey Quarter Sess. 1954-61; JP Surrey. Author of A Lance for Liberty 1961. d. 15th Dec. 1963.

CASTLE, Edward James

s. of Henry James Castle, King's Coll. London. b. 1st May 1842. educ. King's Coll. London. Lieut. RE 1860-67. I.T. Nov. 1868. QC 1888. Bencher 1894. Recorder of Winchester 1888-97, of Bristol 1897; judge of Bristol Tolzey and Pie Poudre Cts. 1897. Author of Law of Rating, and Law of Commerce in time of War. d. 27th April 1912.

CAUTLEY, Henry Strother (Lord Cautley)

s. of Henry Cautley, Bramley, Leeds (d. 1897). b. 9th Dec. 1863. educ. Charterhouse; King's Coll. Camb. BA 1884. M.T. May 1886. KC 1919. Bencher 1925, Reader 1934. MP Leeds (East) 1900-06, Sussex (East Grinstead) 1910-36; Recorder of Sunderland 1918-35; Director of Pig Production 1918; member of bar council; Chmn. East Sussex Quarter Sess. 1927; JP Sussex; member Ecclesiastical Committee of H of L; Baronet 1924; Baron Cautley of Lindfield 1936. d. 21st Sept. 1946.

CAVE, Edward Watkins

s. of Cave J. b. 1st Aug. 1871. educ. Rugby; King's Coll. Sch.; Oriel Coll. Oxf. 1890. I.T. Nov. 1897. KC 1921. Bencher 1928. Recorder of Birmingham 1932-37; Cty. Ct. judge 1937-46. d. 24th April 1948.

CAVE, George (Lord Cave)

s. of Thomas Cave MP, Queensbury House, Richmond, Surrey (d. 1894). b. 23rd Feb. 1856. educ. Merchant Taylors; St. John's Coll. Oxf. BA 1878, MA 1912, Hon. Fellow 1916, Hon. DCL 1924. I.T. June 1880. KC 1904. Bencher 1912. Recorder of Guildford 1904-13; member of Royal Comm. on Land Transfer 1908; standing counsel to Oxf. Univ. 1913-15; Att-Genl. to Prince of Wales 1914-15; MP Surrey (Kingston) 1906-18; Sol-Genl., PC and knighted 1915; Chmn. Contraband Committee 1915; Home Secy. 1916-19; Viscount 1918; Chmn. Southern Rhodesia Comm. 1919; L of A 1919; Chmn. of committee on Trade Boards, and of Munitions Inquiry Trib. 1921; LC 1922-24 and 1924-28; GCMG 1921; adjudicated in Privy Council on rival claims of Canada and Newfoundland concerning boundaries in Labrador 1927; Hon. Col. and comdt. 2nd Vol. Battn. East Surrey Regt.; Chmn. Surrey Quarter Sess. 1894-1911; DL, JP Surrey and Vice-Lieut.; Hon. Freeman Kingston, Guildford, Richmond (Surrey), Merchant Taylors' Co.; Chan. Oxf. Univ. 1925. Brother of Edmund Cave, Master of the Supreme Ct. (Taxing Office) 1923. d. 29th March 1928.

CAVE, Sir Lewis William

s. of William Cave, Desborough, Northamptonshire. b. 3rd July 1832. educ. Rugby; Lincoln Coll. Oxf. BA 1855, MA 1877. I.T. June 1859. QC 1875. Bencher 1877. Recorder of Lincoln 1873-81; Commr. of Assize 1877; Commr. to inquire into corrupt election practices at Oxford 1880; QB judge 1881-97; Knight 1881; judge in bankruptcy 1883-91; edited C.G. Addison's treatises on the law of contracts, and the law of torts; edited (with T. Bell) Stone's Practice of the Petty Sessions; an editor of reports of the Court for the consideration of Crown Cases Reserved 1861-65; part editor of Burn's Justice of the Peace. d. 7th Sept. 1897.

CECIL, Edgar Algernon Robert Gascoygne (Lord Cecil of Chelwood)

s. of 3rd Marquess of Salisbury. b. 14th Sept. 1864. educ. Eton; University Coll. Oxf. BA 1886, MA 1910, Hon. DCL 1919, Hon. Fellow. I.T. Nov. 1887. QC 1899. Bencher 1910. Practised at parliamentary bar; MP East Marylebone 1906-10, Hitchin 1911-23; Parliamentary under-secy. foreign affairs 1915-18; Minister of Blockade 1916-18; Pres. League of Nations Union 1923-45; Chan. and Vicar-Genl. York 1915; Lord Privy Seal 1923-24; Chan. Duchy of Lancaster 1924-27; Chmn. Hertfordshire Quarter Sess. 1911-20;. Pres. Nat. Assoc. of Building Societies 1928-36; Nobel Peace prize 1937; PC 1915; Viscount 1923; CH 1956; Rector Aberdeen Univ.; Chan. Birmingham Univ. 1918-44; Hon. LLD. Camb., Edin., Manchester, Liverpool, St. Andrews, Aberdeen, Princeton, Columbia and Athens. Published autobiography 1941. d. 24th Nov. 1958.

CHADWICK-HEALEY, Sir Charles Edward Heley, Bt.

s. of Edward Charles Healey JP, Crawley, Surrey (d. 1906). b. 26th Aug. 1845. L.I. Jan. 1872. QC 1891. Bencher. Chmn. Admiralty Volunteer Committee 1903-14. Hon. Capt. RNR 1914; Admiralty Transport Arbitration Board 1914-18; commanded hospital ship Queen Alexandra 1915-18. Chan. of dioceses of Salisbury, Bath and Wells, and Exeter; High Sheriff, Somerset 1911-12; Chmn. Somerset Quarter Sess.; DL, JP Somerset; JP Surrey; FSA; CB 1905; KCB 1909; Baronet 1919. d. 5th Oct. 1919.

CHALMERS, Sir Mackenzie Dalzell

s. of Rev. Frederick Skene Courtenay Chalmers, Nonington, Kent. b. 7th Feb. 1847. educ. King's Coll. London; Trinity Coll. Oxf. BA 1868, MA 1876. Bengal Civil Service 1869-72. I.T. Jan. 1869. Standing counsel to Bd. of Trade 1882; Cty. Ct. judge 1884-96; Acting Chief Justice, Gibraltar, 1893; Commr. of Assize 1895; legal member Viceroy's Council 1896; First parliamentary counsel 1902;

Permanent Under-Secy. of State Home Dept. 1903-08; CSI 1898; CB 1904, KCB 1906; JP Warwickshire. Author of Digest of the Law of Bills of Exchange 1878, on which Bills of Exchange Act 1882 was based; draftsman of Sale of Goods Act 1894, and Marine Insurance Act 1906. d. 22nd Dec. 1927.

CHAMBERS, Montagu

s. of George Chambers, Harford, Huntingdonshire. b. 1799. Ensign, Grenadier Guards 1815-18, then on half-pay. L.I. Feb. 1828. QC 1845. Bencher 1845, Treasurer 1868. MP Greenwich 1852-57, Devonport 1866-74. Edited Law Journal reports 1835-65. d. 18th Sept. 1885.

CHAMBERS, Sir Thomas

s. of Thomas Chambers, Hertford. b. 17th Dec. 1814. educ. Clare Coll. Camb. LLB 1836, BA 1840. M.T. Nov. 1840. QC 1861. Bencher 1861, Reader 1863, Treasurer 1871. MP Hertford 1852-57, Marylebone 1865-85; Common Serjeant 1857-78; Recorder of London 1878-91; Steward of Southwark 1884-91; Knight 1872. Joint author of treatises on law of buildings, and law of railway companies. d. 24th Dec. 1891.

CHANCE, George

s. of William Chance, Birmingham, merchant. b. 22nd Dec. 1818. educ. Trinity Coll. Camb. BA 1843, 23rd Wrangler, MA 1846. L.I. Nov. 1846. Commr. to inquire into trade union outrages in Sheffield and Manchester 1867; metrop. magistrate Lambeth 1870-89; JP Middlesex and Home Counties. d. 17th Feb. 1903.

CHANDLESS, Thomas

s. of Thomas Chandless, London. b. 1798. G.I. June 1822. QC 1851. Bencher 1847, Treasurer 1850. Father of Thomas Chandless (I.T.

1853). d. 22nd Feb. 1883.

CHANNELL, Sir Arthur Moseley

s. of W.F. Channell, Exch. Baron. b. 13th Nov. 1838. educ. Harrow; Trinity Coll. Camb. BA 1861, 26th Wrangler, MA 1864; rowing blue. I.T. June 1863. QC 1885. Bencher 1891. Specialised in local govt. cases; Recorder of Rochester 1888-97; Vice-Chmn. bar council 1895; QB judge 1897-1914; Knight 1897; Vice-Chmn. Council of Legal Educ. 1909; tried Richard Arthur Prince, murderer of William Terriss, the actor, 1898; PC 1914; sat in Prize Ct. appeals 1916-27, and as temporary KB judge 1921; JP Somerset. Father of Walter Thornton Trevelyan Channell (solicitor 1904), Herbert Mitford Trevelyan Channell (I.T. 1911) and Arthur Willoughby Trevelyan Channell (I.T. 1904). d. 4th Oct. 1928.

CHANNELL, Sir William Fry

s. of Pike Channell, officer in Royal Navy, afterwards a merchant in London. b. 31st Aug. 1804. educ. Palace Sch. Enfield. Articled to solicitor in London. I.T. May 1827. Serjeant 1840. Shared with Serjeant Talfourd leading business of Ct. of Common Pleas 1840-46; patent of precedence 1845. Leader of Home circuit 1845-57; Commr. of Assize 1856; Exch. Baron 1857-73; Knight 1857; nominated PC 1873 but did not live to be sworn in. d. 26th Feb. 1873.

CHAPMAN, Cecil Maurice

s. of Henry Chapman, Wanstead, Essex. b. 24th June 1852. educ. Tonbridge; Balliol Coll. Oxf. BA 1875. I.T. July 1878. Member of LCC 1896-98; metrop. magistrate 1899, finally at Westminster 1917-24; JP London and Home Counties. Author of The Poor Man's Court of Justice 1925, From the Bench 1932; editor of Cunningham's Indian Law of Evidence Act. d. 23rd. June 1938.

CHAPMAN, Edward Henry

s. of Joseph John Chapman JP, Whitby, Yorkshire, barrister. b. 5th Feb. 1874. educ. Eton; Magdalen Coll. Oxf. BA 1897, MA 1901. I.T. June 1900. Cty. Ct. judge 1923-33. d. 21st July 1933.

CHAPPELL, Robert Kingsley

s. of George Chappell JP, Wimbledon. b. 29th Nov. 1884. educ. Leeds Gr. Sch.; Merchant Taylors' (Crosby); Liverpool Univ. LLB. Qualified as solicitor 1906. I.T. Nov. 1909. KC 1929. WWI Lieut. RGA (despatches twice); Courts Martial Officer (Temp.Capt.). Judge of Appeal, Isle of Man 1934; acting Deemster, Isle of Man 1934. d. 11th Aug. 1937.

CHARLES, Sir Arthur

s. of Robert Charles, London and Carisbrooke, Isle of Wight. b. 23rd Jan. 1839. educ. Univ. Coll. Sch.; University Coll. London BA 1858. I.T. Jan. 1862 (Cert. of Hon.). QC 1877. Bencher 1880. A leader on Western circuit; Recorder of Bath 1878-87; Commr. for corrupt practices in Canterbury election 1880; Commr. to inquire into constitution of ecclesiastical cts. 1881; examr. in common law, London Univ. 1877-82; Chan. of diocese of Southwell 1884-87; Commissary of Westminster 1884-87; QB judge 1887-97; Knight 1887; judge of Ct. of Arches of Canterbury, and of Chancery Ct. of York 1899-1903; member Council of Legal Educ. and Inc. Council of Law Reporting; PC 1903; Hon. MA Cantuar.; Hon. DCL Durham; Pres. of Senate, University Coll. London 1889-96. d. 20th Nov. 1921.

CHARLES, Sir Ernest Bruce

s. of Charles J. b. 15th June 1871. educ. Clifton Coll.; New Coll. Oxf. BA 1895, MA. I.T. June 1896. KC 1913. Bencher 1922. WWI Director of Wounded and Missing Dept., Br. Red Cross in France and hon. legal adviser to Red Cross; civil member of Claims Comm. in France; CBE 1919. Chan. of dioceses of Wakefield and Hereford 1912-28, Chelmsford 1922-28; Commissary-Genl. diocese of Canterbury; Recorder of Bournemouth 1915-24, of Southampton 1924-28; KB judge 1928-47; Knight 1928; KSt J; Freeman of Deal 1931. d. 3rd May 1950.

CHARLEY, Sir William Thomas

s. of Matthew Charley, Finaghy House, Belfast. b. 5th March 1833. educ. Elstree House Sch.; Belmont Lee, Kent; St. John's Coll. Oxf. BA 1856, BCL and DCL 1868. I.T. June 1865. QC 1880. MP Salford 1868-80; Common Serjeant 1878-92; Knight 1880; Officer commanding 3rd Vol. Batt. Royal Fusiliers, City of London Regt. 1883-89; Hon. Col. 1889; VD; Master of Loriners' Co.; DL London. Author of works on Real Property Acts and Judicature Acts. d. 8th July 1904.

CHARTERIS, Sir Evan Edward

s. of Francis Richard Charteris, 10th Earl of Wemyss. b. 29th Jan. 1864. educ. Eton. Lieut. Coldstream Gds. 1885-87. I.T. June 1891. WWI Staff Capt. RFC and Tank Corps. KC 1919. Bencher 1924. Practised at parliamentary bar; Chmn. Trustees of National Portrait Gall. 1928; Chmn. Tate Gallery 1934-40; Trustee of National Gallery 1932-39; Trustee of Wallace Collection; Chmn. Standing Committee on Museums and Galleries; Knight 1932; JP East Lothian. d. 16th Nov. 1940.

CHAYTOR, Alfred Henry

s. of John Clervaux Chaytor, Marshlands, Spring Creek, New Zealand (d. 1920). b. 28th Oct. 1869. educ. Durham Sch.; Clare Coll. Camb. BA 1892, LLB 1892, MA 1896, Fellow 1894. I.T. June 1894. KC 1914. WWI Capt. 8th City of London Regt. Father of

Alfred Drewett Chaytor (I.T. 1925). d. 12th July 1931.

CHILTON, George

s. of George Chilton, Chancery Lane, London, solicitor. b. 10th April 1796. educ. Charterhouse; Queen's Coll. Oxf. BA 1818. I.T. June 1820. QC 1837. Bencher 1837, Reader 1848, Treasurer 1849. Recorder of Hereford and Gloucester 1837-52; Cty. Ct. judge 1847-52. Edited R.B. Comyn's treatise on law of landlord and tenant 1830. d. Boulogne, 2nd Nov. 1852.

CHITTY, Sir Joseph William

s. of Thomas Chitty, special pleader (d. 1878). b. 28th May 1828. educ. Eton (captain); Balliol Coll. Oxf. BA 1851, Vinerian Scholar 1852, MA 1855; rowed against Camb.; Petrean Fellow, Exeter Coll. 1852-58. L.I. April 1856. QC 1874. Bencher 1875, Treasurer 1895. Leader in Rolls Ct.; MP Oxford 1880-81; Chancery judge 1881-97; Knight 1881; LJ 1897-99; PC 1897; appeals from his judgments rare and seldom successful; nominated judge under Benefices Act 1898; Major, Inns of Ct. Rifle Vol. 1869-76; umpire at Oxf. and Camb. boat race 1857-81. Father of Arthur John Chitty (L.I. 1885), Sir Joseph Henry Pollock Chitty 1861-1942, (solicitor 1887), Chief Master in Chancery, and Herbert Chitty FSA (I.T. 1889), bursar of Winchester Coll. d. 15th Feb. 1899.

CHITTY, Sir Thomas Willes, Bt.

s. of Thomas Edward Chitty, barrister (d. 1868). b. 24th June 1855. educ. Winchester; I.T. June 1877. KC 1927. Bencher 1925. Held substantial practice at common law bar; Master in the Supreme Ct. 1901-20; Senior Master and King's Remembrancer 1920-26, Knight 1919; Baronet 1924; member of Judicature Committee 1908, Br. and Foreign Legal Procedure Committee 1918, Committee on Crown procedure 1922, Arbitration Committee 1926, and others. Edited Archbold's Practice, Chitty's Forms, Smith's Leading Cases,

Bullen and Leake's Pleadings; managing editor of Halsbury's Laws of England; editor-in-chief, English and Empire Digest. Father of Sir Thomas Henry Willes Chitty 2nd Bt. (I.T. 1914) and Robert Michael Willes Chitty (Canadian bar). d. 15th Feb. 1930.

CHRISTIE, Harold Alfred Hunter

s. of Sir William Henry Mahoney Christie KCB, FRS, astronomer royal (d. 1922). b. 1st Oct. 1884. educ. Marlborough; Trinity Hall Camb. BA. I.T. Nov. 1913; L.I. 1929. KC 1934. Bencher 1940, Treasurer 1960. WWI Capt. West Kent Yeo.; Major 1931; TD; WWII Sqn. Leader RAFVR. Equity draftsman and conveyancer; vice-chmn. bar council 1949-53; Master of Clockmakers' Co. 1939. d. 23rd Oct. 1960.

CLARK, Sir Andrew Edmund James, Bt.

s. of Sir James Richardson Andrew Clark, 2nd Bt. b. 18th July1898. educ. Eton. WWI Capt. RFA (MC). I.T. June 1928; L.I. 1930. KC 1943. Bencher (I.T.) 1950. WWII Lt.Col. and Hon. Brig. Regular Army, R.O.; acting chief of legal divn., Control Comm. for Germany 1944-45; MBE 1941. Conducted Crichel Down Inquiry 1954; OStJ; succeeded father 1948. Father of Jennifer Jane Clark (I.T. 1955) and Susan Mary Clark (I.T. 1958). d. 19th May 1979.

CLARK, Andrew Rutherfurd

s. of Rev. Thomas Clark DD, Edinburgh. b. 1828. educ. Edin. Univ. Hon. LLD. Scottish bar 1849; advocate depute 1851-52, 1853-58, 1859-60; Sheriff of Inverness 1860, of Haddington and Berwick 1862-69; QC 1869; Sol-Genl. Scotland 1869-74; Dean of Faculty of Advocates 1874; Lord of Session 1875-96. d. 26th July 1899.

CLARK, Charles

s. of William Clark, Clerkenwell, London. M.T. May 1830. QC 1874. Bencher 1872, Reader 1878. Official reporter to House of Lords 1840; Secy. to Channel Islands criminal law comm. 1846; Secy. to Juridical Socy. 1855-58. Author of A summary of colonial law 1834; reported H of L cases 1849-66; reported (with P.Dow) H of L cases 1827-32, (with W. Finnelly) H of L cases 1835-47. d. 28th June 1881, age 78.

CLARK, James William

s. of James Clark, Winchmore Hill, London, Secy. of Colonial Bank. b. 30th May 1851. educ. Brentwood Gr. Sch.; Trinity Hall. Camb. BA 1874, MA 1877, Fellow 1874. L.I. May 1879. KC 1904. Conveyancing counsel to Office of Woods and Forests 1894-95; counsel to Att-Genl. in charity matters 1894-95; legal adviser to Bd. of Agriculture and Fisheries 1895-1915. Joint author of Elphinstone, Norton and Clark on Interpretation of Deeds, and of Elphinstone and Clark on Searches; joint editor of Goodeve's Real Property and Goodeve's Personal Property. d. 21st July 1921.

CLARK, Thomas James

s. of William Clark, Edmonton, Middlesex, crop merchant. b. 1822. educ. University Coll. London BA 1842. I.T. Nov. 1845. QC 1866. Bencher 1867. d. 17th March 1877.

CLARKE, Sir Edward George

s. of Job Guy Clarke, London, jeweller. b. 15th Feb. 1841. educ. College House, Edmonton; City Commercial Sch.; City of London Coll. Assisted father 1854-58; Clerk in India Office 1859-60; supported himself by journalism while reading for bar. L.I. Nov. 1864. QC 1880. In Penge case (murder of Harriet Staunton) 1877, Adelaide Bartlett case (murder of husband) 1886, Baccarat case (cheating at cards) 1891, Jameson case (Transvaal) 1896; MP

Plymouth 1880-1900; Sol-Genl. 1886-92; Knight 1886; MP City of London 1906; PC 1908; Hon. Col. 2nd Batt. Middlesex Vol. Regt.; retired from practice 1914. Author of treatise on law of extradition 1866, and The Story of My Life 1918. Father of Edward Percival Clarke, Recorder of Exeter (L.I. 1894) and William Francis Clarke OBE (LI. 1906). d. 26th April 1931.

CLARKE, Nathaniel Richard

s. of Nathaniel Gooding Clarke KC, Handsworth, Staffordshire (d. 1833). b. 11th May 1785. educ. Ashbourne Gr. Sch.; Trinity Coll. Camb. BA 1808, MA 1811 (Christ's Coll.), Fellow 1808-10. M.T. Nov. 1811. Recorder of Lincoln, Newark, Northampton and Walsall to 1859; Serjeant 1843; Cty. Ct. judge 1847-59; DL, JP Staffordshire, Derbyshire, Warwickshire. d. 31st July 1859.

CLARKSON, Eugene Comerford

s. of Frederick Clarkson, proctor and notary. b. 1831. educ. King's Coll. London. L.I. Jan. 1854. QC 1881. Practised in Ct. of Admiralty. Father of Harold Comerford Clarkson (I.T. 1885). d. 19th Aug. 1881.

CLAUSON, Albert Charles (Lord Clauson)

s. of Charles Clauson, London, merchant, and nephew of Lord Wrenbury. b. 14th Jan. 1870. educ. Merchant Taylors; St. John's Coll. Oxf. BA 1891, Hon. Fellow 1927. L.I. Jan. 1891. KC 1910. Bencher 1914, Treasurer 1937. Leading equity practitioner; standing counsel to Oxf. Univ. and Royal Coll. of Physicians 1923-26; legal member of Controller's staff, Admiralty during WWI; CBE 1920; member Lord Southborough's Indian Reforms Comm. 1918; Chancery judge 1926-38; Knight 1926; LJ 1938-42; PC 1938; Baron 1942; JP Hertfordshire; twice Master of Merchant Taylors' Co. d. 15th March 1946.

CLAYTON, Edward

s. of James Clayton, Hornsey, North London. b. 1856. educ. Dr. Samuel Kinn's Sch., Highbury. Articled to solicitor 1874. G.I. Jan. 1885. KC 1909. Bencher 1904, Treasurer 1911. Equity draftsman and conveyancer. d. 5th May 1938.

CLEASBY, Sir Anthony

s. of Stephen Cleasby, Cragg House, Westmoreland, Russia broker (d. 1844). b. 27th Aug. 1804. educ. Eton; Trinity Coll. Camb. BA 1827, 3rd Wrangler, MA 1830, Fellow 1828-36. I.T. June 1831. QC 1861. Bencher 1861-68. Had flourishing commercial practice; unsuccessful as parliamentary candidate; Exch. Baron 1868-79; Knight 1868. Father of Richard Digby Cleasby (I.T. 1864), Sheriff of Brecon. d. 6th Oct. 1879.

CLEMENTS, Arthur Frederick

s. of Rev. John Clements, Newark-on-Trent. b. 21st Jan. 1877. educ. privately; Univ. of Wales. Solicitor 1899. M.T. May 1911. Recorder of Tewkesbury 1927-30; member of bar council 1922-30; Cty. Ct. judge 1930-50; Chmn. East Kent Quarter Sess. 1940-47; Commr. High Ct. (matrimonial causes) 1947-50; JP Kent; FSA 1939. d. 20th Jan. 1968.

CLERK, John

s. of Sir George Clerk PC, FRS, DCL, 6th Bt. (d. 1867). b. 16th April 1816. I.T. June 1841. QC 1868. Bencher 1868, Treasurer 1885. JP Leicestershire. Author of works on election law. Father of John Frederick Clerk, (I.T. 1874). d. 10th April 1900.

CLEVELAND-STEVENS, William Cleveland

s. of William Richard Stevens DL, JP, Winchet Hall, Goudhurst, Kent, solicitor. b. 21st Oct. 1880. educ. Westminster; Christ Church

Oxf. BA 1904, MA and BCL 1907. L.I. June 1907. KC 1930. Bencher 1935, Treasurer 1955. WWI Lieut. RNVR; signal officer in HMS New Zealand at Jutland (despatches); Asst. to Director of Signal Divn. Admiralty. Equity draftsman and conveyancer; Chan. of diocese of Birmingham 1937, Truro 1940, Gloucester 1946; Director Council of Legal Educ., and Head of Inns of Ct. Sch. of Law 1939; Dep. Chmn. Enemy Exports Committee 1939, Contraband Committee 1940; CMG 1953; JP Essex. Father of William Herbert Carnegie Cleveland-Stevens (L.I.1948), and Robert Victor Carnegie Cleveland-Stevens (L.I.1949). d. 10th June 1957.

CLIFFORD, Frederick

s. of Jesse Clifford, Brompton, Kent. b. 22nd June 1828. educ. privately. On parliamentary staff of Times 1852, Asst. Editor 1877-83. M.T. June 1859. QC 1894, Bencher 1900. Author of The History of Private Bill Legislation. d. 30th Dec. 1904.

CLIVE, George

s. of Edward Bolton Clive MP, Whitfield, Herefordshire (d. 1845). b. France, Oct. 1806. educ. Harrow; Brasenose Coll. Oxf. BA 1826, MA 1829. L.I. June 1830. Metrop. magistrate, Kensington and Wandsworth 1840-47; Cty. Ct. judge 1847-58; Recorder of Wokingham 1849-58; MP Hereford 1857-69 and 1874-80; Under-Secy. of State for Home Dept. 1859-62; Chmn. Herefordshire Quarter Sess. 1871-80; DL, JP Herefordshire. Father of Archer Anthony Clive (I.T. 1868). d. 8th June 1880.

CLODE, Sir Walter Baker

s. of Charles Mathew Clode CB, legal under-secy. War. Dept. (d. 1893). b. 10th July 1856. educ. Winchester; Oriel Coll. Oxf. BA 1879, MA 1887. I.T. Jan. 1881. KC 1912. Bencher 1920. Pres. Ry. Rates Tribunal 1922-32; Master Merchant Taylors' Co.; Knight

1928. Author of works on the law relating to Petition of Right, rating of railways, tenement houses and flats. d. 27th Feb. 1937.

CLOTHIER, Wilfrid

s. of William Charles Clothier, Yeovil, senior surveyor HM Customs. b. 19th Feb. 1887. educ. privately; Liverpool Univ. LLB 1908, LLM 1909. Solicitor 1909, practised in Liverpool. WWI Private HAC, and legal asst. to Director-Genl. of Recruiting, Min. of Nat. Service. I.T. Jan. 1920. KC 1933. Bencher 1941, Treasurer 1965. Recorder of Blackburn 1944-47; Cty. Ct. judge 1947-59. Brother of Henry Williamson Clothier CBE (G.I. 1914), Director of Accounts, Air Ministry. d. 9th Feb. 1967.

CLUER, Albert Rowland

s. of John Thomas Townsend Cluer, London. b. 3rd Dec. 1852. educ. Balliol Coll. Oxf. BA 1876. L.I. June 1877. Recorder of Deal 1894-95; metrop. magistrate 1895, finally at Worship St. 1896-1911; Cty. Ct. judge 1911-34; JP London and Home Counties. Father of Reginald Montagu Cluer, puisne judge Jamaica 1944. d. 12th Jan. 1942.

COCK, Alfred

s. of James Cock, Shrewsbury, tanner. b. 4th May 1849. educ. Shrewsbury; London Univ. M.T. Nov. 1871. QC 1886. Bencher 1891. FSA 1893. d. 20th April 1898.

COCKBURN, Sir Alexander James Edmund, Bt.

s. of Alexander Cockburn, Hertford St., Mayfair, diplomat (d. 1852). b. 24th Dec. 1802. educ. abroad; Trinity Hall Camb. LLB 1829, Fellow 1829, LLD 1874. M.T. Feb. 1829. QC 1841. Bencher 1841, Reader 1847, Treasurer 1852. Member comm. on municipal corporations 1834; defended Daniel M'Naughten who assassinated Edward Drummond, mistaking him for Sir Robert Peel (acquitted as insane) 1843; Recorder of Southampton 1840-46, of Bristol 1854-56; MP Southampton 1847-56; noted for his support of Palmerston's foreign policy 1850; Sol-Genl. 1850; Knight 1850; Att-Genl. 1851-52 and 1852-56; led prosecution of William Palmer, the Rugeley poisoner 1856; PC 1857; CJ of Common Pleas 1856; LCJ of QB 1859-80; presided at trial of Tichborne claimant 1873-74; GCB 1873 for services in Alabama Arbitration; Freeman of City of London 1876; succeeded uncle as 10th baronet of Nova Scotia 1858; reported election cases (with W.C. Rowe) 1832. d. 20th Nov. 1880.

COCKBURN, Archibald William

s. of Henry Cockburn, Collingham Road, London S.W.5. b. 6th June 1887. educ. Eton; New Coll. Oxf. BA 1911, MA 1913. I.T. Jan. 1913. KC 1938. Bencher 1935, Treasurer 1959. WWI 2nd. Lieut. RGA. Secy. Royal Comm. on Cattle Importation 1921; Secy. Arbitral Trib. (USA and Peru) 1922; member of bar council 1919-27 and 1930-38; member Supreme Ct. Rule Committee 1930-38; Recorder of Ludlow 1934-36, of Oxford 1936-38; Chmn. Hope Reorganisation committee for England 1938; Chmn. Home Office Advisory Committee (Defence Regulation 18B) 1940-45; Dep. Chmn. London Sessions 1938-54, Chmn. 1954-59; Chmn. London Magistrates Courts Committee 1954. Joint editor of Pratt and MacKenzie's Law of Highways. d. 19th Sept. 1969.

COHEN, Arthur

s. of Benjamin Cohen, London. b. 18th Nov. 1830. educ. University Coll. London; Magdalen Coll. Camb. BA 1856, 5th Wrangler, MA 1879, Hon. Fellow 1883. I.T. Nov. 1857. QC 1874. Bencher, Treasurer 1894. Junior counsel for GB in Alabama arbitration at Geneva 1872; MP Southwark 1880-87; standing counsel to Camb. Univ. 1879; refused High Ct. judgeship 1881; standing counsel to India Office 1893; PC 1905; Chmn. Royal Comm. on Shipping

Combinations 1906; member Senate, London Univ.; judge of the Cinque Ports 1875-1914; FBA. d. 3rd Nov. 1914.

COHEN, Sir Benjamin Arthur

s. of Arthur Cohen KC. b. 20th Dec. 1862. educ. Rugby; Balliol Coll. Oxf. BA 1886. I.T. Nov. 1887. KC 1914. Bencher 1923. Junior counsel to Admiralty 1910; Senior Referee under Contributory Pensions Act; Knight 1929. Father of Nathaniel Arthur Jim Cohen, Cty. Ct. judge 1955. d. 22nd Dec. 1942.

COHEN, Lionel Leonard (Lord Cohen)

s. of Sir Leonard Lionel Cohen KCVO, banker (d. 1938). b. 1st March 1888. educ. Eton; New Coll. Oxf. BA 1909, MA 1913, Hon. Fellow 1946. I.T. Jan. 1913. KC 1929. Bencher (L.I.) 1934, Treasurer 1954. WWI Capt. 13th Princess Louise's Kensington Battn., London Regt. and on staff. Acquired extensive practice in company law; with Min. of Economic Warfare 1939-43; Chancery judge 1943-46; Knight 1943; LJ 1946-51; PC 1946; Chmn. Company Law Amendment Committee, largely responsible for drafting Companies Act 1948; L of A 1951-60; Baron 1951; Chmn. Royal Comm. on awards to inventors during WWII, including radar and the jet engine 1946-56; one of the "3 Wise Men" appointed by Harold Macmillan to devise an incomes policy 1957; member of trib. to assess compensation for assets vested in NCB on nationalisation; Pres. Jewish Bd. of Guardians; Vice-Pres. Jewish Bd. of Deputies 1934-39; Capt. Royal and Ancient Golf Club; Pres. Council of St. Mary's Hosp. Medical Sch. 1961-66; Fellow of Eton 1950-60; Chmn. College Committee, Univ. Coll. London 1953-63. Father of Leonard Harold Lionel Cohen (L.I. 1948). d. 9th May 1973.

COLAM, Robert Frederick

s. of John Colam, Croydon, Surrey, Secy. to RSPCA (d. 1910). b.

1859. M.T. June 1884. KC 1912. Special pleader. Bencher 1921-25. Recorder of Croydon 1900-39; Assoc. of Surveyors Instit. d. 3rd May 1942.

COLDRIDGE, Ward

s. of Charles Sharman Coldridge. b. 1864. educ. Exeter Gr. Sch.; Emmanuel Coll. Camb. BA 1887, MA 1891. L.I. Nov. 1892. KC 1912. Bencher 1917. Registrar in bankruptcy 1926. Joint author of manual on law of gambling. d. 3rd April 1926.

COLE, Henry Thomas

s. of George Cole, Capt. Cornwall Militia. b. 2nd Feb. 1816. M.T. Nov. 1842. QC 1866. Bencher 1867, Reader 1873, Treasurer 1883. Leader of Western circuit; Recorder of Penzance 1862-72, of Plymouth and Devonport 1872-85; MP Falmouth and Penryn 1874-80. d. 5th Jan. 1885.

COLE, Henry Warwick

s. of William Nicholas Cole, Islington, solicitor. b. 12th Oct. 1812. educ. University Coll. London. I.T. June 1836. QC 1861. Bencher 1861, Reader 1873, Treasurer 1874. Cty. Ct. judge 1872-76. Author of Law of domicile of Englishmen in France 1857. d. 19th June 1876.

COLEFAX, Sir Henry Arthur

s. of Joseph Samuel Colefax JP, Bradford. b. 1866. educ. Bradford Gr. Sch.; Postmaster Merton Coll. Oxf.; Christ Church BA 1888, MA 1892; Strasburg Univ. Ph.D. L.I. Nov. 1894. KC 1912. Bencher 1916. Authority on patent and trademark law; MP Manchester (South West) 1910; Sol-Genl. Cty. Palatine of Durham 1918-30,

Chan. 1930-36; KBE 1920 for war work with Min. of Munitions and the Admiralty; presided at Ct. of Inquiry into London bus strike 1924, and Ct. of Inquiry into loss of HMS Glatton 1918. d. 19th Feb. 1936.

COLERIDGE, Bernard Seymour John (Lord Coleridge)

s. of Coleridge LCJ. b. 19th Aug. 1851. educ. Eton; Trinity Coll. Oxf. BA 1875, MA 1878, Hon. Fellow 1910. M.T. June 1877. QC 1892. Bencher 1894, Reader 1907, Treasurer 1918. MP Sheffield (Attercliffe) 1885-94; succeeded father as 2nd Baron 1894; Commr. of Assize, Midland circuit 1906-07; KB judge 1907-23; Chmn. Conciliation Bd. for Coal Trade of Federated Districts 1912-18; Chmn. Devon Quarter Sess.; JP Devon; FRSL 1916. Author of The Story of a Devonshire House 1905, This for Remembrance 1925. d. 4th Sept. 1927.

COLERIDGE, John Duke (Lord Coleridge)

s; of Coleridge J. b. 3rd Dec. 1820. educ. Eton; Balliol Coll. Oxf. BA 1842, Petrean Fellow Exeter Coll. 1843-46, MA 1846, DCL 1877, Hon. Fellow 1882. M.T. Nov. 1846. QC 1861. Bencher 1861, Reader 1864, Treasurer 1890. Leader of Western circuit; Recorder of Portsmouth 1855-66; MP Exeter 1865-73; Sol-Genl. 1868-71; Knight 1868; Att-Genl. 1871-73; leading counsel for trustees of Tichborne estates in action brought against them by the claimant, Orton, 1871-72; CJ of Common Pleas 1873-75, and Pres. of CP Divn. 1875-80; PC 1873; Baron Coleridge of Ottery St. Mary 1874; LCJ 1880-94; presided at trial of Dudley and Stephens (cannibalism by shipwrecked mariners); opened the new Royal Cts. of Justice 1883; member of Public Schools, Judicature, and Cathedral Comms.; first pres. of Bach Choir 1876-85; FRS 1877. Father of Stephen William Buchanan Coleridge (M.T. 1886), clerk of assize, South Wales circuit, and Gilbert James Duke Coleridge (M.T. 1886), asst. Master in Crown office. d. 14th June 1894. Biography by E.H. Coleridge 2 vols. 1904.

COLERIDGE, Sir John Taylor

s. of James Coleridge JP, Ottery St. Mary, Devon, Capt. 6th Foot (d. 1836). b. 9th July 1790. educ. Eton; Corpus Christi Coll. Oxf. BA 1815, MA 1817, Vinerian law scholar 1812, Fellow of Exeter Coll. 1817-18, Hon. DCL 1852. Special pleader. M.T. June 1819. Commr. in Bankruptcy 1827; Recorder of Exeter 1832; Serjeant 1832; member of Inns of Ct. and Chancery Comm. 1834; declined recorderships of Southmolton and Barnstaple; KB judge 1835-58; Knight 1835; PC and member Judicial Committee 1858; member Law Courts Comm. 1858, Oxf. Univ. Comm. and Educ. Comm. Edited Quarterly Review 1824; edited Blackstone's Commentaries 1825. d. 11th Feb. 1876.

COLLIER, John Francis

s. of John Collier MP, Plymouth, shipowner. b. 19th June 1829. educ. Winchester. I.T. June 1859. Recorder of Poole 1870-73; Cty. Ct. judge 1873-1907; JP Lancashire. Joint author (with Col. Pipon) of a manual of military law. d. 10th Dec. 1913.

COLLIER, Robert Porrett (Lord Monkswell)

s. of John Collier, MP for Plymouth (d. 1849). b. 21st June 1817. educ. Plymouth Gr. Sch.; Trinity Coll. Camb. BA 1843. Member of Anti-Corn Law League. I.T. Jan. 1843. QC 1854. Bencher. Leader of Western circuit; obtained pardon for Brazilian pirates (murder of ten Englishmen at sea) 1845; Recorder of Penzance 1848-56; MP Plymouth 1852-71; counsel to Admiralty and Judge Adv. of the Fleet 1859-63; Sol-Genl. 1863-66; Knight 1863; Att-Genl. 1868-71; Recorder of Bristol 1870; PC 1871; appointed as Judge of Common Pleas Nov. 1871, simply to enable Gladstone a few days later to make him a judicial member of the Privy Council, referred to at the time as the "Colliery Scandal"; Baron Monkswell 1885; DL Devon. Exhibited many landscapes at RA; author of a manual on the railways clauses, companies clauses, and lands clauses consolidation

Acts 1845, and treatises on the law relating to mines 1849, and on reform of the superior courts of common law 1851. Father of Robert Collier, 2nd Baron (I.T. 1869), lord-in-waiting to Queen Victoria. d. nr. Cannes, 27th Oct. 1886.

COLLINGWOOD, Sir Charles Arthur

s. of Charles Meadows Collingwood, schoolmaster. b. 2nd Nov. 1887. educ. Exeter Sch.; Downing Coll. Camb. MA, LLB, Hon. Fellow 1950. L.I. May 1912. WWI Lieut. Northumberland Fusiliers; Courts-martial officer (Captain). Asst. Judge Adv-Genl. 1943-45; Cty. Ct. judge 1945-50; presided as a judge-advocate at trial in Hamburg of FM von Manstein, 1949; P D and A judge 1950-62; Knight 1950. d. 23rd May 1964.

COLLINS, Sir Arthur John Hammond

s. of John Collins, Parkstone, Dorset, HM Coastguard Service. b. Feb. 1834. G.I. June 1860. QC 1877. Bencher 1877, Treasurer 1883 and 1905. Recorder of Poole 1873-79, of Exeter 1879-85; Chief Commr. to inquire into corrupt election practices in Chester 1880; member Council of Legal Educ.; member of bar committee 1883; CJ Madras 1885-99; Knight 1885; V-C. Madras Univ. 1889-99. d. 12th Sept. 1915.

COLLINS, Richard Henn (Lord Collins)

s. of Stephen Collins QC, Merrion Square, Dublin (d. 1843). b. 1st Jan. 1842. educ. Royal Sch. Dungannon; Trinity Coll. Dublin. Hon. LLD 1898; Downing Coll. Camb. BA 1865, MA 1868, Fellow 1865, Hon. Fellow 1885, LLD 1902. M.T. Nov. 1867. QC 1883. Bencher 1886, Reader 1895, Treasurer 1905. Expert in municipal and railway law; QB judge 1891-97; Knight 1891; judicial member and chmn. Ry. and Canal Comm. 1894; an arbitrator in Venezuela Boundary dispute 1899; LJ 1897-1901; PC 1897; MR 1901-07; Chmn. of Comm. of Inquiry which led to Criminal Appeal Act 1907; Chmn.

Historical Manuscripts Comm. 1901-07; Baron Collins of Kensington 1907; a trustee of Br. Museum 1908; DCL Oxf. 1904; DLitt. Manchester. Joint editor of Smith's Leading Cases. Brother of John Stephen Collins JP (Irish bar 1858). d. 3rd Jan. 1911.

COLLINS, William Anthony

s. of Charles Collins, Brixworth Hall, Northamptonshire. b. 1801. educ. Christ's Coll. Camb. BA 1824, 6th Wrangler, MA 1827, Fellow 1828-30. L.I. Nov. 1829. QC 1861. Bencher 1861. d. 30th March 1875.

COLLYER, John

s. of Ven. John Bedingfeld Collyer, Norwich (d. 1857). b. 15th July 1801. educ. Charterhouse; Clare Coll. Camb. BA 1822, MA 1825, Fellow 1828-31. L.I. Feb. 1827. Commissary of Norwich 1842; Cty. Ct. judge 1847-70; JP Norfolk. Author of a treatise on partnership; reported cases in Chancery 1841-46, and (with E. Younge) Exch. cases 1833-41. Father of John Monsey Collyer (L.I. 1869) and William Robert Collyer (I.T. 1869), puisne judge Straits Settlements. d. 1st Sept. 1870.

COLQUHOUN, Sir Patrick MacChombaich

s. of James Colquhoun, Consul-general in London for Saxony. b. 13th April 1815. educ. Westminster; St. John's Coll. Camb. BA 1837, MA 1844, LLD 1851, Hon. Fellow 1886; LLD Heidelberg 1838. I.T. May 1838. QC 1868. Bencher 1869, Treasurer 1888. Common law secy. of Juridical Socy. 1855-58; member Supreme Council of Justice at Corfu 1858; CJ Ionian Islands 1861-64; Knight 1861; Grand Commander of the Saviour of Greece 1847; Knight of Civil Merit of Saxony 1850; Knight of Merit of Oldenburg 1856; Pres. Royal Socy. of Lit.; a noted oarsman, pres. of Leander Boat Club. Author of treatise on Roman civil law 1849. d. 18th May 1891.

COLTMAN, Sir Thomas

s. of John Coltman, Beverley, Yorkshire. b. 9th July 1781. educ. Charterhouse; Rugby; Trinity Coll. Camb. BA 1803, 13th Wrangler, MA 1806, Fellow 1805. L.I. May 1808. KC 1832. Bencher (I.T.) 1831. Judge of Common Pleas 1837-49; Knight 1837. Father of William Bacheler Coltman JP (I.T. 1854), and Francis Joseph Coltman (I.T. 1860). d. 11th July 1849.

COMBE, Boyce

s. of Harvey Christian Combe, Cobham Park, Surrey, Lord Mayor of London (d. 1818). b. 2nd Oct. 1789. educ. Harrow. L.I. Nov. 1813. Bencher. Metrop. magistrate 1833, finally at Southwark 1851-64. Father of Matthew Combe LLD (G.I. 1847). d. 7th Jan. 1864.

COMPSTON, John Albert

s. of Rev. John Compston, Barnsley, Yorkshire (d. 1889). b. 1862. Solicitor 1890, practised in Leeds. M.T. May 1895. KC 1912. Bencher 1921. Recorder of Leeds 1919-28; member of bar council; Fellow Commoner Trinity Hall Camb. 1917. d. 27th Sept. 1930.

CONWAY, Conway Joseph

s. of Asher Wertheimer, London. b. 22nd Sept. 1881. educ. Harrow; Balliol Coll. Oxf. BA 1906, MA 1908. I.T. Jan. 1906. KC 1927. Bencher 1935. Dep. Chmn. Buckinghamshire Quarter Sess. 1939-46; JP Buckinghamshire; changed name to Conway 1916. d. 2nd Nov. 1953.

COOKE, Edward

s. of Edward Cooke, Midleton, Cork. M.T. Nov. 1819. Cty. Ct. judge 1854-61. Author of treatise on law of insolvent debtors. d. 6th

Feb. 1862, age 70.

COOKE, William Henry

s. of Rev. William Cooke, Ullingswick, Herefordshire. b. 1811.
educ. Brasenose Coll. Oxf. BA 1834, MA 1847. I.T. June 1837. QC
1863. Bencher 1863, Reader 1878, Treasurer 1879. Recorder of
Oxford 1866-94; Cty. Ct. judge 1868-88; DL, JP Herefordshire; JP
Norfolk. Author of works on election law, and edited lists of
students admitted to I.T. d. 20th Oct. 1894.

COOKE, William Major

s. of John Cooke, Newport, Isle of Wight. b. 16th May 1825. educ.
London Univ.; Trinity Coll. Camb. 1842. M.T. Nov. 1848. Recorder
of Poole 1857-60, of Southampton 1860-62; metrop. magistrate
1862, finally at Marylebone 1877-95; JP Isle of Wight, Middlesex
and Home Counties. Father of Temple Cooke (M.T. 1874), Recorder
of Southampton. d. 27th April 1895.

COOPER, Charles Purton

s. of Charles Cooper, St. Dunstan's, London. b. 1793. educ. Wadham
Coll. Oxf. BA 1814, MA 1817; LLD Louvain and Kiel. L.I. Nov.
1816. QC 1837. Bencher 1836, Treasurer 1855. Master of the
Library 1856, to which he presented over 2000 volumes. Equity
draftsman and conveyancer; Secy. to Record Comm. 1831-37;
Queen's Serjeant, Lancaster 1834-73; FRS 1832, FSA; reported
cases decided by Brougham 1835, decided by Cottenham, Langdale,
and Shadwell, 1841, decided by Cottenham 1847. Wrote numerous
political pamphlets. d. Boulogne, 26th March 1873.

COOPER, Frank Shewell

s. of Lt. Col. Henry Fallowfield Cooper, RMLI, Rochester. b. 20th May 1864. educ. Clifton Coll.; Pembroke Coll. Camb. BA 1886, MA 1890. Asst. master Lancaster Gr. Sch. 1886-91. I.T. Jan. 1893. Dep. stip. magistrate, West Ham 1917-22; judge of Mayor's and City of London Ct. 1922-36; Master of Fanmakers' Co. 1932. Author of Debentures 1920. d. 7th Dec. 1949.

COPE, William (Lord Cope)

s. of Matthew Cope JP, St. Mellons, nr. Cardiff (d. 1934). b. 18th Aug. 1870. educ. Repton; Clare Coll. Camb. BA 1891, MA 1895. I.T. April 1894. KC 1933. MP Glamorgan (Llandaff and Barry) 1918-29; Civil Commr. for London and Home Counties in General Strike 1926; junior Lord of Treasury 1923-24, and 1924-28; Comptroller of Royal Household 1928-29; Sheriff of Glamorganshire 1932; Dep. Chmn. of Quarter Sess. 1933-39; Major, Glamorgan Yeo.; TD; director of colliery companies; KStJ; DL, JP Glamorgan; Baronet 1928, Baron Cope of St. Mellons 1945; played rugby for Wales 1896. d. 15th July 1946.

COPLEY, John Singleton (Lord Lyndhurst)

s. of John Singleton Copley, London, portrait painter (d. 1815). b. Boston, USA, 21st May 1772. educ. Trinity Coll. Camb. BA 1794, 2nd Wrangler, MA 1796, Junior Fellow 1795, Senior Fellow 1797-1804; travelling bachelor of the univ. 1795-98; High Steward 1840. Special pleader. L.I. June 1804. Serjeant 1813. Leader of Midland circuit; specially retained for the Crown in indictments against Brandreth, Turner and others for high treason, 1817; MP Yarmouth IOW 1818, Ashburton 1818-26, Camb. Univ. 1826-27; King's Serjeant 1818; CJ of Chester 1818-19; Sol-Genl. and knighted 1819; prosecuted Cato Street conspirators 1820, and represented Crown in trial of Queen Caroline in same year; Att-Genl. 1824-26; MR 1826-27; Recorder of Bristol 1826-27; LC 1827; resigned 1830;

Baron 1827; Chief Baron of Exch. 1831-34; on return of Tory government, LC 1834-35; took leading part in H of L debates 1835-41; again LC 1841-46; declined a fourth tenure of that office 1852. d. 18th Oct. 1863. Biography by Sir Theodore Martin 1883.

CORBETT-WINDER, Uvedale

s. of Ven. Joseph Corbett, Longnor Hall, Shropshire. b. 15th Nov. 1792. educ. Pemb. Coll. Oxf. 1809. L.I. Feb. 1815. Commr. in Bankruptcy; Recorder of Bridgnorth 1844-71, of Wenlock to 1871; Cty. Ct. judge 1847-65; DL, JP; assumed additional surname of Winder 1869. Father of Uvedale Corbett JP (M.T. 1844). d. 7th Feb. 1871.

CORRIE, William

s. of Adam Corrie, Wellingborough, Northamptonshire. b. 1806. Practised as attorney in London. I.T. June 1836. Metrop. magistrate 1851, finally at Bow St. 1860-64; Remembrancer of City of London 1864-78; DL London. d. 24th March 1881.

CORSER, Haden

s. of Charles Corser, Wolverhampton, solicitor. b. 9th Oct. 1845. educ. Cheltenham Coll.; Christ Church Oxf. BA 1869. M.T. June 1870. Dep. magistrate, Wolverhampton 1879-80; Recorder of Wenlock 1888-89; metrop. magistrate, North London 1889-1906; JP Middlesex and Home Counties. d. 9th March 1906.

COTES-PREEDY, Digby

s. of Rev. Digby Henry Cotes-Preedy, King's Norton, Worcestershire. b. 1875. educ. privately; Emmanuel Coll. Camb. BA 1899, MA 1902, LLM 1910. Licentiate of Socy. of Apothecaries; house physician St. George's Hosp. London 1903. I.T.

April 1904. KC 1925. Bencher 1932. Recorder of Smethwick 1919-32, of Oxford 1932-36; Cty. Ct. judge 1936-41; Chan. of diocese of Worcester 1935-42; Chmn. Buckinghamshire Quarter Sess. 1937-42; Secy. to committee on administration of R.F.C. 1916; Master of Glaziers' Co. 1927; JP Buckinghamshire. Author of The Law relating to Hospital Authorities, their Staff and Patients. d. 16th Sept. 1942.

COTTINGHAM, John

s. of Thomas Cottingham, Little Neston, Cheshire. b. 1789. educ. Trinity Hall Camb. BA 1812, MA 1815, Fellow 1820-49. L.I. June 1815. Special pleader. Recorder of Chester 1836; metrop. magistrate, Southwark 1841-49. d. 31st July 1849.

COTTON, Sir Henry

s. of William Cotton, Walwood House, Leytonstone, a director of Bank of England (d. 1866). b. 20th May 1821. educ. Eton; Christ Church Oxf. BA 1843, MA 1845, DCL 1877. L.I. Jan. 1846. QC 1866. Bencher 1867. Practised in Chancery; standing counsel to Oxf. Univ. 1872-77, and to Bank of England; engaged in the case of Overend Gurney bank failure; joint leader with W.B. Glasse in V-C Malin's Ct.; LJ 1877-90; Knight and PC 1877; Vice-Chmn. Council of Legal Educ.; active member of Inns of Ct. Rifle Vol. 1866-77. d. 22nd Feb. 1892.

COULSON, Walter

s. of Thomas Coulson, master painter in Devonport dockyard. b. 1794. Amanuensis to Jeremy Bentham. Parliamentary reporter on Morning Chronicle; editor of Traveller 1822, Globe and Traveller 1823. G.I. Nov. 1828. QC 1851. Bencher 1851. Recorder of Penzance 1836-38; parliamentary draftsman for the Home Office; a registration and conveyancing commr. 1847; member Royal Comm. for Great Exhibition 1851. d. 21st Nov. 1860.

COURTHOPE-MUNROE, Sir Harry

s. of Major Lewis Henry Isaacs MP, JP, FRIBA,London. b. 28th May 1860. On baptism named Courthope-Munroe. educ. Trinity Hall Camb. BA 1881, MA 1887. I.T. June 1883. KC 1914. Practised at parliamentary bar; Recorder of Sudbury 1927-46; member Chairmen's Panel set up by Min. of Labour under Industrial Courts Act 1919; Chmn. committee on release of railwaymen for military service in WWI; Chmn. Ry. Police Force Central Confce.; hon. standing counsel to Imperial Socy. of Knights Bachelor; member Council of Surveyors' Inst. to 1940; member Estate Management Degree Committee, London Univ.; member Rating Appeal Committee for East Suffolk 1929-39; Knight 1919; JP Suffolk. d. 8th April 1951.

COUSINS, John Ratcliffe

s. of Edward Ratcliffe Cousins, FRCS. b. 22nd Aug. 1863. educ. University Coll. London; St. John's Coll. Camb. BA 1884, LLB 1886. I.T. Nov. 1887. Stip. magistrate, West Ham 1917-22; metrop. magistrate 1922, finally at West London 1925-28; member LCC 1898-1903. d. 12th March 1928.

COVENTRY, Millis

s. of Millis Coventry, Wandsworth, London, corn factor. b. 3rd Nov. 1838. educ. King's Coll. Sch.; Trinity Hall Camb. BA 1862; rowing blue. I.T. Jan. 1864. Cty. Ct. judge 1886-1905; JP Lancashire; known as "father of the Boat Race". d. 5th Nov. 1930.

COVENTRY, Sir Reginald William

s. of George William, 9th Earl of Coventry (d. 1930). b. 29th Aug. 1869. educ. Eton; New Coll. Oxf. BA. I.T. April 1896. KC 1921. Bencher 1928. Director of Personnel Dept. of Joint Committee of

Red Cross and Order of St. John 1914-19; Recorder of Stoke-on-Trent 1921-40; member of bar council 1897-1938; Lieut. 4th Vol. Battn. Oxfordshire L.I. 1888-89; Chmn. Worcestershire Quarter Sess. 1927; Dep. Chmn. Middlesex Quarter Sess. 1936-40; Knight 1923; DL, JP Worcestershire. d. 3rd Dec. 1940.

COWARD, Sir John Charles Lewis

s. of Rev. John Henry Coward, St. Peter-le Poer, London E.C. b. 19th April 1852. educ. St. Paul's; Corpus Christi Coll. Camb. BA 1875, MA 1903. G.I. and M.T. June 1877. KC 1901. Bencher (G.I.) 1891, Treasurer 1898. Recorder of Folkestone 1886-1921; Hon. Freeman Folkestone 1921; Commissary to Dean and Chapter of St. Paul's Cath. 1914-30; member Inc. Council of Law Reporting 1898-1921; Chmn. Bd. of Legal Studies 1914-20; Vice-Chmn. Council of Legal Educ. 1920; Ry. and Canal Commr. 1921; Knight 1918. d. 7th Feb. 1930.

COWIE, Hugh

s. of Alexander Cowie, Auchterless, co. Aberdeen. b. June 1829. educ. King's Coll. London; Trinity Coll. Camb. BA 1851, 26th Wrangler, MA 1860; rowing blue. G.I. Jan. 1862. QC 1882. Bencher 1880. M.T. April 1875. Recorder of Maldon and Saffron Walden 1873-86; Chan. of diocese of Durham 1876; Secy. to criminal code comm. 1878; common law examr. to Inns of Ct 1881 and 1885; counsel to PO at Central Criminal Ct. 1879; a commr. in Oxford election inquiry 1880; reporter in Ct of Exch. for Law Journal Reports 1864-71. d. 20th July 1886.

COWIE, Thomas Hardwicke

s. of John Cowie, Streatham, Surrey. educ. King's Coll. London. BA 1842. M.T. Nov. 1845. QC 1873. Bencher 1875, Reader 1883, Treasurer 1893. Standing counsel to Govt. of Bengal 1858-62; Adv-

Genl. Bengal 1862-71. d. 14th Aug. 1897, age 75.

COX, Edward William

s. of William Charles Cox, Taunton, manufacturer. b. 1809. educ. Taunton Sch. M.T. May 1843. Recorder of Helston and Falmouth 1857-68; Serjeant 1868; Recorder of Portsmouth 1868-79; MP Taunton 1868-69; Chmn. Second Ct Middlesex Sess. 1870-79; established Law Times 1843, County Courts Chronicle and Gazette of Bankruptcy, The Magistrate, The Advocate, and other journals; reported cases in criminal and company law; founded Psychological Socy. of Great Britain 1875. d. 24th Nov. 1879.

COX, Homersham

s. of Edward Treslove Cox, London. b. 1821. educ. Tonbridge; Jesus Coll. Camb. BA 1844, MA 1852. I.T. June 1851. Cty. Ct. judge 1871-93; a commr. in Beverley election inquiry 1869; JP Kent. Author of works on government, Christianity, and other subjects. d. 10th March 1897.

COZENS-HARDY, Herbert Hardy (Lord Cozens-Hardy)

s. of William Hardy Cozens-Hardy JP, Letheringsett Hall, Norfolk, solicitor (d. 1895). b. 22nd Nov. 1838. educ. Amersham Hall Sch.; Univ. Coll. London BA 1858, LLB 1863, Fellow. LI. April 1862 (Cert. of Hon.). QC 1882. Bencher 1885, Treasurer 1909. Practised in Chancery; examr. to London Univ. in equity and real property 1871-76; MP North Norfolk 1885-99; Chmn. of bar council 1899; Chancery judge 1899-1901; Knight 1899; LJ 1901-07; PC 1901; MR 1907-18; Baron 1914; Chmn. of Historical Manuscripts Comm. 1907; Chmn. Norfolk Quarter Sess. 1907; JP Norfolk; a commr. of Great Seal 1913, whilst LC in Canada; Chmn. Council of Legal Educ.; member Senate London Univ. d. 18th June 1920.

COZENS-HARDY, William Hephurn (Lord Cozens-Hardy)

s. of Cozens-Hardy MR. b. 25th March 1868. educ. New Coll. Oxf. BA 1891, MA 1894. L.I. April 1893. KC 1912. Bencher 1916. WWI Cdr. RNVR. Secy. to father 1907-18; MP Norfolk (South) 1918-20; succeeded father 1920; JP Norfolk; Officer of Order of St. Maurice and St. Lazarus, Italy. k. in motor accident at Buchhof, Bavaria, 25th May 1924.

CRACKANTHORPE, Montague Hughes

s. of Christopher Cookson HEICS, Wellington, Somerset. b. 24th Feb. 1832. educ. Merchant Taylors'; St. John's Coll. Oxf. BCL 1856, DCL 1860, Hon. Fellow. L.I. June 1859. QC 1875. Bencher 1878. Lecturer and Reader to Inc. Law Socy. 1862-66; examr. in civil law to Oxf. Univ. 1872; counsel to Oxf. Univ. 1893-99; Chmn. Westmorland Quarter Sess. 1893-1908; DL, JP Westmorland; assumed name of Crackanthorpe 1888. d. 16th Nov. 1913.

CRAIG, Norman Carlyle

s. of William Simpson Craig MD, Bedford. b. 15th Nov. 1868. educ. Bedford Sch.; Peterhouse Camb. BA 1890, MA 1899. I.T. June 1892. KC 1909. Bencher 1919. MP Kent (Isle of Thanet) 1910-19; Lt Cdr. RNVR. d. 14th Oct. 1919.

CRAIG, Richard Davis

s. of Rev. Thomas Craig, Bocking, Essex. b. 2nd Nov. 1810. educ. London Univ. Private secy. to E.J. Littleton, Chief Secy. for Ireland 1833. L.I. Nov. 1834. QC 1851. Bencher 1851. Author of treatise on rights and liabilities as to trees and woods; published (with J.W. Mylne) reports of cases in Chancery 1835-41, and (with T.J. Phillips) reports of cases in Chancery 1840-41. d. 8th May 1884.

CRANE, Robert Newton

s. of Rev. John Newton Crane, New Jersey, USA. b. 1848. educ. Wesleyan Univ. Middleton, Conn. DCL 1921. Founded with R.W. Gilder, Newark (N.J.) Morning Register 1869; editor St. Louis Globe-Democrat 1873; Consul for U.S.A. at Manchester 1874-80; U.S. Supreme Ct. bar 1881; Chan. of diocese of Missouri 1882. M.T. Jan. 1894. KC 1921. Bencher 1919. Chmn. American Socy. in London 1898; agent for U.S. Govt. in Samoan Arbitration Award 1903-04. U.S. Govt. Despatch agent 1904-27. Chmn. London Branch of American Navy League. d. 6th May 1927.

CRANSTOUN, James

s. of James Cranstoun, Anerley, Surrey, uncovenanted service, India. b. 1855. G.I. Jan. 1880. M.T. 1890. KC 1913. d. 4th March 1931.

CRAWFORD, John Dawson

s. of Joseph Dawson Crawford, MD, FRCS (Edin.), Liverpool. b. 4th Aug. 1861. educ. Trinity Coll. Camb. BA 1883. I.T. Jan. 1884. Cty. Ct. judge 1918-34; JP Hertfordshire. Author of A Ministry of Justice, and Reflections and Recollections 1936. d. 28th June 1946.

CRESSWELL, Sir Cresswell

s. of Francis Easterby (who assumed name of Cresswell), Blackheath, Kent, an elder brother of Trinity House (d. 1834). b. 20th Aug. 1794. educ. Charterhouse; Emmanuel Coll. Camb. BA 1814, MA 1818; tutored by William Henry Maule (later his colleague on the bench). I.T. June 1819. KC 1834. Bencher 1834. Joint leader of Northern circuit with Robert Alexander; Recorder of Hull 1830; MP Liverpool 1837-42; judge of Common Pleas 1842-58; Knight 1842; organiser and judge of new Probate and Divorce Ct. 1858-63; only one of his judgments reversed; PC 1858; reported (with R.V. Barnewall) KB cases 1822-30. d. (result of street accident) 29th July 1863.

CRESWELL, William Thomas

s. of Henry John Creswell, Alresford, Hampshire. b. 11th Nov. 1872. educ. privately; King's Coll. London; Birkbeck Coll. Architectural and engineering assistant. WWI Capt. RE, and Army Educ. Corps.; intelligence and education officer, and member of military ct. Alexandria, Egypt 1914-23. G.I. June 1921. KC 1933. Arbitrator under Electricity (Supply) Acts; hon. member Inst. of Arbitrators; Chmn. RSI 1942-45; Hon. ARIBA; Liveryman Plumbers' Co.; Freeman, City of London. Author of works on building and engineering contracts, arbitration, dilapidations, and fixtures; legal editor of Building Encyclopaedia. d. 10th Oct. 1946.

CRIPPS, Charles Alfred (Lord Parmoor)

s. of Henry William Cripps QC. b. 3rd Oct. 1852. educ. Winchester; New Coll. Oxf. BA 1874, BCL 1879, MA 1879; Fellow St. John's Coll. 1875-81. M.T. June 1877. QC 1890. Att-Genl. to Princes of Wales 1895-1914; MP Stroud 1895-1900, Stretford 1901-06, Wycombe 1910-14; Lord Pres. of Council in Labour Govts. 1924, 1929-31; Vicar-Genl. Canterbury 1902-24, York 1900-14; First Chmn. House of Laity 1920-24; KCVO 1908, Baron and PC 1914. d. 30th June 1941.

CRIPPS, Henry William

s. of Rev. Henry Cripps, Preston, nr. Cirencester. b. 20th March 1815. educ. Winchester; New Coll. Oxf. BA 1837, MA 1842, Fellow 1836-45. M.T. May 1840. QC 1866. Bencher 1866, Reader 1870, Treasurer 1880. Recorder of Lichfield 1852-99; a leader at parliamentary bar; Chmn. diocese of Oxford 1883-99; Chmn. Buckinghamshire Quarter Sess. 1889-99; Chmn. Buckingham-shire Cty. Council 1889; JP Buckinghamshire. Author of treatise on clergy law; reported cases in chancery, common law and ecclesiastical cts. 1846-49. d. 14th Aug. 1899.

CRIPPS, Sir Richard Stafford

s. of Baron Parmoor. b. 24th April 1889. educ. Winchester; University Coll. London. Fellow 1930. M.T. April 1913. KC 1927. Bencher 1930. WWI with Red Cross in France, and as Superintendent of Queensferry Explosives factory. Had extensive practice in patent and compensation cases; Sol-Genl. 1930-31; Knight 1930; MP East Bristol 1931-50; Ambassador to Russia 1940-42; PC 1941; Leader of H of C and Lord Privy Seal 1942; Minister of Aircraft Production 1942-45; Pres. Bd. of Trade 1945-47; Minister for Economic Affairs 1947; Chan. of Exchequer 1947-50; Pres. Fabian Socy. 1951; CH 1951; FRS 1948; JP; Rector, Aberdeen Univ. 1942-45; Hon. DCL Oxf. 1949; Hon. LLD Liverpool 1949. Uncle of Matthew Anthony Leonard Cripps (QC 1958). d. 21st April 1952.

CRISPE, Thomas Edward

s. of Thomas Edward Crispe, Town Malling, Kent. b. 1833. educ. privately. Surveyor, and semi-professional actor. M.T. Jan. 1874. KC 1901. Author of Reminiscences of a KC., 1909. d. 11th July 1911.

CROMPTON, Charles

s. of Crompton J. b. 4th Feb. 1833. educ. Univ. Coll.Sch.; University Coll. London; Trinity Coll. Camb. BA 1855, 4th Wrangler, MA 1858, Fellow 1856-63. I.T. June 1864. QC 1882. Bencher 1887. MP Staffordshire (Leek) 1885-86; member Council of Univ. Coll. London 1874-76. d. 25th June 1890.

CROMPTON, Sir Charles John

s. of Peter Crompton MD, Derby. b. 12th June 1797. educ. Trin. Coll. Dublin BA 1818, MA 1821. Articled to a solicitor. I.T. Nov. 1821. Tubman and postman in Ct. of Exch.; counsel to Bd. of Stamps and Taxes; Assessor of Liverpool Ct. of Passage 1836-52; a commr. of inquiry into functions of Ct. of Chancery 1850; QB judge 1852-65; Knight 1852; reported cases in Ct. of Exch., with John Jervis 1830-32, with Roger Meeson 1832-34, with Meeson and Henry Roscoe 1834-36. Father of Henry Crompton (I.T. 1863), Clerk of North Wales and Chester Assize. d. 30th Oct. 1865.

CROOM-JOHNSON, Sir Reginald Powell

s. of Oliver Croom-Johnson, Clifton, Gloucestershire. b. 27th July 1879. educ. Bristol Cathedral Sch.; London Univ. LLB. Solicitor 1901. I.T. June 1907. KC 1927. Bencher 1935. WWI Lieut. KOYLI, and in JAG's Dept. on Mesopotamia Comm. (despatches). Recorder of Bath 1928-38; MP Somerset (Bridgwater) 1929-38; KB judge 1938-54; Knight 1938; Dep. Chmn. Somerset Quarter Sess.; JP Somerset; Chmn. Committee for foundation of Stowe Sch.; member Council of the Men of the Trees. Joint author of Income Tax Law 1932; published books on philately. Father of Sir David Powell Croom-Johnson (LJ 1984). d. 29th Dec. 1957.

CROSS, John

s. of James Cross, Mortfield nr. Bolton, solicitor. b. 18th Jan. 1807. educ. Bolton Gr. Sch. Solicitor 1829, practised in Bolton 1829-33. G.I. and M.T. June 1836. Serjeant 1858; Chmn. Bd. of directors of Londonderry and Coleraine Ry. Author of treatise on lien and stoppage in transitu. d. 1st June 1861.

CROSSLEY, John Thomas

s. of John Thomas Crossley, King's Coll. London, schoolmaster. b. 24th Sept. 1840. educ. King's Coll. London. I.T. June 1863. QC 1880. Bencher 1885. d. 3rd January 1892.

CROSSMAN, Sir Charles Stafford

s. of Edward Crossman MD, Hambrook, nr. Bristol. b.8th Dec. 1870. educ. Winchester; New Coll. Oxf. BA 1893, MA 1896. Asst. master at Winchester 1893-94. L.I. Jan. 1897. Bencher 1927. Equity draftsman and conveyancer; junior counsel to IR 1926-27; junior equity counsel to Treasury 1927-34; counsel to Royal Coll. of Physicians 1927-34; Chancery judge 1934-41; Knight 1934. d. 1st Jan. 1941.

CROSTHWAITE, Arthur Tinley

s. of Arthur Crosthwaite JP, Liverpool. b. 6th May 1880. educ. Winchester; New Coll. Oxf. BA 1904. I.T. Nov. 1906. WWI temp. major DAAG, 4th army and army of Rhine (despatches twice). OBE 1918; Dep. Recorder of Liverpool 1926-28; Cty. Ct. judge 1928-51; JP Lancashire. d. 28th Nov. 1951.

CROWDER, Sir Richard Budden

s. of William Henry Crowder, Montague Place, London. b. 1795. educ. Eton; Trinity Coll. Camb. L.I. May 1821. QC 1837. Bencher (M.T.) 1837, Reader 1841, Treasurer 1844. Special pleader. Recorder of Bristol 1846-54; MP Liskeard 1849-54; counsel to Admiralty and Judge Adv. of the Fleet 1849-54; judge of Common Pleas 1854-59; Knight 1854. d. 5th Dec. 1859.

CRUMP, Frederick Octavius

s. of Rev. Henry John Crump, Mill Hill, Middlesex. b. 1st Nov. 1840. educ. Queen Elizabeth's Coll. Guernsey; Queens' Coll. Camb 1864. M.T. April 1867. QC 1885. Bencher 1892. Originated Bar Committee 1883, which became General Council of the Bar in 1894; editor of Law Times 1879-1900. Author of works on sale and pledge by factors and agents, and marine insurance. Father of Basil Woodward Crump, journalist (M.T. 1892). d. 15th April 1900.

CUNLIFFE, Sir Joseph Herbert

s. of Thomas Cunliffe JP, Bolton, Lancashire, newspaper proprietor (d. 1891). b. 1st July 1867. educ. Bolton Gr. Sch. M.T. and L.I. April 1896. KC 1912. Bencher (L.I.) 1919, Treasurer 1941. Att-Genl. Cty. Palatine of Lancaster 1921-46; MP Bolton 1923-29; Chmn. of bar council 1932-46; member Council of Legal Educ. 1920-46; Chmn. Inc. Council of Law Reporting 1942-48; Chmn. Joint Committee of Four Inns of Ct. 1933-48; Chmn. Departmental Committee on supervision of charities 1925-27; Chmn. Essex Quarter Sess. 1937-46; JP Essex; Knight 1926, KBE 1946; Chmn. of govrs. of Brentwood Sch. 1939-56. Father of Thomas Cunliffe (1895-1966) Chief registrar in bankruptcy. d. 9th April 1963.

CURTIS-BENNETT, Frederick Henry

s. of Sir Henry Honywood Curtis-Bennett KC. b. 29th Feb. 1904. educ. Radley; Trinity Coll. Camb. BA 1925. M.T. Nov. 1926. KC 1943. Northern Rhodesia bar 1950. Recorder of Tenterden 1940-42, of Guildford 1942-56; Committee Chmn. London Police Ct. Mission 1947-49; Dep. Chmn. Essex Quarter Sess. 1952-55, Chmn. 1955-56; Appeal Steward, Br. Boxing Bd. of Control 1953. Author of The Life of Sir Henry Curtis-Bennett KC ("Curtis") 1937, and The Trial of Mary Court 1939 (both with Roland Wild). d. 23rd July 1956.

CURTIS-BENNETT, Sir Henry Honywood

s. of Sir Henry Curtis Bennett, chief metrop. magistrate. b. 31st July 1879. educ. Radley; Trinity Coll. Camb. BA 1900. M.T. Nov. 1902. KC 1919. Bencher 1926. WWI Lieut. RNVR (secret service). Attached to Scotland Yard 1917-19; Dep. Chmn. Essex Quarter Sess. 1923, Chmn. 1935-36; Chmn. London Sess. 1936; Recorder of Colchester 1929-36; MP Essex (Chelmsford) 1924-26; Knight 1922; JP Essex; winner of one and ten mile ACA championships 1901; Steward of Br. Boxing Bd. of Control. d. 2nd Nov. 1936.

CUTLER, Edward

s. of Edward Cutler, surgeon. b. 4th May 1831. educ. Eton; Paris, Dresden; Balliol Coll. Oxf. L.I. Jan. 1857. QC 1886. Bencher 1888. On Imperial Comm. for copyright 1909; JP Middlesex. Author of works on musical copyright. d. 22nd Dec. 1916.

CUTLER, John

s. of Rev. Richard Cutler, Dorchester, Dorset. b. 9th Jan. 1839. educ. King's Coll. Sch. London; Edin. Univ.; Exeter Coll. Oxf. BA 1861, MA. L.I. Jan. 1863. QC 1897. Bencher 1903. Editor, Reports of Patent Design and Trade Mark cases, published by HM Patent Office; emeritus prof. of law King's Coll. London. Author of treatises on Law of Naturalisation 1871, and on Passing Off, 1904. d. 19th March 1924.

DALE, Sir Edgar Thorniley

s. of William Dale, London. b. 25th March 1886. educ. privately. M.T. May 1909. Cty. Ct judge 1937-59; Divorce Commr.; Chmn. Buckinghamshire Quarter Sess. 1959-61; Chmn. Brill Petty Sess. 1942; Chmn. Prime Minister's Committee on Industrial Health Services and Nat. Health Service 1949-50; Knight 1956; JP Warwickshire and Buckinghamshire. Editor of Annual Cty. Ct

Practice. d. 15th Dec. 1966.

DANCKWERTS, William Otto Adolph Julius

s. of Adolph Victor Danckwerts MD, Somerset East, Cape Province, South Africa. b. 1853. educ. Gill Coll. Cape Colony; Bedford Sch.; St Peter's Coll. Camb. BA 1877, MA 1911. I.T. July 1878. QC 1900. Bencher 1910. Counsel to Commrs. of Public Works and Buildings, and I.R. 1895; specialist in revenue and local government cases; known as "Danky". Father of Danckwerts LJ (1888-1978). d. 25th April 1914.

DANIEL, William Thomas Shave

s. of William Daniel, Burton-on-Trent, cheese factor. b. 17th March 1806. educ. Repton. Articled to solicitor 1822. L.I. Feb. 1830. QC 1851. Bencher 1851. Recorder of Ipswich 1842; originated system of law reports adopted by Council of Law Reporting 1865; member Law Digest Comm. 1868; Cty. Ct judge 1867-84. Author of The History and Origin of the Law Reports 1884. Father of Arthur William Trollope Daniel, d. 1873 (LI. 1867). d. 9th June 1891.

DARLING, Charles John (Lord Darling)

s. of Charles Darling, Langham Hall, Essex (d. 1862). b. 6th Dec. 1849. educ. privately. Articled to solicitor in Birmingham. I.T. Jan. 1874. QC 1885. Bencher 1892. Journalist for St James's Gazette, and other periodicals; MP Deptford 1888-97; Commr. of Assize, Oxford circuit 1896; QB judge 1897-1923; Knight 1897; a political appointment; member of Royal Comm. on the working of the King's Bench 1912; deputised for LCJ 1914-18; PC 1917; Pres. committee on Courts Martial 1919, on moneylenders 1925; presided in cases of Crippen 1910, and Casement 1916, in Ct. of Criminal Appeal; indulged in undue levity on bench; Baron 1924. Author of Scintillae Juris 1877, Meditations in the Tea Room, Seria Ludo 1910, On the

113

Oxford Circuit 1909, A Pensioner's Garden 1926, Reconsidered Rimes 1930, Autumnal Leaves 1933. d. 29th May 1936. Biogs. by Evelyn Graham 1929, Dudley Barker 1936, Derek Walker-Smith 1938.

DASENT, John Bury

s. of John Roche Dasent, Att-Genl. St. Vincent (d. 1832). b. Madras, 22nd Dec. 1806. educ. Rugby; Westminster; Trinity Hall Camb. LLB 1830. M.T. April 1833. Cty. Ct. judge 1858-84. Half-brother of Sir George Webbe Dasent, 1817-96 (M.T. 1852). d. 7th April 1888.

DAVEY, Horace (Lord Davey)

s. of Peter Davey, Horton, Buckinghamshire (d. 1879). b. 29th Aug. 1833. educ. Rugby; University Coll. Oxf. BA 1856, MA 1859, Eldon law scholar, Fellow 1854, Hon. Fellow 1884, Hon. DCL 1894. L.I. Jan. 1861. QC 1875. Bencher 1878, Treasurer 1897. Practised in Rolls Ct; standing counsel to Oxf. Univ. 1877-93; MP Christchurch 1880-85, Stockton-on-Tees 1888-92; Sol-Genl. 1886; Knight 1886; member of bar committee 1883, and of Inc. Council of Law Reporting; LJ 1893-94; PC 1893; L of A 1894; Baron Davey of Fernhurst 1894; Chmn. comm. to make statutes for London Univ. 1898; largely responsible for Street Betting Act 1906; FBA 1905; FRS. d. 20th Feb. 1907.

DAVID, Alexander Jones

s. of Alexander David, Dudley, Worcestershire, Inland Revenue officer. b. 1st Aug. 1851. educ. St. John's Coll. Camb. BA and LLB 1884, LLM 1887. Solicitor 1875, practised in Newport, Monmouth. I.T. Jan. 1883. KC 1910. Recorder of Newcastle-under-Lyme 1909-27; FRGS. d. 1st Feb. 1929.

DAVIDSON, Sir William Edward

s. of William Davidson, Mount House, Braintree, Essex. b. 17th April 1853. educ. London Univ. 1870; Balliol Coll. Oxf. BA 1875, MA 1879. I.T. May 1879. QC 1892. Bencher 1901. One of the standing counsel to Bd. of Trade in bankruptcy 1884, and in shipping matters 1885; private secy. to Lord Chancellor 1886; legal adviser to Foreign Office 1886-1918; commissioned as Acting Counsellor of Embassy in diplomatic service 1910; Pres. Alpine Club 1911-14; CB 1897, KCMG 1907; FSA. d. 12th July 1923.

DAVIES, Clement Edward

s. of Moses Davies, Llanfyllin, Montgomery, auctioneer. b. 19th Feb. 1884. educ. Llanfyllin Cty. Sch.; Trinity Hall Camb. BA and LLB 1907; Hon. Fellow 1950. Law lecturer Univ. Coll. of Wales 1908-09. L.I. May 1909 (Cert. of Hon.). KC 1926. Bencher 1953. Adviser to procurator-genl. on enemy activities in neutral countries and on the high seas 1914; junior Treasury counsel 1919-25; secy. to Pres. of P D and A Division 1918-19, to MR 1919-23; MP Montgomeryshire 1929-62; member of many govt. committees; Leader of Liberal Party in H of C 1945-56; Pres. Parliamentary Assoc. for World Govt. 1951; Chmn. Montgomeryshire Quarter Sess. 1935-62; PC 1947; Hon. LLD Wales 1955; JP Montgomeryshire. Published works on agricultural law, and the law affecting auctions. d. 23rd March 1962.

DAVIES, Sir David

s. of James Davies. b. 14th Sept. 1889. educ. Winchester; New Coll. Oxf. BA 1913. Home Civil Service 1913-19. Asst. Priv. Secy. to Prime Minister 1914-16. I.T. Nov. 1919. KC 1935. Cty. Ct. judge 1937-47; Nat. Insce. Commr. 1947-61; Knight 1952. d. 23rd April 1964.

DAVIES, Francis Maurice Russell

s. of Rev. Septimus Russell Davies. b. 7th Nov. 1871. educ. King's Coll. Sch. London; Selwyn Coll. Camb. BA 1896, MA 1900. Deacon 1897, Priest 1898. M.T. April 1910. KC 1930. Junior counsel to Bd. of Trade 1919-29; Mayor of Hastings 1929-30; Recorder of Worcester 1931-37; Rural Dean of Hastings 1953-56. d. 22nd June 1956.

DAVIES, Herbert Edmund (Lord Edmund-Davies)

s. of Morgan John Davies, Mountain Ash, Glamorgan. b. 15th July 1906. educ. Mountain Ash Gr. Sch.; King's Coll. London LLB 1926, LLD 1928; Exeter Coll. Oxf. Vinerian scholar, BCL 1929; Hon. Fellow. G.I. Nov. 1929. KC 1943. Bencher 1948, Treasurer 1965. Lecturer and examr. in law, London Univ. 1930-31; WWII Lt Col. Royal Welch Fus., and AJAG; Recorder of Merthyr Tydfil 1942-44, of Swansea 1944-53, of Cardiff 1953-58; hon. standing counsel to Univ. of Wales 1947; Foreign Office observer, Cairo Espionage Trials 1957; QB judge 1958-66; Knight 1958; Chmn. Transport Users Consultative Committee for Wales 1959, committee on Limitation of Actions 1961, Inquiry into Aberfan disaster 1966; LJ 1966-74; PC 1966; Chmn. Inc. Council of Law Reporting 1967, Criminal Law Revision Committee 1969; L of A 1974-81; Baron 1974; member Comm. on Penal Reform 1964; Chmn. Police Inquiry Committee 1977; Chmn. Denbighshire Quarter Sess. 1953; Pres. London Welsh Assoc. 1982; FRSoc.Med.; Life Govr. and Fellow King's Coll. London; Hon. LLD Wales 1959, Pro-Chancellor 1974. Author of Law of Distress for Rent and Rates 1931. d. 27th Dec. 1992.

DAVIES, John Bowen

s. of Henry Harries Davies, Llandyssul, Cardigan, surgeon. b. 1876. educ. Epsom Coll.; Downing Coll. Camb. BA and LLB 1897, MA 1902. M.T. June 1898. KC 1926. Bencher 1930, Reader 1942. WWI

Lieut. Pembroke Yeo., and Royal West Surrey Regt.; DJAG Northern Command, and court-martial officer (Capt.). Chmn. Llandyssul Petty Sess. 1924; Recorder of Merthyr Tydfil 1933-36; stip. magistrate Merthyr Tydfil 1935-43; Vice-Chmn. Carmarthenshire Quarter Sess. 1936; lay rector of St. Peter's, Carmarthen; Master of Vale of Clettwr Fox Hunt 1937; JP Carmarthen, Cardigan, Glamorgan, Monmouth, Brecon. d. 12th Oct. 1943.

DAVIES, Joshua David

s. of Rev. Joshua Davies, Llanllwni, Carmarthen. b. 11th Feb. 1889. educ. Llandovery Coll.; St. John's Coll. Oxf. I.T. Jan. 1919. KC 1939. Recorder of Swansea 1942-44; stip. magistrate Merthyr Tydfil 1944-61. d. 3rd Jan. 1966.

DAVIES, William Frank de Rolante

s. of James Davies JP, Ucheldin, Carmarthenshire. b. 1886. educ. Llandovery Coll.; Hertford Coll. Oxf. BA 1909, MA 1927. M.T. April 1913 (Cert. of Hon.). WWI Capt. 4 Battn. Welch Regt (despatches). Cty. Ct. judge 1926-42; Chmn. Carmarthenshire Quarter Sess.; Chmn Haverfordwest Quarter Sess. d. 7th March 1942.

DAVIS, Richard Bramwell

s. of Richard Powell Davis, Bedwellty House, Tredegar, Monmouthshire. b. 1847. educ. privately; Trinity Hall Camb. BA 1872. I.T. June 1873. QC 1895. Practised in chancery. d. 25th Aug. 1923.

DAVISON, John Robert

s. of Rev. Edward Davison, Harlington, Middlesex. b. 15th April 1826. educ. Houghton and Durham Gr. Schs.; Corpus Christi Coll. Oxf. BA 1845, MA 1847. M.T. Nov. 1849. QC 1866. Bencher 1866, Reader 1870. Chmn. Durham Quarter Sess. 1868; MP Durham 1868-71; Judge Adv-Genl. 1870-71; PC 1871. d. 15th April 1871.

DAY, Sir John Charles Frederic Sigismund

s. of Capt. John Day, 49th Regt., Englishbatch, Somerset. b. 20th June 1826. educ. in Fribourg; Downside Coll. London Univ. BA 1845. M.T. Jan. 1849. QC 1872. Bencher 1873, Reader 1879, Treasurer 1889. Very successful in breach of promise and libel cases; QB judge 1882-1901; Knight 1882; Chmn. Royal Comm. to inquire into Belfast Riots 1886; member Parnell Comm. 1888; PC 1901; known as "Judgment Day". Joint editor of Roscoe's Evidence at Nisi Prius, and annotated Common Law Procedure Act 1852. Father of Samuel Henry Day (M.T. 1876), a Master of the Supreme Ct. d. 13th June 1908. Biog.: Recollections of Sir John Charles Frederic Day by Judge William Willis.

DAYMAN, Charles Orchard

s. of John Dayman, Torrington, Devon. b. 9th July 1803. educ. Blundell's; St. John's Coll. Camb. BA 1824, MA 1828. LI. Nov. 1829. Metrop. magistrate, Hammersmith 1856-71; FRAS 1845. d. 22nd Jan. 1892.

DAYNES, John Norman

s. of John William Crook Daynes, Brundall, Norfolk, solicitor. b. 1884. educ. Norwich Sch.; Magdalen Coll. Oxf. BA 1906, MA and BCL 1909. L.I. June 1910. KC 1931. Bencher 1935, Treasurer 1956. WWI Lieut. RAOC. Cty. Ct. judge 1945-57; Dep. Chmn. Norfolk

Quarter Sess. 1939-59; JP Norfolk; Dir. of Cement, Min. of Works 1942-44; Chmn. govrs. Norwich Sch. 1954; Liveryman, City of London 1922; Prime Warden Dyers' Co. 1945-47; Chmn. St. Mark's Hospital, London, 1939-48; Chmn. bar library committee 1959; Divorce Commr. d. 1st June 1966.

DEANE, Sir Henry Bargrave Finnelly

s. of Sir James Parker Deane QC. b. 28th April 1846. educ. Winchester; Balliol Coll. Oxf. BA 1869, MA 1875. I.T. Nov. 1870. QC 1896. Bencher 1895, Treasurer 1917. Secy. Of Royal Comm. on Wellington Coll. 1879; official principal of the archdeaconries of Middlesex, Rochester, and St. Albans 1884-1905; Recorder of Margate 1885-1905; P D and A judge 1905-17; Knight 1905; Lt. Col. and Hon. Col. 21st Middlesex Rifle Vol. 1888-98; VD; Pres. Socy. of Knights Bachelor 1908-11. Author of treatise on the Law of Blockade. d. 21st April 1919.

DEANE, Sir James Parker

s. of Henry Boyle Deane, Hurst Grove, Berkshire. b. 25th June 1812. educ. Winchester; St. John's Coll. Oxf. BCL 1834, DCL 1839, Fellow 1829-41. Advocate Nov. 1839. I.T. Jan. 1841. QC 1858. Bencher 1858, Treasurer 1873. HM's Admiralty Advocate 1868; Vicar-Genl. of Archbishop of Canterbury 1872; Chan. of Salisbury 1868; legal adviser to Foreign Office 1872-86; leading counsel in case of Lord St. Leonard's Will 1876; Knight 1885; PC 1892. d. 3rd Jan. 1902.

DE COLYAR, Henry Anselm

s. of Augustine de Colyar FRSE. b. 1846. educ. Oratory Sch., Edgbaston, Birmingham. M.T. June 1871. KC 1905. Bencher 1914. Gold Staff officer at coronations of Edward VII and George V; a Nat. Service representative on Mil. Service committees 1918;

Master of Poulters' Co. Author of The Law of Guarantees and of Principal and Agent. d. 31st Jan. 1925.

DE GEX, Sir John Peter

s. of John De Gex, Leicester Place, London, hotelkeeper. b. 1809. educ. Jesus Coll. Camb. BA 1831, MA 1834, Fellow. L.I. Jan. 1835. QC 1865. Bencher 1865, Treasurer 1882. Had large practice in bankruptcy; Knight 1882; reported (with B. Montagu and E. Deacon) bankruptcy cases 1842-45, (with J. Smale) chancery cases 1849-53, (with Macnaghten and Gordon) chancery appeal cases 1851-57; director Legal and General Insce. Office 1871. Author (with R.H. Smith) of Arrangements between debtors and creditors 1861. d. 14th May 1887.

DE GREY, John Augustus (Lord Walsingham)

s. of 5th Baron Walsingham. b. 21st March 1849. educ. Eton; Trinity Coll. Camb. BA 1872. I.T. April 1874. Recorder of Sudbury 1896-97, of King's Lynn 1897-1905; metrop. magistrate 1905, finally at West London 1914-19; Chmn. East Suffolk Quarter Sess.; JP Suffolk, London and Home Counties; succeeded 1919, as 7th Baron. d. 21st March 1929.

DE GRUYTHER, Leslie Edward

s. of William de Gruyther ICS. b. Delhi, Dec. 1862. M.T. June 1885. KC 1908. Bencher 1917, Reader 1927, Treasurer 1931. Practised in North West Provinces India 1886-98, later before Privy Council. d. 11th Nov. 1937.

DENMAN, George

s. of Denman LCJ. b. 23rd Dec. 1819. educ. Felsted; Repton; Trinity

Coll. Camb. BA 1842, MA 1845, Fellow 1843-52, Auditor 1852-65; rowed against Oxf. L.I. Nov. 1846. QC 1861. Bencher 1861-72. Counsel to Camb. Univ. 1857-72; MP Tiverton 1859-65 and 1866-72; initiated the Evidence Further Amendment Act 1869, known by his name; judge of Common Pleas 1872-80; QB judge 1880-92; PC 1893; member of Juridical Socy.; member Council of Univ. Coll. London. Father of Sir Arthur Denman (I.T. 1881), Clerk of Assize on South Eastern circuit. d. 21st Sept 1896.

DENMAN, George Lewis

s. of Denman J. b. 15th May 1854. educ. Rugby; Trinity Coll. Camb. LLB 1876, LLM 1879. L.I. Jan. 1877. Clerk of Assize, South Eastern Circuit; Recorder of Queenborough 1882-85; metrop. magistrate 1890, finally at Marlborough St. 1899-1922; JP London and Home Counties. Editor of Broom's Constitutional Law. d. 26th May 1929.

DENMAN, Thomas (Lord Denman)

s. of Thomas Denman, Golden Square, London, physician (d. 1815). b. 23rd Feb. 1779. educ. in Kensington (Rev. Dr. Thompson); Eton; St. John's Coll. Camb. BA 1800, MA 1803. Special pleader until 1806. L.I. May 1806. KC 1828. Bencher 1820. Defended the Luddites 1817; Dep. Recorder of Nottingham 1818; MP Wareham 1818, Nottingham 1820-26, and 1830-32; Sol-Genl. to Queen Caroline 1820-21; Freeman of City of London 1821; Common Serjeant 1822-30; Att-Genl. 1830-32; Knight 1830; drafted Reform Bill 1831; PC 1832; LCJ of King's Bench 1832-50 (the first to attend H of L without judicial robes); Baron Denman of Dovedale 1834; Speaker of H of L 1835; carried two bills abolishing death penalty for forgery and other offences 1837; presided as Lord High Steward when Earl of Cardigan indicted in H of L for duelling with Capt. Tuckett 1841. Father of Richard Denman (L.I. 1838), Clerk of Assize on South Eastern circuit. d. 22nd Sept. 1854. Biography by Sir Joseph Arnould, 2 vols. 1873.

DENNING, Alfred Thompson (Lord Denning)

s. of Charles Denning, Whitchurch, Hampshire, draper (d. 1941). b. 23rd Jan. 1899. educ. Andover Gr. Sch.; Magdalen Coll. Oxf. BA 1920, Eldon scholar 1921, MA 1937, Hon. Fellow 1948, Hon. Fellow Nuffield Coll. 1982, Hon. DCL 1965. WWI Lieut. RE. L.I. June 1923. KC 1938. Bencher 1944, Treasurer 1964. Chan. diocese of Southwark 1937-44, London 1942-44; Recorder of Plymouth 1944; P D and A judge 1944-45; Knight 1944; KB judge 1945-48; Chmn. Committee on Matrimonial Causes 1946-47; judge for War Pensions Appeals 1945-48; LJ 1948-57; PC 1948; L of A 1957-62; Baron 1957; Chmn. Comm. on Historical MSS 1962-82; presided at Inquiry into resignation of J.D. Profumo, Secy. of State for War 1963; Chmn. Committee on Legal Educ. for students from Africa 1960, Br. Instit. of Intern. and Comparative Law 1959-86; MR 1962-82; DL Hampshire; Pres. Birkbeck Coll. 1952-83; Hon. Bencher M.T. 1972, G.I. 1979, I.T. 1982; Hon. FBA 1979; OM 1997; hon. degrees of many univs. in addition to Oxf.; joint editor of Smith's Leading Cases 1929, and of Bullen and Leakes Precedents 1935. Author of Freedom under the Law 1949, The Changing law 1953, The Road to Justice 1955, The Discipline of Law 1979, The Due Process of Law 1980, The Family Story 1981, What Next in the Law 1982, The Closing Chapter 1983, Landmarks in the Law 1984, Leaves from my Library 1984. Biogs. by E. Heward 1990, Iris Freeman 1993.

DERBYSHIRE, Sir Harold

s. of James Derbyshire, Cherry Tree, Blackburn, Lancashire. b. 1886. educ. Blackburn Gr. Sch.; Sidney Sussex Coll. Camb. BA 1908, MA 1926, LLB. G.I. Nov. 1911 (Cert. of Hon). KC 1928. Bencher 1931, Treasurer 1948. WWI Hon. Major RA, liaison officer with RAF, MC. Judge of Appeal, Isle of Man 1933-34; CJ High Ct. Calcutta 1934-46; Knight 1934; Fellow, Calcutta Univ.; Trustee, Victoria Memorial; Chmn. of Mayo Hospital. d. 14th Sept. 1972.

DE RUTZEN, Sir Albert Richard Francis Maximilian

s. of Charles Frederick, Baron de Rutzen, Slebech Park, Pembrokeshire. b. 27th Jan. 1830. educ. Eton; Trinity Coll. Camb. BA 1852; rowing blue. I.T. April 1857. Stip. magistrate Merthyr Tydfil 1872-76; Dep. Chmn. Glamorganshire Quarter Sess.; metrop. magistrate 1876, finally at Bow St. 1899-1911; chief magistrate and knighted 1901; JP Glamorganshire, Pembrokeshire, Middlesex and Home Counties; DL. Brother of Rudolph William Henry Ehrard, Baron de Rutzen (I.T. 1864). d. 22nd Sept. 1913.

DE SILVA, Lucian Macull Dominic

s. of G. de Silva, Ceylon. b. Ceylon, 25th April 1893. educ. Royal Coll. Colombo; Trinity Coll. Kandy; St. John's Coll. Camb. Hon. Fellow 1955. Ceylon bar 1916; KC 1931; G.I. Nov. 1916. KC 1938. Bencher 1953. Sol-Genl. Ceylon 1931-34; acting Att-Genl. 1932; acting puisne judge 1933-34; Chmn. Bribery Enquiry Comm., Ceylon 1941-43; Chmn. Comm. on law relating to Mortgage, Credit Facilities, and Protection of Lands of Agriculturalists, Ceylon 1943-45, Delimitation Comm., Ceylon 1946, Comm. on company law, Ceylon 1948; Ceylon delegate to Commonwealth Relations Confce., Canada 1949; PC 1953, and member of Judicial Committee. d. 28th Nov. 1962.

DEVLIN, Patick Arthur (Lord Devlin)

s. of William John Devlin ARIBA. b. 25th Nov. 1905. educ. Stonyhurst; Christ's Coll. Camb. BA 1927, MA 1961, Hon. Fellow 1958, Hon. LLD 1966, High Steward 1966. G.I. June 1929. KC 1945. Bencher 1947, Treasurer 1963. Pros. counsel to the Mint 1931-39; Legal Dept. Min. of Supply 1940-42; junior counsel to Mins. of War, Transport, Food, and Supply 1942-45; Att-Genl. Duchy of Cornwall 1947; KB judge 1948-60; Knight 1948; Chmn. Inquiry into Dock Labour Scheme 1955, Nyasaland Inquiry Comm. 1959; Pres. Restrictive Practices Ct. 1956; LJ 1960-61; PC 1960;

L of A 1961-64; Baron 1961; Chmn. committee of inquiry into Port Transport Industry 1964, Press Council 1964, committee on identification in criminal cases 1974; a judge of the administrative Trib. of the ILO 1964-86; Chmn. Wiltshire Quarter Sess. 1955; Chmn. Assoc. of Average Adjusters 1966; Pres. Br. Maritime Law Assoc. 1962-76; Chmn. Council of Bedford Coll. London Univ. 1953-59; FBA 1963; Hon. DCL Oxf. and hon. degrees from Glasgow, Toronto, Durham, Leicester, Sussex, Liverpool, St. Louis. Author of Trial by Jury 1956, The Criminal Prosecution in England 1957, Samples of Lawmaking 1962, The House of Lords and the Naval Prize Bill (1911), 1968, The Judge 1979, The Trial of Dr. J.B. Adams 1985. d. 9th Aug. 1992.

DIBDIN, Sir Lewis Tonna

s. of Rev. Robert William Dibdin (d. 1887). b. 19th July 1852. educ. St. John's Coll. Camb. BA 1874, MA 1878, Hon. Fellow. L.I. May 1876. KC 1901. Bencher 1908. Chan. diocese of Exeter 1888-1903, Rochester 1886-1903, Durham 1891-1903; counsel to Att-Genl. in chancery matters 1895-1903; judge of Ct. of Arches and Chancery Ct. York 1903-34; gave judgment in Deceased Wife's Sister case 1908; First Church Estates Commr. 1905-30; lay ecclesiastical commr. 1930-38; Vicar-Genl. Canterbury 1924-34; hon. member, Surveyors Institution; Knight 1903; JP Surrey; Hon. DCL Durham. Author of works on church law. d. 12th June 1938.

DICEY, Albert Venn

s. of Thomas Edward Dicey, Claybrook, Leicester, newspaper proprietor. b. 4th Feb. 1835. educ. King's Coll. Sch. London; Balliol Coll. Oxf. BA 1858, MA 1861, BCL 1877, Fellow 1886; Fellow Trinity Coll. 1860-73; Fellow All Souls Coll. 1882-1909. I.T. Jan. 1863. Junior counsel to C.I.R. 1876-90. QC 1890. Vinerian prof. of common law Oxf. 1882-1909. Author of Introduction to the study of the Law of the Constitution 1885, Digest of Law of England 1896, Law and Public opinion in England 1905, and numerous other works. d. 7th April 1922.

DICKENS, Sir Henry Fielding

s. of Charles Dickens, the author. b. 16th Jan. 1849. educ.
Wimbledon Sch.; Trinity Hall Camb. BA 1872, 29th Wrangler. I.T.
Nov. 1873. QC 1892. Bencher 1899, Treasurer. Recorder of Deal
1883-92, of Maidstone 1892-1918; Common Serjeant 1917-32;
Knight 1922. His recollections published 1934. d. 21st Dec. 1933.

DICKINSON, James

s. of Nodes Dickinson, FRCS, staff surgeon to HM's forces. b. 1811.
L.I. Nov. 1835. QC 1866. Bencher 1866, Treasurer 1883. JP
Buckinghamshire. Brother of Sir John Nodes Dickinson (1806-82),
CJ New South Wales. d. Beaulieu, Alpes Maritimes, 14th March
1895.

DICKINSON, James

s. of John Dickinson, Liverpool, solicitor. Practised as solicitor in
London from 1912. I.T. April 1920; M.T. Nov. 1925. KC 1930.
Commissioned officer in WWI. Practised in commercial ct. d. 4th
Oct. 1933, age 47.

DICKINSON, Sir John

s. of Joseph Dickinson, MD, FRS, Liverpool. b. 17th Nov. 1848.
educ. Collegiate Sch. Liverpool; Cheltenham Coll.; Trinity Coll.
Camb. LLB 1870, LLM 1874. I.T. Nov. 1871. Dep. stip. magistrate,
Liverpool 1880-89; metrop. magistrate 1890, finally at Bow St.
1913-20; chief magistrate and knighted 1913; JP London and Home
Counties. d. 29th Oct. 1933.

DICKSON, Charles Scott

s. of John Robert Dickson MD, Glasgow. b. 13th Sept. 1850. educ. Edin. Univ.; Glasgow Univ. MA, LLD; Aberdeen Univ. LLD. Law agent in Glasgow 1875-76; Scottish bar 1877; Advocate-Depute 1892-95; Sol-Genl. for Scotland 1896-1903; QC 1896; Lord Advocate 1903-05; PC 1903; MP Glasgow (Bridgeton) 1900-06, Glasgow (Central) 1909-15; Lord Justice Clerk and Pres. of 2nd Divn. of Ct. of Session, as Lord Scott Dickson 1915-22; Dean of Faculty of Advocates 1908-15; DL, JP; Hon. Lt. Col. 2/1 Battn. City of Edin. Vol. Regt. 1918. d. 5th Aug. 1922.

DICKSON, William Everard

s. of Thomas Andrew Dickson. b. Geelong, Australia. educ. in Geelong. G.I. Nov. 1914. WWI Major, Infantry and Machine Gun Corps, MC and bar, (despatches). Military legal staff Ireland 1921; metrop. magistrate 1933, finally at Thames St. to 1945; hon. legal editor, Medico-Legal Socy. 1925-37. d. 10th Nov. 1945, age 52.

DIGBY, Edward Aylmer

s. of Sir Kenelm Edward Digby GCB, KC. b. 3rd Oct. 1883. educ. HMS Britannia 1897; RN Colls. Greenwich and Portsmouth. Lieut. 1903. Served in HMS Bulwark, flagship, Mediterranean 1904-05; invalided out 1906. M.T. June 1909. KC 1927. Bencher 1934. WWI Acting. Cdr. RN, Paravane Dept. 1916; Head of Otter Dept. 1918; Cdr. 1919; practised in Admiralty cts.; JP Essex. d. 14th Nov. 1935.

DIGBY, Sir Kenelm Edward

s. of Rev. Canon the Hon. Kenelm Henry Digby, Tittleshall, Norfolk. b. 9th Sept. 1836. educ. Corpus Christi Coll. Oxf. BA 1859, MA 1861, Fellow 1864-70. L.I. Jan. 1865. KC 1904. Bencher 1891. Vinerian Common Law Reader at Oxf. 1868-74; Cty. Ct.

judge 1892-95; Permanent Under-Secy. of State, Home Office 1895-1903; KCB 1898; GCB 1906; JP Essex. d. 21st April 1916.

DINSDALE, Frederick Trotter

s. of Henry Trotter, Staindrop, Durham. educ. Christ's Coll. Camb. LLB 1829, LLD 1835. M.T. May 1834. Judge of Ct. of Requests, Oldham 1843-47; Cty. Ct. judge 1847-72; JP Warwickshire; FSA; adopted name of Dinsdale 1848. d. 7th July 1872, age 69.

DISNEY, Henry William

s. of Rev. William Henry Disney, Winnick, Northamptonshire. b. 5th Jan. 1858. educ. Christ's Coll. Finchley; Hertford Coll. Oxf. BA 1880; rowing blue. L.I. Nov. 1884. Recorder of Gt. Grimsby 1914-18; metrop. magistrate 1918, finally at Thames St. 1922-25; member of bar council; lecturer in law, London Sch. of Economics. Published works on commercial law, and carriage by railways. d. 16th Jan. 1925.

DISTURNAL, William Josiah

s. of Thomas Disturnal, Walsall, Staffordshire, miller and corn merchant. b. 1863. educ. Leys Sch.; Trinity Hall Camb. BA and LLB 1884, MA 1916. I.T. Nov. 1885. KC 1913. Bencher 1921; the first recorder of Dudley, 1908-23. d. 2nd March 1923.

DOBB, Henry

s. of Henry Dobb, Kiligarth, Felixstowe, merchant. b. 15th Aug. 1867. educ. Merchant Taylors'; Pembroke Coll. Camb. BA 1888. L.I. Nov. 1891. Equity draftsman and conveyancer; Cty. Ct. judge 1921-28; JP Leicestershire. d. 23rd March 1928.

DODD, Cyril

s. of Rev. Joseph Dodd, Hampton Poyle, Oxfordshire. b. 1844. educ. Shrewsbury; Merton Coll. Oxf. BA 1866. I.T. June 1869. QC 1890. Bencher 1896. MP East Essex 1892-95; Cty. Ct. judge 1906-13. Joint author of works on law of light railways, and Private Bill legislation. d. 29th Jan. 1913.

DODSON, Sir Gerald

s. of John Dodson JP, Sheriff of Norwich. b. 28th Aug. 1884. educ. privately; Downing Coll. Camb. BA 1905, MA, LLM, Hon. Fellow 1945. I.T. April 1907. Bencher 1938. WWI Lieut. RNVR. Treasury counsel at Central Criminal Ct. 1925-34; Recorder of Tenterden 1932-34; judge of Mayor's and City of London Ct. 1934-37; Recorder of London and High Steward of Southwark 1937-59; Commr. at Central Criminal Ct. 1959-63; DL London; Knight 1939; JP Surrey; Order of Menelik (Ethiopia) 1954, Comendador de Christo (Portugal) 1955, Order of Al Rafidain (Iraq) 1956, Order of Merit (Italy) 1958, Order of Homayoun (Persia) 1959. Joint author (with Montague Phillips) of the light musical opera comedy The Rebel Maid 1921; joint author of The Law Relating to Motor Cars, and a commentary on Road Traffic Act 1929. Consider Your Verdict (memoirs) published 1967. d. 2nd Nov. 1966.

DODSON, Sir John

s. of Rev. John Dodson, Hurstpierpoint, Sussex (d. 1807). b. 19th Jan. 1780. educ. Merchant Taylors; Oriel Coll. Oxf. BA 1801, MA 1804, DCL 1808. Advocate, Doctors' Commons Nov. 1808. Commissary to Dean and Chapter of Westminster; MP Rye 1819-23; advocate to Admiralty Ct. 1829; King's Adv-Genl. 1834; Knight 1834. M.T. Nov. 1834. Bencher 1835, Reader 1838, Treasurer 1841. Master of the Faculties 1841; Vicar-Genl. to Abp. of Canterbury 1849; judge of Prerogative Ct. of Canterbury, and Dean of the Arches 1852-57; PC 1852; reported admiralty cases 1811-22. d. 27th April 1858.

DONE, William Edward Pears

s. of William Done, Groombridge, Sussex. b. 10th March 1883. educ. Elizabeth Coll. Guernsey; Pembroke Coll. Oxf. I.T. June 1910. WWI Capt. Royal Sussex Regt., MC (despatches), Croce di Guerra. Cty. Ct. judge 1945-55; JP Middlesex, West Sussex, Hertfordshire; FSA. Author of books on Sussex history. d. 27th May 1976.

DONOVAN, Terence Norbert (Lord Donovan)

s. of Timothy Cornelius Donovan, London, political agent (d. 1906). b. 13th June 1898. educ. Brockley Gr. Sch. WWI commissioned in Bedfordshire Regt. and Lieut. RAF. Civil Service (Revenue Dept.) 1920-32. M.T. July 1924. KC 1945. Bencher 1950, Treasurer 1970; Southern Rhodesia bar 1937. Specialised in revenue cases; MP Leicester (East) 1945-50, Leicester (North East) 1950; Chmn. parliamentary Labour Party's legal and judicial group; Chmn. Br. Govt. legal mission to Greece; member of committees on divorce procedure, and court-martial system 1946; KB judge 1950-60; Knight 1950; member LC's Law Reform Committee, and standing committee on criminal law revision; LJ 1960-64; PC 1960; L of A 1964-71; Baron 1964; Chmn. Criminal Appeals Committee 1964, Comm. on Trade Unions and Employers Assocs. 1965; expert on industrial relations; Dep. Chmn. appeals committee, Hampshire Quarter Sess. 1949-56; JP Hampshire. Father of Hugh Desmond Donovan (M.T. 1959). d. 12th Dec. 1971.

DOUGHTY, Sir Charles

s. of Charles Doughty JP, Lincoln. b. 27th July 1878. educ. Oatlands, Harrogate; Rugby; Corpus Christi Coll. Oxf. BA 1900, BCL 1901. I.T. April 1902. KC 1925. Bencher 1931, Treasurer 1953. Bd. of Trade arbitrator in industrial disputes 1915-19; Chmn. Sugar Confectionery Trade Bd. 1919, Milk Distribution Trade Bd. 1922, Hertfordshire Agricultural Committee 1924, Cotton Conciliation Committee; Independent Chmn. Lancs. and Cheshire joint committee under Coalmines (Minimum Wage) Act 1912; Recorder of Canterbury 1929-37, Guildford 1937-39, Brighton 1939-55; Chmn. of bar council; Knight 1941. Father of Charles John Addison Doughty QC, MP (1902-73). d. 2nd May 1956.

DOUGLAS, Horace James

s. of Henry William Douglas, Peebles, St. Alban's, and London. b. 5th March 1866. educ. privately. G.I. Jan. 1900; M.T. 1920. KC 1939. Served in ranks of Middlesex Regt. Rifle Vol. for ten years. d. 16th April 1962.

DOWDALL, Harold Chaloner

s. of Thomas Dowdall, Liverpool. b. 7th March 1868. educ. Rugby; Trinity Coll. Oxf. BA 1890, MA and BCL 1891. I.T. Jan. 1893. Practised at Liverpool bar until 1917; KC 1920; Lord Mayor of Liverpool 1908-09; Chan. diocese of Liverpool 1913-48, of Bristol 1919-48; Cty. Ct. judge 1921-40; Pres. Socy. of Public Teachers of Law 1929. Author of Local Development law 1919, Estatification 1930. d. 8th April 1955.

DOWDESWELL, George Morley

s. of William Dowdeswell, Recorder of Bombay. b. 5th Sept. 1809. educ. Pembroke Coll. Oxf. BA 1830, MA 1833. I.T. June 1834. QC 1866. Bencher 1867, Reader 1882, Treasurer 1883. Recorder of Newbury 1856-93; Official Referee 1876-89; JP Sussex. Author of works on insurance, and on merchant shipping; edited Bayley's Bills of Exchange, Smith's Compendium of Mercantile Law, and Starkie on Evidence. d. 3rd Dec. 1893.

DOWLING, Alfred Septimus

s. of Vincent Dowling, London, bookseller. G.I. June 1828. Serjeant 1842. Cty. Ct. judge 1849-68; Commr. for inquiring into state of county courts 1853; reported cases in KB, CP and Exch. 1830-43, and (with J.J. Lowndes) 1844-49. Brother of Sir James Dowling, CJ New South Wales (d. 1845). d. 3rd March 1868, age 63.

D'OYLEY, Thomas

s. of Ven. Matthias Doyley, Archdeacon of Lewes. b. 16th Nov. 1774. educ. Westminster; Christ Church Oxf. BA 1795, BCL 1800, DCL 1804; Fellow of All Souls 1800-20. M.T. Nov. 1798. Serjeant 1819; patent of precedence 1834; Chmn. West Sussex Quarter Sess.; edited (with E.V. Williams) Burn's Justice of the Peace. d. 14th Jan. 1855.

DRAKE, Robert James

s. of John Drake, Dromore, co. Down, Ireland. b. 1861. educ. privately; Trinity Coll. Dublin BA LLB, King's Inns Dublin. M.T. June 1887. KC 1914. d. 8th July 1916.

DREWE, Basil

s. of Julius Charles Drewe JP, Castle Drogo, Drewsteignton, Devon (d. 1931). b. 4th April 1894. educ. Eton; Christ Church Oxf. WWI Lieut. Devonshire Regt. and RGA, MC and bar. I.T. June 1920. KC 1945. Bencher 1952. WWII Wing Cdr. RAF; OBE 1943. d. 9th June 1974.

DRUCE, George

s. of Charles Druce, London, solicitor. educ. Shrewsbury; St. Peter's Coll. Camb. BA 1843, MA 1846, Fellow 1846. L.I. Nov. 1846. QC 1866. Bencher 1867. One of standing counsel to Camb. Univ. 1867-69. Brother of Charles Claridge Druce, Pres. Law Society 1881. d. (riding accident) 15th April 1869, age 48.

DRUCQUER, Maurice Nathaniel

s. of Jonas Drucquer, London. b. 9th Dec. 1876. educ. City of London Sch.; London Univ. MA, LLB. Stockbroker's clerk. M.T. June 1904. WWI Brevet Major RASC. Cty. Ct. judge 1928-50. Asst. editor Hallech's International Law. d. 21st July 1970.

DRUMMOND, Lister Maurice

s. of Maurice Drummond CB. b. 23rd Aug. 1856. educ. privately. I.T. June 1879. Secy. to Evicted Tenants Comm. Dublin 1892-93; Commr. to try municipal election petitions Grimsby 1904, Gloucester 1907; Secy. to Worcester Royal Comm. 1906; metrop. magistrate, South Western 1913-16; Knight of Papal Order of St. Gregory the Great 1901. d. 27th Feb. 1916.

DRURY, George Thorn

s. of George John Drury, Canterbury, ironfounder. b. 1860. educ. Worcester Coll. Oxf. BA 1883, Hon. MA, Hon. Fellow. I.T. and M.T. Jan. 1885. KC 1913. Special pleader. Recorder of Dover 1920-31. d. 14th Jan. 1931.

DUBE, Bhugwandin

s. of Pundit Parmeshwari Das Dube. b. 1st Sept. 1876. educ. Meerut Coll.; Muir Central Coll. Allahabad MA and LLB 1898. M.T. July 1908. KC 1931. Member of Allahabad bar; practised before judicial committee of privy council. d. 10th Dec. 1938.

DUGDALE, John Stratford

s. of William Stratford Dugdale MP, Merevale Hall, Warwickshire (d. 1871). b. 30th July 1835. educ. Eton; Merton Coll. Oxf. BA 1858, MA 1886. I.T. June 1862. QC 1882. Bencher 1888. Chmn.

Warwickshire Quarter Sess. 1883; Chmn. Warwickshire CC 1889-1919; Recorder of Grantham 1874-77, of Birmingham 1877; Chan. of dioceses of Worcester and Coventry; MP Warwickshire North East 1886-92; DL, JP Warwickshire. Author of Punishments and Conviction at Quarter Sessions. Brother of William Stratford Dugdale DL, JP (L.I. 1858). d. 27th Oct. 1920.

DUGMORE, William

s. of John Dugmore, Swaffham, Norfolk, Commr. of Inclosures. b. 1800. L.I. June 1828. QC 1861. Practised as conveyancer. d. Cannes, 1st. July 1872.

DUKE, Henry Edward (Lord Merrivale)

s. of William Edward Duke, Merrivale, Devon, granite merchant. b. 5th Nov. 1855. educ. privately. Journalist in provinces; in press gallery of H of C 1880. G.I. April 1885. QC 1899. Bencher 1899, Treasurer 1908 and 1927. Recorder of Devonport 1897-1914, of Plymouth 1897-1900; Chmn. of Gt. Western Ry. Conciliation Bd. 1909; MP Plymouth 1900-06, Exeter 1910-18; Att-Genl. 1915; PC 1915; Chmn. Royal Comm. on Defence of the Realm Losses 1915; Chief Secy. for Ireland after Easter Rebellion 1916-18; PC (Ireland) 1916; member Council of Legal Educ. 1921; LJ and knighted 1918; Pres. P D and A Division 1919-33; Baron 1925. Author of The House of Lords 1935, Marriage and Divorce: the English Point of View 1936. d. 20th May 1939.

DUMAS, Hugh Charles Sowerby

s. of Henry John Philip Dumas JP of Lloyd's. b. 9th Dec. 1865. educ. St. Leonard's Sch.; Winchester; Trinity Hall Camb. BA 1887, MA 1891. M.T. Jan. 1892. Bencher 1925, Reader 1936. Cty. Ct. judge 1931-39; an arbitrator under Lloyd's salvage agreements 1925. d. 3rd Nov. 1940.

DUMMETT, Sir Robert Ernest (formerly Peter Ernest)

s. of Robert Dummett. b. 1872. educ. Leys Sch.; Clare Coll. Camb. 1891. G.I. Nov. 1895. Bencher 1918, Treasurer 1928. Junior counsel to Mint at Central Criminal Ct 1914; Recorder of South Molton 1911-23, of Barnstaple and Bideford 1923-25; metrop. magistrate 1925, finally at Bow St. to 1941; chief magistrate and knighted 1940. d. 17th Oct. 1941.

DUNDAS, Sir David

s. of James Dundas, Ochtertyre, Perth. b. 1799. educ. Westminster; Christ Church Oxf. BA 1820, MA 1822. Scottish bar. I.T. Feb. 1823. QC 1840. Bencher 1840, Reader 1852, Treasurer 1853. MP Sutherlandshire 1840-52 and 1861-67; Sol-Genl. 1846-48; Knight 1847; Judge Adv-Genl. 1849-52; PC 1849; FRS; Trustee of Br. Museum 1861-67. d. 30th March 1877.

DUNLOP, Charles Robertson

s. of Prof. James Dunlop MD, Glasgow. b. 9th Jan. 1876. educ. High Sch. Glasgow; King William's Coll. Isle of Man; Glasgow Univ., prizeman in Scots law; Balliol Coll. Oxf. BA 1897, MA and BCL 1903. I.T. May 1901. KC 1919. Bencher 1927. Reader and lecturer at Inc. Law Socy. 1903-10; junior counsel to the Admiralty 1911-19. Edited Abbott's Law of Merchant Ships and Seamen. d. 19th July 1932.

DUNNE, Arthur Mountjoy

s. of Arthur Disney Dunne, Benfield, Queen's Co. and Dacca, Bengal (d. 1872). b. 1859. educ. Arlington House, Portarlington; Trinity Coll. Dublin BA, LLB. M. T. June 1881. KC 1917. Bencher 1925, Reader 1933. Practised in Calcutta 1881-1905, and later before Privy Council; member of bar council 1933; JP Wiltshire and Berkshire. d. 18th June 1947.

DUNNE, Sir Laurence Rivers

s. of Arthur Mountjoy Dunne KC. b. 1893. educ. Eton; Magdalen Coll. Oxf. BA 1921. WWI Brevet Major, MC (despatches thrice), 60th Rifles. I.T. Nov. 1922. Bencher 1948. Metrop. magistrate 1936, finally at Bow St. to 1960; chief magistrate and knighted 1948; Chmn. Berkshire Quarter Sess. 1964-66; JP Berkshire. d. 30th June 1970.

DU PARCQ, Herbert (Lord du Parcq)

s. of Clement Pixley du Parcq, St. Helier, Jersey, printer and stationer. b. 5th Aug. 1880. educ. Victoria Coll. Jersey; Exeter Coll. Oxf. BA 1903, BCL 1908, MA, Hon. Fellow Exeter and Jesus Colls. 1935. M.T. June 1906. KC 1926. Bencher 1931. Jersey bar 1906. Pres. Hardwicke Socy. 1910; member of bar council 1928-32; Recorder of Portsmouth 1928-29, of Bristol, and judge of Tolzey Ct. 1929-32; Commr. of Assize Northern circuit 1931; member Home Office committee on persistent offenders 1931; headed enquiry into disturbances at Dartmoor prison 1932; KB judge 1932-38; Knight 1932; LJ 1938-46; PC 1938; Chmn. Channel Is. Refugees Committee 1940; member Permanent Ct. of Arbitration, The Hague 1945; L of A 1946-49; Baron 1946; Chmn. Royal Comm. on Justices of the Peace 1946-48; Chmn. Council of Legal Educ. 1947-49; Hon. LLD Birmingham 1947. d. 27th April 1949.

DYER, Charles Edward

s. of Charles Robinson Dyer, London. b. 1864. educ. Oundle; Jesus Coll. Camb. BA 1886, LLM 1891. M.T. June 1890. KC 1919. Bencher 1925. Recorder of Northampton 1918-27; one of the chmn. of the Industrial Ct. 1924-27; Cty. Ct. judge 1927-37; JP Warwickshire. d. 19th Jan. 1937.

EADY, Charles Swinfen (Lord Swinfen)

s. of George John Eady, Chertsey, Surrey, surgeon (d. 1892). b. 31st July 1851. educ. privately; London Univ. LLB 1874, LLD 1878. Solicitor 1874, practised in London. I.T. June 1879 (Cert. of Hon.). QC 1893. Bencher 1901. Equity draftsman and conveyancer. Chancery judge 1901-13; Knight 1901; LJ 1913-18; PC 1913; MR 1918-19; Baron Swinfen of Chertsey 1919; member Senate, London Univ. Father of Charles Swinfen Eady, 2nd Baron (I.T. 1931). d. 15th Nov. 1919.

EAGLE, Francis King

s. of Robert Eagle, Lakenheath, Suffolk. b. 15th Nov. 1784. educ. Bury St. Edmunds Gr. Sch.; Charterhouse; Trinity Coll. Camb. LLB 1809. M.T. Nov. 1809. Bencher 1839, Reader 1843, Treasurer 1847. Recorder of Thetford; Cty. Ct. judge 1847-56; FLS 1807; reported (with E. Yonge) cases relating to tithes, 1826. d. 8th June 1856.

EALES, John Frederick

s. of William Eales, Luton, Bedfordshire. b. 19th Jan. 1881. Solicitor 1904, practised in Coventry. M.T. Jan. 1910. KC 1929. Bencher 1936. Recorder of Coventry 1928-34, of Nottingham 1934-36; MP Birmingham (Erdington) 1931-36; member of bar council 1932. d. 6th Aug. 1936.

EARDLEY-WILMOT, Hugh Eden

s. of Sir John Eardley Eardley-Wilmot Bt., Cty. Ct. judge. b. 7th Nov. 1850. educ. Charterhouse. L.I. Nov. 1871. Counsel to Mint at Central Criminal Ct.; Cty. Ct. judge 1891-1920. d. 10th March 1926.

EARDLEY-WILMOT, Sir John Eardley, Bt

s. of Sir John Eardley Eardley-Wilmot, Bt., MP (d. 1847). b. 16th Nov. 1810. educ. Winchester; Balliol Coll. Oxf. BA 1831. L.I. Jan. 1842. Recorder of Warwick 1852-74; Cty. Ct. judge 1853-71; MP South Warwickshire 1874-85; DL, JP Warwickshire. Author of a digest of the law of burglary 1851; edited his father's abridgement of Blackstone's Commentaries 1853. d. 1st Feb. 1892.

EARENGEY, William George

s. of James Earengey, Cheltenham. b. 1876. educ. Cheltenham Gr. Sch.; London Univ. BA, LLD. Solicitor 1897, practised in Cheltenham. M.T. Nov. 1919 (Cert. of Hon.). WWI Temp. Capt. General List. KC 1931. Recorder of Tewkesbury 1930-31, of Dudley 1931-34; Cty. Ct. judge 1934-49; member Senate London Univ. 1950-58. Author of The Law of Hire Purchase 1938, and edited Mayne on Damages. d. 12th April 1961.

EASTHAM, Sir Tom

s. of James Cook Eastham CE, Hadfield, Derbyshire. b. 22nd Feb. 1879. educ. Manchester Gr. Sch.; Owen's Coll.; Victoria Univ.; St. Bartholomew's Hosp. London, MB, ChB 1902. Resident MO Royal Boscombe and West Hants. Hosp. 1902. L.I. Jan. 1904. KC 1922. Bencher 1927, Treasurer 1948. Recorder of Oldham 1924-36; Official Referee 1936-44, Senior Referee 1944-54; Dep. Chmn. Surrey Quarter Sess. 1940-54; Chmn. Dorking Petty Sess. 1943-54; Chmn. Royal Corps of Naval Constructors Committee 1946; Chmn. Admiralty Manpower Committee 1947; Commr. of Assize, Chester and Welsh circuit 1948; Knight 1948; DL, JP Surrey. Father of Sir Thomas Michael Eastham, Judge of Family Divn. 1978. d. 11th April 1967.

EASTWOOD, John Francis

s. of John Edmund Eastwood, Gosden House, Bramley, Surrey (d. 1940). b. 13th Oct. 1887. educ. Eton; Trinity Coll. Camb. BA. I.T. May 1911. Lived four years in Canada. WWI Lieut. Grenadier Guards, Courts Martial officer (Major) 1918-20; Legal Officer, Ireland 1920-22; OBE 1922; KC 1937; MP Kettering 1931-40; Recorder of Tenterden 1935-40; metrop. magistrate 1940, finally at Bow St. to 1952. d. 30th Jan. 1952.

EDDIS, Arthur Shelly

s. of Eddis S. Eddis, Somerset House, London. b. 11th Jan. 1817. educ. St. Paul's (captain); Trinity Coll. Camb. BA 1839, MA 1842, Fellow 1840-44. Asst. tutor 1840-43. L.I. June 1845. QC 1869. Bencher 1869. Examr. in equity and real property London Univ. 1863; prof. of equity to Inns of Ct. 1876-82; Cty. Ct. judge 1883-93. Author of Principles of the administration of assets in payment of debts 1880. d. 23rd May 1893.

EDDY, John Percy

s. of Edward Eddy, Kidderminster, Worcestershire. b. 19th May 1881. educ. privately; King Charles I Sch. Kidderminster. Newspaper reporter; present at Siege of Sidney Street 1911. M.T. May 1911. KC 1936. WWI Lieut. Special List, with Min. of Nat. Service; judge of High Ct. Madras 1929-30; Recorder of West Ham 1936-49; stip. magistrate, East and West Ham 1949-54; with Claims Comm. 1941-43; member of bar council 1946-48; Divorce Commr. 1947; council member Medico-Legal Socy. and Inst. for Study and Treatment of Delinquency; lectured at univs. in USA 1952, Canada 1953, India 1963; Pres. West Ham Probation Hostel for youths 1953-56. Author of Guide to National Insurance 1911, Law of Distress for Rent, The Justices' Handbook 1947, Law of Copyright 1957, Scarlet and Ermine: Famous Trials as I saw them 1960, The New Law of Betting and Gaming (with L.L. Loewe) 1961, JPs

Yesterday and Tomorrow 1963, India and the Privy Council: the Last Appeal 1950. d. 10th July 1975.

EDGE, James Broughton

s. of Adam Edge, Bolton, Lancashire. b. 3rd Nov. 1836. educ. privately. Solicitor 1858. M.T. June 1871 (Cert. of Hon.). Coroner for Lancashire 1869-88; Counsel to Mint, Lancashire 1872-88; Cty. Ct. judge 1888-1911; Chmn. Devon Quarter Sess. 1895-98; JP Devon; Hon. Capt. 5th Battn. Loyal North Lancs. Regt. d. 23rd Oct. 1926.

EDGE, Sir John

s. of Benjamin Booker Edge JP, Clonbrock House, Queen's Co., Ireland. b. 28th July 1841. educ. Trinity Coll. Dublin BA 1861, LLB 1862. Irish bar 1864. M.T. April 1866. QC 1886. Bencher 1898, Reader 1909, Treasurer 1919. CJ North West Provinces, India 1886-98; Knight 1886; V-C. Allahabad Univ. 1887-93; member of Council of India 1898-1908; member of Home Office committee to inquire into the convictions in 1896 and 1904 of Adolf Beck (victim of mistaken identity); PC 1909, and member Judicial Committee 1909-26; Lt. Col. Comdt. Allahabad Rifle Corps, and Hon. Col. North West Provinces Vol.; Hon. ADC to Govr-Genl. 1895. d. 30th July 1926.

EDLIN, Sir Peter Henry

s. of Edward Colsill Edlin, Mortlake, Surrey. b. 29th June 1819. educ. privately. M.T. June 1847. Resident in India 1848-50. QC 1869. Bencher 1870, Reader 1876. Recorder of Bridgwater 1872-98; asst. judge Middlesex Sess. 1874-89; Chmn. London Sess. 1889-96; Knight 1888; Chmn. Joint Bd. of Examiners Inns of Ct. 1877; DL, JP Middlesex; JP London. d. 17th July 1903.

EDMUNDS, Lewis Humfrey

s. of James Edmunds MD, London. b. 2nd March 1860. educ. Univ. Coll. Sch.; University Coll. London DSc 1881, Fellow; St. John's Coll. Camb. BA 1883, LLB 1884, MA and LLM 1896. I.T. June 1884. QC 1895. Leader of Oxford Circuit; proprietor and editor Law Journal 1893-1907, Saturday Review, National Observer. Author of works on copyright, patents, and trademarks. Father of Humfrey Henry Edmunds (M.T.1915), Recorder of Bath. d. 27th April 1941.

EDWARDS, John

s. of John Edwards, Lower Broughton, nr. Manchester. b. 1836. educ. Owen's Coll. Manchester; London Univ. 1857. G.I. Jan. 1860 (Cert. of Hon.). Practised as conveyancer in Manchester. QC 1874. Bencher 1874. d. 15th Sept. 1885.

ELLICOTT, Arthur Becher

s. of Rt. Rev. Charles John Ellicott, Bishop of Gloucester and Bristol (d. 1905). b. 24th Sept. 1849. educ. Eton; Trinity Coll. Camb. BA 1872, MA 1891. M.T. Jan. 1875. Chan. of dioceses of Gloucester and Bristol 1891-1919; Secy. to Cathedral Estabs. Comm. 1891-1919; Cty. Ct. judge 1892-1920; JP Gloucestershire. d. 3rd June 1931.

ELLIOTT, Adshead

s. of John Matthews Elliott, Cheadle, Cheshire. b. 1869. educ. Manchester Gr. Sch.; Oriel Coll. Oxf. MA. I.T. Nov. 1894. Pres. of Pensions Appeal Tribunal 1918-19; Cty. Ct. judge 1919-22; JP Yorkshire West Riding. Author of treatise on Workmen's Compensation. d. 7th Sept. 1922.

ELLIOTT, George

s. of George Elliott, Buxton Lodge, Luton, Bedfordshire. b. 24th
Oct. 1860. educ. Mill Hill. Special pleader. I.T. Jan. 1882. KC 1909.
Defended George Chapman, publican who poisoned three barmaids,
Samuel Dougal the Moat Farm murderer 1903, Arthur Devereux (the
trunk murders) 1905, Horace Rayner, murderer of William Whiteley
1907. Author of The Law of Newspaper Libel 1883. d. 27th Oct.
1916.

ELLIOTT, George Percy

s. of Rev. Luther Graves Elliott, Ottery St. Mary, Devon. b. 1800.
educ. Winchester; St. Mary Hall Oxf. BA 1822, MA 1825. M.T.
May 1829. Metrop. magistrate Lambeth 1845-70. Author of treatise
on qualifications of parliamentary electors 1839. d. 12th July 1874.

ELLIS-McTAGGART, Francis

s. of Thomas Flower Ellis, barrister and law reporter (d. 1861). b.
13th Dec. 1823. educ. Trinity Coll. Camb. BA 1846, MA 1849. I.T.
May 1849. Cty. Ct. judge 1861-72; assumed additional name of
McTaggart 1868. d. 15th March 1872.

ELLISON, Cutbert Edward

s. of George Ellison, London, attorney. b. 29th Nov. 1817. educ.
Westminster; Trinity Coll. Camb. BA 1840, MA 1843. I.T. Jan.
1845. Stip. magistrate Newcastle 1854, Manchester 1860; metrop.
magistrate 1864, finally at Lambeth 1870-83; previously equity
draftsman and conveyancer. d. 26th May 1883.

ELLISON, Thomas

s. of Michael E. Ellison, Sheffield. b. 27th Sept. 1818. educ. St. Mary's Coll. Oscott. G.I. Jan. 1844. Cty. Ct. judge 1863-96. d. 7th April 1896.

ELMSLEY, William

s. of William Elmsley, Bristol. b. 1797. educ. Eton; Trinity Coll. Camb. BA 1819, MA 1822. M.T. Nov. 1825. QC 1851. Bencher 1852, Reader 1854, Treasurer 1858. Master of the Library 1861; Cty. Ct. judge 1862-66; JP Derbyshire. d. 20th Dec. 1866.

ELSLEY, Charles Heneage

s. of Rev. Heneage Elsley. b. 14th Aug. 1792. educ. privately; Peterhouse Coll. Camb. BA 1813, MA 1816, Fellow 1815. M.T. Jan. 1819. Commr. in Bankruptcy; Clerk of the Peace for Yorkshire West Riding 1827-65; Recorder of Richmond, Yorkshire 1827-65, of York 1834-65, of Scarborough 1836-44; Cty. Ct. judge 1847-54. Author of Reports of Cases by Sir W. Blackstone, revised, 1828. d. 3rd Aug. 1865.

ELTON, Charles Isaac

s. of Frederick Bayard Elton, HEICS, Southampton. b. 6th Dec. 1839. educ. Cheltenham Coll.; Balliol Coll. Oxf. BA 1862; Fellow Queen's Coll. 1862-64. L.I. Nov. 1865. QC 1885. Bencher 1887. MP West Somerset 1884-85, 1886-92; Lord of manor and patron of White Staunton; JP Somerset; FSA 1883. Author of treatise on copyholds and customary tenures 1874. d. 23rd April 1900.

EMANUEL, Samuel Henry

s. of Henry Herschel Emanuel, Brighton. b. 1865. educ. Univ. Coll. Sch.; Trinity Hall Camb. BA 1885, LLB 1886, LLM 1889, LLD 1895. I.T. July 1886. KC 1919. Bencher. Equity draftsman and conveyancer; Recorder of Winchester 1915-25. d. 15th May 1925.

EMDEN, Alfred Charles Richard

s. of William Samuel Emden, Hampstead, theatre manager. b. 1849. educ. King's Sch. Canterbury, and Paris. I.T. April 1880. First registrar in companies winding-up under new procedure of 1892; Cty. Ct. judge 1894-1911. Author of works on building law, and winding-up of companies. d. 18th Feb. 1911.

ENGELBACH, Archibald Frank

s. of Francis William Engelbach, Richmond, Surrey. b. 1st Jan. 1881. educ. Dulwich. M.T. Jan. 1906 (Cert. of Hon.). WWI Capt. Middlesex Regt. Cty. Ct. judge 1940-55. Won All England Men's Doubles Badminton Championship 1920; Vice-pres. Badminton Assoc. of England 1935-61; Steward, Br. Boxing Bd. of Control 1957-61. d. 14th Dec. 1961.

ENTWISTLE, Sir Cyril Fullard

s. of Joe Entwistle, St. Anne's and Bolton, Lancashire, cotton manufacturer. b. 23rd Sept. 1887. educ. Bolton Sch.; Victoria Univ. Manchester LLB 1908. WWI Major, 235 siege battery RGA, MC (despatches). Solicitor 1909. I.T. Nov. 1919. KC 1931. MP Kingston-upon-Hull (South West) 1918-24, Bolton 1931-45; Dep. Chmn. Committee of Ways and Means 1924; a H of C assessor appointed under Parliament Act 1911; Chmn. of standing committees, and temp. Chmn. H of C; Chmn. Nigel Finance and Investment Ltd., and Decca Record Co. Ltd.; director of several other companies; Knight 1937. d. 9th July 1974.

ERLE, Peter

s. of Rev. Christopher Erle, Gillingham, Dorset. bapt. 17th Nov. 1796. educ. Winchester; New Coll. Oxf. BA 1816, MA 1821, Fellow 1812-25. M.T. June 1821. QC 1854. Bencher 1854, Reader 1857, Treasurer 1863. Chief Charity Estate Commr. 1853-72; PC 1872. d. 29th Jan. 1877.

ERLE, Sir William

s. of Rev. Christopher Erle, Gillingham, Dorset. b. 1st Oct. 1793. educ. Winchester; New Coll. Oxf. BCL 1818, DCL 1857, Fellow 1811-34, Hon. Fellow 1870-80. M.T. Nov. 1819; I.T. June 1822. KC 1834. Bencher 1834, Reader 1843, Treasurer 1844. MP City of Oxford 1837-41; one of the counsel of the Palace Ct. Westminster; counsel to Bank of England 1844; judge of Common Pleas 1844; Knight 1845; QB judge 1846-59; CJ of Common Pleas 1859-66; PC 1859; FRS 1860; member of Trades Union Comm. 1867-68. Author of The Law relating to Trades Unions 1869. d. 28th Jan. 1880.

ERSKINE, Thomas

s. of 1st Baron Erskine, Lord Chancellor (d. 1823). b. 12th March 1788. educ. Hampstead Gr. Sch.; Harrow; Trinity Coll. Camb. MA 1811. Secy. of presentations at father's installation as LC, 1806. Special pleader 1810-13. L.I. May 1813. KC 1827. Chief judge in bankruptcy 1831-42; PC 1831; judge of Common Pleas 1839-44; tried the Chartists, with Coleridge J, 1840; member Judicial Committee of Privy Council; a Commr. for the Duchy of Cornwall; Pres. Trinitarian Bible Socy. 1840. Brother of David Montague Erskine (2nd Baron), MP, (L.I. 1802). d. 9th Nov. 1864.

ESPINASSE, James

s. of Isaac Espinasse, Bexley, Kent, barrister (d. 1834). b. 1798. educ. Balliol Coll. Oxf. BA 1820. G.I. June 1827. Recorder of Rochester 1842-67; Cty. Ct. judge 1847-67; Asst. Chmn. West Kent Quarter Sess.; JP Kent. Author of a treatise on bankrupts. d. 16th March 1867.

ESSENHIGH, Reginald Clare

s. of Henry Streeter Essenhigh, Warrington, Lancashire. b. 7th Sept. 1890. educ. Warrington Secondary Sch.; Christ's Hospital; Manchester Sch. of Art. WWI Capt. Manchester Regt. G.I. Jan. 1922. MP Lancashire (Newton) 1931-35; Cty. Ct. judge 1936-55; member Faculty of Law, Sheffield Univ.; member Appeals Committee Yorkshire West Riding Quarter Sess.; JP Yorkshire West Riding. Joint author of Benas and Essenhigh on pleadings in common law and chancery. d. 1st Nov. 1955.

EVANS, Ernest

s. of Evan Evans, Laura Place, Aberystwyth, solicitor (d. 1933). b. 1885. educ. Llandovery Coll.; University Coll. of Wales; Trinity Hall Camb. BA and LLB 1908. L.I. June 1910. WWI Capt. RASC. Private secy. to David Lloyd George 1918-20; KC 1937; MP Cardiganshire 1921-23, Univ. of Wales 1924-42; Cty. Ct. judge 1942-57; Chmn. Cardiganshire Quarter Sess. 1941; Chmn. Anglesey Quarter Sess. 1945; JP; member Council of Univ. Coll. of Wales. Author of works on agricultural law. d. 18th Jan. 1965.

EVANS, John

s. of Rev. John Evans, Haverfordwest, Pembrokeshire. educ. Glasgow Univ. BA, and Geneva. I.T. June 1820. QC 1837. Bencher 1837, Reader 1849, Treasurer 1850. MP Haverfordwest 1847-52; FSA 1853. d. 17th Oct. 1864, age 68.

EVANS, Sir Samuel Thomas

s. of John Evans, Skewen, nr. Neath, Glamorgan, merchant. b. 1859. educ. Coll. Sch. Swansea; University Coll. Aberystwyth; London Univ. BA. Solicitor 1883. M.T. June 1891. KC 1901. Bencher 1908. Recorder of Swansea 1906-08; MP Mid-Glamorgan 1890-1910; Sol-Genl. 1908-10; Knight 1908; Pres. P D and A Divn. 1910-18; PC 1910; of high repute for his judgments in prize cases during WWI, GCB 1916; JP Glamorgan, Breconshire, Pembrokeshire; hon. freeman of Swansea and Neath; Hon. LLD Wales; Hon. Fellow Jesus Coll. Oxf. d. 13th Sept. 1918.

EVANS, William

s. of James Evans, Merthyr Tydfil. b. 27th Dec. 1847. educ. Jesus Coll. Oxf. BA 1873. I.T. June 1874. Served on commissions to France and Spain 1879, Australia 1893, South Africa 1894; Cty. Ct. judge 1897-1918. Author of works on agency. d. 15th Feb. 1918.

EVE, Arthur Malcolm Trustram (Lord Silsoe)

s. of Sir Herbert Trustram Eve KBE, chartered surveyor (d. 1936). b. 8th April 1894. educ. Winchester; Christ Church Oxf. BA 1919, MA 1927. WWI Major 6th Royal Welch Fusiliers, MC; WWII AA and QMG, Brigadier 1940. I.T. Jan. 1919. KC 1935. Bencher 1942, Reader 1965, Treasurer 1966. Chmn. of Air Transport Licensing Authority 1938-39, War Damage Comm. 1941-49, Local Govt Bdy. Comm. 1945-49, War Works Comm. 1945-49, Central Land Bd. 1947-49, St George's Hosp. 1952-54, Burnham Committees on Teachers' Salaries 1950-53; Chmn. Police Council on Police Salaries 1951, Road Haulage Disposal Bd. 1953-56; First Church Estates Commr. 1954-69; First Crown Estates Commr. 1954-62; Independent Chmn. Cement Makers' Fed. 1951-70; Chmn. Boundaries Comm. Mauritius 1957, Fiji Sugar Inquiry Comm. 1961, Fiji Coconut Industry Inquiry 1963; Gentleman Usher of the Purple Rod in Order of Br. Empire 1960; Pres. Ski Club of G.B. 1950-54; hon. member RICS; Hon. FIOB; GBE 1950; TD; Baronet 1943; Baron

1963. Father of David Malcolm Trustram Eve, 2nd Lord Silsoe (QC 1972). d. Isle of Man, 3rd Dec. 1976.

EVE, Sir Harry Trelawney

s. of Henry Thomas Eve, Jamaica, merchant. b. 13th Oct. 1856. educ. privately; Exeter Coll. Oxf. BA and MA 1883, Hon. Fellow 1918. L.I. June 1881. QC 1895. Bencher 1899. Equity draftsman and conveyancer; MP Devon (Ashburton) 1904-07; Chancery judge 1907-37; Knight 1907; expert in charitable trusts; PC 1937; JP Devon. d. 10th Dec. 1940.

EVERETT, Edward

s. of Joseph Everett, Salisbury. b. 13th May 1798. educ. Winchester; Balliol Coll. Oxf. BA 1820, MA 1824. M.T. May 1824. Conveyancer in Salisbury; judge of Salisbury Ct. of Requests; Cty. Ct. judge 1847-67; JP. d. 24th Jan. 1870.

EVERITT, Francis William Everitt

s. of William Stiffe, Stuttgart and Swansea. b. 1830. L.I. June 1855. QC 1882. Bencher 1884. Equity draftsman and conveyancer; assumed name of Everitt by Royal Licence 1860. d. 9th March 1904.

EVERSHED, Francis Raymond (Lord Evershed)

s. of Frank Evershed, Stapenhill, Burton-on-Trent, solicitor. b. 8th Aug. 1899. educ. Clifton Coll. (captain); Balliol Coll. Oxf. BA 1921, Hon. Fellow 1947, Hon. DCL 1955. WWI 2nd Lieut Royal Engineers. L.I. Jan. 1923 (Cert of Hon.). KC 1933. Bencher 1938, Treasurer 1958. Member of bar council; Chmn. Central Price Regn. Committee 1939-42; Regional Controller, Nottinghamshire, Derbyshire and Leicestershire coal producing area 1942-44; member committee on Compensation and Betterment 1941; Chancery judge 1944-47; Knight 1944; Chmn. Comm. on Wages in Cotton Spinning Industry 1945-46; LJ 1947; Chmn. committee on practice and procedure in Supreme Ct. 1947-53; MR 1949-62; Baron Evershed of Stapenhill 1956; L of A 1962-65; Br. member Permanent Ct. of Arbitration, The Hague 1950; Pres. Bar Musical Socy. 1952-66; Chmn. Pilgrim Trust 1959-65; Chmn. Br. Council Law Committee 1956-66; FSA 1950; Pres. Clifton Coll. 1951; Hon. Freeman, Burton-on-Trent 1950; awarded many honorary degrees. d. 3rd Oct. 1966.

FALCONER, Thomas

of Rev. Thomas Falconer, Bath. b. 25th June 1805. educ. in Edinburgh. L.I. Feb. 1830. One of arbitrators appointed to settle boundary of Canada and New Brunswick 1850; Colonial secy. of Western Australia 1851; Cty. Ct. judge 1851-81; JP Monmouthshire, Glamorganshire, Brecknockshire. Author of On Surnames and the rules of law affecting their change 1862. d. 28th Aug. 1882.

FARRANT, Henry Gatchell

s. of Robert Farrant, Cullompton Court, Devon. b. 10th May 1864. educ. Repton; New Coll. Oxf. BA 1888, MA 1924, MA Corpus Christi Coll. Camb. 1920. I.T. Jan. 1890. Member of bar council 1914; Cty. Ct. judge 1918-37; Chmn. Isle of Ely Quarter Sess. 1921-41; Chmn. Cambridgeshire Quarter Sess. 1929-41; Chmn. Cambridge Div. Justices 1927-41; Pres. Socy. of Chairmen of Quarter Sess. 1930; DL, JP Cambridgeshire and Isle of Ely; JP Worcestershire; a govr. of Repton Sch. d. 16th April 1946.

FARWELL, Sir Christopher John Wickens

s. of Farwell LJ and g.s. of Wickens V-C. b. 26th Dec. 1877. educ. Winchester; Balliol Coll. Oxf. 1896. L.I. April 1902. KC 1923.

Bencher 1928. Chancery judge 1929-43; Knight 1929; edited Haynes' Outlines of Equity 1906, and Farwell on Powers 1916. d. 15th April 1943.

FARWELL, Sir George

s. of Frederick Cooper Farwell, Tettenhall, Staffordshire, land agent. b. 22nd Dec. 1845. educ. Rugby; Balliol Coll. Oxf. BA 1869, Hon. Fellow 1912. L.I. Nov. 1871. QC 1891. Bencher 1895. Chancery judge 1899-1906; Knight 1899; Chmn. Royal Comm. on purchase of supplies and disposal of surplus in South African War, 1905; his decision in leading case of Taff Vale Ry. Co. (trade union law) supported by H of L 1900; LJ 1906-13; PC 1906; Hon. LLD Edin. 1908. Author of concise treatise on powers, 1874. d. 30th Sept 1915.

FENWICK, Christian Bedford

s. of Bedford Fenwick MD, Upper Wimpole St, London W. b. 15th Sept 1888. educ. Eton; Magdalen Coll. Oxf. BA 1909, MA. I.T. Jan. 1911. KC 1945. WWI Capt 8th Battn. London Regt. Recorder of Doncaster 1933-46, of Halifax 1946-47, of Hull 1947-50; Sol-Genl. Cty. Palatine of Durham 1946-47; Att-Genl. 1947-50; Cty. Ct. judge 1950-61; Chmn. Cumberland Quarter Sess. 1953-63. d. 5th Oct. 1969.

FENWICK, Edward Nicholas Fenwick

s. of Edward Matthew Fenwick MP, Burrow Hall, Kirkby Lonsdale, Lancashire, barrister. b. 1846. educ. Highgate; Trinity Hall Camb. BA 1869. I.T. Jan. 1873. Stip. magistrate Bradford 1885-87; metrop. magistrate 1887, finally at Bow St. 1901-08; JP Middlesex and Home Counties. d. 25th May 1908.

FERGUSON, William Bates

s. of Pearson Biggs Ferguson JP, Manchester. b. 1853. educ. Manchester Gr. Sch.; Christ Church Oxf. BA 1874, MA 1878. L.I. June 1882. QC 1900. Joint author of Ambrose and Ferguson's Land Transfer Acts; FIC; photographic inventor, and medallist of Royal Photographic Socy., and Société Française de Photographie; member of Univs. of London, Edin. and Geneva. d. 7th Oct. 1937.

FFOULKES, William Wynne

s. of Lt. Col. John Powell Ffoulkes, Eriviat, Denbighshire (d. 1826). b. 14th July 1821. educ. Shrewsbury; Jesus Coll. Oxf. BA 1844, MA 1847. L.I. Nov. 1847. Cty. Ct. judge 1875-99; JP Cheshire. d. 27th June 1903.

FIELD, Henry St. John

s. of Henry Field, Leamington, Warwickshire, solicitor. b. 22nd Nov. 1883. educ. Rugby; Balliol Coll. Oxf. I.T. May 1908. M.T. May 1928. WWI Lieut. RA. KC 1936. Recorder of Warwick 1937-45. d. 9th Dec. 1949.

FIELD, William Ventris (Lord Field)

s. of Thomas Flint Field, Fielden, Bedfordshire. b. 21st Aug. 1813. educ. Burton Gr. Sch. Solicitor in London. Special pleader 1847-50. I.T. May 1850. QC 1864. Bencher 1864. Had large commercial practice on Midland circuit; QB judge 1875-90; Knight 1875; PC 1890; Baron Field of Bakeham 1890; served in H of L in judicial capacity. d. 23rd Jan. 1907.

FINLAY, Robert Bannatyne (Lord Finlay)

s. of William Finlay FRCP, Cherrybank, nr. Newhaven, Edinburgh

(d. 1886). b. 11th July 1842. educ. Edin. Acad.; Edin. Univ. MD 1863, Hon. LLD. M.T. Nov. 1867. QC 1882. Bencher 1884, Reader 1896, Treasurer 1902. MP Inverness Burghs 1885-92 and 1895-1906, Edin. and St. Andrews Univs. 1910-16; Sol-Genl. 1895-1900; Knight 1895; Att-Genl. 1900-05; led for GB and Canada in Alaska Bdy. Arb. 1903, for GB at Hague Trib. on Venezuelan Bdy. Arb. 1903, for Canada in Newfoundland Fisheries Arb. 1910; member of bar council; GCMG 1904; PC 1905; LC 1916-19; Baron 1916; Viscount 1919; Br. member of Permanent Ct. of Arb., The Hague 1920; intern. judge (League of Nations) 1921-28; JP Invernessshire; DL Nairnshire; Lord Rector of Edin. Univ. 1902; Hon. LLD Camb. and St. Andrews. d. 9th March 1929.

FINLAY, William (Lord Finlay)

s. of Finlay LC. b. 15th Oct. 1875. educ. Eton; Trinity Coll. Camb. BA 1897. M.T. June 1901. KC 1914. Bencher 1924, Reader 1933. Junior counsel to IR 1905-14; in Procurator-Genl.'s Dept. (Intelligence) 1915; Chmn. Contraband Committee, Foreign Office 1916 and 1939; Vice-Chmn. Allied Blockade Committee 1917-19; temp. legal adviser Foreign Office 1918-19; KBE 1920; Commr. of Assize 1921-24; KB judge 1924-38; Commr. under Ry. and Canal Traffic Act. 1888, from 1937; LJ 1938-45; PC 1938; a Br. rep. on UN War Crimes Comm. 1945; GBE 1945; succeeded father as 2nd Viscount 1929; Chmn. Wiltshire Quarter Sess. 1937; Officer, Legion of Honour, and Order of St. Maurice and St. Lazarus (Italy). d. 30th June 1945.

FINNEMORE, Sir Donald Leslie

of William Finnemore, Birmingham. b. 13th June 1889. educ. King Edward's Sch. Birmingham; Pembroke Coll. Oxf. BA 1911, MA 1916, Hon. Fellow 1948; Hon. LLD Birmingham 1966. I.T. Jan. 1914. Bencher 1947. WWI Br. Red Cross Socy. officer. Cty. Ct. judge 1940-47; P D and A judge 1947-48; KB judge 1948-64; Knight 1947; Chmn. Warwickshire Quarter Sess. 1950; JP

Warwickshire; hon. legal adviser to Midland Regional Commr. for civil defence 1940-45; life governor Birmingham Univ. 1945; Governor King Edward's Sch. 1946. d. 10th May 1974.

FISCHER, Thomas Halhed

s: of Capt. Thomas Fischer HEICS. b. 1830. educ. Merchant Taylors'. L.I. June 1851. QC 1872. Bencher 1872. Examr. in real and personal property law to Inns of Ct. 1882-3; equity prof. to Inns of Ct. 1883. d. 1st Nov. 1914.

FISHER, Robert Alexander

s. of John Fisher, Fulham, London. M.T. Jan. 1850. Dep. judge City of London Ct. Secy. to the Judicature Comm. 1872-74. Cty. Ct. judge 1874-79. Author (1870) of a digest of decisions of cts. of common law, bankruptcy, probate, admiralty and divorce, from 1756. d. 30th Sept. 1879, age 62.

FITZGERALD, Gerald Augustus Robert

s. of Ven. Augustus Otway Fitzgerald, Charlton Mackerell, Somerset, archdeacon of Wells (d. 1897). b. 22nd Sept. 1844. educ. Sherborne; Corpus Christi Coll. Oxf. BA 1866; St. John's Coll. MA 1869, Fellow 1867-75. L.I. May 1871. KC 1909. Parliamentary counsel and draftsman of private bills; light ry. commr. 1896-1901; JP Wiltshire. Editor of Thring's Joint Stock Companies, and a manual of Ballot Act. 1872. d. 1st Aug. 1925.

FITZGERALD, John David (Lord Fitzgerald)

s. of David Fitzgerald, Dublin, merchant. b. 1st May 1816. educ. in Williamstown, nr. Dublin; Trinity Coll. Dublin MA, Hon. LLD 1870. Irish bar 1838. QC 1847. Bencher 1855. Leader on Munster circuit; MP Ennis 1852-60; Sol-Genl. Ireland 1855-56, Att-Genl.

1856-58 and 1859-60; PC (Ireland) 1856; declined Chief Secretaryship; successfully introduced bill to establish Ct. of Chancery Appeal in Ireland 1856; QB judge, Ireland 1860-82; L of A, Baron and PC 1882; the first Irish judge to be appointed L of A; Hon. Bencher G.I. 1883; Commr. for Nat. educ. in Ireland; a govr. of the Hibernian Military Sch. d. 16th Oct. 1889.

FITZGERALD, John Donohoe

s. of Rt. Hon. Lord Fitzgerald. b. 20th Jan. 1848. educ. Oscott Coll.; King's Coll. London; Christ's Coll. Camb. LLB 1870, LLM 1873. I.T. June 1872. QC 1896. Had large parliamentary practice; substantially involved in the formation of the Port of London Authority. d. 11th May 1918.

FITZGERALD, Maurice Pembroke

s. of John Donohoe Fitzgerald KC. b. 1887. educ. Harrow; Trinity Coll. Camb. BA 1909, MA 1913. I.T. June 1912. KC 1938. Bencher 1945. WWI Capt. RFA (despatches). Leader of parliamentary bar; Dep. Chmn. Essex Quarter Sess. 1943; Master of Skinners' Co. 1941 and 1948; govr. Tonbridge and Felsted Schs.; JP Essex. d. 13th March 1952.

FLEMING, Charles James

s. of Edmond Lionel Fleming, Sheffield, paper manufacturer. b. 26th Nov. 1839. educ. privately. Chief Asst. to Accountant-Genl. Bombay 1865-71. G.I. June 1872. QC 1893. Bencher 1893. MP Doncaster 1892. d. 25th Dec. 1904.

FLEMING, Edward Lascelles

s. of Thomas Fleming, Blackburn, Lancashire. educ. London Univ. WWI Lieut. 4th Battn. East Lancashire Regt. and attached RFC. G.I.

Jan. 1921. KC 1932. MP Manchester (Withington) 1931-50. WWII
Sq. Leader RAF. d. 17th Feb. 1950, age 58.

FLEMING, James

s. of Valentine Fleming, Tuam, co. Galway, Capt. 9th Regt. M.T.
June 1836. QC 1858. Chief Commr. West Indian encumbered
estates ct. 1865-87; Chan. Cty. Palatine of Durham 1871-87. Author
of Rules and Orders of Chancery Court, Durham 1878. Brother of
Sir Valentine Fleming, CJ Tasmania 1854-70. d. 23rd July 1887,
age 80.

FLEMING, Samuel

s. of Frederick Green Fleming. b. 24th May 1865. educ. Univ. Coll.
London; Edin. Univ. MB. CM 1890; DPH Camb. 1893. G.I. and
M.T. June 1897. WWI Lieut. RAMC. Legal adviser and judge-
advocate Aldershot Command 1915-18; legal adviser at War Office
to Army Medical Dept. 1918-19; Dep. Asst. Director-Genl. Army
Medical Dept. 1918-19; Brevet Lt Col. 1919; member of bar council
1920; Recorder of Doncaster 1920-21; metrop. magistrate 1921,
finally at Lambeth 1924-25; JP Surrey. d. 20th Dec. 1925.

FLOWERS, Frederick

s. of Rev. Field Flowers, Partney, Lincolnshire. b. 1810. educ. Louth
Gr. Sch. L.I. Nov. 1839. Recorder of Stamford 1862-64; metrop.
magistrate, Bow St. 1864-86; JP Middlesex and Home Counties.
d. 26th Jan. 1886.

FLOWERS, John

s. of George Arthur Flowers, Hove, Sussex, solicitor. b. 1882. educ.
New Coll. Eastbourne; Trinity Coll. Oxf. BA 1905. I.T. July 1908.

KC 1929. Bencher 1937. WWI Lieut. RASC. Recorder of Guildford 1928-38, of Southend-on-Sea 1938. d. 8th May 1968.

FOLLETT, Brent Spencer

s. of Benjamin Follett, Topsham, Devon, timber merchant. b. 1810. L.I. June 1833. QC 1851. Bencher 1851, Treasurer 1872. MP Bridgwater 1852-57; member Council of Legal Educ.; Chief Registrar of Land Registry Office 1862-87. Father of William Webb Spencer Follett 1848-1934 (L.I. 1874), examr. to High Ct. d. 23rd Jan. 1887.

FOLLETT, Sir William Webb

s. of Benjamin Follett, Topsham, Devon, timber merchant. b. 2nd Dec. 1798. educ. Exeter Gr. Sch.; Trinity Coll. Camb. BA 1818, MA 1830. Special pleader 1821. I.T. May 1824. KC 1834. Bencher 1835, Reader 1845. MP Exeter 1835-45; Sol-Genl. 1834-35 and 1841-44; Att-Genl. 1844; Knight 1835; counsel to Camb. Univ. 1836; defended Lord Cardigan in House of Lords on charge of duelling; represented G.C. Norton (q.v.) in action for criminal conversation against Lord Melbourne. d. 28th June 1845.

FOOKS, William Cracroft

s. of Thomas Broadley Fooks, Dartford, Kent, attorney and solicitor. b. 1812. Clerk with East India Co. G.I. June 1843. QC 1869. Bencher 1869, Treasurer 1876. Member Council of Legal Educ., and Council of Law Reporting; JP Kent. Father of Courtenay Cracroft Spurrell Fooks JP (G.I. 1884). d. 2nd Aug. 1899.

FOOTE, John Alderson

s. of Capt. John Foote RN, Plymouth. b. 15th Dec. 1848. educ.

Charterhouse (captain); St John's Coll. Camb. BA 1872, MA 1885. L.I. Jan. 1875. QC 1897. Bencher 1905. Recorder of Exeter 1899-1922; counsel to PO on Western Circuit 1893; Commr. of Assize, North East Circuit 1913; counsel to Camb. Univ. 1915. Author of treatise on Private International Jurisprudence 1878 and Pie Powder (anon.) by "A Circuit Tramp" 1911. d. 26th April 1922.

FORBES, Arthur Harold

s. of Henry Bracey Forbes, London, solicitor. b. 29th Oct. 1885. educ. Birmingham Univ. LLM. M.T. Nov. 1906. WWI Capt. Salonika army (despatches). Cty. Ct. judge 1941-56; Chmn. Northamptonshire Quarter Sess. 1946-60; govr. Birmingham Univ. d. 15th April 1967.

FORBES, John

s. of James Forbes, Aberdeen, merchant. b. 4th Feb. 1838. educ. Gr. Sch. and Marischal Coll. Aberdeen; Aberdeen Univ. Read for Scottish bar, Brown Prize for conveyancing 1858, for Scots law 1858-59. L.I. June 1862 (Cert. of Hon.). QC 1881. Bencher 1884. Sol-Genl. Cty. Palatine of Durham 1886-87, Att-Genl. 1887-1901; Recorder of Hull 1887; member of bar committee; Commr. for trial of municipal election petitions 1885-93; Royal Commr. of Assize 1896 and 1902. Author (with W.W. Mackeson QC) of The Judicature Acts and Rules, with Forms of Pleadings etc. 1875. d. 8th March 1904.

FORDHAM, Edward Snow

s. of Edward King Fordham DL, JP, Ashwell Bury, Hertfordshire, brewer and farmer (d. 1889). b. 15th Jan. 1858. educ. Caius Coll. Camb. BA 1881, MA, LLM 1884. I.T. Nov. 1883. Metrop. magistrate 1898, finally at West London 1910-17; Chmn. Cambridgeshire Quarter Sess. 1901-12; DL, JP Cambridgeshire,

Bedfordshire, Hertfordshire; JP London and Home Counties. d. 28th
Jan. 1919.

FORSTER, Sir Thomas Edwards

s. of Thomas Forster, Etherston House, Putney, company director.
b. 23rd Oct. 1859. M.T. Jan. 1905. KC 1924. Dep. Chmn. Middlesex
Quarter Sess. 1932-34, Chmn. 1934-36; responsible for much social
and philanthropic work in Chiswick; Knight 1927; JP Middlesex.
d. 13th April 1939.

FORSYTH, William

s. of Thomas Forsyth, Liverpool. b. 25th Oct. 1812. educ. Sherborne;
Trinity Coll. Camb. BA 1834, MA 1837, Fellow 1835-43. LLD
Edin. 1871. I.T. Nov. 1839. QC 1857. Bencher 1857, Reader 1871,
Treasurer 1872. Standing counsel to Secy. of State for India 1859-
74; MP Cambridge 1865-66, Marylebone 1874-80; Commissary of
Camb. Univ. 1868-99; member Council of Legal Educ. 1860.
Author of treatise on law relating to composition with creditors,
1841, and historical works; edited the Annual Register 1842-68. d.
26th Dec. 1899.

FORTESCUE, Matthew

s. of Joseph Fortescue, Capt. Scots Greys, Lyndhurst, Hampshire.
b. 18th May 1805. educ. Queens' Coll. Camb. BA 1828, MA 1831.
M.T. Nov. 1839. Cty. Ct. judge 1857-83; JP Devon. d. 27th March
1883.

FOSTER, Thomas Campbell

s. of John Foster, newspaper proprietor. b. 6th Oct. 1813. Sub-editor
of Liverpool Standard; parliamentary reporter for The Times.
Special pleader 1842. M.T. Jan. 1846. QC 1875. Bencher 1878.

Recorder of Warwick 1874-82; leading counsel for Crown at trial in Leeds of Charles Peace, 1879. Published treatise on writ of Scire Facias, 1851; reported (with W.F. Finlason) cases at nisi prius 1860-67. d. 1st July 1882.

FOX, John Scott

s. of Rev. William Fox, Preston, Lancashire. b. 17th Jan. 1852. educ. Bedford Gr. Sch.; University Coll. Oxf. BA 1875, MA and BCL 1877. M.T. and L.I. Nov. 1877. QC 1898. Bencher 1905 (M.T.), Reader 1917. Examr. to the High Ct. 1884-94; Sol-Genl. Cty. Palatine of Durham 1901, Chan. 1905-15; Recorder of Sheffield 1903-15; Cty. Ct. judge 1915-16. d. 3rd March 1918.

FOX-ANDREWS, Norman Roy

s. of Stephen Fox-Andrews, Bath. b. 15th April 1894. educ. Leys Sch.; Trinity Hall Camb. BA 1919. WWI 2nd Lieut. DCLI. L.I. April 1921. KC 1945. Bencher 1950. WWII with RAF. Recorder of Bridgwater 1945, of Bournemouth 1945-61, of Bristol 1961; member Royal Comm. on capital punishment 1949. Step-father of James Roland Blake Fox-Andrews (QC 1968). d. 31st July 1971.

FRANCILLON, James

s. of Francis Francillon, Harwich. b. 21st Nov. 1802. educ. King's Sch. Rochester. Attorney 1824, practised in Gloucester. G.I. Nov. 1833. Cty. Ct. judge 1847-66. Author of Lectures elementary and familiar on English law 1860-61. d. Lausanne, 3rd Sept. 1866.

FRANCIS, Charles King

s. of Frederick Francis, East Molesey Court, Surrey. b. 3rd Feb. 1851. educ. Rugby; Brasenose Coll. Oxf. BA 1873. I.T. Jan. 1876. Metrop. magistrate 1896, finally at Westminster 1908-25; JP London and Home Counties; played cricket for Essex and Middlesex. d. 28th Oct. 1925.

FRANKLAND, Cecil James

s. of William Frankland, Leeds. b. 21st Oct. 1884. educ. Leeds Church Sch.; Leeds Univ. LLB. M.T. June 1915. WWI Capt. RGA 17th Corps (despatches). Cty. Ct. judge 1933-42. d. 18th June 1942.

FRASER, Sir Hugh

s. of Thomas Fraser, Blackheath, London, manager of Life Assoc. of Scotland. b. 26th April 1860. educ. Charterhouse; Leamington Coll.; Trinity Hall Camb. BA 1882, LLM 1886, MA 1885, LLD 1892, Hon. Fellow 1925. I.T. Nov. 1886. Bencher 1918. Special pleader; lecturer on equity at Inc. Law Socy. 1888-91; Reader and examr. in common law at Inns of Ct. 1897-1924; examr. for honours in law at Oxf., Camb. and London; arbitrator in Building Trade Dispute 1923; member Irish Deportees Compensation Trib. 1923, and committee dealing with claims of police strikers 1924; KB judge 1924-27; Knight 1917; JP Ross and Cromarty. Author of Law of Torts, Law of Libel and Slander, and Law of Parliamentary Elections and Election Petitions; annotated Representation of the People Act 1918. d. 8th July 1927.

FRASER, John Farquhar

s. of Robert Fraser, Invernesshire. educ. Trinity Coll. Camb. 1806. L.I. May 1817. Cty. Ct. judge 1847-65. Edited reports of Sir Edward Coke, 1826. d. 2nd Feb. 1865, age 75.

FRASER, Patrick

s. of Patrick Fraser, Perth, merchant. b. 1819. educ. Perth Gr. Sch.; St. Andrew's Univ.; LLD Edin. 1871. Scottish bar 1843; Sheriff of

Renfrewshire 1864; Dean of Faculty of Advocates 1878; QC 1880; Lord of Session 1881-89, as Lord Fraser; Lord Ordinary in Exch. cases 1881-89. d. 27th March 1889.

FREEMAN, George Mallows

s. of Robert Freeman, Kensington, London. b. 1850. educ. Kensington Gr. Sch.; Corpus Christi Coll. Oxf. BA 1872. I.T. June 1874. QC 1896. Bencher 1907. Chmn. East Sussex Quarter Sess.; JP Buckinghamshire and East Sussex; High Sheriff, East Sussex 1919-20; Mayor of Winchelsea 1911-19 and 1928. d. 7th March 1934.

FRENCH, Daniel O'Connell

s. of Bartholomew French, Maghull, nr. Liverpool, shipowner. b. 1843. educ. Jesuit Coll., Tournai, Belgium. Solicitor in Liverpool. M.T. April 1872 (Cert. of Hon.). QC 1885. Bencher 1888, Reader 1899. Cty. Ct. judge 1892-1902. d. 5th Aug. 1902.

FRY, Sir Edward

s. of Joseph Fry, Bristol (d. 1879). b. 4th Nov. 1827. educ. Bristol Coll.; University Coll. London BA 1851, Fellow. In business in Bristol 1843-48. L.I. June 1854. QC 1869. Had large practice in chancery and at parliamentary bar; examr. in law to London Univ. and Council of Legal Educ.; Chancery judge 1877-83; Knight 1877; much involved in Rule Committee of Judges; LJ 1883-92; PC; judge of Hague Trib. 1900; arbitrator at Hague between USA and Mexico in Pious Funds of California dispute 1902-03; Br. legal assessor on comm. appointed to deal with Dogger Bank incident 1904; actively concerned in second Hague Confce. 1907; GCB 1907; arbitrator between France and Germany in Casablanca incident 1908-09; declined peerage; Chmn. Somerset Quarter Sess.; FRS 1883; FBA; on Council of Clifton Coll. 1895-1902; Hon. DCL Oxf. and Hon.

Fellow Balliol Coll.; Hon. LLD Aberdeen, Camb., Edin., Bristol. Author of a treatise on the specific performance of contracts 1858, and the doctrine of election 1864. d. 18th Oct. 1918.

FRY, Theodore Wilfred

s. of Sir Theodore Fry, Bt. (d. 1912). b. 6th May 1868. educ. Clifton; New Coll. Oxf. BA 1889. I.T. June 1893. Stip. magistrate, Middlesbrough 1908-20; metrop. magistrate 1920, finally at Bow St. 1926-41; Chmn. Tees District Maritime Bd. 1918; OBE (civil) 1918; JP Yorkshire North Riding; FSA 1892. d. 1st June 1947.

FULLARTON, Ralph Wardlaw Macleod

s. of Arhcibald Fullarton, Glasgow. b. 1835. educ. Edin. High Sch., and in France and Germany; Queens' Coll. Camb. BA 1862. I.T. Nov. 1865. QC 1891. Practised chiefly before Privy Council; unsuccessful parliamentary candidate 1886-95. d. 29th May 1896.

FULTON, Sir James Forrest

s. of Lt. Col. James Forrest Fulton, KH. b. Ostend, 12th July 1846. educ. Norwich Gr. Sch.; London Univ. BA 1867, LLB 1873. M.T. April 1872. QC 1892. Bencher 1898, Reader 1910, Treasurer 1921. Counsel to Treasury at Middlesex Sess. and Central Criminal Ct.; counsel to Mint, Hertfordshire; senior counsel to PO; MP West Ham (North) 1886-92; Recorder of Maidstone 1892; Common Serjeant 1892-1900; Knight 1892; Recorder of London 1900-22; DL, JP London. Father of Eustace Cecil Fulton (M.T.1904), Recorder of Rye. d. 25th June 1925.

FURNER, William

s. of John Furner, Brighton. b. 1790. Attorney 1815, practised in Brighton. Commr. in Bankruptcy; judge of Cts. of Request, Brighton and Shoreham 1840-47. G.I. May 1851. Cty. Ct. judge 1847-77; JP Surrey and Sussex. d. 25th Nov. 1877.

FYFE, David Patrick Maxwell (Lord Kilmuir)

s. of William Thomson Fyfe, Mornington Drive, Edinburgh, schools inspector. b. 29th May 1900. educ. Geo. Watson's Coll. Edin.; Balliol Coll. Oxf. BA 1922, MA, Hon. DCL 1953, Hon. Fellow 1954; Visitor, St. Anthony's Coll. 1953. WWI commissioned in Scots Guards. G.I. June 1922. KC 1934. Bencher 1936, Treasurer 1949, Vice-Treasurer 1950. Practised in Liverpool until 1934; member of bar council 1936; Recorder of Oldham 1936-42; Major, and Dep. Judge Adv. 1940; MP Liverpool (West Derby) 1935-45; Sol-Genl. 1942-45; Knight 1942; PC 1945; Att-Genl. 1945; Dep. Chief Prosecutor at Nuremberg War Trials 1945-46; Chmn. Conservative Party committee on Post-War Reconstruction; Home Secy. 1951; member Council of Europe 1949; GCVO 1953; LC 1954-62; Viscount 1954; dismissed from Cabinet (with earldom) by Harold Macmillan 1962; Chmn. Thomson Foundation (education), and Wolfson Foundation 1962; Chmn. Plessey Co.; Rector, St. Andrews Univ. 1955-58; Hon. LLD Liverpool 1947, and several other univs.; hon. member Canadian and American Bar Assocs.; Hon. FRCSE 1955. Published Political Adventure (memoirs) 1964. d. 27th Jan. 1967.

GALBRAITH, James Francis Wallace

s. of Hugh James Galbraith. b. 1872. educ. Blackheath Proprietary Sch.; Oriel Coll. Oxf. L.I. June 1895 (Cert. of Hon.). KC 1919. Bencher 1922. Member of bar council 1921-35; MP Surrey (East) 1922-35; equity draftsman and conveyancer; Pres. Hardwicke Socy. 1909; Cty. Ct. judge 1935-45; JP Surrey. d. 29th Jan. 1945.

GALE, Charles James

s. of Charles Gale. b. April 1805. educ. Birmingham Gr. Sch. M.T.

June 1832. Cty. Ct. judge 1847-74. Author of the well-known work on easements; reported (with H. Davison) cases in QB 1841-43; JP. d. 5th Aug. 1876.

GAMON, Hugh Reece Percival

s. of John Gamon, Chester, solicitor. b. 9th Jan. 1880. educ. Hartford House, Hartley Wintney; Harrow; Exeter Coll. Oxf. BCL, MA. M.T. June 1906. Practised in Cty. Palatine of Lancaster; Cty. Ct. judge 1936-53. Author of The London Police Court Today and Tomorrow 1907. d. 26th Jan. 1953.

GANE, John Lawrence

s. of Edward Gane, Devizes, timber merchant. b. 1837. educ. Wesleyan Coll. Taunton. Asst. to a surgeon in London. M.T. June 1870. QC 1885. MP East Leeds 1886-95; member Leeds School Bd.; paired with Lord Randolph Churchill, both going abroad in 1894 for health reasons. d. on way home from New Zealand, 7th Feb. 1895.

GARDINER, William Dundas

s. of William Gardiner, Capt. RN. b. 3rd Aug. 1830. educ. Royal Naval Coll.; King's Coll. Sch. London; St. Peter's Coll. Camb. BA 1853, 15th Wrangler, MA 1856, Fellow 1858-63. L.I. April 1859. Equity draftsman and conveyancer; examr. to Inns of Ct. 1869; Cty. Ct. judge 1897-1900. d. 13th Sept. 1900.

GARRETT, Edmund William

s. of Henry Garrett, Cromac House Antrim (d. 1859). b. 1st Feb. 1850. educ. Shrewsbury; St. John's Coll. Camb. BA 1873, MA 1877. I.T. April 1875. Member of bar council; metrop. magistrate 1899, finally at Bow St. 1916-20; JP London and Home Counties; Cty. alderman Middlesex 1895. Author of a treatise on nuisances. Father of Henry Grimshaw Garrett, Senior Chancery Registrar. d. 4th March 1936.

GARTH, Sir Richard

s. of Rev. Richard Lowndes, Lasham, Hampshire. b. 11th March 1820. educ. Eton; Christ Church Oxf. BA 1842, MA 1845; captain of cricket. Assumed the name of Garth 1835. L.I. Nov. 1847. QC 1866. Bencher 1866. Counsel to Inc. Law Socy.; MP Guildford 1866-68; CJ of Bengal 1875-86; Knight 1875; frequently in conflict with Bengal Govt.; PC 1888, but not appointed to judicial committee. d. 25th March 1903.

GARTH, Sir William

s. of Sir Richard Garth KC. b. 26th Aug. 1854. educ. Eton; Merton Coll. Oxf. BA 1876. M.T. June 1877. KC 1919. Advocate, High Ct. Calcutta 1885-1913; Knight 1914. d. 20th Feb. 1923.

GASELEE, Stephen

s. of Sir Stephen Gaselee, judge of Common Pleas (d. 1839). b. 1st Sept. 1807. educ. Winchester; Balliol Coll. Oxf. BA 1828, MA 1832. I.T. June 1832. Serjeant 1840. MP Portsmouth 1865-68; Treasurer of Serjeants' Inn 1866; asst. judge at Middlesex Sess.; JP Middlesex; a director of London and South Western Ry. Co. d. 20th Oct. 1883.

GATES, Philip Chasemore

s. of George Gates, Steyning, Sussex, brewer. b. 19th Aug. 1824. educ. in Midhurst and Le Havre, Caius Coll. Camb. BA 1847. I.T. Nov. 1850. QC 1874. Bencher 1877, Treasurer 1897. Recorder of Brighton 1879; Cty. Ct. judge 1885-96; JP Yorkshire West Riding.

Father of Percy George Gates MP, (1863-1940), solicitor. d. 25th Feb. 1914.

GATEY, Joseph

s. of Joseph Gatey, Keswick, Cumberland. b. 9th Sept. 1855. educ. Windermere Coll.; London Univ. 1873. Solicitor 1877. M.T. June 1880 (Cert. of Hon.). KC 1910. Equity draftsman and conveyancer. d. 11th Dec. 1912.

GATTIE, Vernon Rodney Montagu

s. of Walter Montagu Gattie. b. 29th May 1885. educ. Tonbridge; Worcester Coll. Oxf. BA 1909, MA 1912. L.I. Jan. 1911. WWI Major and DAAG HQ Staff (despatches twice). CBE 1919. Member Mil. Delegation to Peace Confce. 1919; member Committee of Inquiry into breaches of laws of war 1920; Treasury counsel at Middlesex Sess. 1920; metrop. magistrate Greenwich and Woolwich 1925-28; Dep. Chmn. Surrey Quarter Sess. 1956; JP Surrey and Middlesex. d. 23rd May 1966.

GENT, John

s. of William Gent, Stanhope, Durham. b 19th July 1844. educ. Durham Sch.; Trinity Coll. Oxf. BA 1868, MA 1870, Fellow 1869-86. L.I. June 1874. Equity draftsman and conveyancer; Cty. Ct. judge 1906-19. d. 14th March 1927.

GERMAINE, Robert Arthur

s. of Charles Germaine, London. b. 25th June 1854. educ. Univ. Coll. Sch.; University Coll. London BA 1882; Brasenose Coll. Oxf. BA 1878, MA 1882. Coach and journalist. I.T. Nov. 1882. KC 1902. Recorder of Lichfield 1901-05; member LCC 1889-92; with Sir

Robert Reid (Att-Genl.) represented Br. claim in Franco-Chilian arbitration before Swiss Trib. d. 4th June 1905.

GERRARD, Sir Albert Denis

s. of Samuel Gerrard, Southport, Lancashire. b. 27th May 1903. educ. Merchant Taylors, Crosby; Gonville and Caius Coll. Camb. BA 1925, MA 1928, LLB 1925. G.I. May 1927. KC 1945. Bencher 1948. With Min. of Home Security 1941-44; Recorder of Salford 1945-48; judge of Salford Hundred Ct. of Record 1948-53; judge of appeal, Isle of Man 1950-53; QB judge 1953-56; Knight 1953. d. 23rd Jan. 1965.

GIBBONS, Sir Thomas Clarke Pilling

s. of Benjamin Gibbons JP, Oxton, Cheshire. b. 2nd Aug 1868. educ. St. Peter's Coll., Radley nr. Oxford. Solicitor 1891. I.T. Nov. 1897. KC 1913. Adv-Genl. Bengal 1917-22; member Racial Distinctions Committee (India); Knight 1923. d. 2nd June 1934.

GIBBS, Frederick Waymouth

s. of Samuel Newcomen Gibbs, Plymouth. b. 1821. educ. King's Coll. Sch. London; Trinity Coll. Camb. BA 1843, MA 1846, Fellow 1845-53; Fellow of King's Coll. London 1849. L.I. Jan. 1848. QC 1880. Bencher 1882. Tutor to Prince of Wales 1852-58. CB 1858. Author of English law and Irish tenures 1870. d. 18th Feb. 1898.

GIFFARD, Sir George Markham

s. of Admiral John Giffard RN (d. 1855). b. 4th Nov. 1813. educ. Winchester; New Coll. Oxf. BCL 1841, Fellow 1832-54. L.I. Nov. 1840. QC 1859. Bencher 1859. Leading junior in chancery; V-C 1868-69; Knight 1868; LJ 1869-70; PC 1869. d. 13th July 1870.

GIFFARD, Hardinge Goulburn (Lord Halsbury)

s. of Halsbury LC. b. 20th June 1880. educ. Eton; New Coll. Oxf. BA 1904. I.T. Jan. 1906. KC 1923. Recorder of Carmarthen 1923-35. WWI Lt.Cdr. RNVR, Major RAF. Succeeded father as second earl 1921. d. 15th Sept. 1943.

GIFFARD, Hardinge Stanley (Lord Halsbury)

of Stanley Lees Giffard LLD, barrister, editor of the Standard and St. James's Chronicle (d. 1858), and nephew of Sir Ambrose Giffard, CJ Ceylon. b. 3rd Sept. 1823. educ. at home; Merton Coll. Oxf. BA 1855, MA 1857, Hon. DCL 1891, Hon. Fellow 1903. I.T. Jan. 1850. QC 1865. Bencher 1865, Treasurer 1881. Junior prosecuting counsel at Central Criminal Ct. 1859; leading counsel for Govr. Eyre following his forcible suppression of riots in Jamaica 1867; Sol-Genl. and knighted 1875; led for Crown in Franconia case 1876 (collision between German and Br. vessels, resulting in death of Br. passenger); MP Launceston 1877; took active part in the Cts. and parliament over case of Charles Bradlaugh (refusal of right to affirm instead of swearing on bible when elected MP); Chmn. Carmarthen Quarter Sess. 1873-85; JP Carmarthen; LC 1885-86, 1886-92, 1895-1905; PC; Baron 1885; Earl 1898; largely responsible for Land Transfer Act 1897, and Criminal Evidence Act 1898; presided over production of complete digest of Laws of England 1905-16; led "diehards" among the peers opposing Parliament Bill 1911; Constable of Launceston Castle 1883-1919; Hon. LLD Camb. 1908; High Steward Oxf. Univ. 1896; FRS; FSA. Half-brother of Harry Stanley Giffard, Registrar in Bankruptcy 1885. d. 11th Dec. 1921.

GIFFARD, Sir Henry Alexander

s. of Col. Henry Giffard RGA, The Braye, Guernsey. b. 1838. educ. Elizabeth Coll. Guernsey; Corpus Christi Coll. Oxf. BA 1861; Christ Church MA 1863. L.I. Jan. 1865. QC 1882. Bencher 1885. Asst. commr. on Schools Inquiry Comm. 1865-66; Reader in equity to

Inns of Ct. 1888-91; Bailiff of Guernsey 1902-08; Knight 1903. d. 1st July 1927.

GIFFARD, John Walter de Longueville

s. of Stanley Lees Giffard LLD, Dromartin, co. Dublin, barrister (d 1858). b. 1817. educ. privately; Merton Coll. Oxf. BA and MA 1843. I.T. Nov. 1843. Reporter in Ct. of Stuart V-C, 1852-65; Cty. Ct. judge 1875-88. Brother of Lord Halsbury. Father of Hardinge Frank Giffard (I.T. 1887). d. 20th Oct. 1888.

GILES, Sir Charles Tyrrell

s. of Alfred Giles MP, Pres.ICE, Godalming, Surrey (d. 1895). b. 2nd Feb. 1850. educ. Harrow; King's Coll. Camb. BA 1875, MA 1884. I.T. Nov. 1874. KC 1908. MP Cambridgeshire (Wisbech) 1895-1900; Chmn. Wimbledon and Putney Commons Conservators 1892; Chmn. Wimbledon Petty Sess. 1904-17; Pres. League of Mercy, Wimbledon Div. 1899; Hon. Lt. Col. 3rd Vol. Battn. East Surrey Regt. 1917; High Sheriff, Surrey 1915; Freeman, Borough of Wimbledon 1937; Knight 1922; DL, JP Surrey; KStJ. Edited Cunningham on Elections 1885. d. 16th Jan. 1940.

GILL, Arthur Edmund

s. of Charles Gill, Dublin. b. 19th March 1864. educ. King's Coll. Sch.; Magdalene Coll. Camb. BA 1885, MA 1889. G.I. and M.T. May 1886. Bencher (G.I.) 1906, Treasurer 1912. Treasury counsel at North London and Middlesex Sess. 1894; counsel to PO at Central Criminal Ct. 1898; counsel to London Bankers Protection Assoc. 1899; Treasury counsel at Central Criminal Ct. 1901-08; Recorder of Faversham 1905-08; metrop. magistrate 1908, finally at Westminster 1926-32. d. 18th May 1932.

GILL, Sir Charles Frederick

s. of Charles Gill, Dublin, and The Elms, Clapham Common, Surrey. b. 10th June 1851. educ. Royal Sch. Dungannon. M.T. April 1874. QC 1899. Bencher 1905, Reader 1918. Counsel to PO 1886-89; counsel to Treasury 1889-99; counsel to London Bankers Assoc. 1889-1901; Recorder of Chichester 1890-1921; counsel to Jockey Club 1903-22; Knight 1921. d. 22nd Feb. 1923.

GLASSE, William Bulkeley

s. of Rev. John Glasse, Burnham, Norfolk. b. 12th July 1806. educ. Charterhouse. L.I. Nov. 1834. QC 1851. Bencher 1851, Treasurer 1873. Member Inc. Council of Law Reporting; vice-chmn. of bar committee 1884. d. 30th Dec. 1890.

GLEN, Alexander

s. of William Cunningham Glen, barrister. b. 4th Feb. 1850. educ. Charterhouse (captain); Christ's Coll. Camb. BA 1872, 35th Wrangler, MA 1875, LLB 1873, LLM 1906. M.T. April 1873. KC 1903. Bencher 1911. Equity draftsman and conveyancer. Col. commdg. Inns of Ct. R.V. 1905; Brigade signalling officer South London V. Brigade 1891-96; VD 1899. Author of several works on local govt. law. Admitted to M.T. at age of nine. Brother of Reginald Cunningham Glen (M.T. 1879). Father of Randolph Alexander Glen (M.T. 1898), Recorder of Penzance. d. 18th March 1913.

GLOVER, Henry Percy

s. of William James Glover, St. Helen's, Lancashire. b. 1877. educ. Cowley Sch. St Helen's. L.I. Nov. 1907. KC 1936. WWI with Nat. Service Dept. Equity draftsman and conveyancer; Recorder of Preston 1935-38; Chmn. Preston, Manchester, and Liverpool Quarter Sess. Father of William James Glover (QC 1969). d. 29th April

1938.

GLOVER, William

s. of William Glover, Limerick, smith. educ. Trinity Coll. Dublin
BA 1825, MA 1828, LLB and LLD 1840. M.T. Jan. 1829. Serjeant
1840. Proprietor of Morning Chronicle 1854-60. Author of treatise
on municipal corpns. 1836. d. 21st Dec. 1870, age 68.

GLUCKSTEIN, Sir Louis Halle

s. of Joseph Gluckstein OBE, Regents Park, London, NW. b. 23rd
Feb. 1897. educ. St Paul's; Lincoln Coll. Oxf. BA 1920, MA 1925,
Hon. Fellow 1968. WWI Lieut. 5th Battn. Suffolk Regt.
(despatches). L.I. June 1922. KC 1945. Bencher 1952, Treasurer
1970. MP Nottingham (East) 1931-45. WWII Col. Suffolk Regt.
(TA), (despatches); TD 1950. Member LCC 1955-64, GLC 1964-67,
Chairman 1968; Pres. St. Marylebone Conservative Assoc. 1967;
Chmn. Bd. of Army Kinema Corpn. 1956-68; director Br. Transport
Hotels Ltd. 1962; Pres. Royal Albert Hall 1965; govr. St Paul's
School; DL London; Knight 1953; Commendatore, Italian Order of
Merit 1969. d. 27th Oct. 1979.

GLYN, Lewis Edmund

s. of William Glyn (formerly Ginger), one of the Clerks of the House
of Commons. b. 1849. educ. Magdalen Hall Oxf. 1870. M.T. Nov.
1871. KC 1901. Bencher 1907. d. 27th Feb. 1919.

GLYN-JONES, Sir Hildreth

s. of Sir William Samuel Glyn-Jones MP, barrister (d. 1927). b. 19th
March 1895. educ. City of London Sch. WWI Lieut. 10th Battn.
Middlesex Regt. and Machine Gun Corps. Qualified as pharmacist

1920. M.T. Jan. 1921. KC 1943. Bencher 1951. WWII Middlesex Regt, JAG's Office and Quartering Comdt. Recorder of Merthyr Tydfil 1944-45, of Cardiff 1945-53; QB judge 1953-68; Knight 1953; Dep. Chmn. Berkshire Quarter Sess. 1951-62; JP Berkshire; TD 1950; FPS 1975. d. 30th April 1980.

GODDARD, Rayner (Lord Goddard)

s. of Charles Goddard, South Sq., Gray's Inn, solicitor (d. 1922). b. 10th April 1877. educ. Marlborough; Trinity Coll. Oxf. BA 1898, MA 1931; athletics blue; Hon. Fellow 1940, Hon. DCL 1947. I.T. and G.I. Jan. 1899. KC 1923. Bencher (I.T.) 1929. Specialised in banking and other commercial cases; legal adviser to Bd. of Trade 1916-19; Recorder of Poole 1917, of Bath 1925, of Plymouth 1928-32; member of bar council; hon. secy. Barristers' Benevolent Assoc. 1912-17 and 1928-29; KB judge 1932-38; Knight 1932; LJ 1938-44; PC 1938; L of A 1944-46; Baron 1944 (declined hereditary peerage); LCJ 1946-58; secured improvements in administration, and speeding-up of trials; supporter of corporal and capital punishment; presided at controversial trial of Craig and Bentley (murder of police officer) 1953; the first non-political holder of the office of LCJ; GCB 1958; Hon. LLD Camb., Sheffield, Montreal, New York, and William and Mary Coll. Virginia. d. 29th May 1971. Biographies by E. Grimshaw and G. Jones 1958, Arthur Smith 1959, Fenton Bresler 1977.

GODLEY, Hugh John (Lord Kilbracken)

s. of Sir Arthur Godley GCB, 1st Baron Kilbracken. b. 12th June 1877. educ. Eton; Balliol Coll. Oxf. BA 1901, MA 1909. L.I. Jan. 1902. KC 1924. Br. rep. at confce. on maritime law, Brussels 1909; asst. parl. counsel to the Treasury 1917-22; member Central Control Bd. (liquor traffic) 1917-21; counsel to Chmn. of Committees, H of L 1923-44; CB 1931; succeeded father as second baron 1932. d. 13th Oct 1950.

GODSON, Richard

s. of William Godson, Tenbury, Worcestershire, attorney. b. 19th June 1797. educ. in Worcester; Caius Coll. Camb. BA 1818, 26th Wrangler, MA 1821. L.I. July 1821. QC 1841. Bencher. Counsel to the Admiralty 1845; Judge-Advocate of the Fleet. MP St. Albans 1831-32, Kidderminster 1832-49 (except 1835-36). Author of works on patents and copyright. d. 1st Aug. 1849.

GOFF, Sir Park, Bt.

s. of Col. Bruce Goff MD, VD, DL, JP, Bothwell, Lanarkshire. b. 12th Feb. 1871. educ. Marlborough; Trinity Coll. Oxf. BA 1892, BCL and MA 1898. I.T. Jan. 1896. KC 1925. Hon. King's foreign service messenger 1914; gold staff officer at coronations of Edward VII and George V; MP Yorkshire North Riding (Cleveland) 1918-23, 1924-29, Rochester (Chatham) 1931-35; asst parliamentary private secy. to 1st Lord of Admiralty 1919; Chmn. H of C Olympic Games Committee; Chmn. Private Bill committees 1920-24; member Paris Parliamentary Confce. 1920, Lisbon and Stockholm 1921, Paris and Bordeaux 1922, Copenhagen 1923; Hon. Registrar Imp. Socy. of Knights Bachelor; Pres. Men of Sussex 1930-33; Knight 1918, Baronet 1936; FRGS, FRAS; JP Lanarkshire. d. 14th April 1939.

GOLDIE, Sir Noel Barré

s. of John Henry Goldie, Southfields, Lillington, Leamington. b. 26th Dec. 1882. educ. Rugby; Trinity Coll. Camb. BA 1905, LLB 1904. I.T. July 1905. KC 1928. Bencher 1935, Reader 1958. WWI Capt. RA 57th (West Lancashire) Divn. (despatches). Recorder of Burnley 1929-35, of Manchester 1935-56; Commr. of Assize, South Eastern circuit 1947; Divorce Commr. 1947-48; member of bar council 1932-46; MP Warrington 1931-45; Chmn. United Club 1935-37; Knight 1945. d. 4th June 1964.

GOLDSMID, Sir Francis Henry, Bt.

s. of Sir Isaac Lyon Goldsmid Bt. b. 1st May 1808. educ. privately. L.I. Jan. 1833. QC 1858. Bencher 1858. First Jew to be called to English bar. Pres. Senate of Univ. Coll. London; Treasurer of Univ. Coll. Hospital 1857-68; MP Reading 1860-78; founded Anglo-Jewish Assoc. 1871; succeeded father as second baronet 1859. d. 2nd May 1878.

GOODHART, Arthur Lehman

s. of Philip Julius Goodhart, New York, stockbroker. b. New York, 1st March 1891. educ. Hotchkiss Sch.; Yale Univ.; Trinity Coll. Camb. BA and LLB 1914, Hon. Fellow, MA, LLM, LLD. WWI rejected for service with Br. Forces; Capt. US army 1917. I.T. May 1919. KC 1943. Hon. Bencher (L.I.) 1938. Lecturer in law Camb. 1919-31; prof. of jurisprudence Oxf. 1930-51; prof. emeritus 1951; Master of Univ. Coll. Oxf. 1951-63; editor of Cambridge Law Journal and Law Quarterly Review; member Law Revision Committee, Monopolies Comm., Royal Comm. on police, company law revision committee, law reports committee; Chmn. Southern Region Price Regulation Committee 1940-51; Pres. Socy. of Public Teachers of Law 1950; Chmn. Intern. Law Assoc.; Hon. Fellow Corpus Christi Coll. Camb, Univ. Coll. and Nuffield Coll. Oxf; hon. degrees from 20 univs.; FBA 1952; Hon. KBE 1948; retained American nationality. Author: Essays in Jurisprudence and the Common Law 1931, Precedent in English and Continental Law 1934, English Contributions to the Philosophy of Law 1949, Five Jewish Lawyers of the Common Law 1950, English Law and the Moral Law 1953; edited Pollock's Jurisprudence and Essays 1961. d. 10th Nov. 1978.

GOODMAN, Sydney Charles Nichols

s. of Albert Goodman FCA, Taunton, Somerset. b. 27th March 1868. educ. Taunton Sch.; London Univ. BA. G.I. Jan. 1898. KC 1932.

Recorder of South Molton 1923-36; JP South Molton. d. 8th Feb. 1936.

GORDON, Edward Strathearn (Lord Gordon)

s. of John Gordon, Major 2nd Regt., Griamachcorry, Sutherland. b. 10th April 1814. educ. Royal Acad. Inverness; Edin. Univ. LLB, Glasgow Univ. LLB. Scottish bar 1835; Sheriff of Perthshire 1858-66; Sol-Genl. Scotland 1866-67; QC 1868; Lord Advocate 1867-68 and 1874-76; Dean of Faculty of Advocates 1868-74; MP Thetford 1867-68, Glasgow and Aberdeen Univs. 1869-76; PC 1874; L of A 1876-79; Baron Gordon of Drumearn 1876. d. Brussels, 21st Aug. 1879.

GORDON, John William

s. of John Lewis Gordon, Clapton, London, manufacturers' agent. b. 1853. M.T. May 1884. KC 1914. Senior member of comm. to inquire into the Pitch Industry of Trinidad, and draft the Asphalt Ordinance 1902; concerned in drafting of Patent Act 1907; Hon. Secy. Royal Microscopical Socy. 1909-11; hon. chemical adviser, High Explosives Dept., Min. of Munitions, during WWI; gold medal of Socy. of Engineers for his paper on railway surveying by photography, 1924; Clerk to Br. Life Assoc. Ltd. Author of works on patents, and optics. d. 21st Sept 1936.

GORDON, Robert Abercromby

s. of R.J. Abercromby, South Kensington, London. b. Wiesbaden, 6th Sept 1874. educ. St Paul's; Peterhouse Camb. BA 1897, MA 1901, LLM 1907. I.T. Nov. 1904. KC 1924. Bencher 1931. WWI Military Intelligence abroad. Mil. Service Civil Liabilities Commr.; lecturer to Law Socy. on commercial law 1921-23; member House of Laity Church Assembly for Chichester 1934-41; Recorder of Margate 1936-44; JP Eastbourne. Author of Compulsory

Acquisition of Land and Compensation 1929; edited Cripps on Compensation. d. 5th Nov. 1954.

GORE-BROWNE, Sir Francis

s. of Col. Sir Thomas Gore-Browne KCMG, CB (d. 1877). b. 7th March 1860. educ. Harrow; New Coll. Oxf. BA 1882. I.T. June 1883. KC 1902. Bencher 1911. Chmn. Civil Service Arbitration Bd. 1918-20; Chmn. Rates Advisory Committee, Min. of Transport 1919-21; Knight 1921; JP Berkshire. d. 2nd Sept 1922.

GORMAN, Sir William

s. of William Gorman, Wigan, Lancashire, iron merchant. b. 1891. educ. Wigan Gr. Sch. WWI with 7th Divn. RA. Secy. Wigan Committee, Min. of Pensions 1919. M.T. June 1921. KC 1932. Bencher 1938, Treasurer 1959. MP Lancashire (Royton) 1923-24; Recorder of Wigan 1934-38, of Liverpool 1948-50. WWII Wing Cdr. RAFVR, and AJAG. Member Nat. Arbitration Trib. 1944-50; KB judge 1950-64; Knight 1950; Hon. Freeman of Wigan 1954; Pres. Caterham Sch. 1953; Hon. LLD Manchester. d. 21st Dec. 1964.

GORST, Sir John Eldon

s. of Edward Chaddock Lowndes (formerly Gorst). b. 24th May 1835. educ. Preston Gr. Sch.; St John's Coll. Camb. BA 1857, 3rd Wrangler, MA 1860, Fellow 1857-60, Hon. Fellow 1890. I.T. May 1865. Civil Commr. Waikato, N. Zealand 1861-63. QC 1875. Sol-Genl. 1885-86; Under Secy. of State for India 1886-91; Financial Secy. to Treasury 1891-92; MP Cambridge 1866-68, Chatham 1875-92, Camb. Univ. 1892-1906; Lord Rector Glasgow Univ. 1893-94; Knight 1885; FRS 1896; PC 1890. Father of Sir John Lowndes Gorst KCB (I.T. 1884); brother of Thomas William Gorst (I.T. 1864). d. 4th April 1916.

GOULBURN, Edward

s. of Munbee Goulburn, Amity Hall, Jamaica and Portland Place, London (d. 1790). b. 1787. Cornet, Royal Horse Guards 1803, Lieut. 1804-05. Sold out after prosecution for libelling fellow officers. M.T. June 1815; a Welsh judge; Recorder of Leicester to 1835, of Lincoln, and of Boston. Serjeant 1829; patent of precedence 1840. MP Leicester 1835-37; Commr. in Bankruptcy 1842-68; Hon. DCL Camb. 1845. d. 24th Aug. 1868.

GOULD, Charles

s. of Thomas Gould, Sheffield, solicitor. Solicitor 1855, in practice with father. I.T. Jan. 1870. QC 1893. JP Surrey, Yorkshire West Riding. d. 31st July 1909, age 75.

GOVER, John Mahan

s. of John Richard Gover, Bromley, Kent. b. 1867. educ. London Univ. LLD. M.T. Jan. 1889. KC 1919. Bencher 1925, Reader 1935. Equity draftsman and conveyancer; member of bar council 1921; member Senate, London Univ. d. 18th April 1947.

GRAHAM, John Cameron

s. of John Graham, Royal Mint. b. 1847. educ. University Coll. London. Studied engineering with Sir William Siemens. M.T. May 1879. KC 1906. Cty. Ct. judge 1909-22; JP Stirlingshire. Edited Blackburn on Sales. d. 6th Aug. 1929.

GRAHAM, Joseph

s. of Maj.-Genl. Joseph Graham, Bengal Army. b. 4th Sept 1828. educ. in Yelden, Bedfordshire; Trinity Hall Camb. BA 1855. M.T.

Nov. 1852. QC 1880. Bencher 1884, Reader 1893, Treasurer 1901. Member of Legislative Council Bengal 1863; Att-Genl. Bengal 1870-73 (acting 1863-65); standing counsel to Calcutta Govt; Chmn. Devon Quarter Sess.; JP Devon. d. 20th Dec. 1902.

GRAHAM-CAMPBELL, Sir Rollo Frederick

s. of John Graham-Campbell DL, JP, Shirvan, co. Argyll (d. 1889). b. 2nd Jan. 1868. educ. Eton; Trinity Coll. Camb. LLB 1891, LLM 1894. I.T. Nov. 1892. Counsel for Att-Genl. in legitimacy cases 1901-08; junior counsel for DPP at Central Criminal Ct. 1908-13; metrop. magistrate 1913, finally at Bow St 1933-40; chief magistrate and knighted 1933; JP London and Home Counties. d. 3rd June 1946.

GRAHAM-HARRISON, Sir William Montagu

s. of Capt. Thomas Arthur John Harrison RA. b. 4th Feb. 1871. educ. Wellington; Magdalen Coll. Oxf. BA 1895, BCL 1897, DCL 1932; Hon. Fellow 1938; Fellow of All Souls Coll. 1895, MA 1897. L.I. Jan. 1897. KC 1930. Member London Sch. Bd. 1900-03; entered parliamentary counsel office 1903; acting legal adviser to Insce. Commrs. 1912-13; solicitor to Customs and Excise 1913-17; Second parliamentary counsel to Treasury 1917, First 1928-33; Chmn. National Mark Committee 1937; Northern Ireland Civil Service Committee 1937; Chan. of diocese of Durham 1934-40, Truro 1935-40, Portsmouth 1938-40, Gloucester 1937-49; KCB 1926; changed name to Graham-Harrison on marriage 1900. d. 29th Oct. 1949.

GRANGER, Thomas Colpitts

s. of Joseph Granger, Durham. b. 1802. educ. Durham Sch. I.T. May 1830. Bencher 1850. QC 1850. Recorder of Hull 1847-52; MP Durham 1841-52. Author of a supplement to The Statutes by Sir W. D. Evans, 1836; reported (with R.P. Tyrwhitt) Exch. cases 1835-37, (with J. Manning) cases in Common Pleas 1840-45. d. 6th Aug 1852.

GRANGER, Sir Thomas Colpitts

s. of Thomas Colpitts Granger QC. b. 30th Aug. 1852. educ. privately. I.T. Jan. 1874. Cty. Ct. judge 1891-1927; Joint Chmn. Cornwall Quarter Sess.; Knight 1921; JP Cornwall. d. 13th Jan. 1927.

GRANT, Alexander

s. of Alexander Grant, Bolton, Lancashire. b. 5th Sept. 1866. educ. Manchester Gr. Sch. (captain); Merton Coll. Oxf.; Postmaster, All Souls Coll. BCL 1890, MA 1891, Fellow 1890-97. I.T. June 1894. KC 1908. Bencher 1918, Treasurer 1940. Equity draftsman and conveyancer; lecturer in Roman law, and jurisprudence, Manchester Univ. 1892. d. 21st March 1941.

GRANT, Corrie

s. of James Brighton Grant, Kettleburgh, Suffolk. b. 14th Nov. 1850. educ. City of London Sch. M.T. Nov. 1877. KC 1906. MP Warwickshire (South East) 1900-10. Author of Notes on the Agricultural Holdings Act 1883 and A Short Treatise on the Ground Game Act 1880. d. 27th Dec. 1924.

GRANT, Frederick

s. of John Grant, Craigmills, Dundee. b. 25th April 1890. educ. Fettes; Oriel Coll. Oxf. BA 1915, MA 1918. WWI Staff Capt. Tay Defences; Adj. 45th Heavy Artillery Group; commanded 94th Siege Battery, MC. I.T. Nov. 1925 (Cert. of Hon.). KC 1943. Bencher 1951. Member Monopolies and Restrictive Practices Comm. 1949-

52; Chmn. Purchase Tax (Valuation) Committee 1952-53; independent Chmn. Executive Committee, Br. Iron and Steel Federation 1953. d. 19th Sept 1954.

GRANTHAM, Sir William

s. of George Grantham, Barcombe Place, nr. Lewes, Sussex (d. 1849). b. 23rd Oct 1835. educ. King's Coll. Sch. London. I.T. Jan. 1863. QC 1877. Bencher 1880, Treasurer 1904. MP East Surrey 1874-85, Croydon 1885-86; politics his main interest; QB judge 1886-1911; Knight 1886; his decisions in election petition cases, particularly Great Yarmouth severely criticised 1906; rebuked by prime minister for indiscreet speech from bench at Liverpool 1911; a good judge of horses; Chmn. East Sussex Quarter Sess.; JP Sussex; Lord of the manors of Camois Court and Balneth; Hon. DCL Durham. Father of Frederick William Grantham (I.T. 1894). d. 30th Nov. 1911.

GRANTHAM, William Wilson

s. of Grantham J. b. 7th Jan. 1866. educ. Harrow; Trinity Coll. Camb. BA 1889, MA 1895. I.T. Jan. 1890. KC 1923. Recorder of Deal 1905-42. Hon. Capt. in the army 1900; Adjt. City Imp. Vol.'s depot 1900; Major, Inns of Ct. R.V. 1888-1913; Major, 6th (Cyclist) Battn. Royal Sussex. Regt. 1913; VD 1907. Licensed lay reader, diocese of Chichester 1911; Master of Grocers' Co. 1906, (compiled list of wardens 1345-1907); Dep. Chmn. LCC 1935; DL London; JP Sussex; Lord of the manors of Camois Court, and Balneth. d. 18th Feb. 1942.

GRAY, Sir Albert

s. of George Gray, Bowerswell, Perth, Scotland. b. 10th Oct 1850. educ. Rugby. Ceylon C.S, 1871-75. I.T. May 1879. KC 1905. Bencher 1914. Chan. of diocese of Ely 1893-97; counsel to Chmn. of committees, H of L 1896-1922; Pres. Hakluyt Socy. 1908; Mayor of Chelsea 1924; CB 1916; KCB 1919. d. 27th Feb. 1928.

GRAY, James Hunter

s. of William Gray, Edinburgh. b. 3rd Sept. 1867. educ. Glasgow Univ. MA. BSc. Associated in laboratory work and research with Lord Kelvin. M.T. May 1895. KC 1918. An authority in patent and trade mark law; MIEE. d. 1st June 1925.

GRAY, James Neville

s. of James Gray, Montagu Sq., London W. 1., solicitor. b. 1885. educ. Rugby; University Coll. Oxf. BA 1909. L.I. Nov. 1909. KC 1938. Bencher 1944. WWI Major, Inns of Ct. Regt. and attached to Gen. Staff, DSO 1917. WWII Major, Hertfordshire Home Guard. Chan. of diocese of Southwell 1936, Worcester 1943, Wakefield 1944, Cty. Palatine of Durham 1958; commissary gen. diocese of Canterbury 1944; Dep. Chmn. Hertfordshire Quarter Sess. 1947; a Church Commr. 1953; Vice-Chmn. of bar council 1953-55; Grand Registrar, Grand Lodge of England 1950; JP Hertfordshire. d. 20th April 1959.

GRAY, John

s. of George Gray, Aberdeen. b. 1807. educ. Gordon's Hospital. Employed with solicitors in London. M.T. Jan. 1838. QC 1863. Bencher 1863, Reader 1866. Solicitor to the Treasury 1871; conducted prosecution of Tichborne claimant 1873. Author of Country Attorney's practice 1836, Country Solicitor's practice 1837, Law of Costs 1853. d. 22nd Jan. 1875.

GRAZEBROOK, Henry Broome Durley

s. of Henry Durley Grazebrook, Guildford, barrister (d. 1947). b. 6th

June 1884. educ. Tonbridge; St. John's Coll. Oxf. BA 1907, MA 1910. G.I. and M.T. Nov. 1908. KC 1939. Bencher (G.I.) 1945, Treasurer 1960. WWI Lieut. RFC and RAF. Recorder of Penzance 1940-56; Divorce Commr. 1946-57. d. 25th March 1969.

GREAVES, Charles Sprengel

s. of William Greaves MD, Mayfield Hall, Staffordshire. b. 18th July 1801. educ. Rugby; Queen's Coll. Oxf. BA 1823, MA 1825. L.I. Nov. 1827. QC 1850. Bencher 1850. A secy. to Criminal Law Comm. 1878; DL, JP Staffordshire; JP Derbyshire. Author of a review of statutes etc. relating to vestments 1867; edited Sir W.O. Russell's treatise on crimes and misdemeanours 1843. d. 3rd June 1881.

GREAVES-LORD, Sir Walter

s. of Simeon Lord, Southport, Lancashire. b. 21st Sept 1878. educ. Wigan Gr. Sch.; University Coll. Liverpool; Manchester Univ. LLB 1899. G.I. June 1900. KC 1919. Bencher 1920, Treasurer 1933, Vice-Treasurer 1934. Member Council of Legal Educ. 1924; Recorder of Manchester 1925-35; MP Lambeth (Norwood) 1922-35; Chmn. Primrose League 1926; Knight 1927; Vice-Chmn. of bar council 1932; KB judge 1935-40; Master of Feltmakers' Co. 1933; Freeman of City of London; JP Sussex; assumed additional surname of Greaves 1910. d. 18th June 1942.

GREENE, Henry David

s. of Benjamin Buck Greene JP, Governor of Bank of England (d. 1902). b. 16th Aug. 1843. educ. Wellesley House, London; Trinity Coll. Camb. BA 1865, MA 1868, LLB 1866, LLM 1871. Fellow of Downing Coll. 1902. M.T. Jan. 1868. QC 1885. Bencher 1890, Treasurer 1910. Recorder of Ludlow 1892; MP Shrewsbury 1892-1906; member of Senate, London Univ.; Commr. in Lunacy 1908-

14; DL, JP Shropshire. d. 11th Oct. 1915.

GREENE, John Arch

s. of John Greene, Leeds, solicitor. b. 1876. educ. Giggleswick Sch., New Coll. Oxf.BA 1897. L.I. Jan. 1900. KC 1927. Dep. Commr. for Nat. Service 1917; Commr. North East Division, Min. of Food 1917-19; CBE 1919; Cty. Ct. judge 1928-33. d. 31st March 1934.

GREENE, John Stock Turner

s. of Thomas Greene, Bedford, Lancashire, attorney. b. 12th Dec. 1803. educ. Pembroke Coll. Camb. BA 1826. M.T. Nov. 1829. Cty. Ct. judge 1847-72; JP Lancashire. d. 16th June 1874.

GREENE, Thomas Webb

s. of Thomas Webb Greene, Lichfield, Staffordshire, surgeon. b. 1804. educ. Repton; Trinity Hall Camb. LLB 1833, LLM 1859, Fellow 1833-39. M.T. Nov. 1832. QC 1858. Bencher 1858, Reader 1860, Treasurer 1869. Equity draftsman and conveyancer; leader in V-C Stuart's Ct. 1868-75; Chmn. of Inc. Council of Law Reporting; DL, JP Essex. d. 14th Nov. 1875.

GREENE, Wilfrid Arthur (Lord Greene)

s. of Arthur Weguelin Greene, Beckenham, Kent, solicitor. b. 30th Dec. 1883. educ. Westminster; Christ Church Oxf. BA 1906, MA 1912, Vinerian scholar 1908, Fellow of All Souls Coll. 1907, Hon. DCL 1935. I.T. July 1908. KC 1922. Bencher 1925. WWI Capt. Oxf. and Bucks. L.I., Major on Gen. Staff 1918, OBE, MC, Croix de Guerre, Cavalieri Order of Crown of Italy, Crown of St Olaf (Norway). Standing counsel to Oxf. Univ. 1926-35; had very substantial chancery practice; Chmn. of committees on company law

1925, trade practices 1930, intern. communications 1931, beet-sugar industry 1935; LJ 1935-37; Knight 1935; MR 1937-49; Baron Greene of Holmbury St. Mary 1941; L of A 1949-50; Pres. Br. Records Assoc. 1937; Chmn. Royal Comm. on Historical Manuscripts, and Nat. Buildings Record Office 1941-45; Principal, Working Men's Coll. St Pancras 1936-44; Hon. FRIBA; Hon. LLD Birmingham 1936, Sheffield 1946, Wesleyan Univ. USA 1941, St Andrews 1948. d. 16th April 1952.

GREENHOW, William Thomas

s. of Thomas Michael Greenhow MD, FRCS, Newcastle-on-Tyne. b. 6th Feb. 1831. educ. Edgbaston Proprietary Sch.; Univ. Coll. London LLB 1852, BA 1850. M.T. May 1854. Recorder of Berwick-on-Tweed 1870-99; Cty. Ct. judge 1880-1916; member Convocation, London Univ. Author of Shipping Law Manual. d. 30th April 1921.

GREENWELL, Sir Francis John

s. of Francis Greenwell JP, Durham (d. 1894). b. 20th Oct 1852. educ. Durham Sch.; Balliol Coll. Oxf. BA 1877, MA 1879. I.T. Nov. 1877. Recorder of Durham 1883-1924; Cty. Ct. judge 1895-1931; Chmn. Durham Quarter Sess.; DL, JP Durham; JP Northumberland; CBE 1918, Knight 1928. d. 2nd Feb. 1931.

GREENWOOD, Hamar (Lord Greenwood)

s. of John Hamar Greenwood, barrister. b. Ontario, 7th Feb. 1870. educ. Public Sch. Whitby, Ontario; Toronto Univ. BA, Hon. LLD 1938. Eight years in Canadian militia; employed in Dept of Agriculture, Ontario; moved to England 1895. G.I. June 1906. KC 1919. Bencher 1917, Treasurer 1930. New Brunswick bar 1913, New South Wales and South Australia bars 1913. WWI Temp. Lt.Col. commdg. 10th Service Battn. South Wales Borderers;

DAAG 1916. Hon. Col. Winnipeg Grenadiers. MP York 1906-10 (parliamentary secy. to Winston Churchill 1906-10), Sunderland 1910-22, East Walthamstow 1924-29; Secy. Overseas Trade Dept. 1919-20; Chief Secy. for Ireland 1920-22; Chan. of Order of St Patrick 1920; Hon. Treasurer, Conservative Party 1933-38; Baronet 1915; PC 1920; Baron 1929, Viscount 1937. d. 10th Sept 1948.

GREENWOOD, John

s. of William Greenwood, Brookwood Park, Hampshire. b. 24th July 1800. educ. Eton; Jesus Coll. Camb. BA 1822, 13th Wrangler, MA 1825, Fellow. L.I. and M.T. Feb. 1828. QC 1848. Bencher (M.T.) 1849, Reader 1851, Treasurer 1854. Recorder of Portsmouth 1847-48, of Devonport 1848-51; Asst. Solicitor to Treasury 1851-66, Solicitor 1866-71. Author of a digest of cases in Law Journal and Reports 1823, and a treatise on loan societies. d. 12th Feb. 1871.

GREENWOOD, John Beswicke

s. of Abraham Greenwood, Dewsbury, Yorkshire, merchant. b. 30th Dec. 1796. educ. Eton; Caius Coll. Camb. BA 1818, MA 1821. L.I. Nov. 1821. Metrop. magistrate Clerkenwell 1837-47; Chmn. Yorkshire West Riding Quarter Sess. d. 9th Oct. 1879.

GREER, Frederick Arthur (Lord Fairfield)

s. of Arthur Greer, Liverpool, metal merchant. b. 6th Oct 1863. educ. Ormskirk Gr. Sch.; Old Aberdeen Gr. Sch.; Aberdeen Univ. MA 1883, LLD 1926. G.I. Nov. 1886. KC 1910. Bencher 1910, Treasurer 1921. Practised in Liverpool, and was newspaper reporter there, until 1907; lecturer in law Liverpool Univ.; conducted many cases in Prize Ct. 1914-18; KB judge 1919-27; Knight 1919; LJ 1927-38; PC 1927; Chmn. Council of Legal Educ. 1934-36; Baron 1939; Hon. LLD Liverpool 1930. d. 4th Feb. 1945.

GREGORY, Sir Henry Holman

s. of Henry Thomas Gregory, Knowle, Bedminster, Somerset. b. 30th June 1864. educ. Bristol Gr. Sch. Solicitor 1886. M.T. May 1897. KC 1910. Bencher 1920, Reader 1929, Treasurer 1933. Recorder of Bath 1916-24, of Bristol 1924-29; MP Derbyshire (South) 1918-22; Chmn. Departmental Committee on Workmen's Compensation Acts 1918-20; Chmn. Royal Comm. on Unemployment Insce. 1930-32; judge of Mayor's and City of London Ct. 1929-32; Common Serjeant 1932-34, Recorder of London 1934-37; DL London; Knight 1935. d. 9th May 1947.

GREIG, Sir James William

s. of John Borthwick Greig WS, Westminster, parliamentary agent. b. 1859. educ. Univ. Coll. Sch.; London Univ. BA 1878, LLB 1882; Sorbonne, Collège de France, Paris. L.I. June 1882. KC 1913. Bencher 1917. Parliamentary private secy. to Secy. for Scotland 1917-22; equity and parliamentary draftsman; MP Renfrewshire (West) 1910-22; Lt.Col. commdg. 14 Battn. London Regt. (London Scottish) 1904-11, 2/14 Battn. 1914-15, 3/14 Battn. 1915-17; VD; member of convocation, London Univ.; Knight 1921; CB 1911. d. 10th June 1934.

GRIFFITH, Charles Marshall

s. of Rev. Charles Griffith, Worthing. b. 1830. educ. Wadham Coll. Oxf. BA 1852, MA 1855. I.T. Nov. 1855. QC 1877. Bencher 1878. Chmn. Cardiganshire Quarter Sess. 1870-94; Commr. for municipal election petitions 1884; DL, JP Cardiganshire; Lord of the Manor of Llandugwydd. d. 16th Oct. 1894.

GRIFFITH, Sir Ellis Jones Ellis, Bt.

s. of Thomas Morris Griffith, Brynsiencyn, Anglesey (d. 1901). b.

23rd May 1860. educ. University Coll. of Wales; London Univ. BA 1881; Downing Coll. Camb. BA 1884, LLB 1884, MA 1887, Fellow 1888-95, Hon. Fellow 1917. M.T. Nov. 1887. KC 1910. Bencher 1919. Recorder of Birkenhead 1907-12; MP Anglesey 1895-1918, Carmarthen 1923-24; Chmn. of committee on Reformatory and Industrial Schools 1912, and of committee on Industrial Diseases 1912; Under-Secy. of State, Home Dept 1912-15; PC 1914; Baronet 1918; KStJ. d. 30th Nov. 1926.

GRIFFITH, Frank Kingsley

s. of Col. Frank Griffith VD, Bromley, Kent. b. 23rd Dec. 1889. educ. Marlborough; Balliol Coll. Oxf. BA 1912, MA 1916. I.T. June 1915. WWI Capt. 1st Gloucestershire and 2nd Lincolnshire Regts., MC. MP Middlesbrough (West) 1928-40; parliamentary private secy. to Home Secy. 1931-32; Recorder of Richmond, Yorkshire 1932-40; Cty. Ct. judge 1940-56; Chmn. Yorkshire East Riding Quarter Sess. 1947-56; Past Master, Worshipful Co. of Plaisterers. d. 25th Sept. 1962.

GRIFFITH, William Downes

s. of Walter Hussey Griffith, Dublin, barrister. b. 18th July 1829. educ. Royal Sch. Enniskillen; Trinity Coll. Dublin BA 1851. I.T. April 1855. Equity draftsman and conveyancer; Att-Genl. Cape of Good Hope 1866-72; Cty. Ct. judge 1877-98. Author of a treatise on bankruptcy 1868. d. 9th Aug. 1908.

GRIFFITH-JONES, Morgan Phillips

s. of Griffith-Jones JP, Aberllolwyn Hall, Cardigan, barrister. b. 1876. educ. Univ. Coll. Sch.; Trinity Hall Camb. BA 1898. M.T. June 1899. WWI Major Durham Light Inf. (despatches); OBE (Mil.) 1919. Pres. of Pensions Appeal Trib. 1919; stip. magistrate, Middlesbrough 1920-28; metrop. magistrate 1928, finally at

Greenwich 1938-39. Brother of John Stanley Griffith-Jones (G.I. 1899). d. 4th May 1939.

GRIFFITS, James Olliff

s. of John Griffits, High Wycombe, Buckinghamshire, saddler. b. 21st Feb. 1821. educ. High Wycombe Gr. Sch. M.T. June 1848. QC 1875. Bencher 1878, Reader 1888. Recorder of Reading 1870-94; founded free library in Wycombe 1876, and presented it to the town 1882. d. 29th Nov. 1894.

GROTRIAN, Sir Herbert Brent, Bt.

s. of Frederick Brent Grotrian MP, Ingmanthorpe Hall, Wetherby, Yorkshire (d. 1905). b. 29th March 1870. educ. Rossall; Trinity Coll. Oxf. MA 1892, BCL 1895. I.T. Jan. 1894. KC 1925. Recorder of Scarborough 1918-46; MP Kingston-on-Hull (South West) 1924-29; Sheriff of Bedfordshire 1931; Chmn. Bedfordshire Quarter Sess., Dep. Chmn. Hertfordshire Quarter Sess.; JP Hertfordshire and Bedfordshire; Chmn. Argus Press Limited; Baronet 1934. d. 28th Oct 1951.

GROVE, William

s. of Edward Grove DCL, DL, JP, Shenstone Park, Staffordshire. b. 1796. educ. Oriel Coll. Oxf. BA 1819, MA 1821. L.I. June 1821. Metrop. magistrate 1834, finally at Greenwich and Woolwich 1840-46. d. 29th Jan. 1875.

GROVE, Sir William Robert

s. of John Grove DL, JP, St. Mary, Swansea. b. 11th July 1811. educ. in Swansea and Bath; Brasenose Coll. Oxf. BA 1832, MA 1835, DCL 1875. L.I. Nov. 1835. QC 1853. Bencher 1853-71.

Leader on South Wales and Chester circuits; member Royal Comm. on law of patents 1862-64; Pres. Br. Assoc. 1866; judge of Common Pleas 1871-80; Knight 1872; QB judge 1880-87; PC 1887; Vice-Pres. Royal Inst. 1844; invented the Grove gas voltaic battery; an original member of Chemical Socy. 1841; Prof. of experimental philosophy in London Inst. 1840-47; FRS 1840, and royal medallist 1847. Author of Correlation of Physical Forces, establishing theory of mutual convertibility of forces 1846. Member of academies of Rome and Turin; member of Oxf. Univ. Comm.; LLD Camb. 1879; Knight of Brazilian Order of the Rose. Father of Florence Crauford Grove (I.T.1862). d. 1st Aug. 1896.

GULLY, William Court (Lord Selby)

s. of James Manby Gully MD, Great Malvern, Worcestershire. b. 29th Aug. 1835. educ. privately; Trinity Coll. Camb. BA 1856, MA 1859, Hon. LLD 1900, Hon. DCL Oxf. 1904. I.T. Jan. 1860. QC 1877. Bencher 1879. Recorder of Wigan 1886-95; MP Carlisle 1886-1905; Speaker of House of Commons 1895-1905; ordered forcible removal of Irish members from the House 1901; PC 1895; Viscount Selby 1905. d. 6th Nov. 1909.

GURDON, Charles

s. of Rev. Edward Gurdon, Barnham Broom, Norfolk. b. 3rd Dec. 1855. educ. Haileybury; Jesus Coll. Camb. BA 1878, MA 1885. I.T. Nov. 1881. Bencher 1913. Equity draftsman and conveyancer; Cty. Ct. judge 1923-29; played rugby for England 1880-86. d. 26th June 1931.

GURDON, William

s. of Lt.Col. Theophilus Thornhagh Gurdon, Letton, Norfolk. b. 12th Oct 1804. educ. Eton; Downing Coll. Camb. BA 1826, MA 1829, Fellow 1838. I.T. July 1829. Recorder of Bury St. Edmunds 1839-

60; Chmn. Quarter Sess. Ipswich division of Suffolk; Cty. Ct. judge 1847-71; JP. Author of works on highways and bankruptcy. d. 12th Oct 1884.

GURNER, Henry Edward

s. of Henry Field Gurner, Melbourne, Crown solicitor for Victoria. b. Melbourne, 29th July 1853. educ. Cheltenham Coll.; Trinity Coll. Camb. BA 1876, MA 1879. M.T. Nov. 1877. Cty. Ct. judge 1914-15. Brother of John Augustus Gurner KC, Melbourne (I.T. 1877). d. 21st July 1915.

GURNEY, Sir John

s. of Joseph Gurney, Walworth, London, official shorthand writer (d. 1815). b. 14th Feb. 1768. educ. St. Paul's, and in Suffolk. I.T. May 1793. KC 1816. Bencher. Junior defending counsel in state trials of Hardy, Horne Tooke, and Thelwall for high treason 1794; successfully defended Arthur O'Connor, the Irish rebel, charged with treason 1798; leader at Middlesex Quarter Sess.; prosecuted Lord Cochrane, Cochrane-Johnston and others involved in spreading false report of Bonaparte's defeat and death, for the purpose of speculating in the funds 1816; leader of Home circuit; led prosecution and secured conviction of two of the Cato St. conspirators 1820; Exch. Baron 1832-45; Knight 1832. d. 1st March 1845.

GURNEY, Russell

s. of Sir John Gurney, Exch. Baron. b. 2nd Sept 1804. educ. Trinity Coll. Camb. BA 1826. I.T. Nov. 1828. QC 1845. Bencher 1845, Treasurer 1858. Common pleader, City of London 1830-45; judge of Sheriff's Ct. 1850; Common Serjeant 1856; Recorder of London 1857-78; served on several royal commissions 1862-77, including inquiry into the disturbances in Jamaica 1866; PC 1866; FRS 1875; MP Southampton 1865-78; Prime Warden of Fishmongers' Co. d. 31st May 1878.

GUTTERIDGE, Harold Cooke

s. of Michael Gutteridge, Ballindune, Haslemere, Surrey. b. Naples, 16th July 1876. educ. in Naples; Leys Sch.; King's Coll. Camb. BA 1898, MA 1902, LLB 1921, LLD 1941; Fellow of Trinity Hall. M.T. Nov. 1900. KC 1930. Bencher 1936, Reader 1948. WWI Capt. RAOC (despatches). Cassel prof. of industrial and common law, London Univ. 1919-30; Br. delegate to Hague Confce. on private intern. law, and Geneva Confce. on bills of exchange 1930-31; Reader (later prof.) in comparative law Camb. 1930-41; member Law Revision Committee 1932; Pres. League of Nations Committee on Civil Status of Women 1938; Pres. Society of Public Teachers of Law 1928; Associate Inst. of International Law; Senator, London Univ. 1924-30; Dean of Faculty of Laws 1923-27 and 1929-30; LLD London 1928; Hon. docteur en droit Lyons 1927, Grenoble 1939, Paris 1945. Author of Bankers' Commercial Credits 1932, Comparative Law 1946; edited Smith's Mercantile Law, and the Journal of Comparative Legislation. d. 30th Dec. 1953.

GWYER, Sir Maurice Linford

s. of John Edward Gwyer, Kensington, West London, Secretary to Provident Clerks' Life Assce. Assoc. b. 25th April 1878. educ. Highgate Sch.; Westminster (captain); Christ Church Oxf. BA 1901; All Souls Coll. MA 1904, BCL 1908, Fellow 1902-16, Hon. DCL 1939. I.T. Jan. 1903 (Cert. of Hon.). KC 1930. Hon. Bencher 1937. Legal adviser to Insurance Commrs. 1912-16, to Min. of Shipping 1917-19, to Min. of Health 1919-26; HM Procurator-Genl. and Treasury Solicitor 1926-33; first parliamentary counsel to Treasury 1934-37; lecturer in intern. law Oxf. 1912-15; first Br. delegate to Hague Confce. on intern. law 1930; member of Indian States Inquiry committee 1932; CJ India and Pres. of Federal Ct. 1937-43; V-C Delhi Univ. 1938-50; govr. Westminster Sch. 1936; hon. member Surveyors Inst. 1937; CB 1921; KCB 1928; KCSI 1935; GCIE 1947; Hon. LLD Travancore 1943, Patna 1944; Hon. DLitt. Delhi 1950. Edited Anson's Law of Contract, Anson's Law and Custom of the

Constitution (Vol. 1), and Pollock and Mulla's Indian Contract Act. d. 12th Oct 1952.

GYE, Percy

s. of Frederick Gye, London theatre proprietor (d. 1878). b. 25th Nov. 1845. educ. privately. I.T. Jan. 1871. Cty. Ct. judge 1896-1916; JP Hampshire. d. 13th June 1916.

HALCOMBE, John

s. of John Halcombe, Marlborough, Wiltshire, coach proprietor. b. 1790. I.T. June 1823. Serjeant 1840. MP Devon 1833-35. Author of works on the poor laws, and private bills in parliament. d. 3rd Nov. 1852.

HALDANE, Richard Burdon (Lord Haldane)

s. of Robert Haldane WS, Cloanden. Perthshire. b. 30th July 1856. educ. Edin. Acad.; Göttingen 1874; Edin. Univ. MA 1876, LLD. L.I. Nov. 1879. QC 1890. Bencher 1893. Mainly employed in Privy Council and H of L Appeals; MP East Lothian 1885-1911; Lord Rector Edin. Univ. 1905; Secy. of State for War 1905-12; LC 1912-15 and 1924; PC 1902, and member Judicial Committee from 1911; Viscount 1911; KT 1913; OM 1915; FRS 1906; FBA 1914; Hon. LLD Camb., Hon. DCL Oxf. and Durham. d. 19th Aug. 1928. Biog. by Jean Graham Hall and Douglas F. Martin. 1996

HALDIN, Henry Hyman

s. of Philip Victor Haldinstein, Norwich. b. 1863. educ. Norwich Sch.; Balliol Coll. Oxf. BA 1885. I.T. Nov. 1886. KC 1912. Member appeal trib. under Mil. Service Act 1916; Pres. Civil Advisory Bd. with 2nd Army in Germany 1919; JP Buckinghamshire; director of oil and other companies. d. 30th Nov. 1931.

HALKETT, John Gilbert Hay

s. of John Gilbert Halkett, Balendoch, Perthshire (d. 1886). b. 12th May 1863. educ. Cheltenham Coll.; St John's Coll. Camb. BA 1885. I.T. Nov. 1887. Stip. magistrate Hull 1901-15; metrop. magistrate 1915, finally at Westminster 1932-35; JP Perthshire, Yorkshire East Riding, London and Home Counties. d. 31st May 1937.

HALL, Sir Charles

s. of John Hall, Manchester, merchant. b. 14th April 1814. Articled to a solicitor; afterwards a pupil of Lewis Duval, the conveyancer. M.T. Nov. 1838; L.I. 1838. Bencher (M.T.) 1872, Reader 1878. Twice declined silk; succeeded to Duval's practice 1844; counsel in Bridgewater peerage case 1853, Shrewsbury peerage case 1857; leader of chancery bar; conveyancing counsel to Ct. of Chancery 1864-73; V-C 1873-75; Knight 1873; chancery judge 1875-82. d. 12th Dec. 1883.

HALL, Sir Charles

s. of Sir Charles Hall V-C. b. 3rd Aug. 1843. educ. Harrow; Trinity Coll. Camb. BA 1866, MA 1870. M.T. May 1872; L.I. Nov. 1866. QC 1881. Bencher 1884, Reader 1894. Att-Genl. to Prince of Wales 1877-92; Tubman in Ct. of Exch. 1878; MP West Cambridgeshire 1885-92, Finsbury 1892-1900; first Br. delegate to intermaritime confce. at Washington 1889; Recorder of London 1892-1900; PC 1899; KCMG 1890. d. 9th March 1900.

HALL, Sir Edward Marshall

s. of Alfred Hall MD, FRCP, Brighton, and g.s. of Henry Hall, barrister. b. 16th Sept 1858. educ. Rugby; St John's Coll. Camb. BA 1882. I.T. June 1883. QC 1898. Bencher 1910. Recorder of Guildford 1916-27; MP Lancashire (Southport) 1900-06, Liverpool (East Toxteth) 1910-16; Knight 1917; established reputation in defence of Hermann (murder reduced to manslaughter) 1894; career temporarily affected by Ct. of Appeal's disapproval of his conduct in a libel case against Daily Mail 1901; appeared in many sensational cases, his greatest success when acting for petitioner in Russell divorce case 1923. Biography by Edward Marjoribanks 1929. d. 23rd Feb. 1927.

HALL, Sir Samuel

s. of Samuel Hall, Leftwich, Cheshire, farmer. b. 1841. educ. Trinity Coll. Dublin MA. M.T. June 1870. QC 1888. Bencher 1893, Reader 1905. Equity draftsman and conveyancer; Att-Genl. Cty. Palatine of Lancaster 1893-95, V-C 1895-1905; Knight 1902. d. 6th April 1907.

HALL, Thomas James

s. of Cossley Hall, Hyde Hall and Florence Hall, Jamaica. b. Jamaica, 5th December 1788. educ. Harrow; Trinity Coll. Camb. BA 1811, MA 1815. M.T. Feb. 1815. Judge-Adv. and Adv-Genl. of Jamaica 1819 and member House of Assembly; joined Northern circuit 1824; Commr. in Bankruptcy, Liverpool; stip. magistrate Liverpool 1836-39; chief magistrate, Bow St. 1839-64; declined knighthood and baronetcy. Father of William James Fitzwilliam Hall (M.T.1847). d. 20th March 1876.

HALL, Sir William Clarke

s. of Rev. William Hall, Folkestone. b. 1866. educ. privately; Christ Church Oxf. BA 1888. King's Inns 1889; G.I. July 1889. Bencher 1917, Treasurer 1926. Metrop. magistrate 1913, finally at Old St

1914-32; Chmn. Magistrates' Assoc. and Nat. Assoc. of Probation Officers; Knight 1932; JP London and Home Counties. Author of works on law relating to children. d. 28th Oct 1932.

HALLETT, Sir Hugh Imbert Periam

s. of Forbes Ernest Hallett, barrister. b. 12th Dec. 1886. educ. Westminster; Christ Church Oxf. BA 1909, MA 1948. I.T. Nov. 1911. KC 1936. Bencher 1939, Reader 1963, Treasurer 1964. WWI Capt. 1/24th Battn. London Regt., and with army signal services, MC (despatches). Recorder of Newcastle-upon-Tyne 1938-39; KB judge 1939-57; Knight 1939; electoral boundaries commr. for Br. Guiana 1960; Hon. Secy. Junior Imperial League 1909-39; Asst. of Haberdashers' Co. 1939. Uncle of Victor George Henry Hallett (I.T. 1949), Social Security Commr. d. 8th Sept. 1967.

HAMILTON, Henry Best Hans

s. of Ven. George Hans Hamilton DD, Archdeacon of Northumberland (d. 1905). b. 14th Oct. 1850. educ. Durham Sch. I.T. and M.T. April 1873. Private secy. to Earl Fitzwilliam 1886-92; Recorder of Berwick-on-Tweed 1899-1905; Cty. Ct. judge 1905-13; JP Lancashire; Lt.Col. commanding Northumberland RGA 1888-1901. Officer commanding 17th (Reserve) Battn. Co. of London Regt. 1915-16; BEF France 1917-18 (despatches). d. 5th Aug. 1935.

HAMILTON, James Winterbottom

s. of Peter Hamilton, Oldham, merchant. b. 8th Dec. 1849. educ. privately; London Univ. LLB 1875. I.T. June 1873. QC 1895. The first recorder of Oldham 1887-99; member of convocation London Univ. d. 18th Oct 1899.

HAMILTON, John Andrew (Lord Sumner)

s. of Andrew Hamilton, Withington, Manchester, iron merchant (d. 1906). b. 3rd Feb. 1859. educ. Manchester Gr. Sch.; Balliol Coll. Oxf. BA 1882, MA 1883; Fellow of Magdalen Coll. 1882-89, Hon. Fellow 1909, Hon. DCL 1920. I.T. Nov. 1883. KC 1901. Bencher 1909. Standing counsel to Oxf. Univ. 1906-09; inspector in Swansea educ. dispute 1908; had extensive commercial practice, in rivalry with T. E. Scrutton; KB judge 1909-12; Knight 1909; never reserved judgment; LJ and PC 1912; L of A 1913-30; Baron 1913; Chmn. Br. and Foreign Legal Procedure Committee 1918; Br. delegate to Reparation Comm., Paris 1919; Chmn. Royal Comm. on Compensation for War Damage 1921; took leading part in appeals from Prize Ct.; GCB 1920; Viscount 1927; Hon. LLD Edin., Manchester, and Camb.; a voluminous contributor to Dictionary of National Biography. d. 24th May 1934.

HAMILTON, William Frederick

s. of Andrew Hamilton, Southampton. b. 25th Dec. 1848. educ. London Univ. LLD 1883. M.T. June 1879 (Cert. of Hon.). QC 1900. Bencher 1907, Reader 1921. Member of the War Compensation Ct. Author of works on company law, and compulsory arbitration in industrial disputes. d. 17th Sept 1922.

HAMMILL, John

s. of Martin Hammill, Liverpool. b. 13th April 1803. educ. Macclesfield Gr. Sch.; Trinity Coll. Camb. BA 1825, MA 1832. I.T. Jan. 1832. Commr. in Bankruptcy, Liverpool 1840; metrop. magistrate 1847, finally at Marylebone 1860. d. 30th July 1860.

HAMMOND-CHAMBERS, Robert Sharp Borgnis

s. of Robert Hammond JP, Heathers, nr Gt. Marlow,

Buckinghamshire. b. 3rd Feb. 1855. educ. Eton; Magdalen Coll. Oxf. BA 1877. L.I. June 1879. QC 1897. Bencher 1905. d. 25th July 1907.

HANCOCK, Ernest

s. of Robert Hancock, Exeter. b. 30th Nov. 1887. educ. Exeter Sch.; Lincoln Coll. Oxf. I.T. Jan. 1913 (Cert. of Hon.). WWI Lieut. RGA and South African Heavy Artillery, MC. Cty. Ct. judge 1937-50. d. 26th Dec. 1950.

HANNAY, James Lennox

s. of John O. Hannay, WS. b. 20th Sept 1826. educ. privately; St John's Coll. Camb. BA 1848, MA 1851. I.T. June 1852. Recorder of Pontefract; metrop. magistrate 1871, finally at Marlborough St. 1888-1903; counsel to magistrates of Yorkshire West Riding; DL, JP Kirkcudbrightshire; JP Middlesex and Home Counties. d. 7th June 1903.

HANNEN, James (Lord Hannen)

s. of James Hannen, King William St. London, and Dulwich, wine merchant (d. 1857). b. 19th March 1821. educ. St Paul's; Heidelberg Univ. M.T. Jan. 1848. Bencher 1878, Reader 1889. Agent for GB in mixed Br. and American Comm. for settlement of outstanding claims 1853-55; junior counsel to Treasury 1864; prosecuted the "Manchester Martyrs" for murder of Sgt. Brett, when attempting to rescue Fenian prisoners from a police van 1867; QB judge 1868; Knight 1868; Judge of Probate & Divorce Ct. 1872; Pres. of P D & A Divn. 1875-91; Pres. comm. to inquire into charges made by the Times against C.S. Parnell 1888-90; L of A 1891-93; PC 1872; Baron Hannen of Burdock 1891; member Bering Sea Fisheries Arbitration Comm. 1892-93; Hon. DCL Oxf. 1888. Father of James Chitty Hannen (I.T. 1876), Registrar of Probate & Divorce Ct., and

Henry Arthur Hannen (M.T.1891). d. 29th March 1894.

HANSELL, Sir Edward William

s. of Rev. Edward Halifax Hansell, East Isley, Berkshire. b. 2nd Dec. 1856. educ. Charterhouse; Christ Church Oxf. BA 1880, MA 1892. I.T. Nov. 1880. KC 1927. Bencher 1912, Treasurer 1933. Counsel to Bd. of Trade in bankruptcy matters 1905-27; Recorder of Maidstone 1917-27; Commr. of Assize, North Eastern circuit 1932; Chan. of diocese of Oxford 1912, Gloucester and Birmingham 1920, Coventry 1921, Lincoln and Southwark 1923; Official Referee of Supreme Ct. 1927-31; Knight 1930. Editor and part-author of Williams's Bankruptcy Practice. d. 18th April 1937.

HARCOURT, Sir William George Granville Venables Vernon-

s. of Rev. William Vernon-Harcourt, Nuneham Park, Oxfordshire. b. 14th Oct 1827. educ. privately; Trinity Coll. Camb. BA 1851, Hon. Fellow 1904. I.T. May 1854. QC 1866. Whewell prof. of intern. law 1869-87. MP Oxford 1868-80, Derby 1880-95, West Monmouthshire 1895; Sol-Genl. 1873; Home Secy. 1880-85; Chan. of Exch. 1886, 1892-95; a trustee of British Museum; Knight 1873; PC 1880; FRS; declined peerage. d. 1st Oct. 1904.

HARDEN, John William

s. of John Harden, Crea, King's Co., and Brathay Hall, Windermere. b. 11th Dec. 1809. educ. Manchester Gr. Sch.; Edin. Univ. I.T. Nov. 1835. Commr. in Bankruptcy; Cty. Ct. judge 1847-75; JP Cheshire and Lancashire. d. 16th April 1875.

HARDING, Sir John Dorney

s. of Rev. John Harding, Rockfield, Monmouthshire (d. 1861). b.

1809. educ. Charterhouse; Oriel Coll. Oxf. BA 1830, MA 1833, DCL 1837. I.T. Nov. 1835. Advocate Doctors' Commons 1837. QC 1858. Bencher 1852, Reader 1867. Queen's Adv-Genl. 1852-62; Knight 1852. d. 23rd Nov. 1868.

HARDMAN, Sir William

s. of William Bridge Hardman, Chamber Hall, Bury, Lancashire. b. 13th Aug. 1828. educ. Trinity Coll. Camb. BA 1851, MA 1854. I.T. April 1852. QC 1890. Recorder of Kingston-on-Thames 1875-90. Editor of Morning Post 1872-90. Inspector of Woking convict prison; Alderman Surrey CC; Chmn. Surrey Quarter Sess. 2nd Ct. 1871-72, 1st Ct. 1877-90; founder of Primrose League 1882; Knight 1885; DL, JP Surrey. His memoirs (ed. S.M. Ellis) pubd. 1923-25. d. 12th Sept. 1890.

HARDWICK, John

s. of Thomas Hardwick, architect b. 3rd Dec. 1791. educ. Balliol Coll. Oxf. BCL 1815, DCL 1830, Fellow 1808-22. L.I. June 1816. Metrop. magistrate 1821, finally at Gt. Marlborough St. 1841-56; FRS 1838. d. 31st May 1875.

HARDY, Benjamin

s. of Samuel Hardy, Islington. b. 1808. G.I. Nov. 1836. Equity draftsman and conveyancer. QC 1866. Bencher (L.I.) 1867. d. 30th July 1876.

HARGREAVE, Charles James

s. of James Hargreave, Wortley, nr. Leeds, woollen manufacturer. b. Dec. 1820. educ. University Coll. London LLB; Dublin Univ. LLD 1852. I.T. June 1844. QC 1851. Bencher 1851, Reader 1866,

Master of the Library 1865. Prof. of jurisprudence, Univ. Coll. London, 1843-49; Commr. of Incumbered Estates Ct. Ireland 1849-58; judge of Landed Estate Ct. 1858-66; drafted Record of Title Act 1866; FRS 1844. d. 23rd April 1866.

HARGREAVES, Sir Gerald de la Pryme

s. of Thomas Hargreaves, Oakhurst, Birkdale, Lancashire. b. 1881. educ. Eton; Magdalen Coll. Oxf. BA 1903. I.T. July 1905. WWI Capt. Bedfordshire Yeo., and Courts-Martial Officer X Army Corps (despatches), Belgian Croix de Guerre. Cty. Ct. judge 1922-55; Chmn. London Trib. for Conscientious Objectors 1939; served in Home Guard 1942-45; Knight 1944. Author of treatise on Deeds of Arrangement. d. 29th April 1972.

HARINGTON, Edward

s. of Sir Richard Harington Bt., Cty. Ct. judge. b. 25th Oct 1863. educ. Westminster; Christ Church Oxf. BA 1887. I.T. July 1889. Cty. Ct. judge 1905-35; JP Herefordshire. d. 19th Jan. 1937.

HARINGTON, Sir Richard, Bt.

s. of Rev. Richard Harington DD, principal of Brasenose Coll. Oxf. b. 20th May 1835. educ. Eton; Christ Church, Oxf. BA 1857, MA 1860, BCL 1863. Vinerian Law Scholar 1858. L.I. Nov. 1858 (Cert of Hon.). Metrop. magistrate Hammersmith and Wandsworth 1871-72; Cty. Ct. judge 1872-1905; Chmn. Herefordshire Quarter Sess. and Cty. alderman; DL, JP Herefordshire; JP Warwickshire, Worcestershire. Succeeded cousin 1877, as 11th baronet. d. 6th Feb. 1911.

HARKER, Thomas Rowand

s. of Thomas Parkinson Harker, Brighton, solicitor. b. 18th Jan. 1879. educ. in Brighton. Solicitor 1900. M.T. Nov. 1905. KC 1926. WWI in RAOC, later DAAG (Temp. Major, General List). Chmn. South Eastern Area Traffic Commrs. 1931-34; Chmn. Road and Rail Traffic Act 1933 Appeal Trib. 1934-39. d. 1st June 1946.

HARMAN, Sir Charles Eustace

s. of John Eustace Harman, bencher, Lincoln's Inn. b. 22nd Nov. 1894. educ. Eton; King's Coll. Camb. BA 1920, MA 1924. WWI Lieut. Middlesex Regt. (prisoner 1915-18). L.I. June 1921. KC 1935. Bencher 1939, Treasurer 1959. Equity draftsman and conveyancer; Vice-Chmn. bar council 1946; Chancery judge 1947-59; Knight 1947; LJ 1959-70; PC 1959. Father of Sir Jeremiah Le Roy Harman, Chancery judge 1982. d. 14th Nov. 1970.

HARNEY, Edward Augustine St. Aubyn

s. of Richard Harney JP, Kiloteran House, Waterford. b. 31st Aug 1871. educ. Clongowes Wood Coll.; Trinity Coll. Dublin. Irish bar 1892; Australian bar 1897. KC 1904. Senator Commonwealth Parlt. 1901-04. G.I. Nov. 1906. KC 1920. MP South Shields 1922. d. 17th May 1929.

HARRIS, John Henry

s. of James Harris FCA, Campden Hill, London. b. 10th Sept 1875. educ. St. Paul's; Merton Coll. Oxf. BA. I.T. June 1900. Recorder of Portsmouth 1927-28; metrop. magistrate 1928, finally at Thames St. 1930-45. d. 18th March 1962.

HARRIS, Richard

s. of James Harris, Esher, Surrey. b. 1833. educ. privately. M.T. Nov. 1864. QC 1888. Bencher 1892, Reader 1903. Author of Hints on Advocacy, Illustrations in Advocacy, Before Trial, Farmer Bumpkin's Lawsuit, Her Majesty's Judges, Legends of the Temple, and biography of Lord Brampton. d. 11th Sept 1906.

HARRIS, Richard Reader

s. of Richard Reader Harris, Chief Constable of Worcestershire, barrister. b. 5th July 1847. educ. privately. Employed in GWR locomotive works 1864-68. Engineer on GWR and GER 1868-71; chief railway engineer, Republic of Bolivia; MICE. G.I. Nov. 1883. QC 1894. Bencher 1895, Treasurer 1907. Practised at parliamentary bar. d. 30th March 1909.

HARRISON, James Fraser

s. of James Fraser Harrison, Caerwys, Flintshire. b. 7th May 1890. educ. Liverpool Coll., Sedbergh, Liverpool Univ. LLM 1942. I.T. June 1912. WWI Capt. King's Liverpool Regt. Asst. Recorder of Liverpool 1929-40; Cty. Ct. judge 1940-62; Divorce Commr.; Dep. Chmn. Preston, Manchester and Liverpool Cty. Quarter Sess. 1938-40; a Dep. Chmn. Lancashire Quarter Sess. 1940; Commr. of Assize, Northern Circuit 1946; JP Lancashire and Cheshire.
d. 16th Jan. 1971.

HARRISON, William English

s. of John Harrison, Lombard St., London, notary public. b. 1843. educ. King's Coll. London. M.T. Jan. 1867. QC 1897. Bencher 1893, Reader 1904, Treasurer 1916. Commr. of Assize, Stafford and Birmingham 1899, North Wales Circuit 1905, Western Circuit 1907; Chmn. bar council 1907. Known as "Angel Harrison" to distinguish him from William George Harrison. d. 24th Dec. 1933.

HARRISON, William George

s. of Charles Harrison, Sackville St, Piccadilly, London. b. 15th Jan. 1827. educ. King's Coll. London; St. John's Coll. Camb. BA 1850, 18th Wrangler. I.T. Jan. 1853. QC 1877. Bencher 1877. A commercial lawyer. Author (with G.A. Capes) of commentary on Joint Stock Companies Act 1856. Known as "Devil Harrison". d. 5th March 1883.

HART, Heber Leonidas

s. of Percy Matthew Hart, The Pines, Putney Hill, London S.W. b. 1865. educ. London Univ. LLD. M.T. Jan. 1887. KC 1913. Bencher 1923, Reader 1931, Treasurer 1936. Recorder of Ipswich 1915-36; British member of the Anglo-German, Anglo-Austrian, Anglo-Hungarian and Anglo-Bulgarian mixed arbitral tribunals under the Treaties of Peace, until completion of their work in 1931; Hon. Capt. for services during WWI; Pres. Johnson Club 1943; Chmn. of Eighty, and 1920 Clubs. Author of The Law of Banking 1904, The Bulwarks of Peace 1918, Reminiscences and Reflections 1939, The Way to Justice 1941. d. 4th Feb. 1948.

HARVIE-WATT, Sir George Steven, Bt.

s. of James McDougal Watt, Woodlands House, Armadale, West Lothian (d. 1943). b. 23rd Aug. 1903. educ. George Watson's Coll. Edin.; Glasgow and Edin. Univs. I.T. Jan. 1930. KC 1945. MP Yorkshire (Keighley) 1931-35, Richmond, Surrey 1937-59; commissioned in RE (TA) 1924, Lt.Col. 1938; WWII Brig. cding. 6th AA Bde.; Hon. Col. 566 LAA Regt. 1949-62. Asst. Govt. Whip 1938-40; parliamentary secy. to Winston Churchill 1941-45; ADC to George VI 1948-52, to Elizabeth II 1952-58; Pres. Consolidated Goldfields Ltd. 1973-80; director Eagle Star Insce. Co., Clydesdale

Bank Ltd. and other companies; member Royal Co. of Archers; Hon. Freeman of City of London; Baronet 1945; DL Surrey and London; OStJ; TD and 3 bars; JP London. Author of Most of My Life 1980. d. 18th Dec. 1989.

HARWOOD, Charles

s. of Rev. Thomas Harwood DD, headmaster, Lichfield Gr. Sch. (d. 1842). I.T. June 1828. Equity draftsman and conveyancer; Recorder of Shrewsbury 1839-66; Cty. Ct. judge 1847-66; FSA. d. 25th Sept 1866, age 68.

HASTINGS, Graham

s. of John Hastings MD, Albemarle St, London (d. 1874). b. 7th Oct. 1830. educ. in Paris and Edinburgh; King's Coll. London; Worcester Coll. Oxf. BA 1854. L.I. Nov. 1854. QC 1875. Bencher 1877. d. 5th Dec. 1922.

HASTINGS, Sir Patrick Gardiner

s. of Alfred Gardiner Hastings, Kensington, West London. b. 17th March 1880. educ. Charterhouse. Mining engineer 1898-99; served in South African War 1900-01; journalist 1902-03. M.T. June 1904. KC 1919. Bencher 1924, Reader 1934. MP Northumberland (Wallsend) 1922-26; Att-Genl. 1924; Knight 1924; his withdrawal of prosecution of Campbell of Workers' Weekly for sedition caused government's downfall; eminent as leader of common law bar, appearing in many causes célèbres. Wrote plays, also Autobiog. 1948, Cases in Court 1949, Famous and Infamous Cases 1950. Biographies by Patricia Hastings (daughter) 1959, H. Montgomery Hyde 1960. d. 26th Feb. 1952.

HAVERS, Sir Cecil Robert

s. of Daniel Havers, Norwich. b. 12th Nov. 1889. educ. King Edward VI Sch. Norwich; Corpus Christi Coll. Camb. BA 1912, LLB 1913, MA 1943, Hon. Fellow 1975. WWI Capt. 5th Battn. Hampshire Regt. and Royal Tank Corps (despatches). I.T. April 1920 (Cert of Hon.). KC 1939. Bencher 1946, Treasurer 1971. Recorder of Chichester 1939-51; Dep. Chmn. Advisory Committee on Aliens 1940; Commr. in Gold Coast 1944-45; Commr. of Assize, Oxford and Midland circuits 1949; P D and A judge 1951-52; Knight 1951; QB judge 1952-67; Dep. Chmn. West Kent Quarter Sess. Author of manual on Landlord and Tenant Act 1927. Father of Robert Michael Oldfield Havers (Lord Havers), LC 1987. d. 5th May 1977.

HAWKE, Sir John Anthony

s. of Edward Henry Hawke, Tolquilla, Scorrier, Cornwall, merchant. b. 7th June 1869. educ. Merchant Taylors; St John's Coll. Oxf. BA 1891, MA, Hon. Fellow 1931. M.T. Nov. 1892. KC 1913. Bencher 1923, Reader 1932. Recorder of Plymouth 1912-28; MP Cornwall (St.Ives) 1922-23 and 1924-28; Att-Genl. to Prince of Wales 1923-28; Vice-Chmn. bar council 1926; KB judge 1928-41; Knight 1928. Father of Sir Edward Anthony Hawke (M.T.1920), Recorder of London 1959-64. d. 30th Oct. 1941.

HAWKINS, Henry (Lord Brampton)

s. of John Hawkins, Hitchin, Hertfordshire, solicitor. b. 14th Sept 1817. educ. Bedford Sch. Worked with father; special pleader. M.T. May 1843. QC 1858. Bencher 1859, Reader 1862. Successfully defended Simon Bernard (attempted assassination of Napoleon III) 1852; defended Sir John Dean Paul (convicted of bank fraud) 1855; represented Miss Sugden in Lord St. Leonard's will case 1875; appeared against Tichborne claimant in the ejectment case, and on perjury charge 1873-74; leader on Home circuit, and much employed in compensation and election petition cases; QB judge and knighted 1876; Exch. judge 1876; tried the Stauntons for murder (the "Penge case") 1877, and other murder cases, resulting in undeserved nickname of "Hanging Hawkins"; QB judge 1881-98; PC 1898; Baron 1899; member Jockey Club 1889. Published his Reminiscences 1904. d. 6th Oct. 1907.

HAYDON, Thomas Edmett

s. of Thomas Were Haydon, Southsea, Hampshire. b. 15th April 1868. educ. Portsmouth Gr. Sch.; St John's Coll. Camb. BA 1889, MA 1898. I.T. June 1891. KC 1923. Cty. Ct. judge 1925-40. Joint editor of Gore-Browne on Company Law. d. 30th July 1952.

HAYES, Sir George

s. of Sheedy Hayes, Judd Place, Somerstown, London, West India proprietor. b. 19th June 1805. educ. in Highgate, and St Edmund's Coll. Ware. Articled to solicitor in Leamington 1819-24. Special pleader. M.T. Jan. 1830. Serjeant 1856; patent of precedence 1861; leader of Midland circuit; Recorder of Leicester 1861-68; QB judge 1868-69; Knight 1868. Author of an elegy humorously lamenting the extinction of John Doe and Richard Roe in pleadings for ejectment 1854. d. 25th Nov. 1869.

HAYTER, Sir William Goodenough, Bt.

s. of John Hayter, Winterbourne Stoke, Wiltshire. b. 28th Jan. 1792. educ. Winchester; Trinity Coll. Oxf. BA 1814. L.I. Nov. 1819. QC 1839. Bencher 1839, Treasurer 1853. Equity draftsman and conveyancer; retired from practice 1839; MP Wells 1837-65; Judge Adv-Genl. 1847-49; PC 1848; Financial Secy. to Treasury 1849-50; parliamentary and patronage secy. 1850-58; Baronet 1858. Found drowned in the lake at South Hill Park, Easthampstead, Berks. 26th Dec. 1878.

HAYWARD, Abraham

s. of Joseph Hayward, Wilton, nr. Salisbury. b. 22nd Nov. 1801. educ. Tiverton Gr. Sch. (Blundell's). Solicitor 1824. I.T. June 1832. QC 1845. Inn refused to make him a bencher. Secy. of Poor Law Bd. 1854. Editor of Law Magazine 1828-44; author of The Statutes founded on the common law reports 1832, and many other works, particularly essays. Depicted as "Venom Tuft" in Samuel Warren's "Ten Thousand a Year". d. 2nd Feb. 1884.

HAYWARD, Richard Frederick

s. of C.J. Hayward, Lincoln. b. 22nd March 1879. educ. HMS Worcester. Entered merchant navy 1895; Lieut. RNR 1905. I.T. July 1908. KC 1936. Bencher 1943. WWI Major 22nd Battn. London Regt. and MGC; MC (despatches). Served with military mission in USA. Leader of the admiralty bar; acted as a wreck commr. and as an arbitrator for Lloyd's. d. 8th Feb. 1962.

HAZEL, Alfred Ernest William

s. of John Hazel, West Bromwich, builder and contractor. b. 1869. educ. West Bromwich Wesleyan Sch.; King Edward's Sch. Birmingham; Jesus Coll. Oxf. BA 1892, BCL and MA 1895, Fellow, Dean and Bursar; Hon. Fellow Queen's Coll. L.I. June 1898 (Cert. of Hon.). KC 1930. MP West Bromwich 1906-10; the first recorder of Burton-on-Trent 1912-38; Dep. Controller, Priority Dept, Min. of Munitions 1915-19; CBE 1918; Senior Proctor Oxf. 1910-11; Reader in constitutional law at Inns of Ct. 1910-26; lecturer on criminal law and evidence Oxf. 1915-22; All Souls Reader in English law Oxf. 1922-23; Principal of Jesus Coll. 1925-44; Pres. Nat. Education Assoc.; Assessor of Chancellor's Ct. Oxf; examr. in law, Oxf., Camb., Glasgow, London, Wales Univs.; LLD Dublin. d. 20th Aug. 1944.

HEAD, George Herbert

s. of Rev. George Frederick Head, Clifton, Bristol. bapt. 13th April 1869. educ. Repton; Pembroke Coll. Camb. BA 1891, MA 1905. I.T. July 1905. Cty. Ct. judge 1922-27; JP Yorkshire East Riding, and Ouse and Derwent Division. d. 11th Feb. 1927.

HEADLAM, Thomas Emerson

s. of Ven. John Headlam, archdeacon of Richmond, Yorkshire (d. 1854). bapt. 25th June 1813. educ. Shrewsbury; Trinity Coll. Camb. BA 1836, 16th Wrangler, MA 1839. I.T. May 1839. QC 1851. Bencher 1851, Reader 1866, Treasurer 1867. MP Newcastle-on-Tyne 1847-74; carried through parliament Trustee Act 1850; Chan. of diocese of Ripon 1854, of Durham 1854; Judge Adv-Genl. 1859-66; PC 1859; DL, JP Yorkshire North Riding, and Northumberland; FRGS. Edited books on Chancery procedure. d. Calais, 3rd Dec. 1875.

HEALD, Sir Lionel Frederick

s. of James Heald, Parrs Wood, Didsbury, Lancashire. b. 7th Aug. 1897. educ. Charterhouse; Christ Church Oxf. BA 1920. WWI Lieut. RE; Italian Bronze Medal. M.T. Nov. 1923. KC 1937. Bencher 1946. WWII Air Cdre. RAFVR. Junior counsel to Bd. of Trade in technical matters 1931-37; member of St Pancras BC 1934-37; MP Surrey (Chertsey) 1950-70; Att-Genl. 1951-54; Vice-Chmn. of bar council 1957; Knight 1951; PC 1954; JP Surrey; govr. Middlesex Hosp. 1946. d. 7th Nov. 1981.

HEALY, Maurice Francis

s. of Maurice Healy MP, solicitor. b. 16th Nov. 1887. educ. Christian Brothers Coll. Cork; Clongowes Wood Coll.; University Coll. Dublin. Irish bar 1910. G.I. May 1914. KC 1931. Bencher

(I.T.) 1938. WWI Capt. Royal Dublin Fusiliers, and 29th Divn. HQ, MC. Recorder of Coventry 1941. Author of The Old Munster Circuit 1939, Stay me with Flagons 1940. d. 9th May 1943.

HEALY, Timothy Michael

s. of Maurice Healy, Bantry, Co. Cork (d. 1906). b. 1855. educ. by the Christian Brothers. Clerk in Newcastle and London. Irish bar 1884. QC 1899. Bencher, King's Inns 1905. G.I. June 1903. KC 1910. Bencher 1910. MP Wexford Borough 1880-83, Co. Monaghan 1883-85, South Londonderry 1885-86, North Longford 1887-92, North Louth 1892-1910, North East Cork 1910-18; Steward and bailiff of Three Hundreds of Chiltern 1918; first Gov.Genl. of the Irish Free State 1922-28. d. 26th March 1931.

HEATH, Douglas Denon

s. of George Thomas Heath, Dorking, Surrey, serjeant. b. 6th Jan. 1811. educ. Burney's Sch. Greenwich; Trinity Coll. Camb. BA 1832, Senior Wrangler, MA 1835, Fellow 1832-42. I.T. Jan. 1835. Judge of Ct. of Requests, Bloomsbury 1838-47; Cty. Ct. judge 1847-65; cty. clerk of Middlesex 1838-46; JP Surrey. Edited legal remains of Francis Bacon for 1859 ed. of his works. d. 25th Sept 1897.

HEATH, George Thomas

s. of James Heath, Fitzroy Square, London. b. 1778. I.T. Nov. 1807. Serjeant 1830; patent of precedence 1834. Dep. judge Cty. Ct. of Middlesex. d. 21st Jan. 1852.

HEDDERWICK, Thomas Charles Hunter

s. of Robert Hedderwick, Queen's printer and publisher, Glasgow. b. 6th April 1850. educ. Glasgow Univ. MA and Leipzig Univ. M.T.

Nov. 1876. Represented the claimant in Tichborne appeal case; MP Northern Burghs 1896-1900; member Select Committee on election law 1898; Acting Dep. Chmn. London Sess. 1907-10; metrop. magistrate North London 1910-18; founded bar committee; JP London and Home Counties, Lanarkshire, Buckinghamshire. Author of manuals on Parliamentary Election Law 1892, and Sale of Food and Drugs 1894. d. 6th Feb. 1918.

HEDLEY, Walter

s. of John Hedley MD, Cleveland Lodge, Middlesbrough. b. 25th Feb. 1879. educ. Uppingham; King's Coll. Camb. BA 1902, MA 1906. I.T. Nov. 1904. KC 1928. WWI Major RGA, DSO (despatches). Recorder of Richmond, Yorkshire 1920-28, of Middlesbrough 1928-29, of Newcastle-on-Tyne 1929-31, of Sheffield 1931-34; metrop. magistrate 1934, finally at Marlborough St 1941-46. d. 9th Dec. 1951.

HEMMERDE, Edward George

s. of John Hemmerde, manager, Imperial Ottoman Bank. b. 1871. educ. Winchester; University Coll. Oxf. BA 1894, MA. I.T. Jan. 1897. KC 1908. Recorder of Liverpool 1909-48; MP Denbighshire (East) 1906-10, Norfolk (North West) 1912-18, Cheshire (Crewe) 1922-24. Author of plays. d. 24th May 1948.

HEMMING, George Wirgman

s. of Henry Keene Hemming, Grays, Essex (d. 1868). b. 19th Aug. 1821. educ. Clapham Gr. Sch.; St. John's Coll. Camb. BA 1844, Senior Wrangler, MA 1847, Fellow 1844-53. L.I. May 1850. QC 1875. Bencher 1876, Treasurer 1897. Reported cases in ct. of Wood V-C 1859-74; junior counsel to Treasury 1871-75; standing counsel to Camb. Univ. 1875-79; Commr. under Universities Act 1877; equity editor of the Law Reports 1865-94; Official Referee 1877-

1905. Author of pamphlets on income tax, and fusion of law and equity. d. 6th Jan. 1905.

HENDERSON, Arthur (Lord Rowley)

s. of Arthur Henderson, MP, LLD, JP, Newcastle-upon-Tyne (d. 1935). b. 27th Aug. 1893. educ. Central Sch. Darlington; Queen's Coll. Taunton; Trinity Hall Camb. BA and LLB 1921, MA. WWI Private HAC; Lieut. No.4 Middlesex Brigade ASC (TF); WWII Major, General Staff. Secy. Univ. Labour Federation 1920-24. M.T. Nov. 1921. KC 1939. MP Cardiff (South) 1923-24 and 1929-31, Staffordshire (Kingswinford) 1935-50, Rowley Regis and Tipton 1950-66; parliamentary priv. secy. to Att-Genl. 1929-31; standing counsel to Labour Party; joint parliamentary under-secy. War Dept 1942; member Army Council 1942; Financial Secy. War Office 1943-45; parliamentary under-secy. of state for India and Burma 1945-47; Minister of State for Commonwealth Relations 1947; Secy. of State for Air 1947-51; Chmn. parliamentary group for World Government; DL London; PC 1947; Baron Rowley of Rowley Regis 1966. Author of Trade Unions and the Law; joint author of treatise on housing law, and, (with Sir Henry Slesser), Industrial Law. d. 28th Aug 1968.

HENDERSON, Charles Lamond

s. of William Henderson, Auchenblae, Kincardineshire. b. 12th April 1896. educ. Edin. Univ. MA 1919. WWI Capt. Gordon Highlanders, and Bedfordshire Regt. M.T. June 1920. KC 1943. Recorder of Newark 1943-45, of Warwick 1945-49, of Bedford 1949-63; Chmn. Bedfordshire Quarter Sess. 1946-56; JP Hertfordshire and Bedfordshire. d. 16th Jan. 1966.

HENDERSON, John Scott

s. of Matthew Maclaren Henderson, Rosehall, Airdrie, Lanark. b.

28th Sept 1895. educ. Airdrie Acad.; London Univ. BSc(Econ). WWI Royal Dublin Fusiliers, and 2nd Lieut. RASC (despatches). Civil servant, Min. of Health 1920-27; secy. to Br. delegation at Intern. Sanitary Confce. Paris 1926; secy. to inter-departmental committee on Optical Practioners Bill. I.T. Jan. 1927. KC 1945. Bencher 1952. Recorder of Bridgwater 1944, of Portsmouth 1945-62; Chmn. committee on Cruelty to Wild Animals 1949; Chmn. Inquiry into adequacy of security arrangements at Broadmoor 1952 (following escape of Straffen); member of Myxomatosis Advisory Committee 1953; responsible for reports to Home Secy. 1953 on evidence in Evans and Christie murder trials (rejecting Christie's statement that he was responsible for Mrs. Evans' death). d. 5th Nov. 1964.

HENDERSON, William Craig

s. of James Henderson, Glasgow, schoolmaster. b. 2nd June 1873. educ. Glasgow High Sch.; Glasgow Univ. MA 1894, BSc 1895, DSc 1902, Hon. LLD 1943; Trinity Coll. Camb. BA 1900 (for work in Cavendish laboratory). Private secy. to Lord Kelvin 1898-1900. M.T. June 1900. KC 1923. Bencher 1929, Treasurer 1946. Leader of Midland circuit and parliamentary bar; Chmn. Bd. of Trade committee on problems in retail trades, 1941. d. 5th March 1959.

HENN-COLLINS, Sir Stephen Ogle

s. of Collins, L of A. b. 14th Sept 1875. educ. Summer Fields; Winchester; New Coll. Oxf. 1895. M.T. Jan. 1899. KC 1932. Bencher 1924, Reader 1932, Treasurer 1938. Secy. to MR 1901-07; junior common law counsel to Admiralty 1927; P D and A judge 1937-45; Knight 1937; KB judge 1945-48; CBE 1925. d. 16th Oct 1958.

HENNIKER, Aldborough

s. of Aldborough Brydges John Henniker, Catcott, Somerset, barrister. b. 6th July 1821. educ. Charterhouse. G.I. May 1844. QC 1874. Bencher 1874, Treasurer 1877. Member Council of Legal Educ. d. 28th Jan. 1880 from injuries after falling down staircase at King's Cross Station.

HENRIQUES, Henry Straus Quixano

s. of Edward Micholls Henriques JP, Manchester. b. 8th Nov. 1866. educ. Manchester Gr. Sch.; Worcester Coll. Oxf. BA 1889, MA and BCL 1893. Vinerian Law Scholar 1891. Examr. for BCL degree 1897. I.T. May 1892. KC 1921. Special pleader. Pres. Jewish Bd. of Deputies; Pres. Jewish Historical Socy. of England; Pres. West London Synagogue; member executive committees of Grotius Socy. and Intern. Law Assoc. Author of works on Judaism. d. 12th Nov. 1925.

HENRY, Sir Thomas

s. of David Henry, Dublin, government contractor. b. 1807. educ. Von Feinagles Sch.; Trinity Coll. Dublin. BA 1824, MA 1827. M.T. Jan. 1829. Bencher 1872. Metrop. magistrate 1840, finally at Bow St 1846-76; chief magistrate and knighted 1864; draftsman of Extradition Act 1870. d. 16th June 1876.

HERBERT, John Maurice

s. of John Lawrence Herbert, New Hall, Montgomeryshire. b. 15th July 1808. educ. Cathedral Sch. Hereford; St John's Coll. Camb. BA 1830, MA 1833, Fellow 1832-40. L.I. May 1835. Equity draftsman and conveyancer; Cty. Ct. judge 1847-82; JP. d. 3rd Nov. 1882.

HERBERT, Thomas Arnold

s. of Rev. Thomas Martin Herbert, prof. of philosophy and church history at Lancashire Independent Coll. (d. 1877). b. 1st Sept 1863. educ. Mill Hill; Owen's Coll. Manchester; St John's Coll. Camb. BA and LLB 1887. I.T. May 1889. KC 1913. Equity draftsman and conveyancer; MP Buckinghamshire (South) 1906-10; carried the Law of Distress Amendment Act 1908; JP Buckinghamshire. Author of a treatise on the law of prescription. d. 22nd Nov. 1940.

HERBERT-SMITH, Charles

s. of Thomas Smith, York. b. 14th May 1862. educ. Elmfield Coll. York; London Univ. LLD 1888. G.I. and M.T. Jan. 1888. Bencher (G.I.). Cty. Ct. judge 1921-34; Freeman of City of York. d. 7th Jan. 1944.

HERSCHELL, Farrer (Lord Herschell)

s. of Rev. Ridley Haim Herschell, dissenting minister (d. 1864). b. 2nd Nov. 1837. educ. Bonn Univ.; University Coll. London BA 1857. L.I. Nov. 1860. QC 1872. Bencher 1872. Examr. in common law to London Univ.; Recorder of Carlisle 1873-80; MP City of Durham 1874-85; Sol-Genl. 1880-85; Knight 1880; LC 1886 and 1892-95; Baron and PC 1886; Chmn. comms. on Currency, Metropolitan Bd. of Works, and Vaccination 1887-89; GCB 1893; a founder of the Socy. of Comparative Legislation 1894; Pres. Selden Socy.; member Anglo-Venezuelan, and Anglo-American (Alaska Seal Fisheries) Comms. 1898; Captain of Deal Castle 1890-99; Pres. Governing Body of Imperial Inst.; Chan. of London Univ. 1893; DL, JP Kent; DL Durham; Hon. DCL Durham and Oxf.; Hon. LLD Camb. d. Washington, USA 1st March 1899.

HEWART, Gordon (Lord Hewart)

s. of Giles Hewart, Bury, Lancashire. b. 7th Jan. 1870. educ. Bury Gr. Sch.; Manchester Gr. Sch.; Univ. Coll. Oxf. BA 1891, MA 1893, Hon. Fellow 1922. I.T. June 1902 (Cert. of Hon.). KC 1912. Bencher 1917, Treasurer 1938. MP Leicester 1913-22; Sol-Genl. 1916-19; Knight 1916; Att-Genl. 1919-22; attended Peace Confce. in Paris; Cabinet Minister 1921-22; Pres. Comm. on War Criminals; Pres. War Compensation Ct. 1922-29; LCJ 1922-40; PC 1918; Baron 1922; Viscount 1940; hon. member Canadian and American Bar Assocs.; Master of Curriers' Co. 1926; Pres. Classical Assoc. 1926, English Assoc. 1929; Vice-Pres. Oxford Socy.; Freeman of Bury 1922, Hastings 1930; JP Hertfordshire; Hon. LLD Manchester, Toronto, Sheffield, Birmingham, Johannesburg. Author of Essays and Observations 1930, Not Without Prejudice 1937 (autobiog.). d. 5th May 1943.

HEWITT, Edgar Percy

s. of William Henry Hewitt, Purlieu, Hythe, nr. Southampton. b. 1859. educ. St. John's Coll. Oxf. 1877; London Univ. LLB, LLD 1890. L.I. June 1883. KC 1912. Bencher 1916. Equity draftsman and conveyancer. Author of works on the Statutes of Limitations, and Taxes on Land Values; edited Kerr on Injunctions, and White and Tudor's Leading Cases. d. 24th Dec. 1928.

HEWITT, Sir Thomas

s. of Halford Wotton Hewitt JP, Lichfield, Staffordshire, physician (d. 1893). b. 1837. educ. Lichfield Gr. Sch.; High School, Darmstadt. Solicitor 1860, practised in Walton-on-Thames. I.T. May 1884. QC 1899. Practised chiefly in revenue cases. Counsel and Clerk to Commrs. of Taxes for City of London 1882-1916; High Sheriff, Devonshire 1908; Pres. London Chamber of Arbitration 1901-06; Mayor of Kensington 1912; Chmn. Lynton and Barnstaple Ry. Co., and Ocean Accident and Guarantee Insce. Corp.; Capt. 40th

Middlesex R.Vol. 1866-70.; Capt. Nat. Res. Kensington Battn. 1913; Knight 1904; JP London and Devon. Author of Corporation Duty 1892. Father of Copley Delisle Hewitt (I.T. 1897). d. 8th Jan. 1923.

HEYWOOD, George Washington

s. of Abel Heywood, Manchester, bookseller and publisher (d. 1893). b. 6th Jan. 1842. educ. privately. M.T. June 1868. Cty. Ct. judge 1890-94; JP Lancashire. Editor of County Court Practice 1890-95. d. 17th Jan. 1896.

HIGGIN, William Housman

s. of John Higgin, Greenfield, Lancaster. b. 1820. M.T. Jan. 1848. QC 1868. Bencher 1868, Reader 1874, Treasurer 1884. Chmn. Preston Quarter Sess., and Salford Hundred Quarter Sess.; Recorder of Preston 1890-93; QC Cty. Palatine of Lancaster; DL, JP Lancashire; JP Cheshire. d. 30th Jan. 1893.

HIGGINS, Alexander Pearce

s. of Alexander Higgins, Worcester. b. 24th April 1865. educ. Cathedral (King's) Sch. Worcester; Downing Coll. Camb. BA and LLB 1891, MA 1895, LLD 1904, Hon. Fellow 1923; Fellow of Trinity Coll. 1926. Qualified as solicitor 1887. L.I. May 1908. KC 1923. Lecturer on intern. law at RN War and Staff Colleges from 1908; adviser on intern. and prize law in Procurator-Genl.'s Dept 1914-20; adviser to Admiralty on intern. law for Peace Confce. 1919; Pres., Socy. of Public Teachers of Law 1917-18; prof. of intern. law, London Univ. 1919-23; Whewell prof. of intern. law, Camb. Univ. 1920-35; Pres. Institut de Droit International 1929; member Permanent Ct. of Arbitration, The Hague 1930-35; CBE 1917; FBA 1928. Published and edited numerous works on intern. law. d. 2nd April 1935.

HIGGINS, Clement

s. of William Mullinger Higgins, Wrexham, Denbighshire, architect. b. 10th Jan. 1844. educ. in Edmonton, London; Downing Coll. Camb. BA 1869, MA 1874. Asst. master Rossall Sch. 1869. I.T. Nov. 1871. QC 1886. Bencher 1893. Recorder of Birkenhead 1882-1907; MP Mid-Norfolk 1892-95. Author of works on patents, and on watercourses. d. 4th Dec. 1916.

HIGGINS, George Herbert

s. of George Randell Higgins JP, The Croft, Burcote, Oxfordshire. b. 10th Dec. 1878. educ. Dulwich; Balliol Coll. Oxf. BCL, MA. I.T. Nov. 1903. WWI Major Queen's Regt, and Courts-martial officer (despatches). Cty. Ct. judge 1923-37. d. 3rd Feb. 1937.

HIGGINS, Joseph Napier

s. of Joseph Higgins, Glenpatrick, Waterford. b. 1826. educ. Trinity Coll. Dublin. BA 1851. L.I. May 1851. QC 1872. Bencher 1872, Treasurer 1891. Practised in cts. of Malin V-C 1872-82, and North J 1882-91; MRIA; JP Buckinghamshire, Waterford, and Tipperary. d. 17th Dec. 1899.

HILBERY, Sir George Malcolm

s. of Henry Hilbery, 4 South Square, Gray's Inn, solicitor. b. 14th July 1883. educ. Univ. Coll. Sch. G.I. Jan. 1907 (Cert. of Hon.). KC 1928. Bencher 1927, Treasurer 1941. WWI temp. Lieut. RNVR. Member Council of Legal Educ. and Bd. of Studies; Recorder of Margate 1927-35; Commr. of Assize, South Eastern circuit 1935; KB judge 1935-62; Knight 1935; Chmn. Berkshire Quarter Sess. 1946-63; PC 1959; Chmn. govrs. Royal Masonic Hosp.; Chmn. Council of Univ. Coll. Sch. Author of Duty and Art in Advocacy 1946. d. 18th Sept. 1965.

HILDESLEY, Abraham Alfred

s. of Albert Hildesheimer, Chorlton-upon-Medlock, Manchester. b. 5th Sept. 1873. educ. Univ. Coll. Sch.; Pembroke Coll. Oxf. BA 1896, MA 1899. I.T. June 1898. KC 1929. Cty. Ct judge 1931-47; Chmn. East Suffolk Quarter Sess. 1932-47; JP East Suffolk. Author (with Judge Konstam) of Rates and Taxes. d. 31st May 1958.

HILDYARD, Gerard Moresby Thoroton

s. of Gen. Sir Henry John Thoroton Hildyard GCB (d. 1916). b. 3rd June 1874. educ. Eton; Univ. Coll. Oxf. BA 1897. L.I. June 1899 (Cert. of Hon.). KC 1920. Bencher 1924. Master in Lunacy 1923-28; Cty. Ct. judge 1928-43; Chmn. Nottinghamshire Quarter Sess. 1934-47; DL Nottinghamshire. d. 22nd April 1956.

HILDYARD, John

s. of Rev. William Hildyard, Winestead in Holderness, Yorkshire (d. 1842). b. 1796. educ. Shrewsbury (captain); St John's Coll. Camb. BA 1818, MA 1821. L.I. July 1821. Recorder of Stamford, Grantham and Leicester 1835-54; Cty. Ct. judge 1847-55. Brother of Francis Hildyard (I.T. 1838). d. 13th February 1855.

HILDYARD, Robert Charles

s. of Rev. William Hildyard, Winestead in Holderness, Yorkshire (d. 1842). b. 1800. educ. Oakham Sch.; St Catharine's Hall Camb. BA 1823, MA 1826, Fellow 1826. L.I. May 1827; I.T. 1833. QC 1845. Bencher 1844, Reader 1857. Counsel to Duchy of Lancaster 1844-46; MP Whitehaven 1847-57. Brother of Francis Hildyard (I.T. 1838). d. 7th Dec. 1857.

HILL, Alexander Staveley

s. of Henry Hill, Dunstall Hall, Stafford. b. 21st May 1825. educ. King Edward's Sch., Birmingham; Exeter Coll. Oxf. BA 1852, BCL 1854, DCL 1855; Fellow of St John's Coll. 1854-65; Hon. LLD Toronto 1892. I.T. Nov. 1851. QC 1868. Bencher 1868, Treasurer 1886. Recorder of Banbury 1866-1903; MP Coventry 1868-74, West Staffordshire 1874-85, Staffordshire (Kingswinford) 1885-1900; Dep. High Steward Oxf. Univ. 1874-1905; counsel to the Admiralty and Judge-Adv. of the Fleet 1875-1904; PC 1892; DL, JP Staffordshire. Author of Practice of Court of Probate 1859. d. 28th June 1905.

HILL, Sir Edward Maurice

s. of George Birkbeck Hill DCL, schoolmaster and editor (d. 1903). b. 8th Jan. 1862. educ. Haileybury; Balliol Coll. Oxf. BA 1884. I.T. Jan. 1888. KC 1910. Bencher 1917. Temp. Chmn. Ship Licensing Committee, Bd. of Trade 1915-17; Knight 1916; P D and A judge 1917-30. Father of Philip Maurice Hill (solicitor 1922), Secy-Genl. Intern. Chamber of Shipping. d. 6th June 1934.

HILL, Sir Hugh

s. of James Hill, Graig, Doneraile, Cork (d. 1850). b. 1802. educ. Trinity Coll. Dublin BA 1821. Spent two years at King's Inns, Dublin. Special pleader in London 1827-41. M.T. Jan. 1841. QC 1851. Bencher 1852, Reader 1856. QB judge 1858-61; Knight 1859. d. 12th Oct 1871.

HILL, Matthew Davenport

s. of Thomas Wright Hill, schoolmaster. b. 6th Aug. 1792. educ. in Wolverhampton, and at father's school in Birmingham. Asst. in that school until 1815. Ll. Nov. 1819. KC 1834. First recorder of Birmingham 1839-66; Commr. in Bankruptcy, Bristol 1851-69;

defended Nottingham rioters 1831, the Canadian prisoners 1839, Rebecca rioters 1843; leading counsel for Daniel O'Connell 1844; founded, 1827, with Bentham and Brougham, Socy. for Diffusion of Useful Knowledge; MP Hull 1832-35, and had charge of Bill for colonisation of South Australia 1834. Author of Suggestions for Repression of Crime, advocating changes in treatment of criminals, which were adopted in Penal Servitude Acts 1853 and 1864. d. 7th June 1872.

HILLS, Eustace Gilbert

s. of Herbert Augustus Hills JP, Highhead Castle, Cumberland, judge of appeal, International Cts. Egypt (d. 1907). b. 26th July 1868. educ. Eton; Balliol Coll. Oxf. BA 1891. I.T. Nov. 1894. KC 1919. Bencher 1924. Member Council of Legal Educ. 1926-29; Cty. Ct. judge 1929-34; Chmn. Cumberland Quarter Sess. 1930-33. d. 17th Oct. 1934.

HINDMARCH, William Mathewson

s. of William Hindmarch, Sunderland, brewer. b. 10th June 1803. Articled to attorney in Sunderland. G.I. Jan. 1832. QC 1862. Bencher 1862. Att-Genl. Cty. Palatine of Durham 1861; Recorder of York 1865-66. Author on subject of patents. d. Aix-la-Chapelle, 27th Aug 1866.

HOBHOUSE, Arthur (Lord Hobhouse)

s. of Rt. Hon. Henry Hobhouse, Hadspen House, Somerset, barrister, Under-Secy. for Home Dept. (d. 1854). b. 10th Nov. 1819. educ. Eton; Balliol Coll. Oxf. BA 1841, MA 1844. L.I. May 1845. QC 1862. Bencher 1862, Treasurer 1880. Acquired extensive chancery practice; Charity Commr. 1866; Commr. for reorganising Endowed Schools 1869, and for Land Transfer 1869; legal member Council of Viceroy of India 1872-77; responsible for Specific Relief Act

1877; KCSI 1877; arbitrator under Epping Forest Act 1878; member London School Bd. 1882-84; Alderman LCC 1889; PC 1881; delivered decision of Judicial Committee in 200 appeals; Baron 1885 (to enable him to sit in appeal cases in H of L). Author of The Dead Hand, a collection of addresses on endowments and settlements of property 1880. d. 6th Dec. 1904. Biog. by L.T. Hobhouse and J.L. Hammond 1905.

HODGSON, John

s. of John Hodgson, Excise Office, London. L.I. April 1812. QC 1844. Practised as conveyancer; a Commr. for Inquiry into the law of real property. d. 30th Aug. 1849, age 63.

HODSON, Francis Lord Charlton (Lord Hodson)

s. of Rev. Thomas Hodson, Oddington, Gloucestershire (d. 1915). b. 17th Sept. 1895. educ. Cheltenham Coll.; Wadham Coll. Oxf. BA 1920, MA 1938, Hon. Fellow 1939. WWI Capt. 7th Battn. Gloucesterhsire Regt., MC. I.T. June 1921. KC 1937. Bencher 1938, Treasurer 1962. Practised in divorce cases; junior counsel to Treasury (Probate) 1935; P D and A judge 1937-51; Knight 1937; LJ 1951-60; PC 1951; Pres. Br. branch of Intern. Law Assoc. 1955; L of A 1960-71; Baron 1960; member Permanent Ct. of Arbitration, The Hague; JP Oxfordshire; Cavalier of Order of Crown of Italy. Father of Charles Christopher Philip Hodson (I.T. 1947). d. 11th March 1984.

HOGG, Adam Spencer

s. of Adam Hogg, Bowdon, Cheshire. b. 1870. educ. Uppingham; Trinity Coll. Oxf BA. I.T. April 1893. Stip. magistrate, Salford 1911-13; Cty. Ct. judge 1913-37; JP Cheshire and Lancashire. d. 19th Sept 1937.

HOGG, Douglas McGarel (Lord Hailsham)

s. of Quintin Hogg, philanthropist (d. 1903). b. 28th Feb. 1872. educ.
Eton. Eight years with Hogg, Curtis and Campbell, sugar merchants.
Served with Lothian and Berwick Yeo. in South African War (medal
with 4 clasps) 1900-01. L.I. Jan. 1902 (Cert. of Hon.). KC 1917.
Bencher 1920. WWI Capt. and Group Adjt. City of London Vols.
Att-Genl. to Prince of Wales, and member of Council of Duchy of
Cornwall 1920-22; MP St. Marylebone 1922-28; Knight and PC
1922; Att-Genl. 1922-24, 1924-28; acting prime minister 1928; LC
1928-29 and 1935-38; Baron 1928; Viscount 1929; leader of
opposition in H of L 1930; Recorder of Kingston-upon-Thames
1924-28; Secy. of State for War, and leader of H of L 1931-35; Br.
delegate at Ottawa Confce. 1932, World Economic Confce. 1933;
Lord Pres. of the Council 1938; Pres. West India Committee 1943;
Col. Inns of Ct. Regt. 1935-48; JP East Sussex; Chmn. of the
Polytechnic (founded by his father); Hon. LLD Birmingham, Camb.,
Queen's Univ. Belfast; Hon. D.Litt Reading; Hon. DCL Oxf.; edited
Halsbury's Laws of England. Father of Quintin McGarel Hogg,
Baron Hailsham KG, CH, PC, QC. d. 16th Aug. 1950.

HOGGINS, Christopher Argyle

s. of Christopher John Hoggins, Stuarts Grove, Brompton, London.
b. 1793. M.T. Feb. 1830. QC 1850. Bencher 1850, Reader 1852,
Treasurer 1855. d. 19th June 1871.

HOHLER, Sir Gerald. Fitzroy

s. of Henry Booth Hohler DL, JP, Fawkham Manor, Kent (d. 1916).
b. 1862. educ. Eton; Trinity Coll. Camb. LLB 1885. I.T. Jan. 1888.
KC 1906. Bencher 1915. MP Chatham 1910-18, Rochester
(Gillingham) 1918-29; Knight 1924; JP Kent. d. 30th Jan. 1934.

HOLDSWORTH, Sir William Searle

s. of Charles Joseph Holdsworth, Elmers End, Beckenham, Kent, solicitor. b. 7th May 1871. educ. Dulwich; New Coll. Oxf. BA 1893, MA and BCL 1897, DCL 1904; Hon. Fellow, St John's Coll. 1897. L.I. Jan. 1896. KC 1920. Bencher 1924. All Souls Reader in English law 1910; Vinerian prof. in English law 1922-44; member Indian States Inquiry committee 1928, and committee on Ministers' Powers 1929-32; Reader in constitutional law and legal history at Inns of Ct. 1937-44; FBA 1922; Knight 1929; OM 1943; Hon. LLD Camb., N.W. Univ. of Chicago, S. California, Birmingham, Edinburgh, Uppsala; Hon. DL Calcutta. Author of many works including Sources and Literature of English Law 1925, Some Lessons from our Legal History 1928, Charles Dickens as Legal Historian 1928, History of English Law, 13 vols. 1903-52. d. 2nd Jan. 1944.

HOLKER, Sir John

s. of Samuel Holker, Bury, Lancashire, manufacturer. b. 24th March 1828. educ. Bury Gr. Sch. Articled to solicitor in Kirkby Lonsdale. G.I. June 1854. QC 1868. Bencher 1868, Treasurer 1875. Practised in Manchester 1854-64; distinguished himself in parliamentary committee on Stalybridge and Ashton Waterworks Bill; became specialist in patent cases; MP Preston 1872-82; Sol-Genl. and Knight 1874; Att-Genl. 1875-80; introduced Criminal Code Bill and Bankruptcy Bill; carried Summary Jurisdiction and Public Prosecution Acts 1879; LJ 1882. d. 24th May 1882.

HOLL, William Haworth

s. of William Holl, Elderslie House, Worcestershire. Special pleader. I.T. Nov. 1851. QC 1877. Bencher 1877. Cty. Ct. judge 1884-95; JP Berkshire and Buckinghamshire. d. 12th Feb. 1908, age 84.

HOLLAND, Sir Thomas Erskine

s. of Rev. Thomas Agar Holland, Poynings, Sussex (d. 1888). b. 17th July 1835. educ. Brighton Coll.; Balliol and Magdalen Colls. Oxf. BA 1858, MA 1860, BCL 1871, DCL 1876; Fellow, Exeter Coll. 1859-71; Diplomacy Fellow, All Souls Coll. 1875-1926. L.I. Jan. 1863. KC 1901. Bencher 1907. Vinerian Reader in English law 1874. Chichele prof, of intern. law 1874-1910; Assessor of Chancellor's Ct. Oxf. 1876-1910; Pres. Institut de Droit International 1913; hon. member Juristische Gesellschaft zu Berlin, and American Socy. of International law; Br. plenipotentiary at Geneva Confce. 1906; FBA 1902; Knight 1917; Knight Commander Crown of Italy, and Rising Sun of Japan; Hon. LLD Bologna, Glasgow, Dublin, Brussels. Author of legal works on many subjects, the most important being The Elements of Jurisprudence 1880 (13th Ed. 1924). d. 24th May 1926.

HOLMES, Sir Valentine

s. of Rt.Hon. Hugh Holmes, Lord Justice of Appeal, Ireland (d. 1916). b. 24th July 1888. educ. Charterhouse; Trinity Coll. Dublin. I.T. Nov. 1913. KC 1945. Bencher 1934. Junior Treasury counsel 1935-45 in common law matters; specialised in libel cases; legal consultant to Shell Oil Group 1950-56; Knight 1946. d. 19th Nov. 1956.

HOLROYD, Henry

s. of Lieut. George Chaplin Holroyd, Exeter, 29 Bengal N.I. (d. 1871). b. 14th July 1820. Special pleader 1848-53. M.T. June 1853. Reporter for Inc. Council 1865-70; Cty. Ct. judge 1880-94. d. 11th Jan. 1896.

HONYMAN, Sir George Essex, Bt.

s. of Col. Sir Ord John Honyman, 3rd. Bt., and g-s. of Sir William Honyman Bt., a Lord of Session and Justiciary. b. 22nd Jan. 1819. Articled to solicitor in London 1838-40. Special pleader 1842-49. M.T. June 1849. QC 1866. Bencher 1866, Reader 1872. Leading commercial lawyer; Judge of Common Pleas 1873-75; succeeded as 4th baronet 1863. d. 16th Sept. 1875.

HOOPER, James John

s. of Rev. James Hooper, Kingweston, Somerset. b. 7th Nov. 1823. educ. Sherborne; Wadham Coll. Oxf. BA 1847, MA 1849; Fellow of Oriel Coll. 1848-84. I.T. Nov. 1852. Counsel to PO on Western Circuit; I.T. tutor in constitutional law and legal history 1871-75; Cty. Ct. judge 1883-95; Recorder of South Molton 1877-84; JP Somerset. d. 9th Dec. 1895.

HOPE, Collingwood

s. of Thomas Arthur Hope JP, Bebington, Cheshire. b. 10th Nov. 1858. educ. Rugby; in Germany; Pembroke Coll. Oxf. 1877. I.T. June 1882. KC 1901. Member Cheshire CC 1898-1901; Recorder of Bolton 1903-25; High Steward, Borough of Southwold 1905-45; Chmn. Essex Quarter Sess. 1921-35; Chmn. Agricultural Wages Bd.; CBE 1918 for war work with Essex Territorial Assoc., Essex Mil. Appeal Trib. etc.; DL, JP Essex; FRGS. d. 5th May 1949.

HOPE-SCOTT, James Robert

s. of Gen. Sir Alexander Hope, GCB (d. 1837). b. 15th July 1812. educ. Eton; Christ Church Oxf. BA 1832, BCL 1838, DCL 1842; Fellow of Merton Coll. 1833. I.T. Jan. 1838. QC 1849. Bencher 1849, Reader 1862. Leader at parliamentary bar; standing counsel to almost every railway co.; Chan. of diocese of Salisbury 1840-45;

received into RC Church 1851; assumed name of Scott in 1853 on becoming owner of Abbotsford, Melrose. d. 29th April 1873.

HOPKIN, Daniel

s. of David Hopkin, farm labourer. b. July 1886. educ. Elem. Sch. Llantwit Major; Training Coll. Carmarthen; St. Catherine's Coll. Camb. LLB, MA. Schoolmaster. WWI Major, City of London Regt, MC; four years in business in Cairo. G.I. July 1924. MP Carmarthen 1929-31, and 1935-41; rejoined army 1939; metrop. magistrate 1941, finally at Marlborough St. to 1951. d. 30th Aug. 1951.

HOPKINS, Arthur Antwis

s. of John Satchell Hopkins JP, Edgbaston, Birmingham, tin plate worker and japanner (d. 1898). b. 2nd June 1855. educ. Rugby; Trinity Coll. Camb. BA 1877, MA 1880; rugby blue. I.T. Jan. 1879. Reporter for Law Times in Ct. of Appeal; metrop. magistrate 1890, finally at Bow St. 1913-16; JP Middlesex and Home Counties. d. 6th July 1916.

HOPKINSON, Sir Alfred

s. of John Hopkinson, Manchester, mechanical engineer. b. 28th June 1851. educ. Owen's Coll. Manchester; Lincoln Coll. Oxf. BA 1872, Hon. Fellow 1903; University Coll. Oxf. BCL and MA 1876, Stowell Fellow 1873-80. L.I. June 1873. QC 1892. Bencher 1896, Treasurer 1921. Prof. of Law, Owen's Coll. 1875-89, Principal 1898-1904; V-C Manchester Univ. 1900-13; MP Cricklade 1895-98, Combined English Univs. 1926-29; Knight 1910. d. 11th Nov. 1939.

HOPWOOD, Charles Henry

s. of John Stephen Spindler Hopwood, London, solicitor. b. 20th

July 1829. educ. King's Coll. Sch.; King's Coll. London. M.T. June 1853. QC 1874. Bencher 1876, Reader 1886, Treasurer 1895. Recorder of Liverpool 1886-1904; MP Stockport 1874-85, South East Lancashire (Middleton) 1892-95; member Council of Legal Educ.; founded Romilly Socy. 1897. Joint author of Registration cases 1863-67, and 1868-72. Edited Middle Temple Records 1904. d. 14th Oct 1904.

HORNE, Sir William

s. of Rev. Thomas Horne, Chiswick. b. 1774. L.I. June 1798. KC 1818. Bencher 1818. Commr.. in bankruptcy 1806-18; Att-Genl. to Queen Adelaide 1830; Sol-Genl. 1830-32, Att. Genl. 1832-34; declined appointment as Exch. Baron, 1834; Chancery Master 1839-53. Knight 1830. MP Helston 1812-18, Bletchingley 1831, Newton, Isle of Wight 1831-32, Marylebone 1832-34. d. 13th July 1860.

HORRIDGE, Sir Thomas Gardner

s. of John Horridge, Bolton, Lancashire, bleacher. b. 12th Oct. 1857. educ. privately and Nassau Sch. Barnes. Solicitor 1879. M.T. June 1884. KC 1901. Bencher 1909, Reader 1921, Treasurer 1929. Practised initially in Liverpool; member of bar council; MP East Manchester 1906-10; KB judge 1910-37; Knight 1910; judge in bankruptcy 1913-21; PC 1937. d. 25th July 1938.

HORTON-SMITH, Richard Horton

s. of Richard Smith, Littlehampton, merchant. b. 4th Dec. 1831. educ. Univ. Coll. Sch.; University Coll. London; St John's Coll. Camb. BA 1856, MA 1859, Fellow 1859-64. Lecturer on classical literature, King's Coll. London 1857-59. L.I. Jan. 1859. QC 1877. Bencher 1881. Lecturer on conveyancing to Inc. Law Socy. 1865-67; official reporter in cts. of LC and LJs 1862-65. Edited chancery reports (with De Gex, and Jones). d. 2nd Nov. 1919.

HOSACK, John

s. of John R. Hosack, Glenaher, Dumfriesshire. b. 1809. M.T. Jan. 1841. Bencher 1875, Reader 1884. I.T. examr. in intern. and constitutional law; metrop. magistrate, Clerkenwell 1877-87. Author of manual on conflict of English and Scottish law. d. 3rd. Nov. 1887.

HOUGHTON, George Boydell

s. of Boydell Houghton, Handsworth, Staffordshire. b. 1842. educ. St Alban Hall, Oxf. 1875. Previously an accountant. I.T. Jan. 1878. KC 1919. Bencher 1897. Junior counsel to Dept. of Woods and Forests; a well-known arbitrator. d. 16th Jan. 1920.

HOULDSWORTH, Sir Hubert Stanley, Bt.

s. of Albert Edward Houldsworth, Heckmondwike, Yorkshire (d. 1896). b. 20th April 1889. educ. Heckmondwike Gr. Sch.; Leeds Univ. BSc 1911, MSc 1912, DSc 1925; asst. lecturer at the univ. 1919-26. L.I. Nov. 1926 (Cert of Hon.). KC 1937. Bencher 1943. Recorder of Doncaster 1946-48; Chmn. Midlands Coal-Selling Control Committee 1936-42; Regional Controller (Min. of Fuel and Power) South and West Yorkshire 1942-44; Controller-Genl. Min. of Fuel and Power 1944-45; Chmn. East Midland Div. Nat. Coal Bd. 1946-51; Chmn. NCB 1951-56; Dep. Chmn. Yorkshire West Riding Quarter Sess.; Knight 1944; Baronet 1956; Pro-Chancellor Leeds Univ. 1949-56; Hon. LLD Leeds and Nottingham. d. 1st Feb. 1956.

HOWARD, John Morgan

s. of John J. Howard, Swansea, solicitor. M.T. April 1858. QC 1874. Bencher 1877, Reader 1887. An editor of the New Reports 1862-65; Chief Commr. on Norwich Royal Comm. 1875; Recorder of Guildford 1875-91; MP Camberwell (Dulwich) 1885-87; Cty. Ct. judge 1887-91; JP Middlesex and Cornwall. Author of treatise on law of sheriffs. d. 10th April 1891, age 55.

HOWARD, William Reginald

s. of John Howard JP, Bootle, Lancashire. b. 10th June 1879. educ. Bootle Coll.; King's Sch. Chester; Liverpool Univ. Joined family business, Howard Bros. Liverpool and London 1899; director Dey Time Registers Ltd. 1908. M.T. Jan. 1911. WWI Capt. King's (6th) Liverpool Regt. Stip. magistrate East Ham 1935-39; metrop. magistrate, Greenwich and Woolwich 1939-49; JP Surrey. d. 17th Feb. 1966.

HUDDLESTON, Sir John Walter

s. of Thomas Huddleston, captain in merchant service. b. Dublin, 8th Sept 1815. educ. Trinity Coll. Dublin 1835. Schoolmaster in England. G.I. May 1839. QC 1857. Bencher 1857, Treasurer 1859 and 1868. MP Canterbury 1865-68, Norwich 1874-75; counsel to Admiralty and Judge-Adv. of the Fleet 1865-75; had substantial criminal practice; Judge of Common Pleas 1875; Exch. Baron 1875; Knight 1875; created last Exch. Baron; QB judge 1881-90; tried libel action between the sculptors Belt and Lawes 1881-82 (took 43 days and was the last case to be heard in Westminster Hall); represented bar at funeral of Antoine Berryer, and afterwards entertained by French bar in Paris, 1868. d. 5th Dec. 1890.

HUDSON, Alfred Arthur

s. of Henry Hudson, Winchester, merchant. b. 1852. educ. privately, and in Switzerland. I.T. Jan. 1885. KC 1910. Bencher 1919. Pres. Appeal Trib. under London Building Acts 1894-1908; Chmn. South Derbyshire Coal Mines Conciliation Bd. 1912; Commr. under Boiler Explosions Acts 1882 and 1890. Author of works on building and engineering contracts, and compensation. d. 21st Aug. 1930.

HUGHES, Hector Samuel James

s. of Alexander Wilson Hughes, Dublin. b. 1887. educ. Diocesan Sch. Dublin; St. Andrews Coll.; Dublin Univ. Employed with solicitors, and as a civil servant. Irish bar 1915; KC 1927. G.I. June 1923; M.T. 1932. KC 1932. Member of Ghana bar; a founder member of Irish Socialist party 1918; member Nat. Union of General and Municipal Workers, and Union of Seamen; MP Aberdeen (North) 1945-70; member parliamentary delegations to Canada 1952, Nigeria, Malta, and Gibraltar 1957. Author of works on Registration of Title, landlord and tenant, the law relating to road users, and other topics. d. 23rd June 1970 (after being rescued from the sea at Brighton).

HUGHES, Ronw Moelwyn

s. of Rev. Dr. John Gruffydd Moelwyn Hughes, Moderator of Welsh Presbyterian Church. b. 6th Oct 1897. educ. Cardigan Council and Cty. Schs.; University Coll. of Wales BA; Downing Coll. Camb. BA, LLB. WWI 2nd Lieut. Yorkshire Regt, RFC and RAF. I.T. May 1922. KC 1943. Bencher 1950. Lecturer in intern. law at LSE, in commercial law at Law Socy.; examr. to Council of Legal Educ. and London Univ.; Recorder of Bolton 1946-53; MP Carmarthen 1941-45, Islington North 1950-51; Commr. of Inquiry into Bolton football disaster 1946; Chmn. Greater London Water Inquiry 1947; Chmn. Cotton Manufacturing Comm. 1946-49, Catering Wages Comm. 1946-50; member Socy. of Labour Lawyers, Fabian Socy. and Socy. of Public Teachers of Law. d. lst Nov. 1955.

HUGHES, Thomas

s. of John Hughes, Donington Priory, Newbury, author. b. 19th Oct. 1822. educ. Rugby; Oriel Coll. Oxf. BA 1845. I.T. Jan. 1848. QC 1869. Bencher 1870. MP Lambeth 1865-68, Frome 1868-74; Cty. Ct. judge 1882-96; JP Cheshire; FSA; Hon. Col. 19th Middx. Rifle Vol. 1869-77. The author of "Tom Brown's Schooldays" 1857. d. 22nd March 1896.

HUGHES, Sir Thomas Raffles

s. of Edward Hughes, Huyton Hall, Lancashire. b. 28th Jan. 1856. educ. Birkenhead Sch.; Trinity Coll. Camb. BA 1878, MA 1881. L.I. June 1880. QC 1898. Bencher 1905, Treasurer 1928. Chmn. of bar council 1920-31; Knight 1926; JP Surrey. d. 24th Oct 1938.

HUGHES, William Morris

s. of William Hughes, carpenter. b. 25th Sept. 1862. educ. Llandudno Gr. Sch.; St Stephen's C of E Sch., Westminster. Emigrated to Australia 1884. New South Wales bar 1903. Secy. Sydney Wharf Labourers' Union 1899-1915; member New South Wales parliament 1894-1901; member of Federal House of Representatives 1901-52; Min. for External Affairs 1904; Att-Genl. 1908-09, 1910-13, and 1914-15; Prime Minister 1915-23; joined United Australia party 1931, leader 1941-43; Min. for Industry 1939-40; Att-Genl. 1939-41; Min. for the Navy 1940-41. G.I. July 1919. KC 1919. Hon. Bencher. Freeman, City of London; PC 1916; CH 1941; Grand Officier de la Legion d'Honneur; Order of Grand Crown, Belgium; Hon. LLD Edin., Glasgow, Birmingham, Cardiff, Hon. DCL Oxf. d. 28th Oct. 1952.

HULTON, William Adam

s. of Lt. Col. Henry Hulton, Preston (d. 1831). b. 18th Oct. 1802. educ. Manchester Gr. Sch. I.T. June 1827. Assessor of Lancaster Sheriff's Ct. to 1847; Cty. Ct. judge 1847-86; Treasurer of Lancaster Cty. 1831-49; DL, JP Lancashire. Author of On the Law of Convictions, with the Statutes and Forms applicable to summary convictions by justices of the peace 1835.
d. 3rd March 1887.

HUME-WILLIAMS, Sir William Ellis, Bt.

s. of Joseph Williams Hume-Williams, barrister. b. 19th Aug. 1863.

educ. in France and Germany, Trinity Hall Camb. BA, LLB 1881. M.T. June 1881. QC 1899. Bencher 1906, Reader 1918, Treasurer 1928. Recorder of Bury St. Edmunds 1901-05, of Norwich 1905-44; MP Nottinghamshire (Bassetlaw) 1910-29; WWI in Flanders with Munro Ambulance Corps, and in Russia with Red Cross; member of Central Prisoners of War Committee; liaison officer between War Trade Dept. and Comm. Internationale de Ravitaillement; KBE 1918; PC 1929; Baronet 1922; KStJ. Author of The taking of Evidence on Commission; The World, The House, and the Bar 1930; edited Taylor on Evidence (10th Ed.). d. 4th Feb. 1947.

HUMFREY, Lebbeus Charles

s. of Rev. Lebbeus Charles Humfrey, Laughton, Leicestershire (d. 1833). b. 5th Jan. 1798. educ. Christ's Hospital; Trinity Coll. Camb. BA 1820, MA 1823. L.I. June 1823. QC 1845. Bencher 1845. Leader of Midland circuit; counsel to Times newspaper. d. 11th May 1852.

HUMPHREYS, Sir Richard Somers Travers Christmas

s. of Charles Octavius Humphreys, London, solicitor. b. 4th Aug. 1867. educ. Shrewsbury; Trinity Hall Camb. BA 1888, Hon. Fellow. I.T. Nov. 1889. Bencher 1922. Junior Crown counsel at Middlesex and North London Sess. 1905, at Central Criminal Ct. 1908; senior Crown counsel at Central Criminal Ct. 1916-28; Recorder of Chichester 1921-26, of Cambridge 1926-28; appeared in trials of H.H. Crippen, F.H. Seddon, G.J. Smith, Sir R. Casement, and Horatio Bottomley; Knight 1925; KB judge 1928-51; presided at trials of Mrs. E. Barney 1932, Mrs. Rattenbury and George Stoner 1935, J.G. Haig 1949; PC 1946; Médaille du Roi Albert (Belgium). Published Criminal Days 1946, A Book of Trials 1953. Father of Travers Christmas Humphreys QC, addl. judge at Central Criminal Ct. 1968-76. d. 20th Feb. 1956. Biogs. by Bechhofer Roberts 1936, Stanley Jackson 1952, Douglas G. Browne 1960.

HUMPHRY, Joseph

s. of Joseph Humphry, Red House, Sudbury, Suffolk. L.I. July 1821. QC 1846. Master in Chancery 1850-60. d. 18th Nov. 1861, age 66.

HUNTER, Trevor Havard

s. of William Havard Hunter, Briton Ferry House, Glamorganshire. b. 1877. educ. Wilson's Gr. Sch. Clerkenwell. Solicitor 1899. M.T. Nov. 1911 (Cert. of Hon.). KC 1928. Bencher 1936. WWI Lieut. Royal Welch Fusiliers, and Courts-Martial officer. Chan. diocese of Swansea and Brecon 1929-53; Cty. Ct. judge 1939-50. d. 9th May 1960.

HURST, Sir Cecil James Barrington

s. of Robert Henry Hurst MP, Horsham Park, Sussex and Barrington Grove, Gloucestershire, barrister (d. 1905). b. 28th Oct 1870. educ. Westminster; Trinity Coll. Camb. LLB 1892, LLM 1896, Hon. LLD Camb. and Edin. M.T. Nov. 1893. KC 1913. Bencher 1922, Reader 1931, Treasurer 1940. Junior counsel to PO on South East Circuit 1901-02; Asst. legal adviser to Foreign Office 1902-18, legal adviser 1918-29; Br. agent for Pecuniary Claims Arbitration at Washington 1913; judge of permanent Ct. of International Justice at The Hague 1929-45, pres. 1934-36; Member Hague Permanent Ct. of Arbitration 1929-50; Chmn. UN War Crimes Comm. 1943-45; CB 1907; KCB 1920; KCMG 1924; GCMG 1926; JP Sussex. Father of Col. Richard Lumley Hurst (M.T. 1928). d. 27th March 1963.

HURST, Sir Gerald Berkeley

s. of William Martin Hertz, Bradford and Manchester (d. 1912). b. 4th Dec. 1877. educ. Bradford Gr. Sch.; Lincoln Coll. Oxf. BA 1898, MA 1902, BCL 1904. L.I. April 1902. WWI Lt.Col. commdg. 7th Battn. Manchester Regt. Equity draftsman and conveyancer; MP Manchester (Moss Side) 1918-23 and 1924-35. KC 1920. Bencher 1924, Treasurer

1944. Cty. Ct. judge 1937-52; Divorce Commr. 1947-55; Chmn. Home Office committee on adoption 1953; Knight 1929; JP Kent; TD. Author of Closed Chapters 1942, A Short History of Lincoln's Inn 1946, Lincoln's Inn Essays 1949. d. 27th Oct. 1957.

HURST, Sir James Henry Donald

s. of John Gibbard Hurst, KC. b. 1895. educ. King Edward's Sch. Birmingham; Wadham Coll. Oxf. WWI Lieut. Argyll and Sutherland Highlanders. M.T. Nov. 1920. Cty. Ct. judge 1937-62; Chmn. Oxfordshire Quarter Sess. 1944-62; Knight 1954; JP Warwickshire. d. 21st June 1980.

HURST, John Gibbard

s. of Henry Hurst, Birmingham. b. 1865. educ. in Birmingham. Solicitor 1891, practised in Birmingham. M.T. May 1903. KC 1919. Bencher 1926. Recorder of Warwick 1916-31, of Birmingham 1931. d. 30th Nov. 1931.

HUTCHINSON, Christopher Clarke

s. of William Hutchinson, Burnside, Westmoreland. b. 1854. educ. Royal Coll. of Science, Dublin. Practised as engineer and chemical engineer in GB and USA. M.T. Jan. 1896. KC 1910. Parliamentary draftsman; JP Essex; MICE; FIC; FCS. d. 7th March 1914.

HUTCHINSON, Geoffrey Clegg (Lord Ilford)

s. of Henry Ormerod Hutchinson VD, JP, Elderslie, Prestwich, Lancashire (d. 1912). b. 14th Oct 1893. educ. Cheltenham Coll.; Clare Coll. Camb. MA 1919. WWI Major Lancashire Fusiliers, MC. I.T. Nov. 1920. KC 1939. Bencher 1946. WWII with BEF, and Dep. Asst. Mil. Secy. War Office 1941-42. MP Ilford 1937-45, Ilford (North) 1950-53;

Alderman LCC 1945, Pres. Br. Waterworks Assoc. 1947, Assoc. of Municipal Corporations 1944-54; member Select Committee on Nat. Expenditure 1942-45; Hon. Col. 5th Battn. Lancashire Fusiliers 1948-54; Chmn. East Surrey Water Co. 1952-54; Chmn. Nat. Assistance Bd. 1953-64; Chmn. Church Assembly Comm. on pastoral legislation 1955; TD 1939; Hon. Freeman Ilford 1954; Knight 1952; Baron 1962. d. 20th Aug. 1974.

HUTCHINSON, St. John

s. of Sir Charles Hutchinson MP, Mayfield, Sussex (d. 1907). b. 8th April 1884. educ. Elstree Sch.; Winchester; Magdalen Coll. Oxf. BA. M.T. May 1909. KC 1935. Member LCC (Poplar) 1912-16; asst. legal adviser to Min. of Reconstruction 1917; pros. counsel to PO at Central Criminal Ct. 1931-35; Recorder of Hythe 1928-30, of Hastings 1930-42. Father of Jeremy Nicolas Hutchinson, Baron Hutchinson of Lullington (QC 1961). d. 24th Oct. 1942.

HUTTON, Arthur Edward Hill

s. of John Hutton Hill Hutton, Houghton Hall, Durham. b. 17th March 1859. M.T. Nov. 1882. MP Yorkshire West Riding (Morley); metrop. magistrate Greenwich and Woolwich 1906-15; JP London and Home Counties. d. 12th Jan. 1922.

HUTTON, Crompton

s. of Robert O. Hutton, MP, Putney Park, Roehampton, Surrey (d. 1870). b. 5th Dec. 1822. educ. Rugby; Trinity Coll. Camb. BA 1846. I.T. June 1853. Junior counsel to IR; Cty. Ct. judge 1872-89; JP Lancashire and Gloucestershire. Father of Stamford Hutton OBE, JP (I.T. 1891), Chmn. Gloucestershire Quarter Sess. d. 5th Jan. 1910.

IDELSON, Vladimir Robert

s. of Robert Idelson, Taganrog, Russia. b. Russia, 1881. educ. Taganrog Classical Gymnasium; Kharkov Univ. (1st class law degree); Berlin Univ. DPhil., MCL. Russian bar 1906; practised there until 1918; Dozent, Imperial Polytechnic Inst. until 1918; member Council of Russian and English Bank, and committee of Union of Russian Banks 1914-17; with Russian Treasury 1917; practised in London as expert on Russian and Intern. Law 1919-26. G.I. June 1926. KC 1943. Bencher (L.I.) 1947. Member executive councils of Grotius Socy. and Socy. of Comparative Legislation; member Law Advisory Committee of Br. Council. Author of Contract of Insurance in Russian Law 1903 (in Russian), Taxation of Insurance 1905 (in German). d. 29th Nov. 1954.

INCE, Henry Bret

s. of Edward Bret Ince, publisher of the Law Journal (d. 1882). b. 1830. In business related to shipping; a leader writer with the Daily News. I.T. Jun. 1855; L.I. Nov. 1859. QC 1875. Bencher 1878. Reported for "The Jurist" in ct. of Wood V-C.; member of bar committee 1883; MP Hastings 1883-85, Islington (East) 1885-86. d. 7th May 1889.

INDERWICK, Frederic Andrew

s. of Capt. Andrew Inderwick RN, Brompton, London. b. 23rd April 1836. educ. privately; Trinity Coll. Camb. 1853. I.T. Jan. 1858. QC 1874. Bencher 1877, Treasurer 1898. Commr. in Lunacy 1903-04; MP Rye 1880-85; Mayor of Winchelsea 1892-93, 1902-03; DL, JP Sussex. FSA 1894. Author of The Law of Wills 1866, The King's Peace 1895; edited Inner Temple Records 1896-1901. Father of Walter Andrew Inderwick (I.T. 1894), senior probate registrar. d. 16th Aug, 1904.

INGHAM, Sir James Taylor

s. of Joshua Ingham, Blake Hall, Yorkshire (d. 1816). b. 17th Jan. 1805.

educ. Trinity Coll. Camb. BA 1829, MA 1832. I.T. June 1832. Metrop. magistrate 1849, finally at Bow St. 1876-90; chief magistrate and knighted 1876; JP. d. 5th March 1890.

INGHAM, Robert

s. of William Ingham, Newcastle-on-Tyne, surgeon. b. 1793. educ. Harrow; Oriel Coll. Oxf. BA 1815, MA 1818, Fellow 1816-26. L.I. June 1820; I.T. 1825. QC 1851. Bencher 1850, Reader 1862, Treasurer 1863. MP South Shields 1832-41 and 1852-68; Recorder of Berwick-on-Tweed 1832-70; Att-Genl. Cty. Palatine of Durham 1846-61. d. 21st Oct. 1875.

INGHAM, Robert Wood

s. of Sir James Taylor Ingham, metrop. magistrate. b. 1846. educ. Rugby; Corpus Christi Coll. Oxf. BA 1869. I.T. June 1873. Cty. Ct. judge 1892-1928; DL, JP Herefordshire. d. 10th Jan. 1928.

INGHAM, Theophilus Hastings

s. of Ignatius Ingham, East Marton, nr. Skipton, Yorkshire. b. 15th July 1808. educ. privately. I.T. May 1834. Commr. in Bankruptcy; judge of Burnley Ct. of Requests 1842-46; Recorder of Clitheroe 1859-91; Cty. Ct. judge 1847-91; Chmn. Yorkshire West Riding Quarter Sess; DL, JP Yorkshire West Riding; JP Cumberland, Westmorland and Lancashire. d. 5th Jan. 1900.

INGPEN, Arthur Robert

s. of Robert Frederick Ingpen, Chancery Lane, London. b. 1857. educ. in France; Univ. Coll. Sch.; London Univ. LLB 1882. M.T. Nov. 1879; L.I. 1893. QC 1900. Bencher (M.T.) 1907. Member Convocation London Univ. Author of treatise on executors and administrators, and joint editor of Williams thereon; joint editor of Seton on judgments and orders; editor of Master Worsley's Book on the Middle Temple, and of Middle Temple Bench Book (1st Ed.). d. 5th Sept. 1917.

INMAN, Arnold

s. of Thomas Frederic Inman, Bath. b. 3rd Nov. 1867. educ. Clifton Coll.; Magdalen Coll. Oxf. BA 1890. I.T. Nov. 1892. KC 1931. WWI Commander X Divn. Metrop. Special Constabulary; OBE 1920. Pres. appeal trib. under London Building Acts 1930-40. Joint editor of Hudson on Building Contracts. d. 26th Feb. 1951.

INSKIP, Thomas Walker Hobart (Lord Caldecote)

s. of James Inskip, Clifton Park House, Bristol, solicitor. b. 5th March 1876. educ. Clifton Coll.; King's Coll. Camb. BA 1897, MA. I.T. April 1899. KC 1914. Bencher, Treasurer 1943. Recorder of Kingston-upon-Thames 1928-39. Naval Intelligence Divn., Admiralty 1915-18; Head of Naval Law Branch, Admiralty 1918; Admiralty rep. on War Crimes Committee; CBE 1920. MP Central Bristol 1918-29, Fareham 1931-39; Sol-Genl. 1922-24, 1924-28, 1931-32; Knight 1922; Att-Genl. 1928-29, 1932-36; Minister for Coordination of Defence 1936-39; obt.ained transfer of naval aircraft from Air Force to Navy as Fleet Air Arm; Secy. of State for Dominion Affairs 1939, 1940; LC 1939-40; Leader of H of L 1940; LCJ 1940-46; Chan. of diocese of Truro 1920-22; Chmn. Council of Legal Educ. 1942-47; PC 1932; Viscount 1939; JP Wigtownshire; Hon. LLD Bristol 1933. Brother of Sir John Hampden Inskip (1879-1960), solicitor. d. 11th Oct 1947.

ISAACS, Gerald Rufus (Lord Reading)

s. of 1st Marquess of Reading. b. 10th Jan. 1889. educ. Rugby; Balliol Coll. Oxf BA 1911. M.T. June 1912. KC 1929. Bencher 1936, Treasurer 1958. WWI Capt. Royal Fusiliers, and on staff, MC, Croix de Guerre, (despatches); DAAG 1918; Lieut.Col. commdg. Inns of Ct.

237

OTC (TA) 1923-25; Lieut.Col. Pioneer Corps 1939-41; Col. on staff 1941-43; Brig., Director of Labour HQ, 21st Army Group 1943-44; Hon. Col. Inns of Ct. Regt. 1947-59. Chmn. Central Valuation Bd. under Coal Act 1938; Chmn. Departmental Committee on London Govt. 1945-46; Parl. Under-Secy. of State for Foreign Affairs 1951-53; Minister of State for Foreign Affairs 1953-57; Chmn. Council on Tribunals 1958; DL London; KStJ; CBE 1945; TD 1945; PC 1953; KCMG 1957; GCMG 1958; succeeded father as 2nd Marquess 1935. Published The South Sea Bubble 1933, and biography of father, 2 vols. 1943-45. d. 19th Sept 1960.

ISAACS, Rufus Daniel (Lord Reading)

s. of Joseph Michael Isaacs, Belsize Park, London, fruit merchant. b. 10th Oct 1860. educ. Univ. Coll. Sch. London; Brussels, and Hanover. Entered family business at 15; ship's boy on Blair Atholl 1876-77; jobber on Stock Exchange 1880-84. M.T. Nov. 1887. QC 1898. Bencher 1905, Reader 1917, Treasurer 1927. Notably successful in Taff Vale litigation (trade unions) 1902, and prosecution of Whittaker Wright (financier) 1904; MP Reading 1904-13; Sol-Genl. 1910; Knight 1910; Att-Genl. 1910-13; secured conviction of Seddon (murderer) 1912; PC and KCVO 1911; member Cabinet 1912; LCJ 1913-21; Baron 1914; Pres. Anglo-French Loan Mission to USA 1915; Viscount 1916; Special Envoy to USA 1917; High Commr. for Finance in USA and Canada 1917; Earl 1917; Ambassador and High Commr. in USA 1918-19; Viceroy of India 1921-26; supervised early application of Montagu-Chelmsford reforms; Marquess of Reading 1926; Foreign Secy. 1931; Capt. of Deal Castle 1926; Lord Warden of Cinque Ports 1934-35; Pres. Imperial Chemical Industries; FRCI 1921; GCB 1915; GCSI and GCIE 1921; GCVO 1922; Hon. LLD Toronto, Harvard, Yale, Princeton, Columbia. d. 30th Dec. 1935. Biog. by 2nd Marquess 1943-45.

JACKSON, Frank Stather

s. of John Harding Jackson, Bemerton, Salisbury. b. Nov 1853. educ.

Sherborne. Solicitor 1875. M.T. June 1884. Registrar of Mayor's Ct. 1890; Asst. judge Mayor's Ct. 1900-21; judge of Mayor's and City of London Ct. 1921-22. Author (with L. Glyn KC) of Mayor's Court Practice. d. 17th Oct 1922.

JACKSON, Sir Henry Mather, Bt.

s. of Sir William Jackson MP, 1st Bt. b. 23rd July 1831. educ. Harrow; Trinity Coll. Oxf. BA 1853, MA 1859. L.I. Nov. 1855. QC 1873. Bencher 1875. Leader in Palatine Ct. of Lancaster; MP Coventry 1867-68, and 1874-81; practised in V-C Bacon's Ct. 1873-81; QB judge 2nd March 1881, but died before taking seat; succeeded father 1876. d. 8th March 1881.

JACKSON, Joseph Cooksey

s. of George Jackson, Westwood, Lancashire. b. 1879. educ. Royal Gr. Sch. Lancaster; Clare Coll. Camb. BA 1900. M.T. May 1909. KC 1924. Bencher 1929. Recorder of Bolton 1925-38; MP Lancashire (Heywood and Radcliffe) 1931-35. d. 26th April 1938.

JACKSON, Lawrence Colville

s. of Sir Charles Jackson, judge of High Ct, Calcutta (d. 1874). b. 1851. educ. privately and abroad. Solicitor 1875. L.I. May 1879. QC 1896. Examr. to High Ct; judicial commr. Federated Malay States 1896. d. 29th Jan. 1905.

JAMES, Abraham Thomas

s. of Evan James, New Quay, Cardiganshire, master mariner. b. 27th April 1883. Solicitor in Pontypridd 1904-11. M.T. June 1911 (Cert. of Hon.). KC 1928. WWI Capt. Royal Welch Fusiliers. Chmn. Cardiganshire Quarter Sess. 1929-40; Chmn. South Wales Traffic

Commrs. 1931-40; JP Cardiganshire. d. 13th Dec. 1940.

JAMES, Sir Arthur Gwynne Gwynne-

s. of John Gwynne James, Hereford, solicitor, and nephew of Lord James of Hereford. b. 10th April 1855. educ. Cheltenham Coll.; Trinity Coll. Camb. LLB 1878. M.T. Jan. 1881. Recorder of Hereford 1894-1935; Cty. Ct judge 1900-35. Knight 1935; JP Somerset, Gloucestershire, and Wiltshire. d. 17th March 1936.

JAMES, Charles Ashworth

s. of John Henry James, Watford, solicitor. b. 9th Jan. 1859. educ. Rugby (captain); Balliol Coll. Oxf. BA 1881; Fellow, Hertford Coll. 1881-92. L.I. June 1884. KC 1926. Bencher. Equity draftsman and conveyancer. d. 12th March 1937.

JAMES, Edward

s. of Frederick William James, Manchester, merchant b. 1807. educ. Brasenose Coll. Oxf. BA 1831, MA 1834. Employed commercially in Manchester for two years. L.I. June 1835. QC 1853. Bencher 1853. Leader of Northern circuit; Assessor of Liverpool Ct. of Passage 1852-67; Att-Genl. and Queen's serjeant of Cty. Palatine of Lancaster 1863-67; MP Manchester 1865-67. d. Paris, 3rd Nov. 1867.

JAMES, Edwin John

s. of John James, London, attorney. b. 1812. educ. privately. I.T. Jan. 1836. QC 1850. Recorder of Brighton 1855-61; MP Marylebone 1859-61; bankrupt and disbarred for unprofessional conduct 1861; practised law in New York, and played on American stage 1861-72; returned to England 1872; engaged in cases of Palmer (poisoning)

1856, and Anderson (runaway slave) 1861. Author of Bankruptcy Law of United States 1867. d. 4th March 1882.

JAMES, Henry (Lord James)

s. of Philip Turner James, Hereford, surgeon. b. 30th Oct 1828. educ. Cheltenham Coll. (first boy on the roll). M.T. Jan. 1852. QC 1869. Bencher 1870, Reader 1876, Treasurer 1887. Postman in Ct.of Exch. 1867-69; MP Taunton 1869-85, Bury 1885-95; Sol-Genl. and knighted 1873; Att-Genl. 1873, and 1880-85; drafted and carried Corrupt Practices Bill 1883; PC 1885; opposed Gladstone's Irish policy; appeared for The Times before Parnell Comm. 1888; Att-Genl. to Prince of Wales 1892-95; Chan. of Duchy of Lancaster 1895-1902; Baron James of Hereford 1895; member Judicial Committee of Privy Council 1896; Chmn. Coal Conciliation Bd. 1898-1909; GCVO 1902; declined Lord Chancellorship 1886; Hon. LLD Camb. 1892; member Council of Cheltenham Coll. d. 18th Aug. 1911. Biog. by Lord Askwith 1930.

JAMES, Richard Bush

s. of Alfred B. James, North Petherton, Somerset. b. 27th Sept 1889. educ. Harrow; Christ Church Oxf. BA 1911. WWI Capt. Royal Horse Guards (despatches). I.T. Nov. 1919. KC 1939. Bencher 1946. d. 20th June 1970.

JAMES, Sir William Milbourne

s. of Christopher James, Swansea. b. 29th June 1807. educ. Glasgow Univ. MA 1828, Hon. LLD 1873. L.I. June 1831. QC 1853. Bencher 1853, Treasurer 1873. Junior equity counsel to Treasury; counsel to Dept. of Woods and Forests, IR, and Bd. of Works; secured reinstatement of Colenso, Bishop of Natal, after he had been excommunicated by Bishop of Capetown 1864; leading counsel for plaintiff in Lyon v. Home (widow inveigled by spiritualist into parting with property) 1868; served on Indian Code comm., Abolition of Purchase in Army Comm., and Judicature Comm.; V-C Cty. Palatine of Lancaster 1853-69; V-C 1869-70; Knight 1869; LJ 1870-81; PC 1870; the perfect colleague for Mellish LJ in the Ct. of Appeal; arbitrator in matter of European Assce. Socy. 1875. Author of The British in India 1882. d. 7th June 1881.

JARDINE, David

s. of Rev. David B. Jardine, unitarian minister. b. 1792. M.T. Feb. 1823. One of the twenty municipal corp. commrs. for England and Wales 1833-35; Recorder of Bath 1837-60; metrop. magistrate, Bow St. 1839-60. Author of a General Index to Howell's State Trials 1828, and A Narrative of the Gunpowder Plot 1857. d. 13th Sept 1860.

JARDINE, James

s. of William Jardine MP, Dunstable Park, Bedfordshire. b. 6th June 1846. educ. Dunstable Sch.; Caius Coll. Camb. BA 1867, 8th Wrangler, MA 1870, Fellow. I.T. Jan. 1871. QC 1894. Bencher. Terry prof. of jurisprudence, Bombay Univ. 1877-84; Dean of Faculty, Bombay Univ. 1893. d. St. Moritz, 6th Jan. 1909.

JARDINE, James Willoughby

s. of James Jardine KC. b. 29th Oct 1879. educ. Eton; King's Coll Camb. BA 1902, LLB 1903, MA 1907. I.T. June 1904 (Cert. of Hon.). KC 1927. Bencher 1935. WWI Major, RAF. Recorder of Halifax 1923-31, of Newcastle-on-Tyne 1931-32, of Leeds 1932-40; Sol-Genl. Cty. Palatine of Durham 1932-39, Att-Genl. 1939-40; Cty. Ct. judge 1940-45. d. 15th Oct 1945.

JEEVES, William, John

s. of William Jeeves, Hitchin, Hertfordshire. b. 20th Dec. 1864. educ. privately. Solicitor 1886. Town Clerk of St Helen's, Lancs. 1891-99, of Leeds 1899-1903. L.I. Nov. 1903. KC 1920. Bencher 1926. Parliamentary draftsman; assoc. member Surveyors' Inst; CBE 1920 for war work with Red Cross and Order of St. John; Hon. Organiser of Searching for information in all provincial hospitals in GB and Ireland. d. 15th Dec. 1932.

JELF, Sir Arthur Richard

s. of Rev. Richard William Jelf DD, canon of Christ Church, Oxford (d. 1871). b. Pankow, nr. Berlin, 1837. educ. Eton; Christ Church Oxf. BA 1860, MA 1863. I.T. April 1863. QC 1880. Bencher 1885. Recorder of Shrewsbury 1879-1901; KB judge 1901-10; Knight 1901. d. 24th July 1917.

JENKINS, Charles Elliott Edward

s. of Charles Jenkins, Indian Civil Service, Dacca. b. 1859. educ. Lancing; Lincoln Coll. Oxf. BA 1883. L.I. Nov. 1885. QC 1897. Bencher 1904, Treasurer 1927. d. 23rd Sept 1946.

JENKINS, David Llewelyn (Lord Jenkins)

s. of Sir John Lewis Jenkins KCSI (d. 1912). b. 8th April 1899. educ. Charterhouse; Balliol Coll. Oxf. BA 1922, MA 1928, Hon. Fellow 1950. WWI Lieut. 12th Battn. Rifle Brigade. LI. Nov. 1923. KC 1938. Bencher 1945. Equity draftsman and conveyancer. WWII Major RASC, and with Political Warfare Exec. Att-Genl. Duchy of Lancaster 1946-47; Chancery judge 1947-49; Knight 1947; Chmn. of Company Law Committee; LJ 1949-59; PC 1949; Chmn. of Committee of Inquiry into liability of insce. cos.; L of A 1959-63; Baron 1959; Chmn. LC's Law Reform Committee; Chmn. Tancred studentship trustees; govr. Sutton's Hospital in Charterhouse 1953-65. d. 21st July 1969.

JENKINS, George Kirkhouse

s. of Richard Jenkins, Llansamlet, Glamorgan, mining engineer. b. 1884. educ. Swansea Gr. Sch. Solicitor 1907. M.T. Nov. 1914. WWI Lieut. Welch Regt. KC 1931. Cty. Ct. judge 1935-57; Divorce commr.; Chmn. Somerset Quarter Sess.; Chmn. Bath Licensing Planning Committee; JP Somerset, Wiltshire and Berkshire. Editor Bullen and Leake's Precedents of Pleadings. d. 10th May 1957.

JENNER-FUST, Sir Herbert

s. of Robert Jenner, proctor (d. 1810). b. 4th Feb. 1778. educ. in Reading and Trinity Hall Camb. LLB 1798, LLD 1803. G.I. Nov. 1800. Advocate Doctors' Commons July 1803; King's Adv-Genl. 1828-34; Knight 1828; Vicar-Genl. to Abp. of Canterbury 1832-34; judge of Prerogative Ct. of Canterbury, and Dean of the Arches 1834-52; PC 1834; Master of Trinity Hall Camb. 1843-52; presiding judge in Gorham v. Bishop of Exeter (1847-49), concerning the bishop's refusal to instal Gorham as vicar of Brampford Speke. Assumed additional name of Fust on succeeding to property of his cousin Sir John Fust. d. 20th Feb. 1852.

JENNINGS, Sir Raymond Winter

s. of Sir Arthur Oldham Jennings, solicitor (d. 1934). b. 12th Dec. 1897. educ. Rugby; RMC; Oriel Coll. Oxf. MA, BCL. WWI Lieut. Royal Fusiliers. I.T. May 1922. KC 1945. Bencher (L.I.) 1951. Master of the Ct. of Protection 1956-70; Knight 1968; JP. d. 6th March 1995.

JEREMY, Henry

s. of Thomas Jeremy, Covent Garden, London. educ. Honiton Sch.; Trinity Coll. Camb. BA 1809, 8th Wrangler, MA 1812. M.T. Feb. 1818. Recorder of Wokingham; metrop. magistrate 1835, finally at Greenwich and Woolwich 1840-49. d. 15th Feb. 1849, age 61.

JERVIS, Sir John

s. of Thomas Jervis KC (d. 1838). b. 12th Jan. 1802. educ. Westminster; Trinity Coll. Camb. 1819. Commissioned in 6th Dragoon Guards. M.T. Feb. 1824. Bencher 1837-50, Reader 1841. Postman in Ct. of Exch.; leader of North Wales and Chester circuit; MP Chester 1832-50; was offered, but refused silk gown; patent of precedence 1837, with rank after R.B. Crowder KC; requested, but was not granted, Indian judgeship; Sol-Genl. 1846, for a few days; Att-Genl. 1846-50; Knight 1846; advised Crown on Chartist Riots 1848; introduced legislation in 1848 relating to magistrates, and known by his name; Pres. Comm. of Inquiry into system of pleading in common law cts. 1850; PC 1850; CJ of Common Pleas 1850-56; an originator of the weekly journal "The Jurist" 1837; edited several editions of Archbold's Pleading and Evidence in Criminal Cases. Author of treatise on coroners 1829; reported Exch. cases (with E. Younge) 1828-30, (with C. Crompton) 1832-33. Father of John Jervis (M.T.1849). d. 1st Nov. 1856.

JESSEL, Albert Henry

s. of Henry Jessel, London, barrister. b. 31st Oct 1864. educ. Clifton Coll.; Balliol Coll. Oxf. BA 1887, MA 1891. I.T. and L.I. Jan. 1889. KC 1906. Bencher (L.I.) 1911. Equity draftsman and conveyancer; V-Pres. United Synagogue 1899; Pres. South London Jewish Schools; Hon. Secy. Jewish Voluntary Schools Assoc. d. 2nd Jan. 1917.

JESSEL, Sir George

s. of Zadok Aaron Jessel, Savile Row, London, diamond merchant (d. 1865). b. 13th Feb. 1824. educ. in Kew; University Coll. London BA 1843, MA 1844; Senator 1862-83, V-C 1880-83. L.I. May 1847. QC 1865. Bencher 1865, Treasurer 1883. Practised as conveyancer; leading junior in Rolls Ct.; MP Dover 1868-73; Sol-Genl. 1871-73; Knight 1872; PC 1873; MR 1873-83, the first Jewish judge; Commr. of Patents 1873-83; FRS 1880. Father of Sir Charles James Jessel Bt. (L.I. 1885), who was created a baronet in recognition of his father's services. d. 21st March 1883.

JEUNE, Francis Henry (Lord St. Helier)

s. of Francis Jeune, bishop of Peterborough (d.1868). b. Jersey, 17th March 1843. educ. Harrow; Balliol Coll. Oxf. BA 1865, MA 1874; Fellow, Hertford Coll. 1874; Bursar. Employed with London solicitors. I.T. Nov. 1868. QC 1888. Bencher 1891. Went to Australia for evidence in support of Tichborne claimant, and appeared for him, 1871; Chan. of dioceses of Gloucester and Bristol, Bangor, Durham, St Davids, St Albans, St Asaph and Peterborough; Commissary to Dean and Chapter of Westminster; had extensive ecclesiastical practice; member Royal Comms. on Eccles. Patronage 1874, Sandwich Election 1880, Eccles. Cts. 1881; P D and A judge 1891-92; Knight 1891; Pres. of P D and A Divn. 1892-1905; ensured efficiency and dispatch; PC 1892; Judge Adv-Genl. (without payment) 1892-1904; KCB 1897; GCB 1902; Baron 1905; JP Essex and Berkshire; Hon. DCL Durham. d. 9th April 1905.

JOHNES, Arthur James

s. of Edward Johnes MD, Garthmyl Isaf, nr. Montgomery. b. 4th Feb. 1808. educ. Oswestry Gr. Sch.; London Univ. 1828. L.I. Jan. 1835. Cty. Ct. judge 1847-70. Author of books on chancery reform, and law of imprisonment for debt. d. 23rd July 1871.

JOHNES, John

s. of John Johnes, Dolancothy, Carmarthenshire (d. 1815). b. 6th Feb. 1800. educ. Carmarthen and Lampeter Gr. Schs.; Brasenose Coll. Oxf. BA and MA 1829. I.T. Nov. 1831. Cty. Ct. judge 1847-61; Recorder of Carmarthen 1851-72; Chmn. Carmarthenshire Quarter Sess. 1853-72; DL, JP. Murdered by his butler, 19th Aug. 1876.

JOHNSON, John James

s. of William Johnson, Chichester, Sussex. b. June 1812. educ. Winchester. M.T. June 1836. QC 1864. Bencher 1864, Reader 1868, Treasurer 1876. Recorder of Chichester 1863-90; Vice-Chmn. Sussex Quarter Sess., Western Division; JP Sussex. d. 22nd July 1890.

JOLLY, John Catterall

s. of Thomas Jolly JP, Preston, Lancashire, cotton manufacturer. b. 1887. educ. Aldenham Sch.; King's Coll. Camb. BA 1909. I.T. June 1911 (Cert. of Hon.). KC 1939. Bencher 1946. External lecturer in law Manchester Univ.; Recorder of Preston 1938-50; Chmn. Preston, Liverpool, and Manchester Quarter Sess. 1938-50; Chmn. Lancashire Quarter Sess. 1944-50; member Home Secy.'s Advisory Council on Treatment of Offenders 1945; Chmn. Agricultural Land Trib. Lancashire; Chmn. Unemployment Assistance Bd. Trib. Manchester (South & East). d. 22nd Jan. 1950.

JONES, Sir Austin Ellis Lloyd

s. of Rev. Thomas Evans Jones, Hope, Flintshire. b. 27th April 1884. educ. Haileybury; Liverpool Univ. LLB, Hon. LLD 1951. I.T. June 1907 (Cert. of Hon.). Bencher 1945. WWI Capt. RFA, MC (despatches twice). Unsuccessful as parliamentary candidate; Chmn.

Tithe Arrears Investigation Committee 1937; Chmn. Committee on Cty. Ct. Procedure 1947; Cty. Ct. judge 1931-45; P D and A judge 1945-48; Knight 1945; KB judge 1948-61; Chmn. Flintshire Quarter Sess. 1948. d. 31st March 1967.

JONES, Charles Chadwick

s. of Robert Watkin Jones, Kerney Cross, nr. Wrexham, Denbighshire. b. 1800. M.T. June 1830. Special pleader; Serjeant 1844. d. 7th July 1852.

JONES, Chester

s. of John Henry Jones, Elmwood, Streatham, London, warehouseman. b. 1854. educ. Wesleyan Coll. Taunton; University Coll. London; Trinity Hall. Camb. BA 1876. M.T. Nov. 1879. Metrop. magistrate 1907, finally at Bow St. 1920-22; member Vice-regal comm. on loss of Dublin Crown Jewels; JP Essex. d. 9th July 1922.

JONES, Sir David Brynmor

s. of Rev. Thomas Jones, Swansea. b. 12th May 1852. educ. University Coll. London, LLB 1874. M.T. June 1876. QC 1893. Bencher 1899, Reader 1911. Recorder of Merthyr Tydfil 1910-14, of Cardiff 1914-15; Cty. Ct. judge 1885-92; MP Mid-Gloucestershire 1892-95, Swansea 1895-1914; Counsel of Wales Univ.; member Welsh Land Comm. 1893; Welsh Church Comm. 1907; Chmn. Metrop. Police Comm. 1906; Master in Lunacy 1914. Knight 1906; PC 1912; member Convocation London Univ.; Hon. LLD Wales. d. 6th Aug. 1921.

JONES, Edwin

s. of Thomas Jones, Bogrood, Radnorshire. b. 21st June 1841. educ. Owen's Coll. Manchester. M.T. June 1875. Cty. Ct. judge 1889-1900; JP Lancashire and Isle of Man. d. 18th Feb. 1900.

JONES, George Morgan Edwardes

s. of John Morgan Edwardes Jones, Garthmill Hall, Montgomeryshire (d. 1903). b. 16th July 1858. educ. Brighton Coll.; Pembroke Coll. Camb. BA 1881, 4th Wrangler, MA 1884, Fellow 1883-89; Fellow of King's Coll. London. I.T. June 1883. KC 1925. Alderman Surrey CC. Author of Law of Public Education; edited Blunt's Book of Church law. d. 5th Feb. 1936.

JONES, Sir George William Henry

s. of George Jones, Stamford Hill, North London. b. 1874. educ. London Univ. LLB. G.I. April 1907 (Cert. of Hon.). KC 1943. Recorder of Colchester 1937-47; member, LCC (North Hackney) 1910-18; MP Stoke Newington 1918-23, and 1924-45; Knight 1928. d. 3rd Jan. 1956.

JONES, Herbert George

s. of Calvert Richard Jones, Heathfield, Glamorganshire. b. 1805. L.I. May 1828. Att-Genl. Tasmania. Serjeant 1842; Cty. Ct. judge 1849-66. Author of The Court of Exchequer and the County Courts 1858. d. 17th Feb. 1866.

JONES, Herbert Riversdale Mansel

s. of Herbert George Jones, serjeant. b. 1836. educ. Eton; Trinity Coll. Camb. LLB 1862; captain, Univ. Boat Club. L.I. June 1859.

Commr. for mun. election petitions 1884; Cty. Ct. judge 1902-07. d. 2nd Feb. 1907.

JONES, Thomas

(of Heathcote St, Mecklenburgh Sq., Middlesex). b. 1812. Special pleader. M.T. May 1846. QC 1866. Bencher 1866. d. 17th Oct 1869.

JONES, Sir Thomas Artemus

s. of Thomas Jones, Denbigh, stonemason. b. 1871. educ. privately; Bedford Coll. London Univ. Hon. LLD 1938. On parliamentary staff of Daily Telegraph and Daily News. M.T. Nov. 1901. KC 1919. Bencher 1926, Reader 1937. Represented GB in Anglo-Mexican Claims Comm. 1928-29; Cty. Ct. judge 1929-42; Chmn. Carnarvonshire Quarter Sess; Knight 1931; Freeman of City of London. Autobiog. Without my Wig 1944. d. 15th Oct 1943.

JONES, William. Everard Tyldesley

s. of Everard Whiting Jones, Swansea. b. 20th Jan. 1874. educ. Clifton Coll. L.I. Jan. 1905 (Cert. of Hon.). KC 1920. Bencher 1926. WWI Capt. RGA (MBE). Hon. standing counsel to Univ. of Wales; member Council of Legal Educ. 1905; member of bar council 1911; FSA. d. lst Jan. 1938.

JONES, William Hugh

s. of Hugh Jones, Cardiff (d. 1901). b. 1866. educ. University Coll. Cardiff; London Univ. G.I. Nov. 1892. KC 1924. Stip. magistrate, Cardiff 1931-45; Chmn. Ct. of Referees under Unemployment Insce. Act for Rhymney Valley District, Glamorgan and Monmouth 1928-31; Dep. Cty. Ct. judge; Dep. Recorder of Cardiff and Carmarthen; Commr. of Assize, South Wales and Chester circuit; hon. legal adviser to Regional Commrs. for Wales Civil Defence 1941-45. Author of a Guide to the Liquor Licensing Acts. d. 21st Sept. 1960.

JORDAN, Thomas Hudson

s. of William Jordan, Manchester, journalist. b. 1828. Journalist on staff of Manchester Courier; reporter in London for Manchester Examiner 1859-62. G.I. June 1862. Cty. Ct. judge 1883-99; JP Lancashire and Staffordshire. d. 3rd Nov. 1899.

JOWITT, William Allen (Lord Jowitt)

s. of Rev. William Jowitt, Stevenage, Hertfordshire. b. 15th April 1885. educ. Marlborough; New Coll. Oxf. BA 1906, Hon. DCL, Hon. Fellow 1945. M.T. June 1909. KC 1922. Bencher 1929, Treasurer 1952. Member Comm. on Lunacy 1924; MP The Hartlepools 1922-24, Preston 1929-31, Ashton-under-Lyne 1939-45; Att-Genl. 1929-32; Knight 1929; PC 1931; Sol-Genl. 1940-42; Paymaster-Genl. 1942; Minister without Portfolio 1943-44; Minister of Nat. Insce. 1944-45; Baron 1945; LC 1945-51; Viscount 1947; Earl 1951; Trustee of Nat. Gallery 1946-53, and Tate Gallery 1947-53 (Chmn. 1951-53); Master of Curriers' Co. 1955; Pres. Queen Charlotte's Hosp.; Hon. LLD Columbia, Chicago, Toronto, New York, Sao Paulo, Sydney. Author of The Strange Case of Alger Hiss 1953, Some were Spies 1954; general editor of Dictionary of English Law. d. 16th Aug. 1957.

JOY, Henry Holmes

s. of John Holmes Joy MD, Manor House, Tamworth, Staffordshire. b. 1875. educ. Sherborne; Trinity Hall. Camb. BA 1897. I.T. Nov. 1900. KC 1924. OBE for war work as Asst Secy. and legal adviser to Min. of Nat. Service; Recorder of Nottingham 1927-34. d. 22nd March 1934.

JOYCE, Sir Matthew Ingle

s. of John Hall Joyce, Blackfordby, Leicestershire, yeoman farmer. b. 17th July 1839. educ. Ashby de la Zouch Gr. Sch.; Caius Coll. Camb. BA 1862, 8th Wrangler, MA 1865, Fellow 1862-75, Hon. Fellow 1900. L.I. Nov. 1865 (Cert. of Hon.). Bencher 1886. Equity draftsman and conveyancer; junior equity counsel to Treasury 1886-1900; Chancery judge 1900-15; Knight 1900; PC 1915; FSA; JP Leicestershire. d. 10th March 1930.

JOYCE, Samuel

s. of James Joyce, Pentonville, London. b. 1818. educ. private academy. G.I. and M.T. Jan. 1846. QC 1874. Bencher (G.I.) 1874. Standing counsel to London Brighton and South Coast Ry; served as deputy Cty. Ct. judge, and as a judge in City of London Ct. d. 6th Jan. 1876.

KARMINSKI, Sir Seymour Edward

s. of Eugène Karminski, Portland Place, London W. b. 28th Sept 1902. educ. Rugby; Christ Church Oxf. BA 1923, MA 1946. I.T. May 1925. KC 1945. Bencher 1951. WWII Lt.-Cmdr. RNVR. P D and A judge 1951-69; Knight 1951; Dep. Chmn. Bedfordshire Quarter Sess. 1951-57; LJ 1969-73; PC 1967; Dep. Chmn. East Suffolk Quarter Sess. 1961-71. d. 29th Oct 1974.

KARSLAKE, Edward Kent

s. of Henry Karslake, London, solicitor (d. 1857). b. 1820. educ. Harrow; Christ Church Oxf. BA 1841, MA 1846; Fellow of Balliol Coll. 1841-50. L.I. May 1846. QC 1866. Bencher 1867, Treasurer 1892. MP Colchester 1867-68. d. 31st May 1892.

KARSLAKE, Sir John Burgess

s. of Henry Karslake, London, solicitor (d. 1857). b. 13th Dec. 1821. educ. Harrow. Articled to father. M.T. Jan. 1846. QC 1861. Bencher 1861, Reader 1864, Treasurer 1873. Leader of Western circuit; Sol-Genl. 1866; Knight 1866; Att-Genl. 1867-68, and 1874; MP Andover 1867-68, Huntingdon 1873-76; member Judicature Comm.; PC 1876. d. 4th Oct 1881.

KARSLAKE, Sir William Wollaston

s. of Rev. William Heberden Karslake, prebendary of Exeter Cathedral (d. 1878). b. 10th June 1834. educ. Harrow. L.I. April 1857. QC 1881. Bencher 1884. Junior equity counsel to Dept. of Woods and Forests, IR, and Office of Works 1860-81; equity examr. to Inns of Ct. 1882; controller of legacy and succession duties 1886-99; patron of rectories of Meshaw and Creacombe, Devon; Knight 1895. d. 25th Sept 1913.

KAY, Sir Edward Ehenezer

s. of Robert Kay, Brookshall Bury, Lancashire (d. 1834). b. 2nd July 1822. educ. Patricroft Sch. nr. Salford; Trinity Coll. Camb. BA 1844, MA 1847. L.I. June 1847. QC 1866. Bencher 1867, Treasurer 1888. Leader in V-C Bacon's Ct. and from 1878 practised only before H of L and Privy Council; Chancery judge 1881-90; Knight 1881; LJ 1890-97; PC 1890; Chmn. Norfolk Quarter Sess; JP Norfolk; reported chancery cases 1853-54, and (with H.R.V. Johnson) chancery cases 1854-58; gave funds to endow Lady Kay studentships in theology at Jesus Coll. Camb. d. 16th March 1897.

KAY, Joseph

s. of Robert Kay, Brookshall House, nr. Bury, Lancashire (d. 1834). b. 27th Feb. 1821. educ. Patricroft, Lancashire; Trinity Coll. Camb.

BA 1845, MA 1849. I.T. May 1848. QC 1869. Bencher 1870. Judge of Salford Hundred Ct. of Record 1862-78; Sol-Genl. Cty. Palatine of Durham 1872-78. Author of The Law relating to Shipmasters and Seamen 1875. d. 9th Oct 1878.

KEANE, David Deady

s. of James Keane, London. b. 1810. educ. Harrow; Trinity Coll. Camb. 1827; Göttingen Univ. PhD 1831. A parliamentary reporter. M.T. June 1835. QC 1864. Bencher 1864, Reader 1867. Reported cases in Ct. of CP 1854-62; Recorder of Bedford 1861-70. Author of works relating to Cts. of Requests, gaols and houses of correction, and nuisances. d. 20th June 1870.

KEATING, Sir Henry Singer

s. of Lieut.-Genl. Sir Henry Sheehy Keating KCB (d. 1847). b. Dublin, 13th Jan. 1804. educ. Trinity Coll. Dublin BA 1828, MA 1832, Hon. LLD 1871. I.T. May 1832. QC 1849. Bencher 1849-59 and 1877-88. MP Reading 1852-59; successfully introduced Bills of Exchange Act 1854; Sol-Genl. 1857-58 and 1859; Knight 1857; judge of Common Pleas 1859-75; PC 1875; edited (with J.S. Willes) Smith's leading cases in common law 1849. Father of Henry Sheehy Keating (I.T. 1879). d. 1st Oct. 1888.

KEKEWICH, Sir Arthur

s. of Samuel Trehawke Kekewich MP, Peamore, Devon (d. 1873). b. 26th July 1832. educ. Eton; Balliol Coll. Oxf. BA 1854, MA 1856; Fellow of Exeter Coll. 1854-58. L.I. June 1858. QC 1877. Bencher 1881, Treasurer 1902. Had large practice as junior, but unsuccessful as leader; junior standing counsel to Bank of England; Chancery judge 1886-1907; Knight 1886; JP; judgments often reversed on appeal. Father of Charles Granville Kekewich DL (solicitor 1885). d. 22nd Nov. 1907.

KEKEWICH, George Granville

s. of George Kekewich, Dartmouth. b. 1802. educ. Exeter Coll. Oxf. BA 1824, MA 1827. M.T. Nov. 1827. Cty. Ct. judge 1847-57. d. 7th Jan. 1857.

KELLY, Sir Fitzroy Edward

s. of Capt. Robert Hawke Kelly RN. b. 9th Oct 1796. Employed with solicitors in London. Special pleader. L.I. May 1824 (call expedited by benchers to enable him to accept a brief awaiting his attention). KC 1834. Bencher 1838-66. MP Ipswich 1838-41, Cambridge 1843-47, East Suffolk 1852-66; frequently retained by the early railway cos.; defended Tawell, the poisoner, in which his attempted defence of prussic acid in apples eaten by deceased gained him the sobriquet of "Applepip Kelly", 1845; counsel to Bank of England and East India Co.; appeared in Shrewsbury and Crawford peerage cases; Sol.Genl. 1845-46 and 1852; Knight 1845; Att-Genl. 1858-59; Chief Baron of Exchequer 1866-80; PC 1866; permitted to retain the title of Chief Baron after 1875, by Act of Parliament. d. 17th Sept 1880.

KELLY, Sir Stanley Anthony Hill

s. of Samuel William Kelly JP, The Elms, Llandaff Road, Cardiff, colliery proprietor. b. 22nd Nov. 1869. G.I. Nov. 1893. Legal adviser to Seychelles Govt. 1903; Cty. Ct. judge 1910-39; Knight 1936. d. 21st Oct 1949.

KEMP, Henry Thomas

s. of Rev. Henry William Kemp, master of the Charterhouse, Hull, and Hon. Canon of York. b. 7th Dec. 1852. educ. Shrewsbury; St John's Coll. Camb. LLB 1878, BA 1880, LLM 1881, MA 1885. I.T. Nov. 1879. M.T. June 1892. KC 1904. Bencher 1912, Reader 1923. Recorder of York 1911-17, of Hull 1917-28; JP London. d. 12th Jan.

1943.

KEMP, Thomas Richardson

s. of Thomas Reginald Kemp, London, banker. b. 1836. educ. Trinity Hall Camb. BA 1858. M.T. April 1858. QC 1877. Bencher 1881, Reader 1891, Treasurer 1899. Recorder of Deal 1892, of Norwich 1892-1905. d. 30th April 1905.

KEMPLAY, James

s. of Richard Kemplay, Leeds. b. 1810. educ. Leeds Gr. Sch.; Trinity Coll. Camb. BA 1833, 4th Wrangler, MA 1836. Special pleader. M.T. Jan. 1852. QC 1872. Bencher 1874. d. 4th June 1882.

KENEALY, Edward Vaughan Hyde

s. of William Kenealy, Cork, merchant. b. 2nd July 1819. educ. privately; Trinity Coll. Dublin BA 1840, LLB 1846, LLD 1850. Irish bar 1840 G.I. May 1847. QC 1868. Bencher 1868. MP Stoke-upon-Trent 1874-80; junior counsel in defence of Palmer, the Rugeley poisoner 1856; led prosecution of bankers Overend Gurney & Co. 1869; leading counsel for Arthur Orton, the Tichborne claimant 1873; disbarred 1874 for his violent conduct of that case, and libellous articles about it in his periodical The Englishman. Published The Trial at Bar of Sir R.C.D. Tichborne Bart., 5 vols. 1875-78. d. 16th April 1880.

KENNEDY, Alfred Ravenscroft

s. of Kennedy LJ. b. 15th Feb. 1879. educ. Eton; King's Coll. Camb. BA 1903. L.I. May 1903. KC 1919. Bencher 1922. Legal adviser at Foreign Office during WWI. Recorder of Burnley 1924-29; MP Preston 1924-29; Cty. Ct. judge 1929-43; Commr. of Assize 1933 and 1934; Chmn. Gloucestershire Quarter Sess.; Pres. Corpn. of Certified Secretaries 1927-37. Author of treatise on Contracts of Sale C.I.F.; edited Kennedy's Law of Civil Salvage, and Benjamin on Sale. d. 10th Feb. 1943.

KENNEDY, Gilbert George

s. of John Kennedy, HM Diplomatic Service. b. 9th May 1844. educ. Harrow; Trinity Coll. Camb. BA 1868, MA 1871; athletics blue. I.T. April 1870. Recorder of Grantham 1883-89; metrop. magistrate 1889, finally at Marlborough St. to 1907; JP Middlesex and Home Counties. Author (with J.S. Sandars) of Law of Sewers; joint editor of Roscoe's Criminal Evidence. d. 2nd Jan. 1909.

KENNEDY, Sir William. Rann

s. of Rev. William James Kennedy, Barnwood, Gloucestershire. b. 11th March 1846. educ. Eton; King's Coll. Camb. BA 1868, MA 1871, Fellow of Pembroke Coll. 1868-74, Hon. Fellow 1893. Asst. master at Harrow; priv. secy. to George Goschen at Poor Law Bd. 1870-71. L.I. Jan. 1871. QC 1885. Bencher. Practised in Liverpool 1873-82; QB judge 1892-1907; Knight 1892; frequently sat in commercial ct.; LJ 1907-15; PC 1907; Pres. Intern. Law Assoc. 1908-10; member of Inst. de Droit Intern. 1913; FBA 1909; Hon. LLD Victoria. Author of The Law of Civil Salvage 1891. d. 17th Jan. 1915.

KENRICK, George Harry Blair

s. of George Kenrick, Nant Clwyd Hall, Denbighshire (d. 1877). b. 29th Nov. 1869. educ. Cheltenham Coll., London Univ. LLB, LLD 1899. M.T. Jan. 1893 (Cert. of Hon.). KC 1909. Parliamentary draftsman; examr. to London Univ. and for bar final; asst. legal adviser to Foreign Secy. at Hague Confce. 1907; Adv-Genl. Bengal 1909-16; member Legislative Council of Viceroy of India 1910-16;

member Senate and Syndicate, Calcutta Univ. 1910. Joint author of Strahan and Kenrick's Digest of Equity. d. 23rd Aug. 1952.

KENT, Charles Weller

s. of George Weller Kent, Tunbridge Wells, grocer. b. 19th Sept. 1864. educ. privately. Parliamentary journalist on staff of The Times; member Inst. of Journalists. M.T. Jan. 1895. KC 1922. Director City Lands Investment Corpn.; life member Socy. of Sussex Downsmen. d. 5th June 1952.

KENYON, John Robert

s. of Hon. Thomas Kenyon, and g.s. of Kenyon LCJ. b. 13th Jan. 1807. educ. Charterhouse; Christ Church Oxf. BA 1828, BCL 1831, DCL 1836; Fellow of All Souls Coll. 1828. M.T. May 1834. QC 1862. Bencher 1862, Reader 1865, Treasurer 1873. Judge and assessor of Chancellor's Ct. of Oxf. Univ. 1840-59; Recorder of Oswestry 1842-80; Vinerian prof. of common law Oxf. 1843-80; Chmn. Shropshire Quarter Sess. 1871. Father of Robert Lloyd Kenyon (M.T. 1873), Chmn. Shropshire Quarter Sess. d. 17th April 1880.

KERLY, Sir Duncan Mackenzie

s. of Alexander Kerly, London, solicitor. b. 5th Jan. 1863. educ. Merchant Taylors'; St John's Coll. Camb. BA 1884, 9th Wrangler, LLB 1885, MA 1888, Fellow 1886-92. I.T. Jan. 1887. KC 1914. Bencher 1923. Equity draftsman and conveyancer; Chmn. Bd. of Referees for excess profits duty 1915; Knight 1921; JP Surrey. Author of works on law of trade marks and merchandise marks, and a Short History of Equity. d. 5th Oct 1938.

KERR, Robert Malcolm

s. of John Kerr, WS, Glasgow. b. 5th June 1821. educ. Tillicoultry Acad.; Glasgow Univ. LLD 1857. Scottish bar 1843. L.I. Jan. 1848. M.T. April 1860. Dep. Cty. Ct. judge, North Wales circuit; judge of Sheriffs Ct. London 1859-67, of City of London Ct. 1867-1901; a Commr. at Central Criminal Ct.; DL, JP Middlesex; DL London; JP Dumbarton and Westminster; Master of Tallow Chandlers Co. 1897-98. Edited Blackstone's Commentaries. Father of Robert Malcolm Napier Kerr (I.T. 1882). Biography by G. Pitt-Lewis KC 1903. d. 21st Nov. 1902.

KERSHAW, John Felix

s. of Sir Louis Addin Kershaw QC. b. 20th Nov. 1873. educ. Shrewsbury; Balliol Coll. Oxf. BA 1896. I.T. Nov. 1897. Judge in Khartoum 1902-05; judge and military legal adviser, Cairo 1905-26; resigned in consequence of adverse verdict in case of instigators of Sirdar's murder; Cty. Ct. judge 1927; Order of Nile 2nd Class; Order of Medjidieh 3rd Class. Author of Hints on Criminal Investigation 1907. d. 16th June 1927.

KERSHAW, Sir Louis Addin

s. of Matthew Kershaw, Philadelphia Pa., and Luddenden, nr. Halifax. b. 1845. educ. Bradford; Pembroke Coll. Oxf. BA 1869. I.T. Nov. 1872. QC 1895. CJ Allahabad 1898; Knight 1898; CJ Bombay 1898-99. d. Bombay, 17th Feb. 1899.

KETTLE, Sir Rupert Alfred

s. of Thomas F. Kettle, Birmingham, merchant. b. 9th Jan. 1817. Articled to an attorney in Wolverhampton. M.T. June 1845. Bencher 1882. Cty. Ct. judge 1859-92; Asst. Chmn. Staffordshire Quarter Sess.; Knight 1880; DL, JP Staffordshire; JP Hereford,

Worcestershire and Merioneth. Author of works on employment, and arbitration. Known as "The Prince of Arbitrators". d. 6th Oct. 1894.

KETTLE, Rupert Edward Cooke

s. of Sir Rupert Kettle, Cty. Ct. judge. b. 25th Dec. 1854. educ. Wolverhampton Gr. Sch.; Rugby; St. John's Coll. Oxf. BA 1878. M.T. May 1879. Recorder of Lichfield 1899-1901; metrop. magistrate Greenwich and Woolwich 1901-06. d. 15th Oct 1908.

KINDERSLEY, Sir Richard Torin

s. of Nathaniel Edward Kindersley, HEICS, Sunning Hill, Berkshire. b. Madras, 5th Oct 1792. educ. Haileybury; Trinity Coll. Camb. BA 1814, MA 1817, 4th Wrangler, Fellow 1815-24. L.I. Feb. 1818. KC 1835. Practised in chancery; declined to be Sol-Genl. 1841; Chan. of Cty. Palatine of Durham 1846; Master in Chancery 1848; V-C 1851-66; Knight 1851; PC 1866. d. 22nd Oct. 1879.

KING, Cyril Lander

s. of George Lander King, Sutton, Surrey. b. 1883. Solicitor 1908, practised in London. M.T. Nov. 1919. KC 1937. Bencher 1943. d. 24th June 1972.

KINGDON, Thomas Kingdon

s. of Samuel Kingdon, Exeter, ironmonger. b. 1812. educ. Exeter Coll. Oxf. BA 1834, MA 1837. Special pleader for nine years. I.T. Jan. 1848. QC 1866. Bencher 1867. Recorder of Bristol 1872-79. d. 2nd Dec. 1879.

KINGLAKE, John Alexander

s. of Robert Kinglake, MD, Taunton, Somerset. b. 25th June 1802. educ. Eton; Trinity Coll. Camb. BA 1826, MA 1829. L.I. Feb. 1830. Serjeant 1844; patent of precedence 1849; Recorder of Exeter 1851-56, of Bristol 1856-70; MP Rochester 1857-70. Father of Robert Alexander Kinglake (M.T. 1867), Recorder of Penzance. d. 9th July 1870.

KINNEAR, Alexander Smith (Lord Kinnear)

s. of John Kinnear, Glasgow, merchant. b. 3rd Nov. 1833. educ. Glasgow Univ.; Edin. Univ. Scottish bar 1856. QC 1881. Dean of Faculty of Advocates 1881; Lord Ordinary 1882-90; member of First Division 1890-1913; Chmn. Scottish Universities Comm. 1889-97; Baron 1897. d. 20th Dec. 1917.

KNIGHT, George Wilfrid Holford

s. of George Thomas Knight, Kensington, West London. b. 23rd April 1877. educ. privately; London Univ. Employed in local govt. until 1903. M.T. Jan. 1903. KC 1930. Senior counsel to Mint at Central Criminal Ct. 1911-30; Recorder of West Ham 1930-36; MP Nottingham (South) 1929-35; conducted Rights of Way Act 1932; member Wheelwrights' Co., and Freeman of City of London; initiated movement to open English bar to women 1913. d. 26th April 1936.

KNOWLES, Charles James

s. of James Knowles, Greenhead, Yorkshire. b. 1798. M.T. Nov. 1823. QC 1841. Bencher 1841, Reader 1846, Treasurer 1851. Att-Genl. Duchy of Lancaster 1846-61. d. 12th Feb. 1867.

KNOX, Alexander Andrew

s. of George Knox, Jamaica. b. 5th Feb. 1818. educ. Blundell's; Trinity Coll. Camb. BA 1844, MA 1847. L.I. Nov. 1847. Wrote leading articles for The Times 1846-60; metrop. magistrate 1860, finally at Marlborough St. 1862-78; FRGS. d. 5th Oct 1891.

KNOX, Edmund Francis Vesey

s. of Vesey Edmund Knox, Shimnah, Newcastle, co. Down (d.1879). b. 23rd Jan. 1865. educ. Keble Coll. Oxf. BA 1886; Fellow All Souls Coll. 1886-93. G.I. and M.T. Jan. 1889. KC 1906. Bencher (G.I.) 1906, Treasurer 1913. MP Cavan (West) 1890-95, Londonderry 1895-98; parliamentary draftsman. d. 15th May 1921.

KOE, John Herbert

s. of John Heide Koe, London. b. 1783. L.I. Nov. 1810. QC 1842. Bencher 1842, Treasurer 1860. Cty. Ct. judge 1847-60. Editor (with S. Miller) of Law of Bankruptcy 1844. d. 3rd Sept 1860.

KONSTAM, Edwin Max (previously Kohnstamm)

s. of Henry Konstam, London and Mauritius. b. 10th June 1870. educ. Marlborough; King's Coll. Camb. 1888. I.T. June 1899. Indian Civil Service 1890-1902, acting judge at Cuttack. KC 1919. Bencher 1925, Treasurer 1948. Bd. of Agriculture 1917-19; OBE 1918, CBE 1920; Cty. Ct. judge 1932-45; member Treasury committee on codification of income tax law 1927-36. Author of The Law of Income Tax, and books on allied topics. d. 7th April 1956.

KOTZÉ, Sir John Gilbert

s. of Petrus Johannes Kotzé MLA, Cape Town. b. Cape Town, 5th

Nov. 1849. educ. South African Coll.; London Univ. LLB 1873; Hon. LLD. Univ. of Capetown 1927; Cape of Good Hope Univ. 1912. I.T. April 1874. KC 1902. Judge Transvaal High Ct. 1877-81; CJ South African Republic 1881-98; Pres. Imperial and Boer Judicial Comm., Swaziland 1890; Att-Genl. Southern Rhodesia 1900-03; judge president Cape eastern districts Ct. 1904-13; judge, Supreme Ct. Cape Town 1913-20, judge president thereof 1920-22; judge of appeal 1922-27; Knight 1917; Chmn. Bd. of Examrs. in literature and science, South African Republic 1890-98; Chmn. Rhodes Univ. Coll. council 1904-13; Order of the Immaculate Conception (Portugal) 1896. d. 1st April 1940.

LAILEY, Barnard

s. of James Lailey, Hambleden, Bucks. (d. 1915). b. 1860. M.T. Jan. 1890. KC 1914. Cty. Ct. judge 1916-39. Examr. in law, Surveyors Inst. 1915; civil adjutant, Holloway internment camp 1915; held Harrogate aliens inquiry 1918; Pres. Council of Cty. Ct. judges 1932; Chmn. Hampshire Quarter Sess. 1932-38; JP Cheshire, Lancashire, Hampshire and Surrey; Commr. of Assize, South Wales and Chester circuit 1924. Author of Extraordinary Traffic on Highways 1912, Jottings from a Fee Book 1932. Father of Guy Patrick Barnard Lailey 1888-1946 (M.T. 1912), Recorder of Wenlock. d. 9th Feb. 1944.

LAING, Frederick Ninian Robert

s. of Robert Laing, Jedburgh, Co. Roxburgh, solicitor. b. 11th July 1856. educ. Ushaw Coll. M.T. April 1883. QC 1899. Bencher 1907, Reader 1920. Retired from practice 1925. d. 10th March 1931.

LANE, Richard Ouseley Blake

s. of Rev. Jeremiah Lane, Killashee, Co. Kildare. b. 1842. educ. Trinity Coll. Dublin BA. I.T. Nov. 1870. QC 1890. Metrop.

magistrate 1893, finally at West London 1895-1910; JP London and Home Counties. Father of Richard Ouseley Blake Lane (I.T. 1892). d. 28th Feb. 1914.

LANGDON, Adolph Max Lazarus

s. of H.M. Lazarus, Manchester. b. 10th March 1861. educ. Manchester Gr. Sch.; Pembroke Coll. Oxf. BA 1883, MA and BCL 1886. Assumed name of Langdon 1892. I.T. May 1886. KC 1904. Bencher 1913, Treasurer 1934. Recorder of Burnley 1909-15, of Salford 1915-41; Commr. of Assize 1923 and 1924; member of bar council; member Royal Comm. for awards to inventors 1924-35; Head of Inns of Ct. school of Law, and director of legal studies 1925-39; hon.. secy. Manchester Jewish Bd. of Guardians. d. 1st March 1949.

LANGLEY, Frederick Oswald

s. of Frederick Theobald Langley, Wolverhampton. b. 9th May 1883. educ. Uppingham; Caius Coll. Camb. BA 1905, LLB 1905. I.T. April 1907. WWI Capt. 6th South Staffordshire Battn. MC (despatches twice); GS03 (Intelligence) 1917; Legion of Honour. Asst. Mil. Attaché Br. Legation, Berne 1918-20; law officer Straits Settlements 1921-23; Recorder of Oswestry 1926-32; Chan. diocese of Lichfield 1928, Ripon 1932; metrop. magistrate, Old St. 1932-47. d. 22nd Jan. 1947.

LANGMAN, Thomas Witheridge

s. of Joseph Langman, Tavistock, Devonshire. b. 1882. educ. Llandovery Sch.; Jesus Coll. Oxf. BA 1905. G.I. Jan. 1910. WW1 Capt. 5th Battn. Welch Regt. (despatches); OBE 1919. Hon. Freeman, Carmarthen 1926; Cty. Ct. judge 1929-55; Chmn. Lincolnshire (Kesteven) Quarter Sess. 1932-46; Chmn. Lincolnshire (Lindsey) Quarter Sess. 1938-45; Chmn. Herefordshire Quarter Sess.

1951-57; JP Herefordshire. d. 14th Aug. 1960.

LANGTON, Sir George Philip

s. of Francis Albert Romuald Langton, Danganmore, Kilkenny, civil servant. b. 22nd April 1881. educ. Beaumont Coll.; Stonyhurst; New Coll. Oxf. BA 1902. Employed with stockbrokers and solicitors in London. I.T. Jan. 1905. KC 1925. Bencher 1930. Specialised in maritime law. WWI Capt. RGA, Garrison Adjt. Queenstown Harbour; Director, War Office Intelligence, Labour Dept. and Commr. for Labour Disputes, Min. of Munitions 1916-18. Controller, Demobilisation Dept., Min. of Labour 1918-19; OBE 1917. Secy. and adviser, Br. Maritime Law Committee 1922-30; joint Genl-Secy. Comité Maritime Intern.; P D and A judge 1930-42; Knight 1930; Vice-Chmn. Council of Legal Educ., and Chmn. of Bd. of Studies; Chmn. Exec. Committee of All England Lawn Tennis and Croquet Club. d. 9th Aug 1942.

LANKESTER, Edward Forbes

s. of Edwin Lankester MD, coroner for Central Middlesex (d. 1874) and nephew of Samuel Pope QC. b. 31st Jan. 1855. educ. St. Paul's; Lincoln Coll. Oxf. BA 1878. M.T. July 1878. KC 1905. Bencher 1915, Reader 1926. Parliamentary counsel; Registrar of Lincoln 1913, York 1915; metrop. magistrate 1919, finally at West London 1921-25. d. Biarritz, 20th April 1934.

LASKI, Neville Jonas

s. of Nathan Laski JP, Manchester, India merchant (d.1941). b. 18th Dec. 1890. educ. Manchester Gr. Sch.; Clifton Coll.; Corpus Christi Coll. Oxf. BA 1912, MA. I.T. Nov. 1913. KC 1930. Bencher 1938. WWI Capt. 6th Lancashire Fusiliers. Practised in Manchester; Recorder of Burnley 1935-56, of Liverpool 1956-63; Judge of Appeal, Isle of Man 1953-56; member of bar council 1950-56,

Chmn. prof. conduct committee 1952-56; Hon. Treasurer 1955-56; Pres. London committee of Deputies of British Jews 1933-39; Chmn. Manchester Victoria Memorial Jewish Hosp.; Vice-Pres. Anglo-Jewish Assoc.; Hon. LLD Liverpool. d. 24th March 1969.

LATHAM, William

s. of Alfred Latham, Hollow Dene, Frensham, Farnham, Surrey, Governor of Bank of England (d. 1885). b. 9th Dec. 1836. educ. Harrow; Trinity Coll. Camb. BA 1859, MA 1862. L.I. April 1860. QC 1886. Bencher 1889. d. 29th July 1915.

LATTER, Arthur Malcolm

s. of Rev. Arthur Simon Latter, Outwell Rectory, Wisbech. b. 27th June 1875. educ. Marlborough; Balliol Coll. Oxf. BA 1897. L.I. Jan. 1900. KC 1922. Bencher 1926, Treasurer 1946. Practised in Shanghai 1901-03; lecturer for Law Society 1904-12; Dep. Chmn. West Sussex Quarter Sess. 1931, Chmn. 1952; JP Sussex. Joint author of Contracts, 1909. d. 22nd Aug. 1961.

LAW, Charles Ewan

s. of Ellenborough LCJ. b. 14th June 1792. educ. St. John's Coll. Camb. MA 1812, LLD 1847. I.T. Feb. 1817. KC 1829. Bencher 1829, Reader 1838, Treasurer 1839. Common pleader of City of London 1823; Commr. in Bankruptcy; judge of Sheriff's Ct. London 1828; Common Serjeant 1830; Recorder of London 1833-50; MP Camb. Univ. 1835-50. d. 13th Aug. 1850.

LAWES, Edward Hobson Vitruvius

s. of Edward Lawes, attorney, and nephew of Serjeant Vitruvius Lawes (d. 1836). b. 1782. educ. St. Paul's. Special pleader. I.T. Feb.

1810. Serjeant 1827; chief registrar of Ct. of Bankruptcy 1832. Author of treatises on pleading, on charterparties and bills of lading, and other works. Father of Edward Lawes, barrister (d. 1852). d. 27th Nov. 1849.

LAWRANCE, Sir John Compton

s. of Thomas Munton Lawrance, Dunsby Hall, Lincolnshire (d. 1856). b. 30th May 1832. L.I. June 1859. QC 1877. Bencher 1879. Recorder of Derby 1880-90; MP South Lincolnshire 1880-85, Stamford 1885-90; QB judge 1890-1912; Knight 1890; a political appointment; PC 1912; DL, JP Lincolnshire. Father of Thomas Dalton Lawrance (I.T. 1891). d. 5th Dec. 1912.

LAWRANCE, William Thomas

s. of John Lawrance, Truro, Cornwall. b. 1859. educ. privately. M.T. Jan. 1895. KC 1920. Bencher 1928. Recorder of Poole 1924-28, of Bournemouth 1928-32; private secy. to Rt.Hon. Baron Henry de Worms MP at Bd. of Trade and Colonial Office; attaché to Intern. Confce. 1887 at Foreign Office to consider Sugar Bounties, which were abolished in the following year. Author of The Land Laws and Cornish Mining, and The Life-Lease System. d. 23rd June 1932.

LAWRENCE, Alfred Tristram (Lord Trevethin)

s. of David Lawrence, Wainwern House, Pontypool, Monmouth, surgeon. b. 24th Nov. 1843. educ. Mill Hill; Trinity Hall Camb. LLB 1867. M.T. Jan. 1869. QC 1897. Bencher 1892, Reader 1903, Treasurer 1914. Junior counsel to Admiralty 1882; Recorder of Windsor 1885-1904; Commr. of Assize, North Eastern circuit 1903, Northern circuit 1904; KB judge 1904-21; Knight 1904; Pres. War Compensation Ct. 1920-22; LCJ 1921-22; PC 1921; Baron 1921; Pres. Admiralty Transport Arbitration Bd. 1922; DL, JP Co. Nairn; JP Monmouth. Father of Alfred Clive Lawrence (M.T. 1902), HM

Procurator Gen. and Solicitor to Treasury. d. 3rd Aug. 1936.

LAWRENCE, Aubrey Trevor

s. of Sir Trevor Lawrence 2nd Bt. (d. 1913). b. 15th Jan. 1875. educ. Summer Fields; Shrewsbury; Christ Church Oxf. BA 1898, MA 1914. I.T. June 1899. KC 1927. Secy. East Coast Raid Committee 1915; with Min. of Munitions 1915-19; MBE. Chan. of diocese of Sheffield 1914, Worcester 1920, Peterborough 1922, Southwell 1922, Winchester 1924, Leicester 1927, Portsmouth 1927; Hon. Secy. Lord Cave's Comm. on Property and Revenue of the Church; member House of Laity, Church Assembly 1925; hon.. secy. Old Salopian Club 1909-24; editor of Cripps on Law of Church and Clergy, and Cripps on Compensation. d. 23rd March 1930.

LAWRENCE, Geoffrey (Lord Trevethin and Oaksey)

s. of Trevethin LCJ. b. 2nd Dec. 1880. educ. Summer Fields; Haileybury; New Coll. Oxf. BA 1901, MA 1946, Hon. Fellow 1944, Hon. DCL 1947. I.T. Jan. 1906. KC 1925. Bencher 1932, Treasurer 1955. WWI Hertfordshire RFA, DSO (despatches twice); Col. RA (TA) 1926, TD. Counsel to Jockey Club 1922-32; Recorder of Oxford 1924-28; examr. in Eccles. Causes 1927-32; Commr. of Assize, Oxford circuit 1931; Att-Genl. to Prince of Wales, and member of Council of Duchy of Cornwall 1928-32; KB judge 1932-44; Knight 1932; LJ 1944-47; PC 1944; L of A 1947-57; Br. Pres. at Intern. Mil. Trib., Nuremberg 1945-46; Baron Oaksey 1947; Chmn. Police Inquiry Comm. 1948; Pres. of Haileybury and Imperial Service Coll. 1948; Pres. Br. Dairy Farmers Assoc. 1953; Chmn. Wiltshire Quarter Sess. 1945; DL, JP Wiltshire, and Vice-Lieut. 1954; succeeded brother as 3rd Baron Trevethin 1959. d. 28th Aug 1971.

LAWRENCE, Sir Paul Ogden

s. of Philip Henry Lawrence, solicitor to Bd. of Works, afterwards a barrister (d. 1895). b. 8th Sept 1861. educ. Malvern Coll. and abroad. L.I. Nov. 1882. KC 1896. Bencher 1900. Practised in Liverpool until 1896; member Rule Committee of Supreme Ct. 1910-27; Chmn. of bar council 1913-18; Chmn. Inc. Council of Law Reporting 1917-19; Chancery judge 1918-26; Knight 1919; LJ 1926-34; PC 1926; a Conservator of Wimbledon Common 1901; Chmn. Council of Malvern Coll. 1918; helped his sisters to found Roedean School 1885. d. 26th Dec. 1952.

LAWRENCE, Roger Bernard

s. of Philip Henry Lawrence, solicitor to Bd. of Works, afterwards a barrister (d. 1895). b. 1869. educ. London Univ. BA. L.I. Jan. 1891. KC 1913. Bencher 1919. Equity draftsman and conveyancer; Registrar of Chancery of Lancashire 1914-19; V-C of Cty. Palatine of Lancaster 1919-25. d. 8th Dec. 1925.

LAWRIE, Allan James

s. of James Dundas Lawrie JP, Monkrigg, East Lothian. b. 1873. educ. Fettes; Trinity Coll. Oxf. 1892. L.I. Jan. 1899. KC 1924. Treasury counsel at Middlesex Quarter Sess. 1908; Dep. Chmn. London Sess. 1911-26; JP London. d. 1st Feb. 1926.

LAYTON, John Henry

s. of George Layton, Liverpool. b. 19th Sept 1876. educ. Charterhouse. I.T. May 1898. KC 1922 (revoked at his own request 1923). WWI Major, RFA. d. 29th Jan. 1952.

LEA, George Harris

s. of George Butcher Lea, The Larches, Kidderminster, manufacturer (d. 1859). b. 2nd April 1843. educ. in Worcester; Trinity Coll. Camb. BA 1865, MA 1868. M.T. Nov. 1868. L.I. Dec. 1874. Re-admitted M.T. 1886; Cty. Ct. judge 1891-1915; DL, JP Herefordshire. d. 3rd May 1915.

LEAHY, David

s. of Thomas Leahy, Newcastle, Co. Limerick, merchant. b. 1799. educ. Trinity Coll. Dublin. G.I. Jan. 1831. Cty. Ct. judge 1847. d. 21st June 1847.

LE BRETON, Clement Martin

s. of Very Rev. William Corbet Le Breton, Dean of Jersey (d. 1888). b. 1852. educ. Victoria Coll. Jersey; RMC Sandhurst. Lieut. Northumberland Fusiliers 1871-74. I.T. June 1879. KC 1904. Recorder of Sudbury 1918-27; Mil. Service (Civil Liabilities) Commr. 1916; trade disputes arbitrator for Min. of Labour 1917; Chmn. Shirtmaking and Tailoring Trade Bds. 1918; OBE 1918. d. 1st July 1927.

LECK, David Calder

s. of Rev. Alexander Leck, Kilmalcolm, Renfrewshire. b. 22nd Oct 1857. educ. Glasgow Univ. MA, LLB. M.T. Jan. 1884. KC 1912. Bencher 1921. Practised in commercial and shipping cases. d. 18th March 1927.

LEDGARD, Frederick Thomas Durell

s. of George Durell Ledgard, Bournemouth. b. 1837. educ. Brighton

Coll.; Trinity Coll. Camb. BA 1859. I.T. Jan. 1863. QC 1883. Bencher 1890. d. 21st July 1899.

LEE, John

s. of John Fiott, London, merchant. b. 28th April 1783. educ. St John's Coll. Camb. BA 1806, 5th Wrangler, MA 1809, LLD 1816, Fellow 1808-15. Assumed mother's name of Lee 1815. Advocate Doctors' Commons Nov. 1816, Librarian 1826, Treasurer 1828. G.I. July 1863. QC 1864. Bencher 1864. Pres. Numismatic Socy. 1837; Pres. Royal Astronomical Socy. 1861; FSA 1828, FRS 1831. d. 25th Feb. 1866.

LEE, William

s. of William Lee, Lothbury, London. I.T. July 1813. QC 1845. Bencher 1845, Reader 1858. An expert in real property law, but lacking in business habits; his opinions valued by Ct. of Chancery; often called upon by Knight-Bruce LJ to give an opinion as amicus curiae. d. 7th July 1869, age 83.

LEECH, Samuel Chetwynd

s. of Samuel Leech, Derby, solicitor. b. 13th Aug. 1872. educ. Charterhouse; New Coll. Oxf. BA 1894, MA 1902. Solicitor 1897. L.I. Jan. 1906. Cty. Ct. judge 1925-31. OBE 1918, as Commr. in South London Mil. Service (Civil Liabilities) Dept. d. 2nd May 1931.

LEESE, Sir Joseph Francis, Bt

s. of Joseph Leese, Altrincham, Cheshire, cotton-spinner (d. 1906). b 28th Feb. 1845. educ. Regent's Park Coll.; London Univ. BA 1864; St John's Coll. Camb. 1864. I.T. April 1868. QC 1891. Bencher 1899. Recorder of Manchester 1893-1914; MP North East

Lancashire (Accrington) 1892-1910; member Convocation, London Univ.; Capt. 3rd Royal Lancaster Militia; Knight 1895; Baronet 1908; JP Manchester, Lancashire and Surrey. d. 29th July 1914.

LEFROY, Thomas Edward Preston

s. of Capt. (65th Regt.) Anthony Lefroy, Falford, Yorkshire, and nephew of Rt. Hon. Thomas Lefroy, LCJ Ireland. b. 30th Aug. 1815. M.T. June 1844. Reported cases relating to railways and canals 1840-50; dep. judge Bloomsbury Cty. Ct. 1857-65; Cty. Ct. judge 1868-80. Father of William Chambers Lefroy (L.I. 1876). d. 25th July 1887.

LEIGH, Sir Edward Chandos

s. of 1st Baron Leigh, Stoneleigh Abbey, Warwickshire. b. 22nd Dec. 1832. educ. Harrow; Oriel Coll. Oxf. BA 1855, MA 1858; Fellow of All Souls Coll. 1855-71, and Sub-Warden. I.T. Jan. 1859. QC 1881. Bencher 1886. Recorder of Stamford 1864-81, of Nottingham 1881-1909; counsel to Speaker of House of Commons 1884-1907; CB 1895, KCB 1901; JP Warwickshire; reported (with Cave) Crown Cases Reserved. Author of Bar, Bat and Bit 1914, and (with Le Marchant) of Election Law. d. 18th May 1915.

LEIGH, John

s. of John Leigh, Consall Hall, Staffordshire. b. 1809. educ. privately; Trinity Coll. Camb. 1826. I.T. May 1835. Judge of Ct. of Appeal, Jamaica 1840-46; stip. magistrate, Wolverhampton 1846-60; metrop. magistrate Worship St. 1860-64; bankrupt 1864. d. 24th Oct. 1880.

LEIGH, Thomas Bowes

s. of William Leigh JP, Stockport. b. 22nd may 1867. educ. Manchester Gr. Sch.; Manchester Univ. BSc. 1885, Hon. LLD. M.T. Nov. 1901. WWI Capt. 8th Vol. Battn. Cheshire Regt. Recorder of Burnley 1921-25; Cty. Ct. judge 1925-42; Pres. Manchester and District Medico-Legal Socy. 1937-41; JP Lancashire. d. 20th July 1947.

LEITH, John Farley

s. of James Urquhart Murray Leith, Capt. 68th Regt. b. 5th May 1808. educ. Marischal Coll.; Aberdeen Univ. MA 1825. M.T. June 1830. QC 1872. Bencher 1874, Reader 1882. Advocate in Supreme Ct. Calcutta 1840-49; prof. of law, East India Coll. Haileybury 1853; practised before Judicial Committee of Privy Council; MP Aberdeen 1872-80. Father of Edward Tyrrell Leith (M.T. 1866), professor of law, Bombay. d. 4th April 1887.

LEONARD, Patrick Marcellinus

s. of Stephen John Leonard, Queen's Fort, Tuam, Co. Galway, solicitor. b. June 1821. educ. privately; Trinity Coll. Dublin BA 1843, MA 1846. L.I. Jan. 1847. Equity draftsman and conveyancer; Cty. Ct. judge 1874-96; JP Hampshire. Author of Precedents of Pleading in Equity in the County Courts. d. 5th April 1901.

LE QUESNE, Charles Thomas

of Charles John Le Quesne, St. Helier, Jersey. b. 3rd Nov. 1885. educ. Victoria Coll. Jersey; Exeter Coll. Oxf. BA 1908. I.T. Jan. 1912. KC 1925. Member of Jersey bar; practised mainly in commercial ct.; Commr. of Assize; Master of I.T. Library when it was bombed in 1941, and organised rescue of books etc.; Pres. Baptist Union of GB and Ireland 1946-47; Commander of Order of

Orange Nassau. d. 22nd Nov. 1954.

LEVETT, Ernest Laurence

s. of Benjamin Levett, Hull, broker. b. 24th Aug. 1846. educ. Cheltenham Coll.; St. John's Coll. Camb. BA 1870, 3rd Wrangler, MA 1873, Fellow 1870-80. L.I. June 1873. QC 1891. Bencher 1895. Practised in chancery. d. 3rd Oct. 1916.

LEVY, Richard Francis

s. of David Levy, London, fruiterer. b. 13th July 1892. educ. Hackney Downs Secondary Sch; King's Coll. London LLB. Clerk in Estate Duty office 1911. WWI probationary pilot RNAS; 2nd Lieut. Army Printing and Stationery Services. M.T. June 1918. KC 1937. Bencher 1947. Recorder of Margate 1953-56; Chmn. Monopolies Comm. 1956-65, Workmen's Compensation (Supplementation) Bd. 1956-62, Pneumoconiosis and Byssinosis Benefit Bd. 1956-62, Committee of Inquiry into precautions against anthrax 1957. d. 16th Dec. 1968.

LEWIN, Sir Gregory Allnutt

s. of Richard Lewin, Eltham, Kent, Capt. HEIC Navy. educ. Christ's Coll. Camb. MA 1821. Midshipman, and Lieut. RN 1808-18. M.T. April 1822. QC 1843. Bencher 1843. Recorder of Doncaster 1842-45; Commisssary of Camb. Univ.; Knight (Irish) 1820; FSA. Author of works on Poor Laws and their administration. d. 12th Oct. 1845, age 51.

LEWIS, David

s. of John Lewis, Swansea, iron merchant. b. 1849. educ. Llandovery Coll.; Caius Coll. Camb. BA 1872. I.T. Nov. 1873. The first recorder of Swansea 1891-93; Cty. Ct. judge 1893-97; JP. Joint author (with J.K. Fowles) of treatise on law relating to collieries. d. 9th Sept. 1897.

LEWIS, Sir Wilfrid Hubert Poyer

s. of Arthur Griffith Poyer Lewis JP, Henllan, Narbeth, Pembrokeshire, Recorder of Carmarthen (d. 1909). b. 9th Feb. 1881. educ. Eton; University Coll. Oxf. BA 1903, MA 1914, Hon. Fellow 1943. I.T. Jan. 1908. Bencher 1929. WWI Capt. Glamorgan Yeo., OBE (despatches twice). Practised in Cardiff until 1914; Chan. Of dioceses of Llandaff 1914, Monmouth 1921, Manchester and Blackburn 1929, Worcester 1930; regularly briefed by leading London newspapers in libel actions, and by Great Western Ry.; prominent in prize cases arising from WWI; junior counsel to Treasury (common law) 1930; KB judge 1935-50; Knight 1935; WWII served in Home Guard; an authority on eccles. law; Chmn. Pembrokeshire Quarter Sess.; DL, JP Pembrokeshire; Fellow of Eton Coll.; Trustee of Llandovery Coll.; devoted much time to affairs of Welsh Church. d. 15th March 1950.

LEWIS, William David

s. of Rev. George William Lewis, Ramsgate (d. 1858). b. 1823. Pupil of John Rudall, conveyancer 1838. Conveyancer in London 1842. L.I. Jan. 1844. QC 1859. Bencher 1859. Reader on law of real property and conveyancing at G.I. 1847-52; a Commr. on registration of title to land 1854; founded Juridical Socy. 1855. Author of treatise on law of perpetuities 1843. Brother of Sir Charles Edward Lewis Bt., MP, solicitor. d. 24th Jan 1861.

LEYCESTER, Willaim Hamilton

s. of William Leycester, barrister and chief of The Times parliamentary staff. b. 17th Dec. 1864. educ. King's Coll. Sch.;

Peterhouse Camb. BA 1888, 18th Wrangler, MA 1892. M.T. Nov. 1888. Treasury counsel at Central Criminal Ct.; law reporter for The Times; metrop. magistrate 1912, finally at Bow St. 1922-25. d. 23rd Oct. 1925.

LIAS, William John

s. of Rev. John James Lias, The Lodge, Abington, nr. Cambridge. b. 13th March 1868. educ. Haileybury; Jesus Coll. Camb. BA 1889, MA 1898. Headmaster Downs Sch. Clifton 1894-99. L.I. May 1901. Lieut. RNVR 1905-13. WWI Capt. Lancashire Fusiliers and RE (despatches). Prof. of international law Sheffield Univ.; Cty. Ct. judge 1922-40. d. 20th July 1941.

LIDDELL, Sir Adolphus Frederick Octavius

s. of 1st Baron Ravensworth (d. 1855). b. 15th Jan. 1818. educ. Eton; Christ Church Oxf. BA 1839, MA 1844; Fellow of All Souls Coll. 1840-46. I.T. Jan. 1844. QC 1861. Bencher 1861, Reader 1875, Treasurer 1875. Permanent Under-Secy. of State, Home Dept. 1867-85; KCB 1880. d. 27th June 1885.

LIDDELL, Sir Frederick Francis

s. of Very Rev. Henry George Liddell, dean of Christ Church Oxf. (d. 1898). b. 7th June 1865. educ. Eton; Christ Church Oxf. BA 1888, MA 1892; Fellow of All Souls Coll. 1891-1906. Private secy. to Sir Arthur Gordon, Govr. of Ceylon 1888-90. L.I. June 1894. KC 1929. First parliamentary counsel 1917-28; counsel to Speaker of H of C 1928-43; an eccles. commr. for England 1944-48; KCB 1916, CB 1911. Edited the Manual of Military Law. d. 19th March 1950.

LILLEY, Cecil William

s. of Joseph Edward Lilley JP, Wealdstone, Middlesex, barrister. b. 23rd March 1878. educ. Harrow. M.T. June 1900. Bencher 1932. Junior counsel to Min. of Labour1921; Cty. Ct. judge 1934-45. d. 31st March 1953.

LINDLEY, Nathaniel (Lord Lindley)

s. of John Lindley LLD, PhD, FRS, Prof. of Botany, Univ. Coll. London (d. 1865). b. 29th Nov. 1828. educ. Univ. Coll. Sch. and University Coll. London. M.T. Nov. 1850. QC 1872. Bencher 1874, Reader 1881, Treasurer 1891. Distinguished himself as junior counsel for Overend Gurney & Co. (bank failure) 1866; appeared for Frederick Gye in Knox v. Gye (whether partnership subsisted in a business at Covent Garden Theatre) 1871; judge of Common Pleas and knighted 1875; LJ 1881-97; MR 1897-1900; Baron Lindley of East Carleton 1900; L of A 1900-05; PC 1881; FRS 1897; Hon. LLD Edin. and Camb.; Hon. DCL Oxf. Author of An Introduction to the Study of Jurisprudence 1855, and a treatise on partnership, including its application to companies 1860. d. 9th Dec. 1921.

LINDLEY, Walter Barry

s. of Lord Lindley, L of A. b. 31st Dec. 1861. educ. Winchester; University Coll. Oxf. BA 1883, MA 1887. L.I. Nov. 1887. Equity draftsman and conveyancer; Cty. Ct. judge 1902-34; Chmn. Derbyshire Quarter Sess. 1909-12; Chmn. Somerset Quarter Sess. 1920-31; Temp.Lieut. 3rd Battn. Somerset Vol. Regt.; JP Somerset. d. 29th March 1944.

LINDON, John Benjamin

s. of M. Lindenbaum, Maida Vale, London. b. 14th Sept. 1884. educ.

Harrow; Gonville & Caius Coll. Camb. BA and LLB 1906, MA 1910, LLM 1910. I.T. Nov. 1909 (Cert. of Hon.). KC 1943. Bencher (L.I.) 1946. WWI Chief Intelligence Officer, War Trade Intelligence Dept., OBE 1919. With Min. of Economic Warfare 1939-44. d. 13th July 1960.

LINDSAY, William Alexander

s. of Hon. Colin Lindsay JP, Deer Park, Honiton, Devon (d. 1892). b. 8th June 1846. educ. Eton; Trinity Coll. Camb. BA 1868, MA 1872. Member of Lloyd's 1867. M.T. April 1873. QC 1897. Bencher 1906, Reader 1919. Peerage counsel; Portcullis pursuivant 1882-94; Windsor Herald 1894-1919; Norroy King of Arms 1919-22; Clarenceux King of Arms 1922-26; CVO 1924; DL, JP Devon; FSA. Published work on genealogical subjects. d. 13th Sept. 1926.

LITTLE, George

s. of George Little, Blackburn, Lancashire. b. 1815. Articled to solicitor in Manchester. M.T. May 1840. QC 1866. Bencher 1867, Reader 1873. Judge of Chancery Ct. of Cty. Palatine of Lancaster 1871-81. d. 27th Jan. 1881.

LITTLER, Sir Ralph Daniel Makinson

s. of Rev. Robert Littler, Matlock Bath, Derbyshire. b. 2nd Oct. 1835. educ. Univ. Coll. Sch.; University Coll. London BA 1854. I.T. June 1857. M.T. April 1870. QC 1873. Bencher 1882, Reader 1892, Treasurer 1901. Chmn. Middlesex Sess. 1889-1908; Middlesex CC 1889-1908; Chmn. Alexandra Park Trustees; CB 1890; knight 1902; DL, JP London; AMICE. Author of works on practice and evidence in divorce, on the duties of justices, and of a digest of cases before referees in parliament. d. 23rd Nov. 1908.

LLOYD, Edward Honoratus

s. of Sir Horatio Lloyd, Cty. Ct. judge. b. 7th May 1860. educ. Dulwich; London Univ. 1878; Trinity Coll. Oxf. BA 1882, MA 1888. M.T. Nov. 1882. KC 1904. Bencher 1912, Reader 1924. Recorder of Chester 1921-27; JP Cheshire. d. 7th Dec. 1930.

LLOYD, Edward John

s. of Thomas Gore Lloyd, Clapham, London, accountant-general of HEIC. b. 25th Feb. 1799. educ. in Blackheath; Trinity Coll Camb. BA 1822, MA 1825. L.I. Feb. 1825. QC 1849. Bencher 1849. Cty. Ct. judge 1863-74. d. 1st June 1879.

LLOYD, Horace

s. of John Horatio Lloyd MP, barrister (d. 1884). b. Aug 1828. educ. University Coll. London; Caius Coll. Camb. BA 1850, 20th Wrangler. M.T. June 1852. QC 1868. Bencher 1868. d. 30th March 1874.

LLOYD, Sir Horatio

s. of Edward Watson Lloyd, The Mount, Chester, Prothonotary and Clerk of the Crown. b. 29th Sept. 1829. educ. Rossall; Caius Coll. Camb. BA 1850. M.T. May 1852. Counsel to Mint, IR and PO; Recorder of Chester 1866; Cty. Ct. judge 1874-1906; Chmn. Cheshire Quarter Sess. 1883; Knight 1890; JP Cheshire, Flintshire, Denbigh and Carnarvon. Author of The Law of Quarter Sessions 1875; edited Chitty's Statutes. d. 24th Dec. 1920.

LLOYD, Morgan

s. of Morris Lloyd, Cefngellgwm, Merionethshire. b. 14th July 1822.

educ. Bala Sch.; Edin. Univ. A land surveyor. M.T. Jan. 1847. QC 1873. Bencher 1875, Reader 1884. MP Beaumaris 1874-85; JP Merionethshire. Author of works on law of prohibition, and practice of county courts and supreme court. d. 5th Sept. 1893.

LLOYD-JACOB, Sir George Harold

s. of John Lloyd Jacob, Wood Green, London, civil servant. b. 1st Oct. 1897. educ. in Southgate; King;s Coll. London; Christ Church Oxf. BA 1921, BCL and MA 1923. WWI Lieut. RFC, and Flight-Lieut. RAF 1918-21. M.T. Jan. 1923. KC 1945. Bencher 1950. Junior counsel to Bd. of Trade in patent matters 1938-45; Chancery judge 1950-69; Knight 1950. d. 3rd Dec. 1969.

LOCH, George

s. of James Loch MP, Drylaw, Midlothian, barrister (d. 1855). b. 6th July 1811, educ. Charterhouse. M.T. May 1847. QC 1863. Bencher 1863, Reader 1866, Treasurer 1874. MP Wick Burghs 1868-72; Att-Genl. to Prince of Wales 1873-77. d. 18th Aug. 1877.

LOCK, Benjamin Fossett

s. of Henry Lock, Dorchester, Dorset, solicitor. b. 13th Dec. 1847. educ. Dorchester Gr. Sch.; Eton; King's Coll. Camb. BA 1871, MA 1877. L.I. June 1873. Equity draftsman and conveyancer; commissioned in Royal Naval Artillery Volunteers 1890-92; hon. secy. Selden Socy. 1895-1913; examr. to Council of Legal Educ. 1896-1906; Cty. Ct. judge 1913-22. d. 11th Aug. 1922.

LOCKE, John

s. of John Locke, Herne Hill, Surrey, surveyor. b. 1805. educ. Dulwich; Trinity Coll. Camb. BA 1829, MA 1832. I.T. May 1833.

QC 1857. Bencher 1857, Reader 1870, Treasurer 1871. One of common pleaders of City of London 1845-57; counsel to IR; Recorder of Brighton 1861-79; MP Southwark 1857-80. Author of a treatise on the game laws. Father of John Henry Locke (I.T. 1872). d. 28th Jan. 1880.

LOCKWOOD, Sir Frank

s. of Charles Day Lockwood, Doncaster, stone quarrier. b. 15th July 1846. educ. Manchester Gr. Sch.; Caius Coll. Camb. BA 1869. L.I. Jan. 1872. QC 1882. Bencher 1887. Defended Charles Peace 1879; Recorder of Sheffield 1884-94; Sol-Genl. 1894-95; Knight 1894; MP York 1885-97. Published sketches in Punch from 1893; illustrated Darling's "Scintillae Juris" 1889; author of The Law and Lawyers of Pickwick 1894. The Frank Lockwood Sketchbook published 1898. d. 19th Dec. 1897.

LOFTHOUSE, Samuel Hill Smith

s. of John Lofthouse, Sheffield. b. 25th March 1843. educ. Trinity Hall Camb. LLB 1869. L.I. June 1869. KC 1902. Bencher. Asst. Recorder of Sheffield 1881-1915; Recorder of Doncaster 1902-15; hon. secy. bar committee and bar council 1883-97; Col. Inns of Ct. Rifle Volunteers 1896-1910; VD 1902. d. 23rd Dec. 1915.

LONG, Alfred James

s. of Alfred Long, West Bromwich, Staffordshire. b. 1890. educ. King Edward's Sch. Birmingham; London Univ. LLB. WWI Lieut. North Staffordshire Regt. and attached as liaison officer Portuguese Contingent. L.I. June 1915. KC 1938. Bencher 1946. Recorder of Smethwick 1937-39, of West Bromwich 1939-51, of Wolverhampton 1951. d. 7th July 1952.

LONG, George

s. of Joseph Long, Shopwick, nr. Chichester. b. 1780. Special pleader 1809-11. G.I. Feb. 1811. Bencher 1834, Treasurer 1837. Dep. Steward of the Palace Ct. 1825-33; Commr. for inquiry into the state of municipal corporations 1833; metrop. magistrate 1839, finally at Marylebone 1841-59; Recorder of Coventry 1836-42. Author of a treatise on the sale of personal property 1821. d. 26th June 1868.

LONGSON, Edward Harold

s. of James Edward Longson, Bowdon, Cheshire. b. 1872. educ. privately; New Coll. Oxf. I.T. Nov. 1895. Practised in Cty. Palatine Ct. of Lancaster; Cty. Ct. judge 1931-41. d. 21st March 1941.

LONGSTAFFE, Amyas Philip

s. of John Lawrance Longstaffe, Upper Westbourne Terr., West London. b. 28th Sept. 1858. educ. Westminster and abroad. I.T. June 1880. Asst. Recorder of Leeds 1905; junior counsel to Bd. of Trade in Wreck Inquiries 1905; Cty. Ct. judge 1911-14. d. 13th june 1914.

LONSDALE, James John

s. of James Lonsdale, London, portrait painter (d. 1839). b. 5th April 1810. educ. Univ. Coll. London. L.I. Nov. 1836. Secy. to criminal law comm. 1842; Recorder of Folkstone 1847-86; Cty. Ct. judge 1855-84; DL, JP Yorkshire West Riding. Author of a treatise on criminal law. d. 11th Nov. 1886.

LOPES, Henry Charles (Lord Ludlow)

s. of Sir Ralph Lopes MP, 2nd Bt. (d. 1854). b. 3rd Oct. 1828. educ.

Winchester; Balliol Coll. Oxf. BA 1849. I.T. June 1852. QC 1869. Bencher 1870, Treasurer 1890. Recorder of Exeter 1867-76; MP Launceston 1868-74, Frome 1874-76; judge of Common Pleas 1876-81; Knight 1876; QB judge 1881-85; LJ 1885-97; PC 1885; Baron Ludlow of Heywood 1897; Chmn. Wiltshire Quarter Sess. 1896-99; DL, JP Wiltshire and Somerset. Father of Henry Ludlow Lopes, 2nd Baron (I.T. 1890). Brother of Ralph Ludlow Lopes (I.T. 1847), Recorder of Devizes. d. 25th Dec. 1899.

LORT-WILLIAMS, Sir John Rolleston

s. of Charles William Williams, Walsall, Staffordshire, solicitor. b. 14th Sept. 1881. educ. Merchant Taylors'; London Univ. Served in Middlesex Imp. Yeo. 1902-08. I.T. and L.I. Jan. 1904. Member LCC 1907-10; Pres. Hardwicke Socy. 1911. KC 1922. Recorder of West Bromwich 1923-24, Walsall 1924-28; MP Rotherhithe 1918-23; judge of High Ct. Calcutta 1927-41; acting CJ 1939-40; Knight 1936; Pres. Royal Asiatic Socy. of Bengal 1940-42. d. 9th June 1966.

LOSH, James

s. of James Losh, recorder of Newcastle (d. 1833). b. 1803. educ. Durham Sch.; Trinity Coll. Camb. BA 1826, MA 1829. L.I. Nov. 1829. Cty. Ct. judge 1853-58; an alderman of Newcastle. d. 1st Oct. 1858.

LOVELAND, Richard Loveland

s. of John Perry Loveland JP, Pembridge Villas, West London. b. 18th July 1841. educ. Kensington Gr. Sch.; Pembroke Coll. Oxf. I.T. and L.I. Nov. 1865. QC 1897. Dep.Chmn. Middlesex Sess. 1889-96; Dep. Chmn. London Sess. 1896-1911; DL, JP Middlesex; JP London; KStJ; editor of Sir John Kelyng's Crown Cases 1873, Shower's Cases in Parliament, Hall's Seashore Rights. d. 21st Sept. 1923.

LOW, Sir Frederick

s. of Stephen Philpot Low DL, JP, Round Hill Villa, Sydenham, Kent, banker. b. 21st Nov. 1856. educ. Westminster. Solicitor 1878; practised in London. M.T. April 1890. KC 1902. Bencher 1911. Recorder of Ipswich 1906-15; Knight 1909; MP Norwich 1910-15; Commr. of Assize, Western and Midland circuits 1913 and 1915; KB judge 1915-17; Capt. 4th Vol. Battn. Royal West Surrey Regt. and 22nd Middlesex R. Vol. 1880-90. Father of Sir Stephen Philpot Low (M.T. 1906), Solicitor to Bd. of Trade. d. 4th Sept. 1917.

LOWENTHAL, Charles Frederick

s. of Joseph Lowenthal JP, The Grange, Huddersfield. b. 29th June 1862. educ. Marlborough. M.T. Jan. 1888. KC 1926. bencher 1919, Reader 1929, Treasurer 1932. Junior counsel of Commrs. of Works 1908-26; the first recorder of Huddersfield 1919-28; Recorder of Kingston-upon-Hull 1928-33. d. 10th Feb. 1933.

LOWNDES, Sir George Rivers

s. of Rev. Richard Lowndes, canon of Salisbury (d. 1898), and g.s. of William Loftus Lowndes QC. b. 1862. educ. Winchester; New Coll. Oxf. 1880, MA 1905. L.I. Nov. 1892. KC 1917. Bencher 1922. Legal member Council of Gov-Genl. India 1915-20; KCSI 1918; PC 1929; member Judicial Committee 1929-34. d. 18th Sept. 1943.

LOWNDES, William

s. of Richard Lowndes, Liverpool. b. 1791. educ. Harrow; Brasenose Coll. Oxf. BA 1814, MA 1817. L.I. Feb. 1818. Equity draftsman and conveyancer; Cty. Ct. judge 1847-50. Drowned at Liverpool, 31st March 1850.

LOWNDES, William Loftus

s. of Richard Lowndes, Dorking, Surrey. b. April 1793. L.I. Feb. 1818. QC 1842. Bencher 1842. Published W.P. Williams' reports of Chancery cases, with reference to modern cases, 1826. d. 6th April 1865.

LOYD, Archie Kirkman

s. of Thomas Kirkman Loyd, Cheapside, London and Bengal Civil Service (d. 1857). b. 22nd Jan. 1847. educ. Brighton Coll. Indian Civil Service 1867-69. M.T. Nov. 1868. QC 1892. Bencher 1894, Reader 1907. MP Berkshire (North) 1895-1906 and 1916-18; DL, JP Berkshire, and alderman of CC. d. 1st Dec. 1922.

LUDLOW, Ebenezer

s. of Ebenezer Ludlow, Chipping Sodbury, Gloucestershire. b. 1777. educ. Oriel Coll. Oxf. BA 1795, MA 1821. G.I. Nov. 1805. Town Clerk of Bristol 1819-36. Serjeant 1827; patent of precedence 1840. Commr. in Bankruptcy 1842-51; Chmn. Gloucestershire Quarter Sess. 1842-49. d. 14th March 1851.

LUMLEY, William Golden

s. of William Lumley, London. b. 1802. educ. Christ's Hosp.; Trinity Hall Camb. LLB 1825, LLM 1859, Fellow 1825-40. M.T. May 1827. QC 1868. Prof. of English law, London Univ. 1834-38; reporter for Law Journal 1835; Secy. of Poor Law Bd. 1839-47; Asst. Secy. Local Govt. Bd. 1847-71; counsel to Local Govt. Bd. 1872. Author of Works on poor law and local govt., particularly public health. Father of Edmund Lumley (M.T. 1865), Recorder of Grantham. d. 8th May 1878.

LUSH, Sir Charles Montague

s. of Lush LJ. b. 7th Dec. 1853. educ. Westminster; Trinity Hall Camb. BA 1876, Hon. Fellow 1911-30. G.I. May 1879. KC 1902. Bencher 1893, Treasurer 1901. Member Joint Bd. of Examrs. at Inns of Ct. 1880; KB judge 1910-25; Knight 1910; Pres. Ry and Canal Comm.; PC 1925. Author of Law of Husband and Wife 1884. Father of Montague Arthur Lush (G.I. 1924) and Harold Charles Lush (G.I. 1924). d. 22nd June 1930.

LUSH, Sir Robert

s. of Robert Lush, Shaftesbury, Dorset. b. 25th Oct 1807. Employed in a solicitor's office. Special pleader 1839. G.I. Nov. 1840. QC 1857. Bencher 1857-65, Treasurer 1859. QB judge 1865-80; Knight 1865; one of the three judges who tried the Tichborne claimant for perjury 1873-74; member Judicature Comm., and comm. on draft penal code, 1878; PC 1879; LJ 1880-81. Author of the Act for the abolition of arrest on mesne process, with notes, 1838, Practice of the Superior Courts of Law at Westminster in actions and proceedings over which they have a common jurisdiction 1840 (became the standard work on common law practice); edited J. Chitty's The Practice of the Law in all its departments 1842, and Saunders' Law of Evidence and Pleading in civil actions 1851. d. 27th Dec 1881.

LUSH-WILSON, Sir Herbert William

s. of Lush LJ. b. 2nd April 1850. educ. Westminster; Trinity Hall Camb. BA 1872. I.T. April 1873. QC 1895. Assumed additional name of Wilson 1879. Cty. Ct. judge 1901-22; Knight 1923; DL, JP Herefordshire; JP Devon. Brother of Robert Christopher Lush(G.I. 1865). d. 19th Nov. 1941.

LUSHINGTON, Sir Franklin

s. of Edmond Henry Lushington, Park House, Kent, puisne judge
Ceylon (d. 1839). b. 4th Jan. 1823. educ. Rugby; Trinity Coll. Camb.
BA 1846, MA 1849, Fellow 1847. I.T. Jan. 1853. Member Supreme
Council of Justice, Ionian Islands 1855-58; examr. to Inns of Ct.;
metrop. magistrate 1869, finally at Bow St. 1890-1901; chief
magistrate and knighted 1899; JP Middlesex and Home Counties.
d. 10th Nov. 1901.

LUSHINGTON, Stephen

s. of Sir Stephen Lushington Bt., East India director (d. 1807). b.
14th Jan. 1782. educ. Eton; Christ Church Oxf. BA 1802, MA 1806,
BCL 1807, DCL 1808; Fellow of All Souls Coll. 1802. I.T. Feb.
1806. Bencher 1840, Reader 1850, Treasurer 1851. Advocate
Doctors' Commons, Nov. 1808. MP Great Yarmouth 1806-08,
Ilchester 1820-26, Tregony, Cornwall 1826-30, Winchelsea 1831,
Tower Hamlets 1832-41; an executor of Queen Caroline 1821;
Freeman of City of London 1821; judge of Consistory Ct. of London
1828-58; Admiralty judge 1838-67; PC 1838; Dean of the Arches
1858-67; Chan. of diocese of Rochester 1826-56, of London
1828-58; served on many royal comms.; active supporter of Sir T.F.
Buxton in anti-slavery movement. Father of William Bryan
Lushington, barrister, and Sir Godfrey Lushington GCMG, KCB
(I.T. 1858). d. 19th Jan. 1873.

LUSHINGTON, Vernon

s. of Stephen Lushington, Dean of the Arches. b. 8th March 1832.
educ. Trinity Coll. Camb. LLB 1859, LLM 1885. I.T. Jan. 1857. QC
1868. Bencher 1869. Examr. to Inns of Ct.; Dep. Judge Adv-Genl.
1865-69; Recorder of Richmond (Yorkshire) 1866; Secy. to the
Admiralty 1869-77; Cty. Ct. judge 1877-1900; JP; reported cases
decided in the Admiralty Ct. and on appeal in Privy Council. d. 24th
Jan. 1912.

LUXMOORE, Sir Arthur Fairfax Charles Coryndon

s. of Arthur Coryndon Hansler Luxmoore, Danescliffe, St. Lawrence, Thanet, artist. b. 27th Feb. 1876. educ. King's Sch. Canterbury; Jesus Coll. Camb. BA 1900; played rugby for Camb. and for England 1900-01; Hon. Fellow 1938. L.I. Nov. 1899. KC 1919. Bencher 1922. Equity draftsman and conveyancer; member of bar council; expert in patent and trademark law; Chmn. Rating Appeal Committee, East Kent 1929-40; Chancery judge 1929-38; Knight 1929; LJ 1938-44; PC 1938; Chmn. Committee on Post-War Agricultural Educ. 1941-43; Chmn. East Kent Quarter Sess. 1931-40; JP Kent; Pres. Kent Cty. Cricket Club; Mayor of New Romney 1920-26; Speaker of the Cinque Ports. d. 25th Sept. 1944.

LYNSKEY, Sir George Justin

s. of George Jeremy Lynskey, Liverpool, solicitor (d. 1921). b. 5th Feb. 1888. educ. St. Francis Xavier's Coll. and Liverpool Univ. LLB 1907, LLM 1908, Hon. LLD 1951. Solicitor 1910. I.T. Jan. 1920 (Cert. of Hon.). KC 1930. Bencher 1938. Leader of Northern circuit; judge of Salford Hundred Ct. of Record 1937-44; KB judge 1944-57; Knight 1944; Chmn. Bd. of Trade Inquiry into alleged payments to Ministers or public servants in return for licences or permissions, or withdrawal of prosecutions 1948. d. 21st Dec. 1957.

LYONS, Abraham Montagu

s. of Rabinavitch Lyons, West Bridgford, Nottinghamshire, commission agent. b. 1894. educ. Old Clee Gr. Sch. Lincolnshire. Solicitor 1916, practised in Leeds and Lincoln. WWI 2nd. Lieut. Durham Light Infantry, and legal dept. Min. of Food. M.T. Jan. 1922. KC 1933. Leader of Midland circuit; Recorder of Great Grimsby 1936-61; member of bar council; MP East Leicester 1931-45. WWII Sqn. Leader AAF 1939; Major and Dep. Asst. Director War Office 1941, Colonel 1944. Master of Pattenmakers' Co. 1959-60. d. 29th Nov. 1961.

LYTTELTON, Alfred

s. of George William, 4th Baron Lyttelton. b. 7th Feb. 1857. educ. Eton; Trinity Coll. Camb. BA 1879, MA 1899; cricket and assoc. football blue; Hon. MA Oxf. Univ. I.T. June 1881. QC 1900. Bencher 1899. Legal private secy. to Sir Henry James, Att-Genl. 1882-86; Recorder of Hereford 1893-94, of Oxford 1895-1903; Chan. of diocese of Rochester 1903; Secy. of State for Colonies 1903-05; MP Leamington 1895-1906, St. George's, Hanover Sq. 1906-13; Chmn. Transvaal Concessions Comm. 1900; Royal Commr. on Port of London, and Alien Immigration; Dep. High Steward Camb. Univ.; PC 1903; FRCI 1906; cricketer for England and amateur tennis champion; Pres. MCC 1898. d. 4th July 1913.

MACASKIE, Nicholas Lechmere Cunningham

s. of Stuart Cunningham Macaskie KC. b. 19th Aug. 1881. educ. Uppingham; Belgium; Paris Univ. Bachelier ès lettres 1901. G.I. July 1905. KC 1930. Bencher 1930, Treasurer 1943. WWI Lieut. RGA. Recorder of York 1930-41, of Sheffield 1941-57; member Council of Legal Educ. and Bd. of Legal Studies 1935-45; head of legal divn. Control Comm. Germany 1945-49; Chmn. Appeal Trib. under Road and Rail Traffic Act 1949-51; member special panel of Transport Trib. 1951-61; from 1952, standing arbitrator under The Railways Act 1921; Commr. of Assize 1954; judge of Cinque Ports 1954-67; appeal steward of Br. Boxing Bd. of Control 1950; director, London General Investment Trust Ltd. d. 1st Jan. 1967.

MACASKIE, Stuart Cunningham

s. of George Macaskie, Berwick-upon-Tweed. b. 1853. educ. Berwick Gr. Sch. Journalist until 1875. G.I. July 1878 (Cert. of Hon.). KC 1901. Bencher 1893, Treasurer 1899. Member of bar council 1895; Recorder of Doncaster 1901-02, of Sheffield 1902-03; a commr. to inquire into the uprising in Trinidad 1903. Author of Law of Executors, Law of Bills of Sale. Joint author of the Law of

Corrupt Practices at Elections. d. 2nd Nov. 1903.

MACASSEY, Sir Lynden Livingston

s. of Luke Livingston Macassey MICE, Holywood, Co. Down, barrister. b. 14th June 1876. educ. Upper Sullivan Sch. Holywood; Bedford; London Univ.; Trinity Coll. Dublin LLB and BA 1898, MA 1903, LLD 1903. Assoc. member of Inst. CE, Surveyors' Inst. and Inst. of Patent Agents. M.T. Nov. 1899. KC 1912. Bencher 1922, Reader 1930, Treasurer 1934. Capt. London Irish Rifles. Lecturer in economics and law LSE 1901-09; secy. Royal Comm. on London traffic 1903-06; Bd. of Trade arbitrator in shipbuilding and engineering cases 1914-16; director, shipyard labour, Admiralty 1917-18; member, War cabinet committees on labour 1917-18, on women in industry 1918-19; labour assessor for GB, Permanent Ct. of International Justice 1920; chmn. govnrs. Queen Mary Coll. London Univ. 1922-44; Master of Drapers' Co. 1932; Pres. Inst. of Arbitrators; Pres. Scottish Amicable Life Assce. Socy.; KBE 1917. d. 23rd Feb. 1963.

MACAULAY, Kenneth

s. of Rev. Aulay Macaulay, Rothley Temple, Lancashire. b. 1815. educ. in Plymouth, Jesus Coll. Camb. BA1835, MA 1839. I.T. May 1839. QC 1850. Bencher 1850, Reader 1864, Treasurer 1865. Leader of Midland circuit; MP Cambridge 1852-54 and 1857-65. d. 29th July 1867.

McCALL, Sir Robert Alfred

s. of Hugh McCall, Lisburn, Antrim, newspaper editor. b. 9th July 1849. educ. Queen's Univ. Belfast MA, LLD. M.T. June 1871. QC 1891. Bencher 1894, Reader 1906, Treasurer 1917. Att-Genl. Cty. Palatine of Lancaster; Queen's Attorney and Serjeant, Lancaster 1899-1921; Vice-Chmn. Council of Legal Educ. 1917; Commr. of

Assize, Wales and Chester circuit 1919; Registrar, Ry. and Canal Comm. 1921; Pres. Huguenot Socy. 1923; member Senate, London Univ.; KCVO 1921; JP Kent and Cinque Ports. d. 6th April 1934.

McCARDIE, Sir Henry Alfred

s. of Joseph William McCardie, Wellington Grove, Edgbaston, merchant. b. 18th july 1869. educ. King Edward's Sch. Birmingham. M.T. April 1894. Bencher 1916, Reader 1927. KB judge 1916-33; Knight 1916; his judgments prolix, with tendency to enter into consideration of social problems; his removal sought following libel case involving Brig-Genl. Dyer, in which McCardie recorded his opinion that Dyer's action in quelling civil disturbance at Amritsar was justified, 1919. d. (suicide) 26th April 1933. Biog. by George Pollock 1934.

McCARTHY, John William

s. of Jeremiah McCarthy, Kilworth, Co. Cork, merchant. b. 19th Sept. 1854. educ. Kilkenny Coll., Queen's Coll. Cork, Dublin Univ. British consular service, Japan 1876; private secy. to Japanese Minister for Foreign Affairs 1879-82. G.I. and M.T. Nov. 1886. Bencher (G.I.) 1909. Standing counsel to Chinese legation in London 1892-1902; Cty. Ct. judge 1914-29; Asst. Chmn. Yorkshire West Riding Quarter Sess.; Chmn. Yorkshire North Riding Quarter Sess. 1929; JP Durham, Yorkshire North and West Ridings. d. 19th July 1935.

McCLEARY, Robert

s. of George McCleary, Manchester. b. 2nd Dec. 1869. educ. privately; Trinity Hall. Camb. BA 1891. M.T. May 1895. Cty. Ct. judge 1926-36. Author of works on Cty. Ct. procedure. d. 27th Sept. 1936.

McCLURE, George Buchanan

s. of James Howe McClure. b. 21st April 1887. educ. Kelvinside Acad.; Trinity Coll. Oxf. WWI Capt. 9th London Regt. (despatches). I.T. Nov. 1917. Bencher 1938. Junior pros. counsel to Treasury, Central Criminal Ct. 1928-34, senior 1937-42; Recorder of Rochester 1933-39, of Guildford 1939-42; Chmn. Hertfordshire Quarter Sess. 1939-50; judge of Mayor's and City of London Ct. 1942-53. Joint editor of Russell on Crimes and Misdemeanours. d. 22nd Feb. 1955.

McCONNELL, William Robert

s. of David McConnell JP, Charleville, nr. Belfast. b. 2nd July 1837. educ. Royal Acad. Inst. Belfast; London Univ. BA. I.T. April 1862. QC 1896. Counsel in Goncourt frauds, case of Mrs. Florence Maybrick (poisoning of husband) 1889, and other notable trials; junior counsel to Bd. of Trade 1875, to Bd. of Customs 1876; Commr. to inquire into corrupt election practices in Gloucester; Chmn. London Sess. 1896-1906; member of bar committee 1883; DL, JP London; JP Co. Down; FRGS. d. 21st Dec. 1906.

McCURDY, Charles Albert

s. of Rev. Alexander McCurdy, Loughborough, Leicestershire. b. 13th March 1870. educ. Loughborough Gr. Sch.; Pembroke Coll. Camb. BA 1891. I.T. June 1896. KC 1919. MP Northampton 1910-23; parliamentary secy. to Min. of Food 1919-20, Food Controller 1920-21; joint parliamentary secy. to Treasury 1921-22; a founder of the League of Nations Union; PC 1920; Chmn. United Newspapers (1918) Ltd., and Edinburgh Evening News Ltd. 1922-26; director, Equity and Law Insce. Co. Ltd.; Chmn. Bedford General Insce. Ltd. d. 10th Nov. 1941.

MACDONALD, Sir John Hay Athole

s. of Matthew Norman Macdonald-Hume WS, Ninewells. b. 28th
Dec. 1836. educ. Edin. Acad.; Univs. of Edin. and Basle. Scottish
bar 1859. Sheriff, Ross, Cromarty and Sutherland 1874-76;
Sol-Genl. Scotland 1876-80; QC 1880; Sheriff, Perthshire 1880-85;
Dean of Faculty of Advocates 1882-85; Lord Adv. 1885-86,
1886-88; Lord Justice Clerk 1888 (as Lord Kingsburgh); Pres. of
2nd Div. of Ct. of Session 1888-1915; PC 1885; KCB 1900, GCB
1916; FRS; Brig-Genl. commanding Forth Vol. Infy. Brigade
1888-1901. d. 9th May 1919.

MACGEAGH, Sir Henry Davies Foster

s. of Thomas Foster Macgeagh, Hadlow Castle, Kent, and g.s. of
Benjamin Foster Macgeagh, barrister. b. 21st Oct. 1883. educ. St.
Paul's; Magdalen Coll. Oxf. BA 1905. M.T. June 1906. KC 1924.
Bencher 1931, Reader 1943, Dep. Treasurer 1949 (during Queen's
treasurership), Treasurer 1950. WWI Brev. Major London Rifle
Brigade (despatches); mil. asst. to JAG 1916-22; AAG War Office
1918-23; Dep. JAG Br. forces in China (Shanghai Defence Force)
1927; Col. in charge of Mil. and Air Force Dept. of JAG's office
1923-34; JAG 1934-54; Chmn. Council of Legal Educ. 1953-62;
member Council of Socy. of Comparative Legislation; Medal of
Freedom with gold palms, USA; GCVO 1950; KCB 1946; KBE
1930; CBE 1919; TD. d. 29th Dec. 1962.

MACGILLIVRAY, Evan James

s. of William MacGillivray WS, Edinburgh. b. 14th Sept 1873. educ.
Edin. Acad.; Trinity Coll. Camb. BA 1894, LLB 1895. I.T. June
1896. KC 1939. Scottish bar 1897. WWI Lieut. RNVR,
Anti-Aircraft Corps, Dover Patrol and London Defences. Author of
Law of Copyright 1902, Insurance Law 1912, and manual on
Copyright Act 1911. d. 18th Oct. 1955.

McILWRAITH, Sir Robert Malcolm

s. of Robert McIlwraith, Hans Place, London S.W.1., and Bombay. b. 18th July 1865. educ. Marlborough; Berlin Univ.; graduated at Paris Sch. of Law 1887. L.I. Nov. 1890. KC 1914. Bencher 1922. Judicial adviser to Egyptian Govt. 1898-1916; instituted criminal assize cts. in Egypt 1905; CMG 1904; KCMG 1905; Grand cordon, Orders of Medjidie and the Nile. d. 18th March 1941.

McINTYRE, Aeneas John

s. of Aeneas McIntyre LLD, FLS, Hackney, London. b. 1821. M.T. Nov. 1846. QC 1872. Bencher 1873, Reader 1879. Member of bar committee 1883-89; MP Worcester 1880-85; Cty. Ct. judge 1889. d. 19th Sept. 1889.

MACKARNESS, Frederick Michael Coleridge

s. of Rt. Rev. John Fielder Mackarness, Bishop of Oxford. b. 31st Aug. 1854. educ. Marlborough; Keble Coll. Oxf. BA 1879, MA. M.T. June 1879. Advocate, Cape Colony 1882; Recorder of Newbury 1894-1904; MP Berkshire (South) 1906-10; prof. of Roman-Dutch law, Univ. Coll. London 1905-06; Cty. Ct. judge 1911-20. d. 23rd Dec. 1920.

McKENNA, Harold

s. of Leopold McKenna, Waltham St. Lawrence, Berkshire. b. 16th July 1879. educ. Westminster; Christ Ch. Oxf. BA 1902, MA 1905. I.T. Nov. 1903. Metrop. magistrate 1927, finally at Bow St. 1936-46; Chmn. Berkshire Quarter Sess. 1945-46; JP Berkshire. d. 19th Dec. 1946.

MACKENZIE, William Warrender (Lord Amulree)

s. of Robert Mackenzie, Pickston Hill, Scone, Perthshire (d. 1898). b. 19th Aug. 1860. educ. Perth Acad.; Edin. Univ. MA 1885, Hon. LLD 1936; L.I. May 1886. KC 1914. One of the chairmen of the Committee on Production 1917-18; first pres. of the Industrial Ct. 1919-26; Chmn. Railway National Wages Bd. 1920-26; Chmn. of Royal Comms. on Licensing 1929-31, and Newfoundland 1933, and of many tribunals and committees; Secy. of State for Air 1930-31; PC 1930; CBE 1917; KBE 1918; GBE 1926; Baron 1929. Joint author of Pratt and Mackenzie's Law of Highways; edited Paterson's Licensing, and books on local govt. law. d. 5th May 1942.

MACKESON, William Wyllys

s. of John Mackeson, Blue Mountain, Jamaica. b. 1813. educ. Queen's Coll. Oxf, BA 1836. I.T. Feb. 1836. QC 1868. Bencher 1868, Treasurer 1884. Edited Coote on Mortgages; edited (with J. Forbes QC) the Judicature Acts 1873 and 1875. d. 4th March 1892.

MACKINNON, Sir Frank Douglas

s. of Benjamin Thomas MacKinnon, Lingfield, Surrey, underwriter. b. 11th Feb. 1871. educ. Highgate Sch.; Trinity Coll. Oxf. BA 1894, MA 1895, Hon. Fellow 1931. I.T. June 1897. KC 1914. Bencher 1923, Treasurer 1945. Leader in commercial cases; successfully argued Re Polemis and Furness Withy and Co. Ltd. 1921; KB judge 1924-37; Knight 1924; LJ 1937-46; PC 1937; introduced "the officious bystander" concept into contract law; Chmn. Average Adjusters Assoc. 1935; Chmn. Buckinghamshire Quarter Sess.; JP; FSA. Author of The Murder in the Temple and other Holiday Tasks 1935, Grand Larceny (trial of Jane Austen's aunt) 1937, On Circuit 1940; edited Scrutton's Charterparties and Bills of Lading; annotated Charles Lamb's The Old Benchers of the Inner Temple 1927. d. 23rd Jan. 1946.

MACKINTOSH, William

s. of William Mackintosh, Inshes House, Inverness. b. 9th April 1842. educ. Edin. Acad.; Edin. Univ. MA, LLD. Scottish bar 1865. Procurator, Church of Scotland 1880. Sheriff, Ross, Cromarty and Sutherland 1881; QC 1886; Dean of Faculty of Advocates 1886-89; Senator of Coll. of Justice, (as Lord Kyllachy) 1889; judge of Ct. of Session and Justiciary to 1907; DL, JP Edin.; DL Invernesshire. d. 9th Dec. 1918.

MACKLIN, Albert Romer

s. of Albert Macklin, clerk in civil service. b. 14th Nov. 1863. educ. City of London Sch.; Caius Coll. Camb. BA 1886, LLB 1888. Asst. master, Chigwell Sch. 1903. L.I. July 1889. Legal adviser to War Trade Dept. 1915; Cty. Ct. judge 1916-19; JP Lancashire. Father of Sir Albert Sortain Romer Macklin (1890-1976), puisne judge, Bombay. d. 18th Aug. 1921.

MACKONOCHIE, James

s. of Col. George Mackonochie, HEICS. b. 1823. Scottish bar 1845. I.T. June 1855. Recorder of Winchester 1880-88; Cty. Ct. judge 1888-92. d. 18th Dec. 1892.

McLAREN, Charles Benjamin Bright (Lord Aberconway)

s. of Duncan McLaren MP, Newington House, Edinburgh (d. 1886). b. 12th May 1850. educ. Edin. Univ. MA; Bonn and Heidelberg Univs. L.I. Nov. 1874. QC 1897. MP Stafford 1880-86, West Leicestershire 1892-1910; industrialist from 1897; Chmn. Metropolitan Ry, Co., director Harland and Wolff Ltd., and of various steel and colliery undertakings; JP Denbighshire, Surrey, Flintshire, Middlesex; PC 1908; Baronet 1902; Baron Aberconway of Bodnant 1911; AINA; Japanese Order of the Sacred Treasure (3rd

Cl.); Serbian Order of the Takova (3rd Cl.); Greek Order of the Redeemer. Father of Henry Duncan McLaren MP, 2nd Baron (L.I. 1905). d. 23rd Jan. 1934.

McLAREN, John

s. of Duncan McLaren MP, Newington House, Edinburgh (d. 1886). b. 17th April 1831. educ. privately; Edin. Univ. Hon. LLD 1882. Scottish bar 1856. Sheriff of Chancery 1869-80; QC 1880; Lord Advocate 1880; Lord of Session with title of Lord McLaren 1881; Lord of Justiciary 1885; MP Wigtown District 1880, Edin. 1881; DL, JP Edin.; Hon. LLD, Glasgow 1883, Aberdeen 1906. Author of several works on Scottish law. d. 6th April 1910.

MACLEAN, Sir Francis William

s. of Alexander Maclean, Barrow-Hedges, Carshalton, Surrey. b. 13th Dec. 1844. educ. Westminster; Trinity Coll. Camb. BA 1866, MA 1871. I.T. April 1868. QC 1886. Bencher 1892. MP Mid-Oxfordshire (Woodstock) 1885-91; Master in Lunacy 1891-96; CJ Bengal 1896-1909; KCIE 1898; Chmn. Indian Famine Relief committees 1897, 1900, 1907; V-C Calcutta Univ. 1898-1900; Kaisar-i-Hind Gold Medal 1900. d. 11th Nov. 1913.

MACLEOD, Joseph Addison

s. of Joseph Addison Macleod, London, solicitor. b. 1839. educ. in Brentwood; Trinity Hall Camb. LLB 1861. I.T. Nov. 1863. QC 1882. d. 14th April 1883.

MACLEOD, Simon John Fraser

s. of William Macleod MD, CB, RN, Insp-Genl. of hospitals and fleets (d. 1904). b. 29th Aug. 1857. educ. London Univ. LLB. M.T.

Jan. 1881. KC 1905. Senior Commr. Bd. of Control to 1936. d. 7th Sept. 1938.

MACMILLAN, Hugh Pattison (Lord Macmillan)

s. of Rev. Hugh Macmillan DD, LLD, Free Church Minister, Glasgow and Greenock (d. 1903). b. 20th Feb. 1873. educ. Collegiate Sch. Greenock; Edin. Univ. MA 1893, Hon. LLD 1924; Glasgow Univ. LLB 1896, Hon. LLD 1930. Scottish bar 1897. KC 1912. Examr. in law to Glasgow Univ. 1899-1904; Lord Advocate 1924; standing counsel for Convention of Royal Burghs 1923-30, for Canada 1928, for Australia 1929; PC 1924; Hon. Bencher I.T. 1924; L of A 1930-39 and 1941-47; Baron 1930; Minister of Information 1939-40; Chmn. Royal Comm. on Lunacy and Mental Disorder 1924, Home Office Committee on Street Offences 1927, Treasury Finance and Industry Committee 1929-31, Royal Comm. on Canadian Banking and Currency 1933, Pilgrim Trust 1935-52, Political Honours Committee 1935-52, Ct. of London Univ. 1929-43, BBC Advisory Council 1936-46. and of numerous other tribunals; GCVO 1937; awarded hon. degrees by many other univs.; Freeman of City of London; Hon. Burgess Edin. 1938. Published Law and Other Things, and A Man of Law's Tale (autobiog.) 1952. d. 5th Sept. 1952.

MACMORRAN, Alexander

s. of Thomas Macmorran, Newton Stewart, Wigtonshire, clothier. b. 5th Nov. 1852. educ. Edin. Univ. MA 1872. M.T. Nov. 1875. QC 1896. Bencher 1903, Reader 1915, Treasurer 1926. Recorder of Hastings 1915-30; Commr. of Assize, North Eastern Circuit 1921; editor, Justice of the Peace 1879; Fellow, Instit. of Hygiene 1906; Fellow, Sanitary Instit. 1908; JP Middlesex; AMICE 1899; FRMetS 1908. Edited Lumley's Public Health, and published numerous works on local govt., poor law, and public health. d. 17th Dec. 1933.

MACMORRAN, Kenneth Mead

s. of Alexander Macmorran KC. b. 29th Nov. 1883. educ. Westminster; King's Coll. Camb. BA 1905, MA 1909, LLB 1907. M.T. April 1907. KC 1932. Bencher 1937, Reader, Treasurer 1956. WWI 2nd Lieut. 5th Battn. East Surrey Regt.; staff captain to JAG 1919; Chan. of diocese of Chichester and St. Albans 1922, Ely 1924, Guildford 1927, Lincoln 1937, Newcastle 1942; member of House of Laity, Church Assembly 1930-37; Referee under Widows and Orphans etc. Pensions Acts, Nat. Insce. Acts, Family Allowances Act, 1926-50; member Interned Enemy Aliens Trib. (Home Office) 1940, Advisory Committee on Probation (Home Office) 1946; Dep. Chmn. Surrey Quarter Sess. 1940-44, Asst. Chmn. 1944-49; JP Surrey. Author of works on public health and church law; edited Cripps' Law of Church and Clergy. d. 9th Jan. 1973.

MACNAGHTEN, Edward (Lord Macnaghten)

s. of Sir Edmund Charles Workman-Macnaghten, Dundarave, Antrim, 2nd Bt., receiver of Ct. of Chancery, Calcutta. b. 3rd Feb. 1830. educ. Dr. Cowan's Sch. Sunderland; Trinity Coll. Dublin 1847; Trinity Coll. Camb. BA 1852, MA 1859, Fellow 1853, Hon. Fellow 1902; rowing blue. L.I. Jan. 1857. QC 1880. Bencher 1883, Treasurer 1907. Practised in chancery; Secy. to Charity Funds Comm. 1858; MP Co. Antrim 1880-85, Co. Antrim (Northern Division) 1885-87; declined chancery judgeship 1883, and Home Secretaryship 1886; L of A and Baron 1887; Chmn. Council of Legal Educ. 1895-1913; PC 1887; chmn. arbitral trib. in boundary dispute between Chile and Argentina 1899; GCMG 1903; GCB 1911; DL, JP Antrim; succeeded brother as 4th baronet 1911; Hon. LLD Dublin. Father of Sir Frederic Fergus Macnaghten, 9th Bt. (Solicitor 1891). d. 17th Feb. 1913.

MACNAGHTEN, Sir Edward Charles, Bt.

s. of Macnaghten L of A. b. 9th Oct. 1859. educ. Trinity Coll. Camb.

BA 1883. L.I. June 1885. QC 1897. Bencher 1904. Leader of chancery bar; DL Antrim; succeeded as 5th baronet 1913. Brother of Sir Frederick Fergus Macnaghten Bt. (solicitor 1891). d. 31st Dec. 1914.

MACNAGHTEN, Sir Malcolm Martin

s. of Macnaghten L of A. b. 12th Jan. 1869. educ. Eton; Trinity Coll. Camb. BA 1891, MA 1895. L.I. and I.T. Jan. 1894. KC 1919. Bencher (L.I.) 1915. Secy. to Adolf Beck Inquiry Committee (wrongful conviction for defrauding women) 1904; Director of Foreign Claims Office 1915-19; KBE 1920; MP Londonderry Cty. (North Derry) 1922, Londonderry City and Cty. 1922-28; Recorder of Colshester 1924-28; Commissary of Camb. Univ. 1926; KB judge 1928-47; PC 1948. d. 24th Jan. 1955.

McNAIR, Arnold Duncan (Lord McNair)

s. of John McNair, Paisley, Renfrewshire, member of Lloyd's. b. 4th March 1885. educ. Aldenham Sch.; Gonville and Caius Coll. Camb. BA and LLB 1909, LLM 1913, MA 1919, LLD 1925, Fellow 1912; senior tutor. Solicitor 1906. G.I. May 1917. KC 1945. Bencher 1936, Treasurer 1947. Secy. Coal Industry Comm. 1919; Reader in intern. law London Univ. 1926-27; Whewell Prof. of intern. law Camb. 1935-37; prof. of comparative law Camb. 1945; Tagore Prof. Calcutta Univ. 1931; judge of Intern. Ct. of Justice, The Hague 1946, Pres. 1952-55; Chmn. Burnham Committees 1956-58; first Pres. European Ct. of Human Rights 1959-65; Pres. Socy. of Public Teachers of Law 1933; Pres. Inst. de Droit Intern. 1949-50; Commissary of Camb. Univ. 1955; CBE 1918; FBA 1939; Knight 1943; Baron 1955; V-C Liverpool Univ. 1937-45; Hon. LLD Glasgow, Liverpool, Birmingham, Salonika; Hon. DCL Oxf.; Hon. Litt.D. Reading. Author of Legal Effects of War 1920, Law of the Air 1932, Law of Treaties 1938 and 1961, Dr. Johnson and the Law 1949, The Expansion of International Law 1962; edited Oppenheim's International Law. d. 22nd May 1975.

McNAIR, Sir William Lennox

s. of John McNair, Court Lane, Dulwich, Lloyd's underwriter. b. 18th March 1892. educ. Aldenham Sch.; Gonville and Caius Coll. Camb. BA and LLB 1914, Whewell Exhibitioner 1919, LLM 1920, Hon. Fellow 1951. WWI Capt. Royal Warwickshire Regt. (despatches). G.I. Jan. 1918. KC 1943. Bencher 1938, Treasurer 1951, Vice-Treasurer 1952. Legal adviser to Min. of Shipping, and Min. of War Transport 1939-45; Knight 1946; KB judge 1950-66; joint editor of Temperley's Merchant Shipping Acts, and Scrutton's Charterparties and Bills of Lading. d. 19th Feb. 1979.

MACNAMARA, Henry Tyrwhitt Jones

s. of Capt. Frederick Hayes Macnamara, 47th Foot. b. 1820. educ. in Ealing; Lichfield Gr. Sch. Founder of Hardwicke Debating Socy. Special pleader 1841-49. L.I. Nov. 1849. Recorder of Reading 1864-70; Cty. Ct. judge 1872-73; legal member Ry. Comm. Ct. 1873-77. Author of a treatise on pleadings in civil proceedings 1844, and The Complete Practice of the Law of England, 1855; edited R.P. Collier's Railway Consolidation Acts, and Paley's Law of Summary Convictions. d. 2nd Feb. 1877.

MACPHERSON, Alan

s. of Allan Macpherson, Blairgowrie, Perthshire, and MLA, New South Wales (d. 1891). b. 11th Jan. 1857. educ. Winchester; Exeter Coll. Oxf. BA 1881, MA 1886. L.I. Nov. 1881. Cty. Ct. judge 1913-29. d. 23rd June 1930.

MACPHERSON, James Ian (Lord Strathcarron)

s. of James Macpherson JP, Newtonmore, Inverness, merchant (d. 1922). b. 14th May 1880. educ. George Watson's Coll.; Edin. Univ. MA, LLB, Hon. LLD 1933. M.T. June 1906. KC 1919. Bencher

1930. Recorder of Southend 1930-37; MP Inverness-shire (Ross and Cromarty) 1911-35; parliamentary private secy. to Under-Secy. of State for War 1914-16, Under-Secy. 1916-18; Vice-Pres. Army Council 1918 (Dep. Secy. of State); Chief Secy. for Ireland 1919-20; Minister of Pensions 1920-22; Chmn, Scottish Land Enquiry Committee; Chan. of the Order of St. Patrick; Lt. Col. City of London Vol. Regt.; Freeman Royal Borough of Dingwall 1936; JP Southend; PC 1918; Baronet 1933; Baron 1936. d. 14th Aug. 1937.

MACQUEEN, John Fraser

s. of Donald Macqueen, Corrybrough, Inverness. b. 1803. L.I. June 1838. QC 1861. Bencher 1861. Secy. of the Divorce Comm. 1851; official reporter of Scottish and divorce appeals in House of Lords 1860. Author of works on jurisdiction of House of Lords, and Privy Council, and on matrimonial law. d. 6th Dec. 1881.

MACQUISTEN, Frederick Alexander

s. of Rev. Alexander Macquisten DD, Inverkip, Renfrewshire. b. 23rd July 1870. educ. privately; Glasgow Univ. LLB. Solicitor in Glasgow 1892. Scottish bar 1910; KC 1920. G.I. June 1920. KC 1931. MP Glasgow (Springburn) 1918-22, Argyllshire 1924-40; Chmn. of Globe and Phoenix gold Mining Co. Ltd. d. 29th Feb. 1940.

MACRORY, Edmund

s. of Adam John Macrory, Duncairn, Belfast, advocate. b. 1831. educ. Trinity Coll. Dublin BA 1850, MA 1857. M.T. Jan. 1853. QC 1890. Bencher 1878, Reader 1888, Treasurer 1897. Chmn. Bd. of Examiners, Inns of Ct. 1890; JP. Author of works on patents. d. 18th April 1904.

MADDEN, William

s. of William Madden, Liverpool. b. 1853. educ. St. Francis Xavier Coll. Liverpool; Stonyhurst. Solicitor 1879, practised in Liverpool. G.I. Nov. 1888. KC 1922. Recorder of Blackburn 1924-25; specialised in criminal cases; successfully defended, 1902, John McKeever charged with murder of John Kensit, Protestant leader, Birkenhead. d. 10th Aug. 1925.

MADDOCKS, Sir Henry

s. of William Maddocks, Wem, Shropshire. b. 26th April 1871. educ. Wem Gr. Sch. Solicitor 1893. I.T. June 1904 (Cert. of Hon.). KC 1920. Member of bar council; Recorder of Stamford 1924-25, of Birmingham 1925-31; MP Warwickshire (Nuneaton) 1918-23; member Imperial War Graves Comm.; Knight 1923. Father of Henry Hollingdrake Maddocks (1898-1969), metrop. magistrate. d. 9th June 1931.

MALINS, Sir Richard

s. of William Malins, Ailston, Warwickshire. b. 9th March 1805. educ. privately; Caius Coll. Camb. BA 1827. I.T. May 1830. QC 1849; Bencher (L.I.) 1849, Treasurer 1871. MP Wallingford 1852-56; leader in V-C Stuart's Ct.; Infants' Marriage Settlement Act 1855, and Married Women's Reversionary Property Act 1857, known by his name; equity draftsman and conveyancer; V-C 1866-75; Knight 1867; Chancery judge 1875-81; PC 1881. d. 15th Jan. 1882.

MALKIN, Sir Herbert William

s. of Herbert Charles Malkin JP, Corrybrough, Inverness, chief clerk in H of L (d. 1913), and g.s. of Sir Benjamin Heath Malkin , puisne judge, Calcutta. b. 17th April 1883. educ. Charterhouse; Trinity

303

Coll. Camb. BA 1905, MA 1913. I.T. Nov. 1907. KC 1931. Bencher 1941. Joined Foreign Office 1911; asst. legal adviser 1914-29; legal adviser 1929-45; CMG 1918; CB 1923; KCMG 1930; GCMG 1937. d. 4th July 1945.

MALTBY, Edward Harvey

s. of Rt. Rev. Edward Maltby, Buckden, Huntingdonshire, Bishop of Durham (d. 1859). educ. Pembroke Coll. Camb. BA 1820, MA 1823. L.I. May 1824. Recorder of Buckingham 1836-40; metrop. magistrate, Marlborough St. 1841-46. d. 24th March 1867, age 69.

MANISTY, Sir Henry

s. of Rev. James Manisty, Edlingham, Northumberland. b. 13th Dec. 1808. educ. Durham Cath. Gr. Sch. Solicitor in London 1830-42. G.I. April 1845. QC 1857. Bencher 1859, Treasurer 1861. QB judge 1876-90; Knight 1876; presided at R v. Bishop of Oxford (failure of bishop to prosecute for ritualistic practices) 1879. d. 31st Jan. 1890.

MANISTY, Herbert Francis

s. of Manisty J. b. 2nd March 1853. educ. Westminster; Trinity Hall Camb. LLB 1875. I.T. and G.I. Nov. 1877. KC 1901. Bencher (G.I.) 1904, Treasurer 1910. Recorder of Rotherham 1904-05, of Berwick-on-Tweed 1905-39; Sol-Genl. Cty. Palatine of Durham 1905-15, Att-Genl. 1915-39. Edited Broom's Legal Maxims. d. 10th May 1939

MANNING, James

s. of James Manning, Exeter, Unitarian minister. b. 1781. L.I. June 1817. Leader of Western circuit; Recorder of Sudbury 1835-66, of

Oxford and Banbury 1837-66; Serjeant 1840; patent of precedence 1845; Queen's ancient serjeant 1846; Cty. Ct. judge 1847-63. Treasurer of Serjeants' Inn. Edited various series of law reports. d. 29th Aug. 1866.

MANNING, John Westley

s. of William Manning, London. b. 1866. educ. Univ, Coll. Sch.; University Coll. London MA 1887. L.I. Nov. 1891. KC 1920. Bencher 1923. Equity draftsman and conveyancer. d. 19th Dec. 1954.

MANSFIELD, John Smith

s. of John Edward Mansfield, Diggleswell House, Hertfordshire, barrister (d. 1841). b. 22nd May 1813. educ. Eton; Trinity Coll. Camb. BA 1836, MA 1839, Fellow 1838. M.T. Jan. 1842. Metrop. magistrate, Marlborough St. 1860-88. JP Middlesex and London. Brother of Horatio Mansfield (I.T. 1853), dep. magistrate Liverpool. d. 20th June 1905.

MARCHANT, James Robert Vernam

s. of Rev. Job Marchant, Lower Tooting. b. 1853. educ. City of London Sch.; Wadham Coll. Oxf. BA 1876, MA 1879. G.I. June 1884. Cty. Ct. judge 1920-25. d. 11th July 1936.

MARLOWE, Anthony Alfred Harmsworth

s. of Thomas Marlowe, Osborne Cottage, Cowes, Isle of Wight, Chairman, Associated Newspapers Ltd. (d. 1935). b. 25th Oct. 1904. educ. Marlborough; Trinity Coll. Camb. BA. I.T. Jan. 1928. KC 1945. Bencher 1953. WWII Lt. Col. on staff of JAG. MP Brighton 1941-50, Hove 1950-65. d. 8th Sept. 1965.

MARRIOTT, Charles Bertrand

s. of Sir Charles Hayes Marriott FRCS, MD, DL, JP (d. 1910). b. 1st Oct. 1868. educ. Uppingham; Trinity Coll. Oxf. BA. I.T. June 1892. KC 1926. Bencher 1934. Counsel to Port of London Auth. and Thames Conservancy; Recorder of Northampton 1928-46; Chmn. Rutland Quarter Sess; Dep. Chmn. Northamptonshire and Leicestershire Quarter Sess.; JP Rutland and Northamptonshire. Brother of Harold Henry Marriott (solicitor 1909). d. 11th May 1946.

MARRIOTT, Sir William Thackeray

s. of Christopher Marriott, Crumpsall, nr. Manchester, merchant. b. 1834. educ. St. John's Coll. Camb. BA 1858. Deacon 1858. L.I. Jan. 1864. QC 1877. Bencher 1879. Judge Adv-Genl. 1885-86, 1886-92; counsel for ex-Khedive Ismail in claims against Egyptian Govt. 1887; large practice in railway and compensation cases; MP Brighton 1880-93; Chan. of Primrose League 1892; PC 1885; Knight 1888. d. Aix-la-Chapelle, 27th July 1903.

MARSHALL, Frederic

s. of William Marshall, Northampton. b. 13th March 1839. educ. London Univ. BA 1862, LLB 1870. I.T. Nov. 1870. QC 1893, Bencher 1900. Member Convocation London Univ. d. 1st Aug. 1910.

MARSHALL, Kenneth McLean

s. of Francis Marshall, Edinburgh. b. 16th May 1874. educ. Rugby; Trinity Coll. Camb. BA 1896, LLB 1896. I.T. May 1900. WWI DJAG (Home). CBE 1920. Metrop. magistrate 1922, finally at Westminster to 1944; JP London and Home Counties. d. 21st Nov. 1954.

MARSHALL, Thomas Horncastle

s. of Rev. Thomas Horncastle Marshall, Pontefract, Yorkshire. b. 1st March 1800. G.I. Nov. 1821. Bencher 1850, Treasurer 1851. Dep. judge and steward of Ct. of Honour of Pontefract; Cty. Ct. judge 1847-75. d. 18th Feb. 1875.

MARSHAM, Robert Henry Bullock

s. of Robert Bullock Marsham DCL, Warden, Merton Coll. Oxf. b. 3rd Sept. 1833. educ. Merton Coll. Oxf. BA 1855, MA 1858. I.T. June 1860. Recorder of Maidstone 1868-79; metrop. magistrate 1879, finally at Bow St. to 1913; JP London and Home Counties. d. 5th April 1913.

MARTELLI, Ernest Wynne

s. of Charles Henry Ansley Martelli, barrister. b. 13th Feb. 1862. educ. King's Sch. Ely; Queens' Coll. Camb. BA 1884, MA 1899. L.I. Jan. 1888. KC 1908. Bencher 1913. Equity draftsman and conveyancer; Cty. Ct. judge 1916-17. d. 2nd May 1917.

MARTEN, Sir Alfred George

s. of Robert Giles Marten, Plaistow, Essex. b. 9th Nov. 1829. educ. Mill Hill; St. John's Coll. Camb. BA 1856, MA 1859, LLB and LLM 1874, 19th Wrangler, LLD 1879, Fellow 1865. I.T. Jan. 1857 (Cert. of Hon.). QC 1874. Bencher 1874, Treasurer 1893. Law lecturer and examr. in law, Camb. 1867-68; member Council of Legal Educ. 1874; MP Cambridge 1874-80; Cty. Ct. judge 1896-1906; knight 1896; JP. Father of Sir Amberson Barrington Marten (1870-1962), CJ Bombay. d. 22nd June 1910.

MARTIN, Sir Samuel

s. of Samuel Martin, Culmore, Newton Limavady, Londonderry. b. 23rd Sept. 1801. educ. trinity Coll. Dublin BA 1821, MA 1832, Hon. LLD 1857. Special pleader1828-39. M.T. Jan. 1830. QC 1843. Bencher 1843, Reader 1850. MP Pontefract 1847-50; acquired extensive mercantile practice; Exch. Baron 1850-74; Knight 1850; tried Franz Muller for murder of Briggs on a train 1864; Common Law Commr. 1857; PC 1874, but took no part in proceedings of Judicial Committee; LLD Durham 1857; hon. member of Jockey Club. Author of treatise on The Statute of Frauds Amendment Act 1828. d. 9th Jan. 1883.

MARTINEAU, Alfred

s. of Philip R. Martineau, Taxing Master in Chancery (d. 1860). b. 1820. educ. Univ. Coll. Sch.; Trinity Coll. Camb. BA 1841, MA 1844, Fellow 1843. L.I. Nov. 1846. Cty. Ct. judge 1872-77; JP Sussex. Father of Alfred Edward Martineau (1868-1926), puisne judge in Punjab. d. 30th Sept. 1903.

MASTERMAN, William

s. of Henry Masterman, Wanstead, Essex, solicitor. b. 28th April 1846. educ. Winchester; Wadham Coll. Oxf. BA 1868, BCL and MA 1871, DCL 1881. M.T. June 1870. Cty. Ct. judge 1891-1903; Master of Skinners' Co. 1889; JP Nottinghamshire. Author of handbook on statutes relating to parliamentary elections. d. 14th Jan. 1903.

MATHEW, Charles James

s. of Mathew LJ. b. 24th Oct. 1872. educ. Oratory Sch. Birmingham; Trinity Hall Camb. BA 1893. L.I. Jan. 1897. KC 1913. Bencher 1918. CBE 1917 for war work. Alderman LCC 1919. Father of Sir

Theobald Mathew (1898-1964), Director of Public Prosecutions. d. 8th Jan. 1923.

MATHEW, Sir James Charles

s. of Charles Mathew, Lehenagh House, Cork. b. Bordeaux, 10th July 1830. educ. in Cork; Trinity Coll. Dublin BA 1850, Hon. LLD 1881. L.I. Jan. 1854. Bencher 1881. A founder of Hardwicke Socy.; acquired vast city practice, but did not apply for silk; member Law Procedure Committee 1880; QB judge 1881-1901; Knight 1881; obtained institution of the Commercial Ct. 1895; member Council of Legal Educ. and Chmn. Bd. of Studies 1890; as Chmn. of Royal Comm. concerning evictions in Ireland refused to allow cross-examination by counsel, which led to resignation of many members of the Comm., and withdrawal of Edward Carson who was representing the landlords 1892; LJ 1901-05; PC. Father of Theobald Mathew(L.I. 1890), Recorder of Maidstone. d. 9th Nov. 1908.

MATHEWS, Wilkinson

s. of John Mathews, Stokesley in Cleveland, Yorkshire, solicitor. b. 9th March 1784. educ. Barnard Castle, Hadleigh, Suffolk; Trinity Coll. Camb. BA 1805, 9th Wrangler, MA 1808, Fellow 1806-15. L.I. May 1810. QC 1842. Bencher 1841, Treasurer 1859. A Charity Commr. 1818-30. d. 12th May 1866.

MATTHEWS, Henry (Lord Llandaff)

s. of Henry Matthews, Belmont, Herefordshire, and puisne judge, Ceylon. b. Ceylon, 13th Jan. 1826. educ. Paris Univ. Bachelier ès lettres 1844; London Univ. BA 1847, LLB; Fellow, Univ. Coll. L.I. May 1850. QC 1868. Bencher 1868. MP Dungarvan 1868-74, East Birmingham 1886-95. Home Secy. 1886-92; examr. in common law to Council of Legal Educ. 1872-76; commuted the sentence of death on Mrs. Maybrick to penal servitude for life 1889; his refusal to offer a reward for the discovery of Jack the Ripper gave rise to much comment; Viscount 1895; PC. d. 3rd April 1913.

MATTHEWS, Joseph Bridges

s. of John Matthews, Worcester. b. 29th Nov. 1861. educ. Worcester Cathedral Sch. Solicitor in Worcester 1884-95. M.T. June 1896. KC 1913. Bencher 1924. Recorder of Tewkesbury 1912-23, of Dudley 1923-28; Sheriff of Worcester 1895; Royal Humane Socy's Bronze Medal. Author of Covenants in Restraint of Trade, The Law of Moneylending, The Law relating to Married Women; edited Hayes and Jarman on Wills. Joint editor of the Annual Practice, and Pritchard's Quarter Sessions. d. 5th Aug. 1928.

MATTHEWS, Richard

s. of Richard Matthews, Histon, Cambridgeshire. M.T. April 1828. Serjeant 1852. d. 24th Feb. 1854, age 57.

MATTINSON, Sir Miles Walker

s. of Thomas Mattinson, Newcastle-on-Tyne. b. 26th Dec. 1854. G.I. Jan. 1877 (Cert. of Hon.). QC 1896. Bencher 1891. Recorder of Blackburn 1886-1922; MP Liverpool (Walton) 1888-92; Knight 1922. Author of The Law of Corrupt Practices at elections, and Selection of Precedents in Pleading. d. 29th Feb. 1944.

MAUDE, Daniel

s. of Francis Maude, Hatfield Hall, Yorkshire, barrister. b. 1801. educ. Southwell Sch. Notts.; Caius Coll. Camb. BA 1825, MA 1828, 25th Wrangler, Fellow 1826-38. G.I. Nov. 1829. Stip. magistrate Manchester 1838-60; metrop. magistrate Greenwich 1860-74. d. 27th March 1874.

MAUDE, John Cyril

s. of Cyril Maude, actor-manager (d. 1951). b. 3rd April 1901. educ.
Eton; Christ Church Oxf. MA. M.T. Jan. 1925. KC 1943. Bencher
1952. Counsel to PO at Central Criminal Ct. 1935-42; junior pros.
counsel to Treasury at Central Criminal Ct. 1942-43; Recorder of
Devizes 1939-44, of Plymouth 1944-54; temp. civil asst. General
Staff, War Office 1939. WWII Acting major, Intelligence Corps,
Offices of War Cabinet 1942. MP Exeter 1945-51; Chan. of diocese
of Bristol 1948-50; member of bar council 1952; addl. judge,
Mayor's and City of London Ct. 1954; addl. judge Central Criminal
Ct. 1964-68; director, Old Vic Trust Ltd. 1951-54; Chmn. Br. Drama
League 1952-54; member Middlesex Hospital Bd. 1952-62; govr.
Royal Victoria Hall Foundation 1953; FRSL 1952. d. 16th Aug.
1986.

MAUGHAM, Frederic Herbert (Lord Maugham)

s. of Robert Ormond Maugham, solicitor (d. 1884). b. 20th Oct.
1866. educ. Dover Coll.; Trinity Hall Camb. BA 1889, Hon. Fellow
1928, Hon. LLD 1938; rowing blue. L.I. Nov. 1890. KC 1913.
Bencher 1915. Equity draftsman and conveyancer; Chancery judge
1928-34; Knight 1928; LJ 1934-35; PC 1934; L of A 1935-38 and
1939-41; Baron 1935; LC 1938-39; took leading part in enacting
of Coal Act, and Law of Evidence Act 1938; Viscount 1939. Author
of The Case of Jean Calas 1928, The Tichborne case 1936, At the
End of the Day (autobiog.) 1954. Father of Robert Cecil Romer
Maugham, 2nd Viscount (L.I. 1945). d. 23rd March 1958.

MAULE, Sir John Blossett

s. of George Maule, solicitor to the Treasury (d. 1851). b. 29th May
1817. educ. Westminster; Christ Church Oxf. BA 1839, MA 1846.
I.T. Jan. 1847. QC 1866. Bencher 1866, Reader 1881, Treasurer
1882. Member comm. of inquiry into Jamaica rebellion 1866;
Recorder of Leeds 1861-80; Director of Public Prosecutions 1880-

84; Knight 1882; edited Burn's Justice of the Peace and Parish Officer 1869. d. 20th Oct. 1889.

MAULE, Sir William Henry

s. of Henry Maule, Edmonton, Middlesex, surgeon. b. 25th April 1788. educ. in Greenford; Trinity Coll. Camb. BA 1810, Senior Wrangler, MA 1813, Fellow 1811-20; a coach in mathematics; refused to accept professorship in that subject at Haileybury. L.I. May 1814. KC 1833. Bencher 1835-39. An authority on marine insurance; counsel to Bank of England 1835; MP Carlow 1837-39; accidentally set fire to his chambers at Paper Buildings, and destroyed large part of the Temple 1838; Exch. Baron 1839; Knight 1839; judge of Common Pleas 1839-55; PC 1855, and member Judicial Committee. d. 16th Jan. 1858. Memoir of his early life by E. Leathley 1872 (his niece).

MAXWELL, Alexander Hyslop

s. of Maxwell Hyslop Maxwell, Dumfries and Liverpool. b. 10th May 1864. educ. Uppingham. Solicitor. M.T. July 1889. Cty. Ct. judge 1920-37. d. 7th March 1957.

MAYER, Sylvain

s. of Michael Leopold Mayer, London. b. 9th Aug. 1863. educ. Univ. Coll. Sch.; University Coll. London BA 1882; Heidelberg Univ. PhD 1884. M.T. and G.I. June 1887. KC 1913. Published A Code of the Law of Rating, The Law of Agricultural Holdings, The Law of Compensation, Reminiscences of a K.C., Theatrical and Legal 1924, and several theatre comedies; also commentaries on the French Code of Commerce, and The Representation of the People Act 1918. d. 13th Sept. 1948.

MEAD, Frederick

s. of George Edward Mead, Chelsea, solicitor. b. 22nd July 1847. educ. King's Coll. London (Fellow). M.T. June 1869. Treasury counsel 1879-89. Metrop. magistrate 1889, finally at Marlborough St. 1907-33; JP London and Home Counties; Chmn. Marine Socy.; joint editor of Archbold's Quarter Sessions. d. 14th Dec. 1945.

MEEK, William Alfred

s. of Sir James Meek, Middlethorpe Lodge, nr. York, banker (d. 1891). b. 17th May 1850. educ. St. Peter's Sch. York; Harrow; Trinity Coll. Camb. BA 1873, MA 1876, Fellow 1875-83. I.T. and M.T. Jan. 1876. KC 1903. Recorder of York 1898-1911; JP Yorkshire North Riding. d. 10th March 1929.

MELLISH, Sir George

s. of Edward Mellish, Dean of Hereford (d. 1830). b. 19th Dec. 1814. educ. Eton; University Coll. Oxf. BA 1837, MA 1839, DCL 1874, Hon. Fellow 1872-77. Special pleader 1840-48. I.T. June 1848. QC 1861. Bencher 1861, Reader 1875. Leader of Northern circuit; "his opinion as counsel was equal in weight to a judgment of the Court of Exchequer Chamber"; declined puisne judgeship; LJ 1870-77; PC 1870; the perfect colleague for James LJ in the Ct. of Appeal. Uncle of Henry Mellish CB, DL, JP (I.T. 1882). d. 15th June 1877.

MELLOR, Francis Hamilton

s. of Mellor J. b. 13th May 1854. educ. Cheltenham Coll.; Trinity Coll. Camb. BA 1877, MA 1889. I.T. Nov. 1880. KC 1903. Recorder of Preston 1898-1921; member of bar council 1898-1911; Cty. Ct. judge 1911-25; CBE 1918; JP Cheshire and Lancashire. Brother of Sir James Robert Mellor, Senior Master of Supreme Ct.

(1839-1926). d. 26th April 1925.

MELLOR, Sir James Gilbert Shaw

s. of Sir James Robert Mellor, Eastgate, Tenterden, Kent, King's Remembrancer (d. 1926). b. 29th March 1872. educ. Charterhouse; Trinity Hall. Camb. BA 1893, LLB 1894. I.T. Nov. 1896. KC 1920. Served in South African War 1900, with City Imperial Vol. Mounted Inf. Secy. of Royal Comm. on Martial Law Sentences, South Africa 1902; Br. agent in Venezuelan Claims Comm. 1903; Dep. Judge-Adv. 1907-14; DJAG 1914-32. WWI Col. Res. of Off., CB, CMG, Chev. Legion of Honour, (despatches). Hon. Brig-Genl. 1919; KBE 1923; Dep. Chmn. West Kent Quarter Sess. 1944; Chmn. Bearsted Petty Sessions; JP Kent. d. 16th April 1947.

MELLOR, Sir John

s. of John Mellor JP, Leicester, merchant (d. 1861). b. 1st Jan. 1809. educ. Leicester Gr. Sch. Employed with an attorney in Leicester. I.T. June 1833. QC 1851. Bencher 1851-61 and 1877-87. Leader of Midland circuit; Recorder of Warwick 1848-52, of Leicester 1855-61; MP Great Yarmouth 1857-59, Nottingham 1859-61; QB judge 1861-79; Knight 1862; member special comm. which tried Fenian prisoners at Manchester 1867; one of the judges who tried Tichborne claimant for perjury 1873-74; frequently acted as arbitrator in important cases; PC 1879. Author of The Life and Times of John Selden 1859, Suggestions as to Oaths 1882. d. 26th April 1887.

MELLOR, John William

s. of Mellor J. b. 26th July 1835. educ. Trinity Hall Camb. BA 1857, MA 1860. I.T. June 1860. QC 1875. Bencher 1877. Recorder of Grantham 1871-74; MP Grantham 1880-86, Yorkshire (Sowerby) 1892-1904; Judge Adv-Genl. 1886; Chmn. Committees 1893-95; member Royal Comms. on Tweed and Solway Fisheries 1896,

Water Supply to London 1897, Patriotic Fund 1898; PC 1886; Dep. Chmn. Somerset Quarter Sess.; DL, JP Somerset; JP Devon. Father of Sir John Paget Mellor, Bt. (I.T. 1886), Treasury Solicitor and King's Proctor. d. 13th Oct. 1911.

MELVILLE, Sir James Benjamin

s. of William Melville, Clapham, London, S.W., police superintendent. b. 1885. Clerk with Eagle Insurance Co. M.T. June 1906. KC 1927. Bencher 1929. WWI Major ASC (despatches). MP Gateshead 1929; Sol-Genl. 1929-30; resigned due to ill health; Knight 1929; Serbian Order of St. Sava. d. 1st May 1931.

MELVILLE, Robert

s. of Michael Linning Melville, barrister, judge in Sierra Leone (d. 1878). b. 1841. educ. Magdalen Coll. Oxf. BA 1861, MA 1864. L.I. Nov. 1864. Cty. Ct. judge 1889-91. d. 1st Sept. 1891.

MEREWETHER, Charles George

s. of Francis Merewether, Rector of Cole Orton, Leicestershire. b. 20th Aug. 1823. educ. Wadham Coll. Oxf. BA 1845. I.T. Jan. 1848. QC 1877. Recorder of Leicester 1868-84; MP Northampton 1874-80; counsel for PO on Western circuit; Commr. to inquire into corrupt practices at elections 1880. Wrote for Anthony Trollope the legal opinion as to heirlooms in "The Eustace Diamonds" 1872. d. 26th June 1884.

MEREWETHER, Henry Alworth

s. of Henry Merewether, Calne, Wiltshire. b. 1780. educ. Reading Sch. I.T. May 1809. Serjeant 1827; patent of precedence 1832. Recorder of Great Yarmouth 1832-35, of Reading 1830-64; Sol-

Genl. to Queen Adelaide 1832, Att-Genl. 1845-64; Town Clerk of London 1842-59; Hon.DCL Oxf. 1839. Author of A New System of Police 1816, and works on municipal corporations. d. 22nd July 1864.

MEREWETHER, Henry Alworth

s. of Henry Alworth Merewether, serjeant. b. 23rd April 1812. educ. Winchester; Trinity Coll. Camb. 1830. I.T. June 1837. QC 1853. Bencher 1853, Reader 1867, Treasurer 1868. Leader of parliamentary bar; Recorder of Devizes 1844-77; Chmn. Wiltshire Quarter Sess. to 1875. d. 29th Aug. 1877.

MERRIMAN, Frank Boyd (Lord Merriman)

s. of Frank Merriman JP, Hollingford House, Knutsford, Cheshire (d. 1920). b. 28th April 1880. educ. Winchester. I.T. June 1904. KC 1919. Bencher 1927, Dep. Treasurer 1949. WWI Major 22nd Battn. Manchester Regt, DAAG (despatches thrice), OBE. Pupil of Gordon Hewart. Recorder of Wigan 1920-28; member of bar council; MP Manchester (Rusholme) 1924-33; Sol-Genl. 1928-29 and 1932-33; Knight 1928; Pres. P D and A Divn. 1933; PC 1933; Baron 1941; made recommendations to Denning committee on divorce 1946; Pres. of Bishop of London's comm. concerning bombed churches in the City 1941-46; GCVO 1950; hon. member American and Canadian Bar Assocs.; Hon. LLD McGill Univ. d. 18th Jan. 1962.

METCALFE, Herbert

s. of James Metcalfe, Walton-le-Dale, Lancashire. b. 10th Oct 1887. educ. privately. Newspaper journalist. G.I. June 1914. WWI Lieut. Lancashire Fusiliers and East Lancs. Regt. Metrop. magistrate 1929, finally at Old St. to 1940. d. 30th Oct. 1940.

METCALFE, William James

s. of Rev. William J. Metcalfe, Fowlmere, Cambridge. b. 1818. educ. St John's Coll. Camb. BA 1842, MA 1845. I.T. May 1845. QC 1873. Recorder of Ipswich 1866-74, of Norwich 1874-92; Cty. Ct. judge 1879-92; JP Somerset. Brother of Robert Metcalfe (solicitor 1852). d. 8th Dec. 1892.

MEYNELL, Edgar John

s. of Thomas Meynell, Kilvington Hall, Thirsk, Yorkshire. b. 1st Feb. 1825. educ. Ampleforth. M.T. May 1852. Recorder of Doncaster 1870-1901; Cty. Ct. judge 1873-1901; JP Durham. Father of Edgar Meynell (M.T. 1884), Recorder of Doncaster. d. 15th Jan. 1901.

MEYSEY-THOMPSON, Albert Childers

s. of Sir Harry Stephen Meysey-Thompson, 1st Bt. b. 13th July 1848. educ. Eton; Trinity Coll. Camb. BA 1871. I.T. June 1872. QC 1892. Parliamentary counsel. d. 20th March 1894.

MICHAEL, William Henry

s. of Lewin Michael, Swansea, merchant. b. 6th Sept. 1821. M.T. Jan. 1864. QC 1878. Bencher 1882. A leader at parliamentary bar; JP Glamorgan. Author of works on public health. d. Meran, Tyrol, 15th Feb. 1892.

MICKLEM, Nathaniel

s. of Thomas Micklem JP, Cookham, Berkshire, solicitor (d. 1901). b. 1853. educ. New Coll. Oxf. BA 1877, BCL and MA 1881; London Univ. BA, LLB; Fellow, Univ. Coll. 1881. L.I. June 1881

(Cert. of Hon.). QC 1900. Bencher 1906, Treasurer 1930. MP Hertfordshire (West) 1906-10; member Royal Comm. on Lunacy 1924; JP Middlesex and Hertfordshire. d. 19th March 1954.

MICKLETHWAIT, St John Gore

s. of John Pollard Micklethwait JP, Chepstow, Monmouthshire, barrister (d. 1909). b. 29th April 1870. educ. Clifton Coll.; University Coll. Oxf. BA 1892, BCL and MA 1896. M.T. Nov. 1893. KC 1927. Bencher 1921, Reader 1930, Treasurer 1933. Recorder of Reading 1923-51; Chan. of diocese of Monmouth; Chmn. Merchandise Marks Act Committee, Min. of Agriculture 1933; Dep. Chmn. Middlesex Quarter Sess. 1934, Chmn. 1936-45; Dep. Chmn. Monmouthshire Quarter Sess. 1935-50; leader of Oxford circuit 1940-46; Chmn. Aliens Advisory Committee for Southern Area 1940; JP Middlesex and Monmouthshire. Father of Sir Robert Gore Micklethwait (QC 1956). d. 26th April 1951.

MIDDLETON, Noel

s. of Clement Alexander Middleton. b. 1875. educ. Eton; New Coll. Oxf. BA 1897. G.I. Jan. 1900. KC 1936. Bencher 1930, Treasurer 1942. Consulting editor for Rayden on Divorce. d. 24th June 1955.

MILLAR, Frederick Charles James

s. of Frederick George Millar, HM Ordnance Office. b. 1828. educ. privately; University Coll. London BA 1854, LLB 1856. I.T. Jan. 1856 (Cert. of Hon.). QC 1880. Bencher 1881. d. 18th Nov. 1899.

MILLAR, John (Lord Craighill)

s. of John Hepburn Millar, Glasgow, merchant. b. 1817. educ. Glasgow and Edin. Univs. LLD Glasgow. Scottish bar 1842;

advocate depute 1858, 1859, and 1866; Sol-Genl. Scotland 1867 and 1874. QC 1868. Lord of Session 1874, as Lord Craighill; Lord Justiciary 1876. d. 22nd Sept. 1888.

MILLER, Sir Alexander Edward

s. of Alexander Miller, Ballycastle, Antrim. b. 29th Aug. 1828. educ. Rugby; Trinity Coll. Dublin BA 1852, Hon. LLD 1875. L.I. Nov. 1854. QC 1872. Bencher 1872. Equity and real property examr. London Univ. 1873-78; Ry. Commr. 1877-88; Master in Lunacy 1889-91; legal member Gov-Genl.'s Council, India 1891-96; CSI; Knight 1889; JP Middlesex and London. d. 14th Sept. 1903.

MILLER, Alexander Thomas

s. of Alexander Allen Miller, Liverpool, solicitor. b. 14th Oct. 1875. educ. Parkfield Sch., Liverpool; Brighton Coll. Solicitor 1899. Lecturer at Liverpool Univ. M.T. July 1908. KC 1919. Bencher 1927. d. 1st March 1942.

MILLER, Robert

s. of John Charles Miller, Dublin. educ. Trinity Coll. Dublin BA 1822, MA 1827. M.T. Nov. 1826. Serjeant 1850; Cty. Ct. judge 1856-76. d. 5th Aug. 1876, age 78.

MILLER, Sir Thomas Frederick Dawson

s. of Thomas Robson Miller, London. b. 20th Dec. 1867. educ. Durham Sch.; Trinity Coll. Oxf. BA 1890. I.T. Nov. 1891. KC 1912. CJ High Ct. Patna, India 1917-28; Knight 1918. d. 3rd Oct. 1942.

MILLS, Henry

s. of Hon. John Colkoun Mills, Nevis, West Indies. b. 1819. M.T. Nov. 1843. QC 1861. Bencher 1861, Reader 1863. Recorder of Buckingham 1858-63; judge of High Ct. Calcutta 1863-64. Father of Henry Maynard Mills (I.T. 1875). d. Calcutta, 19th March 1864.

MILVAIN, Sir Thomas

s. of Henry Milvain JP, North Elswick Hall, Northumberland (d. 1890). b. 4th May 1844. educ. Durham Sch.; Trinity Hall Camb. LLB 1867, LLM 1873; athletics blue. M.T. June 1869. QC 1888. Bencher 1893, Reader 1904, Treasurer 1915. Recorder of Bradford 1892-1905; Chan. of Cty. Palatine of Durham 1892-1905; MP Durham 1885-92, Hampstead 1902-05; Judge Adv-Genl. 1905-16; CB 1912; Knight 1913; JP Durham. d. 23rd Sept. 1916.

MILWARD, Clement

s. of Rear-Admiral Clement Milward, Chewton House, Somerset. b. 20th Aug. 1821. M.T. Nov. 1846. QC 1865. Bencher 1865, Reader 1869, Treasurer 1879. A leader on Northern circuit, and at parliamentary bar. Author of a treatise on Cty. Ct. practice. d. 26th Oct. 1890.

MIREHOUSE, John Campbell

s. of John Mirehouse, High Sheriff of Pembrokeshire. b. 26th June 1789. educ. Harrow; Trinity Coll. Camb. BA 1812, MA 1817. L.I. May 1817. Special pleader. Common Serjeant 1833-50; DL, JP Middlesex and Pembrokeshire. Author of works on advowsons and tithes. Father of John Mirehouse, barrister (d. 1864). d. 18th Feb. 1850.

MITCHELL-INNES, Edward Alfred

s. of Gilbert Mitchell-Innes, Inverleith Place, Edinburgh. b. 21st Dec. 1863. educ. Wellington; Balliol Coll. Oxf. BA and MA 1899. M.T. April 1894. KC 1908. Bencher 1918, Reader 1928. Recorder of Middlesbrough 1915-28, of Leeds 1928-32; Chmn. of bar council 1931; Sol-Genl. Cty. Palatine of Durham 1930-32; Chmn. Hertfordshire Quarter Sess. 1924; Chan. of diocese of Ripon 1929-32; Commr. of Assize, South Wales, Western and Midland circuits 1930 and 1931; CBE 1918; DL, JP Hertfordshire. d. 6th March 1932.

MONCKTON, Walter Turner (Lord Monckton)

s. of Frank William Monckton, Ightham Warren, Kent (d. 1924). b. 17th Jan. 1891. educ. Harrow; Balliol Coll. Oxf. BA and MA 1918, Hon. Fellow 1957, Visitor 1957, Hon. DCL 1951. WWI Major 9th Battn. West Riding Regt., MC (despatches). I.T. May 1919. KC 1930. Recorder of Hythe 1930-37; Chan. diocese of Southwell 1930-36; Att-Genl. to Prince of Wales 1932-36; Att-Genl. Duchy of Cornwall 1936-51; Chmn. Aliens Advisory Committee 1939; Director-Genl. Press and Censorship Bureau 1939-40, Min. of Information 1940-41, Propaganda and Information Services, Cairo 1941; Acting Minister of State 1942; Sol-Genl. 1945; MP Bristol (West) 1951-57; Minister of Labour and Nat. Service 1951-55; Minister of Defence 1955-56; Paymaster-Genl. 1956-57; standing counsel Oxf. Univ. 1938-51; Pres. MCC 1957; Chmn. Midland Bank 1957-64; Chmn. Iraq Petroleum Co. 1958-65; govr. Harrow Sch.; Hon. LLD Bristol 1954, Sussex 1963 (first Chancellor); KCVO 1937, KCMG 1945; PC 1951; GCVO 1964; Viscount Monckton of Brenchley 1957. d. 9th Jan. 1965.

MONCREIFF, James Wellwood (Lord Moncreiff)

s. of Sir James Wellwood Moncreiff Bt., Lord of Session. b. 29th Nov. 1811. educ. Edin. High Sch.; Edin. Univ. LLD 1858. Scottish bar 1833; Sol-Genl. Scotland 1850-51; Lord Advocate 1851-58 and 1859-66 and 1868-69; MP Leith 1851-59, Edin. 1859-68, Univs. of Glasgow and Aberdeen 1868-69. QC 1868. Dean of Faculty of Advocates 1859-69; Lord Justice Clerk 1869-88; Hon. Col. Edin. Rifle Volunteer Corps 1873-95; PC 1869; Baronet 1871; Baron 1874; Lord Rector Edin. Univ. 1868-71; LLD Glasgow 1879. d. 27th April 1895.

MONK, John

s. of John Monk, Belper, Derbyshire. b. 1802. Solicitor in Manchester. M.T. Nov. 1839. QC 1857. Bencher 1857, Reader 1860, Treasurer 1868. Dep. Recorder of Manchester. d. 29th Jan. 1874.

MONTAGU, Basil

natural s. of 4th Earl of Sandwich. b. 24th April 1770. educ. Charterhouse; Christ's Coll. Camb. BA 1790, 6th Wrangler, MA 1793. G.I. May 1798. KC 1835. Commr. in Bankruptcy 1806; Accountant-Genl. in Bankruptcy 1836-46. Author of manuals on partnership, and bankruptcy; edited works of Francis Bacon 1825-34; reported bankruptcy cases (with W.S. Ayrton) 1833-38, (with R. Bligh) 1832-33, (with E. Chitty) 1838-40, (with E.C. Deacon and J. de Gex) 1840-44. d. Boulogne, 27th Nov. 1851.

MONTAGU, Ewen Edward Samuel

s. of 2nd Baron Swaythling (d. 1927). b. 29th March 1901. educ. Westminster; Trinity Coll. Camb. BA and LLB 1923, MA 1948; Harvard Univ. M.T. May 1924. KC 1939. Bencher 1948, Treasurer 1968. Recorder of Devizes 1944-51, of Southampton 1951-60. WWII Lt.Cdr. RNVR, Naval Intelligence; responsible for Operation Mincemeat to mislead enemy as to landing place for invasion of Italy 1943, OBE 1944. Judge-Adv. of the Fleet 1945-73; Dep.

Chmn. Hampshire Quarter Sess. 1948-51, Chmn. 1951-60; Dep. Chmn. Middlesex Quarter Sess. 1954, Chmn. 1956-65; Chmn. Middlesex Area, Greater London Quarter Sess. 1965-69; judge from 1969; Chmn. Central Council of Magistrates' Cts. Committees 1963-70; Chmn. Pioneer Health Centre; Vice-Pres. Nat. Addiction and Research Inst.; Pres. United Synagogue 1954-62; Chmn. GP committee RYA 1960-68; RYA Award 1971; Founder-Commodore Royal Ocean and Bar Yacht Club; Hon. Capt. RNR 1973; CBE 1950; DL, JP Hampshire; Order of Crown of Yugoslavia (3rd class) 1943. Author of The Man Who Never Was 1953, Beyond Top Secret U 1977. d. 19th July 1985.

MONTGOMERY, Robert Mortimer

s. of Rev. J.K. Montgomery, Chester. b. 1869. educ. King's Sch. Chester; St. Catherine's Soc. Oxf. MA. I.T. Nov. 1893. KC 1914. Bencher 1923, Treasurer 1944. Recorder of Chester 1926-48; independent member Committee on Holidays with Pay 1938. Author of Licensing Practice 1895, Excess Profits Duty 1916, and manuals on War Damage Acts 1941 and 1943. d. 31st Dec. 1948.

MOON, Arthur

s. of Sir Ernest Robert Moon KC. b. 1882. educ. Eton; New Coll. Oxf. BA 1906. I.T. Nov. 1907. KC 1928. Bencher 1936. WWI Capt. 8th Battn. London Regt. (TF), MC. Parliamentary draftsman; Chmn. General Claims Tribunal under Compensation (Defence) Act 1945-59. d. 4th April 1961.

MOON, Sir Ernest Robert

s. of Sir Richard Moon, 1st Bt. (d. 1899). b. 21st June 1854. educ. Winchester; Trinity Coll. Camb. LLB 1877. I.T. Nov. 1878. KC 1902. Bencher 1910. During WWI Pres. Munitions Trib. South West Midland Dist., and Enemy Trading Committee; mainly concerned in parliamentary committees, arbitrations, and railway cases; counsel to Speaker of H of C 1907-29; KCB 1919; CB 1915. d. 31st May 1930.

MOORE, Edmund Fitz

s. of Richard Moore, Hampton Court Palace. b. 17th Nov. 1801. educ. Charterhouse; Caius Coll. Camb. BA 1824, MA 1827. M.T. Nov. 1827. QC 1868. Bencher 1869. Authorised reporter for Judicial Committee of Privy Council, of appeal cases 1836-62, and appeals from India 1836-72. d. 11th Aug. 1873.

MOORE, Robert Ernest

s. of William Baker Moore, Hampstead, stockbroker. b. 16th Dec. 1863. educ. Malvern Coll.; Trinity Coll. Camb. BA and LLB 1885. M.T. June 1887. WWI Major commdg. 2nd Battn. City of London Volunteer Regt. Cty. Ct. judge 1919-34. d. 18th June 1934.

MOORSOM, James Marshall

s. of Vice-Admiral Constantine Richard Moorsom, Birmingham (d. 1861). b. 1838. educ. King Edward's Sch. Birmingham; Trinity Coll. Camb. BA 1860. I.T. Jan. 1863. QC 1885. Bencher 1892, Treasurer 1914. Examr. in common law to Inns of Ct. 1884; MP Great Yarmouth 1892-95; JP Cumberland. d. 26th March 1918.

MORGAN, George Hay

s. of Walter Morgan, Wernwilk House, Hay-on-Wye, Breconshire. b. 1866. educ. Pontypool Coll.; Cardiff Univ. Coll.; London Univ. BSc. Schoolmaster until 1887. I.T. June 1899. KC 1913. Member Tottenham Sch. Bd. 1897-1900; MP Cornwall (Truro) 1906-18; Whip of Nonconformist Party. d. 24th Jan. 1931.

MORGAN, Sir George Osborne, Bt.

s. of Rev. Morgan Morgan, Conway, Carnarvon. b. Gothenburg, 8th May 1826. educ. Shrewsbury; Worcester Coll. Oxf. BA 1848; Fellow Univ. Coll. 1850-57, MA 1850. L.I. June 1853. QC 1869. Bencher 1869, Treasurer 1890. Equity draftsman and conveyancer; MP Denbighshire 1868-85, Denbighshire (East) 1885-97; PC 1880; Judge Adv-Genl. 1880-85; Under-Secy. of State for the Colonies 1886; Baronet 1892. Author of works on chancery procedure, and a joint editor of the New Reports. d. 25th Aug. 1897.

MORGAN, Hopkin Trevor

s. of Hopkin Morgan JP, Pontypridd, South Wales. b. 19th June 1892. educ. Mill Hill; Gonville and Caius Coll. Camb. BA 1917, MA and LLB 1920. WWI Capt. 5th Battn. Welch Regt. and 1st Battn. Wiltshire Regt., MC (despatches). I.T. June 1920. KC 1936. Chmn. Traffic Commrs. (West Midland) 1938, Western Area 1938, Wales 1941; Cty. Ct. judge 1948-76; Dep. Chmn. Glamorganshire Quarter Sess. 1948-59; Dep. Chmn. Pembrokeshire Quarter Sess. 1950-53; Chmn. Carmarthenshire Quarter Sess. 1951; DL, JP Glamorgan; JP Somerset and Carmarthen. d. 25th Oct. 1976.

MORGAN, John Hartman

s. of Rev. David Morgan, Ystrad Rhondda. b. 20th March 1876. educ. Caterham Sch.; University Coll. of Wales; Balliol Coll. Oxf. BA 1905; London Univ. MA 1896; Berlin Univ. Lecturer at Toynbee Hall 1902-04; journalist with Daily Chronicle and Manchester Guardian. I.T. Nov. 1915. KC 1926. WWI Home Office rep. with BEF to inquire into conduct of Germans in the Field 1914-15; Staff Capt. on JAG's staff (despatches); DAG on Inter-Allied military comm. of control, Germany 1919-23; Hon. Brig-Genl. 1923. Defended Sir Roger Casement 1916; Reader in constitutional law at Inns of Ct. 1926-36; prof. of constitutional law, Univ. Coll. London 1923-41; examr. in law, London Univ. and Civil Service

Comm.; legal adviser to American War Crimes Comm. 1947-49; DL, JP Wiltshire; legal editor of Encyclopaedia Britannica. Author of The House of Lords and the Constitution 1910, War, its Conduct and Legal Results (with T. Baty) 1915, Gentlemen at Arms 1918, Assize of Arms 1945, The Great Assize 1948, The Law Merchant, The Legal and Political Unity of the Empire. d. 8th April 1955.

MORGAN, John Lloyd

s. of Rev. Prof. William Morgan, Carmarthen. b. 13th Feb. 1861. educ. Tettenhall Coll.; Owen's Coll. Manchester; Trinity Hall Camb. BA 1884. I.T. May 1884. KC 1906. Recorder of Swansea 1908-11. MP Carmarthenshire (West) 1889-1910; Cty. Ct. judge 1910-26; JP Carmarthenshire, Pembrokeshsire, Glamorganshire. d. 17th May 1944.

MORITZ, Rudolph

s. of Hermann Moritz, Highgate, London, stockbroker. b. 11th July 1878. educ. Highgate Sch.; Zurich Univ.; London Univ. BSc. L.I. Jan. 1902. KC 1925. Bencher 1931. Alderman, Hornsey Borough Council 1907; member Metrop. Water Bd. 1908-19; Middlesex CC 1909-12. d. 22nd Aug. 1940.

MORLEY, Arthur

s. of William James Morley, Bradford. b. 19th Nov. 1881. educ. Bradford Sch.; Christ Church Oxf. BA 1903, MA. M.T. Jan. 1913. KC 1933. Bencher 1938. OBE 1920 for hospital administrative services. Recorder of Richmond, Yorkshire 1928, Huddersfield 1928-34, Sheffield 1934-41, Leeds 1940-43; member of bar council; Chan. of diocese of Bradford 1941-46; metrop. magistrate 1943-44; Chmn. Middlesex Sess. 1945-46; JP Sussex. Father of Sir Godfrey William Rowland Morley OBE (1909-87), solicitor. d. 11th Jan. 1946.

MORRIS, Sir Harold Spencer

s. of Sir Malcolm Alexander Morris KCVO, surgeon (d. 1924). b.
21st Dec. 1876. educ. Clifton Coll.; Magdalen Coll. Oxf. BA 1897.
I.T. Jan. 1899. KC 1921. Bencher 1934. WWI Special constable;
Coldstream Guards and attached RAF (Major); MBE 1919,
(despatches). Recorder of Folkestone 1921-26; MP Bristol (East)
1922-23; Chmn. Nat. Wages Bd. for Railways 1925; Dep. Chmn.
Middlesex Quarter Sess.; Pres. of Industrial Ct. 1926-45; Knight
1927; JP Middlesex; CStJ. Published The Barrister 1932, and Back
View (autobiog.) 1960. Father of Malcolm John Morris (QC 1959).
d. 11th Nov. 1967.

MORRIS, John William (Lord Morris)

s. of Daniel Morris, Liverpool, bank manager. b. 11th Sept. 1896.
educ. Liverpool Inst.; Trinity Hall Camb. LLB 1920, Hon. Fellow
1951, Hon. LLD 1967; Choate Fellow, Harvard Univ. WWI Capt.
Royal Welch Fus., MC. I.T. Nov. 1921. KC 1935. Bencher 1943,
Treasurer 1967. Practised initially in Liverpool; appeal judge, Isle
of Man 1937-45; hon. standing counsel to Univ. of Wales 1938-45;
KB judge 1945-51; Knight and CBE 1945; LJ 1951-60; PC 1951;
L of A 1960-75; Baron Morris of Borth-y-Gest 1960; CH 1975;
Chmn. several committees, including Home Office Committee on
Jury Service 1963; Chmn. Carnarvonshire Quarter Sess. 1943; DL,
JP Carnarvonshire; hon. member Canadian and American Bar
Assocs.; Pres. London Welsh Assoc. 1951; Chmn. Bd. of Govrs.
Charing Cross Hospital 1948-68; Pro-Chan. Univ. of Wales 1956-
74; Hon. LLD Liverpool, Wales, and Br. Columbia. d. 9th June
1979.

MORRIS, Michael (Lord Killanin)

s. of Martin Morris JP, Spiddal, Galway (d. 1862). b. 14th Nov.
1826. educ. Erasmus Smith's Sch. Galway; Trinity Coll. Dublin BA
1847, Hon. LLD 1887, Visitor 1887. Irish bar 1849. QC 1863.

Bencher 1866. High Sheriff of Galway 1850; Recorder of Galway 1857-65; MP Galway 1865-67; Sol-Genl. Ireland July 1866, Att-Genl. 1866-67; PC (Ireland) 1866; judge of Common Pleas 1867-76, CJ thereof 1876-87; LCJ Ireland 1887; Baronet 1885; L of A 1889-1900; PC 1889; Baron (life) 1889; Hon. Bencher L.I. 1890; Commr. of Irish Nat. educ.; Senator and V-C Royal Univ. of Ireland 1899; Baron (hereditary) 1900; JP Galway and Cavan. Father of Martin Henry Fitzpatrick Morris, 2nd Baron (L.I. 1892). d. 8th Sept. 1901.

MORRIS, Sir Owen Temple

s. of Dr. Frederick Temple Morris, Cardiff (d. 1942). b. 18th Sept. 1896. Solicitor 1919. G.I. Jan. 1925. KC 1937. Pros. counsel to PO South Wales 1931-37; Chan. diocese of Llandaff 1935; MP Cardiff (East) 1931-42; Recorder of Merthyr Tydfil 1936-42; Cty. Ct. judge 1942-69; Acting Recorder of Swansea 1940-42; Chmn. of Quarter Sess. Carmarthenshire 1942-50, Town and Cty. of Haverfordwest 1942-48, Brecknockshire 1948-55, Monmouthshire 1950; Dep. Chmn. of Quarter Sess. Glamorganshire 1938-48, Pembrokeshire 1942-48; judge of Provincial Court Church in Wales; Commr. of Assize Oxford circuit 1946, Welsh circuit 1960-61; member Royal Comm. on Police 1960-62; Knight 1967. Father of Peter Temple-Morris MP (I.T. 1962). d. 21st April 1985.

MORRIS, Sir Rhys Hopkin

s. of Rev. John Morris, Maesteg, Glamorgan. b. 1888. educ. London Univ.; Univ. of Wales Hon. LLD. M.T. July 1919. KC 1946. WWI Lieut. Royal Welsh Fusiliers; MBE, (despatches). MP Cardiganshire 1923-32; member Palestine Comm. 1929; metrop. magistrate South Western 1932-36; BBC Regional Director for Wales 1936-45; MP Carmarthen 1945-56; Dep. Chmn. Ways and Means 1951; Knight 1954; JP Middlesex. d. 22nd Nov. 1956.

MORRISON, William Shepherd (Lord Dunrossil)

s. of John Morrison, Torinturk, Argyll. b. 10th Aug. 1893. educ.
George Watson's Coll. Edin.; Edin. Univ. MA 1920. WWI Capt.
RFA, MC, (despatches thrice). I.T. Nov. 1923. KC 1934. Bencher
1951. Recorder of Walsall 1935-36; MP Cirencester and
Tewkesbury 1929-59; parliamentary private secy. to Financial Secy.
to Treasury 1931, to Att-Genl. 1931-35; Financial Secy. to Treasury
1935-36; Minister of Agr. and Fisheries 1936-39; Chmn. 1922
Committee 1932-36; Minister of Food 1939-40; Postmaster-Genl.
1940-43; Minister of Town and Country Planning 1943-45; Speaker
of H of C 1951-59; member Medical Research Council 1932-35,
and Industrial Health Research Bd. 1931-36; Chan. of Duchy of
Lancaster 1939-40; Govr-Genl. Australia 1960-61; PC 1936; KStJ;
GCMG 1959; Viscount Dunrossil 1959; Hon. LLD Edin, Leeds, St.
Andrews, London; Hon. FRCS Edin.; Hon. MIMunE. d. 3rd Feb.
1961.

MORTEN, Edward

s. of Thomas Honnor Morten, Hampstead, London. b. 23rd Dec.
1845. educ. Manchester Gr. Sch.; Christ's Coll. Camb. BA 1867.
I.T. Jan. 1871. KC 1909. Bencher 1915. Special pleader. The first
recorder of West Ham 1894-1929. d. 15th Feb. 1929.

MORTIMER, George Frederick Lloyd Jones

s. of Rev. Mortimer Lloyd Jones Mortimer, Norton, Stockton-on-
Tees. b. 9th Sept. 1866. educ. Birkenhead Sch.; Balliol Coll. Oxf.
BA 1889, MA 1892. I.T. June 1891. KC 1919. Bencher 1924.
Recorder of Rotherham 1905-28. d. 5th Sept. 1928.

MORTON, Fergus Dunlop (Lord Morton)

s. of George Morton, Henryton, Ayrshire, stockbroker (d. 1927). b.

17th Oct. 887. educ. Kelvinside; St John's Coll. Camb. BA 1909, MA and LLB 1910; Hon. Fellow 1940; played golf for univ. Employed in solicitor's office. I.T. Nov. 1912; L.I. 1914. KC 1929. Bencher 1932, Treasurer 1953. WWI Capt HLI and Royal Fus., MC. At War Office 1918-19; Chancery judge 1938-44; Knight 1938; Dep. Chmn. Contraband Committee 1939; Chmn. Black List Committee (Min. of Economic Warfare) 1941-46; LJ 1944-47; PC 1944; L of A 1947-59; Baron 1947; Chmn. Council of Legal Educ. 1949-53, Committee on Law of Intestate Succession 1950, Comm. on Marriage and Divorce 1952; hon. member of Faculty of Advocates (Scotland), and Canadian and American Bar Assocs.; Dep. High Steward Camb. Univ.; Hon. LLD Camb. and Glasgow 1951, St. Andrews 1956, Sydney 1957; Grand Cross of Order of Orange Nassau, and US Medal of Freedom; Pres. Oxf. and Camb. Golfing Socy. 1953. d. 18th July 1973.

MOSS, Samuel

s. of Enoch Moss, Broad Oak, Rossett, Denbigh. b. 13th Dec. 1858. educ. privately; Worcester Coll. Oxf. BA 1878, BCL and MA 1883. L.I. April 1880. Asst. boundary commr. for Wales 1887; MP Denbighshire (East) 1897-1906; Chmn. Denbighshire CC; Cty. Ct. judge 1906-18; JP Denbighshire and Cheshire. Author of a treatise on land law 1886. d. 14th May 1918.

MOSSOP, Leonard

s. of Charles Mossop, Chelsea. b. 1869. educ. Bath Coll.; Trinity Coll. Oxf. BA, BCL. L.I. Jan. 1893 (Cert. of Hon.). Equity draftsman and conveyancer; Cty. Ct. judge 1924-26; JP Middlesex; played hockey and lawn tennis for Middlesex. d. 7th April 1933.

MOTTERAM, James

s. of Charles Motteram, Edgbaston, Birmingham, merchant. b. 16th

May 1817. educ. Solihull Gr. Sch. M.T. Nov. 1851. QC 1875. Bencher 1880. Cty. Ct. judge 1876-84; JP Staffordshire and Warwickshire. d. 20th Sept. 1884.

MOULTON, John Fletcher (Lord Moulton)

s. of Rev. James Egan Moulton, Madeley, Shropshire, Wesleyan minister. b. 18th Nov. 1844. educ. by father; Kingswood Sch.; London Univ. BA 1865, MA 1868; St John's Coll. Camb. BA 1868, Senior Wrangler (with highest total of marks ever gained), MA; Fellow of Christ's Coll. 1868-75; Hon. Fellow St John's Coll. M.T. Nov. 1874. QC 1885. Bencher 1889, Reader 1900, Treasurer 1910. Specialised in patent actions; MP Battersea (Clapham) 1885-86, South Hackney 1894-95, North East Cornwall 1898-1906; organised and directed War Dept. in supply of high explosives 1914-18; KCB 1915, GBE 1917; Chmn. Medical Research Committee under Nat. Insce. Act; LJ, Knight and PC 1906; L of A 1912; Baron 1912; Fellow and member Senate of London Univ.; FRS; FRAS; Hon. LLD Edin. 1911, Camb. 1914; Grand Officer of Order of Etoile Noire (France); Commander of Legion of Honour, of Order of Leopold of Belgium, and White Eagle (Russia). Father of Hugh Fletcher Moulton MC (M.T. 1899). d. 9th March 1921.

MOYLAN, Denis Creagh

s. of Denis Moylan, Cork. educ. Stonyhurst. L.I. Nov. 1829. Assessor of Ct. of Requests, Westminster 1845; Cty. Ct. judge 1847-49. Author of The Opinions of Lord Holland as recorded in the Journals of the House of Lords 1841. Published pamphlets (1843) on the Right of Search, and the law of Registration of Voters and parliamentary elections. d. 19th Nov. 1849, age 55.

MUIR-MACKENZIE, Kenneth Augustus (Lord Muir-Mackenzie)

s. of Sir John Muir-Mackenzie, Bt. b. 29th June 1845. educ. Charterhouse; Balliol Coll. Oxf. BA 1868, MA 1873. L.I. April 1873. QC 1886. Bencher 1891, Treasurer 1917. Permanent princ. secy. to Lord Chancellor, and Clerk of the Crown in Chancery 1880-1915; High Bailiff of Westminster 1912; Warden of Winchester Coll. 1904-15; govr. Winchester, Charterhouse, Bradfield and Bedford Schools; Lord-in-Waiting 1924; PC 1924; CB 1893, KCB 1898, GCB 1911; Baron 1915; JP London, Middlesex, Surrey and Sussex. Father of William Montague Muir-Mackenzie, barrister (d. 1901). Brother of Montague Johnstone Muir-Mackenzie (L.I. 1873), Official Referee. d. 22nd May 1930.

MULHOLLAND, William

s. of Joseph Stevenson Mulholland MD, Belfast. b. 19th Jan. 1843. educ. Queen's Coll. Galway; Royal Univ. of Ireland MA. Irish bar 1865. L.I. June 1875. QC 1894. Bencher 1897. Cty. Ct. judge 1899-1907. d. 21st Aug. 1907.

MULLIGAN, James

s. of David Mulligan, Annaclone, Co. Down. b. 1847. educ. Queen's Univ. Ireland MA. G.I. Jan. 1874 (Cert of Hon.). QC 1897. Bencher 1891, Treasurer 1896. Member Council of Legal Educ. 1891-1917; Cty. Ct. judge 1906-21. Author of The Riddle of Justice, Justice in the After-Life, Notes on Bacon's Historia Vitae et Mortis, Thoughts of an Octogenarian on Overcrowding. d. 15th Dec. 1937.

MULLINS, Claud William

s. of Edwin Roscoe Mullins, Finchley, sculptor (d. 1907). b. 6th Sept. 1887. educ. Univ. Coll. Sch.; Mill Hill. Employed by LCC

1907-12. G.I. Jan. 1913 (Cert of Hon.). WWI Lieut. RAOC Mesopotamia and India; member Br. Comm. war criminal trials at Leipzig 1921 (Interpreter). Metrop. magistrate 1931, finally at South Western to 1947; Vice-Pres. London Marriage Guidance Council; Vice-Pres. Family Planning Assoc. Author of In quest of Justice; Marriage, Children and God, Wife v. Husband in the Courts, Crime and Psychology, Why Crime?, One man's Furrow (autobiog.) 1963. d. 23rd Oct. 1968.

MUNDELL, William Adam

s. of Alexander Mundell, Leatherhead, Surrey. b. 1815. educ. Tonbridge; St John's Coll. Oxf. 1832. Solicitor's clerk in Leicester and London. M.T. May 1847. QC 1866. Bencher 1866, Reader 1872. Practised mainly at parliamentary bar; known as "the shilling whist player". Author of a digest of criminal statutes and cases 1846-48. d. 15th July 1875.

MURISON, Alexander Falconer

s. of Alexander Murison, Brucklay, Aberdeenshire, cart- and wheelwright. b. 3rd March 1847. educ. Aberdeen Gr. Sch.; Aberdeen Univ. MA, Hon. LLD. English master at Aberdeen Gr. Sch. 1869-77. M.T. June 1881. KC 1924. On political and literary staff, Daily Chronicle, India; prof. of Roman law 1883-1925 (emeritus from 1925) and of jurisprudence 1901-25, Univ. Coll. London; dep. prof. of Roman-Dutch law 1914-24; Dean of the Faculty of Laws, London Univ. 1912-24; dep. prof. of civil law and dep. reader in Roman law, Oxf. Univ. 1916-19; Pres. Society of Teachers of Public Law 1916-17; Senator, London Univ. 1921-24; editor of the Educational Times 1902-12. Author of numerous educational works, particularly translations from the classics. Father of Sir James William Murison (1872-1945), CJ Straits Settlements. d. 8th June 1934.

MURPHY, Francis Stack

s. of Jeremiah Murphy, Cork, merchant. b. 1807. educ. Clongowes Wood Coll.; Trinity Coll. Dublin BA 1829, MA 1832. L.I. Jan. 1833. Assisted "Father Prout" (F.S. Mahony) in Fraser's Magazine 1834. Depicted in Prout Papers as Frank Cresswell of Furnival's Inn. MP Cork 1841-46 and 1851-53. Serjeant 1842; patent of precedence 1846; Commr. in Bankruptcy 1853-60. Reported (with E.T. Hurlstone) exchequer cases 1836-37. d. 17th June 1860.

MURPHY, Harold Lawson

s. of James Murphy, QB judge in Ireland (d. 1901). b. 12th Dec. 1882. educ. Charterhouse, Trinity Coll. Dublin BA 1903, MA. Irish bar 1906; Barrington Lecturer in Political Economy 1910. I.T. Jan. 1910. KC 1936. WWI Capt. RAF. d. 5th Jan. 1942.

MURPHY, John Harvey Joseph

s. of John Patrick Murphy KC. b. 1862. educ. Downside Sch. Bath; Trinity Hall Camb. 1881. M.T. June 1887. KC 1920. Chief reporter to The Times in Probate and Divorce Ct. 1895-1909. d. 20th Dec. 1924.

MURPHY, John Patrick

s. of Patrick Mathias Murphy QC, Dublin. b. 17th March 1831. educ. Stonyhurst; Trinity Coll. Dublin BA 1853, MA 1859. Lieut. Cavan Militia. M.T. Nov. 1856. QC 1874. Bencher 1876, Reader 1886, Treasurer 1897. One of counsel for The Times in Parnell Comm. 1889; Commr. of Assize 1881. Sang as a tenor in first Handel Festival at Crystal Palace. d. 24th July 1907.

MURRAY, Andrew Graham, (Lord Dunedin)

s. of Thomas Graham Murray WS, Stenton, Perthshire, Crown-Agent for Scotland. b. 21st Nov. 1849. educ. Harrow; Edin. Univ.; Trinity Coll. Camb. BA 1872, MA 1875. Scottish bar 1874; senior advocate depute 1888-90; Sheriff of Perthshire 1890-91; Sol-Genl. for Scotland 1891-92, 1895-96; Lord Advocate 1896-1903. QC 1891. PC 1896; MP Buteshire 1891-1905; Secy. for Scotland 1903-05; Lord Justice-Genl. of Scotland and Lord Pres. of Ct. of Session 1905-13; L of A 1913-32; Keeper of Great Seal of principality of Scotland 1900-36; KCVO 1908, GCVO 1923; Baron 1905; Viscount 1926. d. 21st Aug. 1942.

MYBURGH, Philip Albert

s. of Francois Gerard Myburgh, civil service, Cape of Good Hope (d. 1868). b. 24th Feb. 1841. educ. South African Coll.; London Univ. BA 1860. I.T. Nov. 1862. QC 1882. Bencher 1886. HM standing counsel in Supreme Ct., China and Japan; practised in Admiralty Ct. London; member Convocation, London Univ. d. 4th July 1892.

NALDRETT, Edward James

s. of Edward Naldrett, Lodsworth, Petworth, Sussex, yeoman. educ. privately. Asst. clerk and accountant, Walthamstow Local Bd. M.T. Nov. 1894. KC 1928. Hon. Associate RIBA; JP Sussex. Author of works on local govt. and public health. Father of Harold Carter Naldrett (M.T. 1917). d. 15th March 1930, age 73.

NAPIER, Thomas Bateman

s. of Richard Clay Napier, Knutsford, Cheshire. b. 1854. educ. Rugby; London Univ. LLD; Fellow Univ. Coll. 1895-1905. I.T. Nov. 1883 (Cert. of Hon.). Member of LCC 1893-1906; MP Kent

(North East) 1906-10; Cty. Ct. judge 1912-13; a governor of Rugby Sch. 1927; JP Middlesex. d. 6th Nov. 1933.

NASMITH, David

s. of David Nasmith, founder of London City Mission. b. 1829. educ. London Univ. LLB 1870. M.T. Jan. 1865. QC 1888. Translated J.L.E. Ortolan's History of Roman Law 1871; author of works on public law 1873, private law 1875, adjective law 1879; member of Convocation, London Univ.; Hon. LLD St. Andrew's Univ.; FSS. d. 10th July 1894.

NEAL, John

s. of Arthur Neal MP, Ryegate, Sheffield (d. 1933). b. 17th Aug. 1889. educ. Leys Sch.; King's Coll. Camb. BA 1910, LLB 1911, MA 1914. WWI Major RA, MC. I.T. April 1920. Cty. Ct. judge 1942-61; Dep. Chmn. Yorkshire West Riding Quarter Sess. 1942-45; with Min. of Economic Warfare and Min. of Food 1940-42. d. 8th Sept. 1962.

NEEDHAM, Sir Raymond Walter

s. of Herbert Needham, Canford Cliffs, Dorset, schoolmaster. b. 1877. educ. Dronfield Gr. Sch.; Sheffield Univ. Technical Sch. Employed with IR 1897. M.T. July 1908. KC 1928. Bencher 1936, Reader 1945, Treasurer 1953. Seconded to War Office and Lord Lieut. of Ireland 1915-16; private secy. to Minister of Information 1917-19; Controller of Aerodromes and Aerial Licensing, Air Min. 1919; Director, Min. of Information 1939; member, Air Supply Bd. 1940-46; Director of Priorities, Min. of Aircraft Production 1940-42; General Commr. of Taxes M.T. 1938; Dep. Chmn. Kent Quarter Sess. 1946-52; JP Hertfordshire, Dorset, Hampshire, Kent; Knight 1957; FSA. Author of manuals on death duties and income tax. d. 16th March 1965.

NEILSON, Alexander

s. of John N. Neilson WS, Edinburgh. b. May 1868. educ. Fettes; Edin. Univ. MA.; rugby blue. M.T. Nov. 1893. KC 1919. Bencher 1925. Practised in Commercial Ct. d. 9th April 1929.

NELSON, Henry Ince

s. of Henry Nelson OBE, Liverpool. b. 29th May 1897. educ. Aldenham Sch.; Pembroke Coll. Camb. BA and LLB 1921. WWI Lieut RFA. I.T. Jan. 1922. KC 1945. Bencher 1952. WWII in Home Guard. Judge of Salford Hundred Ct. of Record 1947-48; judge of Liverpool Ct. of Passage 1948-50; Recorder of Liverpool 1950-54; Commr. under Nat. Insce. and Nat. Insce. (Industrial Injuries) Acts 1959. d. 1st Aug. 1981.

NEVE, Eric Read

s. of David Edgar Neve, Blackheath, Kent, artist. b. 11th March 1887. educ. Brighton Gr. Sch. Newspaper editor 1908-14. WW1 Lieut. RASC (Mechanised Transport). M.T. Jan. 1921. KC 1939. Bencher 1948. Recorder of Canterbury 1938-52; Chmn. West Sussex Quarter Sess. 1943, East Sussex Quarter Sess. 1947; Chmn. Middlesex Quarter Sess. 1946-56. d. 12th Jan. 1958.

NEVILLE, Sir Ralph

s. of Henry Neville, MRCS, Esher, Surrey. b. 13th Sept. 1848. educ. Tonbridge; Emmanuel Coll. Camb. BA 1871, MA 1874, Hon. Fellow 1906-18. L.I. April 1872. QC 1888. Bencher 1892. Equity draftsman and conveyancer; MP Liverpool (Exchange) 1887-95; Chancery judge 1906-18; Knight 1906; Pres. Garden City Assoc. Joint author of Railway and Canal cases. Father of Ralph Neville OBE (M.T. 1899), judge in Egypt. d. 13th Oct. 1918.

NEWBOLT, Sir Francis George

s. of Rev. Henry Francis Newbolt, Bilston, Staffordshire. b. 21st Nov. 1863. educ. Clifton Coll.; Balliol Coll. Oxf. BA 1887, MA 1900. I.T. Jan. 1890. KC 1914. Recorder of Doncaster 1916-20; member of bar council; Chan. of diocese of Exeter 1919, Bradford 1920; Chmn. Devon Quarter Sess. 1920-36; Official Referee of High Ct. 1920-36; hon. prof. of law in Royal Acad. 1928; Master of Art Workers' Guild 1927; Master of Clockmakers' Co. 1932; hon. member Land Agents Socy.; Pres. Norwegian Club 1920-26; Knight 1919; JP Devon; Hon. RA; FCS 1885; ARE 1897. Author of Summary Procedure in the High Court, and commentary on Sale of Goods Act 1893. Brother of Sir Henry Newbolt, the poet (L.I. 1887). d. 5th Dec. 1940.

NEWELL, Harold

s. of Joseph Newell, Pudsey, Yorks. b. 3rd Jan. 1866. educ. Bradford Gr. Sch.; Durham Univ. BA, BCL. M.T. June 1895. Cty. Ct. judge 1920-28. d. 5th Nov. 1937.

NEWTON, Robert Milnes

s. of William S. Newton MP, Elvedon, Suffolk. b. 2nd July 1821. educ. Eton; Trinity Coll. Camb. BA 1843, MA 1847. L.I. May 1847. Recorder of Cambridge 1858-66; metrop. magistrate 1866, finally at Marlborough St. 1871-96; JP Middlesex and Liberty of the Tower. d. 29th Oct. 1900.

NICHOLS, William

s. of William Nichols, Dawes Green, nr. Reigate, Surrey. b. 1793. educ. Colchester Sch.; Trinity Coll. Camb. BA 1817. L.I. Feb. 1818. Commr. for relief of insolvent debtors 1860; Registrar of Manchester Ct. of Bankruptcy 1862; Cty. Ct. judge 1862-64. d.

Mentone, Savoy, 29th Dec. 1864.

NIELD, Sir Basil Edward

s. of Charles Edwin Nield JP, Upton Grange, Upton by Chester, solicitor (d. 1941). b. 7th May 1903. educ. Harrow; Magdalen Coll. Oxf. BA 1924, MA 1936. I.T. May 1925. KC 1945. Bencher 1952, Reader 1976, Treasurer 1977. Recorder of Salford 1948-56; Chan. diocese of Liverpool 1948-56; Recorder and judge of Crown Ct. Manchester 1956-60; MP Cheshire (City of Chester) 1940-56; WWII Lt. Col. in JAG's Office; Pres. Palestine Mil. Cts. 1941, ADJAG Middle East Forces 1942, MBE (despatches). Member of bar council 1951; CBE 1956; Knight 1957; QB judge 1960-78; sponsored as Private Members Bill, Adoption of Children Act 1949; hon. parliamentary Chmn. of Dock and Harbour Authorities Assoc.; member Magistrates' Rules Committee 1952, Legal Bd. of Church Assembly 1952, Home Secy.'s Advisory Committee on Treatment of Offenders 1957; Chmn. Chester Conservative Assoc. 1930-40; member Ct. of Liverpool Univ.; govr. Harrow Sch.; Freeman, City of London 1963; DL Chester. Author of Farewell to the Assizes 1972. d. 4th Dec. 1996.

NIELD, Sir Herbert

s. of William Robert Nield, Saddleworth, Yorkshire. b. 20th Oct. 1862. educ. privately. Solicitor 1885, practised in London. I.T. Nov. 1895. KC 1913. MP Middlesex (Ealing) 1906-18, Ealing Borough 1918-31; Recorder of York 1917-32; Alderman Middlesex CC 1906; Dep. Chmn. Middlesex Quarter Sess. 1909; Chmn. Lea Catchment Bd.; Chmn. Council of Nat. Union of Conservative Assocs. 1923-24; Chmn. United Club 1923-24; Knight 1918; PC 1924; DL, JP Middlesex. d. 11th Oct. 1932.

NOAD, Lewis

s. of William John Noad. b. 8th Oct. 1865. educ. privately; St. Mary's Coll. Went to sea at age 15, and became master mariner. L.I. Jan. 1894. KC 1933. Bencher 1935. Practised in admiralty and commercial cts.; arbitrator to Lloyd's; FRMS. d. 17th Dec. 1950.

NOBLE, William James

s. of John Noble, Little Over, nr. Derby, director Midland Ry. Co. (d. 1896). b. 31st July 1855. educ. Keble Coll. Oxf. BA 1879, MA 1883. I.T. Jan. 1882. KC 1905. Recorder of Newark 1899-1914. d. 1st Nov. 1914.

NORRIS, John Freeman

s. of Robert E. Norris, Clifton, Gloucestershire. b. 15th Oct. 1842. educ. privately; University Coll. London. I.T. Nov. 1865. QC 1882. Puisne judge, High Ct. Calcutta 1882-95. d. 15th May 1904.

NORTH, Sir Ford

s. of John North, Liverpool, solicitor (d. 1877). b. 10th Jan. 1830. educ. Winchester; University Coll. Oxf. BA 1852. I.T. April 1856. QC 1877. Bencher 1881. Equity draftsman and conveyancer; QB judge 1881-83; Knight 1881; Chancery judge 1883-1900; PC 1900; FRS; FRMS. d. 12th Oct. 1913.

NORTON, George Chapple

s. of Fletcher Norton, Exch. Baron (Scotland) (d. 1820). b. 31st Aug. 1800. educ. Winchester; Edin. Univ. M.T. Nov. 1825. Commr. in Bankruptcy 1827-31; MP Guildford 1826-30; Recorder of Guildford 1827-75; metrop. magistrate 1831, finally at Lambeth 1845-67. d.

24th Feb. 1875.

NORTON, Robert Frederick

s. of Frederick Norton, principal clerk in Chancery Taxing Office. b. 1854. educ. City of London Sch.; London Univ. BA 1874, LLB 1887. L.I. June 1879. QC 1900. Hon. legal adviser to Foreign Trade Dept., Foreign Office; CBE 1918; VD; member Convocation, London Univ. Joint author of manual on Interpretation of deeds. d. 8th Aug. 1929.

O'BRIEN, Michael William

s. of William O'Brien, Nenagh, Tipperary, farmer. b. 29th Sept. 1813. educ. privately; Trinity Coll. Dublin BA 1835, MA 1842. L.I. May 1842. Serjeant 1862; Recorder of Lincoln 1872-73. d. 2nd June 1873.

O'CONNOR, Arthur

s. of William O'Connor MD, Dingle, Co. Kerry. b. 1st Oct. 1844. educ. Ushaw Coll. Clerk in War Office 1863-79. M.T. Jan. 1883. KC 1899. MP Queen's Co. 1880-85, East Donegal 1885-1900; Chmn. Public Accounts Committee 1895-1900; Cty. Ct. judge 1901-20; served on several Royal Comms. d. 30th March 1923.

O'CONNOR, Sir James

s. of Michael O'Connor, Wexford, Co. Leinster. b. 1st April 1872. educ. Blackrock Coll. Dublin. Irish bar 1900. KC 1908. Bencher 1915. Sol-Genl. for Ireland 1914-16; Att-Genl. 1916-18; Chancery judge 1918; LJ 1918-24; PC (Ireland) 1917. M.T. May 1925. KC 1925 (revoked at own request 1929); re-admitted as solicitor, Dublin 1929. Author of The Licensing Laws of Ireland, The Motor Car

Acts, The Irish Justice of the Peace. d. 29th Dec. 1931.

O'CONNOR, John

s. of William O'Connor, Cork, soldier. b. 10th Oct. 1850. educ.
Christian Brothers' Sch. Cork. Commercial agent and merchant.
M.T. Jan. 1893. KC 1919. MP South Tipperary 1885-92, North
Kildare 1905-18. d. 27th Oct. 1928.

O'CONNOR, Sir Terence James

s. of James O'Connor, Bridgnorth, Shropshire. b. 13th Sept. 1891.
educ. Sherborne; New Coll. Oxf. I.T. Jan. 1919. KC 1929. Bencher
1936. WWI Capt. 4th Battn. Highland L.I. and West African
Frontier Force. MP Bedford (Luton) 1924-29, Nottingham (Central)
1930-40; Sol-Genl. 1936; Knight 1936; Dep. Chmn. Oxfordshire
Quarter Sess.; member of Law Revision Committee; JP Oxfordshire;
FRGS. d. 8th May 1940.

ODGERS, Walter Blake

s. of William Blake Odgers KC. b. 14th Dec. 1880. educ. Sedbergh;
Balliol Coll. Oxf. BA 1904, MA 1907. M.T. Jan. 1906. KC 1938.
WWI Capt. General List; Courts-martial officer 1918-19. Member
of bar council 1925-41; Recorder of Southampton 1937-41; metrop.
magistrate 1941, finally at North London to 1954. Author, with
father, of Odgers on Common Law; edited Odgers on Libel and
Slander, Odgers on Pleading and Practice, and Warburton's Criminal
Cases. d. 25th April 1969.

ODGERS, William Blake

s. of Rev. William James Odgers, Belvedere, Bath. b. 15th May
1849. educ. Bath Gr. Sch; University Coll. London; Trinity Hall

Camb.BA 1871, 32nd Wrangler, MA and LLM 1874, LLD 1880. M.T. Nov. 1873. QC 1893. Bencher 1900, Reader 1912. Recorder of Winchester 1897-1900, of Plymouth 1900-12, of Bristol 1912-24; director of legal studies, Inns of Ct. 1905; prof. of law, Gresham Coll. 1907; Hon. LLD Tufts Coll. Massachusetts. Author of works on libel and slander, pleading and practice, local govt. and common law. d. 16th Dec. 1924.

OLIVER, Sir Roland Giffard

s. of Edmund Ward Oliver, Orlestone, Ashford, Kent. b. 5th May 1882. educ. Marlborough; Corpus Christi Coll. Oxf. BA. I.T. June 1909. KC 1925. Bencher 1934. WWI 2nd Lieut. RFA, (MC). Pupil of Travers Humphreys; junior pros. counsel for Crown at Central Criminal Ct. 1921; Recorder of Folkestone 1926-38; led for Crown in Leopold Harris case (fire-raising for purpose of fraudulent claims) 1933; member committee to investigate leakage of budget secrets 1936; chmn. committee on the courts-martial system 1938; KB judge 1938-57; Knight 1938; chmn. committee to inquire into treatment of men under sentence in naval and military prisons 1943. d. 14th March 1967.

O'MALLEY, Peter Frederick

s. of Charles O'Malley, The Lodge, Co. Mayo. b. 1804. educ. Trinity Coll. Dublin MA 1828. L.I. May 1834. QC 1850. Bencher (M.T.) 1850, Reader 1852, Treasurer 1856. Leader of Norfolk circuit; Recorder of Norwich 1859-74. Father of Sir Edward Loughlin O'Malley (1842-1932), CJ British Guiana. d. 10th Dec. 1874.

ORMEROD, Sir Benjamin

s. of John Aspden Ormerod JP, North Bank, Blackburn (d.1947). b. 7th Sept. 1890. educ. Blackburn Gr. Sch.; Manchester Univ. LLB, Hon. LLD 1949. Solicitor 1913. WWI Capt. 4th Battn. East

Lancashire Regt. L.I. July 1924. Bencher 1948. Cty. Ct. judge 1944-48; P. D. and A. judge 1948; KB judge 1950-57; LJ 1957-63; Knight 1948; PC 1957; JP Lancashire; Director, Royal Acad. of Music. d. 21st Sept. 1974.

ORMEROD, Herbert Eliot

s. of Charles Ormerod, Brighton. b. 1831. educ. Merton Coll. Oxf. 1850; St. Mary Hall BA 1854, MA 1857. I.T. Nov. 1855. KC 1902. d. 13th Aug. 1911.

OSBORNE, John

s. of Jeremiah Osborne, Bristol. b. 10th Oct. 1810. educ. Shrewsbury; Trinity Coll. Oxf. BA 1831, MA 1834. L.I. June 1835. QC 1862. Bencher 1863. Cty. Ct. judge 1871-72. d. 23rd Nov. 1872.

O'SULLIVAN, Richard

s. of Richard D. O'Sullivan, Cork, marine engineer. b. 1888. educ. Our Lady's Mount, Cork; London Univ. Examr. in HM Exchequer and Audit Dept. M.T. June 1914 (Cert. of Hon). KC 1934. Bencher 1940, Reader 1952. WWI Lieut. RA. Recorder of Derby 1938-62; member of bar council 1939-53; member LC's committee on defamation 1939-47; hon. lecturer in common law London Univ. 1946-60; Reader in common law at Inns of Ct. 1949-56, senior master tutor, post-final course 1959-60; hon. secy. Thomas More Socy. and Grotius Socy. Author of On Military Law and the Supremacy of the Civil Courts 1921, Christian Philosophy in the Common Law 1947, The Inheritance of the Common Law 1950, Under God and the Law 1949, Edmund Plowden 1953; edited Gatley on Libel and Slander. d. 18th Feb. 1963.

OSWALD, James Francis

s. of William Oswald, Stepney. b. 21st Nov. 1838. educ. Stepney
Gr. Sch.; Islington Proprietary Sch.; St. Edmund Hall Oxf. 1868.
Solicitor 1861. M.T. Nov. 1869. QC 1893. Bencher (G.I.) 1893.
Member of bar committee, and bar council 1883-97; member Inc.
Council of Law Reporting 1894-97; MP Oldham 1895-99; ten years
service in HAC of City of London; published a treatise on contempt
of court. d. 14th Sept. 1908.

OULTON, William Harold Stowe

s. of William Oulton LLD., JP, Liverpool (d. 1913). b. 1st Feb.
1869. educ. Royal Institution Liverpool; Leys Sch.; Christ's Coll.
Camb. BA and LLB 1892, MA and LLM 1896. I.T. April 1893.
Commr. for Liverpool and Isle of Man under Civil Liabilities Dept.
1914-19; Asst. Recorder and dep. stip. magistrate, Liverpool to
1925; metrop. magistrate 1925, finally at Tower Br. 1928-40; JP
West Sussex. d. 25th July 1941.

OVENS, Edward

s. of Hugh Ovens, St. Catherine's, Co. Fermanagh. b. 1817. educ.
Trinity Coll. Dublin BA 1838. M.T. Nov. 1845. Chmn. of Salford
(Hundred) Quarter Sess. 1858-62; Cty. Ct. judge 1862-69; JP
Lancashire and Cheshire. d. 19th Feb. 1869.

OVEREND, William

s. of Hall Overend, Sheffield, surgeon. b. 1809. educ. Sheffield Gr.
Sch. L.I. Nov. 1837. QC 1855. Bencher 1855. MP Pontefract 1859-
60; Chief Commr. to assess damage from bursting of Bradfield
reservoirs 1864, when 250 lives were lost. d. 24th Dec. 1884.

OWEN, William Stevenson

s. of William Owen, Withybush, Haverfordwest. b. 1834. educ. London Univ. BA 1852. I.T. June 1856. Cty. Ct. judge 1884-1909; Chmn. Pembrokeshire and Haverfordwest Quarter Sess.; DL, JP Pembrokeshire; JP Glamorganshire, Monmouthshire and Haverfordwest. d. 20th Oct. 1909.

PAGE, Sir Arthur

s. of Nathaniel Page JP, Carshalton, Surrey. b. 1876. educ. Harrow; Magdalen Coll. Oxf. BA 1899. I.T. Jan. 1901. KC 1922. WWI Capt. Royal Marine Artillery. Judge of High Ct. Calculta 1923-30; CJ High Ct. Burma 1930-36; Knight 1930; Chmn. Evidence Section, Blockade Intelligence, Min. of Economic Warfare 1939-40; Chmn. North Staffordshire Regional Coal Valuation Bd. 1941. Author of Licensing Bill; is it Just? 1908, and several other political works. d. 1st Sept. 1958.

PAGE, Ernest

s. of William Bousfield Page FRCS, JP, Carlisle. b. 6th July 1848. educ. High Sch. Carlisle; Rossall. Solicitor 1872. I.T. July 1878. QC 1898. Bencher 1909. Recorder of Carlisle 1904-29; prominent in railway cases, and as an arbitrator in labour disputes; Hon. Freeman Carlisle 1926. d. 24th Oct. 1930.

PAGET, John

s. of Thomas Paget, Humberston, Leicestershire, banker. b. 14th May 1811. Clerk in father's bank. M.T. Nov. 1838. Private secy. to Lord Truro 1850-52, to Lord St. Leonards 1852; metrop. magistrate 1864, finally at Hammersmith 1888-92; JP Middlesex and Home Counties. Author of Paradoxes and Puzzles: historical, judicial and literary, 1874. d. 28th May 1898.

PAGET, Sir John Rahere, Bt.

s. of Sir James Paget FRS, LLD, DCL, 1st Bt., Surgeon to Queen Victoria (d. 1899). b. 9th March 1848. educ. Royal Inst. Liverpool; London Univ. 1865; Trinity Hall Camb. BA 1870, LLB 1871. I.T. April 1873. KC 1902. Bencher 1908. Gilbart lecturer on banking 1888; Hon. Fellow Inst. of Bankers 1928. Author of The Law of Banking. d. 20th Aug. 1938.

PALMER, Arthur

s. of John Jordan Palmer, Bristol. b. 1783. G.I. May 1821. Commr. in Bankruptcy; Cty. Ct. judge 1847-54. d. 19th Nov. 1856.

PALMER, John Hinde

s. of Samuel Palmer DL, JP, Dulwich Common, Surrey. b. 1808. L.I. Jan. 1832. QC 1859. Bencher 1859, Treasurer 1880. MP Lincoln 1868-74 and 1880. DL, JP Surrey. d. 2nd June 1884.

PALMER, Roundell (Lord Selborne)

s. of Rev. William Jocelyn Palmer, Mixbury, Oxfordshire (d. 1853). b. 27th Nov. 1812. educ. Rugby; Winchester; Trinity Coll. Oxf. BA 1834, Eldon law scholar 1834; Fellow, Magdalen Coll. 1834-48, MA 1836, Hon. Fellow and DCL 1862; Hon. Student, Christ Church Oxf. 1867. L.I. June 1837. QC 1849. Bencher 1849. MP Plymouth 1847-52 and 1853-57, Richmond, Yorkshire 1861-72; leader in the Rolls Ct.; Sol-Genl. and knighted 1861; counsel to Oxf. Univ. 1861-63; Att-Genl. 1863-66; counsel before trib. at Geneva for decision on Br. claims under Washington Treaty 1871; declined Lord Chancellorship 1868; LC 1872-74 and 1880-85; Baron 1872; Earl 1882; introduced Supreme Court of Judicature Bill 1873, enacted that year; Chmn. comm. for reform of Oxf. Univ. 1876-80; Master of Mercers' Co. 1876; Lord Rector of St. Andrews Univ. 1877; PC

1872; Hon. LLD Camb. FRS 1860. Author of theological works. d. 4th May 1895. His Memorials of his Life, 2 vols. published 1896.

PARFITT, James John Alexander

s. of James John Parfitt, Brecon, South Wales. b. 23rd Dec. 1857. educ. Prior Park Coll. Bath; London Univ. BA 1884. Schoolmaster in Edgbaston. M.T. May 1887. KC 1908. Bencher 1918. Junior counsel to PO on Midland circuit; standing counsel to Assay Authorities in Birmingham; Recorder of Northampton 1916-18; Cty. Ct. judge 1918-26; member of bar council; Commr. of Assize, Manchester 1921, South Wales and Oxford circuits 1924; member Convocation, London Univ.; played cricket for Somerset, Surrey and Warwickshire. d. 17th May 1926.

PARHAM, Benjamin

s. of Benjamin Parham, Ashburton, Devon (d. 1851). b. 1793. Attorney in Ashburton. M.T. May 1827. Cty. Ct. judge 1847-59. JP Worcestershire and Herefordshire. d. 16th Aug. 1861.

PARKE, James (Lord Wensleydale)

s. of Thomas Parke, Highfield, nr. Liverpool, merchant. b. 22nd March 1782. educ. Macclesfield Free Gr. Sch.; Trinity Coll. Camb. BA 1803, 5th Wrangler, MA 1806, Fellow 1804-17, LLD 1835. Special pleader. I.T. July 1813. Assisted Crown officers in conducting case against Queen Caroline in H of L 1820; KB judge 1828-34; Knight 1828; Exch. Baron 1834-56; PC and member Judicial Committee 1833; to assist in the hearing of appeals in H of L, created Baron Wensleydale of Wensleydale Jan. 1856 (life peerage), but it was decided this did not entitle him to sit, and vote in Parliament; received new patent as Baron Wensleydale of Walton, July 1856; was known as "Green Park", to distinguish him from Mr. Justice James Alan Park, who was referred to as "St. James's Park".

d. 25th Feb. 1868.

PARKER, Sir James

s. of Charles Steuart Parker, Blochairn, nr. Glasgow. b. 1803. educ.
Glasgow Gr. Sch. and Coll.; Trinity Coll. Camb. BA 1825, 7th
Wrangler, MA 1828. L.I. Feb. 1829. QC 1844. Equity draftsman and
conveyancer. Member Chancery Comm. 1850; V-C 1851-52; Knight
1851; "gave promise of a most brilliant career, but died after only
ten months in office". d. 13th Aug. 1852.

PARKER, Kenyon Stevens

s. of Adamson Parker, Langley, Yorkshire. b. 1789. 2nd. Lieut. RM
1805; half-pay lieut. 1814. G.I. Nov. 1819. QC 1841. Bencher (L.I.)
1841. Examr. in Ct. of Chancery 1853-66. Father of Kenyon Charles
Shirecliffe Parker (L.I. 1862), Examr. to High Ct. Run over by a cab
in Chancery Lane and d. 2nd June 1866.

PARKER, Robert John (Lord Parker)

s. of Rev. Richard Parker, Claxby, Lincolnshire. b. 25th Feb. 1857.
educ. Summer Fields; Westminster; Eton; King's Coll. Camb. BA
1880, MA 1883, Fellow 1881. L.I. Nov. 1883. Bencher. Equity
draftsman and conveyancer; specialised in patent cases; junior equity
counsel to Treasury 1900-06; Chancery judge 1906-13; Knight 1906;
L of A 1913-18; Baron Parker of Waddington and PC 1913; expert
in prize appeals during WWI; brought before H of L detailed scheme
for formation of League of Nations 1918. Father of Hubert Lister
Parker (Lord Parker of Waddington, and LCJ 1958-71). d. 12th July
1918.

PARR, Thomas Henning

s. of Rev. John Parr, hon. canon of Salisbury. b. 12th Nov. 1864. educ. Marlborough; Worcester Coll. Oxf. BA 1888, MA 1890. I.T. Jan. 1892. KC 1922. Acting counsel to IR 1914-20; counsel to PO on Western Circuit; Recorder of Salisbury 1918-37. Chan. of diocese of Portsmouth 1930-37; Vice-Chmn. Wiltshire Quarter Sess. and Hampshire Quarter Sess.; JP Wiltshire and Hampshire. d. 31st March 1937.

PARRY, Sir Edward Abbott

s. of John Humffreys Parry, serjeant. b. 2nd Oct. 1863. educ. King's Coll. Sch. M.T. Jan. 1885. Cty. Ct. judge 1894-1927. Chmn. West Kent Appeal trib. for nat. service 1916; Pres. Pensions Appeal trib. 1917-18; Knight 1927; JP Lancashire and Kent. Author of many books, including Judgments in Vacation 1911, What the Judge saw 1912, The Law and the Poor 1914, The Law and the Woman 1916, What the Judge thought 1922, The Drama of the Law 1924, The Overbury Mystery 1925, Vagabonds All 1926, The Bloody Assize 1929, Queen Caroline 1930, The Persecution of Mary Stewart 1931, My Own Way 1932. d. 1st Dec. 1943.

PARRY, John Billingsley

s. of James Parry, Preston Montford Hall, Shropshire. b. 1798. educ. Shrewsbury. L.I. Nov. 1824. QC 1845. Equity draftsman; Cty. Ct. judge 1847-74; JP. d. 28th March 1876.

PARRY, John Humffreys

s. of John Humffreys Parry, barrister and Welsh antiquary (d. 1825). b. 24th Jan. 1816. educ. Philological Sch. Marylebone. Employed in printed book dept. of Br. Museum 1839-43. M.T. June 1843. Serjeant 1856; patent of precedence 1864. Bencher 1878. Leader of

Home circuit; appeared in trials of Mr. and Mrs. Manning (murder of O'Connor) 1849, Franz Muller (murder of Briggs in railway carriage) 1864, Overend Gurney (bank frauds) 1869, Tichborne claimant 1873-74, and Whistler v. Ruskin (libel concerning picture) 1878. d. 10th Jan. 1880.

PARSONS, Albert

s. of Robert Parsons, Bradford, Yorkshire. b. 1865. educ. Bedford Sch.; London Univ. M.T. June 1891. KC 1914. Recorder of Merthyr Tydfil 1915-17; Cty. Ct. judge 1917-37; JP Cheshire and Gloucestershire. Author of works on liability of railway companies, and workmen's compensation. d. 7th April 1938.

PARTRIDGE, William

s. of John Partridge, Monmouth. b. 2nd Jan. 1818. educ. Winchester; Christ Church Oxf. BA 1840, MA 1860. M.T. Nov. 1843. Stip. magistrate, Wolverhampton 1860-63; metrop. magistrate 1863, finally at Marylebone 1890-91; director of Ross and Monmouth Ry. DL, JP Herefordshire and Monmouthshire; JP Gloucestershire, Sussex and Staffordshire. d. 10th Sept. 1891.

PASHLEY, Robert

s. of Robert Pashley, Harness Grove, Nottinghamshire. b. 4th Sept. 1805. educ. in Mansfield, Notts.; Trinity Coll. Camb. BA 1829, MA 1832, Fellow 1830-53. I.T. Nov. 1837. QC 1851. Bencher 1851. Asst. judge Middlesex Sess. 1856-59. Author of works on the poor laws. d. 29th May 1859.

PATCHETT, William

s. of George Patchett, Manchester, distiller. b. April 1827. educ.

Manchester Gr. Sch.; St. John's Coll. Camb. BA 1853, MA 1855. I.T. June 1855. QC 1877. Bencher 1878, Treasurer 1900. JP Essex. d. 19th Jan. 1915.

PATERSON, William

s. of William Paterson, London. b. 2nd Oct. 1815. G.I. Jan. 1843. M.T. June 1846. Bencher (G.I.) 1891, Treasurer 1894. Cty. Ct. judge 1886-1901; JP Somerset. d. 3rd Nov. 1903.

PATTESON, James Henry

s. of Patteson J. and nephew of Coleridge J. b. 1828. educ. Eton; Balliol Coll. Oxf. BA 1850, MA 1853. M.T. Jan. 1853. Secy. of Ct. of Probate 1858-63; metrop. magistrate, Greenwich and Woolwich 1868-77. d. 4th July 1904.

PATTESON, Sir John

s. of Rev. Henry Patteson, Drinkstone, Suffolk. b. 11th Feb. 1790. educ. Eton; King's Coll. Camb. BA 1813, MA 1816, Fellow 1812. Special pleader. M.T. July 1821. One of the legal commrs. on the reform of the Welsh Judicature 1829; KB judge 1830-52 (no previous instance of barrister of only 9 years standing being raised to bench); Knight 1830; PC 1852 and member Judicial Committee; a commr. to examine into the state of the City of London 1853; arbitrator in disputes between the Crown and the Duchy of Cornwall, between PO and Great Western Ry. and between the Univ. and town of Cambridge. Edited (with E.V. Williams) Sir E. Saunders' reports of KB cases, 1824. d. 28th June 1861.

PAULL, Sir Gilbert James

s. of Alan Paull FSI, JP, Wembley, Middlesex. b. 18th April 1896.

educ. St Paul's; Trinity Coll. Camb. 1915. I.T. Jan. 1920. KC 1939. Bencher 1946, Reader 1968, Treasurer 1970. Recorder of Leicester 1944-57; member Council of Legal Educ. 1947-66; QB judge 1957-71; Knight 1957. d. 13th Nov. 1984.

PAYNE, John Horne

s. of Reuben Craven Payne, Bridgwater, Somerset. b. 12th Nov. 1837. educ. University Coll. London MA 1860. Special correspondent of Morning Herald and Standard in Hungary 1861. I.T. Nov. 1863. Jamaican bar 1866. QC 1886. Commr. for Spanish Govt. to take evidence in England; member Convocation, London Univ. d. 9th Sept. 1920.

PAYNE, William

s. of William Payne, London. b. 1799. Chief Clerk at Guildhall, London 1833-43. G.I. Nov. 1843. Serjeant 1858; coroner of London and Southwark 1829-72; High Steward of Southwark and judge of Borough Ct. of record 1850-72. Father of William John Payne (L.I. 1844), Recorder of Buckingham. d. 25th Feb. 1872.

PAYNTER, Thomas Camborne

s. of James Paynter, Boskenna, Cornwall (d. 1800). b. 24th July 1794. educ. Blundell's; Trinity Coll. Camb. BA 1816, MA 1824. L.I. Nov. 1824. Recorder of Falmouth, Helston, and Penzance 1838-41; metrop. magistrate 1840, finally at Westminster 1855-63. Author of The Practice at Elections 1837. d. 20th April 1863.

PEACOCK, Sir Barnes

s. of Lewis H. Peacock, London, solicitor. b. 1805. Special pleader 1831-36. I.T. Jan. 1836. QC 1850. Bencher 1850, Reader 1864.

Legal member, Supreme Council of India 1852-59; V-Pres. Legislative Council of India 1859; CJ Bengal 1859-70; Knight 1859; PC 1870; member Judicial Committee of Privy Council 1872-90. Father of Frederick Barnes Peacock CSI (I.T. 1880). d. 3rd Dec. 1890.

PEARCE, Edward Holroyd (Lord Pearce)

s. of John William Ernest Pearce FSA, schoolmaster (d. 1951). b. 9th Feb. 1901. educ. Charterhouse; Corpus Christi Coll. Oxf. BA 1923, MA 1950, Hon. Fellow 1950. L.I. Jan. 1925. KC 1945. Bencher 1948, Treasurer 1966. Dep. Chmn. East Sussex Quarter Sess. 1947-48; Chmn. Committee on Shipbuilding Costs 1947-49; P D and A judge 1948-54; Knight 1948; member Royal Comm. on Marriage and Divorce 1951; QB judge 1954-57; LJ 1957-62; PC 1957; L of A 1962-69; Baron 1962; Chmn. Press Council 1969-74, Appeals Committee, Take-Over Panel 1969-76, Comm. to test Rhodesian approval of proposed Br. Rhodesian settlements 1971-72, Committee on organisation of Bar and Inns of Ct. 1971-73; hon. member of Senate, 4 Inns of Ct. 1974; independent Chmn. of Press discussions on Charter of Press Freedom 1976-77; a painter of landscapes; RBA 1940; Hon. FRBS; Pres. Artists League of GB 1950-74; Pres. Council of Imp. Arts League; Prof. of Law, R. Acad. of Arts 1971; past Master of Skinners' Co.; govr. Charterhouse, Tonbridge Sch. and Sutton's Hosp. in Charterhouse. Father of Richard Bruce Holroyd Pearce (QC 1969), and James Edward Holroyd Pearce (QC 1979). d. 26th Nov. 1990.

PEARSON, Sir Charles John

s. of Charles Pearson CA, Edinburgh. b. 6th Nov. 1843. educ. Edin. Acad.; Edin. and St. Andrews Univs.; Corpus Christi Coll. Oxf. BA 1865, MA 1868; Hon. LLD Edin. 1894. Scottish bar 1870. I.T. June 1870. QC 1890. Sheriff of Chancery 1885-88; Procurator of Church of Scotland 1886-90; Sheriff of Renfrew and Bute 1888, of Perthshire 1889; Sol-Genl. Scotland 1890; MP Edin. and St.

Andrews Univs. 1890-96; Lord Advocate for Scotland 1891-92, 1895-96; Dean of Faculty of Advocates 1892-95; judge of Supreme Ct. of Scotland 1896-1909; Knight 1887; PC 1891; DL Edin. d. 15th Aug. 1910.

PEARSON, Sir John

s. of Rev. John Norman Pearson, Bower Hall, Essex (d. 1865). b. 5th Aug. 1819. educ. Islington Proprietary Sch.; Gonville and Caius Coll. Camb. BA 1841, MA 1844. L.I. June 1844. QC 1866. Bencher 1867, Treasurer 1884. Chancery judge 1882-86; Knight 1882; member Council of Legal Educ., and Inc. Council of Law Reporting. Author of The Duty of Laymen in the Church of England 1856. d. 13th May 1886.

PEARSON, William

s. of Thomas Pearson, Huttons Ambo, Yorkshire. b. 28th Oct. 1824. educ. Edin. Univ. 1843. I.T. Jan. 1853. QC 1874. Bencher 1874, Treasurer 1892. Practised at chancery bar. Father of Arthur Beilby Pearson-Gee (I.T. 1879). d. 15th Oct. 1907.

PEEL, Robert

s. of William Peel JP, Knowlmere Manor, Clitheroe, Lancashire (d. 1926). b. 3rd Feb. 1881. educ. Winchester; New Coll. Oxf. BA 1904, MA 1910. L.I. June 1906. WWI Brevet major 16th London Regt. and GHQ (DJAG) Salonika, OBE 1917 (despatches). KC 1930. Cty. Ct. judge 1933-53; Dep. Chan. Duchy of Lancaster 1933-59; JP Lancashire; Order of White Eagle, Serbia 4th Class. d. 28th April 1969.

PEMBER, Edward Henry

s. of John Edward Rose Pember, Clapham, Surrey. b. 28th May 1833. educ. Harrow; Christ Church Oxf. BA 1854, MA 1857. L.I. Jan. 1858. QC 1874. Bencher 1876, Treasurer 1906. Practised at parliamentary bar; successful conduct of bill for creation of Manchester Ship Canal 1885; counsel for Cecil Rhodes in investigation of Jameson raid 1897; JP Hampshire; Joint Secy. of Dilettanti Socy. 1896-1911. Father of Francis William Pember (L.I. 1889), V-C Oxf. Univ. d. 5th April 1911.

PEMBERTON-LEIGH, Thomas (Lord Kingsdown)

s. of Robert Pemberton, Bispham Hall, Lancashire, barrister. b. 11th Feb. 1793. educ. in Chiswick, West London (Dr. Horne). L.I. Nov. 1816. KC 1829. Bencher 1830. Leader in the Rolls Ct.; declined appts. as Sol-Genl. and High Ct. judge; MP Rye 1831-32, Ripon 1835-43; Att-Genl. to Prince of Wales 1841-43; Chan. of Duchy of Cornwall 1843-61; took additional name of Leigh 1843, on inheriting property from a relative; PC 1843; member of Judicial Committee 1843-63; declined Lord Chancellorship 1858; Baron 1858. Brother of Edward Leigh Pemberton (1795-1877), Pres. Inc. Law Socy. d. 7th Oct. 1867.

PEPYS, Charles Christopher (Lord Cottenham)

s. of Sir William Weller Pepys, 1st Bt., Master in Chancery (d. 1825). b. 29th April 1781. educ. Harrow; Trinity Coll. Camb. LLB 1803. L.I. Nov. 1804. KC 1826. Bencher 1826. Practised in chancery; Sol-Genl. to Queen Adelaide 1830; MP Higham Ferrers 1831, Malton 1831-36; Sol-Genl. 1834; Knight 1834; MR 1834-36; PC 1834; Baron Cottenham 1836; first Commr. of Great Seal 1835; LC 1836-41; instituted chancery reforms; assisted while out of office in hearing appeals to H of L and Privy Council; LC 1846-50; Trustees Relief Act 1847 known by his name. Succeeded brother as 3rd baronet 1845 (cr. 1801); succeeded cousin as 4th baronet

1849 (cr. 1784); Viscount Crowhurst and Earl of Cottenham 1850. Father of George Pepys (L.I. 1857) and Walter Courtenay Pepys (L.I. 1877). d. Lucca, 29th April 1851.

PETERSDORFF, Charles Erdman

s. of Christian Frederick Petersdorff, London, furrier. b. 4th Nov. 1800. Special pleader. I.T. Jan. 1833. Counsel to the Admiralty; serjeant 1858; Cty. Ct. judge 1865-85. Author of an abridgment of cases in KB, CP, Exch., and at Nisi Prius, from the Restoration 15 vols. 1825-30, an abridgment of the common law 1841-44, and several other works. By order of the Admiralty compiled complete collection of statutes relating to the navy, shipping, ports and harbours. d. 29th July 1886.

PETERSON, Sir Arthur Frederick

s. of William Peterson, St. Kilda, Melbourne, Australia (d. 1898). b. 12th Oct. 1859. educ. Dulwich Coll.; Corpus Christi Coll. Oxf. BA 1883, MA 1886. L.I. and I.T. Jan. 1886. KC 1906. Bencher (L.I.) 1911. Equity draftsman and conveyancer; Chancery judge 1915-22; Knight 1915. d. 12th May 1922.

PETHERAM, Sir William Comer

s. of William Petheram, Wellington, Somerset (d. 1870). b. 1834. Special pleader 1862. M.T. Jan. 1869. QC 1880. Bencher 1883. CJ North West Provinces, India 1884-86, Bengal 1886-96; Knight 1884; V-C. Calcutta Univ. Author of Law of Interrogatories. d. 15th May 1922.

PHILBRICK, Frederick Adolphus

s. of Frederick Blomfield Philbrick, Colchester, attorney. b. 1836. educ. London Univ. BA 1853. M.T. June 1860. QC 1874. Bencher

1877, Reader 1887. Recorder of Colchester 1870-1910; examr. in common law, London Univ. 1882; Cty. Ct. judge 1895-1910; JP Somerset, Wiltshire, Hampshire, Dorset; member Convocation, London Univ. Father of Arthur James Philbrick CBE, (M.T. 1889) 1866-1941, Colonial Service. d. 25th Dec. 1910.

PHILLIMORE, John George

s. of Joseph Phillimore DCL, FRS, MP (d. 1855). b. 5th Jan. 1808. educ. Westminster; Christ Church Oxf. BA 1828, MA 1831. Clerk in Bd. of Control for India 1827-32. L.I. Nov. 1832. QC 1851. Bencher 1851. Reader on civil law and jurisprudence M.T. 1851; Reader on constitutional law and history to Inns of Ct. 1852; MP Leominster 1852-57. Author of works on Roman law, evidence and jurisprudence. d. 27th April 1865.

PHILLIMORE, Sir Robert Joseph, Bt.

s. of Joseph Phillimore DCL, FRS, MP (d. 1855). b. 5th Nov. 1810. educ. Westminster; Christ Church Oxf. BA 1832, MA 1834, BCL 1835, DCL 1838. Clerk in Bd. of Control Office 1832-35; Advocate Doctors' Commons Nov. 1839, Steward 1847-50, Librarian 1850 and 1853, Treasurer 1851. M.T. May 1841. QC 1858. Bencher 1858, Reader 1861, Treasurer 1869. Commissary of the deans and chapters of St. Paul's and Westminster to 1867; Chan. of dioceses of Chichester 1844-67, Salisbury 1845-67, Oxford 1855-67; judge of the Cinque Ports 1855-75; Admiralty advocate 1855; Queen's Adv-Genl. 1862-67; Knight 1862; MP Tavistock 1853-57; Dean of the Arches 1867-75; Admiralty judge 1867-83; PC 1867; temp. Judge Adv-Genl. 1871-72; Master of the Faculties 1873-75; Baronet 1881; Pres. Assoc. for reform and codification of law of nations 1879; member comms. on Neutrality 1868, Naturalisation 1868, Ritual 1867, building of cts. of justice 1859, judicature and eccles. cts. 1867. Author of law of domicil 1847, Commentaries on Intern. Law 1854-61, The Ecclesiastical Law of the Church of England 1873. d. 4th Feb. 1885.

PHILLIMORE, Walter George Frank (Lord Phillimore)

s. of Phillimore J. b. 21st Nov. 1845. educ. Westminster (captain); Christ Church Oxf. BA 1867, Vinerian law scholar 1868, DCL 1875; Fellow of All Souls Coll. M.T. Nov. 1868. Bencher 1888, Reader 1898, Treasurer 1907. Granted patent of precedence 1883; leader in Admiralty Ct.; Chan. of diocese of Lincoln 1872-97; succeeded to father's baronetcy 1885; QB judge 1897-1913; LJ 1913-16; PC 1913; Chmn. committee on a League of Nations 1917-18; Baron Phillimore of Shiplake 1918; Pres. English Church Union 1919; govr. of Westminster; Mayor of Kensington 1909-10; Commander of the Order of the Crown of Belgium; JP Oxfordshire; FBA 1922; Hon. LLD Edin. and Birmingham; a great intern. and eccles. jurist. Edited his father's Ecclesiastical Law of the Church of England, and J.H. Blunt's Church Law. Father of Robert Charles Phillimore (M.T. 1895). d. 13th March 1929.

PHILLIPS, Sir Thomas

s. of Thomas Phillips, Llanellan House, Monmouthshire. b. 1801. Solicitor in Newport, Monmouthshire 1824-40; Mayor of Newport 1838-39; read riot act when 7000 Chartists entered town 1839, and was wounded; Knight 1839; Freeman of City of London 1840. I.T. June 1842. QC 1865. Bencher 1865. Parliamentary counsel and frequently employed as arbitrator. d. 26th May 1867.

PHINN, Thomas

s. of Thomas Phinn, Exeter, surgeon. b. 1814. educ. Eton (captain); Exeter Coll. Oxf. BA 1838. I.T. Nov. 1840. QC with patent of precedence 1854. Bencher 1854. Recorder of Portsmouth 1848-52, of Devonport 1852-55; counsel to Bd. of Stamps and Taxes in the Exchequer 1852; MP Bath 1852-55; counsel to Admiralty and Judge-Adv. of the Fleet 1854; Second Secy. to Admiralty 1855-57. d. 31st Oct. 1866.

PHIPPS, Edmund

s. of 1st Earl of Mulgrave. b. 7th Dec. 1808. educ. Harrow; Trinity Coll. Oxf. BA 1828, MA 1831. I.T. June 1832. QC 1857. Recorder of Scarborough 1844-57, of Doncaster 1857; Chief Commr. of West Indian incumbered estates ct. 1857. d. 28th Oct. 1857.

PHIPSON, Thomas Weatherley

s. of Joseph Weatherley Phipson, Selley Hall, Worcestershire. b. 8th Sept. 1807. educ. Shrewsbury; Glasgow Univ. Special pleader. L.I. June 1845. QC 1862. Bencher 1862. d. 15th Jan. 1875.

PICCIOTTO, Cyril Moses

s. of James Picciotto, London. b. 1888. educ. St. Paul's; Trinity Coll. Camb. BA 1910. I.T. Nov. 1913. KC 1938. Military Dept. India Office 1915-19; Referee under Widows, Orphans and Old Age Contributory Pensions Acts, 1930-32; member Council of Jewish Historical Socy. of England. Author of The Relation of International Law to the Law of England and the United States 1914, and The Legal Position of the Jews in England as shown in the Plea Rolls of the Jewish Exchequer. d. 9th Feb. 1940.

PICKERING, Percival Andrew

s. of Edward Rowland Pickering, London, solicitor. b. 1811. educ. Eton; Trinity Coll. Camb. BA 1832; St. John's Coll. MA 1835, Fellow 1833-41. I.T. May 1838. QC 1855. Bencher 1855, Reader 1869, Treasurer 1870. Recorder of Pontefract 1853-65; judge of Liverpool Ct. of Passage 1867-76; Queen's attorney and serjeant, Lancaster 1868-76. d. 7th Aug. 1876.

PICKFORD, William (Lord Sterndale)

s. of Thomas Edward Pickford, Manchester, merchant. b. 1st Oct. 1848. educ. Liverpool Coll.; Exeter Coll. Oxf. BA 1873, MA 1908, Hon. Fellow 1916. I.T. Nov. 1874. QC 1893. Bencher 1902. Leader of Northern circuit; Recorder of Oldham 1901, of Liverpool 1904; leading counsel for GB at Inquiry into Dogger Bank incident 1905; Commr. of Assize 1906; member Confce. on Unification of Maritime Law at Brussels 1905, 1909, 1910; KB Judge 1907; Knight 1907; LJ and PC 1914; Chmn. Dardanelles Comm. 1917; Pres. P D and A Divn. and Baron 1918; MR 1919. d. 17th Aug. 1923.

PIGOTT, Sir Gillery

s. of Paynton Pigott, Archer Lodge, Hampshire (d. 1862). b. 1813. educ. in Putney (Rev. William Carmalt). M.T. May 1839. Counsel to IR 1854; Serjeant 1856; patent of precedence 1857; Recorder of Hereford 1857-62; MP Reading 1860-63; Exch. Baron 1863-75; Knight 1863. Reported (with B.B.H. Rodwell) cases in Common Pleas on appeal from the decisions of revising barristers 1844-46. Uncle of Sir Paynton Pigott (M.T. 1866), Chief Constable of Norfolk, and father of Cecil Ernest Pigott (M.T. 1885) and Arthur Gough Pigott (M.T. 1873). d. 28th April 1875.

PILCHER, Sir Gonne St. Clair

s. of Maj-Genl. Thomas David Pilcher CB (d. 1929). b. 19th Sept. 1890. educ. Wellington; Trinity Coll. Camb. BA 1911. WWI Lieut. Special List (Intelligence), MC (despatches). I.T. April 1915. KC 1936. Bencher 1942. Junior counsel to Admiralty 1935; attached officer at War Office 1939-42; P D and A judge 1942-51; Knight 1942; KB judge 1951-61; Vice-Pres. Comité Maritime International 1947-62; Pres. Br. Maritime Law Assoc. 1950-62; Chmn. committee to inquire into administration of justice in naval courts martial 1950-51; head of UK delegation to Brussels Diplomatic Confce. on Intern. Maritime Conventions 1952, 1958, and 1961; Dep. Chmn. Somerset

Quarter Sess. 1938; JP Somerset. d. 3rd April 1966.

PITMAN, Charles Murray

s. of Frederick Pitman WS, Edinburgh. b. 8th Jan. 1872. educ. Eton; New Coll. Oxf. BA 1895; rowing blue. I.T. May 1897. KC 1925. Bencher 1926. Recorder of Rochester 1924-33; Judge-Adv. of the Fleet 1924-33; Official Referee of Supreme Ct. 1933-45; Chmn. Berkshire Quarter Sess. 1927-45; JP Berkshire. d. 13th Oct. 1948.

PITT-LEWIS, George

s. of Rev. George Tucker Lewis, Exminster, Devon. b. 13th Dec. 1845. educ. at father's school. M.T. June 1870 (Cert. of Hon.). QC 1885. Bencher 1892-1904. Recorder of Poole 1885-1904; MP Devon (North West) 1885-92; Dep. Cty. Ct. judge. Author of A Complete County Court Practice, River Law on the Thames, Commissioner Kerr (biography) 1903. Edited Taylor on Evidence, 9th Ed. Assumed additional name of Pitt 1875. d. 30th Dec. 1906.

PLATT, Sir Thomas Joshua

s. of Thomas Platt, Brunswick Square, London, solicitor. b. 1788. educ. Harrow; Trinity Camb. BA 1810, MA 1814. I.T. Feb. 1816. KC 1834. Bencher 1835-45. Leader of Home circuit; Exch. Baron 1845-56; Knight 1845. Father of Charles Platt (I.T. 1840), Clerk of Assize and Associate South Eastern circuit. d. 10th Feb. 1862.

PLOWDEN, Alfred Chichele

s. of Trevor John Chichele Plowden, Bengal Civil Service (d. 1899). b. India, 21st Oct. 1844. educ. Westminster; Brasenose Coll. Oxf. BA 1866. Priv. secy. to Governor of Jamaica 1866-68. M.T. Jan. 1870. Recorder of Wenlock 1878-88; metrop. magistrate 1888, finally at Marylebone 1893-1914; JP Middlesex and Home Counties. Autobiog. Grain or Chaff, 1903. d. 8th Aug. 1914.

POLAND, Sir Harry Bodkin

s. of Peter Poland, Highgate, London, furrier. b. 9th July 1829. educ. St. Paul's. I.T. June 1851. QC 1888. Bencher 1879. Counsel to Treasury and Home Office 1865-88; Recorder of Dover 1874-1901; Crown prosecutor in cases of Sir John Dean Paul (fraudulent banker) 1855, the Lennie (mutiny and murder at sea) 1876, the Wainwrights (murder) 1875, the Franconia 1876 (collision between German and Br. vessels, resulting in death of Br. passenger), the Stauntons (the Penge murder) 1877; defended Governor Eyre (Jamaica rebellion) 1868; Knight 1895; DL, JP London; Alderman LCC. d. 2nd March 1928.

POLLOCK, Sir Charles Edward

s. of Pollock LCB. b. 31st Oct. 1823. educ. St. Paul's. Private secy. to father 1841-44; his marshal 1846. I.T. Jan. 1847. QC 1866. Bencher 1866-73, Reader 1882. Tubman in Ct. of Exch. 1861, Postman 1862-66; practised in mercantile cases; Chmn. Conservators of Wimbledon Common; Exch. Baron 1873-75; Knight 1873; tried Franconia case 1876 (collision between German and Br. vessels, resulting in death of Br. passenger); QB judge 1880-97; JP Surrey. Author of treatise on the power of the courts of common law to compel production of documents for inspection 1851, The Practice of the County Courts 1851; author (with H. Nicol) of The Practice of the County Courts in respect to probate and administration 1858; (with F.P. Maude) of a Compendium of the law of Merchant Shipping 1853; reported (with J.J. Lowndes and P.B. Maxwell) QB cases 1850-51. Father of Herbert Charles Pollock (I.T. 1877). d. 21st Nov. 1897.

POLLOCK, Sir David

s. of David Pollock, Charing Cross, London, saddler. b. 2nd Sept. 1780. educ. St. Paul's; Edin. Univ. Special pleader. M.T. Jan. 1803. KC 1833. Bencher 1833, Reader 1837, Treasurer 1839. Recorder of Maidstone, Tenterden, and Dymchurch 1838; Commr. in Bankruptcy; CJ Bombay 1846-47; Knight 1846. d. Bombay, 22nd May 1847.

POLLOCK, Ernest Murray (Lord Hanworth)

s. of George Frederick Pollock, Queen's Remembrancer (d. 1915), and g.s. of Pollock LCB. b. 25th Nov. 1861. educ. Charterhouse; Trinity Coll. Camb. BA 1884, MA 1887, Hon. LLD. I.T. June 1885. KC 1905. Bencher 1914, Treasurer 1936. MP Warwick and Leamington 1910-23; Chmn. Contraband Committee 1915-17; Controller of Foreign Trade Dept. 1917-19; Recorder of Kingston-on-Thames 1911-19; KBE 1917; Sol-Genl. 1919-22; headed delegation which attended trials in Germany of war criminals; Att-Genl. 1922; PC 1922; Baronet 1922; MR 1923-35; Baron 1926; Viscount 1936; zealous in his duty as custodian of public records; Chmn. of Business of the Courts Committee 1932, and Law Revision Committee 1934; Pres. Dugdale, Grotius and Magna Carta Societies; trustee of Br. Museum; govr. Charterhouse and Wellington; Dep. High Steward of Camb. Univ.; High Steward of Stratford-on-Avon; JP Hertfordshire; Hon. Freeman of Leamington and Warwick; Hon. LLD Warsaw; Officer of Legion of Honour, and of St. Maurice and St Lazarus (Italy). Wrote biography of Pollock LCB 1929. d.22nd Oct. 1936.

POLLOCK, Sir Frederick, Bt.

s. of Sir William Frederick Pollock 2nd Bt., Queen's Remembrancer. b. 10th Dec. 1845. educ. Eton; Trinity Coll. Camb. BA 1867, MA 1870, Fellow 1868, Hon. Fellow 1920; Hon. Fellow, Corpus Christi Coll. Oxf. 1906, DCL 1901. L.I. May 1871. KC 1920. Bencher

1906. Corpus prof. of jurisprudence Oxf. 1883-1903; prof. of common law at Inns of Ct. 1884-89; Chmn. Royal Comm. on public records 1910; judge of Cinque Ports 1914-20; 3rd baronet 1888. Author of many works including Principles of Contract at Law and in Equity 1876, The Land Laws 1883, The Law of Torts 1887, First book of Jurisprudence for students of the Common Law 1896, The Genius of the Common Law 1912, Essays in the Law 1922. Edited Law Quarterly Review, and editor-in-chief of the Law Reports. His correspondence with Oliver Wendell Holmes 1874-1932, published as The Holmes-Pollock Letters, 1942. FBA 1902; PC 1911; FSA; Hon. LLD, Paris, Camb., Edin., Dublin, Harvard, Columbia, Oslo. Father of Sir Frederick John Pollock, 4th Bt., author (L.I. 1907). d. 18th Jan. 1937.

POLLOCK, Sir Jonathan Frederick, Bt.

s. of David Pollock, Charing Cross, London, saddler (d. 1815). b. 23rd Sept. 1783, educ. St. Paul's; Trinity Coll. Camb. BA 1806, Senior Wrangler, MA 1809, Fellow 1807. M.T. Nov. 1807. KC 1827. Bencher (I.T.) 1827-44, Reader 1836, Treasurer 1837. Successfully represented Capt. Blake RN in court-martial of Col. Arthur for involvement in rebellion against Blake as governor of New South Wales; leader of Northern circuit; Commissary of Camb. Univ. 1824-35; MP Huntingdon 1831-44; a commr. for inquiry into practice of the cts. of law 1831; Att-Genl. 1834-35 and 1841-44; Knight 1834; Chief Baron of Exch. 1844-66; PC 1844; Baronet 1866; FRS 1816; FGS 1818. Father of Sir William Frederick Pollock, 2nd Bt. (I.T. 1838) Queen's Remembrancer, George Frederick Pollock (I.T. 1843) Queen's Remembrancer, Henry Pollock, Master of Supreme Ct., Sir Edward James Pollock (I.T. 1872) Official Referee of Supreme Ct., and 21 other children. d. 23rd Aug. 1870. Biography by Lord Hanworth 1929.

POLLOCK, Joseph

s. of Edward Pollock, Co. Down, Ireland, barrister. b 1811. educ.

Armagh Coll.; Trinity Coll. Dublin BA 1834. G.I. June 1842. Judge of Salford Ct. of Record to 1851; Cty. Ct. judge 1851-57. d. 26th May 1858.

POLLOCK, Robert Erskine

s. of Robert John Pollock, barrister, Capt. 8th Madras Cavalry (d. 1853), and g.s. of Pollock LCB. b. 2nd June 1849. educ. St. Paul's; Trinity Hall Camb. LLB 1872. I.T. June 1873. M.T. April 1878. QC 1892. Bencher 1897, Reader 1909. Dep. Chmn. Gloucestershire Quarter Sess. 1904; JP Gloucestershire. d. 4th Jan. 1915.

POOLE, Arthur Ruscombe

s. of Gabriel Stone Poole, Bridgwater, Somerset, solicitor. b. 18th April 1840. educ. Rugby; Trinity Coll. Oxf. BA 1863, MA 1866. Rowing blue. I.T. Nov. 1865. QC 1888. Bencher 1894. Recorder of Bristol, and judge of Bristol Tolzey and Pie Poudre Cts. 1892-97. d. 22nd May 1897.

POPE, Samuel

s. of Samuel Pope, London and Manchester, merchant. b. 11th Dec. 1826. educ. privately; London Univ. Employed in Manchester. M.T. June 1858. QC 1869. Bencher 1870, Reader 1877, Treasurer 1888. Recorder of Bolton 1869; leader of parliamentary bar; DL, JP Merionethshire; temperance advocate and freemason. d. 22nd July 1901.

POPE, Samuel

s. of William Rushton Pope, and nephew of Samuel Pope QC. b. 1868. educ. privately; Trinity Coll. Oxf. BA 1891. M.T. Jan. 1892. Recorder of Burnley 1915-21; Commr. to inquire into various colliery disasters 1908-14; asst. legal adviser Min. of Food 1917-19; metrop. magistrate 1921, finally at Clerkenwell 1926-35; AMIME. d. 8th April 1935.

PORTER, Samuel Lowry (Lord Porter)

s. of Hugh Porter, Headingley, Leeds, warehouse manager. b. 7th Feb. 1877. educ. Perse Sch.; Emmanuel Coll. Camb. BA 1899, MA 1921, Hon. Fellow 1937, Hon. LLD 1947. I.T. May 1905. KC 1925. Bencher. WWI Capt. on general list, with Min. of Nat. Service, MBE. Specialised in commercial cases; Recorder of Newcastle-under-Lyme 1928-32, of Walsall 1932-34; KB judge 1934-38; Knight 1934; Chmn. trib. to inquire into disclosure of budget secrets by J.H. Thomas MP (who resigned) 1936; Chmn. Nat. Reference Trib. of coalmining industry; L of A, PC and Baron 1938; Chmn. committee on law of defamation 1948; GBE 1951; Hon. LLD Birmingham 1940. d. 13th Feb. 1956.

POTTER, William

s. of William Potter, Liverpool, merchant. b. 1838. educ. Trinity Coll. Dublin BA 1859. I.T. April 1861. QC 1880. Bencher 1881. Master of the northern bar lodge of freemasons. d. 5th Dec. 1893.

POWELL, Arthur Charles Joseph

s. of Joseph Martin Powell, St. Bride St., London, newspaper proprietor, and nephew of J.J. Powell QC. b. 3rd Dec. 1853. educ. Stockwell Gr. Sch.; London Univ. Articled to solicitor 1870. M.T. Nov. 1877. KC 1902. Bencher 1910, Reader 1922. Leader of Oxford circuit; Recorder of Wolverhampton 1918-30; Commr. of Assize 1921; proprietor of the Printers' Register. Author of a manual on the law affecting printers and publishers. d. 9th Oct. 1930.

POWELL, Frank John

s. of Francis Cox Powell, Wimbledon. b. 1891. educ. Rutlish Sch. M.T. Jan. 1921. Queen's Westminster Rifles 1910-14. WWI Capt. KOYLI. Metrop. magistrate 1936, finally at Clerkenwell 1942-63. Author of Trial of Jesus Christ, Justice in Magistrates' Courts, and (jointly) The Roots of Crime. d. 31st Oct. 1971.

POWELL, John Joseph

s. of Thomas Powell, Gloucester. b. 3rd Sept. 1816. M.T. April 1847. QC 1863. Bencher 1863, Reader 1867, Treasurer 1875. MP Gloucester 1862-65; the first recorder of Wolverhampton 1864-91; Cty. Ct. judge 1884-91. Uncle of A.C.J. Powell KC. d. 15th Sept. 1891.

POWELL, Ronald Arthur

s. of A.C.J. Powell KC. b. 15th Sept. 1888. educ. Winchester; New Coll. Oxf. BA 1911. M.T. Jan. 1914. WWI Capt. Hampshire Regt. Metrop. magistrate 1926, finally at Marylebone 1944-49. d. 30th Oct. 1966.

POWER, David

s. of David Power, Berbice, and Brompton, Middlesex. b. 1817. educ. London Univ. L.I. May 1840. QC 1858. Bencher (M.T.) 1858, Reader 1861. Recorder of Ipswich 1848-61; leader of Norfolk circuit. Author of works on election law. d. 10th May 1862.

POYSER, Arthur Horatio

s. of Charles Poyser, Summer Hill, nr. Wrexham, Denbighshire. b. 21st Jan. 1849. educ. Shrewsbury; Christ Church Oxf. BA 1872, MA 1876. M.T. and L.I. Nov. 1873. KC 1920. Father of Sir Ronald

Poyser (M.T. 1908), Master in Lunacy. d. 6th June 1923.

PRAED, William Mackworth

s. of William Mackworth Praed, serjeant (d. 1835). b. 24th May 1797. educ. Eton; St. John's Coll. Camb. BA 1819, MA 1822. L.I. May 1822. Recorder of Barnstaple, Bideford and South Molton 1836-57; Cty. Ct. judge 1847-57; Chmn. Devon Quarter Sess. d. 25th Sept. 1857.

PRATT, John Lhind

s. of John Marchant Pratt, Exmouth, Devon. b. 7th Oct. 1885. M.T. Nov. 1909 (Cert. of Hon.). Bencher 1939. WWI Capt. RGA (despatches). Recorder of Bournemouth 1932-44; Judge-Adv. of the Fleet 1943-45; metrop. magistrate 1944, finally at West London 1946-55. d. 23rd Sept. 1960.

PRENDERGAST, Harris

s. of Gen. Sir Jeffrey Prendergast, Tipperary (d. 1856). b. Madras, 31st July 1805. educ. Harrow; Trinity Coll. Camb. BA 1826, LLB 1829. L.I. Nov. 1829. QC 1866. Bencher 1867. Equity draftsman and conveyancer; edited Court Circular from 1856. Author of works on martial law, and (with J. Stewart) Conveyancing Practice 1846. d. 30th Sept. 1878.

PRENDERGAST, Michael

s. of Michael Prendergast, Cloth Fair, London, woollen draper. b. 10th Aug. 1795. educ. Merchant Taylors'; Pemb. Coll. Camb. LLB 1821. L.I. Nov. 1820. QC 1850. Bencher 1850. Recorder of Bedford 1846-48, of Norwich 1848-59; judge of City of London Sheriffs Ct. 1856-59. Father of Sir James Prendergast (1828-1921), CJ New

Zealand, Michael Prendergast (M.T. 1849), Recorder of Bedford, and Philip Prendergast (M.T. 1859). d. 20th March 1859.

PRENTICE, Samuel

s. of Golden Nehemiah Prentice, Rayleigh, Essex. b. 1819. M.T. May 1843. QC 1866. Bencher 1866, Reader 1871, Treasurer 1881. Commr. for mun. election inquiries; common law examr. to Inns of Ct. 1879; Recorder of Maidstone 1879-92; Cty. Ct. judge 1884-92; occasionally sat as Chmn. of Middlesex Sess. Wrote and edited standard works on QB practice, evidence, crime, merchant shipping, and highways. d. 17th Dec. 1893.

PRESTON, Herbert Sansome

s. of Thomas Sansome Preston, Hampstead, London. b. 5th Aug. 1866. educ. Marlborough; London Univ. LLB. Solicitor 1889. L.I. June 1898. KC 1920. Bencher 1924. Equity draftsman and conveyancer. Brother of Arthur Sansome Preston OBE (I.T. 1905), judge in Egypt. d. 24th June 1935.

PRESTON, Richard

s. of Rev. John Preston, Okehampton, Devon. b. 1768. Attorney. I.T. May 1807. KC 1834. Bencher 1834, Reader 1844. Previously practised as certificated conveyancer; MP Ashburton 1812-18; prof. of law King's Coll. London. Author of Treatise on Conveyancing 1806-09, and other works. d. 20th June 1850.

PRICE, Edwin Plumer

s. of Thomas Price, Clementhorpe, Yorkshire. b. 13th March 1818. educ. St. Peter's Sch. York; Lincoln Coll. Oxf. BA 1839. I.T. Jan. 1841. QC 1861. Bencher 1861, Reader 1874. Recorder of York

1866-98; Cty. Ct. judge 1874-95; JP Yorkshire. d. 1st Aug. 1899.

PRIDEAUX, Charles Grevile

s. of Neart Grevile Prideaux, Bristol, solicitor. b. 19th Dec. 1810. educ. Balliol Coll. Oxf. BA 1831, MA 1834. L.I. May 1836; M.T. 1847. QC 1866. Bencher (L.I.) 1867, Treasurer 1884. Recorder of Helston 1868-76, of Exeter 1876-79, of Bristol 1879-92; judge of Bristol Tolzey and Pie Poudre Cts. 1879. Author of Guide to duties of Churchwardens 1841; FRAS. Father of C. Augustin Prideaux (M.T. 1880). d. 18th June 1892.

PRIESTLEY, Sir Joseph Child

s. of Sir William Overend Priestley MP, MD, Westbrook Hall, Horsham (d. 1900). b. 11th Jan. 1862. educ. Marlborough; Pembroke Coll. Camb. BA 1884. I.T. June 1888. KC 1903. Bencher 1917, Reader 1938. Specialised in probate and divorce cases; Chmn. Hertfordshire Quarter Sess. 1926-40, and Chmn. of Cty. Council; Knight 1927; DL, JP Hertfordshire. d. 9th June 1941.

PRINGLE, John MacKay

s. of David Pringle, Leith, Edinburgh. b. 27th April 1888. educ. Fettes; Merton Coll. Oxf. Postmaster, BA 1911. Entered Indian Civil Service 1911. L.I. Nov. 1923. KC 1945. District judge, Bengal 1923-30; practised before Judicial Committee of Privy Council 1930-50. d. 22nd April 1955.

PRITCHARD, Sir Fred Ellis

s. of Fred Pritchard, Liverpool, fruit merchant (d. 1937). b. 23rd June 1899. educ. Shrewsbury; Liverpool Univ. LLM, Hon. LLD 1956. WWI Lieut. RMA. M.T. April 1923. KC 1937. Bencher 1946,

Treasurer 1964; Hon. Bencher (G.I.) 1965. Practised in Liverpool until 1937. WWII Lieut. Col. RA and AJAG, MBE 1942. Judge of Salford Hundred Ct. of Record 1944-47; member Council of Inc. Inns of Ct. Mission; KB judge 1947-53; Knight 1947; member Bd. of Church Army 1956, and House of Laity in Nat. Assembly of Church of England 1955; Chmn. Appellate Trib. for Conscientious Objectors 1956-70; a Church Commr. 1965-68; Chmn. committee on Rating of Charities 1958; Chmn. Special Grants Committee, Min. of Social Security 1960; Commr. under Civil Aviation (Licensing) Regulations 1960; Director Council of Legal Educ., and Head of Inns of Ct. Schools of Law 1958-68; Chmn. govrs. of Shrewsbury Sch. Author of The Common Calendar: a notebook on criminal law for circuiteers. d. 10th Aug. 1982.

PRITT, Dennis Nowell

s. of Henry Walter Pritt, Billericay, Essex, metal merchant. b. 22nd Sept. 1887. educ. Winchester; London Univ. LLB; Switzerland, Spain, Germany. M.T. Nov. 1909. KC 1927. Bencher 1936, declined treasurership. War Office postal censorship dept. 1917; MP Hammersmith (North) 1935-50; Chmn. Howard League for Penal Reform, and Bentham Committee for poor litigants; Lenin Peace Prize 1954; Pres. Socy. for Cultural Relations with USSR, and Br. Peace Committee; Hon. Pres. International Assoc. of Democratic Lawyers; Freeman of Leipzig 1957; prof. of law, Ghana Univ. 1965-66; career damaged by his concentrating on political cases; Hon. LLD Prague, Sofia, Berlin, Moscow. Author of numerous political books and pamphlets, particularly on Russia; also autobiog. in three volumes 1965-66. d. 23rd May 1972.

PROCTER, Sir William

s. of William Procter, Everton, Lancashire, whitesmith. b. 17th Nov. 1871. Solicitor 1899, practised in Liverpool. G.I. Jan. 1905. Cty. Ct. judge 1928-46; Commr. of Assize, Northern circuit 1931, 1936, and 1941; Chmn. Medical Appeal Trib. for North West Region under

Nat. Insce. (Industrial Injuries) Act 1948; Knight 1941; JP Derbyshire and Lanarkshire; Hon. LLM Liverpool Univ. 1936. d. 26th June 1951.

PROFUMO, Albert Peter Anthony

s. of Baron Joseph Alexander Profumo (d. 1911). b. 20th April 1879. educ. City of London Sch. and abroad. I.T. May 1901; M.T. 1907. KC 1919. Member HAC 1897-1901. WWI Capt. United Artists Rifles (1st Battn. City of London Vol. Regt.). Hon. LLM Birmingham Univ; Hon. FRAM; 4th Baron (of Kingdom of Italy) 1911; Commendatore of the Crown of Italy. d. 27th March 1940.

PUGH, Sir John Alun

s. of Dr. John Williamson Pugh, Brighton. b. 23rd Jan. 1894. educ. Brighton Coll.; Queen's Coll. Oxf. BA 1918. I.T. June 1918. WWI Lieut. Welsh Guards. Pres. Hardwicke Socy. 1924; legal adviser Min. of Pensions 1939-42; Cty. Ct. judge 1944-66; Chmn. Norwich Licensing Area Planning Committee 1945-48; Pres. Comm. on Bahamas Police Force 1962; Chmn. governing body of Brighton Coll.; Knight 1959; JP Norfolk. Edited Butterworth's Workmen's Compensation cases 1939-42. d. 24th Nov. 1971.

PUGH, Lewis Pugh Evans

s. of Lewis Pugh Pugh MP, DL, JP, Abermaed, Aberystwyth, barrister (d. 1908). b. Calcutta, 19th April 1865. educ. Winchester; Corpus Christi Coll. Oxf. BA. L.I. May 1889 (re-admitted July 1904). KC 1937. Practised in Calcutta; acting judge there 1910; retired from Calcutta bar 1936, and afterwards practised before Judicial Committee of Privy Council. d. 24th July 1940.

PULLING, Alexander

s. of George Christopher Pulling, Capt. RN. b. 1st Dec. 1813. educ. Merchant Taylors'. I.T. June 1843. Serjeant 1864; leader on South Wales circuit; Senior Commr. under Metropolitan Management Act 1855; a promoter and original member Inc. Council of Law Reporting 1865; Dep. Cty. Ct. judge; JP Gloucestershire. Author of treatises on laws, customs, and regulations of City and Port of London 1842, attornies and solicitors, and joint stock companies. Father of Alexander Pulling CB (I.T. 1881) 1857-1942. d. 15th Jan. 1895.

PURCHASE, Edward James

s. of James Purchase, Chief Constable of Reading. b. 28th Oct. 1868. educ. Kendrick Sch. Reading; Wadham Coll. Oxf. BA 1891, MA. Rector of Owsden, Newmarket 1903-05. M.T. July 1908. KC 1923. Specialised in criminal cases. d. 3rd Feb. 1924.

PURVIS, Thomas

s. of Charles Dalston Purvis (formerly Barker), Windmill Hills, Durham. b. 12th July 1793. educ. in Houghton-le-Spring; Trinity Coll. Camb. BA 1815, 18th Wrangler, MA 1818. G.I. April 1818. QC 1842. Bencher 1842, Treasurer 1844. Leader at Chancery bar. d. 10th May 1849.

PYKE, Lionel Edward

s. of Joseph Pyke, Chatham. b. 21st April 1854. educ. Rochester Cath. Gr. Sch.; Univ. Coll. Sch.; University Coll. London BA 1873, LLB. I.T. June 1877. QC 1892. A leader at admiralty bar; member Convocation, London Univ. d. 26th March 1899.

QUAIN, Sir John Richard

s. of Richard Jones Quain, Fermoy, Cork. b. 1816. educ. Gottingen; University Coll. London LLB 1839, Fellow 1843. Special pleader 1841-51. M.T. May 1851. QC 1866. Bencher 1866-72. Att-Genl. Cty. Palatine of Durham 1868-71; QB judge 1872-76; Knight 1872; examr. in law to London Univ., member of Senate 1860; his law library presented to Univ. Coll. London 1876. Author (with H. Holroyd) of The New System of Common Law Procedure 1852. d. 12th Sept. 1876.

RABAGLIATI, Herman Victor

s. of Andrea Carlo Francisco Rabagliati MD, FRCSE, Bradford (d. 1930). b. 22nd July 1883. educ. Bradford Gr. Sch.; Edin. Univ. MA 1906. L.I. May 1908. KC 1937. Bencher 1942. WWI Capt. RFC and RAF, adjutant 13 Wing. Parliamentary draftsman. WWII Wing-Cdr. RAFVR. Member standing Courts-Martial and permanent pres. of Cts. of Inquiry for investigation of flying accidents etc.; lecturer in Air Force law; Dep. Chmn. Panel of Arbitrators 1947; Chmn. Midland District Valuation Bd. (Coal Ind. Nationalisation Act 1946) 1948-55. d. 16th April 1962.

RADCLIFFE, Cyril John (Lord Radcliffe)

s. of Capt. Alfred Ernest Radcliffe, Royal Lancaster Regt., North Court, Finchamstead, Berkshire. b. 30th March 1899. educ. Haileybury; New Coll. Oxf. BA 1921, MA 1926, Hon. DCL 1961; Fellow of All Souls Coll. 1922-37. WWI comm'd in Labour Corps. Eldon law scholar 1924. I.T. May 1924. KC 1935. Bencher 1943. Outstanding at chancery bar; Director-Genl. Min. of Information 1941-45; Vice-Chmn. bar council 1946-49; Chmn. India and Pakistan Bdy. Comm. 1947; L of A 1949-64; Baron and PC 1949; Chmn. comm. on Taxation of Profits and Income 1952, BBC General Advisory Council 1952, Inquiry into Vassall spying case 1962; Constitutional Commr. Cyprus 1956; Chmn. Committee of

Inquiry into the Monetary and Credit System 1957, of Inquiry into Security Procedures and Practices 1961; Chmn. trustees of Br. Museum 1963; First Chan. of Warwick Univ. 1966; Govr. Royal Shakespeare Theatre; Viscount 1962; GBE 1948; KBE 1944; FBA 1968; Hon. MICE; held many other honorary degrees. Author of The Problem of Power 1958, The Law and its Compass 1961, Government by Contempt, Whitehall's Way with Parliament and People 1968, Not in Feather Beds 1968. d. 1st April 1977. Biog.: The Great and the Good by E. Heward 1995.

RADCLIFFE, Francis Reynolds Yonge

s. of John Alexander Radcliffe, Cobham, Surrey. b. 20th Sept. 1851. educ. Eton; Corpus Christi Oxf. BA 1874, MA 1876; Fellow of All Souls Coll. 1874-82. I.T. June 1876. KC 1904. Bencher 1912. Recorder of Devizes 1887-1904, of Portsmouth 1904-14; Cty. Ct. judge 1914-24; Commr. of Assize 1923; Chmn. Wiltshire Quarter Sess.; JP Wiltshire, Berkshire, Oxfordshire, Northamptonshire, Warwickshire; Chevalier de l'Ordre de Leopold. Father of Geoffrey Reynolds Yonge Radcliffe DCL (L.I. 1913) and John Edward Yonge Radcliffe (I.T. 1911). d. 23rd April 1924.

RAEBURN, Sir William Norman, Bt.

s. of Sir William Hannay Raeburn MP, lst Bt. b. 16th Aug. 1877. educ. Kelvinside Acad.; Uppingham; Glasgow Univ. MA, LLB. M.T. June 1903. KC 1919. Asst. to HM Procurator-Genl. and Treasury Solicitor; CBE 1920; JP Surrey; succeeded father 1934. Edited Blackburn on Sale. d. 5th Feb. 1947.

RAIKES, Ernest Barkley

s. of Rev. Francis Raikes, Carleton Forehoe, Norfolk. b. 18th Nov. 1863. educ. Haileybury; Keble Coll. Oxf. BA 1887, MA 1889. I.T. June 1888. KC 1929. Cty. secy. Norfolk branch of Red Cross 1915-20; OBE 1919; Chmn. East Norfolk Quarter Sess. 1925-31; JP. d. 7th Dec. 1931.

RAIKES, Francis William

s. of Henry Raikes, registrar for diocese of Chester, barrister (d. 1863). b. 2nd Feb. 1842. educ. Shrewsbury; Royal Acad. Gosport; Peterhouse Camb. BA 1871, MA 1874, LLM 1876, LLD 1882. Served for 3 years in merchant navy and for 7 years in RN (navigating officer). I.T. Nov. 1872. QC 1893. Admiralty reporter for Law Times in Ct. of Appeal; election commr. at Gloucester 1880; Cty. Ct. judge 1898-1906. Author of works on maritime law. Brother of Henry Cecil Raikes PC 1838-91 (M.T. 1863). d. 29th Sept. 1906.

RAIKES, Henry St. John Digby

s. of Henry Cecil Raikes PC, MP, DL, JP, Llwynegrin Hall, Flintshire (d. 1891). b. 23rd Dec. 1863. educ. Charterhouse; Trinity Coll. Camb. BA 1886. I.T. June 1887. KC 1921. Bencher 1928. Recorder of King's Lynn 1905-43; Chmn. Derbyshire Quarter Sess. 1912; Chmn. Derbyshire War Savings Committee and 2nd Div. Derbyshire Military Appeal Tribunal; CBE 1920; DL, JP Flintshire and Derbyshire. Edited Sanders's Precedents of Indictments. Father of Sir Henry Victor Alpin Raikes KBE, MP (I.T. 1924). d. 1st May 1943.

RAINES, William

s. of William Raines, Wyton Hall, nr. Hull. b. 1808. educ. privately; Trinity Coll. Camb. 1826. L.I. May 1833. Cty. Ct. judge 1847-74; DL Yorkshire East Riding; JP Yorkshire North and East Ridings; raised company of rifle volunteers (Capt. 1860-72). d. 28th Jan. 1874.

RALEIGH, Sir Thomas

s. of Samuel Raleigh, Edinburgh, actuary. b. 2nd Dec. 1850. educ.

in Edinburgh and Tübingen; Balliol Coll. Oxf. BA 1875; All Souls Coll. MA 1878, BCL 1890, DCL 1896, Fellow 1876. L.I. June 1877. KC 1908. Reader in English law Oxf. 1884-96; Registrar of Privy Council 1896-99; legal member council of Viceroy of India 1899-1904, member 1909-13; Dep. Steward Oxf. Univ. 1906-09; V-C Calcutta Univ. 1900-04; CSI 1902; KCSI 1904; Hon. LLD Edin.; published Outline of the Law of Property 1889. d. 8th Feb. 1920.

RAM, Abel John

s. of Rev. Canon Abel John Ram, Clonatin, Co. Wexford (d. 1883). b. 21st Sept. 1842. educ. Repton; Corpus Christi Coll. Oxf. BA 1866, MA 1869. I.T. June 1872. QC 1899. Bencher 1897. Leader of Oxford circuit; Recorder of Hanley 1891-1900, of Wolverhampton 1900-18; Chmn. Royal Comm. on vivisection 1910; member East Coast Raid Comm. 1915; member of bar council; JP Hertfordshire; KStJ. d. 8th Aug. 1920.

RAM, Sir Lucius Abel John Granville

s. of Abel John Ram KC. b. 24th June 1885. educ. Eton; Exeter Coll. Oxf. BA 1909, MA 1927. I.T. Nov. 1910. KC 1943. WWI Capt. Hertfordshire Yeo., and Adjt. S. Irish Horse. Solicitor to Min. of Labour 1923; third parliamentary counsel to Treasury 1925, second 1929, first 1937-47; head consolidation branch, Parliamentary Counsels' Office 1947-52; Chmn. Statute Law Committee 1947; Church Commr. 1948; Dep. Chmn. Hertfordshire Quarter Sess. 1932-46, Chmn. 1946-52, and of appeal committee and licensing committee; CB 1931; KCB 1938; JP Hertfordshire and Cornwall. Father of Edward David Abel Ram (solicitor 1962). d. 23rd Dec. 1952.

RAMSHAY, William

s. of Rev. Thomas Ramshay, Brampton, Cumberland. b. 1807. educ.

Durham Sch.; Trinity Coll. Camb. BA 1830, MA 1833. I.T. Nov. 1833. Cty. Ct. judge 1850; suspended June 1851, during inquiry into alleged misconduct and incapacity; removed following second inquiry, Nov. 1851. d. 13th June 1853.

RANDOLPH, Joseph Randolph

s. of Capt. Arthur Randolph Randolph, 15th Hussars, Eastcourt, Wiltshire (d. 1885). b. 9th Oct. 1867. educ. Radley; Magdalen Coll. Oxf. BA 1890, MA and BCL 1894. I.T. Nov. 1892. KC 1913. Cty. Ct. judge 1921-36; Chmn. Wiltshire Quarter Sess. 1924; JP Wiltshire. d. 25th Sept 1936.

RAPHAEL, Geoffrey George

s. of Joseph Henry Raphael (d. 1939). b. 21st Dec. 1893. educ. Frinton Coll.; Univ. Coll. Sch. and in Germany. I.T. Nov. 1924. WWI Lieut. Post Office Rifles; Capt. 1920. Junior counsel to Treasury at London Sess. and Ct. of Criminal Appeal 1934. WWII ADJAG (Lt. Col., despatches). Metrop. magistrate 1945, finally at Marylebone to 1965; Pres. Hardwicke Socy. 1930; JP Deal. d. 21st Dec. 1969.

RATTIGAN, Sir William Henry

s. of Bartholomew Rattigan, Athy, Co. Kildare, Ordnance Dept. HEICS. b. Delhi, 4th Sept. 1842. educ. High Sch. Agra; King's Coll. London. L.I. June 1873. QC 1897. Bencher 1903. Advocate, High Ct. North West Provinces; temp. judge Chief Ct. of Punjab 1880-86; additional member Supreme Legislative Council of India 1892-93; member Punjab Legislative Council 1898-99; V-C Punjab Univ. 1887-95; Knight 1895; MP Lanarkshire (North East) 1901-04; DL Göttingen, Hon. LLD Glasgow, Hon. DL Punjab Univ. Author of The Science of Jurisprudence, Private International Law 1895, Digest of civil and customary law of the Punjab 1880, De Jure

Personarum or the Roman Law of Persons 1873. d. 4th July 1904.

RAWLINS, William Donaldson

s. of Samuel Rawlins, Bevere, Worcestershire (d. 1884). b. 20th July 1846. educ. Eton; Trinity Coll. Camb. BA 1868, MA 1871, Fellow 1869. Asst. master at Eton 1868-69. L.I. April 1872. QC 1896. Bencher 1900. Commr. for Income Tax; Mayor of Holborn 1906; JP London and Berkshire. Author of works on specific performance, company law, landlord and tenant, and receivers. d. 21st May 1920.

RAWLINSON, John

s. of John Rawlinson MD, Combe, Hampshire. educ. Emmanuel Coll. Camb. 1797. Steward of the Emmanuel "meeting" in 1804. M.T. April 1818. Metrop. magistrate, Marylebone 1819-47; JP Hampshire. Father of Sir Christopher Rawlinson (1806-88), CJ Madras. d. 25th June 1847, age 69.

RAWLINSON, John Frederick Peel

s. of Sir Christopher Rawlinson, CJ Madras (d. 1888). b. 21st Dec. 1860. educ. Eton; Trinity Coll. Camb. LLB 1883, LLM 1887; Hon. Fellow, Pembroke Coll. Camb., Hon. LLD 1920. I.T. June 1884. QC 1897. Bencher 1907. Recorder of Cambridge 1898-1926; MP Camb. Univ. 1906-26; Commissary of Camb. Univ. 1900-26; Dep. High Steward Camb. Univ. 1918-26; represented Treasury in Inquiry in South Africa concerning Jameson Raid 1896; V-Chmn. of bar council; lecturer and examr. in law, Pembroke Coll.; PC 1923; JP Cambridgeshire; Fellow of Eton Coll. 1919-26; member governing bodies of Eton, Malvern, and Brighton Colls. d. 14th Jan. 1926.

REECE, Francis Bertram

s. of Rev. Canon John Francis Reece, St. Asaph, Flintshire. b. 1888. educ. Rossall; St. John's Coll. Camb. I.T. June 1914. Recorder of Birkenhead 1935-43; metrop. magistrate 1943, finally at Bow St. 1948-61; Chmn. Poisons Bd. (Home Office) 1946-58; CBE 1958. d. 4th April 1971.

REED, Herbert Parker

s. of Herbert Adolphus Reed, solicitor. b. 1851. educ. in Brighton. Solicitor 1873. I.T. Jan. 1877. G.I. 1887. QC 1892. Bencher 1896, Treasurer 1902. Author of The Law of Bills of Sale. d. 30th Jan. 1920.

REES, Griffith Caradoc

s. of Griffith Rees, Cilgerran, Cardigan. b. 1868. educ. Liverpool Inst. Solicitor 1895-1905. M.T. Nov. 1905. MP Carnarvonshire (North) 1915-18; private secy. to Home Secy. 1915-16; Cty. Ct. judge 1921-24. d. 20th Sept. 1924.

REES, John Thomas Tudor

s. of I.J. Rees, Maesteg, nr. Bridgend. b. 1880. educ. Univ. of Wales. Solicitor 1907, practised in Cardiff. WWI Capt. Welch Regt., and Machine Gun Corps. G.I. June 1922. MP Devon (Barnstaple) 1918-22 and 1923-24; Cty. Ct. judge 1939-56; Chmn. Surrey Quarter Sess. 1941; Chmn. Epson Petty Sess.; DL, JP Surrey; Freeman of City of London 1921. Author of Our Jury System, Reserved Judgment (autobiog.). d. 27th Feb. 1956.

REEVE, Raymond Herbert Roope

s. of James William Reeve. b. 1875. educ. Christ's Coll., Hobart, Tasmania. L.I. Nov. 1900. Transvaal bar 1906. WWI Lieut. RFA. KC 1922. Bencher 1927. Member of bar council; served with Comm. on War Stores in South Africa 1905-06; Cty. Ct. judge 1926-45. Edited Gale on Easements. d. 16th Feb. 1952.

REID, Robert Threshie (Lord Loreburn)

s. of Sir James John Reid, Mouswald Place, Dumfries, CJ Corfu. b. Corfu, 3rd April 1846. educ. Cheltenham Coll.; Balliol Coll. Oxf. BA 1869, Hon. DCL 1907, Hon. Fellow 1908, Visitor 1912. I.T. June 1871. QC 1882. Bencher 1890. MP Hereford 1880-85; Dumfries Burghs 1886-1905; successfully arbitrated in boundary dispute between Venezuela and Br. Guiana 1899; Sol-Genl. and knighted 1894; Att-Genl. 1894; standing counsel to Oxf. Univ. 1899-1906; LC 1905; established Ct. of Criminal Appeal 1907; acted as a Counsellor of State during HM's absence abroad 1911-12; resigned 1912; Chmn. Royal Comm. on Railways 1913; GCMG 1899, PC 1905, Baron 1906, Earl 1911; JP Kent and Cinque Ports; Pres. Council of Cheltenham Sch. Author of Capture at Sea 1913. d. 30th Nov. 1923.

REILLY, Sir Francis Savage

s. of James Miles Reilly, Dublin. b. 4th Feb. 1825. educ. Trinity Coll. Dublin BA 1847, MA 1851. L.I. May 1851. QC 1882. Parliamentary draftsman; secy. to comm. of inquiry into law and practice of bankruptcy 1853; assessor in the London, Chatham and Dover Ry. arbitration, Albert Life Assce. Co. arbitration 1871-73, and European Assce. Co. arbitration 1872-79; counsel to the Speaker 1882; KCMG 1882, for services to foreign and colonial departments. d. 27th Aug. 1883.

RENSHAW, Thomas Charles

s. of Henry Grundy Renshaw, Camden Town, North London (d. 1848). b. 4th April 1810. L.I. Jan. 1832. QC 1872. Bencher 1872. d. 26th May 1886.

RENSHAW, Walter Charles

s. of Thomas Charles Renshaw QC. b. 24th Sept. 1840. educ. King's Coll. London; Trinity Hall Camb. LLB 1862, LLM 1868. L.I. Jan. 1864. QC 1886. Bencher 1890. Equity draftsman and conveyancer; member Supreme Ct. Rule Committee, and Council of Law Reporting; Pres. Selden Socy.; member of bar committee, and Baronetage committee; JP Sussex. d. 16th July 1922.

RENTON, Sir Alexander Wood

s. of Rev. John Renton, Auchtermuchty, Fife. b. 24th June 1861. educ. privately; Glasgow Acad.; Edin. Univ. MA, LLB. G.I. April 1885. KC 1923. Bencher 1917, Treasurer 1925. Puisne judge, and Procureur and Adv-Genl. Mauritius 1901-05; puisne judge, Ceylon 1905-14, CJ 1914-18; on special mission for Colonial Office to Nigeria and Gold Coast 1918, and to Egypt for Foreign Office 1919; Vice-Pres. Egyptian Riots Indemnities Comm. 1919; Chmn. Salaries Comm., Ceylon 1921; Chmn. Compensation (Ireland) Comm. 1923; Chmn. Irish Grants Committee 1926-30; Knight 1915; KCMG 1925, GCMG 1930. Author of Law and Practice of Lunacy 1896; editor of H of L and Privy Council series of English Reports, and of Law Journal. d. 17th June 1933.

RENTOUL, Sir Gervais Squire Chittick

s. of James Alexander Rentoul QC. b. 1st Aug. 1884. educ. City of London Sch.; Royal Univ. Ireland; Christ Church Oxf. 1904. G.I. April 1907. Legal asst. War Office 1915-17; Capt. HQ Staff, Eastern

Command 1917-20. KC 1930. Recorder of Sandwich 1929-34; MP Lowestoft 1922-34; Chmn. Conservative 1922 Committee 1922-32; private secy. to Att-Genl. (Sir Douglas Hogg) 1925-29; counsel to Att-Genl. in legitimacy cases, and to IR in licensing matters 1924-30; metrop. magistrate 1934, finally at West London to 1946; Knight 1929. Author of Sometimes I think 1940, Blockade and contraband 1942, This is My Case 1944. d. 7th March 1946.

RENTOUL, James Alexander

s. of Rev. Alexander Rentoul DD, MD, Manor Cunningham, Co. Donegal. b. 1854. educ. Queen's Coll. Galway; Queen's Univ. BA, LLD; Berlin Univ. I.T. Nov. 1884. QC 1895. MP East Down 1890-1902; judge of City of London Ct. 1901-19. d. 12th Aug. 1919.

REWCASTLE, Cuthbert Snowball

s. of Cuthbert Rewcastle JP, Newcastle-on-Tyne. b. 21st Feb. 1888. educ. Rugby; Trinity Coll. Camb. BA 1909, LLB 1910. I.T. June 1912. KC 1935. Referee under Landlord and Tenant Act 1927; Secy. Royal Comm. on Sugar Supply; senior advocate, Federal Ct. of India; Chmn. Comm. on silicosis legislation, Northern Rhodesia 1949, and Comm. on pulmonary disability 1954; Cty. Ct. judge 1952-61; hon. secy. Eighty Club. Edited Mahaffy and Dodson on the law relating to motor cars; joint editor of Hudson on Building Contracts. d. 8th June 1962.

RHODES, George

s. of John Rhodes, Manchester. b. 1851. educ. Owen's Coll. Manchester. Merchant in Manchester until 1889; member of Manchester City Council 1890-92. G.I. June 1892. KC 1909. Bencher 1909. Recorder of Oldham 1914-24; Chmn. Shireoaks Colliery Co. Ltd.; director, Thomas Rhodes and Son Ltd., Hadfield Mills; JP Cheshire and Lancashire. Published Manchester Municipal

Code. d. 23rd Sept. 1924.

RHODES, Harold

s. of George Rhodes KC. b. 1885. educ. Bowdon Coll.; Corpus Christi Coll. Oxf. MA. I.T. June 1910. WWI Capt. 29th Divisional Artillery. Cty. Ct. judge 1942-58; Commr. of Assize, Northern Circuit 1946; Dep. Chmn. Lancashire Quarter Sess. 1942-60; Chmn. Altrincham Petty Sess. 1944-60; JP Cheshire and Lancashire. d. 17th Oct. 1964.

RHYS-WILLIAMS, Sir Rhys, Bt.

s. of Gwilym Williams, Cty. Ct. judge. b. 20th Oct. 1865. educ. Eton; Oriel Coll. Oxf. BA 1887. I.T. Jan. 1890. KC 1913. WWI Lieut.Col. Welsh Guards, DSO (despatches twice); acting military attaché Tehran 1915-16; Asst. Director-Genl. Movements and Railways, War Office 1917-18; Dep. Director Staff duties, Admiralty 1918. Chmn. Glamorganshire Quarter Sess. 1906; Recorder of Cardiff 1922-30; MP Oxford (Banbury) 1918-22; parliamentary secy. to Min. of Transport 1919; Baronet 1918; DL, JP Glamorganshire; Orders of St. Vladimir of Russia, and Lion and Sun of Persia. d. 29th Jan. 1955.

RICE-JONES, Benjamin Rowland

s. of J.E. Rice-Jones, Southport, Lancashire. b. 19th June 1888. educ. Temple Grove, Clifton; Christ's Coll. Camb. BA, LLB. WWI Lieut. RGA (Lancashire and West Riding Batteries). I.T. May 1912 (Cert of Hon.). Asst. judge Liverpool Ct. of Passage; Cty. Ct. judge 1945-60. d. 26th Aug. 1978.

RICHARDS, Edward Lewis

s. of David Lewis Richards, Merthyr Tydfil, Glamorganshire. b. 25th March 1804. educ. Cowbridge, Glamorgan; Christ's Coll. Camb. 1833. L.I. Jan. 1837. Cty. Ct. judge 1847-63; Chmn. Flintshire Quarter Sess. 1851-63; DL, JP Glamorgan. d. 25th June 1863.

RICHARDS, Edward Vaughan

s. of William Parry Richards, wine merchant (d. 1860). b. 18th Nov. 1821. educ. Westminster; Christ Church Oxf. BA 1844, MA 1846; rowed against Cambridge 1841. I.T. April 1847. QC 1868. Bencher 1868. d. 26th Sept. 1884.

RICHARDS, Henry Charles

s. of Frederick Richards JP, West Hill, St. Leonard's-on-Sea. b. 10th April 1851. educ. City of London Sch. and Coll. Employed in commerce for twelve years in London. G.I. and M.T. May 1881. QC 1898. Bencher (G.I.). Counsel to PO at Central Criminal Ct.; Chmn. City Branch, Church Defence Inst. 1877; formed City Church and Churchyard Preservation Socy. 1880; engaged in many compensation cases; MP Finsbury (East) 1895-1905; FSA. Author of works on charities, elections, compensation, and education. d. 1st June 1905.

RICHARDS, Sir Henry Erle

s. of Rev. Prebendary Henry William Parry Richards (d. 1900). b. 6th Dec. 1861. educ. Eton; New Coll. Oxf. BA 1885; All Souls Coll. BCL and MA 1911, Fellow 1911. I.T. May 1887. KC 1905. Bencher 1914. Legal member council of Viceroy of India 1904-09; counsel for GB in Samoa arbitration 1902, Venezuela arbitration 1903, for Newfoundland and Canada in North Atlantic Coast Fisheries arbitration 1910; Chichele prof. of intern. law and diplomacy, Oxf.

Univ. 1911; counsel to India Office 1911-21; KCSI 1909. d. 23rd
April 1922.

RICHARDS, Robert Vaughan

s. of Sir Richard Richards LCB (d. 1823). b. 3rd Nov. 1790. educ.
Westminster; Christ Church Oxf. BA 1812, MA 1814. I.T. Nov.
1819. QC 1839. Special pleader; examr. to I.T.; Bencher 1839.
Brother of Richard Richards, Master in Chancery (1787-1860). d.
2nd July 1846.

RICHARDS, Whitmore Lionel

s. of John Henry Richards, Cty. Ct. judge (Ireland) (d. 1901). b. 12th
Sept. 1869. educ. Rugby; Trinity Coll. Dublin BA 1891. L.I. May
1895. Equity draftsman and conveyancer; Cty. Ct. judge 1922-42;
joint editor of Godefroi's Law of Trusts; JP Cheshire. d. 21st Nov.
1954.

RICHARDSON, Sir Albion Henry Herbert

s. of James Henry Richardson, New Lodge, Hendon, Middlesex. b.
2nd Oct. 1874. educ. privately, and in France and Germany. Solicitor
1899, practised in London. G.I. May 1912. KC 1930. Bencher 1930.
Recorder of Warwick 1931-36, of Nottingham 1937-50; MP
Camberwell (Peckham) 1910-22; Chmn. Law Socy. Section, Appeal
Trib. for London 1916-18; Commr. to report on allegations made
by Col. Wedgwood MP against Govr. of Wandsworth Prison 1918;
a commr. on many occasions to inquire into allegations against the
police; on panel of Chmn. of Grand Committees, H of C; member
standing joint committee of Inns of Ct.; CBE 1918; Knight 1919.
d. 7th July 1950.

RICHARDSON, Thomas

s. of Sir Thomas Richardson MP, Kirklevington Grange, Yarm, Yorkshire (d. 1906). b. 17th Jan. 1880. educ. Rossall; Clare Coll. Camb. BA 1904, LLB 1904. M.T. Jan. 1905. WWI Capt. General List. OBE 1919. Cty. Ct. judge 1927-53; Chmn. Durham Quarter Sess. and Northumberland Quarter Sess.; JP Durham and Northumberland. Father of John David Benbow Richardson MC, a Recorder of the Crown Court 1972. d. 22nd April 1956.

RICKARDS, Arthur George

s. of Sir George Kettilby Rickards KCB, barrister (d. 1889). b. 22nd May 1848. educ. Eton; Brasenose Coll. Oxf. BA 1872, MA 1891. I.T. Jan. 1875. QC 1899. Bencher 1909. Major in Volunteer Forces; VD; served on Executive Committee of Nat. Service League, and of Mil. Appeal Tribs. for London and Gloucestershire; JP Gloucestershire. Author of commentary on Metropolis Water Act 1902, and joint editor of Clifford and Rickard's Locus Standi reports. d. 28th July 1924.

RIDDELL, Sir Walter Buchanan, Bt.

s. of Sir John Buchanan Riddell, 9th Bt. b. 8th Aug. 1810. educ. Eton; Christ Church Oxf. BA 1831, MA 1834. L.I. Nov. 1834. Steward of manorial cts. of Duke of Northumberland 1842; Recorder of Tenterden 1846-59, of Maidstone 1846-68; Cty. Ct. judge 1859-79; JP Kent, Northumberland and Staffordshire; succeeded father 1819. d. 27th Aug. 1892.

RIDLEY, Sir Edward

s. of Sir Matthew White Ridley, 4th Bt. b. Aug. 1843. educ. Harrow; Corpus Christi Coll. Oxf. BA 1866, MA 1869; Fellow of All Souls Coll. 1866-82. I.T. June 1868. QC 1892. MP Northumberland

(South) 1878-80; Official Referee 1887-97; KB judge 1897-1917; Knight 1897; PC 1917. Father of Cecil Guy Ridley CBE (I.T. 1911). d. 14th Oct. 1928.

RIGBY, Sir John

s. of Thomas Rigby, Runcorn, Cheshire. b. 4th Jan. 1834. educ. Liverpool Inst.; Trinity Coll. Camb. BA 1856, 2nd Wrangler, MA 1859, Fellow 1856. L.I. Jan. 1860. QC 1881. Bencher 1884. Junior equity counsel to Treasury; member of bar committee 1883; MP North Cambridgeshire 1885-86, Forfar 1892-94; confined his practice to Ct. of Appeal and H of L; Sol-Genl. 1892; Att-Genl. 1894; Knight 1892; LJ 1894-1901; PC. d. 26th July 1903.

RIGG, Herbert Addington

s. of Jonathan Rigg, Wrotham Hill Park, Kent. b. 7th March 1845. educ. Tonbridge; Trinity Coll. Camb. BA 1868, MA 1871. I.T. June 1871. KC 1906. Practised at parliamentary bar; Dep. Chmn. West Sussex Quarter Sess.; Alderman, West Sussex CC; JP West Sussex; FSA. d. 7th March 1924.

RINGWOOD, Richard

s. of Richard Ringwood, Farrenmurry, Co. Kilkenny. b. 1846. educ. Trinity Coll. Dublin MA. M.T. June 1873. KC 1919. Bencher 1913. Special pleader. Mil. Service (Civil Liabilities) Commr. 1914-18. Author of The Principles of Bankruptcy and The Law of Torts; joint editor of Hazlitt and Ringwood's Bankruptcy Act 1883. d. 17th March 1921.

RISLEY, Sir John Shuckburgh

s. of Shuckburgh Norris Risley, Elmore, Newbury, Berkshire,

barrister. b. 22nd Dec. 1867. educ. Marlborough; Magdalen Coll. Oxf. BA 1890, MA and BCL 1894. L.I. Nov. 1893. KC 1921. Legal Asst. Colonial Office 1901-11; Prin. Legal Adviser Colonial Office 1911-31, and Dominions Office 1925-31; CB 1912, KCMG 1922. Author of The Law of War 1897; edited Dale's Clergyman's Legal Handbook and Waterlow's Companies Acts Manual. d. 22nd Feb. 1957.

ROBERTS, Geoffrey Dorling

s. of Charles Tanner Kingdon Roberts, Exeter, solicitor. b. 27th Aug. 1886. educ. Exeter Gr. Sch.; Rugby; St. John's Coll. Oxf. MA; half-blue lawn tennis; rugby blue, played rugby for England 1907-08. I.T. May 1912. KC 1937. Bencher 1944. WWI Major, Devonshire Regt. and on staff; OBE 1919. Senior treasury counsel at Central Criminal Ct.; Recorder of Exeter 1932-46, of Bristol 1946-61; JP Surrey; director, Balijan Tea Co. Ltd.; Master of Glaziers' and Painters of Glass Co. 1950. Author of Without my Wig 1957, Law and Life 1964. d. 7th March 1967.

ROBERTS, John Bryn

s. of Daniel Roberts, Bryn Adda, Bangor. b. 8th Jan. 1843. educ. Cheltenham Gr. Sch. Solicitor 1868, practised in Bangor. L.I. Jan. 1889. Equity draftsman and conveyancer; MP South Carnarvonshire 1885-1906; Cty. Ct. judge 1906-21; Dep. Chmn. Carnarvonshire Quarter Sess.; DL, JP Carnarvonshire. d. 14th April 1931.

ROBERTS, Richard Owen

s. of William Roberts, Plas Hyfryd, Holyhead. b. 3rd Sept. 1876. educ. Holborn Estate Gr. Sch.; King's Coll. London. M.T. June 1902. Pres. Hardwicke Socy. 1910.; member LCC 1918-25; Cty. Ct. judge 1924-29. Author of The Law of Collisions on Land. d. 12th Sept 1929.

ROBERTS, Sir Walworth Howland

s. of Sir Thomas Howland Roberts, 3rd Bt. b. 30th Aug. 1855. educ. Highgate Sch.; King's Coll.. London. M.T. July 1878. Lieut. 3rd Vol. Battn. Rifle Brigade 1873-78. Cty. Ct. judge 1900-21; Chmn. Cty. Cts. Rules Committee; standing arbitrator under Min. of Transport Act 1922; CBE for war work as a Chmn. of committee on production, and in arbitrations; Knight 1921; JP Staffordshire. d. 21st Dec. 1924.

ROBERTSON, Edmund (Lord Lochee)

s. of Edmund Robertson, Kinnaird, Perthshire. b. 28th Oct. 1845. educ. St. Andrews Univ.; Lincoln Coll. Oxf. BA 1870; Corpus Christi Coll. MA 1874, Fellow 1870; Hon. LLD St. Andrews. L.I. Nov. 1871. QC 1895. Reader in law to Council of Legal Educ.; MP Dundee 1885-1908; Civil Lord of Admiralty 1892-95; Secy. to Admiralty 1905-08; PC 1905; Baron Lochee of Gowrie 1908; DL. d. 13th Sept. 1911.

ROBERTSON, Sir George Stuart

s. of John Abel Robertson, Sutton Court, Sutton, Surrey. b. 25th May 1872. educ. Winchester; New Coll. Oxf. MA 1895, Fellow. I.T. June 1899. KC 1920. Secy. to Lord Alverstone as pres. of Alaska Boundary Trib. 1903; member of bar council 1907-11; Chief Registrar of Friendly Societies 1912-37; Industrial Assce. Commr. 1923-37; Dep. Chmn. Devon Quarter Sess. 1939-46; director Prudential Assce. Co. Ltd. 1937-52; Knight 1928; JP Devon; FSA; Knight of the Order of the Saviour of Greece; threw discus at Olympic Games, Athens 1896. Author of The Law of Tramways and Light Railways, Civil Proceedings by and against the Crown, The Law of Copyright. d. 29th Jan. 1967.

ROBERTSON, James Patrick Bannerman (Lord Robertson)

s. of Rev. Robert John Robertson, Forteviot. b. 10th Aug. 1845.

educ. Royal High Sch. Edin.; Edin. Univ. MA 1864; Hon. LLD 1890. Scottish bar 1867. QC 1885. Sol-Genl. for Scotland 1885 and 1886; MP Buteshire 1885-86, 1886-91; carried Local Government (Scotland) Act 1889; PC 1889; Lord Advocate 1889; Lord Pres. of Ct. of Session 1891; Baron Robertson of Forteviot, and member judicial committee of Privy Council 1899; Lord Rector Edin. Univ. 1893; DL Kincardine and Edin. Father of Robert Bannerman Fraser Robertson (I.T. 1899). d. 1st Feb. 1909.

ROBINSON, Benjamin Coulson

s. of Thomas Robinson, London. b. 21st March 1812. M.T. April 1840. Serjeant 1865. Patent of precedence 1874; Master of Saddlers' Co. 1889. FRGS. Author of the Law of Warrants of Attorney 1844, and Bench and Bar (reminiscences) 1889. d. 4th Jan. 1890.

ROBINSON, William Fothergill

s. of William Fothergill Robinson, Aigburth, Liverpool. b. 1833. educ. Bonn; Trinity Coll. Camb. BA 1854, 24th Wrangler, MA 1864. I.T. Nov. 1856 (Cert. of Hon.). QC 1875. Bencher 1877. Member of bar committee 1883; V-C of Cty. Palatine of Lancaster 1893-95. d. 8th July 1895.

ROBSON, William Snowdon (Lord Robson)

s. of Robert Robson JP, Newcastle-upon-Tyne, merchant (d. 1890). b. 10th Sept. 1852. educ. privately; Caius Coll. Camb. BA 1877, MA 1879, Hon. Fellow 1910. Qualified as solicitor. I.T. June 1880. QC 1892. Bencher 1899. Practised in shipping, industrial and commercial cases; Recorder of Newcastle-upon-Tyne 1895-1905; MP Bow and Bromley 1885, South Shields 1895-1910; Sol-Genl. and knighted 1905; Att-Genl. 1908-10; piloted budget of 1909; largely responsible for legislation on children's working hours; presented Br. case at Atlantic Fisheries Arbitration, The Hague

1910; GCMG 1911; L of A 1910-12; Baron and PC 1910; Hon. DCL Durham 1906. Father of Harold Burge Robson DL, JP (I.T. 1910). d. 11th Sept. 1918.

ROBY, Arthur Godfrey

s. of Henry John Roby MP, LLD, Lancrigg, Grasmere (d. 1915). bapt. 19th Oct. 1862. educ. Manchester Gr. Sch.; St. John's Coll. Camb. BA 1884, MA 1903. I.T. June 1887. KC 1919. Equity draftsman and conveyancer. d. 15th April 1944.

ROCHE, Alexander Adair (Lord Roche)

s. of Dr. William Roche, Seaton, Devon. b. 24th July 1871. educ. Ipswich Gr. Sch.; Wadham Coll. Oxf. BA 1894, Hon. Fellow 1917. I.T. Nov. 1896. KC 1912. Bencher 1917, Treasurer 1939. Had extensive practice in commercial and admiralty cases; KB judge 1917-34; Knight 1917; LJ 1934-35; PC 1934; L of A 1935-38; Baron 1935; Chmn. Agricultural Wages Bd. 1940-43; Chmn. Oxfordshire Quarter Sess. 1932-47; JP Oxfordshire; Hon. DCL Durham. Father of Thomas Gabriel Roche (QC 1955). d. 22nd Dec. 1956.

RODWELL, Benjamin Bridges Hunter

s. of William Rodwell, Woodlands, Holbrook, Suffolk, banker (d. 1878). b. 17th Jan. 1815. educ. Charterhouse; Trinity Coll. Camb. BA 1837, MA 1840. M.T. Nov. 1840. QC 1859. Bencher 1859, Reader 1862, Treasurer 1870. MP Cambridgeshire 1874-81; Chmn. West Suffolk Quarter Sess. 1862; DL, JP Suffolk; reported (with Sir G. Pigott) cases in CP 1846; joint editor of election cases 1847-53. d. 6th Feb. 1892.

RODWELL, Edgar Kedington

s. of William Rodwell, Woodlands, Holbrook, Suffolk, banker (d. 1878). b. 2nd Feb. 1823. educ. Charterhouse. M.T. May 1846. QC 1880. Bencher 1882. JP Sussex. d. 21st Jan. 1903.

ROEBUCK, John Arthur

s. of Ebenezer Roebuck, HEICS. b. Madras, 28th Dec. 1802. educ. in Canada. I.T. Jan. 1831. QC 1843. Bencher 1843, Reader 1856, Treasurer 1857. Agent in England for House of Assembly of Lower Canada 1835; MP Bath 1832-37 and 1841-47, Sheffield 1849-68 and 1874-79; moved, 1855, for comm. of inquiry into conduct of Crimean War, with result that Lord Aberdeen's govt. resigned and Lord Palmerston made Roebuck Chmn. of Sebastopol committee; PC 1878. d. 30th Nov. 1879.

ROGERS, Arundel

s. of Thomas Rogers, Helston, Cornwall, solicitor. b. 1826. educ. Trinity Hall Camb. 1859. Solicitor in Penzance 1849-53. I.T. Jan. 1862. Mining draftsman and special pleader. Cty. Ct. judge 1879-89; JP Herefordshire. Author of the Law relating to Mines, Minerals and Quarries 1864, and the Law and Practice of the Supreme Court 1875. d. 20th Sept. 1889.

ROGERS, Francis James Newman

s. of Rev. James Rogers, Rainscombe, Wiltshire. b. 1791. educ. Eton; Oriel Coll. Oxf. BA 1812, MA 1815. L.I. May 1816. I.T. 1820. KC 1837. Bencher 1837, Reader 1847, Treasurer 1848. Recorder of Exeter 1835-51; DJAG 1842-51. Author of works on election law and ecclesiastical law. d. 19th July 1851.

ROLFE, Robert Monsey (Lord Cranworth)

s. of Rev. Edmund Rolfe, Cockley Cley, Norfolk (d. 1795). b. 18th Dec. 1790. educ. Bury Gr. Sch.; Winchester; Trinity Coll. Camb. BA 1812, 17th Wrangler, MA 1815; Fellow of Downing Coll. L.I. May 1816. KC 1832. Bencher 1832-39. Recorder of Bury St. Edmunds; MP Penryn and Falmouth 1832-39; Sol-Genl. 1834 and 1835-39; Knight 1835; Exch. Baron 1839-50; presided at trial of 59 Chartists for seditious conspiracy 1843; a Commr. of the Great Seal 1850; PC 1850; V-C 1850; LJ in Chancery 1851; LC 1852-58 and 1865-67; Baron Cranworth 1850, the first instance of a V-C receiving a peerage; introduced legislation for the better administration of charitable trusts; presided over Royal Comm. for Consolidation of Statutes 1854; introduced "Cranworth's Act" for shortening of conveyances 1860; a govr. of the Charterhouse 1855. d. 26th July 1868.

ROLT, James

s. of Rolt LJ. b. 27th April 1860. educ. Eton; Univ. Coll. Oxf. BA 1883. I.T. Nov. 1886. KC 1914. Bencher 1922. Equity draftsman and conveyancer. d. 10th Nov. 1938.

ROLT, Sir John

s. of James Rolt, Calcutta, architect and merchant (d. 1813). b. Calcutta, 5th Oct. 1804. educ. in Chipping Norton and Islington. Apprenticed to woollen drapers in London 1818; employed in a Manchester warehouse in Newgate St. 1823-27; Secy. to Dissenters' Sch. Mill Hill; clerk to a proctor in Doctors' Commons 1827. I.T. June 1837. QC 1846. Bencher 1846, Reader 1859, Treasurer 1860. Practised in Chancery; MP West Gloucestershire 1857-67; carried "Rolt's Act" 1862, concerning fusion of law and equity; Att-Genl. 1866; Knight 1866; LJ 1867-68; PC 1867; DL, JP Gloucestershire. d. 6th June 1871. His memoirs, edited by C.T. Le Quesne and others, published 1939.

ROMER, Sir Charles Robert Ritchie

s. of Lord Romer. b. 19th Jan. 1897. educ. Rugby. WWI Capt. King's Royal Rifle Corps, OBE (despatches twice). L.I. Jan. 1921. KC 1937. Bencher 1943. Legal adviser to Regional Commr. North Midland Coal Region 1940-44; Chancery judge 1944-51; Knight 1944; LJ 1951-60; PC 1951; Chmn. Committee of Inquiry into breaches of security at the Underwater Detection Establishment, Portland 1961, following the spy trial earlier that year; JP Kent; Hon. Fellow Trinity Hall Camb. 1957. Father of Mark Lemon Robert Romer, metrop. magistrate 1972, and Ian Lebeau Ritchie Romer (Bencher L.I. 1981). d. 15th Feb. 1969.

ROMER, Mark Lemon (Lord Romer)

s. of Romer LJ. b. 9th Aug. 1866. educ. Rugby; Trinity Hall Camb. BA 1888, MA 1915; Hon. Fellow 1922. L.I. June 1890. KC 1906. Bencher 1910. Counsel to Royal Coll. of Physicians 1914, and to Camb. Univ. 1915; member LC's Law Revision Committee; Chancery judge 1922-29; Knight 1922; Chmn. committee on draft bills on law of real property (enacted 1925); LJ 1929-38; PC 1929; L of A 1938-44; Baron Romer of New Romney 1938. d. 19th Aug. 1944.

ROMER, Sir Robert

s. of Frank Romer, musical composer (d. 1889). b. 23rd Dec. 1840. educ. privately; Trinity Hall Camb. BA 1863, MA 1866, Senior Wrangler, Fellow 1866. Secy. to Baron Lionel Nathan de Rothschild; prof. of mathematics, Queen's Coll. Cork 1865-66. L.I. June 1867. QC 1881. Bencher 1884. Equity draftsman and conveyancer; examr. in civil law, Camb. Univ. 1869-70; member of bar committee 1883; Chancery judge 1890-99; Knight 1890; LJ 1899-1906; PC 1899; Chmn. Royal Comm. on management of military hospitals in South African War 1900; GCB 1901; FRS 1899. d. 19th March 1918.

ROMILLY, John (Lord Romilly)

s. of Sir Samuel Romilly MP, KC (d. 1818). b. 10th Jan. 1802. educ. Trinity Coll. Camb. BA 1823, MA 1826. G.I. June 1827. QC 1843. Bencher 1843, Treasurer 1846. MP Bridport 1832-34 and 1846-47, Devonport 1847-52; Recorder of Ludlow 1836-38; Sol-Genl. 1848; Knight 1848; Att-Genl. 1850-51; carried Encumbered Estates Act through H of C 1849; obtained setting-up of comm. for chancery reform 1852; MR 1851-73, (the last to sit in H of C); PC 1851; promoted preparation and publication of calendars of the Public Records 1856, with free access, (started by his predecessor, Langdale); Baron Romilly of Barry 1866; arbitrator in connection with European Assce. Co. 1872. Brother of Charles Romilly (I.T. 1836), clerk to the Crown in Chancery; father of William Romilly, 2nd Baron (G.I. 1864), clerk of enrolments in Chancery, Edward Romilly (G.I. 1864), Master of Supreme Ct., and Arthur Romilly (G.I. 1871). d. 23rd Dec. 1874.

RONAN, Stephen

s. of Walter Ronan, Cork, solicitor. b. 1848. educ. Queen's Coll. Cork; Queen's Univ. MA. Irish bar 1870. Junior crown pros. for Kerry 1873; counsel to Att-Genl. 1883. I.T. Nov. 1888. Employed on Parnell Comm. as junior counsel for The Times 1888. QC (Ireland) 1889. Bencher, King's Inns 1892. Senior crown pros. Cork City and cty. 1891; Queen's Adv-Genl. for Ireland 1892; KC (England) 1909; LJ of Appeal and PC (Ireland) 1915-24. d. 3rd Oct. 1925.

ROOTH, Henry Goodwin

s. of Goodwin Rooth, Monyash, Derbyshire, West India merchant. b. 25th Feb. 1861. educ. Harrow; Trinity Coll. Camb. BA 1884. I.T. May 1887. Junior Treasury counsel at London Sess. 1916; metrop. magistrate 1917, finally at Lambeth 1922-28; JP London and Home Counties. d. 12th Oct. 1928.

ROSE, Geoffrey Keith

s. of Thomas Harry Rose JP, Oxford. b. 27th Oct. 1889. educ. Dragon Sch. Oxf; Harrow; King's Coll. Camb. BA 1911, LLB 1911, MA 1918. I.T. Nov. 1913 (Cert. of Hon.); L.I. 1940. WWI Major, Oxford and Buckinghamshire L.I., MC and bar (despatches twice). Recorder of Ludlow 1932-34; metrop. magistrate 1934, finally at Lambeth to 1959; JP Essex. Author of History of 2/4th Oxford and Buckinghamshire L.I. 1920. d. 1st June 1959.

ROSE, Sir George

s. of James Rose, London, lighterman. b. 1st May 1782. educ. Westminster; Trinity Coll. Camb. Hon. MA 1835. I.T. May 1809. KC 1827. Bencher 1827, Reader 1834, Treasurer 1835. Judge of Ct. of Review 1831-40; Knight 1831; Master in Chancery 1840-58; first Chmn. of Law Life Inse. Socy. 1844; FRS 1834; Fellow of Geographical Socy; reported cases in bankruptcy 1810-16. d. 3rd Dec. 1873.

ROSE, John

s. of John Randolph Rose, Stoke-upon-Trent. b. 17th June 1841. G.I. June 1868. Bencher 1885, Treasurer 1893. Recorder of Hanley 1890-91; metrop. magistrate 1891, finally at Tower Bridge 1905-12; JP London and Home Counties. d. 5th Feb. 1926.

ROSE-INNES, Sir Patrick

s. of George Rose-Innes, DL, JP, Blachrie, Co. Aberdeen, solicitor (d. 1895). b. 26th Aug. 1853. educ. Aberdeen Univ. L.I. Jan. 1878. KC 1912. Bencher 1915. Equity draftsman and conveyancer; Recorder of Sandwich and Ramsgate 1905-20; Commr. of Assize, South East circuit 1914-15; Cty. Ct. judge 1920-22; Major, West London Rifles; Knight 1918; JP Aberdeen, Kent, Middlesex. Brother of George Rose-Innes, solicitor and alderman of London, Hugh Rose- Innes, solicitor and Cosmo Rose-Innes, barrister. d. 2nd Oct. 1924.

ROSKILL, John Henry

s. of Gustavus Roskill, Manchester. b. 1860. educ. Owen's Coll. Manchester BSc; Corpus Christi Coll. Oxf. BA 1883, MA 1886. I.T. Jan. 1888. KC 1903. Recorder of Burnley 1907-09; judge of Salford Hundred Ct. of Record 1909-37; JP Hampshire. Father of Roskill LJ (b. 1911) and Sir Ashton Wentworth Roskill (QC 1949). d. 19th Aug. 1940.

ROSS, George Edward Aubert

s. of Alexander Ross, Judge of High Ct., Allahabad, North West Provinces. b. Dehra Doon, 22nd March 1847. educ. Wimbledon Sch.; Rugby. M.T. Nov. 1871. KC 1912. Practised in Allahabad from 1872; public pros. there 1885-90; practised before Judicial Committee of Privy Council 1891-1916. d. 18th March 1931.

ROSS-BROWN, James William

s. of James Brown, Isle of Man, newspaper proprietor. b. 29th Sept. 1856. educ. King William's Coll. Isle of Man. Member of parliamentary staff of Daily Telegraph. G.I. April 1888; M.T. Aug. 1904. KC 1920. Bencher (G.I.) 1924. Member Cheshire CC. d. 27th July 1938.

ROTTON, Sir John Francis

s. of Richard Rotton, London. b. 1837. educ. London Univ. MA 1859, LLB 1858. L.I. June 1860 (Cert. of Hon.). QC 1891. Legal asst. Medical Dept., Local Govt. Bd. 1869-76; Asst. Secy. 1876-83; Legal Adviser 1883-98; Vice-Pres. Senate, Univ. Coll. London 1878 and 1882; Knight 1899. d. 9th April 1926.

ROUPELL, Robert Prioleau

s. of George Boone Roupell, Chartham Park, Sussex, barrister. b. 1798. educ. in Greenwich; Trinity Coll. Camb. BA 1821, MA 1828. L.I. June 1822. QC 1842. Bencher 1842, Treasurer 1863. MRI. Brother of John Stuart Roupell LLD (M.T. 1834) and Charles Morris Roupell (L.I. 1842). d. 16th Dec. 1886.

ROWCLIFFE, Henry

s. of Charles Rowcliffe JP, Milverton, Somerset (d. 1874). b. 4th Dec. 1828. educ. Blundell's; St. John's Coll. Oxf. BA 1851, MA 1854. I.T. June 1854; L.I. 1855. QC 1874. Equity draftsman and conveyancer. d. 8th July 1876.

ROWDEN, Aldred William

s. of Rev. George Croke Rowden, DCL, Mortlake, Surrey (d. 1863). b. 1849. educ. Rugby; Balliol Coll. Oxf. 1868. L.I. June 1874. QC 1899. Bencher 1906. JP Surrey. d. 12th Feb. 1919.

ROWE, Sir Michael Edward

s. of John Tetley Rowe, archdeacon of Rochester (d. 1915). b. 24th Dec. 1901. educ. Marlborough; Trinity Coll. Camb. BA and LLB 1923, MA. G.I. May 1925. KC 1945. Bencher 1945, Treasurer 1961. WWII Staff Capt. Queen's Royal Regt. Dep. Secy. War Damage Comm. 1943-45; member of General Claims Trib. 1946; member Committee on Inland Waterways 1956; Dep. Chmn. Local Govt. Comm. for England 1958-65; Pres. Lands Tribunal 1965-73; hon. member RICS Council 1949-60; director Mid-Kent Water Co.; CBE 1946; Knight 1963; edited Ryde on Rating. d. 22nd Dec. 1978.

ROWE, Sir William Carpenter

s. of Coryndon Rowe MD, Launceston, Cornwall. bapt. 28th July 1801. educ. Winchester; Balliol Coll. Oxf. BA 1823, MA 1827; Fellow of Queen's Coll. 1827-38. I.T. Feb. 1830. QC 1850. Special pleader. Recorder of Plymouth 1837-56; CJ Ceylon 1856-59; Knight 1856. Author of works on election law. d. Ceylon, 9th Nov. 1859.

ROWLANDS, Horace John

s. of Joseph Rowlands, Birmingham, solicitor. b. 3rd June 1869. educ. Malvern; Exeter Coll. Oxf. BA 1893, MA; half-blue for athletics. I.T. May 1895. Cty. Ct. judge 1928-44; Chmn. Norfolk Quarter Sess. d. 6th Feb. 1954.

ROWLANDS, Rowland

s. of Moses Rowlands, Porthcawl, Glamorgan, mining engineer. b. 26th Jan. 1869. educ. Cardiff Coll.; St. John's Coll. Camb. LLB 1889. I.T. June 1892. Equity draftsman and conveyancer; Cty. Ct. judge 1918-35. d. 17th Jan. 1935.

ROWLANDS, William Bowen

s. of Thomas Rowlands JP, Glenover, Pembrokeshire. b. 1836. educ. Jesus Coll. Oxf. BA 1859, MA 1865. Headmaster of Gr. Sch. Haverford West 1864; curate of Narbeth, Pembrokeshire 1864. G.I. Jan. 1871 (Cert. of Hon.). QC 1882. Bencher 1882, Treasurer 1889. Leader of South Wales and Chester circuit; MP Cardiganshire 1886-95; Recorder of Swansea 1894; member Council of Legal Educ.; Cty. Ct. judge 1900-06; Master of G.I. Library 1898; DL Cardigan; JP Pembrokeshire, Cardiganshire, Cheshire, Haverford West. Father of Ernest Brown Bowen-Rowlands (G.I. 1889). d. 4th Sept. 1906.

ROWLATT, Sir Sydney Arthur Taylor

s. of Arthur Henry Rowlatt, manager, Bank of Egypt, Alexandria. b. Cairo, 20th July 1862. educ. Fettes; King's Coll. Camb. BA 1884, MA 1888, Fellow 1886-92. I.T. Nov. 1886. Bencher 1908. Junior counsel to IR 1900-05, and to Treasury 1905-12; Recorder of Windsor 1904-12; member of bar council; an expert in revenue cases; KB judge 1912-32; Knight 1912; Chmn. Indian Sedition Committee 1917; KCSI 1918; Chmn. Royal Comm. on Lotteries and Betting 1932; PC 1932; Chmn. General Claims Trib. 1939-45. Brother of John Friend Rowlatt (solicitor 1895); father of Sir John Rowlatt KCB (QC 1954). d. 1st March 1945.

ROXBURGH, Francis

s. of Sir Francis Roxburgh, Cty. Ct. judge. b. 17th July 1850. educ. Harrow; Trinity Hall Camb. BA 1873, LLM 1876. M.T. June 1873. Asst. judge in Mayor's Ct. 1887-1900. Author of Marriage, its Legal Effect on Property 1879, and of works on bankruptcy. d. 19th July 1935.

ROXBURGH, Sir Francis

s. of Francis O. Roxburgh, Haddington, East Lothian. b. 1820. educ. privately. M.T. Nov. 1845; L.I. March 1851. QC 1866. Bencher (M.T.) 1867, Reader 1874, Treasurer 1882. Recorder of Aldeburgh 1878-85; Cty. Ct. judge 1881-91; Knight 1882; JP Suffolk. d. 19th March 1891.

ROXBURGH, Sir Ronald Francis

s. of Francis Roxburgh, assistant judge in Mayor's Ct. b. 19th Nov. 1889. educ. Harrow; Trinity Coll. Camb. BA 1911, Whewell scholar 1912. M.T. June 1914; L.I. 1924. KC 1933. Bencher 1937, Treasurer 1957. Chancery judge 1946-60; Knight 1946. Author of Prisoners of War Information Bureau in London 1915, International Conventions and Third States 1917, The Origins of Lincoln's Inn 1963; edited Oppenheim's International Law. d. 19th Aug. 1981.

RUEGG, Alfred Henry

s. of Edward James Ruegg, Castle Bank, Stroud, Gloucestershire, insurance broker (d. 1889). b. 27th Nov. 1853. educ. privately. M.T. June 1877. QC 1895. Bencher 1903, Reader 1914, Treasurer 1924. Examr. for Council of Legal Educ.; counsel for F.H. O'Donnell MP in 1888 in libel action against The Times, from which arose the Parnell Comm.; Cty. Ct. judge 1907-39; JP Staffordshire; editor of Cty. Ct. Annual Practice. Author of works on employer's liability, factories and workshops. d. 22nd April 1941.

RUSSELL, Arthur Joseph

s. of Lord Russell of Killowen. b. 19th Feb. 1861. educ. Beaumont Coll. Old Windsor; Oriel Coll. Oxf. BA 1886, MA. I.T. Nov. 1886. Secy. to father 1894-1900; editor of Times Law Reports 1890-1900; Cty. Ct. judge 1900-07. d. 22nd Nov. 1907.

RUSSELL, Charles Alfred

s. of John Archibald Russell QC. b. 1855. educ. Univ. Coll. Sch.; University Coll. London LLB. G.I. July 1878. QC 1896. Bencher 1894. d. 21st June 1926.

RUSSELL, Charles Arthur (Lord Russell)

s. of Arthur Russell, Newry, co. Down (d. 1845). b. 10th Nov. 1832. educ. in Newry; St. Vincent's Coll. Castleknock. Solicitor 1854, practised in Belfast; Trinity Coll. Dublin 1856. L.I. Jan. 1859. QC 1872. Bencher 1872, Treasurer 1893. MP Dundalk 1880-85, South Hackney 1885-94; Att-Genl. 1886; vigorous advocate of Home rule;

Knight 1886; defended C.S. Parnell before the commrs. 1888; defended Mrs. Maybrick on charge of poisoning husband (death sentence commuted) 1889; Att-Genl. 1892-94; counsel with Sir R. Webster for GB in Behring Sea Arbitration 1893; GCMG 1893; PC 1894; L of A 1894; Baron Russell of Killowen 1894; LCJ 1894-1900; presided at trial of Jameson Raiders 1896; LLD Dublin 1894, Laval Univ. Canada 1896, Edin. and Camb. 1897. d. 10th Aug. 1900. Biog. by R.B. O'Brien 1901.

RUSSELL, Francis Xavier Joseph (Lord Russell)

s. of Lord Russell of Killowen. b. 2nd July 1867. educ. Beaumont Coll.; Oriel Coll. Oxf. BA 1890, Hon. Fellow 1928. L.I. April 1893. KC 1908. Bencher 1913. Equity draftsman and conveyancer; member of bar council; Chancery judge 1919-28; declined knighthood; LJ 1928-29; PC 1928; Pres. Thomas More Socy. 1928-46; L of A 1929-46; Baron Russell of Killowen 1929; "No judge in recent times had in a higher degree the art of saying in terse and clear language just what he meant and no more". Brother of Sir Charles Russell, Bt. (1863-1928), solicitor, and father of Charles Ritchie Russell (1908-86), L of A. d. 20th Dec. 1946.

RUSSELL, Sir George, Bt.

s. of Sir Henry Russell, 2nd Bt. b. 23rd Aug. 1828. educ. Eton; Exeter Coll. Oxf. BA 1850, MA 1853. L.I. Nov. 1853. Recorder of Wokingham 1860-98; Cty. Ct. judge 1866-84; MP Berkshire (East) 1885-98; Alderman, Berkshire CC 1889-98; Chmn. South Eastern Ry. Co. 1895-98; DL Berkshire; succeeded brother as 4th baronet 1883. d. 7th March 1898.

RUSSELL, George Lake

s. of Sir Henry Russell, Bt. CJ Bengal (d. 1836). b. 19th June 1802. educ. Eton; Christ's Coll. Camb. BA 1823, MA 1826. L.I. Nov. 1826. Equity draftsman and conveyancer; Cty. Ct. judge 1865-78. d. 16th Nov. 1878.

RUSSELL, James

s. of James Russell, Stirling. b. 1790. educ. Glasgow Univ. BA. I.T. June 1822. QC 1841. Reporter in cts. of LC and MR 1823-34; reported Chancery cases 1826-29, (with G. Turner) 1822-24, (with J. Mylne) 1829-32; edited Annual Register for many years with his brother, John Russell. Father of Robert Bruce Russell (I.T. 1871), examiner to High Ct. d. 6th Jan. 1861.

RUSSELL, John Archibald

s. of James Russell, Rutherlglen, nr. Glasgow. b. 25th Nov. 1816. educ. Glasgow Gr. Sch.; Glasgow Univ. BA 1835, Hon. LLB 1851. G.I. Nov. 1841. QC 1868. Bencher 1868, Treasurer 1874. Examr. to Inns of Ct.; prof. of English law, Univ. Coll. London 1850-69; Sol-Genl. Cty. Palatine of Durham 1862-69; Recorder of Bolton 1865-69; Cty. Ct. judge 1869-90; life govr. Univ. Coll. London; JP Lancashire. Author of treatises on factors, brokers, and mercantile agency; edited Chitty's Law of Contract, and Law of Bills of Exchange. d. 18th Nov. 1899.

RUTLEDGE, Sir John Guy

s. of Henry Rutledge, Aughnahoo, Co. Tyrone. b. 18th March 1872. educ. Queen's Coll. Galway; Royal Univ. Dublin MA 1894. I.T. June 1897. KC 1921. Practised in Liverpool until 1908; Secy. to Burma Leglislative Council 1908; Govt. Advocate Burma 1908; acting judge of Chief Ct. Lower Burma 1919 and 1921-22; judge of High Ct. 1922; CJ Rangoon 1925-30; Knight 1926; Fellow, Rangoon Univ. d. 15th Feb. 1930.

RYDE, Walter Cranley

s. of Edward Ryde, Woking, Surrey, land surveyor. b. 25th Oct 1856. educ. Westminster; Christ Church Oxf. BA 1883, MA 1888. I.T. Jan. 1882. KC 1910. Author of Law and Practice of Rating 1900, and other works. Brother of Edward Harrow Ryde (solicitor 1876). d. 27th April 1938.

SACHS, Sir Eric Leopold Otho

s. of Edwin Otho Sachs FRS (Edin.), architect (d. 1919). b. 23rd July 1898. educ. Charterhouse; Christ Church Oxf. BA 1921, MA 1927, hon. student 1971. WWI Lieut. RA. I.T. and M.T. Jan. 1921. KC 1938. Bencher (M.T.) 1947, Treasurer 1967. Recorder of Dudley 1938-43, of Stoke-on-Trent 1943-54; leader of Oxford circuit. WWII re-employed in War Office; MBE 1941; Lt. Col. AAG; Brig. Political Warfare Dept, TD. Member of bar council 1946-53; Gresham lecturer on law 1946; Commr. of Assize, Western circuit 1946; Commr. to inquire into allegations of corruption in Gold Coast 1946; instrumental in drafting scheme of Legal Aid and Advice Act 1949; P D and A judge 1954-60; Knight 1954; QB judge 1960-66; LJ 1966-73; PC 1966. d. 1st Sept. 1979.

SALMON, Cyril Barnet (Lord Salmon)

s. of Montagu Salmon, London. b. 28th Dec. 1903. educ. Mill Hill; Pembroke Coll. Camb. BA 1925, Hon. Fellow 1965; Hon. LLD 1982. M.T. Nov. 1925. KC 1945. Bencher 1953, Treasurer 1972. WWII commissioned in RA; 8th Army HQ staff. Recorder of Gravesend 1947-57; Commr. of Assize, Wales and Chester circuit 1955; QB judge 1957-64; Knight 1957; LJ 1964-72; PC 1964; Chmn. 1966, Royal Comm. on the Working of the Tribunals of Inquiry (Evidence) Act 1921; L of A 1972-80; Baron 1972; Chmn. Royal Comm. on standards of Conduct in Public Life 1974; Commissary of Camb. Univ. 1979; Captain, Royal St. George's, Sandwich 1972; JP Kent; Hon. DCL Kent 1978; govr. of Mill Hill. d. 7th Nov. 1991.

SALTER, Sir Arthur Clavell

s. of Henry Hyde Salter MD, FRS, Harley St., London W. (d. 1871). b. 30th Oct. 1859. educ. Wimborne Gr. Sch.; King's Coll. London MA, LLB. M.T. Jan. 1885. KC 1904. Bencher 1913, Reader 1925. Recorder of Poole 1904-17; MP North Hampshire 1906-17; KB judge 1917-28; Knight 1917; tried Col. Rutherford (murder) 1919, Horatio Bottomley (fraudulent conversion) 1922; Pres. Ry. and Canal Comm. 1928. d. 30th Nov. 1928.

SALTER, William Talfourd

s. of William Davis Salter, Hammersmith, West London. b. 1827. M.T Jan. 1853. QC 1874. Bencher 1877. Senior pros. counsel to PO on South Eastern circuit; a leader in Mayor's Ct. d. Varese, Italy, 5th Oct 1883.

SAMSON, Sir Edward Marlay

s. of Louis Samson DL, JP, Scotchwell, Pembrokeshire, barrister. b. 27th March 1869. educ. Harrow; Trinity Coll. Oxf. BA 1891, MA 1927. I.T. Nov. 1893. KC 1919. Chan. of diocese of St Davids 1909, Swansea and Brecon 1923-29; Recorder of Swansea 1918-23; Chmn. War Pensions Assoc. 1919-21; Esquire of St. John 1919; stip. magistrate, Swansea 1923-49; Chmn. Pembrokeshire and Haverfordwest West Quarter Sess. 1924-43; KBE 1920; CBE 1918; DL, JP Pembrokeshire; JP Glamorganshire. d. 3rd April 1949.

SAMUEL, Howel Walter

s. of Thomas Samuel, Forestfach, Swansea. b. 1881. educ. elementary sch. M.T. April 1915. KC 1931. MP Swansea (West) 1923-24, and 1929-31; Recorder of Merthyr Tydfil 1930-33; Cty. Ct. judge 1933-53; Chmn. Radnorshire Quarter Sess. d. 5th April 1953.

SAMUELS, Herbert David

s. of M. Samuels, London. b. 1880. L.I. May 1908. KC 1933.
Bencher 1937. Recorder of Bournemouth 1944-45; an Official
Referee of the Supreme Ct. 1945-47. d. 11 th Dec. 1947.

SANDBACH, John Brown

s. of Rev. Francis Butterworth Sandbach. b. 1878. educ. Leys Sch.;
King's Coll. Camb. BA 1901, MA 1905. I.T. June 1902. KC 1925.
Metrop. magistrate 1926, finally at South Western to 1947. Author
of the Law of Motor Cars, and This Old Wig (autobiog). d. 27th
Aug. 1951.

SANDERSON, Sir Lancelot

s. of John Sanderson JP, Ward House, Ellel, Lancashire (d. 1908).
b. 24th Oct. 1863. educ. in Elstree; Harrow; Trinity Coll. Camb. BA
and LLB 1885, MA 1895. I.T. Jan. 1886. KC 1903. Bencher 1912.
Recorder of Wigan 1901-15; MP Westmorland (North) 1910-15;
CJ Calcutta 1915-26; Knight 1926; PC and member judicial
committee 1926; V-C Calcutta Univ. 1918; Chmn. Westmorland
Quarter Sess. 1926, Lancashire Quarter Sess. 1927; JP Westmorland
and Lancashire. d. 9th March 1944.

SANDLANDS, Paul Ernest

s. of Rev. John Poole Sandlands, Brigstock, Northamptonshire. b.
25th May 1878. educ. privately; Trinity Coll. Camb. BA 1899.
Served in South African War with City Imp. Volunteers Mounted
Infantry; orderly to Lord Roberts. I.T. Nov. 1900. KC 1935. Bencher
1928, Treasurer 1950. Cdr. in Birmingham Special Constabulary
1916-19; OBE 1920. Recorder of Newark 1915-32, of Leicester
1932-44, of Birmingham 1944-54; Capt. Home Guard 1942-44;
Chmn. Medical Appeal Trib. Midlands Region 1948-57, under Nat.

Insce. (Industrial Injuries Act) 1946; Chmn. Workmen's Compensation (Supplementation) Bd. 1951, Pneumoconiosis and Byssinosis Benefit Bd. 1952-56; Chmn. Newark and Retford Quarter Sess. to 1954; Chmn. Derbyshire Quarter Sess. 1947-54; DL, JP Nottinghamshire. d. 8th March 1962.

SANKEY, John (Lord Sankey)

s. of Thomas Sankey, Moreton-in-March, Gloucestershire, draper. b. 26th Oct. 1866. educ. Lancing; Jesus Coll. Oxf. BA 1889, BCL 1891, MA 1909, Hon. Fellow, Hon. DCL 1930, High Steward. M.T. June 1892. KC 1909. Bencher 1914, Reader 1925. Chanc. of diocese of Llandaff 1909-14; KB judge 1914-28; Knight 1914; Chmn. Enemy Aliens Advisory Committee 1915; GBE 1917; Chmn. Coal Industry Comm. 1919; LJ 1928-29; PC 1928; LC 1929-35; Baron 1929; Viscount 1932; member Permanent Ct. of Arbitration, The Hague 1930; Chmn. Federal Indian Structure Committee (Round Table Confce.) 1930; hon. freeman Cardiff, KStJ; Hon. LLD Wales, Camb., Bristol. d. 6th Feb. 1948.

SARGANT, Sir Charles Henry

s. of Henry Sargant, barrister (d. 1880). b. 20th April 1856. educ. Rugby (captain); New Coll. Oxf. BA 1879, MA 1882, Hon. Fellow 1919. Employed with London solicitors. L.I. May 1882. Bencher 1908. Equity draftsman and conveyancer; junior equity counsel to Treasury 1908-13; Chancery judge 1913-23; Knight 1913; Chmn. Royal Comm. on awards to inventors 1919-23; Chmn. Bd. of Trade Committee on patent law and practice; LJ 1923-28; PC 1923. d. 23rd July 1942.

SARGOOD, Augustine

s. of Timms Kight Sargood, Greenwich. b. 1815. G.I. Nov. 1846. Serjeant 1868; patent of precedence 1872. d. Frankfurt, 14th Sept. 1880.

SAUNDERS, Charles

s. of William Saunders, Southampton. b. 1801. L.I. Nov. 1829.
Recorder of Devonport 1855-72, of Plymouth 1856-72, of Wells
1856-72; Cty. Ct. judge 1856-62. d. 8th April 1872.

SAUNDERS, Herbert Clifford

s. of Charles Alexander Saunders, Kensington, Secy. to Great
Western Ry. Co. b. 14th July 1834. educ. Charterhouse; Christ
Church Oxf. BA 1856, MA 1860. L.I. April 1859. QC 1881. M.T.
June 1871. Bencher 1884, Reader 1893. Chmn. executive
committee, City and Guilds of London Inst. 1887-93. d. 25th Aug.
1893.

SAUNDERS, Thomas William

s. of Samuel E. Saunders, Bath. b. 21st Feb. 1814. M.T. June 1837.
Recorder of Dartmouth 1855-60, of Bath 1860-78; Commr. for
hearing mun. election petitions 1872-78; metrop. magistrate,
Thames 1878-90. Author of works on assault and battery, affiliation
and bastardy, practice of magistrates' courts; reported (with R.G.
Walford) cases on real property 1846; edited Oke's Magisterial
Formulist. Father of William Edgar Saunders (M.T. 1879). d. 28th
Feb. 1890.

SCANLAN, Thomas

s. of Mathew Scanlan, Drumscliff, Co. Sligo. b. 1873. educ. Catholic
Coll. Sligo; St. Andrew's Univ. G.I. Jan. 1912. MP North Sligo
1909-18; metrop. magistrate, South Western 1924-27. d. 9th Jan.
1930.

SCHILLER, Ferdinand Philip Maximilian

s. of Frederick Schiller, Calcutta. b. 28th July 1868. educ. Clifton Coll.; Magdalen Coll. Oxf. BA 1890, MA 1909. I.T. April 1893. KC 1913. Bencher 1922, Treasurer 1942. Recorder of Southampton 1928-35, of Bristol 1935-46; Chmn. Joint Conciliation Bd., South West Coal Trade 1931. d. 19th Jan. 1946.

SCHOLEFIELD, Sir Joshua

s. of John Scholefield, Hemsworth, Yorkshire, solicitor. b. 1865. educ. privately. Solicitor 1887. M.T. June 1900 (Cert. of Hon.). KC 1922. Bencher 1929, Treasurer 1945. Recorder of Middlesbrough 1929-47; Chmn. Railway Assess. Authority 1930-50; Pres. London Passenger Transport Arbitration Trib. 1933-36; Knight 1937; JP Surrey. Joint author or editor of many publications on public health and rating, in particular Lumley's Public Health Acts; edited Encyclopaedia of Local Government Law. d. 11th March 1950.

SCHOMBERG, Joseph Trigge

s. of Isaac Schomberg, Capt. RN (d. 1813). b. 14th Aug. 1805. educ. Winchester. I.T. Feb. 1828. L.I. 1864. QC 1866. Bencher 1875. Commr. in Bankruptcy, Salisbury; Recorder of Aldborough 1845-78; annotated the Act for the commutation of tithes in England and Wales 1836. Father of Reginald Broderick Schomberg (L.I. 1875). d. 28th July 1878.

SCHUSTER, Claud (Lord Schuster)

s. of Frederick Leo Schuster, Manchester, merchant. b. 22nd Aug. 1869. educ. Winchester, New Coll. Oxf. BA 1892, MA 1909. I.T. Jan. 1895. KC 1919. Bencher 1924. Legal asst. Bd. of Educ. 1903-07, prin. asst secy. 1911; Secy. London Govt. Act Comm. 1899-1902; Chief Registrar of Friendly Societies 1911-12; Secy. Nat.

Health Insce. Comm. 1912-13, member 1913-15; Clerk of Crown in Chancery, and perm. secy. LC's Office 1915-44; head legal branch, Allied Control Comm. (Br. Zone) in Austria 1944-46; Pres. Ski Club, and Alpine Club; Knight 1913; CVO 1918; KCB 1920; GCB 1927; Baron 1944; Order of Crown of Belgium; JP London and Dorset; Hon. Fellow, St. Catherine's Coll. Camb. d. 28th June 1956.

SCHUSTER, Ernest Joseph

s. of Francis Joseph Schuster, Harrington Gdns., South Kensington (d. 1906). b. 7th July 1850. educ. Frankfurt; Geneva; LLD Munich. Partner in firm of Schuster, Son and Co., merchants and bankers, London 1873-88. L.I. June 1890. KC 1922. Equity draftsman and conveyancer; member Executive of Socy. of Comparative Legislation; member of Council of Intern. Law Assoc.; lecturer at Inst. of Bankers and School of Economics and Political Science. Author of Principles of German Civil Law, The Effect of War on Commercial Transactions, The Wife in Ancient and Modern Times. Father of Sir George Ernest Schuster KCSI, KCMG (L.I. 1905). d. 16th Dec. 1924.

SCHWABE, Sir Walter George Salis

s. of Maj-Genl. George Salis Schwabe CB (d. 1907). b. 3rd March 1872. educ. Marlborough; Trinity Coll. Oxf. BA. I.T. Jan. 1897. KC 1913. WWI Capt. 19th Battn. City of London Vol. Regt. CJ High Ct. Madras 1921-24; Knight 1922. Joint author of Schwabe and Branson's Law of the Stock Exchange. d. 21st April 1931.

SCOBLE, Sir Andrew Richard

s. of John Scoble, Toronto, member of Provincial Parliament of Canada, and Kingsbridge, Devon. b. 25th Sept. 1831. educ. City of London Sch. L.I. Jan. 1856. Adv-Genl. and member Legislative

Council, Bombay 1872-77. QC 1876. Bencher 1879, Treasurer 1899. Member Council of Gov-Genl. of India 1886-91; MP Hackney Central 1892-1900; KCSI 1890; PC and member Judicial Committee 1901. d. 17th Jan. 1916.

SCOTT, Charles Clare

s. of John Scott, Insp-Genl. of hospitals IMS, Bombay (d. 1859). b. 2nd Sept. 1850. educ. Rugby; King's Coll. London. M.T. June 1874. KC 1910. Bencher 1898, Reader 1910, Treasurer 1920. d. 4th May 1925.

SCOTT, Charles Paley

s. of Henry Venn Scott, York, solicitor. b. 17th June 1881. educ. St. Peter's Sch. York; King's Coll. Camb. BA 1903, MA 1946. I.T. Nov. 1906. KC 1933. Bencher 1930. WWI 2nd Lieut. RGA. Member of bar council 1930; Recorder of Doncaster 1923-33, of Kingston-upon-Hull 1933-43, of Leeds 1943-50; Chan. of Cty. Palatine of Durham 1936-50, Bradford 1946-50. Father of Henry Cooper Scott (QC 1961). d. 30th Jan. 1950.

SCOTT, Harold Claughton

s. of Canon Thomas Scott, Lavenham, Suffolk. b. 10th Nov. 1873. educ. King's Sch. Canterbury; King's Coll. London; Caius Coll. Camb. BA 1895. L.I. Jan. 1900. KC 1923. Legal representative of GB at Geneva 1928; specialist in commercial and marine insurance cases. d. 30th Dec. 1928.

SCOTT, Sir Leslie Frederic

s. of Sir John Scott KCMG, DCL, judicial adviser to the Khedive (d. 1904). b. 29th Oct. 1869. educ. Rugby; New Coll. Oxf. BA 1892,

MA 1895, Hon. Fellow 1939. I.T. June 1894. KC 1909. Bencher. Practised in Liverpool until 1906; represented GB at Intern. Confce. on maritime law, Brussels 1909, 1910, 1922 and 1923; MP Liverpool (Exchange) 1910-29; member committee to inquire into Employment and Land Settlement, for Disabled Soldiers and Sailors in WWI; member Reconstruction Committee 1917; Sol-Genl. and knighted 1922; Chmn. Land Acquisition Committee (leading to Law of Property Act 1922); PC 1927; Chmn. Ministers' powers committee 1931; LJ 1935-48; Chmn. Land Utilisation Committee 1941. Author of The Effect of War on Contracts 1914, The New Law of Property Acts explained (with B. Benas) 1925. d. 19th May 1950.

SCOTT, William Carmalt

s. of Henry Dundas Scott, London. b. 22nd Dec. 1824. M.T. Jan. 1848. Prin. secy. to Chelmsford LC 1858-59, and 1866-69; Gentleman of the Chamber to Cranworth LC 1865-66; Cty. Ct judge 1866-74. d. 3rd March 1874.

SCRIMGEOUR, John Stuart

s. of William Douglas Scrimgeour, Dundee, collector of rates (d. 1935). b. 3rd Feb. 1887. educ. Harris Acad. Dundee; Univ. Coll. Dundee; Edin. Univ. BA. Practised at Canadian bar 1911-16; with Min. of Munitions, and Disposal and Liquidation Comm. 1917-22. M.T. May 1922. KC 1945. OBE 1924; JP Berkshire. d. 30th Aug. 1950.

SCRUTTON, Sir Thomas Edward

s. of Thomas Urquhart Scrutton, Buckhurst Hill, Essex, shipowner. b. 28th Aug. 1856. educ. Mill Hill; Trinity Coll. Camb. BA 1880, four times Yorke prizeman, Hon. LLD. University Coll. London BA 1875, MA 1878, LLB 1881, Fellow. M.T. June 1882. KC 1901.

Bencher 1908. Prof. of constitutional law and history Univ. Coll. London; had extensive practice in commercial Ct. and in copyright business; particular rival of J.A. Hamilton; KB judge 1910-16; Knight 1910; tried George Joseph Smith (brides in bath murders) 1915; LJ 1916-34; PC 1916; engaged in unfortunate dispute with McCardie J, which had to be resolved by intervention of Lord Hanworth MR. Author of works on the law of copyright 1883, Charterparties and Bills of Lading 1886, Mercantile Law 1891, and manual on Merchant Shipping Act 1894. d. 18th Aug. 1934.

SCULLY, James Aloysius

s. of James Scully, Dublin and Tipperary. b. 13th Feb. 1856. educ. Stonyhurst; London Univ. BA. M.T. Jan. 1879. Equity draftsman and conveyancer; Reader and examr.to Inns of Ct. 1898-1903; Cty. Ct. judge 1903-28. d. 5th Feb. 1929.

SECKER, Isaac Onslow

s. of John Secker, New Windsor, Secy. to George III. b. 1799. educ. Eton; St. John's Coll. Camb. BA 1821, MA 1824. L.I. May 1824. Metrop. magistrate 1846, finally at Marylebone 1860-61. d. 21st Feb. 1861.

SEGAR, Robert

s. of William Segar, Kirkham, Lancashire, merchant. M.T. June 1825. Recorder of Wigan 1836-62; QC Cty. Palatine of Lancaster; Judge of Lancaster Insolvent Ct; judge of Salford Ct. of Record 1857; Cty. Ct. judge 1859-62. Father of George Xavier Segar (I.T. 1862), Recorder of Oldham. d. 11 th May 1862, age 61.

SELFE, Henry James Selfe

s. of Rev. James Page, Rose Hill, nr. Worcester. b. 15th Nov. 1810. educ. Glasgow Univ. Assumed name of Selfe 1832. L.I. June 1834. Recorder of Newbury 1842-56; metrop. magistrate 1856, finally at Westminster 1863-70. d. 6th Sept. 1870.

SELFE, Sir William Lucius

s. of Henry James Selfe Selfe, metrop. magistrate. b. 11 th June 1845. educ. Rugby; Corpus Christi Coll. Oxf. BA 1868. I.T. June 1870. Equity draftsman and conveyancer; engaged in drafting, indexing and revision of statutes; secy. to Cairns LC 1880; Cty. Ct. judge 1882-1919; Chmn. East Kent Quarter Sess. 1893-1905; Knight 1897; JP Kent and Breconshire. d. 19th March 1924.

SELLERS, Sir Frederic Aked

s. of John Shuttleworth Sellers, Liverpool. b. 14th Jan. 1893. educ. Silcoates Sch.; Liverpool Univ. BA, LLB, Hon. LLD 1956. WWI Capt. King's (Liverpool) Regt., MC and two bars. G.I. May 1919. KC 1935. Bencher 1938, Treasurer 1952, Vice-Treasurer 1953. Recorder of Bolton 1938-46; WWII with Home Guard; KB judge 1946-57; Knight 1946; LJ 1957-68; PC 1957; Chmn. Criminal Law Revision Committee 1959-69; Chmn. govrs. of Mill Hill Sch.; member of Bd. Silcoates Sch. and New Coll. London. Father of Norman William Malin Sellers (G.I. 1947), circuit judge. d. 20th March 1979.

SELWYN, Sir Charles Jasper

s. of William Selwyn QC. b. 13th Oct. 1813. educ. in Ealing (Dr. Nicholson); Eton; Trinity Coll. Camb. BA 1836, MA 1839, LLD 1862. L.I. Jan. 1840. QC 1856. Bencher 1856. Practised mainly in Rolls Ct.; Commissary of Camb. Univ. 1855-68; MP Camb. Univ.

1859-68; Sol-Genl. and knighted 1867; LJ 1868-69; PC 1868. d. 11th Aug. 1869.

SELWYN, William,

s. of William Selwyn KC (d. 1817). b. 31st March 1775. educ. Eton; St. John's and Trinity Colls. Camb. BA 1797, MA 1800. L.I. Nov. 1807. KC 1827. Bencher 1827, Treasurer 1839. Recorder of Portsmouth 1819-29; instructed Prince Albert in English law 1840. Author of Abridgement of law of Nisi Prius 1808; reported (with G. Maule) cases in KB 1813-17. d. 25th July 1855.

SEYMOUR, William Digby

s. of Rev. Charles Seymour, Kilronan, Co. Roscommon. b. 22nd Sept 1822. educ. Trinity Coll. Dublin BA 1844, LLD 1872. M.T. June 1846. MP Sunderland 1852-54, Southampton 1859-65; Recorder of Newcastle 1854-95; censured by benchers for conduct in commercial transactions 1859, and excluded from bar mess of Northern circuit. QC Cty. Palatine of Lancaster 1860. QC 1861. Drew up Admiralty Reform Act 1861; Cty. Ct. judge 1889-95. d. 16th March 1895.

SEYMOUR-LLOYD, Sir John Hall

s. of Richard Bowerman Lloyd. b. 1873. M.T. April 1899. KC 1923. Pres. Hardwicke Socy. 1908. WWI Lieut. RASC, temp. Lt. Col. and AAG; Dir-Genl. of recruiting at Min. of Nat. Service 1917-18. Practised at parliamentary bar; member council Inns of Ct. Mission; legal adviser to Independent Peers' Assoc.; CMG 1917; KBE 1918. d. 26th July 1939.

SHADWELL, Sir Lancelot

s. of Lancelot Shadwell, barrister. b. 3rd May 1779. educ. Eton; St John's Coll. Camb. BA 1800, 7th Wrangler, MA 1803, Fellow 1801, LLD 1842. Served in Light Horse Vol. 1797. L.I. Feb. 1803. KC 1821. Bencher 1822, Treasurer 1833. Confined his practice to LC's Ct.; MP Ripon 1826-27; V-C 1827-50; Knight and PC 1827; a commr. of the Great Seal 1835-36 and 1850; the last V-C of England; Pres. Socy. of Psychrolutes. Half-brother of Cayley Shadwell (L.I. 1825); father of Alfred Hudson Shadwell, solicitor, Chancery Taxing Master (d. 1884), Lancelot Shadwell (L.I. 1832), equity draftsman and conveyancer, and Louis Henry Shadwell (L.I. 1847). d. 10th Aug. 1850.

SHAND, Sir Charles Lister

s. of Alexander Shand, Liverpool and Doncaster. b. 2nd Dec. 1846. educ. Harrow; Trinity Coll. Oxf. BA 1868, MA 1871. I.T. June 1870. Cty. Ct. judge 1889-1921; Knight 1922; JP Lancashire. d. 4th April 1925.

SHAPTER, John

s. of Thomas Shapter, Exeter. b. 1806. I.T. Feb. 1830; L.I. 1846. QC 1858. Bencher 1858, Treasurer 1872. d. 24th Nov. 1887.

SHARP, William Henry Cartwright

s. of William George Graham Sharp, Highgate, London. b. 1883. educ. King Edward's Sch. Birmingham; St. John's Coll. Camb. MA, LLB. I.T. April 1907; M.T. 1919. KC 1934. Private, Inns of Ct. OTC 1918-19. Recorder of Banbury 1936-37. d. 20th Dec. 1950.

SHARPE, Joseph

s. of Joseph Sharpe, Bankfield House, Ireleth-in-Furness, Lancashire. b. 1859. educ. Liverpool Coll.; New Coll. Oxf. BA 1883, MA. M.T. May 1886. Commr. for Civil Liability, Lancashire 1916-19; stip. magistrate, West Ham 1922-25; metrop. magistrate, Thames St. 1925-30. d. 5th July 1930.

SHARPE, Sir Montagu

s. of Cdr. Benjamin Sharpe RN, JP, Hanwell Park, Middlesex (d. 1883). b. 28th Oct. 1856. educ. Felsted Sch. G.I. Nov. 1889. KC 1920. Bencher 1909, Treasurer 1920. Chmn. Middlesex CC 1889-1909; Vice-Lieut. 1926; Dep. Chmn. Middlesex Sess. 1896-1909, Chmn. 1909-34; Chmn. Brentford Petty Sess. 1897-1909; Pres. Socy. of Chmn. of Quarter Sess. 1913-30; Hon. Lt. Col. 4th Battn. Middlesex Vol. Regt. 1918; member Middlesex Appeal Trib. under Military Service and Profiteering Acts; member Home Office Advisory Committee on Wild Birds' Protection; Knight 1922; Chmn. Egyptian Delta Railways, and Tendring Hundred Water Co. Author of Antiquities of Middlesex. d. 23rd Aug. 1942.

SHAW, Joseph

s. of Joseph Shaw, Celbridge, Co. Kildare. b. 24th Sept. 1856. educ. Malvern; Trinity Coll. Camb. BA 1879, MA 1904. I.T. Jan. 1887. KC 1910. Parliamentary draftsman; Chmn. Powell Duffryn Steam Coal Co. 1897-1928; director Great Western Ry. Co.; JP Herefordshire. d. 14th Dec. 1933.

SHAW, Thomas (Lord Craigmyle)

s. of Alexander Shaw, Dunfermline, baker (d. 1856). b. 23rd May 1850. educ. Dunfermline High Sch.; Edin. Univ. MA 1874, LLB 1875. Scottish bar 1875. Advocate Depute 1886. MP Hawick 1892-

1909; Sol-Genl. for Scotland 1894-95; QC 1894; Lord Advocate 1905-09; PC 1906; L of A 1909-29; Chmn. Royal Comm. on Dublin Riots 1914; Baron 1929; Hon. LLD St. Andrews, Aberdeen, Edin.; Hon. Bencher (M.T.) 1910; DL Edin. Father of Alexander Shaw, 2nd Baron, MP (I.T. 1908). d. 28th June 1937.

SHAW, William

s. of John Shaw, Morton upon Swale, nr. Northallerton, Yorkshire. b. 1816. G.I. May 1844. QC 1880. Bencher 1880, Treasurer 1884. JP Yorkshire West Riding. d. 21st Dec. 1885.

SHAWCROSS, Hartley William (Lord Shawcross)

s. of John Shawcross, Duddleswell, Sussex (d. 1966). b. 4th Feb. 1902. educ. Dulwich; Geneva Univ. G.I. May 1925 (Cert of Hon.). KC 1939. Bencher 1939, Treasurer 1955. Hon. member of American and New York bars; senior law lecturer, Liverpool Univ. 1927-34; MP St. Helens 1945-58; Att-Genl. 1945-51; Pres. Bd. of Trade 1951; Chmn. Catering Wages Committee 1943-45; regional commr. for civil defence North West 1942-45; UK member Permanent Ct. of Arbitration, The Hague 1950; chief pros. for UK at Intern. Military Trib., Nuremberg; Chmn. Medical Research Council 1961-65; Chmn. Royal Comm. on the Press 1961-62; Chmn. Justice and Intern. Law Section of Br. Inst. of Intern. and Comparative Law; Recorder of Salford 1941-45, of Kingston-upon-Thames 1946-61; Asst. Chmn. East Sussex Quarter Sess. 1941; Chmn. of bar council 1952-57; Chmn. Press Council 1974; Chmn. Thames Television Ltd.; director EMI Ltd., Times Newspapers Ltd., HawkerSiddeley Group Ltd. and other companies; Pro-Chan. Sussex Univ. 1959; Chmn. govrs. of Dulwich Coll.; member Council of Eastbourne Coll.; Knight 1945; PC 1946; CBE 1974; Baron 1959; JP Sussex; Hon. DCL Liverpool; Hon. LLD Columbia, Bristol, Michigan, Lehigh, Sussex, New Brunswick. Brother of Christopher Nyholm Shawcross (KC 1949). "Life Sentence" (memoirs) published 1995.

SHEARMAN, Sir Montague

s. of Montague Shearman, Wimbledon, solicitor (d. 1865). b. 7th April 1857. educ. Merchant Taylors; St. John's Coll. Oxf. BA 1880, MA 1884, Hon. Fellow 1916; Pres. OUAC; rowed and played rugby for the Univ.; amateur champion for 100 yds. 1876, quarter mile 1880. I.T. Jan. 1881. KC 1903. Bencher. KB judge 1914-29; Knight 1914; member committee to inquire into origin and causes of Easter Rebellion in Ireland 1916; presided at murder trials of Harold Greenwood (wife poisoning, acquitted) 1920, Frederick Bywaters and Edith Thompson 1922, and Sinn Feiners who assassinated F-M Sir Henry Wilson 1922; PC 1929; Pres. Amateur Athletic Assoc. 1915, in succession to Lord Alverstone. Father of Montague Shearman OBE (I.T. 1908). d. 6th Jan. 1930.

SHEE, Henry Gordon

s. of Shee J. b. April 1847. educ. Ushaw Coll.; Christ Church Oxf. 1864. I.T. April 1870. QC 1892. Bencher 1899. Recorder of Burnley 1893-1907, of Liverpool 1907-09; judge of Salford Ct. of Record 1893; Commr. of Assize, Welsh circuit. d. 13th Feb. 1909.

SHEE, Martin Archer

s. of Sir Martin Archer Shee PRA. b. 14th Nov. 1804. M.T. April 1839. QC 1868. Practised in chancery. Wrote biography of father 1860. d. 13th Sept. 1898.

SHEE, Sir William

s. of Joseph Shee, Thomas-Town, Kilkenny, a London merchant. b. 24th June 1804. educ. St. Cuthbert's Coll. Durham; Edin. Univ. L.I. June 1828. Leader of Home circuit; Serjeant 1840; patent of precedence 1847. Defended William Palmer, the Rugeley poisoner 1856; Queen's Serjeant 1857; MP Kilkenny 1852-57; declined to be CJ of Madras; QB judge 1863-68; Knight 1864; first Roman Catholic judge since the Revolution; edited Lord Tenterden's treatise on the law relative to merchant ships and seamen, and Samuel Marshall's Law of Insurance. Author of Reflections on the trial of the Prince of Polignac before the Chamber of Peers of France 1830. His papers, letters, and speeches privately printed 1862-63. Father of George Darell Shee (M.T. 1867), Recorder of Hythe. d. 19th Feb. 1868.

SHEIL, James

s. of James Sheil QC (Ireland). b. 2nd July 1829. educ. Trinity Coll. Dublin BA 1848. G.I. June 1852. Bencher 1884, Treasurer 1890. Metrop. magistrate 1879, finally at Westminster 1890-1904; JP Middlesex and Home Counties. d. 12th Dec. 1908.

SHELLEY, Kew Edwin

s. of Kamel Krishna Shelley Bonnerjee, Calcutta, barrister. b. 10th Nov. 1894. educ. Rugby; New Coll. Oxf. 1914. WWI Capt. 2/6 Battn. Royal Sussex Regt., and with RFC and RAF (Flying Officer). M.T. Jan. 1921. KC 1937. Changed surname to Shelley 1920. Commissioned in ATC 1941. Joint author of Terrell and Shelley on Law of Patents. d. 1st May 1964.

SHEPHERD, Henry John

s. of Sir Samuel Shepherd LCB (Scotland) (d. 1840). educ. Eton; Trinity Coll. Camb. BA 1807, MA 1823. L.I. Feb. 1809. KC 1834. Bencher 1838. Counsel to Admiralty 1828-45; Recorder of Abingdon 1833-52; Commr. in Bankruptcy, Basinghall St. 1845-50. Author of the Law relative to election of MPs. 1830. d. 21st May 1855, age 71.

SHIELD, Hugh

s. of John Shield, Stotes Hall, Jesmond, Newcastle. b. 12th Oct. 1831. educ. Grange Sch. Bishopwearmouth; King Edward's Sch. Birmingham; Jesus Coll. Camb. BA 1854, MA 1857, Fellow. G.I. Jan. 1860 (Cert. of Hon.). QC 1881. Bencher 1880. MP Cambridge 1880-85; Senior Bursar of Jesus Coll. d. 24th Nov. 1903.

SHORTT, Edward

s. of Rev. Edward Shortt, Woodhorn, Northumberland. b. 10th March 1862. educ. Durham Sch.; Durham Univ. BA 1884, Hon. DCL. M.T. Jan. 1890. KC 1910. Bencher 1919, Reader 1928. Recorder of Sunderland 1907-18. MP Newcastle-on-Tyne (West) 1910-22; Chief Secy. for Ireland 1918-19; Home Secy. 1919-22; Commr. of Assize, Midland circuit 1922; PC 1918; Pres. Br. Bd. of Film Censors 1929-35. d. 10th Nov. 1935.

SHORTT, John S.

s. of William Shortt, Tuam, Co. Galway. b. 1841. educ. Trinity Coll. Dublin BA 1860; London Univ. LLB 1865. M.T. Nov. 1866 (Cert of Hon.). Member of bar committee; Cty. Ct. judge 1894-1922. Author of The Law of Works of Literature and Art. d. 8th May 1932.

SHOVE, Ralph Samuel

s. of Herbert Samuel Shove, Ospringe, Faversham, Kent. b. 31st May 1889. educ. Uppingham; Trinity Coll. Camb. MA; rowing blue (Capt. Leander Crew, Olympic Games, Belgium 1920). I.T. Jan. 1918. WWI Major RFA (despatches). Cty. Ct. judge 1945-60; Vice-Chmn. Parts of Lindsey Quarter Sess. 1945; Chmn. Parts of Kesteven Quarter Sess., and Parts of Holland Quarter Sess. 1946; JP Parts of Lindsey. d. 2nd Feb. 1966.

SIMES, Charles Erskine Woollard

s. of Frederick Albert Woollard Simes, Worcester (d. 1921). b. 1893. educ. Royal Gr. Sch. Worcester; St. John's Coll. Oxf. MA 1918. WWI Lieut. 1/7th Battn. Worcestershire Regt., and HQ Staff, West Midland Region, Min. of Nat. Service. I.T. Nov. 1921. KC 1945. Bencher 1961. Recorder of Banbury 1938-51; Chmn. Inter-departmental Committee on Rating of Site Values 1947-51; member Lands Trib. 1951-67; Dep. Chmn. Parliamentary Bdy. Comm. for England 1952-56, member 1957-66; Chmn. Harlow New Town Licensed Premises Committee 1953-72; Dep. Chmn. Surrey Quarter Sess. 1957-66; JP Surrey; Grand Registrar, United Grand Lodge of England; an editor of Lumley's Public Health. d. 24th March 1978.

SIMON, Sir John

s. of Isaac Simon, Jamaica, merchant. b. Jamaica, 9th Dec. 1818. educ. University Coll. London LLB 1841. M.T. Nov. 1842. Practised in Jamaica 1842-45; Serjeant 1864 (first Jewish); patent of precedence 1868; leader of Northern circuit; successfully defended Simon Bernard for complicity with Orsini in attempt to assassinate Napoleon III, 1858; MP Dewsbury 1868-86; a founder of Anglo-Jewish Assoc. 1871; Knight 1886. d. 24th June 1897.

SIMON, John Allsebrook (Lord Simon)

s. of Rev. Edwin Simon, Bath, congregational minister. b. 28th Feb. 1873. educ. Bath Gr. Sch.; Fettes; Wadham Coll. Oxf. BA 1896, MA 1899, Hon. Fellow 1912; Fellow, All Souls Coll. 1897, Hon. DCL 1926. I.T. Jan. 1899 (Cert. of Hon.). KC 1908. Bencher 1910, Treasurer 1930. WWI Major RAF, OBE 1919 (despatches). Junior counsel in Alaska Bdy. Arb. 1903; MP Walthamstow 1906-18, Spen Valley 1922-40; standing counsel to Oxf. Univ. 1909-10; Sol-Genl. and knighted 1910; PC 1912; Att-Genl. 1913-15; declined Lord Chancellorship 1915; Home Secy. 1915-16, resigned on conscription issue; Chmn. Committee on Street Trading 1909, Indian Statutory

Comm. 1927-30; leading counsel for Newfoundland in Labrador Bdy. Refce. 1926; leader of Liberal National party 1931-40; Pres. R101 Airship Inquiry 1930; Foreign Secy. 1931-35; Home Secy. 1935-37; Chan. of Exch. 1937-40; LC 1940-45; Viscount 1940; Chmn. Population Comm. 1943-46; KCVO 1911; GCSI 1930; GCVO 1937; Pres. of Parliamentary Golfing Socy.; High Steward Oxf. Univ. 1948; JP Oxfordshire and Pembrokeshire; Hon. LLD Edin., Camb, McGill, Toronto, Columbia, Manchester, Leeds, St. Andrews, Sheffield. Author of Simon's Income Tax 1950, Retrospect 1952. d. 11th Jan. 1954.

SIMONDS, Gavin Turnbull (Lord Simonds)

s. of Louis de Luze Simonds, Audleys Wood, Basingstoke, brewer (d. 1916). b. 28th Nov. 1881. educ. Summer Fields; Winchester; New Coll. Oxf. BA 1904, MA 1943, Hon. Fellow 1944, Hon. DCL 1954, High Steward 1954. L.I. Nov. 1906. KC 1924. Bencher 1929, Treasurer 1951. WWI Lieut. Royal Berkshire Regt. (invalided 1916). Had extensive chancery practice; member Donoughmore committee on ministers' powers 1929; Chancery judge 1937-44; Knight 1937; Chmn. Nat. Arbitration Trib. (Industrial Disputes) 1940; member trib. of inquiry on unauthorised disclosure of budget information 1936; PC 1944; L of A 1944-51 and 1954-62; Baron 1944; LC 1951-54; Viscount 1954; carried through first major reform of judicial salaries in 120 years 1954; prof. of law, Royal Acad. of Arts 1951; Fellow of Winchester 1933, Warden 1946; Freeman of Winchester 1963; Hon. FRCOG; Hon. LLD Laval Univ. Quebec; Hon. DLitt. Reading. Father of Gavin Alexander Simonds (L.I. 1945) and John Mellor Simonds (I.T. 1939). d. 28th June 1971.

SIMPKINSON, Sir John Augustus Francis

s. of Rev. John Simpkinson, Geneva. b. Dec. 1780. educ. Westminster; elected to Trinity Coll. Camb. 1798, but attended Christ Church Oxf. BA 1802, MA 1804. L.I. Nov. 1806. KC 1831. Bencher 1832, Treasurer 1845. Knight 1845, on opening of new hall of L.I.; FRS 1847. d. 8th July 1851.

SINGLETON, Sir John Edward

s. of George Singleton, Howick House, Preston, Lancashire. b. 18th Jan. 1885. educ. Royal Gr. Sch. Lancaster; Pembroke Coll. Camb. BA and LLB 1905, MA, Hon. Fellow 1938. I.T. Nov. 1906. KC 1922. Bencher 1929, Treasurer 1952. WWI Capt. RFA (despatches). MP Lancashire (Lancaster) 1922-23; Recorder of Preston 1928-34; appeal judge, Isle of Man 1928-33; KB judge 1934-48; Knight 1934; during WWII concerned in Govt. Inquiries into submarine services, production of stabilised bomb sites, and relative strength of Br. and German Air Forces; Br. Chmn. Anglo-American Palestine Comm. 1945; LJ 1948-57; PC 1948; JP Lancashire; Hon. LLD Liverpool 1949. Author of Conduct at the Bar 1933. d. 6th Jan. 1957.

SINHA, Satyendra Prasanna (Lord Sinha)

s. of Babu Siti Kantha Sinha, Raipur, Bengal. b. 24th March 1864. educ. Birbhum Zilla Sch.; Presidency Coll. Calcutta. Calcutta bar 1886. L.I. July 1886. KC 1918 (first native of India to be appointed). Legal member Council of Governor of Bengal 1909-10; Adv-Genl. 1908-09 and 1915-17; MLC Bengal 1916; member of War Cabinet, London 1917-18; Under-Secy. of State, Indian Dept. 1919-20; Governor of Bihar and Orissa 1920-21; Freeman, City of London 1917; Knight 1915; Baron 1919; PC 1919; member of Judicial Committee 1926; KCSI 1921. Father of Arun Kumar Sinha, 2nd Baron, barrister. d. 6th March 1928.

SKINNER, Allan Maclean

s. of Lt. Genl. John Skinner, London. b. 14th July 1809. educ. Eton; Balliol Coll. Oxf. BA 1832. L.I. June 1834. QC 1857. Bencher 1857, Treasurer 1877. Counsel to the Mint and PO, Hertfordshire and Gloucestershire 1842; Recorder of Windsor 1852-85; Cty. Ct. judge

1859-72; JP Staffordshire and Worcestershire. Father of John Edwin Hilary Skinner (L.I. 1862), war correspondent. d. 22nd May 1885.

SKIRROW, Walker

s. of John Skirrow, Leppotts Hall, Essex, barrister. b. 1784. educ. Little Casterton, Rutland; Trinity Coll. Camb. BA 1806, MA 1809. L.I. May 1810. KC 1834. Bencher 1838. Commr. in Bankruptcy, Manchester 1842-60. Father of Walker Skirrow (L.I. 1853), Inspector of Charities. d. 21st Dec. 1866.

SLADE, Sir Frederick William, Bt.

s. of Genl. Sir John Slade, Bt b. 22nd Jan. 1801. educ. Winchester; Brasenose Coll. Oxf. BA 1824. M.T. June 1830. QC 1851. Bencher 1852, Reader 1855, Treasurer 1859. Unsuccessful parliamentary candidate; succeeded father as 2nd baronet 1859. d. 9th Aug. 1863.

SLADE, George Penkivil

s. of George Slade, London, solicitor. b. 30th June 1899. educ. Eton; Magdalen Coll. Oxf. BA 1922. I.T. Jan. 1923. KC 1939. WWI 2nd Lieut. RE; WWII Acting Cdr. RNVR (Special Branch). Father of Sir Christopher John Slade, Chancery judge 1975. d. 13th Sept. 1942.

SLADE, Sir Gerald Osborne

s. of Sir James Benjamin Slade, auctioneer (d. 1950). b. 14th Oct. 1891. educ. Lindisfarne Coll. Westcliff; Bedford Sch.; Trinity Coll. Camb. BA 1912, MA 1919. WWI Lieut. Essex Regt. M.T. Jan. 1921. KC 1943. Bencher 1948. Chan. of diocese of Chelmsford 1934-48, Southwark 1944-48; Recorder of Tenterden 1942; specialised in libel cases; member LC's committee on defamation

1939; defended William Joyce (Lord Haw-Haw) on treason charge; Chmn. of bar council 1946; Commr. of Assize 1948; KB judge 1948-62; Knight 1948; Chmn. Legal Committee on Medical Partnerships, appointed by Minister of Health 1948; first Chmn. Bar Lawn Tennis Socy.; edited Hugh Fraser's Law of Libel and Slander. d. 10th Feb. 1962.

SLADE, Wyndham

s. of Genl. Sir John Slade, Bt. b. 27th Aug. 1826. educ. Eton; Balliol Coll. Oxf. BA 1848. I.T. Nov. 1850. Commr. to inquire into corrupt election practices at Wakefield 1859, Great Yarmouth 1866, Boston 1875; pros. counsel for PO at Central Criminal Ct.; Recorder of Penzance 1876-77; metrop. magistrate 1877, finally at Southwark 1879-1901; Capt. West Somerset Yeo.; JP Somerset, Middlesex and Home Counties. Father of Wyndham Neave Slade (I.T. 1891), Recorder of Bridgwater. d. 13th March 1910.

SLEIGH, William Campbell

s. of William Willcocks Sleigh MD, Bull House, Buckinghamshire. b. Dublin, 1818. educ. privately; studied medicine St. Mary Hall Oxf. 1843. M.T. Jan. 1846. Serjeant 1868 (last person, not a judge, received into Serjeants' Inn); counsel to Bank of England; counsel for the claimant, Arthur Orton, in action against Tichborne trustees 1871; unsuccessful parliamentary candidate; called to bar of Victoria 1877, and practised in Melbourne until 1886. Author of A Handy Book on Criminal Law 1858, and Personal Wrongs and Legal Remedies 1860. Father of Warner Sleigh, barrister. d. 23rd Jan. 1887.

SLESSER, Sir Henry Herman

s. of Ernest Theodore Schloësser, Layters Cottage, Gerrards Cross, Buckinghamshire (d. 1929). b. 12th July 1883. educ. Oundle; St Paul's; London Univ. Hon. LLD. I.T. June 1906. KC 1924. Bencher

1924. Member of Faculty of Laws, and lecturer on industrial law, London Univ.; MP Leeds (South East) 1924-29; Sol-Genl. 1924; Knight 1924; LJ 1929-40; PC 1929; Chmn. Dartmoor Nat. Park Committee; Ald. Devon CC; JP Buckinghamshire and Devon; Hon. LLD Exeter 1963. Author of Trade Union Law 1922, Law (Heritage Series) 1936, Judgment Reserved 1941, The Judicial Office and Other Matters 1943, Order and Disorder 1945, Administration of the Law 1948, The Art of Judgment and other legal studies 1962. Father of Victor Slesser, solicitor. d. 3rd Dec. 1979.

SMITH, Sir Archibald Levin

s. of Francis Smith JP, Salt Hill, nr. Chichester (d. 1872). b. 27th Aug. 1836. educ. Eton; Trinity Coll. Camb. BA 1858; rowing blue. I.T. Nov. 1860. Bencher 1885. Junior counsel to Treasury 1878-83; QB judge 1883-92; Knight 1883; LJ 1892-1900; PC 1893; Commr. to inquire into The Times' allegations against C.S. Parnell 1888; MR 1900-01; Pres. MCC 1899. "There is a distressing nudity about A.L. Smith's language" (per Lord Bowen). Father of Archibald Francis Fletcher Smith (I.T. 1894). d. 20th Oct. 1901.

SMITH, Edward Francis

s. of William. Smith, Fairy Hall, nr. Eltham, Kent. b. 1813. M.T. Jan. 1839. QC 1865. Bencher 1865. d. 25th Dec. 1877.

SMITH, Frederick Edwin (Lord Birkenhead)

s. of Frederick Smith, Birkenhead, barrister (d. 1887). b. 12th July 1872. educ. Birkenhead Sch.; Wadham Coll. Oxf. BA 1894, Vinerian law scholar 1895, MA and BCL 1897; Fellow and lecturer, Merton Coll. 1896; lecturer, Oriel Coll. 1897, Hon. Fellow 1912, Hon. DCL 1922; examr. in Final Schools 1899-1900. G.I. June 1899. KC 1908. Bencher 1908, Treasurer 1916, 1924. Lecturer in Modern History, Victoria Univ. 1900; first practised in Liverpool; MP Liverpool (Walton) 1906-18, Liverpool (West Derby) 1918-19;

achieved parliamentary reputation by his maiden speech; PC 1911; Sol-Genl. 1915; Knight 1915; Att-Genl. (with seat in Cabinet) 1915, and 1916; LC 1919-22; Baronet 1918; Baron 1919; Viscount 1921; Earl 1922; Director of Govt. Press Bureau Aug-Sept. 1914 (despatches); Maj. Oxfordshire Yeo. and temp. Lt. Col. on General Staff; much involved in prize cases, particularly S.S. Zamora and S.S. Ophelia; accomplished reform of law relating to transfer of land 1922; Secy. of State for India 1924-28; GCSI 1928; Director ICI Ltd. and Tate and Lyle Ltd.; DL Oxfordshire; Hon. DCL Durham; Lord Rector Glasgow Univ. 1922; High Steward Oxf. Univ. 1922. Author of International Law, Points of View, Contemporary Personalities, Fourteen English Judges, Famous Trials of History, Law Life and Letters, More Famous Trials, and other works. d. 30th Sept. 1930. Principal biogs. by Ephesian (C.E. Bechhofer Roberts) 1926, son (2nd Earl) 1933, J. Campbell 1983.

SMITH, Sir Harold

s. of Frederick Smith, Birkenhead, barrister (d. 1887). b. 18th April 1876. educ. Birkenhead Sch. Engaged in cotton industry, then surveyor and valuer in Liverpool until 1908. G.I. Jan. 1911. KC 1923. Bencher 1920. Hon. Lieut. RNVR. Member Select committee on Marconi Agreement 1912; Secy. to Official Press Bureau during WWI; Recorder of Blackburn 1922-24; MP Warrington 1910-22, Liverpool (Wavertree) 1922-23; counsel to Min. of Agr. and Fisheries, and Office of Works 1921; Knight 1921; JP Northamptonshire. d. 10th Sept 1924.

SMITH, Horace

s. of Robert Smith, London, merchant. b. 18th Nov. 1836. educ. Highgate Sch.; King's Coll. London; Trinity Hall Camb. BA 1860. I.T. April 1862. Bencher 1886. Counsel to the Mint; Secy. to Oxford Bribery Comm. 1880; Recorder of Lincoln 1881-88; metrop. magistrate 1888, finally at Westminster 1899-1918; JP Middlesex and Home Counties. Author of treatises on landlord and tenant, and negligence; edited Addison on Contracts, Addison on Torts,

Roscoe's Criminal Evidence, Russell on Crimes. d. 25th Nov. 1922.

SMITH, John George Stapylton

s. of James Gouger Smith, Egham, Surrey, and Naples. I.T. Nov. 1830. Cty. Ct. judge 1847-62. d. 23rd Oct. 1862, age 64.

SMITH, Joseph Grace

s. of Joseph Smith, Bristol. b. 1786. I.T. Nov. 1814. Recorder of Hereford 1837-47; Chmn. of Bath Ct. of Requests; Cty. Ct. judge 1847-59. d. 26th March 1859.

SMITH, Josiah William

s. of Rev. John Smith, Baldock, Hertfordshire. b. 3rd April 1816. educ. Trinity Hall Camb. LLB 1841. L.I. May 1841. QC 1861. Bencher 1861. Equity draftsman and conveyancer; drafted consolidated general orders of Ct. of Chancery 1860; Cty. Ct. judge 1865-79; JP Herefordshire. Author of works on equity, fines and recoveries, conveyancing, common law, and bankruptcy; edited Fearne's Contingent Remainders. d. 10th April 1887.

SMITH, Sir Lumley

s. of Richard Smith, Littlehampton, Sussex, merchant. b. 17th Feb. 1834. educ. Univ. Coll. Sch.; University Coll. London; Trinity Hall Camb. BA 1857, 9th Wrangler, MA 1860, Fellow 1857. I.T. April 1860. QC 1880. Bencher 1881, Treasurer 1906. Recorder of Sandwich 1883-94; Cty. Ct. judge 1892-1901; judge of City of London Ct. 1901-13; Chmn. West Sussex Quarter Sess. 1904-14; Knight 1914; DL London; JP Sussex; Vice-Chmn. Sussex Territorial Force Assoc. 1908-10; joint editor of Mayne on Damages. d. 7th June 1918.

SMITH, Sir Montague Edward

s. of Thomas Smith, solicitor and town clerk of Bideford, Devon. b. 25th Dec. 1809. educ. Bideford Gr. Sch. Attorney. G.I. Nov. 1835; M.T. May 1839. QC 1853. Bencher 1853, Reader 1857, Treasurer 1862. MP Truro 1859-65; a Commr. under Courts of Justice Building Act 1865; judge of Common Pleas 1865-71; Knight 1865; PC and member Judicial Committee 1871-81; member universities committee of Privy Council 1877. Brother of Sir Philip Protheroe Smith (solicitor 1832), Mayor of Truro. d. 3rd May 1891.

SMITH, Philip Howard

s. of Sir William Smith DCL, LLD (d. 1893). b. 27th Dec. 1845. educ. St. Paul's; Trinity Coll. Camb. BA 1868, MA 1873. I.T. Nov. 1870. Special pleader; Recorder of Bridgnorth 1900-05; Cty. Ct. judge 1905-19. Father of Gerald Howard Smith (solicitor 1909). d. 13th May 1919.

SMITH, Reginald John

s. of John Smith, Britwell House, Oxfordshire, barrister. b. 30th May 1857. educ. Eton; King's Coll. Camb. BA 1880, LLB 1881, LLM 1885. I.T. April 1883. QC 1894. Principal of Smith Elder and Co. publishers; Pres. Publishers' Assoc. 1904-05 and 1915-16. d. 26th Dec. 1916.

SMITH, Vernon Russell

s. of Thomas Smith, Highgate, London, attorney. b. 7th April 1849. educ. Highgate Sch.; St. Peter's Coll. Camb. BA 1871, MA 1874. I.T. Nov. 1872. QC 1894. Retired from practice 1904. d. 5th Dec. 1921.

SMYLY, William Cecil

s. of John George Smyly QC, DL, Camus, Castlederg, and Dublin (d. 1866). b. 2nd Jan. 1840. educ. Harrow; Trinity Coll. Camb. LLB 1863; Capt. of Univ. Boat Club 1862. I.T. Jan. 1865. QC 1891. Cty. Ct. judge 1895-1915; JP Derbyshire. d. 4th March 1921.

SNAGGE, Sir Thomas Mordaunt

s. of Sir Thomas William Snagge, KCMG. b. 25th July 1868. educ. Eton; New Coll. Oxf BA 1891, BCL and MA 1893. L.I. June 1893. Standing counsel to Council of Foreign Bondholders 1901; counsel to PO on Oxford circuit 1904-19; Recorder of Ludlow 1915-19; Cty. Ct. judge 1919-43; Knight 1931; JP London. d. 4th Nov. 1955.

SNAGGE, Sir Thomas William

s. of Thomas Samuel Snagg, Leeson Park, Dublin, solicitor. b. 3rd Jan. 1837. educ. Trinity Coll. Dublin BA 1858, MA 1863, Hon. LLD 1904; Hon. MA Oxf. 1895. Added final `e' to surname. M.T. Nov. 1864. Admitted 1875 to privileges of a member of US bar; junior counsel to Bd. of Trade 1881-83; member Council of Foreign Bondholders; Cty. Ct. judge 1883-1914; represented GB at Intern. Diplomatic Confce. on White Slave Traffic, Paris 1902, and at Intern. Congress thereon, Paris 1906; Recorder of Woodstock 1912-14; DL; Knight 1903; KCMG 1912; JP Northamptonshire, Oxfordshire, Berkshire, Buckinghamshire. d. 1st Feb. 1914.

SNELL, Ivan Edward

s. of Edward Snell, Durban, Natal. b. 25th April 1884. educ. Charterhouse; Christ Church Oxf. BA. I.T. June 1909. WWI Brevet Major London Scottish, and Black Watch, MC (despatches four times). Metrop. magistrate 1925, finally at Marylebone to 1948. d. 29th Aug. 1958.

SOMERSET, Granville Robert Henry

s. of Granville Charles Henry Somerset PC, MP (d. 1848). b. 7th Jan. 1824. educ. Westminster; Christ Church Oxf. BA 1845, BCL 1848, DCL 1853; Fellow, All Souls Coll. 1845-58. I.T. Jan. 1851. QC 1868. Bencher 1869. Practised at parliamentary bar; Recorder of Gloucester 1877-81. d. 23rd March 1881.

SOMERVELL, Donald Bradley (Lord Somervell)

s. of Robert Somervell, bursar of Harrow Sch. (d. 1933). b. 24th Aug. 1889. educ. Harrow; Magdalen Coll. Oxf. BA 1911, MA 1915, Hon. Fellow; Fellow of All Souls Coll. 1912, Hon. DCL 1959. I.T. Jan. 1916. KC 1929. Bencher, Treasurer 1957. WWI Staff Capt. 53rd Inf. Brigade, OBE 1919. One of the leading counsel for the Bank in Waterlow v. Bank of Portugal, H of L 1932; MP Crewe 1931-45; Sol-Genl. and knighted 1933; Att-Genl. 1936; PC 1938; Home Secy. 1945; Recorder of Kingston-upon-Thames 1940-46; LJ 1946-54; L of A 1954-60; Baron 1954; Chmn. of Harrow govrs. 1947-53; a trustee of Tate Gallery 1944-49; Hon. LLD St. Andrews. d.18th Nov. 1960.

SOSKICE, Frank (Lord Stow Hill)

s. of David Soskice, foreign correspondent of Manchester Guardian (d. 1943). b. Geneva, 23rd July 1902. educ. St. Paul's; Balliol Coll. Oxf. BA 1924 Naturalised 1924. I.T. Jan. 1926. KC 1945. Bencher 1945, Treasurer 1968. WWII Major, Oxfordshire and Buckinghamshire L.I.; Political Warfare Executive, Cairo. MP Birkenhead (East) 1945-50, Sheffield (Neepsend) 1950-55, Newport, Mon. 1956-66; Sol-Genl. 1945-51; Att-Genl. 1951; UK delegate to UN General Assembly 1950; Home Secy. 1964-65; Lord Privy Seal 1966; Knight 1945; PC 1948; Baron 1966. d. 1st Jan. 1979.

SOUTHGATE, Thomas

s. of Thomas Southgate, Red Lion Square, London, builder. b. 1819.
G.I. Jan. 1843. QC 1862. Bencher 1862, Treasurer 1865. Leader in
the Rolls Ct.; advised judges as to their right to sell Serjeants' Inn
1877. d. 3rd Sept. 1885.

SOWLER, Robert Scarr

s. of Thomas Sowler, Manchester, printer. b. 19th Sept. 1815. educ.
Manchester Free Gr. Sch. M.T. Nov. 1842. QC 1866. Bencher 1866,
Reader 1871. QC Cty. Palatine of Lancaster 1858; dep. judge of
Salford Cty. Ct. Edited Manchester Courier 1842-67. d. 23rd April
1871.

SPEED, William

s. of William Speed, Southwell, Nottinghamshire. b. 1813. M.T.
May 1839. QC 1885. Bencher 1875, Reader 1883. Examr. for the
M.T. scholarships 1880. Father of Francis Elmer Speed JP (M.T.
1883). d. 4th Dec. 1893.

SPENCE, Edward Fordham

s. of James Spence, Liverpool. b. 18th Oct. 1860. educ.
Charterhouse. Solicitor in London 1883-89. M.T. Jan. 1890. KC
1925. Art critic 1881-87; dramatic critic of Westminster Gazette,
The Scotsman and The Sketch; published autobiog. Bar and Buskin
1930. d. 28th May 1932.

SPENCE, George

s. of Thomas Richard Spence, London, dentist. b. 1787. educ. at
Richmond, Surrey; Eton; Glasgow Univ. MA 1805. Articled to a
solicitor. 1. T. June 1811. KC 1834. Bencher 1835, Reader 1845,

Treasurer 1846. MP Reading 1826, Ripon 1829-32. Author of Equitable Jurisdiction of Court of Chancery, and other works. d. (suicide) 12th Dec. 1850.

SPENS, William Patrick (Lord Spens)

s. of Nathaniel Spens JP, Kensington, West London, Royal Co. of Archers (d. 1933). b. 9th Aug. 1885. educ. Rugby; New Coll. Oxf. BA 1907, MA 1942. I.T. Jan. 1910. KC 1925. Bencher 1934, Treasurer 1958. Specialised in company work. WWI Capt. 5th Battn. Royal West Surrey Regt, OBE (despatches). DAAG, Meerut 1918-19; MP Kent (Ashford) 1933-43, Kensington (South) 1950-59; member Imp. War Graves Comm. 1931-43 and 1949-65; CJ of India 1943-47; presided at judicial inquiry into Calcutta racial riots 1946; Chmn. Arbitration Trib. in India 1947-48, on division of assets between India and Pakistan; director Southern Ry. Co. 1938-43, and Prudential Assce. Co. 1949-61; KStJ 1945; PC 1953; Knight 1943; KBE 1948; Baron Spens of Blairsanquhar 1959. Father of William George Michael Spens, 2nd Baron (I.T.1945). d. 15th Nov. 1973.

SPINKS, Frederick Lowten

s. of John Spinks, London, attorney (d. 1850). b. 27th Dec. 1816. educ. King's Coll. London; Magdalene Coll. Camb. BA 1840, MA 1843, 38th Wrangler. I.T. May 1843. Serjeant 1862; MP Oldham 1874-80; Chmn. Faversham Petty Sess.; DL, JP Kent; the last serjeant to be in practice. d. 27th Dec. 1899.

SPINKS, Thomas

s. of William Spinks, Walworth, London. b. 26th Sept. 1819. educ. Merchant Taylors'; St. John's Coll. Oxf. BCL 1845, DCL 1849. Advocate Doctors' Commons 1849; Librarian 1860, Treasurer 1862 and 1868. I.T. Nov. 1858. QC 1866. Bencher 1867, Reader 1883. Registrar of York District Probate Registry 1880-86; reported eccles.

and admiralty cases 1853-55. d. 14th Jan. 1899.

SPOONER, William

s. of Ven. and Rev. William Spooner, archdeacon of Coventry (d.1857). b. 14th July 1811. educ. Oriel Coll. Oxf. BA 1832, MA 1836. L.I. Nov. 1837. Cty. Ct. judge 1863-80. d. 9th May 1880.

STABLE, Sir Wintringham Norton

s. of Daniel Wintringham Stable JP, Plas Llwyn, Llanbrynmair, Montgomeryshire, barrister (d.1929). b. 19th March 1888. educ. Winchester; Christ Church Oxf. BA 1912, MA 1920, hon. student 1960. M.T. Jan. 1913. KC 1935. Bencher 1938. WWI Capt. Montgomeryshire Yeo. and Royal Welch Fus., MC (despatches). Chan. diocese of Portsmouth 1937-38; KB judge 1938-68; Knight 1938; Chmn. Merioneth Quarter Sess. 1944; Chmn. Salop Quarter Sess. 1947-67; PC 1965; JP. Father of Rondle Owen Charles Stable (QC 1963) and Philip Loscombe Wintringham Owen (QC 1963). d. 23rd Nov. 1977.

STANGER, Henry Yorke

s. of George Eaton Stanger, Nottingham, surgeon. b. 11th Nov. 1849. educ. privately; Lincoln Coll. Oxf. BA 1873. L.I. June 1874. QC 1895. Bencher 1898. Recorder of Nottingham 1909-11; MP North Kensington 1906-10; Cty. Ct. judge 1910-22; JP Gloucestershire. d. 19th April 1929.

STANSFELD, James

s. of David Stansfeld, Leeds, merchant. b. 22nd April 1792. educ. privately. Partner in Stansfeld and Craven, solicitors, Halifax; Judge of Ct of Requests, Halifax 1841; Cty. Ct. judge 1847-71; JP

437

Yorkshire West Riding; the last Cty. Ct. judge who was not a barrister. Father of Sir James Stansfeld GCB, MP (I. T. 1849). d. 29th Jan. 1872.

STAPYLTON, Henry Downer

s. of Martin Stapylton (formerly Bree), Myton Hall, Yorkshire (d. 1842). b. 15th Oct. 1802. I.T. Nov. 1826. Recorder of Durham 1835-59, of Hartlepool from 1841; Cty. Ct. judge 1847-73; JP Durham. d. 9th July 1887.

STARKIE, Thomas

s. of Rev. Thomas Starkie, Blackburn, Lancashire. b. 12th April 1782. educ. Clitheroe Gr. Sch.; St John's Coll. Camb. BA 1803, Senior Wrangler, MA 1806; Fellow and tutor, Catherine Hall. L.I. May 1810; I.T. 1819. KC 1835. Bencher (I.T.) 1835, Reader 1846, Treasurer 1847. KC Cty. Palatine of Lancaster; Downing prof. of law, Camb. 1823; counsel to Camb. Univ. 1825; Cty. Ct. judge 1847-49. Author of a treatise on defamation 1813. d. 15th April 1849.

STAVELEY-HILL, Henry Staveley

s. of Alexander Staveley Hill PC, KC, DCL, MP. b. 22nd May 1865. educ. Westminster; St. John's Coll. Oxf. 1884. I.T. April 1891. Recorder of Banbury 1903-22; MP Staffordshire (Kingswinford) 1905-18. WWI Lt.Col. 2/1 Staffordshire Yeo. Cty. Ct. judge 1922-28; DL, JP Staffordshire and Warwickshire; JP Northamptonshire; TD; assumed additional name of Staveley 1906. d. 25th March 1946.

STEAVENSON, David Fenwick

s. of John Carpenter Steavenson JP, Berwick-upon-Tweed. b. 10th Sept 1844. educ. privately; King William's Coll. Isle of Man; Trinity

Hall Camb. BA 1866; rowed for the Univ. I.T. Nov. 1866. Special pleader. Cty. Ct. judge 1891-1912; JP Cumberland, Lancashire and Westmorland. d. 12th March 1920.

STEEL, Allan Gibson

s. of Joseph Steel JP, Kirkwood, Dumfriesshire (d.1880). b. 24th Sept. 1858. educ. Marlhorough; Trinity Hall Camb. BA 1881; cricket blue. I.T. Nov. 1883. KC 1901. Recorder of Oldham 1904-14; played cricket for England against Australia; Pres. MCC 1902. d. 15th June 1914.

STEPHEN, Henry John

s. of James Stephen, Master in Chancery (d. 1832). b. St. Christopher, West Indies, 18th Jan. 1787. educ. St John's Coll. Camb. 1802. I.T. Nov. 1815. Serjeant 1827; member Common Law Comm. 1828, and of committee of inquiry into forgery of Exchequer bills 1842; Commr. in Bankruptcy, Bristol 1842-54. Wrote treatises on pleading in civil actions 1824, and criminal law 1834, also the well-known Commentaries on the Laws of England. Brother of Sir George Stephen 1794-1879 (G.I.1849). d. 28th Nov. 1864.

STEPHEN, James

s. of Henry John Stephen, serjeant. b. 16th Sept 1820. educ. Rugby; Caius Coll. Camb. 1839. M.T. Jan. 1846. Prof. of law, King's Coll. London 1852-65; Recorder of Poole 1860-64; Registrar of Bankruptcy Ct. Leeds 1864-69; Cty. Ct. judge 1871-94; JP Lincolnshire; Hon.LLD Edin. 1856; edited H.J. Stephen's Commentaries on the Laws of England. d. 25th Nov. 1894.

STEPHEN, Sir James Fitzjames, Bt.

s. of Sir James Stephen KCB, colonial under-secretary (d. 1859).

b. 3rd March 1829. educ. Eton; King's Coll. London LLB 1854; Trinity Coll. Camb. BA 1852, MA 1857, Hon. Fellow 1885. I.T. Jan. 1854. QC 1868. Bencher 1868, Treasurer 1887. Contributor to Saturday Review from 1855; Secy. to Educ. Comm. 1858-61; Recorder of Newark 1859-69; chief writer in Pall Mall Gazette 1865-70; counsel for Jamaica committee in prosecution of Govr. Eyre for forcible suppression of native rebellion 1867; legal member Council of India 1869-72, prepared Evidence Act 1872; prof. of common law at Inns of Ct 1875-79; member comms. on fugitive slaves 1876, extradition 1878, copyright 1878; KCSI 1877; Exch. judge 1879-81; QB judge 1881-91; Baronet 1891; Chmn. of Ordnance Comm. 1886; Hon.DCL Oxf.; Hon.LLD Edin.; corresponding member of French Inst. 1888. Author of Essays by a Barrister 1862, A general view of the criminal law of England 1863, Digest of law of Evidence 1876, Digest of Criminal law 1877, History of criminal law 1883, The Story of Nuncomar and Sir Elijah Impey 1885. Father of James Kenneth Stephen (I. T. 1884) clerk of assize, South Wales circuit, Sir Herbert Stephen, 2nd Bt. (I. T. 1881) clerk of assize, Northern circuit, Sir Harry Lushington Stephen, 3rd Bt. (I. T. 1885) judge of High Ct. Calcutta. d. 11th March 1894. Biog. by his brother, Sir Leslie Stephen, 1895.

STEPHENS, Archibald John

s. of William Charles Stephens, civil servant b. 1808. educ. Trinity Coll. Dublin. G.I. May 1832. QC 1859. Bencher 1860, Treasurer 1862. Lecturer on common law and criminal law at Inc. Law Socy. 1843-45; Commr. of inquiry into endowed schools of Ireland 1854-59; Recorder of Andover 1855-57, Winchester 1857-80; Chan. of diocese of Bangor 1864-80, St Davids 1872-80. Author of works on nisi prius, and clergy law. d. 30th Jan. 1880.

STEPHENS, Daniel

s. of Daniel Stephens JP, Ravenstone, Corbridge-on-Tyne, master mariner and steamship owner. b. 11th Feb. 1866. educ. Ashville

Coll. Harrogate; St. John's Coll. Camb. BA 1890. 1. T. Nov. 1891. KC 1919. Bencher 1924. Special pleader; junior counsel for owners of the Olympic, in action concerning collision between Olympic and HMS Hawke. d. 17th March 1932.

STEPHENS, Pembroke Scott

s. of Edward Bell Stephens, Harcourt Lodge, Dublin. b 1834. educ. privately at Namur, Madrid and Dublin. L.I. June 1862. QC 1882. Bencher 1884, Treasurer 1910. Practised mainly at parliamentary bar; Vice-Chmn. Buckinghamshire CC; Vice-Pres. Royal Botanic Socy.; JP Buckinghamshire. d. 14th Jan. 1914.

STEPHENSON, Sir Augustus Frederick William Keppel

s. of Henry Frederick Stephenson MP, Commr. of Excise (d. 1859). b. 18th Oct. 1827. educ. privately; Caius Coll. Camb. BA 1849, MA 1853. I.T. Jan. 1852. QC 1890. Bencher 1892. Recorder of Bedford 1862-65; Registrar of Friendly Societies 1870-75; Solicitor to Treasury, and HM's Procurator-Genl. 1875-94; Director of Public Pros. 1884-94; KCB 1885. Father of Sir Guy Stephenson 1865-1930 (I.T.1888). d. 26th Sept. 1904.

STEVENSON, Sir Aubrey Melford Steed

s. of Rev. John George Stevenson, Oxford. b. 17th Oct. 1902. educ. Dulwich; London Univ. LLB. I.T. June 1925. KC 1943. Bencher 1950, Treasurer 1972. WWII Major, and Dep. Judge-Adv. Recorder of Rye 1944-57, of Cambridge 1952-57; P D and A judge 1957-60; Knight 1957; QB judge 1960-79; member of inter-departmental committee on Human Artificial Insemination 1958; Dep. Chmn. West Kent Quarter Sess. 1949-55; PC 1973. Father of John Melford Stevenson (1. T. 1975). d. 26th Dec. 1987.

STEWART, William

s. of William Henry Stewart, Wakefield, Yorkshire. b. 16th Dec. 1879. educ. Charterhouse. Mining engineer 1898-1905. M.T. Nov. 1908. Recorder of Doncaster 1933; Cty. Ct. judge 1933-52; Chmn. Ripon Quarter Sess. 1935-51, Yorkshire West Riding Quarter Sess. 1942-54; Divorce Commr. 1932; Chmn. Nat. Service Trib. North East Div. 1938-52. d. 27th April 1964.

STEWART-SMITH, Sir Dudley

s. of Alexander Stewart-Smith, Warwick Road, Maida Hill, and Hong Kong. b. 3rd Feb. 1857. educ. Univ. Coll. Sch. London; London Univ. LLB 1886. Solicitor 1879, practised in London. M.T. Jan. 1886; L.I. 1900. KC 1902. Bencher 1911 (M.T.). Chmn. Lancaster Quarter Sess. (Salford Hundred); MP Westmorland (Kendal) 1906-10; V-C Cty. Palatine of Lancaster 1912-19; Knight 1917; council member, Victoria and Liverpool Univs.; JP Westmorland, Lancashire and Cheshire. Author of Law of Winding-Up and Reconstruction of Joint Stock Companies. d. 9th May 1919.

STIRLING, Sir James

s. of Rev. James Stirling, Aberdeen. b. 3rd May 1836. educ. Aberdeen Gr. Sch. and Univ.; Trinity Coll. Camb. BA 1860, Senior Wrangler, MA 1863. LLD Aberdeen. L.I. Nov. 1862. Bencher 1886. Equity draftsman and conveyancer; junior equity counsel to Treasury; member of bar committee 1883; Chancery judge 1886-1900; Knight 1886; LJ 1900-06; PC 1900; FRS; reported chancery cases for Inc. Council of Law Reporting 1865-76. d. 27th June 1916.

STOCK, John Shapland

s. of John Edmunds Stock MD, Clifton, Gloucestershire. b. 1804. educ. Shrewsbury; Peterhouse Camb. BA 1826, MA 1830. M.T.

June 1830. QC 1865. Bencher 1865. Recorder of Winchester 1847-56, Exeter 1856-67; judge of Provost Ct. Exeter 1856-67; published treatise on law of lunacy 1838. d. 7th May 1867.

STONOR, Henry James

s. of Lt.Col. Charles Stonor (in Spanish army, d. 1834). h. 14th March 1820. educ. St. Mary's Coll. Oscott; St. Edmund's Coll. Ware. M.T. Nov. 1842. Chief Commr. of West Indian Incumbered Estates Comm. 1858-65; Cty. Ct. judge 1865-1905; JP Surrey. Brother of Alban Charles Stonor (1817-66), Sol-Genl., Tasmania (L.I. 1839). d. 24th April 1908.

STORKS, Henry

s. of Robert Storks, Nottingham. b. 7th Aug. 1778. educ. Merchant Taylors'; St Peter's Coll. Camb. 1798. L.I. Nov. 1803. Serjeant 1827; patent of precedence 1834. CJ Isle of Ely 1827-41; Recorder of Cambridge 1837-58; Cty. Ct judge 1847-58; JP Middlesex. d. Paris, 4th Nov. 1866.

STORMONTH-DARLING, Moir Tod

s. of James Stormonth-Darling WS, Lednathie, Forfarshire (d. 1866). b. 3rd Nov. 1844. educ. Kelso Gr. Sch.; Edin. Univ. MA, Hon.LLD 1895. Scottish bar 1867; MP Univs. of Edin. and St. Andrews, and Sol-Genl. for Scotland 1888-90; member of Edin. Univ. Ct. 1887-99 and 1901-07; QC 1888; Ry. Commr. for Scotland 1898-1909; Judge of Ct. of Session 1890-1909, with judicial title of Lord Stormonth-Darling; Councillor, Royal Co. of Archers 1895-1909; DL Edin. d. 2nd June 1912.

STRACHAN, John

s. of John Strachan JP, South Shields, Co. Durham, auctioneer. b.

18th June 1838. educ. privately. Journalist and dramatic author. M.T. June 1876. QC 1896. Bencher 1904, Reader 1916. Chmn. and umpire of Conciliation Bd, Northumberland Coal Trade to 1916; District Probate Registrar, Lincoln 1914. d. 3rd June 1918.

STRANGER, Innes Harold

s. of Innes Thomas Stranger, Worthing, Sussex, law clerk. b. 1879. educ. privately. I.T. and M.T. Jan. 1909. KC 1933. MP Berkshire (Newbury) 1923-24; Recorder of Sunderland 1936. d. 28th July 1936.

STRANGMAN, Sir Thomas Joseph

s. of Joseph Strangman DL, JP, Ferrybank House, Kilkenny, Ireland. b. 7th Jan. 1873. educ. Charterhouse; Trinity Hall Camb. BA 1894, LLB 1895. M.T. Jan. 1896. KC 1938. Bencher (L.I.) 1944. Acting prof. Elphinstone Coll., Bombay 1899; prof. Govt. Law Sch., Bombay 1899; Chief Presidency magistrate, Bombay 1901; Adv-Genl., Bombay and member Legislative Council 1908-15, and 1916-22; Knight 1920; Chmn. Eastern Bank Ltd. Father of James Gonville Thomas Joseph Strangman (KC 1950). d. 8th Oct 1971.

STREATFEILD, Sir Geoffrey Hugh Benbow

s. of Major Hugh Sidney Streatfeild JP, Ryhope Hall, Durham, and Barlay, Balmaclellan, Kirkcudbrightshire. b. 28th July 1897. educ. Rugby. WWI Lieut. 4th Battn. DLI, and Capt. RFC and RAF (MC). I.T. June 1921. KC 1938. Bencher 1945. Recorder of Rotherham 1932-34, of Huddersfield 1934-43, of Kingston-upon-Hull 1943-47; Sol-Genl. and Att-Genl. Cty. Palatine of Durham 1939-47; WWII Lt.Col. and AJAG; Commr. of Assize, Western circuit 1946; KB judge 1947-66; Knight 1947; Chmn. Inter-Departmental Committee on the Business of the Criminal Cts. 1958; Dep. Chmn. Somerset Quarter Sess. 1966; lay judge of Chancery Ct. of Province of York 1968; Hon.DCL Durham 1957. d. 7th Oct 1979.

STUART, Sir John

s. of Dugald Stuart, Balachulish, Argyll. b. 1793. educ. Edin. High Sch. and Univ. L.I. Nov. 1819. QC 1839. Bencher 1839, Treasurer 1857. MP Newark 1846-52, Bury St. Edmunds 1852; V-C 1852-71; Knight 1853; PC 1871; reported (with N. Simons) chancery cases 1822-26. d. 29th Oct 1876.

STUART, Sir Robert

s. of Robert Stuart, Annat, Perthshire. b. 1816. educ. Edin. Univ. Scottish bar 1840. L.I. June 1856. QC 1868. Bencher 1868, Treasurer 1889. CJ North West Provinces, India 1871-84; Knight 1871; member of council, Edin. Univ. 1871-84. d. 26th Aug. 1896.

STUART-WORTLEY, James Archibald

s. of 1st Baron Wharncliffe (d. 1845). b. 3rd July 1805. educ. Christ Church Oxf. BA 1826, MA 1831; Fellow of Merton Coll. 1830-46; Sub-Warden 1840. I.T. Jan. 1831. QC 1841. Bencher 1841, Reader 1855, Treasurer 1856. MP Halifax 1835-37, Buteshire 1842-59; counsel to Bank of England 1844; Sol-Genl. to Adelaide, the Queen Dowager 1845; Att-Genl. Duchy of Lancaster 1845; Judge Adv-Genl. 1846-50; PC 1846; Recorder of London 1850-56; Sol-Genl. 1856-57. See also Charles Beilby Stuart Wortley. d. 22nd Aug. 1881.

STURGES, Hugh Murray

s. of Rev. Canon Edward Sturges, Wokingham, Berkshire (d. 1907). b. 26th Aug. 1863. educ. Winchester; Keble Coll. Oxf. BA 1884. L.I. Jan. 1889. KC 1912. Bencher 1926, Treasurer 1945. Equity draftsman and conveyancer; Recorder of Tewkesbury 1912, Windsor 1912-45; Cty. Ct. judge 1913-28; Chmn. Hertfordshire Quarter Sess. 1932-46; JP Lancashire and Hertfordshire; director Legal and General Assce. Socy. d. 12th Oct 1952.

SUGDEN, Edward Burtenshaw (Lord St. Leonards)

s. of Richard Sugden, Duke Street, London, wigmaker and hairdresser. b. 12th Feb. 1781. educ. private sch. Conveyancer under the bar 1803-07. L.I. Nov. 1807. KC 1822. Bencher 1821. Practised as conveyancer until 1817; MP Weymouth and Melcombe Regis 1828-30, St. Mawes 1831-32, Ripon 1837-41; Sol-Genl. 1829-30; Knight 1829; leader in Ct. of Chancery; PC 1834; LC (Ireland) 1835 and 1841-46; LC and Baron 1852; held office for less than a year, but carried important reforms relating to trusts and wills, and continued to take active legal part in Privy Council and H of L; declined to serve again as LC 1859; High Steward of Kingston-upon-Thames; DL Sussex; Hon.DCL Oxf. 1853; Hon.LLD Camb 1835. Author of A Practical Treatise on the Law of Vendors and Purchasers of Estates 1805, A Practical Treatise on Powers 1808, A Handy Book on Property Law 1858; edited Sir Geoffrey Gilbert's Law of Uses and Trusts (1734), 1811. Father of Henry Sugden (L.I.1837), Registrar of Ct. of Chancery in Ireland. d. 29th Jan. 1875. His will, which had been lost, was admitted for probate on the secondary evidence of his daughter, Charlotte Sugden.

SULLIVAN, Alexander Martin

s. of Alexander Martin Sullivan MP, Bantry, Ireland. b. 14th Jan. 1871. educ. Ushaw Coll., Belvedere; Trinity Coll. Dublin. Newspaper journalist. Irish bar 1892; First King's serjeant 1920 (last creation). KC 1908. M.T. Nov. 1899. KC 1919. Bencher 1925, Reader 1936, Treasurer 1944. Defended Sir Roger Casement 1916; represented Dr. Halliday Sutherland in defeat of libel action brought by Dr. Marie Stopes 1924. Author of Old Ireland 1927, and The Last Serjeant 1952 (autobiog.). d. 9th Jan. 1959.

SUMNER, Charles

s. of Charles Richard Sumner, bishop of Winchester (d. 1874). b. 11th May 1819. educ. Balliol Coll. Oxf. BA 1840, MA 1843. M.T. June 1848. Chan. of diocese of Winchester 1856-85; Cty. Ct. judge

1866-85; Chmn. Gloucestershire Quarter Sess.; JP Gloucestershire. d. 23rd Dec. 1885.

SUTTON, Sir Henry

s. of James Sutton JP, Shardlow Hall, Derby (d. 1868). b. 10th Jan. 1846. educ. Rugby; Christ's Coll. Camb. BA 1868. L.I. April 1870. Bencher 1900. Special pleader; junior counsel to Treasury 1890; KB judge 1905-10; Knight 1906. Author of treatise on the Law of Tramways. d. 30th May 1920.

SUTTON, Ralph

s. of Edmund Sutton, Manchester. b. 11th May 1881. educ. Summer Fields; Shrewsbury; Oriel Coll. Oxf. BA 1903, MA 1906. L.I. Jan. 1905. KC 1935. Bencher 1938. OBE 1920, for war work as legal adviser to Central Control Bd. (liquor traffic). Reader in common law to Council of Legal Educ.; editor of the Law Reports 1941-53; judge of Cinque Ports 1937-54. d. 8th Oct 1960.

SWAN, Sir Kenneth Raydon

s. of Sir Joseph Wilson Swan, DSc., FRS (d. 1914). b. 13th March 1877. educ. Rugby; Balliol Coll. Oxf. BA 1900. I.T. and M.T. April 1902. KC 1936. Bencher (M.T.) 1943. WWI Lt. Cdr. RNVR; OBE 1919. Bd. of Education (O Branch) 1919-20; Chmn. Bd. of Trade Patents Committee 1944; Dep. Chmn. Royal Comm. on Awards to Inventors 1946; Pres. British Sailors Socy. 1959, Chmn. 1940-59; Knight 1949; Pres. Ski Club. of GB 1911; Pres. Royal Skating Club 1955. Author of Patents, Designs and Trade Marks 1908, Memoir of Sir Joseph Swan FRS, In the Days of my Youth (autobiog.). d. 15th Aug. 1972.

SWANSTON, Clement Tudway

s. of Sherland Swanston, London. b. 1783. educ. privately. L.I. Nov. 1813. KC 1832. Bencher 1833. Commr. in Bankruptcy 1824-31; Chancery leader; JP Middlesex; FSA; FRS; reported chancery cases 1818-19. d. 19th April 1863.

SWANSTON, Clement Tudway

s. of Clement Tudway Swanston QC. b. 1831. educ. King's Coll. London; Trinity Coll. Camb. BA 1854, MA 1857. L.I. Jan. 1856. QC 1868. Bencher 1868. d. Paris, 22nd Sept. 1879.

SWETENHAM, Edmund

s. of Major Clement Swetenham DL, JP, Somerford Booths, Congleton, Cheshire (d.1852). b. 15th Nov. 1822. educ. Macclesfield Sch.; Brasenose Coll. Oxf. BA 1845, MA 1848. L.I. June 1848. QC 1880. Bencher 1882. Registrar of stamp office at Chester; MP Carnarvon District 1886-90; JP Denbighshire. d. 19th March 1890.

SWIFT, Sir Rigby Philip Watson

s. of Thomas Swift, Liverpool, barrister (formerly solicitor) (d.1899). b. 7th June 1874. educ. Parkfield Sch. Liverpool; London Univ. LLB 1895. L.I. June 1895. KC 1912. Bencher 1916. Practised on Northern circuit until 1910; Recorder of Wigan 1915-20; MP St. Helen's 1910-18; KB judge 1920-37; Knight 1920; Hon.LLD Liverpool 1935. d. 19th Oct. 1937.

SWORDS, William Francis

s. of John George Swords, Woolston, Southampton, schoolmaster.

b. 1873. educ. Hartley Coll. Southampton; Royal Coll. of Science, South Kensington BSc; St. John's Coll. Camb. BA 1908, LLB. Master at Bishop's Sch. Salisbury. M.T. May 1909 (Cert. of Hon.). KC 1930. Equity draftsman and conveyancer. d. 4th March 1964.

SYMMONS, Israel Alexander

s. of Samuel Symmons, London. b. 1862. educ. Univ. Coll. Sch.; London Univ. LLB. M.T. June 1885; the first Jewish metrop. magistrate 1911, finally at Marylebone 1922-23. d. 31st July 1923.

TADDY, William

s. of Christopher Taddy, Broad St., London, merchant. b. 31st Jan. 1773. educ. Eton; St. John's Coll. Camb. BA 1794, 14th Wrangler. I.T. Feb. 1797. Serjeant 1818; King's serjeant 1827; Att-Genl. to Adelaide, the Queen Dowager 1832-45. d. 14th March 1845.

TALBOT, Sir George John

s. of John Gilbert Talbot MP, DL, JP, Falconhurst, Edenbridge, Kent (d.1910). b. 19th June 1861. educ. Winchester; Christ Church Oxf. BA 1885, Fellow of All Souls Coll. 1886, MA 1887; hon. student 1935. I.T. June 1887. KC 1906. Bencher 1914, Treasurer 1936. Chan. of dioceses of Lincoln, Ely, Lichfield, Rochester, Southwark, and Winchester; had extensive parliamentary and ecclesiastical practice; counsel to Oxf. Univ. 1915-23; KB judge 1923-37; Knight 1924; PC 1937; Fellow of Winchester 1930; member Council of Keble Coll. Oxf. Author of Index of Cases Judicially Noted (with H. Fort) 1891, Modern Decisions on Ritual 1894; Law and Practice of Licensing 1896. Father of Thomas George Talbot (QC 1954). d. 11th July 1938.

TALBOT, John Chetwynd

s. of Charles, 2nd Earl Talbot (d. 1849). b. 31st May 1806. educ. Charterhouse; Christ Church Oxf. BA 1827, MA 1829; Dep. Steward Oxf. Univ. 1846-52. L.I. Nov. 1829; M.T. 1836. QC 1843. Bencher 1843, Reader 1849. Recorder of Monmouth 1834-39, Windsor 1836-52; Att-Genl. to Prince of Wales 1844-52. d. 26th May 1852.

TALFOURD, Sir Thomas Noon

s. of Edward Talfourd, Reading, brewer. b. 26th May 1795. educ. Dissenters' Sch. Mill Hill; Reading Gr. Sch. Special pleader 1817. Journalist while reading for the bar. M.T. Feb. 1821. Times reporter on the Oxford circuit, of which he became leader; Serjeant 1833; patent of precedence 1840; Queen's Serjeant 1846-49; Dep. Recorder of Banbury 1832, Recorder 1837; MP Reading 1835-41 and 1847-49; introduced Copyright Act 1841 (extending periods); judge of Common Pleas 1849-54; Knight 1850. Author of Vacation Rambles and Thoughts 1845, and of poems and stage dramas; edited letters of Charles Lamb 1837; Dickens dedicated to him the posthumous papers of the Pickwick Club 1837; DCL Oxf. 1844. Father of Francis Talfourd (M.T.1852), dramatist. d. 13th March 1854.

TANCRED, Henry William,

s. of Sir Thomas Tancred, 5th Bt, barrister (d.1784). b. 1781. educ. Eton; Jesus Coll. Camb. BA 1804, MA 1807, Fellow 1808-60. L.I. May 1804. KC 1831. Bencher 1832, Treasurer 1845. MP Banbury 1832-59. d. 20th Aug. 1860.

TASSELL, Alick James

s. of James Tassell, Faversham, Kent, solicitor. b. 28th Aug. 1865.

educ. Charterhouse; New Coll. Oxf MA 1892. M.T. April 1890. Stip. magistrate, Chatham and Sheerness 1902-24; metrop. magistrate, Clerkenwell 1924-31; Dep. Chmn. East Kent Quarter Sess.; JP London and Home Counties; Chief Scout's Commr. d. 6th Jan. 1932.

TAYLOR, George Paul

s. of George Taylor, Harrington Square, Middlesex. b. 1860. educ. Downside; Catholic Univ. Coll., Kensington. M.T. April 1885. Metrop. magistrate 1895, finally at Marylebone 1905-17; JP London and Home Counties. d. 4th May 1917.

TAYLOR, Henry Gawan

s. of William Taylor, Cloughton, Yorkshire, surgeon. b. 16th Dec. 1855. educ. University Coll. London LLB 1879; Trinity Hall Camb. BA and LLB 1883. L.I. Nov. 1882. Special pleader; Chmn. Joint Committee of Durham Coal Trade 1906-10; Cty. Ct. judge 1912-28; JP Lancashire, Cumberland, Westmorland. d. 9th Dec. 1928.

TAYLOR, John Pitt

s. of Thomas Taylor, Coombe, Surrey, Comptroller of the Customs. b. 30th Dec. 1811. educ. Eton; Christ Church Oxf. BA 1834. M.T. June 1837. Drafted Documentary Evidence Act 1845, and Evidence Law (Amendment) Act 1852; Cty. Ct. judge 1852-85. Wrote treatise on law of evidence 1848. d. 17th July 1888.

TAYLOR, Samuel

s. of Thomas Taylor, Manchester. b. 8th March 1821. educ. Rugby; Brasenose Coll. Oxf BA 1843, MA 1846. I.T. Jan. 1846. QC 1885. Dep. Recorder of Manchester 1874-96. d. 26th Nov. 1896.

TAYLOR, William Francis Kyffin (Lord Maenan)

s. of Ven. William Francis Taylor, archdeacon of Liverpool (d. 1906). b. 9th July 1854. educ. Liverpool Coll.; Exeter Coll. Oxf. BA 1877. I.T. May 1879. QC 1895. Bencher 1905, Treasurer 1926. Recorder of Bolton 1901-03; presiding judge, Liverpool Ct. of Passage 1903-48; judge of appeal, Isle of Man 1918-21; Commr. of Assize, Midland circuit 1919, 1925, Chester and South Wales circuit 1920, Northern circuit 1920, 1929; Commr. for Min. of Transport 1928; Ry. and Canal Commr. 1930; Chmn. Shropshire Quarter Sess. 1927-47; member of bar council 1900-11; Master of the Garden I.T. 1927; Vice-Pres. Liverpool Coll. 1927; DL, JP Shropshire; KBE 1918; GBE 1929; Baron 1948. d. 22nd Sept. 1951.

TEBBS, Herbert Louis

s. of Joseph Tebbs, Leeds, merchant b. 1868. educ. privately. Practised as an accountant. G.I. Nov. 1902 (Cert. of Hon.). Cty. Ct. judge 1919-39. Author of Guide to County Court Practice. d. 9th Dec. 1940.

TEED, John Godfrey

s. of John Teed, Plymouth, MP for Grampound. b. 7th March 1794. G.I. May 1816. Equity draftsman and conveyancer. QC 1841. Cty. Ct. judge 1862-71. Brother of Charles Martin Teed (G.I.1826), Master in High Ct. Madras, and Thomas Teed, of Madras, (G. I. 1839). d. 20th Oct. 1871.

TEMPLE, Christopher

s. of Christopher Temple, Gwernygoe, Montgomeryshire. b. 1784. L.I. May 1810. KC 1834. Bencher 1835, Treasurer 1852. Temporal Chan. of Cty. Palatine of Durham 1851-71; unsuccessful as parliamentary candidate; Cty. Ct. judge 1858-71. Father of

Christopher Temple, puisne judge, Ceylon 1856-73. d. 21st Jan. 1871.

TEMPLE, Leofric

s. of Christopher Temple QC. b. 1819. L.I. May 1843. QC 1872. Bencher 1872. Dep. Recorder of Liverpool 1879-91, Recorder of Carlisle 1880-91. Author of a treatise on attachment of debts; reported (with G. Mew) cases in Ct. of Criminal Appeal 1848-51; a joint editor of Chitty's Precedents in Pleading. Brother of Christopher Temple, puisne judge, Ceylon 1856-73. d. 6th March 1891.

TEMPLE, Robert Griffiths

s. of Christopher Temple, Oswestry, Shropshire. b. 1798. L.I. Feb. 1825. Cty. Ct. judge 1847-59. d. 11th Jan. 1859.

TEMPLE, Stephen

s. of George Temple, Kingston, Jamaica, merchant. b. 1805. I.T. Jan. 1831. QC 1853. Att-Genl. Cty. Palatine of Durham 1866-68; Att-Genl. Cty. Palatine of Lancaster 1867-68. d. 27th July 1868.

TEMPLER, Frederic Gordon

s. of John Charles Templer, Master in Ct. of Exchequer (d. 1874). b. 12th June 1849. educ. Harrow; Trinity Coll. Camb. BA 1871. I.T. Nov. 1872. Prin. Asst. Colonial Secy. Ceylon 1869-82; district judge, Cyprus 1882; Queen's Advocate 1893-98; Cty. Ct. judge 1898-1918; JP Yorkshire North Riding. Brother of John Harvey Templer (I.T. 1876), district judge, Ceylon. d.28th Aug. 1918.

TENNYSON-D'EYNCOURT, Edmund Charles

s. of Louis Charles Tennyson-D'Eyncourt, metrop. magistrate. b. 11th Feb. 1855. educ. Eton; University Coll. Oxf. BA 1879, MA 1882. I.T. May 1881. Metrop. magistrate 1897, finally at Marlborough St. 1922-24; Chmn. Lincolnshire (Lindsey) Quarter Sess.; JP London and Home Counties, Parts of Lindsey; Capt. Lincolnshire Imp. Yeo. 1902. d. 20th Oct. 1924.

TENNYSON-D'EYNCOURT, Louis Charles

s. of Charles Tennyson-D'Eyncourt MP, barrister (d.1861). b.23rd July 1814. educ. Westminster; King's Coll. London. I.T. May 1840. Metrop. magistrate 1851, finally at Westminster 1877-90; JP Lincolnshire (Lindsey), London and Home Counties. d. 11th Dec. 1896.

TERRELL, Henry

s. of Thomas Hull Terrell, Cty. Ct. judge. b. Versailles, 9th May 1856. educ. Christ's Coll. Brecon; St. John's Coll. Camb. 1879. M.T. June 1882. QC 1897. Bencher 1904, Reader 1916. WWI Major 11th Battn. Gloucestershire Regt. MP Gloucester 1910-18; Cty. Ct. judge 1920-29; Master of Glovers' Co. 1918. d. 9th Sept. 1944.

TERRELL, Thomas

s. of Thomas Hull Terrell, Cty. Ct. judge. b. 1852. G.I. June 1879; M.T. June 1890. QC 1895. Bencher (G.I.) 1896, Treasurer 1904. FCS. Father of Sir Courtney Terrell (1881-1938), CJ Patna, and Edward Terrell QC (1902-79). d. 27th April 1928.

TERRELL, Thomas Hull

s. of John Terrell, Exeter, solicitor. b. 23rd Jan. 1809. I.T. June 1835. Cty. Ct. judge 1866-77. Father of Arthur A'Becket Terrell (L.I. 1872). d. Nice, 7th Dec. 1896.

THEOBALD, Sir Henry Studdy

s. of William Theobald, clerk of High Ct. Calcutta, barrister (d. 1870). b. 7th June 1847. educ. Rugby; Balliol Coll. Oxf. BA 1870, MA 1877, Fellow 1871; Hon.Fellow Wadham Coll.; lecturer and senior bursar 1881; examr. in jurisprudence 1884. I.T. Nov. 1873. QC 1899. Master in Lunacy 1907-22; Knight 1923. Author of works on land law, and law relating to wills, lunacy, and railways. d. 8th June 1934.

THESIGER, Alfred Henry

s. of Chelmsford LC. b. 15th July 1838. educ. Eton; Christ Church Oxf. BA 1860, MA 1862; distinguished as cricketer and oarsman. I.T. June 1862. QC 1873. Bencher 1874. Tubman in Ct. of Exch. 1866, Postman 1869; member of comm. on Fugitive Slave circular 1876; Att-Genl. to Prince of Wales 1877; LJ 1877-80; PC 1877. d. 20th Oct. 1880.

THESIGER, Arthur Lionel Bruce

s. of Sir Edward Peirson Thesiger KCB (d. 1928) and g.s. of Chelmsford LC. b. 19th Oct. 1872. educ. Winchester; New Coll. Oxf. Engaged for fourteen years in insurance profession. I.T. June 1899. Did not practise until 1907; Cty. Ct. judge 1931-47; Dep. Chmn. Devon Quarter Sess. d. 20th Feb. 1968.

THESIGER, Frederick (Lord Chelmsford)

s. of Charles Thesiger, collector of customs, St. Vincent, W.I. (d. 1831). b. 15th July 1794. educ. in Greenwich (Dr. Charles Burney) and at a naval acad. in Gosport. Midshipman RN 1807, present at second bombardment of Copenhagen. Pupil of Godfrey Sykes, the well-known special pleader. G.I. Nov. 1818. KC 1834. Bencher (I.T.) 1834, Reader 1842, Treasurer 1843. Leader of Home circuit; standing counsel to Inc. Law Socy.; gained prominence as counsel for petitioners at election committee which inquired into the return of O'Connell and Ruthven for Dublin 1835; purchased a place as counsel in the Palace Ct.; MP Woodstock 1840-44, Abingdon 1844-52, Stamford 1852-58; Sol-Genl. 1844-45; Knight 1844; Att-Genl. 1845-46 and 1852; successfully represented Earl Ferrers in fraudulent claim by Mary Eliza Smith for breach of promise of marriage 1846; LC 1858-59 and 1866-68; Baron and PC 1858; Hon. DCL Oxf. 1842; FRS 1845. d. 5th Oct. 1878.

THOMAS, Abel

s. of Theophilus Evan Thomas JP, Trehale, Pembrokeshire. b. 5th Feb. 1848. educ. Clifton Coll.; London Univ. BA 1870. M.T. Jan. 1873. QC 1892. Bencher 1899, Reader 1911. MP Carmarthenshire (East) 1890-1912; Chmn. Pembrokeshire Quarter Sess.; JP Pembrokeshire. d. 23rd July 1912.

THOMAS, Alfred Patten

s. of William Thomas, Liverpool. b.1860. educ. Liverpool Coll.; University Coll. Liverpool; London Univ. BA 1884, LLB 1886, LLD 1888. Employed in commerce 1877-84. M.T. July 1886. Practised in Liverpool; prof. of commercial law, Liverpool Univ. 1903-07, and hon. prof. of intern. law there; Cty. Ct. judge 1907-31; JP Lancasire. d. 30th March 1931.

THOMAS, Aubrey Ralph

s. of Ralph Thomas, London, solicitor. b. 11th Feb. 1879. educ. Oxf. Univ. (non-collegiate) BA 1898, BCL, MA. M.T. Jan. 1902. Bencher 1934, Treasurer 1951. On instructional staff, School of Musketry, Bisley 1916-18. Hon. junior counsel to Officers' Assoc. 1928-36; Recorder of Gloucester 1932-37; judge of Mayor's and City of London Ct. 1935-54. d. 31st May 1957.

THOMAS, David Rowland

s. of Thomas Thomas, Merthyr Tydfil, Glamorganshire. b. 1881. educ. Merthyr Tydfil High Sch.; London Univ. M.T. Jan. 1909. KC 1931. Bencher 1937. Metrop. magistrate 1941, finally at Marlborough St. to 1954; Recorder of Carmarthen 1935-41. d. 25th Feb. 1955.

THOMAS, Evan Lewis

s. of John Thomas, Kingsland, Middlesex, tea-dealer. b. 18th Dec. 1858. educ. City Middle Sch.; Sidney Sussex Coll. Camb. BA 1882, MA 1885, LLM 1887. L.I. Nov. 1885. KC 1908. Bencher 1913, Treasurer 1934. JP Cornwall; Fellow, Royal Sanitary Inst. d. 3rd June 1935.

THOMAS, Frederic George

s. of Rev. Frederic Thomas, Exeter. b. 12th Aug. 1872. educ. Exeter Sch.; Sidney Sussex Coll. Camb. BA 1894, LLB 1895. I.T. April 1899. KC 1921. Bencher 1928. Practised at parliamentary bar; Ry. and Canal Commr.; CMG 1912, for services in connection with reception of Prime Ministers of Self-Governing Colonies 1911. d. 17th Nov. 1937.

THOMAS, Leonard Charles

s. of John Henwood Thomas, Bodmin, Cornwall, surveyor of customs. b. 18th Oct. 1879. Confidential clerk to Frank Lloyd of Daily Chronicle. M.T. Jan. 1905. Served in Directorate of Mil. Intelligence (censorship) during WWI. Cty. Ct. judge 1926-53; independent Chmn. Pneumoconiosis Bd. for GB; Chmn. Cwmbran New Town Committee. d. 16th Nov. 1964.

THOMAS, Ralph

s. of Ralph Thomas, London. b. 26th March 1803. Shoemaker to age of sixteen; bookseller in London 1820-26; conveyancer 1829. M.T. 1831. Serjeant 1852. Junior counsel in defence of Chartists 1839-40. d. 12th Jan. 1862.

THOMAS, Sir William Bruce

s. of Jabez Thomas FRCS, Swansea. b. June 1878. educ. Christ Coll. Brecon. Solicitor in London 1903-11. M.T. Jan. 1912. KC 1928. Bencher 1936. Pres. Ry. Rates Trib. (later Transport Trib.) 1932-50; Chmn. Rates Advisory Committee 1932, Harbour Docks and Piers Committee 1932, Charges (Railway Control) Consultative Committee 1940; Knight 1941. d. 5th Sept. 1952.

THOMPSON, John Vincent

s. of Thomas Thompson MP, Hull, merchant. b. 1785. educ. Queens' Coll. Camb. BA 1805, MA 1808, Fellow 1806-25. L.I. May 1813. Serjeant 1841. Recorder of Beverley; FSA. Father of Vincent Thomas Thompson (L.I. 1858) and Frederick Thompson (L.I. 1866). d. 12th Dec. 1856.

THOMPSON, Owen

s. of Henry Thompson, Colchester. b. 17th March 1868. educ. Colchester Sch.; Univ. Coll. Sch.; Trinity Coll. Camb. BA 1889, MA 1893. L.I. June 1893. KC 1919. Bencher 1922. Equity draftsman and conveyancer; Cty. Ct. judge 1928-40. d. 16th Jan. 1958.

THOMPSON, Thomas Perronet Edward

s. of Genl. Thomas Perronet Thompson MP, FRS (d. 1869). b. 4th May 1813. educ. Beverley Gr. Sch.; Queens' Coll. Camb. BA 1835, MA 1838. L.I. Nov. 1838. Recorder of Scarborough 1872; Cty. Ct. judge 1872-89; JP Lancashire. d. 25th Aug. 1904.

THORP, Linton Theodore

s. of Frederick William Theodore Thorp, Marlow, Buckinghamshire, solicitor. b. 21st Feb. 1884. educ. Manchester Gr. Sch.; Univ. Coll. London LLB. L.I. June 1906 (Cert. of Hon.). KC 1932. Bencher 1936. WWI with South Wales Borderers, and Major RA. Judge of native cts. Egypt 1919; judge of Supreme Ct. and Prize Ct. Egypt 1921; last Br. judge of Supreme Ct. Constantinople 1921-24; Recorder of Saffron Walden and Maldon 1932-50; MP Nelson and Colne 1931-35; Dep. Chmn. Essex Quarter Sess. 1936, Chmn. 1946-50; Chan. diocese of Chelmsford 1948-50; govr. Felsted Sch. 1946; JP Saffron Walden and Maldon. Author of Law of Moneylending, and Quarter Sessions handbook. d. 6th July 1950.

THORPE, John Henry

s. of Ven. John Henry Thorpe, archedeacon of Macclesfield (d. 1932). b. 7th Aug. 1887. educ. in Leatherhead; Trinity Coll. Oxf. BA 1909. I.T. Jan. 1911. KC 1935. Bencher 1941. WWI Capt. 7th Battn. Manchester Regt., and court-martial officer (despatches).

Legal adviser to Mil. Govt. Cologne 1919; OBE; MP Manchester (Rusholme) 1919-23; Recorder of Blackburn 1925-44; Dep. Chmn. Middlesex Quarter Sess. 1941; JP; member of bar council; Chmn. Appeal Trib. (Architects Registration Act 1931) 1940; Chmn. Central Price Regulation Committee 1942-44. Father of John Jeremy Thorpe PC, MP (I.T. 1954). d. 31st Oct. 1944.

TINDAL, Sir Nicolas Conyngham

s. of Robert Tindal, Coval Hall, nr. Chelmsford, Essex, attorney. b. 12th Dec. 1776. educ. Chelmsford Gr. Sch.; Trinity Coll. Camb. BA 1799, 8th Wrangler, MA 1802, Fellow 1801. Special pleader. L.I. June 1809. Successfully claimed in Ashford v. Thornton (1818) right of wager of battle for his client to prove innocence of murder charge (right abolished in following year); one of the counsel for defence of Queen Caroline 1820; MP Wigtown Burghs 1824, Harwich 1826-27, Camb. Univ. 1827-29; Sol-Genl. 1826-29; Knight 1826; CJ of Common Pleas 1829-46; tried action for criminal conversation brought by G.C. Norton (q.v.) against Lord Melbourne; Hon. DCL Oxf. 1834. Father of Charles John Tindal (L.I. 1842). d. 6th July 1846.

TINNEY, William Henry

s. of William Tinney, Salisbury. b. 1784. educ. Magdalen Coll. Oxf. BA 1805, MA 1808; Fellow of Oriel Coll. 1806-28. I.T. Nov. 1811; L.I. July 1813. Bencher 1830, Treasurer 1840. KC 1829. A real property commr. 1829-33; Master in Chancery 1847-60. d. 30th Nov. 1871.

TOBIN, Sir Alfred Aspinall

s. of James Aspinall Tobin JP, Eastham, Cheshire, merchant. b. 26th Dec. 1855. educ. Rugby; University Coll. Oxf. BA 1878. M.T. June 1880. KC 1903. Bencher 1912, Reader 1923, Treasurer 1930.

Defended Dr. Crippen; Recorder of Salford 1904-15; MP Preston 1910-15; Cty. Ct. judge 1915-35; Commr. of Assize, Northern circuit 1921; Knight 1919. d. 30th Nov. 1939.

TOLLER, Samuel Bush

s. of Edward Toller, proctor in Doctors' Commons. b. 1804. educ. Harrow; Trinity Coll. Oxf. BA 1825, BCL 1830. L.I. May 1830. QC 1858. Bencher 1858. Brother of Charles Toller (proctor and notary 1828). d. 10th May 1868.

TOMLIN, Thomas James Chesshyre (Lord Tomlin)

s. of George Taddy Tomlin, Combe House, Canterbury. b. 6th May 1867. educ. Harrow; New Coll. Oxf. BA 1889, MA and BCL 1892, Hon.Fellow. M.T. April 1891; L.I. 1892. KC 1913. Bencher 1918. Junior equity counsel to IR, Bd. of Trade, Commrs. of Woods and Forests, Charity Commrs.; Chmn. LC's committees on Royal Cts. of Justice, and Probate Registries 1919; counsel to R. Coll. of Physicians 1922; Chancery judge 1923-29; Knight 1923; Vice-Chmn. Trevethin committee 1923; Chmn. Royal Comm. on awards to inventors 1923-33, and on Civil Service 1929; Chmn. Child Adoption Committee 1925, and Home Office Committee on Cruelty to Animals 1928; Chmn. Univ. of London commrs. 1926; L of A 1929-35; Baron and PC 1929; Hon.LLD London, Toronto, Columbia; joint editor of Lindley on Partnership. d. 12th Aug. 1935.

TOPHAM, Alfred Frank

s. of Frank William Warwick Topham RI (d. 1924). b. 6th March 1874. educ. Highgate Sch.; Queens' Coll. Camb. LLB 1896, LLM 1900. L.I. June 1900. KC 1922. Bencher 1926. Equity draftsman and conveyancer; editor of the Law Reports; Reader in real property, Council of Legal Educ.; Cty. Ct. judge 1938-48. Author of works on company law, and real property. d. 18th Jan. 1952.

TORR, John Berry

s. of Rev. John Torr, Westleigh, Devon. b. Nov. 1817. educ. Bideford Gr. Sch. Studied medicine in London and Paris. Editor and part proprietor of Court Gazette, and Salopian Journal. M.T. May 1850. QC 1872. Bencher 1874. Father of James Fenning Torr (M.T. 1873). Recorder of Hastings. d. 9th March 1878.

TOWNSEND, William Charles

s. of William Townsend, Walton, Lancashire. b. 1803. educ. Queen's Coll. Oxf. BA 1824, MA 1827. L.I. Nov. 1828. QC 1850. Bencher 1850. Recorder of Macclesfield 1833. Author of Lives of Twelve Eminent Judges 1846, and Modern State Trials 1850. d. 8th May 1850.

TOZER, John

s. of John Tozer, Woolwich, Kent. b. 1806. educ. in Woolwich, Caius Coll. Camb. BA 1836, 13th Wrangler, MA 1839, LLD 1854, Fellow 1839-77, Bursar 1855-57. L.I. Nov. 1840. Serjeant 1858; Assessor to Chan. of Camb. Univ. 1852-77; Recorder of Bury St. Edmunds 1861-77; Fellow of Camb. Philosophical Socy. d. 8th Dec. 1877.

TRAFFORD, Richard Leigh

s. of Trafford Leigh Trafford, Oughtrington Hall, Cheshire (d. 1859). b. 30th April 1800. educ. Rugby; St. John's Coll. Camb. BA 1822, MA 1826. M.T. May 1826. Commr. in Bankruptcy; Cty. Ct. judge 1847-62; DL, JP Cheshire. Brother of Henry Leigh Trafford (M.T. 1834), stip. magistrate Salford and Manchester. d. 27th Jan. 1864.

TRAILL, James

s. of James Traill, Rattar, Caithness. b. 1794. educ. in Glasgow;

Balliol Coll. Oxf. BCL 1817. M.T. Nov. 1820. Metrop. magistrate 1833, finally at Greenwich 1846-68. Father of James Christie Traill (I.T. 1853), and William Frederick Traill (I.T. 1865). d. 17th Oct. 1873.

TRAPNELL, John Graham

s. of Caleb Trapnell, Stoke Bishop, Bristol, solicitor. b. 1876. educ. Harrogate Coll.; King's Coll. Camb. BA and LLB 1903. I.T. Nov. 1903. KC 1931. Bencher 1938. WWI Lieut. RNVR. Recorder of Plymouth 1932-43; Judge-Adv. of the Fleet 1933-43; Official Referee of Supreme Ct. 1943-49. d. 3rd Nov. 1949.

TRISTRAM, Thomas Hutchinson

s. of Rev. Henry Baker Tristram, Egglingham, Northumberland. b. 25th Sept. 1825. educ. Durham Sch.; Lincoln Coll. Oxf. BCL 1850, DCL 1854. Examr. for BCL degree 1854-57; advocate Doctors' Commons Nov. 1855. QC 1881. Judge of Consistory Ct. London 1872; Chan. of diocese of Hereford, Ripon and Wakefield 1883, Chichester 1892; Commissary-Genl. diocese of Canterbury; law reporter for Inc. Council. Author of a treatise on probate practice. d. 8th March 1912.

TUCKER, Frederick James (Lord Tucker)

s. of Frederick Nugent Tucker, The Grey House, Epsom (formerly MLA, Natal). b. Natal, 22nd May 1888. educ. Winchester; New Coll. Oxf. BA 1911, Hon. Fellow 1946. I.T. Jan. 1914. KC 1933. Bencher 1937, Treasurer 1960. WWI Lieut. on General List. Pupil of Rayner Goddard, to part of whose practice he succeeded; member of bar council 1930-37; Recorder of Southampton 1936; KB judge 1937-45; Knight 1937; presided at trial of William Joyce (Lord "Haw Haw") for treason 1945; LJ 1945-50; PC 1945; candidate for position of LCJ 1945, but Goddard appointed; L of A 1950-61;

Baron 1950. d. 17th Nov. 1975.

TUCKER, Howard Archibald

s. of Henry Howard Tucker, Walsall, Staffordshire. b. 1889. educ. Queen Mary's Sch. Walsall; London Univ. LLB. Solicitor 1911, practised in Walsall. M.T. Jan. 1922 (Cert. of Hon.). Recorder of Worcester 1937-41, of Stoke-on-Trent 1941-43; Cty. Ct. judge 1943-61; Chmn. Staffordshire Quarter Sess. 1949-63. Father of Richard Howard Tucker QC, Crown Ct. Recorder 1972. d. 5th Sept. 1963.

TUCKER, Sir James Millard

s. of William Ive Tucker, Bishop's Stortford and Ilford, schoolmaster. b. 14th Oct. 1892. Chartered accountant in Br. Columbia. WWI with 29th (Vancouver) Battn. CEF; Lieut. 6th Battn. Essex Regt. and attached to Oxford and Buckinghamshire L.I. M.T. Nov. 1920. KC 1932. Bencher 1938, Treasurer 1957. Chmn. Treasury Committee on Taxation of Trading Profits 1949; Chmn. Treasury Committee on Taxation of Pensions etc. 1950; Vice-Chmn. Royal Comm. on Income Tax 1950; Chmn. Treasury Advisory Panel under Income Tax Act 1952; Knight 1955; Freeman of City of London; Master of Glaziers' Co. 1949; director, Prudential Assce. Co. Ltd. d. 9th Sept. 1963.

TURNER, Edmond Robert

s. of Turner LJ. b. 12th May 1826. educ. Charterhouse; Gonville & Caius Coll. Camb. BA 1848, MA 1851. L.I. Jan. 1852. Equity draftsman and conveyancer; Cty. Ct. judge 1868-98; JP Yorkshire North Riding. Author of a manual on Employers' Liability 1882. d. 12th April 1899.

TURNER, Sir George James

s. of Rev. Richard Turner, Great Yarmouth. b. 5th Feb. 1798. educ. Charterhouse; Pembroke Coll. Camb. BA 1819, 9th Wrangler, MA 1822, Fellow 1820-23. L.I. July 1821. QC 1840. Bencher 1840. MP Coventry 1847-51; introduced and carried bill known by his name, enabling Ct. of Chancery to decide upon a special case, questions in which the parties were agreed upon the facts; V-C and knighted 1851; member comm. for reform of chancery practice 1852; PC 1851; LJ 1853-67; FRS; Hon. DCL Oxf. 1853; a govr. of Charterhouse; reported, (with J. Russell), Chancery cases during time of Eldon LC, 1822-24. d. 9th July 1867.

TURNER, Richard Whitbourn

s. of James Smith Turner MRCS, LDS, Ealing, Middlesex. b. 2nd Nov. 1867. educ. Merchant Taylors'; Trinity Hall Camb. BA 1889; athletics blue. M.T. Jan. 1891. Acting secy. to LCJ (Lord Reading) 1915-19; Cty. Ct. judge 1919-32; JP Lancashire, Nottinghamshire, Middlesex. d. 20th Nov. 1932.

TURNER, Sydney George

s. of Arthur James Turner, Kensington, West London, schoolmaster. b. 5th Oct. 1880. educ. Westminster City Sch. A surveyor. M.T. Jan. 1906. KC 1931. Bencher 1937, Reader 1948, Treasurer 1955, Master emeritus 1963. Head of legal section, Lands Directorate, War Office 1915-23; OBE 1920; practised at parliamentary bar; Recorder of Sandwich 1942-51; member, 1948-58, of General Claims Trib. under Compensation (Defence) Act 1939; Dep. Chmn. Essex Quarter Sess. 1946, Chmn. 1950-55; Chmn. Hosp. Management Committee, Battersea and Putney Group, under Nat. Health Service Act, 1948-59; CBE 1956. d. 5th Jan. 1967.

TURNER, Theodore Francis

s, of George Lewis Turner, London. b. 19th Nov. 1900. educ. Downside; Balliol Coll. Oxf. BA 1922. I.T. July 1924. KC 1943. Chmn. Mining Subsidence Committee 1947-48; Regional Controller, Min. of Fuel and Power, North Midland Region; Recorder of Rochester 1946-50; admitted to New York bar 1962. Father of Sir Michael John Turner (QB judge 1985). d. 19th May 1986.

TWISS, Horace

s. of Francis Twiss, Bath, compiler. b. 1787. I.T. June 1811. KC 1827. Bencher 1827, Reader 1837, Treasurer 1838. MP Wootton Bassett 1820-30, Newport, Isle of Wight 1830-31, Bridport 1835-37; counsel to the Admiralty and Judge-Adv. of the Fleet 1825; Under-Secy. for War and Colonies 1828-30; V-C of Duchy of Lancaster 1844. Wrote biography of Eldon LC 1844. d. 4th May 1849.

TWISS, Sir Travers

s. of Rev. Robert Twiss, Trevallyn House, Denbighshire. b. 19th March 1809. educ. University Coll. Oxf. BA 1830, MA 1832, BCL 1835, DCL 1841, Fellow 1830-63, Bursar 1835, Tutor 1836-43, Dean 1837-43. L.I. Jan. 1840. QC 1858. Bencher 1858. Advocate Doctors' Commons 1841; Librarian 1854-60, Treasurer 1860-62. Prof. of political economy Oxf. 1842-47; Commissary-Genl. Canterbury 1849-72; Queen's Advocate 1852; prof. of intern. law King's Coll. London 1852-55; FRS 1838; Regius prof. of civil law Oxf. 1855-70; Adv-Genl. to Admiralty 1862; Chan. of diocese of London 1858-72, of St. Davids 1865-72; Knight 1867. Author of the Law of Nations considered as Independent Political Communities, 1861-63; edited Black Book of the Admiralty, and Bracton. d. 14th Jan. 1897.

TWYFORD, Samuel

s. of Samuel Twyford, Petersfield, Hampshire. b. 1787. educ. Trinity Coll. Oxf. BA 1809, MA 1811. I.T. Nov. 1811. Metrop. magistrate 1822, finally at Bow St. 1837-46. d. 4th July 1863, but remained in Law List until 1882.

TYLOR, Alfred

s. of Joseph John Tylor, Mayfield, Sussex, civil engineer. b. 25th Aug. 1888. educ. Marlhorough; University Coll. Oxf. BA 1910. M.T. June 1913. KC 1943. Bencher 1940. Legal adviser Min. of Food 1939-46; Cty. Ct. judge 1947-58. d. 20th May 1958.

TYNDALE, Geoffrey Clifford

s. of Walter Frederick Roofe Tyndale RI, Brunswick Gdns. London W. (d. 1943). b. 19th Feb. 1887. educ. Epsom Coll.; Keble Coll. Oxf. BA 1909, MA 1932; London Univ. LLB. I.T. Jan. 1913. KC 1943. Bencher 1950. Pres. Hardwicke Socy.; on teaching staff of Law Socy.; practised in P D and A Division; Divorce Commr. d. 6th May 1966.

TYRRELL, John

s. of Timothy Tyrrell, London, City remembrancer (d. 1832). b. 11th Nov. 1789. educ. Merchant Taylors'. L.I. Nov. 1813. Recorder of Tiverton 1837-66, of Barnstaple, Bideford and South Molton 1857-59; Cty. Ct. judge 1847-64. d. 10th July 1868.

TYRWHITT, Robert Philip

s. of Richard Tyrwhitt, Bridgnorth, Shropshire, Recorder of Chester (d. 1836). b. 15th July 1798. educ. Westminster. M.T. Feb. 1825. Metrop. magistrate 1847, finally at Marlborough St. 1860-71.

Author (with T.W. Tyndale) of a Digest of the Public General Statutes 1822; reported Exch. cases 1830-35; reported (with T.C. Granger) Exch. cases 1835-36. d. 18th June 1886.

UNDERDOWN, Emanuel Maguire

s. of Emanuel Underdown, Sidmouth, Devon. b. 1831. educ. privately, and Rome, Paris, Berlin. I.T. June 1861 (Cert. of Hon.). QC 1886. Bencher 1894. Hon. counsel to Socy. of Authors; corresponding member, Acad. of Legislation and Jurisprudence, Madrid; FRGS. Author of treatise on law of art copyright. Father of Harry Charles Baillie Underdown JP (I.T. 1902). d. 11th April 1913.

UNDERHILL, Joseph

s. of George Lees Underhill, Wolverhampton, iron merchant. b. 1839. educ. Brewood Gr. Sch., and Dresden. M.T. Jan. 1862. QC 1880. Bencher 1882. Recorder of Newcastle-under-Lyme 1887-90; the first recorder of West Bromwich 1890-92. First cousin to Sir Arthur Underhill (1850-1939), senior conveyancing counsel of Supreme Ct. d. 13th July 1892.

UPJOHN, Gerald Ritchie (Lord Upjohn)

s. of William Henry Upjohn QC. b. 25th Feb. 1903. educ. Eton; Trinity Coll. Camb. BA 1925, MA 1928. Employed with solicitors and accountants. L.I. Jan. 1929 (Cert. of Hon.). KC 1943. Bencher 1948, Treasurer 1965. WWII Capt. and Technical Adjt. 2nd Battn. Welsh Guards 1940-43; Brig. 1944; legal adviser Allied Control Comm. Italy 1943; Vice-Pres. Allied Control Comm. 1944; CBE 1945 (despatches). Treasurer of bar council 1946-51; Dep. Chmn. Bd. of Referees 1946-51; Att-Genl. Duchy of Lancaster 1947-51; member committee on practice and procedure of Supreme Ct. 1947-53; Chancery judge 1951-60; Knight 1951; member Lynskey Inquiry

(Bd. of Trade) 1948; judge of Restrictive Practices Ct. 1956; a trib. Chmn. under Coal Industry Nationalisation Act., 1947-51; LJ 1960-63; PC 1960; L of A 1963-71; Baron 1963; DL Essex; Officer of US Legion of Merit 1946; govr. of Eton 1963; govr. Felsted Sch.; Chmn. St. George's Hosp. Medical Sch. 1954-64. d. 27th Jan. 1971.

UPJOHN, William Henry

s. of William Bellingham Drew Upjohn, barristers' clerk (d. 1881). b. 31st Aug. 1853. educ. King's Coll. Sch.; London Univ. LLB. G.I. Jan. 1881 (Cert. of Hon.). QC 1897. Equity draftsman and conveyancer; known as "Uppy". Brother of Arthur Ritchie Upjohn (solicitor 1883, L.I. 1920). d. 16th July 1941.

UTHWATT, Augustus Andrewes (Lord Uthwatt)

s. of Thomas Andrewes Uthwatt, Ballarat, Victoria, Australia. b. 25th April 1879. educ. Ballarat Coll.; Melbourne Univ. BA 1899, LLB; Balliol Coll. Oxf. BCL 1903; Vinerian scholar 1905; Hon. Fellow 1947. G.I. Jan. 1904. Bencher 1927, Treasurer 1939, Vice-Treasurer 1941. Legal adviser to Min. of Food 1916-18; declined knighthood; member Council of Legal Educ. 1929; junior equity counsel to Treasury and Bd. of Trade, and to Att-Genl. in charity matters 1934; Chancery judge 1941-46; Knight 1941; Reader at Law Socy.; Chmn. Committee on Compensation and Betterment, "Uthwatt Report" 1941, and of other committees concerning war damage to property; L of A 1946-49; Baron and PC 1946; Chmn. Leasehold Committee 1948. d. 24th April 1949.

VACHELL, Charles Francis

s. of Charles Redwood Vachell MD, FRCS, Cardiff. b. 1854. educ. Milton Abbas Sch. Blandford. Solicitor 1877. M.T. Jan. 1886. KC 1905. Bencher 1915, Reader 1926. Leader of Oxford circuit; Recorder of Gloucester 1905-32; JP Worcestershire and

Warwickshire. d. 5th Nov. 1935.

VAISEY, Sir Harry Bevir

s. of Arthur William Vaisey, Tring, Hertfordshire. b. 22nd June
1877. educ. Shrewsbury; Hertford Coll. Oxf. BA 1900, MA 1903,
Hon. Fellow 1946. L.I. Nov. 1901. KC 1925. Bencher 1929,
Treasurer 1950. Chan. of diocese of Derby 1927, Wakefield 1928,
Carlisle 1930-44; Chan. of diocese and vicar-genl. of York 1934-44;
Commissary-Genl. diocese of Canterbury 1942-44; Chancery judge
1944-60; Knight 1944; Chmn. London Diocesan Fund 1947; Chmn.
Hertfordshire Quarter Sess. 1946-58; DCL Lambeth 1939; member
Council of Keble Coll. Oxf. 1939; govr. Brentwood, and Forest
Schs. d. 24th Nov. 1965.

VAN DEN BERG, Frederick John

s. of Nathaniel Van den Berg, chief criminal magistrate,
Johannesburg, South Africa. b. Johannesburg 1893. educ. St. John's
Coll. Johannesburg. M.T. July 1916. KC 1931. d. 27th Jan. 1957.

VAUGHAN, Sir James

s. of Richard Vaughan, Cardiff. b. 14th March 1814. educ. privately;
Worcester Coll. Oxf. BA 1834. M.T. Nov. 1839. Commr. to inquire
into corrupt election practices at Gloucester 1859, Berwick-upon-
Tweed 1860; metrop. magistrate, Bow St. 1864-99; Chief and
knighted 1897; JP Middlesex and Home Counties. d. 20th May
1906.

VENABLES, George Stovin

s. of Richard Venables DD, Archdeacon of Carmarthen (d. 1859).
b. 18th June 1810. educ. Eton; Charterhouse; Jesus Coll. Camb. BA
1832, MA 1835, Fellow 1832-68, Tutor 1835-38. I.T. June 1836.

QC 1863. Bencher 1873, Reader 1877, Treasurer 1878. Practised at parliamentary bar; Sheriff of Radnorshire 1884; journalist for Saturday Review and the Times; said to be the original of George Warrington in Thackeray's "Pendennis". d. 6th Oct. 1888.

VESEY-FITZGERALD, John Vesey Foster

s. of William Leslie Foster Vesey-Fitzgerald JP, Moyvane, Co. Kerry (d. 1895). b. 25th Feb. 1848. educ. Rugby; Balliol Coll. Oxf. BA 1872, BCL 1873. I.T. June 1873. QC 1895. JP Warwickshire, Clare and Kerry. Author of The Law relating to the Pollution of Rivers, and other works. d. 24th April 1929.

VICK, Sir Godfrey Russell

s. of Richard William Vick JP, West Hartlepool, Durham. b. 24th Dec. 1892. educ. Leys Sch.; Jesus Coll. Camb. MA, LLB. WWI Capt. Durham Light Infantry, and general staff. I.T. May 1917. KC 1935. Bencher 1942. Recorder of Richmond, Yorkshire 1930-32, of Halifax 1932-39, of Newcastle-on-Tyne 1939-56; Chmn. of bar council 1948-52; Co-Pres. intern. Bar Assoc. 1950; Home Guard 1940; Cty. Ct. judge 1956-58; Master of Curriers' Co. 1947-48; Knight 1950. Brother of Cyril Hampton Vick (solicitor 1910). Father of Arnold Oughtred Russell Vick QC, circuit judge 1982, Jacqueline Russell Vick (I.T. 1950), and Clive Compston Russell Vick, solicitor (Master of Curriers' Co. 1967). d. 27th Sept. 1958.

VOS, Philip

s. of Jack Vos, London. b. 1891. educ. Owen's Sch.; London Sch. of Economics; Caius Coll. Camb. BA 1913. WWI Lieut. Norfolk Regt. (Croix de Guerre avec palme); Asst. Director of Priority at War Office 1917-18. I.T. June 1921. KC 1937. Wrote works on economic and political subjects. d. 6th Jan. 1948.

WADDY, Henry Turner

s. of Samuel Danks Waddy, Cty. Ct. judge. b. 12th Feb. 1863. educ. Leys Sch. I.T. June 1885. Member of bar council 1906; Recorder of Scarborough 1913-17; metrop. magistrate 1917, finally at North London 1918. d. 4th Nov. 1926.

WADDY, Samuel Danks

s. of Rev. Samuel Dousland Waddy DD, principal, Wesley Coll. Sheffield. b. 27th June 1830. educ. Wesley Coll.; London Univ. BA 1851. I.T. Nov. 1858. QC 1874. Bencher 1877. Recorder of Sheffield 1894-1902; MP Barnstaple 1874-79, Sheffield 1879-80, Edinburgh 1882-85, Lincolnshire (Brigg) 1886-94; Cty. Ct. judge 1896-1902; member Convocation, London Univ.; director Star Life Assce. Socy. d. 30th Dec. 1902.

WADE, Sir Charles Gregory

s. of William Burton Wade MICE, Singleton, New South Wales. b. Singleton, 26th Jan. 1863. educ. All Saints, Bathurst; King's Sch. Parramatta; Merton Coll. Oxf. BA 1885; Hon.Fellow. I.T. May 1886. KC 1919. Crown pros. NSW 1891; pros. for Western circuit and Central Criminal Ct. 1894-1902; MLA 1903-17; Premier NSW 1907-10; Att-Genl. and Minister for Justice 1904-10; KC (NSW) 1905; Leader of Liberal party in NSW 1907-16; Agent-Genl. for NSW in London 1917-20; judge of Supreme Ct. Sydney 1920-22; Knight 1918; KCMG 1920; FR Hist. Socy. 1918; played rugby for England 1883-86; d. 22nd Sept. 1922.

WAKEFIELD, Daniel

s. of Edward Wakefield, London, merchant (d. 1826). b. 1776. educ. privately. L.I. May 1807. KC 1834. Bencher 1835. Equity draftsman and conveyancer; writer on political economy. d. 19th July 1846.

WALKER, James Douglas

s. of James Ouchterlony Walker, Blairton, Aberdeenshire. b. 1841. educ. Rugby; Univ. Coll. Oxf. BA 1865, MA 1868. L.I. June 1866. QC 1891. Bencher 1887, Treasurer 1913. A commr. of supply for Aberdeenshire; JP Somerset. Author of a treatise on banking law, and wrote preface to Black Books of L.I. d. 24th June 1920.

WALKER, John

s. of John Walker, Bedford Square, London. b. 1795. L.I. Nov. 1819. QC 1841. Bencher 1842. Reported (with E. Jacob) chancery cases 1819-21. d. 6th Nov. 1869.

WALKER, Thomas Hollis

s. of John West Walker MD, JP, Hundleby House, Spilsby, Lincolnshire. b. 22nd Oct. 1860. educ. Epsom Coll.; Christ Church Oxf. BA 1883. Asst. master, Epsom Coll. I.T. July 1886. KC 1910. Bencher 1920, Treasurer 1941. Recorder of Derby 1918-38; Commr. of Assize, Midland circuit 1924, Swansea and Chester circuit 1931, Oxford and South Wales circuits 1932, South Wales and Western circuits 1933; Chmn. Lincolnshire (Parts of Lindsey) Quarter Sess. 1932-38; CMG 1935; JP Lindsey and Buckinghamshire. d. 12th Oct. 1945.

WALKER, William

s. of William Walker, Wilsick Hall, Doncaster, barrister (d. 1830). b. 1807. educ. Repton; Westminster; Trinity Coll. Camb. BA 1829, MA 1832. L.I. Jan. 1834. Cty. Ct. judge 1847-63; DL, JP Yorkshire West Riding. d. 21st April 1881.

WALLACE, George Henry

s. of Rev. Thomas Sneyd Wallace, Bolton, Lancashire. b. 18th Sept. 1854. educ. Clergy Orphan Sch. (St.Edmund's) Canterbury; Jesus Coll. Camb. BA 1876, MA 1881. L.I. May 1879; M.T. Nov. 1901. KC 1910. Bencher 1918-25. Chmn. Bar Benevolent Assoc. Joint author of treatise on employers' liability. d. 24th Nov. 1927.

WALLACE, Sir Robert

s. of Robert Wallace, Stephen's Green, Dublin. b. 1850. educ. Queen's Univ. Dublin BA 1871, LLB 1873; Queen's Univ. Belfast LLD. M.T. June 1874. QC 1894. Bencher 1901, Reader 1913, Treasurer 1923. Examr. to High Ct. 1884-94; MP Perth 1895-1907; Chmn. London Sess. 1907-31; Knight 1916. d. 19th March 1939.

WALLACE, Roger William

s. of Hugh Wallace JP, Dorset Hall, Wimbledon. b. 28th April 1854. educ. London Univ. M.T. Jan. 1882. QC 1896. The first Chmn. of RAC 1897-1904; Chmn. Royal Aero Club 1901-12; director of several electric light companies; AMIEE and member of that Institution's Council. Author of The Law of Letters Patent for Invention. d. 13th Dec. 1926.

WALLER, Frederick

s. of Samuel Waller, Cuckfield, Sussex (d. 1857). b. Feb. 1825. I.T. May 1848. QC 1874. Bencher 1874. Member Council of Legal Educ. 1879-88; Dep. Chmn. Huntingdon Quarter Sess.; DL, JP Huntingdon; JP Middlesex and Sussex. d. 22nd Feb. 1893.

WALLINGER, John Arnold

s. of William Arnold Wallinger, Westminster, merchant (d. 1798).
b. 1797. Special pleader. M.T. Feb. 1824. Serjeant 1848. d. 4th April
1860.

WALLINGTON, Sir Hubert Joseph

s. of James Wallington, Chesham, Buckinghamshire. b. 1st Aug.
1875. educ. privately. Solicitor 1899; practised in London, St.
Albans, and Watford. G.I. Nov. 1910. KC 1934. Bencher 1934,
Treasurer 1946, Vice-Treasurer 1947. Member Nat. Mark
Committee 1936-39; Recorder of Birmingham 1937-44; sat as
Aliens Trib. for Midlands (No.9) Defence Region 1939; Chmn.
Price Regulation Committee, and Aliens Advisory Committee,
Midlands (No.9) 1940; Commr. of Assize, Midland circuit 1939;
Chmn. Home Office Advisory Committee on Internees 1940; P D
and A judge 1944-60; Knight 1944. d. 19th Jan. 1962.

WALPOLE, Spencer Horatio

s. of Thomas Walpole, Stagbury Park, Surrey (d. 1840). b. 11th Sept.
1806. educ. Eton (captain); Trinity Coll. Camb. BA 1828, MA 1831;
Hon. LLD 1860. L.I. June 1831. QC 1846. Bencher 1846, Treasurer
1870. MP Midhurst 1846-56, Camb. Univ. 1856-82; Secy. of State,
Home Dept. 1852, 1858-59, 1866-67; a commr. for Church Estates
1856-58, 1862-66; High Steward Camb. Univ. 1887-98; Chmn. of
Great Western Ry. 1855-56; PC 1852; FRS 1860; FSA; Hon. DCL
Oxf. 1853. d. 22nd May 1898.

WALSH, Sir Cecil Henry

s. of Percival Walsh, Stanton Harcourt, Oxfordshire, solicitor (d.
1905). b. 26th March 1869. educ. Honiton Gr. Sch.; St John's Coll.
Oxf. BA 1890, MA 1910. G.I. and M.T. Jan. 1895. KC 1913.

Bencher (G.I.) 1916, Treasurer 1931. Puisne judge, High Ct. North West Provinces India 1915-28; acting CJ 1924 and 1926; Knight 1926; Mayor of Wimbledon 1909. Author of The Agra Double Murder, Indian Village Crimes 1929, Crime in India 1930. Father of Dennis Cecil Whittington Walsh (solicitor 1927). d. 24th Nov. 1946.

WALTER, Arthur James

s. of James Walter, Gough House, Croxted Road, West Dulwich, solicitor. b. 25th Feb. 1862. educ. Dulwich; London Univ. LLB. I.T. Nov. 1885. KC 1906. Bencher 1914. Mainly engaged in patent and trade mark litigation; manager of the Royal Institution 1919; a founder member of the Automobile Club; a govr. of Dulwich Coll. d. (suicide) 9th April 1919.

WALTON, Sir John Lawson

s. of John Walton, minister in Ceylon and South Africa. b. 4th Aug. 1852. educ. Merchant Taylors' Gt. Crosby; London Univ. 1872. I.T. June 1877. QC 1890. Bencher 1897. Had a flourishing practice in the commercial ct.; defended Whitaker Wright, the financier, 1904; MP South Leeds 1892-1908; Att-Genl. 1905-08; Knight 1905; JP Buckinghamshire; cousin of Sir Archibald Bodkin (DPP 1920-30). d. 18th Jan. 1908.

WALTON, Sir Joseph

s. of Joseph Walton, Fazakerley, Lancashire, merchant b. 25th Sept. 1845. educ. St. Francis Xavier's Coll.; Stonyhurst; London Univ. BA 1865. L.I. Nov. 1868. QC 1892. Bencher 1896. Practised in Liverpool in commercial and shipping cases; Recorder of Wigan 1895-1901; counsel to Jockey Club; Chmn. of bar council 1899; KB judge 1901-10; Knight 1901; Pres. Medico-Legal Socy. 1905; member Liverpool Sch. Bd. Author of Practice and Procedure of

Court of Common Pleas at Lancaster 1870; an editor of the Annual Practice of the Supreme Court d. 12th Aug. 1910.

WARD, Arthur Samuel

s. of James Newman Ward, Aston Park, Birmingham, draper. b. 1881. educ. King Edward's Sch. Birmingham. L.I. May 1906. KC 1943. Recorder of Newark-on-Trent 1935-43, of Coventry 1943-52. d. 6th Feb. 1952.

WARMINGTON, Sir Cornelius Marshall, Bt.

s. of Edward Warmington, Colchester, merchant. b. 5th June 1842. educ. Univ. Coll. Sch. London 1858. Solicitor 1864. M.T. Jan. 1869. QC 1882. Bencher 1885, Reader 1895, Treasurer 1904. MP West Monmouthshire 1885-95; member Senate, London Univ.; Baronet 1908; JP Sussex. Father of Sir Marshall Denham Warmington, 2nd Bt., Registrar in Bankruptcy, High Ct. 1926. d. 12th Dec. 1908.

WARREN, Samuel

s. of Samuel Warren, Rector of All Souls, Ancoats (d. 1862). b. 23rd May 1807. educ. studied medicine at Edin. Univ. 1826-27. Special pleader 1831-37. I.T. Nov. 1837. QC 1851. Bencher 1851, Treasurer 1866. Recorder of Hull 1852-74; MP Midhurst 1856-59; Master in Lunacy 1859-77; FRS 1835; Hon.DCL Oxf. 1853. Author of Popular and Practical Introduction to Law Studies 1835, Ten Thousand a year (fiction) 1839, Duties of attorneys and solicitors 1848, and other works. d. 29th July 1877.

WARRINGTON, Thomas Rolls (Lord Warrington)

s. of Thomas Warrington, London, silversmith and jeweller. b. 29th May 1851. educ. Rugby; Trinity Coll. Camb. BA 1873, MA 1876.

L.I. June 1875. QC 1895. Bencher 1897. Had large chancery practice in ct. of Kekewich J; member of bar committee 1883; Chancery judge 1904-15; Knight 1904; LJ 1915-26; PC 1915; Baron Warrington of Clyffe 1926; member Inns of Ct. Rifle Vol.; JP Wiltshire. d. 26th Oct. 1937.

WARRY, George Deedes

s. of George Warry JP, Shapwick House, Bridgwater, Somerset (d. 1883). b. 7th June 1831. educ. Winchester; Trinity Coll. Oxf. BA 1853, MA 1859. L.I. Nov. 1859. QC 1888. Bencher 1892. Recorder of Portsmouth 1879-1904; JP Somerset. Author of manual on Rating of Railways. Brother of William Taylor Warry ISO (L.I. 1866), Secy. to Charity Comm. d. 4th May 1904.

WATSON, Sir Arthur Townley, Bt.

s. of Sir Thomas Watson MD, FRS, 1st Bt. b. 13th Sept 1830. educ. Eton; St. John's Coll. Camb. BA 1852, MA 1855. L.I. Jan. 1856. QC 1885. Bencher 1887. Succeeded father 1882. d. 15th March 1907.

WATSON, Basil Bernard

s. of John Williams Watson, Olivers, Haslemere, Surrey. b. 5th Dec. 1877. educ. Highgate; Eton; Trinity Coll. Camb. BA 1899. I.T. Jan. 1902. KC 1923. WWI Lieut. Irish Guards; OBE. Metrop. magistrate 1923, finally at North London 1926-41. d. 20th Jan. 1941.

WATSON, Sir John Bertrand

s. of John Wilson Watson JP, Woodlands, Stockton, timber merchant. b. 16th May 1878. educ. Harrogate Coll. Solicitor 1900; Dep. Coroner, Durham 1902-11; MP Stockton-on-Tees 1917-23; member Durham CC 1912-19; Mayor of Stockton 1915-16. G.I.

May 1919. Bencher 1942. Parliamentary private secy. to Edward Shortt KC, MP, Home Secy.; metrop. magistrate 1928, finally at Bow St. 1941-48; Chief and knighted 1942. d. 16th Feb. 1948.

WATSON, William (Lord Thankerton)

s. of Watson L of A. b. 8th Dec. 1873. educ. Winchester; Jesus Coll. Camb. LLB 1895, Hon. Fellow 1929. Scottish bar 1899. KC 1914. MP South Lanarkshire 1913-18, Carlisle 1924-29; member Defence of the Realm Losses Comm. 1918-20; Procurator of Church of Scotland 1918-22; Advocate Depute 1919; Sol-Genl. for Scotland 1922; Lord Advocate 1922-24 and 1924-29; PC 1922; Hon. Bencher (G.I.) 1928; L of A 1929-48; Baron 1929; member Royal Co. of Archers; Hon.LLD Edin. 1929. Brother of Thomas Henry Watson (L.I. 1892); father of David John Watson QC, Scotland (G.I.1934). d. 13th June 1948.

WATSON, William (Lord Watson)

s. of Rev. Thomas Watson, Covington, Lanarkshire. b. 25th Aug. 1827. educ. privately; Edin. and Glasgow Univs. Hon.LLD Edin. 1876. Scottish bar 1851. Defended Dr. Edward Pritchard, the poisoner, 1865; Sol-Genl. for Scotland 1874-76; Dean of Faculty of Advocates 1875; Lord-Advocate, and MP for Glasgow and Aberdeen Univs. 1876-80; PC 1878; member Council for Educ. in Scotland 1878; L of A 1880; Baron 1880; DL. d. Kelso, 14th Sept 1899.

WATSON, Sir William Henry

s. of John Watson, Capt. 76th Foot (d. 1811). b. 1796. educ. Royal Military Coll. Marlow. Lieut. 1st Royal Dragoons 1812-14, served in Peninsular War; Lieut. 6th Dragoons 1815; half-pay 1816; present at Waterloo and entry of allied armies into Paris. Special pleader 1820-32. L.I. June 1832. QC 1843. Bencher 1843-56. Practised on

Northern circuit; MP Kinsale 1841-47, Hull 1854-56; Exch. Baron 1856-60; Knight 1856. Author of treatises on the law of arbitration and awards 1825, and on the law relating to the office and duty of sheriff 1837. d. 13th March 1860.

WATSON, William, Trevor

s. of Rev. William Watson, Kingsbridge, Devon. b. 30th June 1886. educ. Kingsbridge Gr. Sch.; Merton Coll. Oxf. Postmaster, BA 1909. G.I. June 1911 (Cert of Hon.). KC 1930. Bencher 1930. WWI Capt. RAF. Member of bar council; specialised in patent and scientific cases; member Inc. Council of Law Reporting 1935-42; member Comm. on Trade Mark law 1936-37. d. 24th March 1943.

WAUGH, William James

s. of James Waugh, Morecambe, Lancashire. b. 18th Nov. 1856. educ. privately. Articled to solicitor 1872. M.T. Nov. 1880. KC 1904. Bencher 1912, Reader 1924. The first recorder of Middlesbrough 1910-15; Recorder of Sheffield 1915-31. d. 20th Aug. 1931.

WEATHERLY, Frederic Edward

s. of Frederic Weatherly, Portishead, Somerset. b. 4th Oct 1848. educ. Brasenose Coll. Oxf. BA 1871, MA 1874; a coach at the Univ. I.T. May 1887. KC 1925. Known principally as the writer and composer of many popular songs, e.g. Danny Boy, Up from Somerset, Roses of Picardy. Published Piano and Gown (a book of recollections) 1926, and a manual on musical and dramatic copyright d. 7th Sept 1929.

WEBB, Charles Locock

s. of Samuel Webb, Chard, Somerset b. 26th Nov. 1822. educ. private sch. in Chard and Honiton. M.T. April 1850. QC 1875. Bencher 1879, Reader 1889. Junior counsel for Tichborne claimant in chancery suit against trustees; M.T. examr. for scholarships in constitutional and intern. law 1887-92; examr. in equity 1892. d. 15th Aug. 1898.

WEBSTER, Richard Everard (Lord Alverstone)

s. of Thomas Webster QC. b. 22nd Dec. 1842. educ. King's Coll. Sch.; Charterhouse; Trinity Coll. Camb. BA 1865, 35th Wrangler, MA 1868, Hon. LLD 1892. L.I. April 1868. QC 1878. Bencher. Tubman and Postman in Ct. of Exchequer. MP Launceston 1885, Isle of Wight 1885-1900; Att-Genl. 1885-86, 1886-92, 1895-1900; leading counsel for the Times in Parnell Comm. 1888; represented GB with Sir C. Russell in Behring Sea Arbitration 1893; leading counsel in Venezuela Arbitration 1899; MR 1900; member Royal Comm. on Historical MSS. 1900; LCJ 1900-13; one of the arbitrators in the Alaska Boundary Question 1903; Knight 1885; GCMG 1893; Baronet 1900; Baron 1900; PC 1900; Viscount 1913; FRS; KStJ; JP Surrey; Hon. LLD Edin. and Aberdeen; Hon.DCL Oxf. Published Recollections of Bar and Bench 1914. d. 15th Dec. 1915.

WEBSTER, Thomas

s. of Rev. Thomas Webster, Oakington, Cambridgeshire. b. 16th Oct 1810. educ. Charterhouse; Trinity Coll.Camb. BA 1832, 14th Wrangler, MA 1835. Secy. to Inst. of Civil Engineers 1837-41. L.I. May 1841. QC 1865. Bencher 1865. Specialised in scientific cases; FRS 1847. Author of works on patent law. d. 3rd June 1875.

WEDDERBURN, Alexander Dundas Ogilvy

s. of James Alexander Wedderburn, Madras Civil Service, Auchterhouse, Co. Forfar (d. 1854). b. 7th Aug. 1854. educ. Haileybury; Balliol Coll. Oxf. BA 1877. I.T. Jan. 1880. QC 1897. Bencher 1908. Recorder of Gravesend 1897-1921; a leader at parliamentary bar; CBE 1920 for war work with Red Cross; JP Sussex; one of John Ruskin's literary executors. d. 17th July 1931.

WELFORD, Richard Griffiths

s. of Richard Welford, Marlborough, Wiltshire, attorney and solicitor. b. 6th Dec. 1804. educ. in Marlborough; Harrow. I.T. May 1839. Commr. to inquire into corrupt election practices at Gloucester 1859; Cty. Ct. judge 1865-72. Author of treatise on equity 1842. Father of Richard Welford (L.I. 1861), murdered in Queensland 1872. d. 2nd Sept 1872.

WELLS, Henry Bensley

s. of Thomas Edward Wells, Wigod House, Wallingford, Berkshire. b. 12th Jan. 1891. educ. Winchester; Magdalen Coll. Oxf. BA 1913; coxed Univ. crew; coxed Leander crew at Olympic Games 1912. G.I. June 1914. WWI Lieut. 6th London Brigade RFA; MBE 1919. Cty. Ct. judge 1934-58. d. 4th July 1967.

WELLS, Sir Mordaunt Lawson

s. of Samuel Wells, London, barrister. b. 29th Sept. 1817. educ. Huntingdon Gr. Sch. M.T. Jan. 1841. Serjeant 1856; Recorder of Bedford 1856-58; puisne judge of High Ct. Calcutta 1858-63; Knight 1858; member Legislative Council of India 1860; petition presented for his recall after he denounced wholesale forgeries by Bengali litigants, but rejected by Secy. of State. d. 26th Nov. 1885.

WEST, Henry Wyndham

s. of Martin John West, barrister (d. 1870). b. 7th Nov. 1823. educ. Eton; Christ Church Oxf. BA 1844. I.T. May 1848. QC 1868. Bencher 1868. Recorder of Scarborough 1857-65, of Manchester 1865-93; Att-Genl. Duchy of Lancaster 1861-93; judge of Salford Hundred Ct. of Record 1868-93; MP Ipswich 1868-74 and 1883-86; JP Lancashire; director Lands Improvement Co. d. 25th Nov. 1893.

WESTLAKE, John

s. of John Westlake, Lostwithiel, Cornwall, woolstapler. b. 4th Feb. 1828. educ. privately; Trinity Coll. Camb. BA 1850, 6th Wrangler, Fellow 1851-60. L.I. Nov. 1854 (Cert. of Hon.). QC 1874. Bencher 1874. Recorder of Lostwithiel 1879; MP Romford 1885-86; prof. of intern. law Camb. 1888-1908; member Intern. Ct. of Arbitration 1900-06; Hon. Pres. Inst. of Intern. Law; Hon. LLD Edin. 1877; Hon. DCL Oxf. 1908; Japanese Order of Rising Sun (2nd class). Author of several works on intern. law. d. 14th April 1913.

WETHERED, Ernest Handel Cossham

s. of Edward Bestbridge Wethered JP, Totland Bay, Isle of Wight. b. 18th July 1878. educ. Cheltenham Coll.; Pembroke Coll. Camb. BA and LLB 1899, MA 1908. L.I. Nov. 1899. Chmn. Bristol and Swindon munitions tribs. 1914-19; OBE 1920; Chmn. Bristol Ct. of Referees 1919-34; Cty. Ct. judge 1934-50; Commr. for matrimonial causes 1947; Chmn. of trib. under Nat. Service Acts, South West District 1939-47 and 1951-60. d. 17th April 1975.

WETHERELL, Sir Charles

s. of Nathan Wetherell, Dean of Hereford, Master of Univ. Coll. Oxf. (d. 1807). b. 1770. educ. St. Paul's; Magdalen Coll. Oxf. BA 1790, MA 1793, Hon. DCL 1834. I.T. July 1794. KC. 1830. Bencher

1816, Reader 1824, Treasurer 1825. Successfully defended James Watson on charge of high treason 1817; MP Rye 1812, Shaftesbury 1813-18, Oxford 1820-26, Hastings 1826, Plympton Earl 1826-30, Boroughbridge 1830-32; Sol-Genl. 1824; Knight 1824; Att-Genl. 1826 and 1828; Recorder of Bristol; Great Bristol riot caused by his unpopularity 1831. Brother of Nathan Croke Wetherell, barrister (d. 1840). d. 17th Aug. 1846.

WHARTON, Robert

s. of Rev. Robert Wharton. educ. Eton; St. John's Coll. Camb. BA 1823, MA 1826. I.T. June 1832. Cty. Ct. judge 1847-49. d. 27th Oct. 1849, age 48.

WHATELEY, William

s. of William Whateley, Birmingham, solicitor. b. 7th Nov. 1794. educ. Merchant Taylors; New Coll. Oxf. BA 1820, MA 1825. I.T. Nov. 1820. QC 1841. Bencher 1841, Reader 1853, Treasurer 1854. Recorder of Shrewsbury, of Newbury 1832-42; frequently sat as Commr. of Assize. d. 15th Nov. 1862.

WHEELER, Thomas

s. of John Wheeler, Manchester, printer, b. 7th Oct. 1805. educ. Manchester Gr. Sch.; St. John's Coll. Camb. LLB 1853, LLD 1858. Solicitor in Manchester 1827-42. M.T. Jan. 1846. Serjeant 1861; judge of Salford Ct. of Record 1860-62; Cty. Ct. judge 1862-83; JP Lancashire and Cheshire. d. 17th June 1883.

WHEELER, Thomas Whittenbury

s. of Thomas Wheeler, Cty. Ct. judge. b. 28th April 1839. educ. Westminster; Trinity Hall Camb. BA 1863, MA 1878. I.T. Jan.

1865. QC 1886. Bencher 1894. Alderman, Kensington Borough Council; Chmn. Vestry of Kensington 1897; junior counsel to PO 1873-86; Cty. Ct. judge 1905-18; JP Cambridgeshire, Bedfordshire, Northamptonshire. Author of works on contract, betterment, and dilapidations. d. 3rd April 1923.

WHEELHOUSE, Sir William St. James

s. of James Wheelhouse, Snaith, Yorkshire. b. 1821. G.I. May 1844. QC 1877. Bencher 1877, Treasurer 1882. MP Leeds 1868-80; member Council of Legal Educ.; Knight 1882. Author of Law of Election. d. 8th March 1886.

WHIGHAM, James

s. of Robert Whigham, Halliday Hill, Dumfriesshire. b. 1808. educ. Edin. High Sch. and Univ. L.I. Jan. 1832; M.T. May 1838. Counsel to the Admiralty, PO and Mint; Cty. Ct. judge 1860-89; JP Buckinghamshire and Kirkcudbright; member Council of Edin. Univ. d. 9th Aug. 1889.

WHITBREAD, Gordon

s. of Jacob Whitbread, Loudham Park, Suffolk (d. 1838). b. 21st May 1814. educ. Exeter Gr. Sch.; Charterhouse; Brasenose Coll. Oxf. BA 1836, MA 1839. L.I. Jan. 1840. Equity draftsman and conveyancer; counsel to Duchy of Lancaster 1851, to Charity Commrs. 1853; secy. to Hatherley LC 1853-70; Cty. Ct. judge 1870-83; member governing body, Charterhouse 1872-83. d. 28th Jan. 1883.

WHITE, Frederick Meadows

s. of John Meadows White, Lewisham, solicitor. b. 21st Dec. 1829.

educ. Blackheath New Propr. Sch.; Balliol and Magdalen Colls. Oxf. BA 1852, MA 1855; Magdalen Demy 1849-65; Fellow 1865-67; Clerk 1869-73. I.T. Nov. 1853. QC 1877. Bencher 1878. Recorder of Canterbury 1883-93; Cty. Ct. judge 1893-98. d. 21st May 1898.

WHITE, George Rivers Blanco

s. of Thomas Blanco White, Chancery Lane, London, solicitor. b. 8th May 1883. educ. St. Paul's; Trinity Coll. Camb. BA 1905, 2nd Wrangler. L.I. Nov. 1907. KC. 1936. Bencher 1941. WWI Lieut. RGA, and court-martial officer. Recorder of Croydon 1940-56; Divorce Commr. 1948-57. Father of Thomas Anthony Blanco White (QC 1969). d. 26th March 1966.

WHITE, Henry Hopley

s. of James White, Lincoln's Inn, Chancery Lane. b. 1789. educ. Oriel Coll. Oxf. 1807. M.T. Nov. 1818. QC 1866. Bencher 1855, Reader 1858, Treasurer 1865. Practised as conveyancer. Edited Roper's Law of Legacies, and Cruise's Real property digest. d. 10th Dec. 1876.

WHITEHEAD, James

s. of John R. Whitehead, Padiham, Burnley, Lancashire. b. 1878. educ. Royal Coll. of Science; Imp. Coll. of Science London (Fellow). G.I. Nov. 1910. KC. 1923. Bencher 1924. Specialised in patent and trade mark, and other technical litigation; member of bar council 1932; Chmn. Departmental committee on dating of patents; member Senate, London Univ.; govr. Berkhamsted Sch.; JP Hertfordshire. d. 3rd April 1936.

WHITEHEAD, Sir Rowland Edward, Bt.

s. of Sir James Whitehead, 1st Bt. (d. 1917). b.1 st Sept. 1863. educ. Clifton Coll.; University Coll. Oxf. BA 1886, MA 1889. L.I. and

I.T. April 1888. KC. 1910. Bencher (L.I.) 1914. Equity draftsman and conveyancer; lecturer at Inc. Law Socy. 1890; MP Essex (South East) 1906-10; private secy. (unpaid) to Under-Secy. of State for Home Dept. (Rt. Hon. H.L. Samuel) 1906-09; secy. to Att-Genl. (Sir W.S. Robson KC, MP) 1909-10; succeeded brother as third baronet 1931; DL London; JP Berkshire. d. 9th Oct. 1942.

WHITEHORNE, James Charles

s. of James Whitehorne, London. educ. London Univ. BA 1850. M.T. and L.I. Nov. 1853. QC 1881. Bencher (L.I.) 1892. Cty. Ct. judge 1896-1905; member Convocation, London Univ.; JP Warwickshire. d. 28th Nov. 1905, age 74.

WHITEHURST, Charles Howard

s. of John Whitehurst, Derby. b. 1796. educ. Wadham Coll. Oxf. BA 1819. M.T. Feb. 1822. QC 1844. Bencher 1844, Reader 1850, Treasurer 1853. Leader of Midland circuit. d. 13th April 1879.

WHITELEY, George Cecil

s. of George Crispe Whiteley, The Chestnuts, Dulwich Common, London S.E., barrister. b. 10th May 1875. educ. Dulwich; King's Coll. Camb. BA 1897, MA 1898. M.T. June 1900. KC. 1921. Bencher 1928. Junior counsel to Treasury at Central Criminal Ct. 1912-21; Recorder of Sandwich 1920-29, of West Ham 1929-30, of Southend 1930-31; Commr. of Assize 1930; Chmn. Surrey Quarter Sess. 1925-32; Chmn. London Sess. 1931-32; judge of Mayor's and City of London Ct. 1932-34; Common Serjeant 1934-42; DL, JP Surrey; a govr. of Dulwich Coll. Published Whiteley's Licensing Laws, and Brief Life (autobiog.) 1942. d. 15th Oct. 1942.

WHITMARSH, James Francis

s. of James Whitmarsh, Salisbury. b. 1777. G.I. June 1803. KC. 1837. Bencher 1820, Treasurer 1830 and 1853. Commr. in Lunacy 1824-38; Registrar of Joint Stock Companies 1846-57. Author of a treatise on bankruptcy 1811. d. 28th Nov. 1857.

WHITMORE, Charles Shapland

s. of Genl. Sir George Whitmore, Slaughter, Gloucestershire (d. 1862). b. 25th July 1806. educ. Rugby; Trinity Coll. Camb. BA 1827, MA 1830. I.T. Nov. 1830. QC 1855. Bencher 1856, Reader 1868, Treasurer 1869. Recorder of Lichfield 1848-52, of Gloucester 1852-77; Cty. Ct. judge 1857-77; JP Gloucestershire. Father of Charles Algernon Whitmore MP (I.T. 1876). d. 17th May 1877.

WICKENS, Sir John

s. of James Stephen Wickens, Cavendish Sq. London, certificated conveyancer (d. 1858). b. 13th June 1815. educ. Eton; Balliol Coll. Oxf. BA 1836, MA 1839. L.I. May 1840. Bencher 1871. Equity draftsman and conveyancer; equity counsel to Treasury 1843-69 (which precluded him from applying for silk); V-C Cty. Palatine of Lancaster 1869-71; V-C 1871-73; Knight 1871. d. 23rd Oct. 1873.

WIGHTMAN, Sir William

s. of William Wightman, St. Clements, London. b. 1784. educ. University Coll. Oxf. 1801; Queen's Coll. BA 1805, MA 1809, Hon. Fellow 1859-63. Special pleader 1807-21. L.I. Nov. 1821; I.T. 1830. Junior counsel to Treasury; member comms. on practice of common law cts. 1830, and on proposal for a criminal law digest 1833; counsel in prosecutions following Bristol riots of 1831 (sparked off by unpopularity of the Recorder, Sir Charles Wetherell); QB judge 1841-63; Knight 1841. d. 10th Dec. 1863.

WIGHTWICK, Humphrey Wolseley

s. of William Norman Wightwick, Canterbury. b. 30th Sept. 1889. educ. Radley; Oriel Coll. Oxf. BA 1910, I.T. May 1914. WWI Capt. 12th Battn. London Regt., MC. Metrop. magistrate 1944, finally at Lambeth to 1961; JP London. d. 8th May 1962.

WIGRAM, Sir James

s. of Sir Robert Wigram, Bt. (d. 1830). b. 5th Nov. 1793. educ. privately; Trinity Coll. Camb. BA 1815, 5th Wrangler, MA 1818, Fellow 1817-18. L.I. Nov. 1819. KC. 1834. Bencher 1838. Practised in Chancery. MP Leominster 1841; V-C 1841-50; Knight and PC 1842; FRS. Author of An examination of the rules of law respecting the admission of extrinsic evidence in aid of the interpretation of wills 1831, and Points in the Law of Discovery 1836. Father of Arthur James Wigram (L.I. 1859). d. 29th July 1866.

WIGRAM, Loftus Tottenham

s. of Sir Robert Wigram, Bt. (d. 1830). b. 6th Nov. 1803. educ. in Richmond, Surrey; Trinity Coll. Camb. BA 1825, 8th Wrangler, MA 1828. L.I. Nov. 1828. QC 1842. Bencher 1842-84, Treasurer 1865. MP Camb. Univ. 1850-59; standing counsel to Secy. of State in council for India 1859. d. 19th Sept. 1889.

WILBERFORCE, Sir Herbert William Wrangham

s. of Edward Wilberforce, Manor House, St. Margaret's, Ware, Master of Supreme Ct. (d. 1914). b. 8th Feb. 1864. educ. London Intern. Coll.; University Coll. London; Downing Coll. Camb. BA 1885, LLB 1885. I.T. Jan. 1888. Member LCC 1901-04; stip. magistrate Bradford 1908-14; metrop. magistrate 1914, finally at Bow St. 1925-26; Dep. Chmn. London Sess. 1926-38; Knight 1931; JP Middlesex; a tennis champion. d. 28th March 1941.

WILBRAHAM, Edward

s. of Edward Wilbraham, Cirencester, Gloucestershire. b. 1785. educ. Eton. L.I. Feb. 1810. QC 1841. Bencher 1841. Dep. Clerk of the Crown in Chancery 1818-42. d. 15th Sept. 1859.

WILBRAHAM, Sir Philip Wilbraham Baker, Bt.

s. of Sir George Barrington Baker Wilbraham, 5th Bt., barrister. b. 17th Sept. 1875. educ. Harrow; Balliol Coll. Oxf. BA 1898, MA 1901, Fellow of All Souls Coll. 1899-1906; DCL 1936. L.I. June 1901. Bencher 1942. Chan. of diocese of Chester 1913-34, of Truro 1923-34, of Chelmsford 1928-34, of Durham 1929-34; Chan. and Vicar-Genl. of diocese and province of York 1915-34; Vicar-Genl. of province of Canterbury 1934-55; Secy. of Church Assembly 1920-39; Dean of the Arches 1934-55; Auditor of Chancery Ct. of York 1934-55; Master of the Faculties; Commissary of St Paul's Cath. 1942; First Church Estates Commr. 1939-54; KBE 1954; JP Cheshire. Succeeded father 1912. d. 11th Oct. 1957.

WILD, Sir Ernest Edward

s. of Edward Wild JP, Eaton, Norwich (d. 1929). b. 1st Jan. 1869. educ. Norwich Sch.; Jesus Coll. Camb. BA 1890, LLB 1891, LLM 1897. M.T. Jan. 1893. KC. 1912. Member LCC (Holborn) 1907-10; judge of Norwich Guildhall Ct. of Record 1897-1922; Inspector of Metrop. Spec. Constabulary 1915; MP West Ham (Upton) 1918-22; Knight 1918; Recorder of London 1922; High Steward of Southwark 1922; DL London; Hon. Freeman Norwich. Biography by R.J. Blackham 1935. d. 13th Sept. 1934.

WILDE, James Plaisted (Lord Penzance)

s. of Edward Archer Wilde, College Hill, London, solicitor (d. 1871). b. 12th July 1816. educ. Winchester; Trinity Coll. Camb. BA

1838, MA 1842. I.T. Nov. 1839. QC 1855. Bencher 1856-60 and 1877-99. Junior counsel to Excise and Customs 1840-60; leader of Northern circuit; counsel to Duchy of Lancaster 1860; unsuccessful as parliamentary candidate; Exch. Baron 1860-63; Knight 1860; chief judge of Probate and Divorce Ct. 1863-72; PC 1864; Baron Penzance 1869; judge under Public Worship Regulation Act 1874; Dean of the Arches; Master of the Faculties, and Official Principal of Chancery Ct. of York 1875-99; served on numerous royal comms. d. 9th Dec. 1899.

WILDE, Thomas (Lord Truro)

s. of Thomas Wilde, College Hill, London, attorney. b. 7th July 1782. educ. St. Paul's. Attorney 1805, practised in London; special pleader. I.T. Feb. 1817. One of the counsel who defended Queen Caroline 1820 (she later appointed him one of her executors); Serjeant 1824; King's serjeant 1827; leader in Ct. of Common Pleas; MP Newark-on-Trent 1831-32 and 1835-41, Worcester 1841; introduced Rowland Hill's scheme for postal reform; Sol-Genl. 1839; Knight 1840; Att-Genl. for two months in 1841, and for a few days in 1846; PC 1846; CJ of Common Pleas 1846; LC 1850-52; Baron Truro of Bowes 1850; initiated various Chancery reforms, particularly appointment of two Lords Justices; his law library donated to H of L. Father of Charles Robert Claude Wilde, 2nd Baron (I.T. 1842), and Thomas Montague Carrington Wilde (I.T. 1842), registrar of Bristol Bankruptcy Ct.; brother of Sir John Wilde, CJ of Cape Colony (d. 1859), and Edward Archer Wilde, solicitor. d. 11th Nov. 1855.

WILDMAN, Richard

s. of James Wildman, Chilham Castle, Kent (d. 1805). b. 1802. educ. Harrow; Christ Church Oxf. BA 1825. I.T. Nov. 1829. Recorder of Nottingham 1837-81; defended the Sutton-in-Ashfield rioters (Chartists) 1839; judge of Derbyshire Ct. of Requests; Cty. Ct. judge 1847-81. Author of Institutes of International Law 1849-51. d.

Lucerne, 26th Aug. 1881.

WILKINS, Charles

s. of George Wilkins, Shaftesbury, Dorset, surgeon. b. 29th June 1802. Apprenticed to an apothecary; kept a day school in Birmingham; a strolling player in the Midland counties. I.T. June 1835. Serjeant 1845; patent of precedence 1850. Defended William Henry Barber, solicitor, charged with forgery of a will 1844 (transported to Australia, but later declared innocent). d. 4th March 1857.

WILKINSON, George Hutton

s. of Thomas Wilkinson, Walsham le Willows, Suffolk. b. 25th Jan. 1791. educ. Harrow; Trinity Coll. Camb. BA 1811, MA 1814. L.I. June 1814. Mun. Corpn. Commr. 1833; Recorder of Hartlepool 1833, of Newcastle-on-Tyne 1834-54; Cty. Ct. judge 1847-53; DL, JP Durham. d. 23rd Dec. 1859.

WILL, John Shiress

s.of John Will, Hanover (Jamaica), and Dundee. b. 1840. educ. Brechin Gr. Sch.; King's Coll. London. M.T. June 1864. QC 1883. Bencher 1888, Reader 1898. MP Montrose Burghs 1885-96; Cty. Ct. judge 1906-10. Author of manual of law of gas and water; edited Wharton's Law Lexicon. d. 24th May 1910.

WILLCOCK, John William

s. of John Willcock, Bideford, Devon, merchant. b. 1800. I.T. Nov. 1825; L.I. 1841. QC 1851. Bencher 1851. Chancery leader. d. 5th April 1881.

WILLES, Sir James Shaw

s. of James Willes, Cork, physician. b. 13th Feb. 1814. educ. Trinity Coll. Dublin BA 1836, Hon. LLD 1860. I.T. June 1840. Tubman in Ct. of Exch. 1851-55; member comm. on common law procedure 1850; judge of Common Pleas 1855-72; Knight 1855; member Indian law comm. 1861, Irish law comm. 1862; PC 1871; edited (with H.S. Keating) Smith's leading cases in common law 1849; served in Inns of Ct. Vol. Corps from its formation in 1859. d. (suicide) 2nd Oct. 1872.

WILLES, Richard Augustus

s. of William Willes DL, JP, Newbold Comyn, Warwickshire (d. 1885). b. 24th Feb. 1881. educ. HMS Britannia. Midshipman RN; on China Station 1897-1901; served in Boxer rebellion; invalided out; acting sub-lieut. 1901. L.I. May 1905. Bencher 1933. Recorder of Newark 1932-34, of Coventry 1934-41; member Council of Selden Socy. 1934; member Council of Legal Educ. 1936-41; Cty. Ct. judge 1941-53; Dep. Chmn. Warwickshire Quarter Sess. 1921-50; JP Warwickshire. d. 17th Aug. 1966.

WILLES, William Henry

s. of James Willes, Cork, physician. b. 1822. educ. Trinity Coll. Dublin BA 1844, MA 1847. I.T. May 1848. Cty. Ct. judge 1859-63. d. 2nd Feb. 1863.

WILLIAMS, Benjamin Francis

s. of Enoch E. Williams, Merthyr Tydfil, Glamorgan, minister. b. 27th Feb. 1845. educ. Shrewsbury; St. John's Coll. Camb. BA 1866. M.T. Jan. 1867. QC 1885. Bencher 1891, Reader 1901, Treasurer 1903. Recorder of Carmarthen 1878-90, of Cardiff 1890-1914; JP Monmouthshire. d. 28th July 1914.

WILLIAMS, Benjamin Thomas

s. of Rev. Thomas Rayson Williams, Narberth, Pembrokeshire. b. 19th Nov. 1832. educ. Glasgow Univ. BA 1853, MA 1854. G.I. Jan. 1859; M.T. April 1875. QC 1875. Recorder of Carmarthen 1872-78; MP Carmarthen 1878-81; Cty. Ct. judge 1881-85; member Council, Glasgow Univ.; JP Breconshire, Glamorganshire, Pembrokeshire. Author of The Case of George William Gordon 1866, and The Commercial Law Annual 1871. d. 21 st March 1890.

WILLIAMS, Sir Charles Frederick

s. of Richard Williams, Dursley, Gloucestershire. Did not attend university; served in militia. L.I. April 1804. KC. 1828. Bencher. Commr. in Bankruptcy 1832; Recorder of Ipswich to 1842; Knight 1838; JP Hampshire; was less than five feet tall, and known as "Minimus". d. 17th Jan. 1845, age 65.

WILLIAMS, Sir Charles James Watkin

s. of Rev. Peter Williams, Llansannan, Denbighshire. b. 23rd Sept. 1828. educ. Ruthin Gr. Sch.; St. Mary Hall Oxf. 1851; qualified in medicine, Univ. Coll. Hosp. London. I.T. Nov. 1854. QC 1873. Bencher 1873. Tubman in Ct. of Exch. 1869-73. MP Denbigh Boroughs 1868-80, Carnarvonshire 1880; QB judge 1880-84. Author of An examination of the Law of Church Rates, 1854, and An Introduction to the principles and practice of pleading in Civil Actions in the Superior Courts 1857. d. 17th July 1884.

WILLIAMS, Sir Edward Vaughan

s. of John Williams, serjeant (d. 1810). b. 1797. educ. Winchester; Westminster; Trinity Coll. Camb. BA 1820, MA 1823. L.I. June 1823. Recorder of Kidwelly; judge of Common Pleas 1846-65; resignation forced by deafness precluded further advancement; Knight 1847; PC and member judicial committee 1865. Author of treatise on law of executors and administrators 1832; edited (with

J. Patteson) KB reports of Sir Edmund Saunders, 1824, and edited notes to those reports by Serjeant Williams; edited (with Serjeant D'Oyley) Burn's Justice of the Peace and Parish Officer 1836. d. 2nd Nov. 1875.

WILLIAMS, Frederick Sims

s. of Frederick Sims Williams, Penrhyn, Pembrokeshire, barrister (d. 1863). b. 18th Jan. 1855. educ. King's Coll. Sch. London; Trinity Hall Camb. LLB 1878. I.T. Nov. 1879. KC. 1913. Commr. for Bd. of Trade; practised in commercial and insurance cases. d. 27th Dec. 1941.

WILLIAMS, Sir George Clark, Bt.

s. of Samuel Williams, Llanelly, South Wales. b. 2nd Nov. 1878. educ. Bishop's Stortford; University Coll. of Wales LLD 1956; London Univ. BA 1898. Solicitor 1902-09, practised in Llanelly. I.T. May 1909. KC. 1934. WWI Capt. Welch Regt. Cty. Ct. judge 1935-48; Lord Lieut. Carmarthenshire 1949-53; JP Carmarthen; life govr. Univ. Coll. of Wales; Baronet 1955. CStJ 1951. d. 15th Oct. 1958.

WILLIAMS, Gwilym

s. of David J. Williams, Miskin Manor, Llantrissant, Glamorgan (d. 1862). b. 2nd May 1839. I.T. June 1863. Stip. magistrate Pontypridd 1872-84; Cty. Ct. judge 1884-1906; Chmn. Glamorganshire Quarter Sess.; DL, JP Glamorganshire. See also Sir Rhys Rhys-Williams, Bt. d. 25th March 1906.

WILLIAMS, Hubert Llewelyn

s. of Mayberry Williams, Pontypridd, Glamorgan, merchant. b.

1890. educ. Llandovery Coll.; Lincoln Coll. Oxf. MA 1919. WWI
Lieut. 250 Siege Battery RGA. M.T. Nov. 1920. KC. 1938. Bencher
1947. Recorder of Carmarthen 1941-50; Vice-Chmn.
Glamorganshire Quarter Sess. 1939, Chmn. 1949-61; stip.
magistrate Swansea 1950-60; DL, JP Glamorgan; JP Swansea. d.
11th May 1964.

WILLIAMS, Sir John

s. of Rev. William Williams, Bunbury, Cheshire (d. 1813). bapt.
10th Feb. 1777. educ. Manchester Gr. Sch.; Trinity Coll. Camb. BA
1798, MA 1801, Fellow 1800. I.T. Nov. 1804. KC. 1827. Bencher
1827. Junior counsel to Brougham and Denman in defence of Queen
Caroline 1820; MP Lincoln 1823-26, Winchilsea 1830-32; active
in criticism of delays in Chancery; Sol-Genl. and Att-Genl. to Queen
Adelaide 1830; Exch. Baron 1834; Knight 1834; KB judge 1834-46.
d. 14th Sept. 1846.

WILLIAMS, Sir John Fischer

s. of John Williams, Elvaston Place, London S.W. b. 26th Feb. 1870.
educ. Harrow; New Coll. Oxf. BA 1892, MA 1895, Fellow 1892-99.
L.I. Nov. 1894. KC. 1921. Equity draftsman and conveyancer; asst.
legal adviser Home Office 1918-20; Br. legal rep. on Reparation
Comm., Paris 1920-30; Chmn. Royal Comm. which led to Tithe Act
1936; Br. member Permanent Ct. of Arbitration at the Hague
1936-47; member Inst. of Intern. Law, and of Belgian Royal
Academy; Knight 1923; CBE 1917. Published political works. d.
17th May 1947.

WILLIAMS, Joshua

s. of Thomas Williams, Aston, Oxfordshire. b. 23rd May 1813. educ.
privately, University Coll. London. L.I. May 1838. QC 1865.
Bencher 1865. Conveyancing counsel to Ct. of Chancery 1862-64;

prof of law of real and personal property at Inns of Ct. 1875-80; styled "The Gamaliel of Real Property Law". Author of leading works on real and personal property. Father of Sir Joshua Strange Williams, puisne judge, New Zealand 1875. d. 25th Oct. 1881.

WILLIAMS, Montagu Stephen

s. of John Jeffries Williams, barrister (d. 1862). b. 30th Sept. 1835. educ. Eton. Classical master Ipswich Gr. Sch. 1854-55; Lieut. South Lincoln militia 1855; Ensign 96th Foot 1856; resigned 1857; theatrical author (with F.C. Burnand) 1860-63. I.T. April 1862. QC 1888. Junior pros. counsel to Treasury 1879; metrop. magistrate 1886, finally at Marylebone 1891-92; took appointment to bench when throat ailment prevented him continuing as an advocate. Author of Leaves of a Life (reminiscences) 1890, Later Leaves 1891, Round London 1892. d. 23rd Dec. 1892.

WILLIAMS, Robert Griffith

s. of Robert Hubert Williams, Liverpool. b. 1829. educ. Univ. Coll. London MA 1856. M.T. June 1857. QC 1874. Author (with G. Bruce) of Admiralty practice 1869; an editor of Chitty's Precedents in Pleading. d. 18th Oct. 1875.

WILLIAMS, Robert Vaughan

s. of William Williams, Peniarthuca, Merioneth. b. 14th Jan. 1822. educ. Shrewsbury; Christ Church Oxf. BA 1845, MA 1848. L.I. June 1848. Counsel to Mint and PO; Cty. Ct. judge 1863-74; JP Carnarvon, Denbigh, Flintshire, Merioneth, Anglesey. d. 21st June 1878.

WILLIAMS, Roland Edmund Lomax Vaughan

s. of Vaughan Williams LJ. b. 1866. educ. Merton Coll. Oxf 1886. L.I. and M.T. Nov. 1893. KC. 1913. Bencher (L.I.) 1918. Recorder of Carmarthen 1917-23, of Swansea 1923-30, of Cardiff 1930-45; Vice-Chmn. of bar council 1935; Br. member of 1st divn. Anglo-German mixed arbitral trib. 1920-28; Chmn. Aliens Deportation Advisory Committee. d. 22nd Jan. 1949.

WILLIAMS, Sir Roland Lomax Vaughan

s. of Edward Vaughan Williams J. b. 31st Dec. 1837. educ. Westminster; Christ Church Oxf. BA 1860, MA 1863, Fellow. L.I. Nov. 1864. QC 1889. Bencher 1886. QB judge 1890-97; Knight 1890; LJ 1897-1914; PC 1897; JP Surrey; assumed name of Lomax in place of Bowdler 1865. Author of The Law and Practice of Bankruptcy 1870; joint editor of Williams' Law of Executors. Brother of Walter Vere Vaughan Williams (I.T. 1868). d. 8th Dec. 1916.

WILLIAMS, William Llewelyn

s. of Morgan Williams, Brownhill, Carmarthenshire. b. 10th March 1867. educ. Llandovery Coll. Brasenose Coll. Oxf. MA, BCL. L.I. Jan. 1897. KC. 1912. Bencher 1917. MP Carmarthen District 1906-18; Recorder of Swansea 1912-15, of Cardiff 1915-22. d. 22nd April 1922.

WILLINK, Sir Henry Urmston, Bt.

s. of William Edward Willink, FRIBA, Liverpool (d. 1924). b. 7th March 1894. educ. Eton; Trinity Coll. Camb. BA 1919, MA 1933; DCL Lambeth 1955. WWI Capt. RFA, MC (despatches, Croix de Guerre). I.T. Nov. 1920. KC. 1935. Bencher 1942. MP North Croydon 1940-48; special commr. for rehousing homeless of

London 1940-43; Minister of Health 1943-45; Chmn. Royal Comm. on Betting, Lotteries and Gaming 1949-51; Chan. of dioceses of Norwich, St. Edmundsbury and Ipswich 1948-55; member Eastern Area Bd. Br. Transport Comm.; Chmn. Royal Comm. on Police 1961-62; Dean of the Arches, Master of the Faculties, vicar-genl. of Canterbury and auditor of Chancery Ct. of York 1955-69; high bailiff of Westminster 1942-67; Fellow of Eton Coll. 1946-56; Master of Magdelene Coll. Camb. 1948-66, Hon. Fellow 1966, V-C 1953-55; govr. Wellington Coll. 1955-61; PC 1943; Baronet 1957; Major, West Lancashire Regt. (TA) 1923-38; Officer of the Legion of Honour; Hon. LLD, Liverpool and Melbourne; Hon. FRIBA. Hon. liveryman Goldsmiths' Co. 1943. d. 1st Jan. 1973.

WILLIS, Edward Cooper

s. of Thomas Willis MD, Newark, Nottinghamshire. b. 16th March 1831. educ. Brighton Coll.; Tonbridge; London Univ. 1850; Caius Coll. Camb. MB 1858; MRCS Edin. I.T. Nov. 1865. QC 1882. Bencher 1887, Treasurer 1907. Author of Law and Practice in Bankruptcy 1884. d. 26th July 1912.

WILLIS, William

s. of William Willis, Dunstable and Luton, straw-hat manufacturer. b. 29th April 1835. educ. Free Gr. Sch. Dunstable; Huddersfield Coll.; London Univ. BA 1859, LLD 1865. Employed six years in commerce. I.T. June 1861. QC 1877. Bencher 1880. Examr. in common law, London Univ.; Recorder of Maldon and Saffron Walden 1886-1911; MP Colchester 1880-85; Cty. Ct. judge 1897-1911. d. 22nd Aug. 1911.

WILLIS, William Outhwaite

s. of William Willis, Cty. Ct. judge. b. 15th Feb. 1870. educ. Leys Sch.; Emmanuel Coll. Camb. BA 1894. I.T. June 1895. KC. 1924.

Bencher 1930. Practised in P D and A Division. Father of Roger Blenkiron Willis (I.T. 1930), Cty. Ct. judge. d. 22nd Aug. 1940.

WILLMER, Sir Henry Gordon

s. of Arthur Washington Willmer JP, Heathfield, Willaston, Wirral, Cheshire (d. 1940). b. 11th Aug. 1899. educ. Birkenhead Sch.; Corpus Christi Coll. Oxf. BA 1922, MA 1950, Hon. Fellow 1949. I.T. Nov. 1924. KC. 1939. Bencher 1946, Treasurer 1969. Wreck commr. under Merchant Shipping Acts; arbitrator under Lloyd's Salvage Agreement; WWII with Coast Artillery, and Col. with Allied Mil. Govt., Italy; OBE 1945, TD. P D and A judge 1945-58; Knight 1945; Chmn. Shipping Claims Trib. 1946; member General Claims Trib. 1950; Chmn. Inns of Ct. Mission 1950; member Supreme Ct. Committee on Practice and Procedure 1947; LJ 1958-69; PC 1958; Chmn. Committee of Pharmaceutical Socy. of GB 1970; Chmn. Assoc. of Average Adjusters 1971; Chmn. Northern Ireland Detention Appeal Trib. 1972; Hon. LLD Liverpool 1966. Father of John Franklin Willmer (QC 1967). d. 17th May 1983.

WILLMORE, Graham

s. of Joseph Willmore, Birmingham. b. 1804. educ. King Edward's Sch. Birmingham; Trinity Coll. Camb. BA 1825, MA 1828. M.T. Nov. 1829. QC 1851. Bencher 1852, Reader 1854. Recorder of Wells 1853-56; Cty. Ct. judge 1853-56. d. Neuilly, nr. Paris, 19th June 1856.

WILLS, Sir Alfred

s. of William Wills JP, Park Mount, Edgbaston, solicitor (d. 1860). b. 11th Dec. 1828. educ. Proprietary Sch., Edgbaston; University Coll. London BA 1849, LLB 1851, Fellow. M.T. Nov. 1851. QC 1872. Bencher 1874, Reader 1882, Treasurer 1892. Hon. Bencher

1912. The first Recorder of Sheffield 1881-84; QB judge 1884-1905; Knight 1884; Pres. Ry. and Canal Comm. 1888-93; PC 1905; JP Hampshire; one of the founders and Pres. Alpine Club 1863-65; edited his father's work, On the rationale of Circumstantial Evidence. d. 9th Aug. 1912.

WILSON, Clyde Tabor

s. of Dr. Foden Wilson, Birkenhead. b. 21st Sept. 1889. educ. Rugby; Trinity Coll. Camb. BA 1911, LLB. I.T. June 1913. WWI Lieut. 5th London Brigade RFA. MP Liverpool (West Toxteth) 1931-35; member LCC 1925-35; Recorder of Birkenhead 1934-35; metrop. magistrate 1935, finally at Marlborough St. to 1962. d. 13th Nov. 1971.

WILSON, Sir Giffin

s. of Rev. Edward Wilson, Binfield, Berkshire. b. 1766. L.I. Jan. 1789. KC. 1818. Bencher 1819, Treasurer 1830. Counsel to the Ordnance; Recorder of Windsor 1806-36; Commr. in Bankruptcy 1792-1826; MP Yarmouth 1808-12; Vice-Justice of Chester 1825; V-C of Duchy of Lancaster 1822-26; Master in Chancery 1826-48; Knight 1828. d. 4th Aug. 1848.

WILSON, John

s. of William Wilson, Stockton-on-Tees. b. 1785. M.T. May 1811. Recorder of Carmarthen 1836-51; Cty. Ct. judge 1847-51; reported Exch. cases 1805-17, Chancery cases 1818-19. d. 8th Dec. 1851.

WILSON, Sir William Courthope Townshend

s. of Richard Duff Wilson, Liverpool. b. 1865. educ. Birkenhead Coll.; Liverpool Institute. G.I. May 1900 (Cert. of Hon.). KC 1919.

Bencher 1920, Treasurer 1932. Equity draftsman and conveyancer; V-C of Cty. Palatine of Lancaster 1925-36; Knight 1930; Chmn. Liverpool Bd. of Legal Studies; member Court, Liverpool Univ. d. 5th Jan. 1944.

WINCH, Henry

s. of Edward Winch, Chatham, brewer. b. 1840. M.T. Nov. 1872. QC 1888. Bencher 1893. Leader on South Eastern circuit. Author of commentary on Agricultural Holdings Act 1875. d. 13th June 1894.

WINFIELD, Sir Percy Henry

s. of Frederick Charles Winfield, Stoke Ferry, Norfolk, corn merchant. b. 16th Sept. 1878. educ. King's Lynn Gr. Sch.; St. John's Coll. Camb. BA and LLB 1899, LLM 1906, LLD 1918, Fellow 1921. WWI Lieut. Cambridgeshire Regt.; attached to staff at War Office 1919. I.T. June 1903. KC. 1943. Hon. Bencher 1938. Law lecturer, St. John's Coll. 1918-28, Trinity Coll. 1918-26; univ. lecturer in law Camb. 1926-28; Rouse Ball prof. of English law, Camb. 1928-43; Reader in common law to Council of Legal Educ. 1938-49; Pres. Socy. of Public Teachers of Law 1929-30; WWII Home Guard; member Council of Senate, Camb. 1924-32; member LC's Law Revision and Law Reporting Committees; Dep. Cty. Ct. judge; Knight 1949; FBA 1934; JP Cambridge; Hon. LLD Harvard, Leeds, London. Published works on legal procedure, intern. law, legal history, torts, contract, and legal essays; edited Cambridge Law Journal 1927-47, and Law Quarterly Review 1929. d. 7th July 1953.

WING, John William

s. of Rev. John Wing, Thornhaugh, Northamptonshire. b. 21st June 1813. educ. Charterhouse; University Coll. Oxf. BA 1835, MA 1837, Fellow 1837-44. L.I. Nov. 1838. Cty. Ct. judge 1847-55. d.

18th June 1855.

WINGATE-SAUL, Sir Ernest Wingate

s. of William Wingate Wingate-Saul MD, Fenton Cawthorne House, Lancaster. b. 25th March 1873. educ. Rugby; Christ Church Oxf. BA 1895, MA 1898. I.T. May 1897. KC. 1919. Bencher 1925. Recorder of Preston, and judge and assessor of Borough Ct. of Pleas, 1921-28; judge of appeal, Isle of Man 1925-28; umpire under Unemployment Insce. Act 1928, and under Reinstatement in Civil Employment Act 1944; Knight 1933. Father of Bazil Sylvester Wingate-Saul (1906-75) Cty. Ct. judge. d. 13th Dec. 1944.

WINGFIELD-BAKER, William

s. of George Wingfield, Mickleham, Surrey (d. 1858). b. 1772. educ. Christ Church Oxf. BA 1792. L.I. Nov. 1797. KC. 1818. Bencher 1818, Treasurer 1828. MP Bodmin 1806-07; Commr. in Bankruptcy 1803-16; CJ of Brecknock circuit 1816-24; Master in Chancery 1824-49; Lieut. Law Association Volunteers 1803; assumed additional name of Baker 1849. Father of Richard Baker Wingfield MP (1. T. 1827) and Frederick Bassett Wingfield (L.I.1850). d. 20th March 1858.

WINSLOW, Thomas Ewing

s. of Thomas Forbes Winslow, London. b. 1st Feb. 1820. M.T. Nov. 1845. QC 1874. Registrar of Ct. of Bankruptcy, London 1859, Commr. 1865-69. Father of Reginald Winslow (L.I. 1882). d. 23rd Jan. 1896.

WITT, John George

s. of James M. Witt, Swaffham Prior, Cambridgeshire, barrister. b. 24th Sept. 1836. educ. Eton (captain); King's Coll. Camb. BA 1860,

MA 1863, Fellow 1859-88. L.I. Jan. 1864. QC 1892. Bencher 1895. Editor of the Law Journal 1879-94. Author of Then and Now 1897, and Life in the Law. d. 7th Feb. 1906.

WOOD, Charles William

s. of John Wood, Kennington, London, tailor and draper. b. 7th May 1813. educ. Peterhouse Camb. BA 1838. Apprenticed to wholesale druggists in Thames St. London. Special pleader 1840-43. L.I. June 1843. QC 1872. Bencher 1872. Standing counsel to London and South Western Ry. Co. d. 13th Jan. 1884.

WOOD, William Page (Lord Hatherley)

s. of Sir Matthew Wood, Bt., Falcon Square, London, hop merchant (d. 1843). b. 29th Nov. 1801. educ. Woodbridge Free Gr. Sch.; Winchester; Geneva Univ.; Trinity Coll. Camb. BA 1824, 24th Wrangler, MA 1827, Fellow 1824-30, LLD 1864. L.I. Nov. 1827. QC 1845. Engaged in parliamentary practice 1828-41; MP Oxford 1847-53; V-C Cty. Palatine of Lancaster 1849-51, and instituted reforms in that Ct.; Sol-Genl. 1851-52 and 1852-53; Knight 1851; a commr. for reform of Ct. of Chancery 1851; V-C 1853 (having declined in 1851); LJ and PC 1868; LC 1868-72; Baron 1868; acted with Lord Wensleydale and Sir Robert Peel, as arbitrators between Queen Victoria and the King of Hanover with reference to certain Crown Jewels claimed by the latter; FRS 1834; Hon. DCL Oxf. 1851; translated Lord Bacon's Novum Organum 1826. d. 10th July 1881. Memoirs of his life by W. R. Stephens, 2 vols. 1883.

WOOD, William Wightman

s. of Canon Peter Almeric Leheup Wood, Middleham, Yorkshire. b. 21st May 1846. educ. Eton; University Coll. Oxf. BA 1868. I.T. Jan. 1871. Counsel to the Mint in Essex; Cty. Ct. judge 1894-1914; JP Leicestershire. d. 9th Feb. 1914.

WOODCOCK, Hubert Bayley Drysdale

s. of Thomas Woodcock, Antigua, W.I., barrister, Queen's Advocate, Gold Coast. b. Antigua, Sept. 1867. educ. Eastbourne Coll.; City of London Sch. M.T. Jan. 1891. KC. 1923. Member Mauritius Royal Comm. 1909; Recorder of Stamford 1912-24; acting Chmn. Soke of Peterborough Quarter Sess. 1916-42; Cty. Ct. judge 1924-40. d. 12th Feb. 1957.

WOODFALL, Robert

s. of Henry Woodfall, Stanmore, Middlesex. b. 21st April 1855. I.T. Jan. 1883. Victoria bar 1884. Secy. to Pres. of P D and A Division 1892-98; Cty. Ct. judge 1898-1920. Author of a treatise on Law of Railway and Canal Traffic 1889. d. 6th Feb. 1920.

WOODFORDE, Woodforde Ffooks

s. of Thomas Ffooks, Clerk of the Peace for Dorset (d.1822). b. 9th June 1816. educ. Sherborne; Exeter Coll. Oxf. BA 1838, MA 1841. I.T. Jan. 1844. Dep. judge of Bristol Tolzey Ct.; Cty. Ct. judge 1874-89; JP Derbyshire and Suffolk; assumed name of Woodforde 1870. d. 11th Aug. 1896.

WOODROFFE, James Tisdall

s. of Canon John Nunn Woodroffe, Cork (d. 1892). b. 16th March 1838. educ. Trinity Coll. Dublin BA 1859; Senior Moderator. I.T. June 1860. QC 1893. Practised in Calcutta from 1860; Att-Genl. Bengal 1899-1904 (acting 1892-93); member Govr-Genl.'s Legislative Council 1899-1900, Bengal Legislative Council 1899-1904; member Dorset CC; JP Devon and Dorset; decorated by Pope Leo XIII for services rendered to the Catholic Church in India; Knight Commander of St. Gregory. Father of Sir John Woodroffe (1865-1936), puisne judge Calcutta. d. 3rd June 1908.

WOODS, Matthew Grosvenor Snooke

s. of Matthew Snooke, Chichester. b. 14th March 1838. educ. Prebendal Sch. Chichester; Trinity Coll. Camb. BA 1860, 6th Wrangler, MA 1863, Fellow 1860. L.I. June 1865. QC 1894. Bencher 1897. Assumed name of Woods 1864. d. 5th April 1925.

WOOLF, Sidney

s. of Benjamin Woolf, Regent St. London, tailor. b. 16th June 1844. educ. Univ. Coll. Sch. London. Solicitor in London 1867-71. M.T. Nov. 1873. QC 1890. Leader in Bankruptcy Ct. Author of treatise on law of adulteration of food and drink 1874. d. 12th March 1892.

WOOLL, Edward

s. of Rev. Charles William Wooll, Ditton, Lancashire. b. 31st March 1878. educ. Liverpool Coll.; New Coll. Oxf. BA 1901. I.T. Jan. 1903. KC. 1943. WWI Capt. Cheshire Yeo., and Cavalry Corps HQ, BEF (despatches twice), OBE 1919. Recorder of Carlisle 1929-63. WWII Capt. Liverpool Home Guard. Dramatist and novelist, and author of Layman's Guide to Libel. d. 20th May 1970.

WOOLRYCH, Edmund Humphry

s. of Genl. Josiah Allen Woolrych, Weobley, Herefordshire and Monastier, Lombardy-Venetia (d.1849). educ. Hereford Sch.; Bonn. Univ. M.T. Nov. 1839. Clerk to Metrop. Commrs. of Sewers 1849, and to Metrop. Bd. of Works 1856-61; metrop. magistrate 1861, finally at Westminster 1870-79; JP Middlesex, Kent, Essex, Hertfordshire, Surrey. d. 28th Jan. 1883, age 76.

WOOLRYCH, Humphry William

s. of Humphry Cornwall Woolrych, Croxley House, Rickmansworth, Hertfordshire, barrister (d. 1816). b. 24th Sept. 1795. educ. Eton; St. Edmund Hall Oxf. 1816. L.I. July 1821. Serjeant 1855; JP. Author of Lives of Eminent Serjeants-at-Law 1869, and of manuals on rights of common, waters and sewers, and window lights. Father of William Richard Woolrych JP (I.T.1860). d. 2nd July 1871.

WOOTTEN, Aubrey Francis Wootten

s. of William Wootten Wootten, Oxford, banker. b. 19th Sept. 1866. educ. Rugby; Oriel Coll. Oxford BA 1889. I.T. June 1892. KC. 1921. Chief Inspector V Div. Special Constabulary 1914-19; Asst. Commander 1920; OBE 1921; Chmn. Epsom Div. Consitutional Assoc. 1921. d. 4th Aug. 1923.

WORDSWORTH, Charles Favell Forth

s. of Robinson Wordsworth, Harwich, collector of customs (d. 1856). b. 1803. I.T. Jan. 1833. QC 1857. AICE 1861, and hon. counsel to that Institution 1852-74. Author of works on election law, joint stock companies, and compensation under Lands and Railway Clauses Acts. d. 18th Feb. 1874.

WORLLEDGE, John

s. of John Worlledge, Chevington, Suffolk (d. 1862). b. 2nd June 1809. educ. Felsted; Trinity Coll. Camb. BA 1831, MA 1834, Fellow 1836-41. M.T. Nov. 1838. Cty. Ct. judge 1856-80; Chan. of diocese of Norwich 1871-81; JP Suffolk. d. 19th July 1881.

WORSLEY-TAYLOR, Sir Henry Wilson, Bt.

s. of James Worsley JP, The Laund, Accrington, Lancashire (d. 1869). b. 25th July 1847. educ. Harrow; Exeter Coll. Oxf. BA 1870. M.T. May 1871. QC 1891. Bencher 1894, Reader 1906. Recorder of Preston 1893-98; MP North Lancashire (Blackpool) 1900-06; Chmn. Preston Quarter Sess. 1893-1917; DL, JP Lancashire; JP Yorkshire West Riding; assumed additional name of Taylor 1881; Baronet 1917. d. 27th June 1924.

WORTLEY, Charles Beilby Stuart (Lord Stuart)

s. of James Archibald Stuart-Wortley QC, MP. b. 15th Sept. 1851. educ. Rugby; Balliol Coll. Oxf. BA 1875, MA 1879. I.T. Jan. 1876. QC 1892. MP Sheffield (undivided) 1880-85, Hallam Divn. 1885-1916; Under-Secy. of State for Home Dept. 1885-86 and 1886-92; principal govt. delegate at Intern. Confces. on Protection of Industrial Property and the Repression of False Trade Descriptions, Madrid 1890, Brussels 1897 and 1900; temp. Chmn. of H. of C. 1895; an eccles. commr. 1895; director, Great Central Ry.; PC 1896; Baron Stuart of Wortley 1917. d. 24th April 1926.

WRANGHAM, Digby Cayley

s. of Francis Wrangham, archdeacon of Cleveland (d. 1842). b. 16th June 1805. educ. in Ripon; Brasenose Coll. Oxf. BA 1826, MA 1829. Private secy. to Viscount Dudley, and the Earl of Aberdeen at Foreign Office 1827-30. G.I. June 1831. Serjeant 1840; patent of precedence 1843. MP Sudbury 1831-32; Queen's Serjeant (with Shee and Byles) 1857. Father of Walter Francis Wrangham JP (L.I. 1859). d. 10th March 1865.

WRIGHT, Robert Alderson (Lord Wright)

s. of John Wright, South Shields, marine superintendent. b. 15th Oct.

1869. educ. privately; Trinity Coll. Camb. BA 1896, MA 1900, Fellow 1899-1905; Hon. Fellow 1939; Hon. LLD. I.T. June 1900. KC. 1917. Bencher 1923, Treasurer 1946. Specialised in commercial cases; KB judge 1925-32; Knight 1925; presided at trial of Lord Kylsant (false co. prospectus) 1931, and at hearing of Banco de Portugal v. Waterlow and Sons Ltd.; L of A 1932-35 and 1937-47; PC and Baron Wright of Durley 1932; MR 1935-37; Chmn. Law Revision Committee 1935; Chmn. UN War Crimes Comm. 1945; Dep. High Steward Camb. Univ. 1936-54; GCMG 1948; FBA 1940; Hon. LLD London, Birmingham, Toronto. d. 27th June 1964.

WRIGHT, Sir Robert Samuel

s. of Rev. Henry Edward Wright, Litton, Somerset. b. 20th Jan. 1839. educ. King's Sch. Bruton, Somerset; Balliol Coll. Oxf. BA 1862, BCL 1863, MA 1864; Fellow, Oriel Coll. 1861-80, Hon. Fellow 1882. Private tutor until 1865. I.T. June 1865. Bencher 1891. Junior counsel to Treasury 1883; QB judge 1890-1904; Knight 1891; Ry. and Canal Commr., and frequently sat as additional Chancery judge; his judgment in Br. South Africa Co. v. Companhia de Mocambique, confirmed by H of L; one of the judges requested by H of L to give an opinion in Allen v. Flood (whether trade combination unlawful) 1897. Author of The Law of Criminal Conspiracies and Agreements 1873, An Outline of Local Government and Local Taxation (with H. Hobhouse) 1884, An Essay on Possession in the Common Law (with Sir F. Pollock) 1888. d. 13th Aug. 1904.

WROTTESLEY, Sir Frederic John

s. of Rev. Francis John Wrottesley, Denstone, Staffordshire (d. 1922). b. 20th March 1880. educ. Tonbridge; Lincoln Coll. Oxf. BA 1903, MA, Hon. Fellow 1937. I.T. June 1907. KC. 1926. Bencher 1934. WWI Major 46th Divn. RFA (despatches). Practised at parliamentary bar; Recorder of Wolverhampton 1930-37; Chmn. Gas Legislation Committee 1931; conducted inquiry into marketing of sugarbeet 1936; Ry. and Canal Commr. 1938; KB judge 1937-47; Knight 1937; outstanding judge in criminal cases; LJ 1947-48; PC 1947; Chmn. Staffordshire Quarter Sess. 1939; JP Staffordshire. Author of The Examination of Witnesses 1910, Criminal Appeal 1912, Letters to a young Barrister 1930. d. 14th Nov. 1948.

WYNN PARRY, Sir Henry

s. of Robert Henry Wynn Parry FRCSE, Tomlinscote, Frimley, Surrey. b. 15th Jan. 1899. educ. Rugby; New Coll. Oxf. BA 1921, BCL 1922, MA 1925. WWI 2nd Lieut. Worcestershire Regt. L.I. June 1922. KC. 1936. Bencher 1941, Treasurer 1960. Dep. Chmn. Bd. of Referees. WWII 2nd Lieut. RA 1939-40. Chancery judge 1946-60; Knight 1946; Chmn. Committee of Inquiry under Br. Nationality Act 1948-50; Chmn. Hertfordshire Quarter Sess. 1950; Chmn. Permanent committee on private intern. law 1952, Council of Legal Educ. 1963, Comm. on riots in Br. Guiana 1962, Home Office Departmental Committee on conditions of service of Prison Officers. d. 10th Jan. 1964.

YARDLEY, Edward

s. of Edward Yardley, Shrewsbury. b. 1808. educ. Shrewsbury; Magdalene Coll. Camb. BA 1830, MA 1833, 40th Wrangler, Fellow 1830-32. L.I. Nov. 1834. Metrop. magistrate 1846, finally at Marylebone 1860-66. Brother of Sir William Yardley (1811-78), CJ Bombay and father of Arthur Yardley ICS (I.T. 1858). d. 18th Nov. 1866.

YATE-LEE, Lawford

s. of John Yate-Lee, barrister. b. 17th June 1838. educ. Royal Inst. Liverpool; Emmanuel Coll. Camb. BA 1860, 20th Wrangler, MA 1863. L.I. Nov. 1864. Equity draftsman and conveyancer; practised in chancery and bankruptcy 1864-96; Cty. Ct. judge 1896-1901; JP Worcestershire. Author of treatise on bankruptcy. d. 17th May 1901.

YATES, Joseph Maghull

s. of Joseph St.John Yates, Cty. Ct. judge. b. 19th June 1844. educ. Westminster; Trinity Coll. Camb. BA 1867. I.T. Jan. 1869. QC 1893. Recorder of Salford 1889-1904; stip. magistrate, Manchester 1894-1916; Chmn. Lancashire Quarter Sess. 1904; JP Lancashire and Cheshire. Brother of Walter Baldwyn Yates CBE (I.T.1881) and father of Joseph Mervyn St.John Yates (I.T.1903). d. 17th April 1916.

YATES, Joseph St. John

s. of Joseph Yates, Peel Hall, Lancashire, and g.s. of Yates J (d. 1770). b. 16th Oct. 1808. educ. Charterhouse (captain); Christ Church Oxf. 1827. I.T. May 1835. Commr. in Bankruptcy, Manchester; judge of Small Debts Ct., Glossop to 1847; Cty. Ct. judge 1847-82; JP Lancashire, Derbyshire, Cheshire. d. 2nd March 1887.

YOUNG, Alfred

s. of George Young, Longton, Staffordshire. b. 8th July 1837. I.T. Nov. 1858. Practised at Wolverhampton 1858-77, Birmingham 1877-98; Recorder of Gloucester 1881-1900; member of bar committee 1883-95; Cty. Ct. judge 1898-1900. Author of a digest of maritime cases and salvage awards. d. 22nd Nov. 1900.

YOUNG, George

s. of Alexander Young, Rosefield, Kirkcudbrightshire, procurator-fiscal of Dumfriesshire. b. 2nd July 1819. educ. Dumfries Acad.; Edin. Univ. Hon. LLD 1871. Scottish bar 1840. M.T. Nov. 1869. QC 1868. Bencher 1871, Reader 1877. Advocate-depute 1849; Sheriff of Inverness-shire 1853-60, of Haddington and Berwick 1860-62; Sol-Genl. for Scotland 1862-67, 1868-69; Lord Advocate 1869-74; MP Wigtown Burghs 1865-74; judge of Ct. of Session, with title of Lord Young 1874-1905; PC 1872. d. 22nd May 1907.

YOUNG, Hugo Joseph

s. of John Joseph Young JP, Claxby House, nr. Market Rasen, Lincolnshire (d.1893). b. 29th Oct. 1847. educ. Mount St. Mary's nr. Chesterfield; Ushaw Coll.; London Univ. BA 1869. I.T. June 1872. QC 1898. Bencher 1907. Recorder of Lincoln 1905-21, of Nottingham 1921-27; Commr. of Assize, Oxford circuit and Birmingham 1918, Stafford and Birmingham 1920, North Eastern circuit 1921. Author of Conventual and Monastic Institutions, their Legal Position, Property, and Disabilities 1873. d. 22nd March 1929.

YOUNGER, Robert (Lord Blanesburgh)

s. of James Younger, Alloa, Clackmannanshire, brewer (d. 1868). b. 12th Sept. 1861. educ. Edin. Acad.; Balliol Coll. Oxf. BA 1883, MA 1909, Hon. Fellow 1916, DCL 1928, Visitor 1933-46. I.T. Nov. 1884. QC 1900. Bencher (L.I.) 1907, Treasurer 1932. Chancery judge 1915-19; Knight 1915; Chmn. Comm. on Treatment by the Enemy of Br. prisoners, and served on several other tribs. arising from WWI; GBE 1917; LJ 1919-23; PC 1919; L of A 1923-37; Baron 1923; principal Br. rep. on Reparation Comm. 1925-30; Prime Warden of Goldsmiths' Co. 1931; Hon. LLD Edin. 1919, St. Andrews 1929. d. 17th Aug. 1946.